World Development Report 1989

Published for The World Bank
Oxford University Press

Oxford University Press

NEW YORK OXFORD CORBY LONDON TORONTO
NEW DELHI BOMBAY CALCUTTA MADRAS
SELANGOR SINGAPORE HONG KONG TAIPEI
TOKYO BANGKOK KARACHI LAHORE MELBOURNE
AUCKLAND CAPE TOWN JOHANNESBURG DURBAN
NAIROBI DAR ES SALAAM KAMPALA
JAKARTA IBADAN

ISBN 0-19-520787-4 clothbound
ISBN 0-19-520788-2 paperback
ISSN 0163-5085

The Library of Congress has cataloged this serial publication as follows:
World development report. 1978–
[New York] Oxford University Press.
v. 27 cm. annual.
Published for The World Bank.
1. Underdeveloped areas—Periodicals.   2. Economic development—
Periodicals.   I. International Bank for Reconstruction and Development.

HC59.7.W659   330.9'172'4   78-67086

This book is printed on paper that adheres to
the American National Standard for Permanence of Paper
for Printed Library Materials, Z39.48-1984.

Foreword

This Report is the twelfth in the annual series assessing major development issues. Like its predecessors, the Report includes the World Development Indicators, which provide selected social and economic data for more than a hundred countries. Chapter 1 reviews recent trends in the world economy and their implications for the future prospects of developing countries. Chapters 2 through 9 examine the role of financial systems in development, the special topic of this year's Report. The main points of the Report are summarized below.

Economic growth rates among the developing countries have varied considerably. In Asia, where the majority of people live, per capita incomes during the 1980s have risen more rapidly than in the 1960s and 1970s, but in Latin America and the Caribbean, Europe, the Middle East, and North Africa per capita incomes have risen by less than 1 percent a year, and in Sub-Saharan Africa they have actually declined. The external environment has had an adverse impact on growth, but domestic policies have been more important. Countries striving to adjust their economies have had considerable success in reducing external imbalances but less success with internal balance. In the first half of the 1990s, per capita incomes are expected to increase only slowly in Sub-Saharan African countries. The highly indebted countries will grow more rapidly, particularly if there are reductions in their external debt. Growth is expected to slow among Asian countries, although per capita incomes will continue to rise rapidly.

The decline in foreign capital inflows means that countries will need to rely primarily on domestic resources to finance investment. Financial systems can play an important role in this regard: by mobilizing savings and allocating them to the most profitable activities, the financial sector enables society to make more productive use of its scarce resources. The financial systems of many developing countries are in need of restructuring, however. Their present condition reflects the approach to development taken by many countries in the 1960s and 1970s, an approach that emphasized government intervention to promote economic growth. Today many countries are revising their approach to rely more heavily on the private sector and on market forces. For the financial sector this implies a smaller role for government in the allocation of credit, the determination of interest rates, and the daily decisionmaking of financial intermediaries. Relaxation of these economic and operational controls calls for an effective system of prudent regulation and supervision. In most countries improvements in the legal and accounting systems will be required to strengthen the financial structure.

The industrial and financial policies followed in the 1970s and 1980s, together with the economic shocks of the 1980s, have left many developing countries' financial institutions insolvent. Still, many institutions continue to lend to their most impaired customers and to accrue unpaid interest. The allocation of scarce resources to insolvent firms has delayed adjustment. Restructuring the insolvent firms and institutions is an important part of the adjustment process.

Restructuring the financial system provides a unique opportunity to reconsider what sorts of institutions will be best suited to the economic environment of the 1990s. Although commercial banks will continue to dominate financial systems in many developing countries, greater emphasis than in the past should be placed on ensuring the availability of a broad array of financial services. Many countries should develop contractual savings systems, and the more advanced should develop securities markets. Governments should provide a tax and regulatory environment that is neutral with regard to different types of financial activities. Informal financial institutions have proved able to serve the household, agricultural, and microenterprise sectors on a sustained basis. Measures that link informal institutions to the formal financial system will improve that service and ensure a competitive environment.

In recent years some countries have experimented with varying degrees of financial liberalization. Their experience with both domestic liberalization and full or partial decontrol of the capital account has been mixed. Nevertheless, it suggests that the pace and sequencing of liberalization should depend on the initial structure of a country's financial system and the degree of macroeconomic stability. Countries with unstable economies and price systems that do not reflect the scarcity of resources will need to deregulate their financial systems gradually. In countries without fully liberalized markets, policymakers should make sure that interest rates reflect market forces and that directed credit programs are limited to a modest share of total credit. When a country lacks macroeconomic stability, decontrol of external financial transactions may cause destabilizing capital flows. Hence, although the objective is an open market, countries should not remove all capital controls until other economic and financial reforms are in place.

Like previous World Development Reports, this is a study by the staff of the World Bank, and the judgments in it do not necessarily reflect the views of the Board of Directors or the governments they represent.

Barber B. Conable
President
The World Bank

June 1, 1989

This Report has been prepared by a team led by Millard F. Long and comprising Yoon Je Cho, Warren L. Coats, Jr., Eirik Evenhouse, Barbara Kafka, Catherine Mann, Gerhard Pohl, Dimitri Vittas, Robert Vogel, and Robert Wieland. The team was assisted by Anastasios Filippides, Lynn Steckelberg Khadiagala, Clifford W. Papik, Anna-Birgitta Viggh, and Bo Wang. The work was carried out under the general direction of Stanley Fischer.

Many others in and outside the Bank provided helpful comments and contributions (see the bibliographical note). The International Economics Department prepared the data and projections presented in Chapter 1 and the statistical appendix. It is also responsible for the World Development Indicators. The production staff of the Report included Les Barker, Pensri Kimpitak, Cathe Kocak, Victoria Lee, Walton Rosenquist, Nancy Snyder, and Brian J. Svikhart. Library assistance was provided by Iris Anderson. The support staff was headed by Rhoda Blade-Charest and included Trinidad S. Angeles and María Guadalupe M. Mattheisen. Clive Crook was the principal editor.

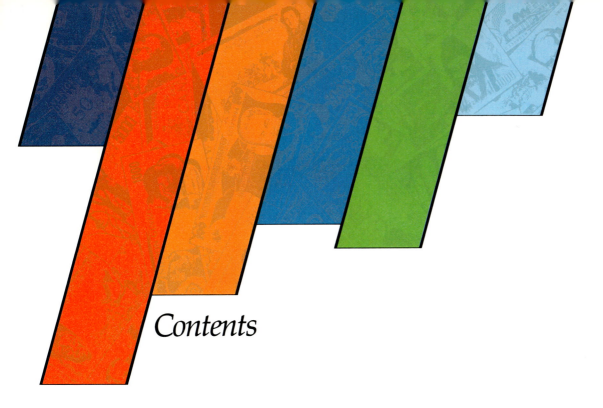

Contents

Boxes

Text figures

Text tables

Statistical appendix tables

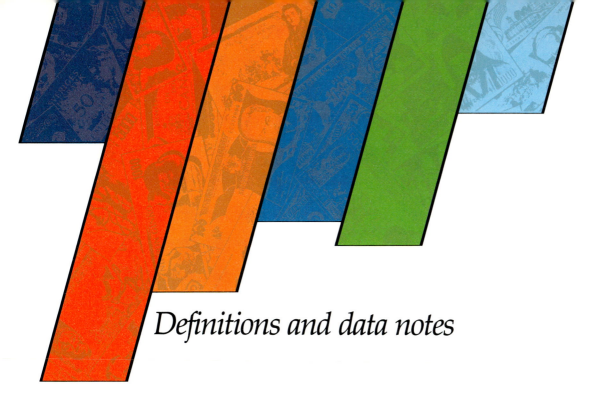

Definitions and data notes

Financial terms

• *Banks.* Financial institutions that accept funds, principally in the form of deposits repayable on demand or at short notice (such as demand, time, and savings deposits). Under the general rubric "banks" come: commercial banks, which engage only in deposit taking and short- and medium-term lending; investment banks, which handle securities trading and underwriting; housing banks, which provide housing finance; and so on. In some countries there are universal banks, which combine commercial banking with investment banking and sometimes with insurance services.

• *Capital market.* The market in which long-term financial instruments, such as equities and bonds, are raised and traded.

• *Commercial bills.* Short-term debt instruments that are used mainly to finance trade. Examples are promissory notes, by which debtors commit themselves to pay to creditors or to their order a stated sum at a specified date, and bills of exchange, which are drawn up by creditors and accepted by debtors. Commercial bills that are also accepted by banks are known as bank acceptances. Promissory notes issued by large corporations to meet their general financial needs are known as commercial paper.

• *Contractual savings institutions.* Occupational pension funds, national provident funds, life in-surance companies, and similar institutions that collect long-term savings on a contractual basis.

• *Curb market.* An unofficial money and capital market.

• *Development finance institutions (DFIs).* Financial intermediaries that emphasize the provision of capital (loans and equity) for development. DFIs may specialize in particular sectors—for example, industry, agriculture, or housing. Although most provide only medium- and long-term capital, some, particularly those that specialize in agriculture, also provide short-term finance.

• *Discount.* A reduction from the face value of a financial contract.

• *Equity finance.* The provision of finance in a form that entitles its owner to share in the profits and net worth of the enterprise.

• *Eurocurrency market.* A market in which assets and liabilities denominated in a particular currency are held outside the country of that currency.

• *Financial savings.* The portion of total wealth held in the form of financial assets.

• *Foreign portfolio investment.* Investment by foreign residents in domestic capital markets, without the investors' provision of technology and management services that usually occurs with foreign direct investment.

• *Forward contract.* An agreement to purchase or sell at a future date a fixed amount of commodities or securities at a preset price.

• *Fractional reserve banking.* The practice by which commercial banks maintain a reserve of highly liquid assets (usually deposits in a central bank) equal to only a fraction of their deposit liabilities.

• *Hedging.* The acquisition of a financial contract designed to protect the purchaser against a future change in the price of a commodity or security in which the purchaser has an interest.

• *Indexation.* A mechanism for periodically adjusting the nominal value of contracts in line with movements in a specified price index.

• *Leverage.* The ratio of debt to equity or of debt to total capital employed.

• *Liquid liabilities.* Money plus highly liquid money substitutes, such as savings deposits.

• *Market capitalization.* The total value of outstanding securities at present market prices.

• *Money.* Currency and other liquid assets. Narrow definitions such as M1 refer to money used as a medium of exchange. Broader definitions such as M2 or M3 add to M1 money used as a store of value.

M1. Currency outside banks plus demand deposits, excluding those held by government and banking institutions.

M2. M1 plus time and savings deposits (other than large certificates of deposit) at commercial banks.

M3. M2 plus deposits at nonbank thrift institutions.

• *Money market.* A market in which short-term securities such as Treasury bills, certificates of deposit, and commercial bills are traded.

• *Nonbank financial intermediaries.* Financial institutions, such as building societies and insurance companies, that hold less-liquid liabilities not normally regarded as part of the money stock.

• *Nonperforming loan.* A loan on which contractual obligations (for example, interest or amortization payments) are not being met.

• *Reserve money.* Currency in circulation plus deposits (of banks and other residents but not the government) with the monetary authorities.

• *Rotating savings and credit association (ROSCA).* An informal group of six to forty participants who regularly (for example, monthly) make a contribution into a fund that is given in rotation to each group member.

• *Seigniorage.* The net revenue derived from money issue.

• *Swaps.* The exchange of future streams of payment between two or more parties.

• *Term finance.* Equity or medium- and long-term loan finance.

Country groupings

For operational and analytical purposes, the World Bank classifies economies according to their per capita GNP. Other international agencies maintain different classifications of developing countries (see the table on pages 250–51 for a comparative listing).

Country classifications have been revised since the 1988 edition of the *World Development Report* and its statistical annex, the World Development Indicators. The principal changes are: (a) the "developing economies" group has been dropped, but references to the specific income groups *low- and middle-income economies* have been retained, (b) all economies with a GNP per capita of $6,000 or more are classified as *high-income economies*, and (c) the subgroups "oil exporters" and "exporters of manufactures" under "developing economies" have been dropped. In addition, "high-income oil exporters" is no longer a separate group; "industrial economies" has been renamed *OECD members*, which is a subgroup of the new category *high-income economies*; and a new aggregate, *total reporting economies*, and its subcategory *oil exporters* have been added. As in previous editions, this Report uses the latest GNP per capita estimates to classify countries. The country composition of each income group may therefore change from one edition to the next. Once the classification is fixed for any edition, all the historical data presented are based on the same country grouping. The country groups used in this Report are defined below.

• *Low-income economies* are those with a GNP per capita of $480 or less in 1987.

• *Middle-income economies* are those with a GNP per capita of more than $480 but less than $6,000 in 1987. A further division, at GNP per capita of $1,940 in 1987, is made between lower- and upper-middle-income economies.

• *High-income economies* are those with a GNP per capita of $6,000 or more in 1987.

The Report has always used a specific level of GNP per capita as the dividing line between low- and middle-income economies. In previous editions the line between middle- and high-income groups was ambiguous. Industrial market economies and high-income oil exporters were shown separately, but some economies remained in the middle-income group although their GNP per capita was higher than that of some countries classified as high income. The cutoff point of $6,000 for high-income economies in this edition removes that anomaly.

Low- and middle-income economies are sometimes referred to as "developing economies." The use of the term is convenient; it is not intended to imply that all economies in the group are experiencing similar development or that other economies have reached a preferred or final stage of development. Classification by income does not necessarily reflect development status. (In this edition of the World Development Indicators, high-income economies classified by the United Nations or otherwise regarded by their authorities as developing are identified by the symbol †.) The use of the term "countries" to refer to economies implies no judgment by the World Bank about the legal or other status of any territory.

• *Nonreporting nonmembers* are Albania, Angola, Bulgaria, Cuba, Czechoslovakia, German Democratic Republic, Democratic People's Republic of Korea, Mongolia, Namibia, and Union of Soviet Socialist Republics.

For analytical purposes, other overlapping classifications based predominantly on exports or external debt are used in addition to geographic country groupings. The economies in these groups with populations of more than 1 million are listed below.

Analytical groupings

• *Oil exporters* are countries for which exports of petroleum and gas, including reexports, account for at least 30 percent of merchandise exports. They are Algeria, Cameroon, People's Republic of the Congo, Ecuador, Arab Republic of Egypt, Gabon, Indonesia, Islamic Republic of Iran, Iraq, Kuwait, Mexico, Nigeria, Norway, Oman, Saudi Arabia, Syrian Arab Republic, Trinidad and Tobago, United Arab Emirates, and Venezuela.

• *Seventeen highly indebted countries* are those deemed to have encountered severe debt servicing difficulties: Argentina, Bolivia, Brazil, Chile, Colombia, Costa Rica, Côte d'Ivoire, Ecuador, Jamaica, Mexico, Morocco, Nigeria, Peru, Philippines, Uruguay, Venezuela, and Yugoslavia.

• *OECD members*, a subgroup of high-income economies, comprises the members of the Organisation for Economic Co-operation and Development except for Greece, Portugal, and Turkey, which are included among the middle-income economies.

Geographic regions (low- and middle-income economies)

• *Sub-Saharan Africa* comprises all countries south of the Sahara except South Africa.

• *Europe, Middle East, and North Africa* comprises eight European countries—Cyprus, Greece, Hungary, Malta, Poland, Portugal, Romania, and Yugoslavia—all the economies of North Africa and the Middle East, and Afghanistan.

• *East Asia* comprises all the low- and middle-income economies of East and Southeast Asia and the Pacific east of and including China and Thailand.

• *South Asia* comprises Bangladesh, Bhutan, Burma, India, Nepal, Pakistan, and Sri Lanka.

• *Latin America and the Caribbean* comprises all American and Caribbean countries south of the United States.

Acronyms and initials

BDC Botswana Development Corporation
BFN Banco de Fomento Nacional
BKK Badan Kredit Kecamatan
BNI Bank Negara Indonesia
CD Certificate of deposit
COOPEC Coopérative d'Epargne et de Crédit
CPI Consumer price index
DFI Development finance institution
DTC Deposit-taking cooperative
EC The European Community (Belgium, Denmark, Federal Republic of Germany, France, Greece, Ireland, Italy, Luxembourg, Netherlands, Portugal, Spain, and United Kingdom)
EMBRAER Empresa Brasileira de Aeronáutica
FOPINAR Fondo de Fomento para la Pequeña Industria y la Artesanía
FSLIC Federal Savings and Loan Insurance Corporation
GATT General Agreement on Tariffs and Trade
GDP Gross domestic product
GNP Gross national product
GRT Gross receipts tax
IBRD International Bank for Reconstruction and Development (The World Bank)
ICOR Incremental capital-output ratio
IDA International Development Association
IFC International Finance Corporation
IFS *International Financial Statistics*, published monthly by the IMF
IMF International Monetary Fund
MFA Multifibre Arrangement

NTB Nontariff barrier

OECD Organisation for Economic Co-operation and Development (Australia, Austria, Belgium, Canada, Denmark, Finland, France, Federal Republic of Germany, Greece, Iceland, Ireland, Italy, Japan, Luxembourg, Netherlands, New Zealand, Norway, Portugal, Spain, Sweden, Switzerland, Turkey, United Kingdom, and United States)

PSBR Public sector borrowing requirement

QR Quantitative restriction

ROSCA Rotating savings and credit association

S&L Savings and loan association

SEC Securities and Exchange Commission

SOE State-owned enterprise

UMOA Union monétaire ouest africaine (West African Monetary Union)

VISA Valores Industriales S.A.

Data notes

- *Billion* is 1,000 million.
- *Trillion* is 1,000 billion.
- *Dollars* are current U.S. dollars unless otherwise specified.

- *Growth rates* are based on constant price data and, unless otherwise noted, have been computed with the use of the least-squares method. See the technical notes of the World Development Indicators for details of this method.
- *The symbol* . . in tables means not available.
- *The symbol* — in tables means not applicable.
- *The number 0 or 0.0* in tables means zero or less than half the unit shown and not known more precisely.

All tables and figures are based on World Bank data unless otherwise specified. The cutoff date for all data in the World Development Indicators is April 30, 1989.

Data from secondary sources are not always available after 1987. Historical data shown in this Report may differ from those in previous editions because of continuous updating as better data become available and because of new group aggregation techniques that use broader country coverage than in previous editions.

Economic and demographic terms are defined in the technical notes to the World Development Indicators.

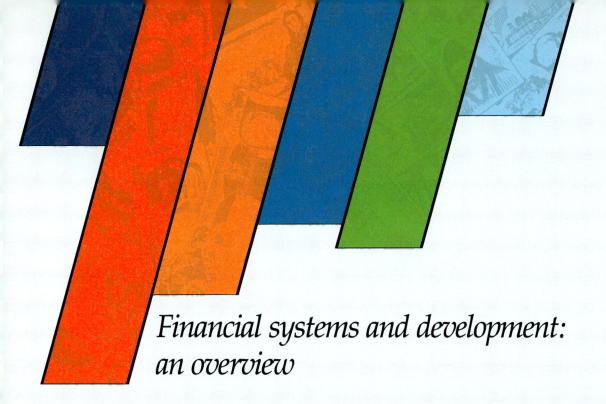

Financial systems and development: an overview

The experiences of the 1980s have led many developing countries to reconsider their approach to development. Although countries differ in the scale of government intervention and in the extent to which they have already stabilized and restructured their economies, most have decided to rely more upon the private sector and market signals to direct the allocation of resources. To obtain all the benefits of greater reliance on voluntary, market-based decisionmaking, they need efficient financial systems.

A financial system provides services that are essential in a modern economy. The use of a stable, widely accepted medium of exchange reduces the costs of transactions. It facilitates trade and, therefore, specialization in production. Financial assets with attractive yield, liquidity, and risk characteristics encourage saving in financial form. By evaluating alternative investments and monitoring the activities of borrowers, financial intermediaries increase the efficiency of resource use. Access to a variety of financial instruments enables economic agents to pool, price, and exchange risk. Trade, the efficient use of resources, saving, and risk taking are the cornerstones of a growing economy.

In the past, governments' efforts to promote economic development by controlling interest rates, directing credit to priority sectors, and securing inexpensive funding for their own activities have undermined financial development. In recent years financial systems came under further stress when, as a result of the economic shocks of the 1980s, many borrowers were unable to service their loans. In more than twenty-five developing countries, governments have been forced to assist troubled intermediaries. The restructuring of insolvent intermediaries provides governments with an opportunity to rethink and reshape their financial systems.

Conditions that support the development of a more robust and balanced financial structure will improve the ability of domestic financial systems to contribute to growth. By restoring macroeconomic stability, building better legal, accounting, and regulatory systems, specifying rules for fuller disclosure of information, and levying taxes that do not fall excessively on finance, governments can lay the foundations for smoothly functioning financial systems. This Report reviews the lessons of experience in both high-income and developing countries and tries to identify the measures that will enable domestic financial systems to provide the services needed in the 1990s.

The economic background

In 1988 conditions were generally favorable for economic growth in the developing countries. High-income countries enjoyed steady growth with low inflation for the sixth consecutive year and grew even faster in 1988 than in 1987. Interest and exchange rates were less volatile than during earlier phases of the recovery from the worldwide recession of 1982, and prices of the principal commodities exported by developing countries rose by an average of 20 percent.

Some developing countries have taken advantage of the favorable world environment. Most countries in Asia did well; in several the gross national product (GNP) grew at an estimated annual rate of 10 percent. Some countries, however, continued to suffer from misdirected domestic policies, excessive indebtedness, and the economic shocks of the 1980s. The growth rates of many African nations remained near zero. The heavily indebted economies also continued to stagnate. The governments of creditor countries agreed at the Toronto summit to grant debt relief to the poorest and most heavily indebted countries, such as the countries of Sub-Saharan Africa, and early in 1989 took the first official steps to sanction debt relief for the middle-income countries. But despite a rise in the disbursement of funds to the highly indebted countries in 1988, net transfers to these countries continued to be negative.

Future growth in the developing countries will depend in part on the policies of high-income countries. By ensuring the success of the Uruguay Round of trade negotiations, the high-income countries can create a favorable environment for the exports of developing countries. Tighter fiscal but easier monetary policy in high-income countries would bring international interest rates down, which would ease the burden of debt. This would benefit developing and high-income countries alike. But far more important will be the policies pursued by the developing countries themselves. They can improve their growth prospects by continuing to seek fiscal balance and trade reforms. The decline in foreign capital flows has placed a premium on policies that encourage domestic saving and investment and direct the flow of resources to profitable activities—in other words, on policies that will improve the performance of domestic financial systems.

Origins of financial distress

When the developing countries set out to modernize their economies in the 1950s and 1960s, their financial systems comprised mainly foreign-owned commercial banks. These provided short-term commercial and trade credit. Governments decided to remodel their financial systems to ensure that resources were allocated in accordance with their development strategies. Toward this end, they created new financial institutions to provide funding at low interest rates to the sectors that were to be at the forefront of industrial development, or they directed existing institutions to do so. The governments themselves borrowed heavily, both from the domestic financial system and from abroad, to finance budget deficits and the needs of state-owned enterprises. In many countries banks were also directed to open rural branches in order to mobilize deposits and provide credit to widely dispersed smallholders.

During the 1960s this development strategy seemed to be working: many developing countries grew rapidly. But economic performance during the 1970s was more mixed. Despite favorable terms of trade and an ample supply of cheap foreign financing, growth in some countries began to slow. Except in Asia, only a few developing countries have grown rapidly in the 1980s.

The interventionist approach was much less successful in promoting financial development. Under government pressure, banks did lend to state enterprises and priority sectors at below-market interest rates, but spreads were often too small to cover the banks' costs. Many of the directed loans were not repaid. Interest rate controls discouraged savers from holding domestic financial assets and discouraged institutions from lending longer term or to riskier borrowers. In some countries, public borrowing from commercial banks displaced lending to the private sector; in others, public borrowing financed by money creation led to rapid inflation. Many countries developed a market for short-term debt, but only a few have more than a rudimentary system for long-term finance. In sum, the financial systems of all but a few developing countries remain small and undeveloped.

In recent years the inability or unwillingness of borrowers to repay their loans has become a serious problem. Its roots lie in the shocks of the early 1980s and in the industrial and financial policies pursued over the past thirty years. Many countries depended on commodity exports and foreign borrowing to pay for the imported inputs essential to their industrialization programs. For the highly indebted countries in particular, foreign borrowing became expensive as interest rates rose in the late 1970s; it became virtually impossible as foreign commercial banks ceased voluntary lending after 1982. Deteriorating terms of trade and international recession in the early 1980s further reduced countries' ability to pay for imports. Many countries were forced to reduce their trade deficits. To promote exports, they devalued their currencies and lowered their tariffs and other trade barriers. Firms in developing countries therefore had to face abrupt changes in relative prices, often alongside recession at home. Many became unprofitable and thus were unable to service their loans.

Instead of foreclosing on bad debts, many bankers chose to accrue unpaid interest and roll over unpaid loans. In some cases this was because the borrowers were linked to the banks through ownership, in others because taking provisions for loan losses would have made the banks insolvent. Collateral was often inadequate, and foreclosure procedures were slow and biased in favor of debtors. So in many countries it was not thought feasible to start bankruptcy proceedings. The practice of rolling over unpaid loans and making new loans to cover unpaid interest has undermined the adjustment process: instead of financing new ventures made profitable by changed relative prices, much new lending has gone to prop up firms that are no longer viable.

Financial institutions in many developing countries have suffered large losses: many are insolvent, and some have actually failed. Bank insolvency is nothing new, but the scale of the problem—the number of insolvent institutions, the size of their losses, and the number of countries affected—is without precedent. Although more than twenty-five developing countries took action during the 1980s to restructure financial institutions, many of them dealt with only the largest or most seriously affected ones; others remain severely impaired. Restructuring banks is politically difficult, particularly when the banks are public or the principal defaulters are public enterprises, but experience shows that delay is costly and that losses mount with time.

Reform needs to go beyond recapitalizing insolvent banks. It must address the underlying causes of bank insolvency as well. Governments can strive to provide macroeconomic stability, which generally means reducing their spending. They can also undertake the structural adjustments that will lead to a more productive use of resources. Restructuring or closing insolvent firms must be part of this process; otherwise the recapitalized intermediaries that continue to lend to them will once again become insolvent.

Prerequisites for financial development

Countries with stable economies and fairly well-developed and competitive financial markets would benefit from giving market forces more influence over interest rates. Where these conditions are not satisfied, governments may choose to control interest rates, but unless that control is flexible enough to take account of inflation and market pressures, it will impede financial development. Proper alignment of interest rates is particularly important for economies that have open capital markets.

In the past, governments have allocated credit extensively. In a world of rapidly changing relative prices, complex economic structures, and increasingly sophisticated financial markets, the risk of mismanaging such controls has increased. Many countries could allocate resources better by reducing the number of directed credit programs, the proportion of total credit affected, and the degree of interest rate subsidization. Governments that continue to direct credit should specify priorities narrowly. An emphasis on credit availability is preferable to interest rate subsidies, which undermine the financial process.

Liberating financial institutions from interest rate or credit controls cannot, by itself, ensure that financial systems will develop as intended. The legal and accounting systems of most developing countries cannot adequately support modern financial processes. Legal systems are often outdated, and laws concerning collateral and foreclosure are poorly enforced. Because collecting debts can be difficult, and because borrowers are hard to monitor and control, lenders have been unwilling to enter into certain types of financial contract. If governments overcome such reluctance by directing banks to make loans that the banks consider too risky, losses can result. Governments can increase the supply of long-term loans and other types of financing by reducing the risks to lenders—for instance, by requiring fuller disclosure of financial information and defining and enforcing the lenders' rights. To ensure the stability of the financial system and discourage lenders from fraud, it is equally important for governments to supervise financial markets and institutions. In the past, supervisors have spent too much time checking banks' compliance with directives on credit allocation and too little time inspecting the quality of their loans and the adequacy of their capital.

Institutions and markets

Commercial banks are likely to remain the dominant institutions for some time. Banks can be made more efficient by improving their management systems and increasing the competition they face. Better management requires new lending policies, better loan recovery procedures, more sophisticated information systems, and better-trained staff. The entry of new banks, domestic or foreign, can stimulate competition.

Countries also need to develop other financial institutions, whose services compete with and complement those of commercial banks. Nonbank financial intermediaries, such as development finance institutions, insurance companies, and pension funds, are potentially important sources of long-term finance. Most of the existing development banks are insolvent, however. Where they are to be restructured, rather than closed or merged with commercial banks, thought must be given to their future role and viability. Any diversification should build on the experience of their staffs and on their existing client relationships. As more of the population becomes able to and desires to make provision for retirement, contractual savings institutions will grow in size. Permitting pension funds and insurance companies to invest in financial instruments other than low-interest government bonds can greatly increase the supply of long-term finance to the private sector.

Many developing countries have benefited from the creation of money and capital markets. Money markets can provide competition for banks, a flexible means for managing liquidity, a benchmark for market-based interest rates, and an instrument of monetary policy. Capital markets can be a source of long-term finance—both debt and equity—and can help to foster sounder corporate capital structures.

Most developing countries have a long-established informal financial sector that provides services to the noncorporate sector—households, small farmers, and small businesses. Although family and friends are usually the most important source of credit, pawnbrokers provide a substantial amount of credit to those with marketable collateral, and moneylenders to those without. Merchants provide financing to their customers, and purchasing agents advance funds to their suppliers. Rotating savings and credit associations are ubiquitous in the developing world.

Financial institutions have often been weakened by being forced to channel credit to small-scale borrowers. Because such borrowers do not maintain financial accounts, formal lenders find it difficult to predict who is likely to repay. Moreover, if the borrower is in a group favored by government, formal intermediaries may find it difficult to collect. The informal sector, in contrast, has been able to serve such borrowers. Informal lending has se-

vere drawbacks, however. The scale of lending is small, the range of services is limited, markets are fragmented, and interest rates are sometimes usurious. Nevertheless, these institutions help clients that formal institutions often find too costly or risky to serve. Some countries have recognized this and have established programs to link informal markets more closely with formal markets. The most successful formal programs for the noncorporate sector utilize rather than suppress indigenous systems, take deposits as well as lend, and levy charges that cover costs.

As the developing countries move toward more sophisticated financial systems, they can draw on the experience of the high-income countries in the design of instruments and institutions. Some of the lessons are cautionary. One lesson is that competitive financial markets, although efficient at mobilizing and allocating funds and managing risk, can still make mistakes—witness the excessive lending to developing countries that took place in the 1970s and the current savings and loan crisis in the United States. Another is that market-based financial systems can be unstable and susceptible to fraud. This underlines the importance of adequate regulation and supervision. Because finance evolves rapidly, regulators must continually strive for the right balance between stimulating competition and growth and limiting fraud and instability.

The path to reform

Many developing countries have taken steps toward financial liberalization during the past decade. In perhaps a dozen countries, interest rates have been fully liberalized; in many more, interest rates are managed more flexibly than before. Many countries have curtailed their directed credit programs, although few have eliminated them entirely. Competition among financial institutions has been promoted by opening the domestic market to foreign banks and by authorizing charters for new banks and nonbank financial intermediaries. Several centrally planned economies aim to stimulate competition by extensively restructuring their banking systems.

In a few countries financial liberalization has been quite comprehensive. Argentina, Chile, and Uruguay, for example, carried out extensive reforms in the mid-1970s, including the elimination of directed credit programs, interest rate controls, and exchange controls. Several Asian countries have also moved toward deregulation, but the reforms were introduced more gradually and were less comprehensive. Financial liberalization has sometimes proved difficult. In the Southern Cone countries—Argentina, Chile, and Uruguay—liberalization ended in disarray: the government of Argentina had to reimpose controls, and all three governments had to deal with widespread bank failures. Turkey's government had to restore interest rate controls when real rates rose too high. But in Asia, where macroeconomic conditions were more stable and reforms were implemented more gradually, there has been no need to reintroduce controls.

Experience suggests that financial liberalization needs to be undertaken alongside macroeconomic reform. Countries that attempted financial liberalization before undertaking other reforms suffered destabilizing capital flows, high interest rates, and corporate distress. Although certain measures should be taken at an early stage, such as the alignment of interest rates with market forces, overall liberalization cannot succeed unless it is accompanied by the restructuring of insolvent banks and firms and by adequate regulation and supervision. Domestic financial markets need to be competitive to ensure that intermediaries are efficiently run. And to avoid the destabilizing capital flows that proved so difficult to manage in several countries attempting deregulation, care must be taken in opening the capital account.

The change in many countries' approach to development implies important changes in their financial sectors. Countries that wish to rely more upon private decisionmaking need financial systems that operate on a more consensual basis. For that, confidence is needed—confidence that the value of financial contracts will not be eroded by inflation and that contracts will be honored. Getting the prices—interest rates—right is important for financial development, but this must be complemented by other policies as well. Countries also need to create appropriate financial institutions, develop better systems of prudential regulation and supervision, improve the flow of financial information, develop human skills for managing complex financial operations, and promote good financial habits. None of these changes will be easily or quickly accomplished.

Outline of the Report

Chapter 1 describes the global macroeconomic environment that has confronted developing coun-

tries in recent years and discusses two scenarios for prospects to the end of the century. Even under the more optimistic of these, the developing countries face serious economic challenges.

Chapter 2 introduces the main body of the Report and examines the role of finance in development. It argues that finance matters in more ways than might be immediately apparent. Efficient financial systems help to allocate resources to their best uses and are indispensable in complex, modern economies. In many developing countries, as some of their governments have begun to realize, the financial sector is in urgent need of reform.

Reform will not be easy, but the difficulties faced by developing countries as they seek to improve their financial systems are not new. Chapter 3 charts the history of financial institutions in the industrial countries. It shows an often unsatisfactory mixture: innovation in response to the needs of growing economies, but many disruptive episodes of financial instability. Failures and fraud in their financial systems have led governments to intervene extensively.

Chapter 4 shows that for several decades after World War II, regulation of the financial systems in developing countries was designed to control the economy rather than foster the safety and soundness of banks. More than in the high-income countries, governments used the financial system to pursue their development objectives. This left their financial institutions weak, and as a result many were unable to withstand the worldwide economic shocks of the 1970s and early 1980s. Chapter 5 describes the difficulties of financial institutions in many countries and the steps taken by some governments to address the problems of their financial sectors.

This experience has led the developing countries to reassess their financial policies. A search is under way for policies that will strengthen the financial sector so that it can make its full contribution to the efficient use of resources, while keeping its tendency toward instability in check. Chapter 6 examines the legal and institutional changes that should be part of this reappraisal. Chapters 7 and 8 report in more detail on the current provision of financial services to the corporate and noncorporate sectors and explore ways in which these services might be improved. Chapter 9 discusses the lessons that can be learned from the developing countries that have already begun to liberalize their financial sectors.

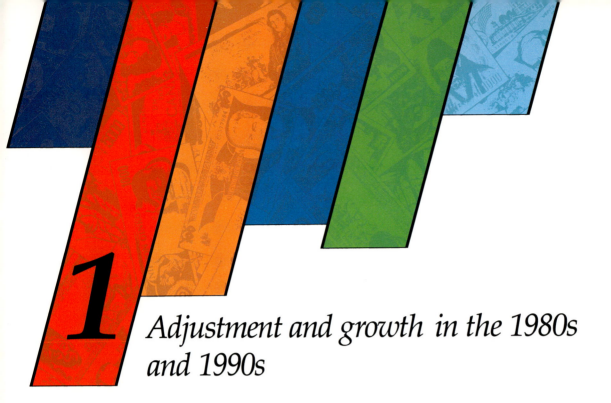

1 Adjustment and growth in the 1980s and 1990s

Economic performance in the 1980s has varied widely among countries and continents. After a sharp recession at the beginning of the decade, the industrial countries are well into their seventh year of uninterrupted growth, although at rates lower than those of the 1950s and 1960s. In parts of Asia, where much of the world's poverty is concentrated, economic growth in the 1980s has been faster than in earlier decades. But in Africa and Latin America hundreds of millions of people have seen economic decline and regression rather than growth and development (see Figure 1.1). In some countries in Latin America real per capita GNP is less than it was a decade ago (see Figure 1.2); in some African countries it is less than it was twenty years ago.

Why have some countries fared so much better than others during the 1980s? Economies differ greatly in their structures, in their domestic development strategies and policies, and in the extent to which they have been affected by external shocks. Higher real interest rates, reduced international capital flows, and lower commodity prices have made adjustment both necessary and difficult, particularly for the highly indebted countries. But some governments have been more successful than others in pursuing short-term adjustment and longer-term structural reform. In addition, markets and agents have varied in the speed with which they responded to new policies and to changed incentives.

The prospects for growth in the developing countries in the coming decade depend primarily on their own actions, but also on the environment created by the actions of the industrial countries. The industrial countries can promote growth in the developing economies in three ways: by adopting fiscal and monetary policies to maintain their own growth while reducing real interest rates, by ensuring the success of the Uruguay Round of trade negotiations and thereby keeping the international trading system open and the volume of trade expanding, and by ensuring that the international community provides the external resources that the developing countries need for growth and adjustment.

The international economic environment

The world economy in the 1980s was dominated first by sharp recession, then by steady and prolonged growth in the industrial countries, high real interest rates, declining real commodity prices, massive movements in exchange rates, and the collapse of voluntary private lending to many developing countries. The recovery of the industrial countries from the recession of 1982 has been strong and so far without interruption—the second longest recovery since World War II. But the mix of fiscal and monetary policies and the resulting pattern of trade and growth have changed over the past eight years.

Figure 1.1 Growth of real GNP in developing countries by region, 1965 to 1988
(average annual percentage change)

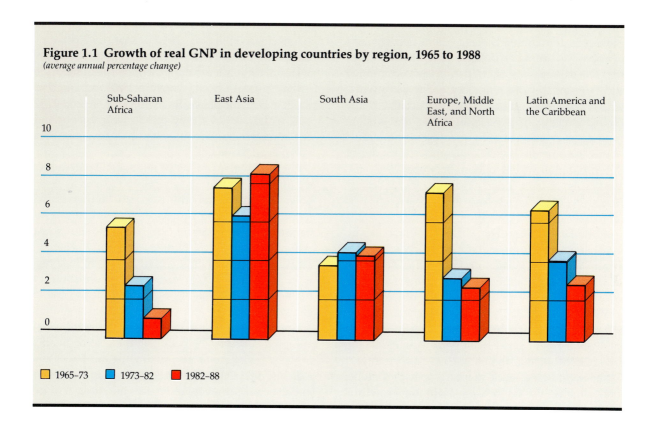

☐ 1965–73   ☐ 1973–82   ☐ 1982–88

Figure 1.2 Real GNP per capita in developing countries by region, 1965 to 1988
(period average in 1980 dollars)

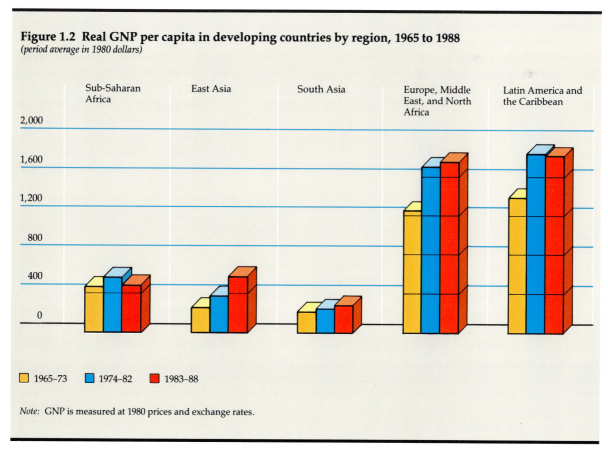

☐ 1965–73   ☐ 1974–82   ☐ 1983–88

Note: GNP is measured at 1980 prices and exchange rates.

The early years of the recovery were led by brisk growth in the United States, where tax cuts and increased spending on defense provided the impetus. The expansionary U.S. fiscal policy, combined with anti-inflationary monetary policy worldwide, led to high real interest rates (especially in the United States), an appreciating dollar, and a boom in imports and consumer spending in the United States. As a result, the U.S. current account deficit deteriorated by $100 billion between 1982 and 1984. This, in turn, led to expectations of a decline in the dollar, which were fulfilled between 1985 and 1987.

In the Federal Republic of Germany and Japan, expansionary policies in 1987 and 1988 were consistent with low inflation because of the decline in oil prices and the appreciations of the yen and the deutsche mark. The transition to domestic-led growth was particularly successful in Japan, where the growth of consumption, imports, and especially investment (a rise of 11 percent in 1988) supported continued growth in the world economy.

The worldwide stock market crash of October 1987 clouded the outlook for economic growth at the beginning of 1988. But vigorous and concerted responses to the crash by monetary authorities in the leading financial centers, some fiscal adjustment in the United States, and cheaper oil all combined to permit steady growth with low inflation in the industrial countries in 1988. Indeed, growth in the high-income countries of the Organisation for Economic Co-operation and Development (OECD) was markedly higher in 1988 than in 1987 (4.2 percent compared with 3.4 percent). Only at the end of the year—as fears grew that pressures on capacity would increase inflation and that the new U.S. administration would not attack the budget deficit—did exchange and interest rates show some of the volatility that had characterized the earlier stages of recovery.

Interest rates

Real interest rates in the 1980s have been higher than at any time since the Great Depression. They climbed during the early part of the decade, as monetary restraint brought down inflation while raising nominal interest rates. One explanation for the persistence of high interest rates is that nominal rates are affected by the fear that inflation will return. This may help to account for high long-term nominal interest rates, but it cannot explain the persistence of high short-term rates.

Another explanation for high interest rates is the decline in the world's saving rate, which appears to have fallen (the data are imprecise) by 2 percentage points in the 1980s, to 11 percent in 1987. Part of this decline is a result of the increase in the U.S. federal budget deficit, which in 1987 amounted to about 8 percent of world saving of just under $2 trillion. Lower saving by other governments and declining private saving rates in many countries also played a role.

World growth can now be maintained with a policy mix in which monetary policy loosens as fiscal policy tightens, with the extent of monetary expansion determined by concerns about future inflation. This combination, including a significant reduction in the U.S. budget deficit and other increases in world saving, would help to reduce real interest rates. That, in turn, would contribute to higher investment and thus to growth led from the supply side.

Lower interest rates would assist growth in developing countries by reducing the cost of financing new investments and easing the burden of the existing debt. The low interest rates of the 1950s and 1960s are unlikely to return, however; real interest rates on safe government bonds may be expected to remain well above the postwar average of 1 percent.

High interest rates have reduced the extent to which developing countries can rely on foreign borrowing to finance development. Higher real interest rates lower the ratio of debt stock to exports that a country can sustain and thereby make net transfers of resources to lenders necessary sooner. Ratios of debt stock to exports that may have been sustainable at the interest rates of the 1970s are not sustainable at the interest rates of the 1980s.

More than in the past, developing countries will have to rely on their own saving to finance investment. This underlines the need for greater efficiency in their financial systems—both to encourage saving and to allocate investment more effectively.

World trade

Growth in the developing world has been affected not only by the growth of imports by the industrial countries but also by the changing source and composition of import demand. Figure 1.3 shows the relationship between world economic growth and world trade. The recession of 1982 hurt world trade overall, but developing country trade fell proportionately more. In general, the volume of world trade fluctuates more than world growth, and developing country trade is even more volatile. Resilient economies can absorb these shocks and rebound rapidly. For example, open economies that depend on manufactured exports, such as some of the newly industrialized economies of East Asia, were particularly hard hit by the slump in world trade in 1982. But these outward-oriented countries experienced faster export growth during the 1980s, and their economies have grown much more quickly than those of countries that pursued more inward-oriented policies.

Export growth not only contributes directly to economic growth but, more important, also permits more imports and a rapid modernization of production. The result is efficient domestic industry that meets the market test of international competition. High export growth among East Asian countries and low export growth in Latin America and Africa have significantly changed the regional distribution of developing country exports during the 1980s (see Figure 1.4).

The volume of world trade increased by more than 9 percent in 1988—the fastest growth in the 1980s. Trade patterns have been strongly affected by the expansion of domestic demand in Japan and the delayed effects of exchange rate movements. Import volume in Japan was up by 17 percent in 1988, compared with an 8 percent increase in the European countries; the yen moved significantly more against the dollar than did the European currencies. The middle-income countries of East Asia sharply increased their exports to Japan, and East Asian intraregional trade increased by 30 percent.

Oil and commodity prices

Massive swings in the price of oil and a prolonged decline in the real prices of other commodities have posed short- and long-term adjustment problems for producers and consumers alike in the 1980s. The real price of oil (deflated by the unit value of manufactures) more than doubled from 1978 to 1981, peaking at six times its 1973 level. It then drifted downward for several years, collapsing to its pre-1973 level late in 1988, when the market price dipped below $11, before quickly rebounding to $20 in the first part of 1989. The real prices of most other commodities continued to decline during the 1980s, except for minor price run-ups such as the revival of metal prices in 1988 (see Figure 1.5).

The large swings in the relative prices of commodities (especially oil) have made it harder for governments (especially in commodity-producing

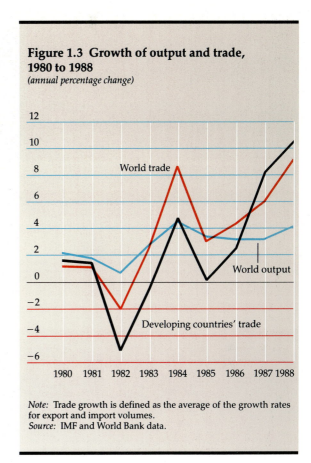

Figure 1.3 Growth of output and trade, 1980 to 1988
(annual percentage change)

World trade

World output

Developing countries' trade

Note: Trade growth is defined as the average of the growth rates for export and import volumes.
Source: IMF and World Bank data.

countries) to manage demand and exchange rates. Oil price increases and the surge in the value of oil exports put upward pressure on the producers' exchange rates and thereby harmed non-oil exports and encouraged imports. This difficulty—known as the Dutch disease—has been faced by high-income countries (such as the Netherlands and the United Kingdom) and low-income countries (such as Nigeria and Egypt) alike. When the commodity boom passed, trade deficits followed. Moreover, in some countries oil taxes supported public spending programs that have since been difficult to curb. As a result of the decline in the price of oil since 1982, gross domestic product (GDP) in the oil-exporting countries grew by only 1.6 percent annually between 1982 and 1988, compared with 5.0 percent between 1973 and 1982.

Countries that depend on commodity exports should save more—run larger current account surpluses or smaller deficits—while export revenues are temporarily high. It is difficult, however, to distinguish between temporary and permanent changes in commodity prices. Was the upturn in metal prices in 1988 part of a medium-term trend,

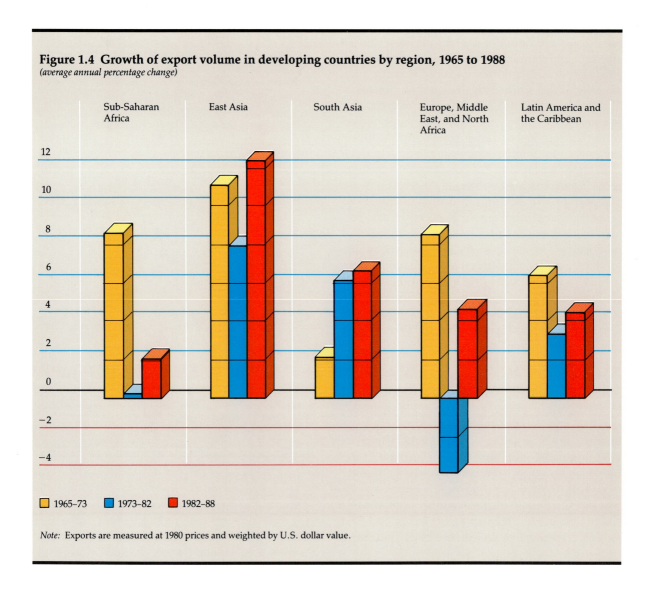

Figure 1.4 Growth of export volume in developing countries by region, 1965 to 1988
(average annual percentage change)

Legend: 1965–73 | 1973–82 | 1982–88

Note: Exports are measured at 1980 prices and weighted by U.S. dollar value.

or was it a temporary blip? Moreover, despite the uncertainties, it may be politically difficult for poor producers to take a conservative view of the likely course of commodity prices. Some exporters of oil and other commodities, such as Chile, Indonesia, Kuwait, and Morocco, have succeeded in spreading risk, both by diversifying production and through financial and fiscal management. But many others, to their detriment, have not.

Structural adjustment policies and challenges

The setback to development in Africa, Latin America, and Eastern Europe in the 1980s followed two decades of rapid growth. Yet this growth was often founded on development strategies that failed to emphasize economic efficiency and international

competitiveness and that drew finance from abroad by distorting the domestic financial system. External shocks precipitated the crisis of the 1980s. But internal structure determined how countries would respond. Faced with changed circumstances, countries now have no choice but to adjust. During the 1980s governments of countries at all income levels and, remarkably, of all ideological stripes have come to recognize the need for reforms to increase economic efficiency and flexibility.

At the most abstract level, adjustment programs use changes in fiscal, monetary, and sectoral policies, in regulations, and in institutions to alter relative prices and the level of spending and thereby redirect economic activity. The real exchange rate and the real interest rate are key relative prices.

They affect both economic activity and saving, as well as exports and imports and the rate of investment. Changes in taxes, subsidies, and quantitative controls move resources between sectors. Ensuring that adjustment achieves a balanced change in spending and an appropriate sectoral reallocation is critical for growth and development. The domestic financial system plays an important role. It mobilizes domestic saving and directs it to the most profitable investments.

Structural adjustment is complicated and slow. It is especially difficult now—and all the more necessary—because many developing countries are in dire financial straits. Countries need external resources to offset the costs of adjustment. In the 1980s both the International Monetary Fund (IMF) and the World Bank have helped finance economic programs contributing to the adjustment process. Fifty-nine countries received long-term structural adjustment loans from the World Bank between 1980 and 1988. The programs consist of a series of operations, worked out with the borrower, that are conducted within a medium-term macroeconomic framework which is often supported by the IMF.

Many governments have made progress toward restructuring their economies, especially with regard to trade reform and exchange rate policy. But further reforms will be necessary. In some cases industrial policies in support of earlier import-substitution strategies have maintained a protectionist stance, despite trade reform. In other cases inefficient financial systems continue to distort interest rates. In many countries the failure of fiscal reforms is undermining the adjustment achieved so far and preventing further progress. Unsustainable fiscal deficits create economic uncertainty, contribute to high inflation, and subvert the domestic financial system.

In East Asia the newly industrialized economies and several others have pursued sound macroeconomic policies and maintained the competitiveness of their exports. They have generally adapted well to the shocks of the 1970s and early 1980s. The populous economies of South Asia have also achieved good results. Their success has more to do with macroeconomic stability, prudent fiscal and external borrowing policies, and rural modernization than with internationally competitive trade policies. But economies are not prisoners of their geography. Chile has pursued one of the most wide-ranging programs of economic liberalization, despite setbacks in the early 1980s, and seems to be shedding the problems that beset many of its neighbors.

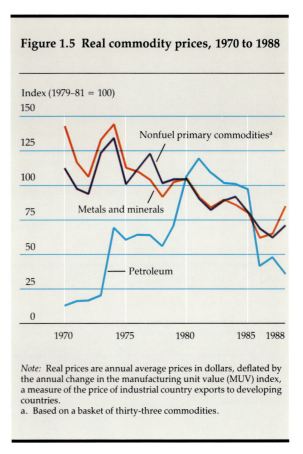

Figure 1.5 Real commodity prices, 1970 to 1988

Index (1979–81 = 100)

Nonfuel primary commodities[a]

Metals and minerals

Petroleum

Note: Real prices are annual average prices in dollars, deflated by the annual change in the manufacturing unit value (MUV) index, a measure of the price of industrial country exports to developing countries.
a. Based on a basket of thirty-three commodities.

Challenges for successful adjusters

Successful adjusters, especially those in East Asia, not only increased domestic saving and maintained high investment during the 1980s (see Figure 1.6) but also achieved export-led growth. In the future their growth will need to depend less on external demand; domestic consumers should reap some of the fruits of successful investment in manufacturing. Domestic saving rates may therefore return to their somewhat lower levels of the 1970s.

Maintaining competitiveness requires support for the development of infrastructure and human capital. In most countries such programs are government funded. They call for long-term investment strategies. Sound fiscal policy is a prerequisite.

Moreover, as the successful adjusters become more integrated with the international capital markets, and as they compete with the next generation of exporters of manufactured goods, the efficient allocation of domestic saving will become even more important. A domestic financial system

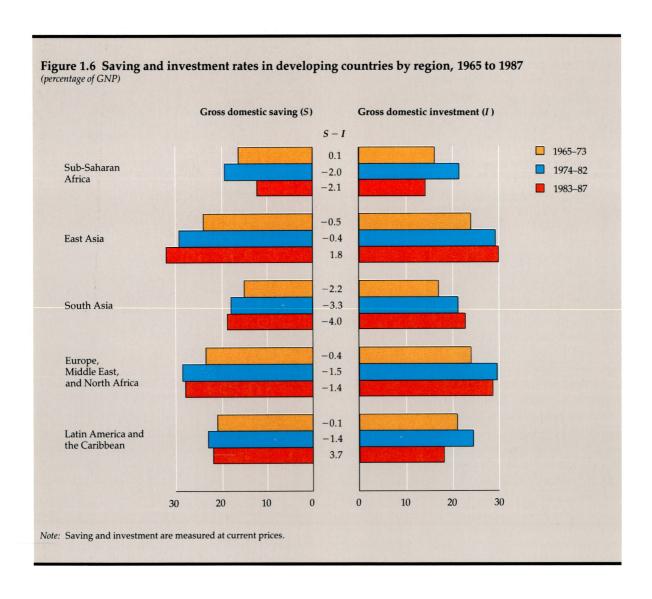

Figure 1.6 Saving and investment rates in developing countries by region, 1965 to 1987
(percentage of GNP)

Gross domestic saving (S)   Gross domestic investment (I)

S − I

Region					

Sub-Saharan Africa: 0.1, −2.0, −2.1

East Asia: −0.5, −0.4, 1.8

South Asia: −2.2, −3.3, −4.0

Europe, Middle East, and North Africa: −0.4, −1.5, −1.4

Latin America and the Caribbean: −0.1, −1.4, 3.7

Legend: 1965–73, 1974–82, 1983–87

Note: Saving and investment are measured at current prices.

based on market principles will contribute to this end.

Adjustment in Sub-Saharan Africa

The gravest development problems are in Sub-Saharan Africa. Unfavorable external conditions (including a prolonged fall in the terms of trade of primary goods exporters) and inadequate domestic policies have caused economic, social, and environmental decline.

After reasonable growth in the 1960s and early 1970s, the region's economic performance deteriorated. Export growth was robust before the 1973 oil shock but stalled thereafter; it has recovered somewhat but not to previous levels. Saving and investment rates fell sharply in the early 1980s (Figure 1.6) and are today less than two-thirds of the developing country average. The collapse in saving is partly attributable to fiscal deficits, which expanded during the 1980s. Private saving did not increase either—but it is extremely difficult to increase saving when income is falling. Most important, the combination of slow growth and rapidly expanding populations reduced per capita incomes and left many people close to starvation. Average caloric intake is no higher than twenty years ago.

Nevertheless, some adjustment—painfully slow and not always sustained—is occurring. Many governments have started to reduce their role in the economy and are focusing their spending on priority areas. This means curbing spending on the civil service, on subsidies, and on state-owned enterprises. Some African governments (for example, in Ghana) have cut spending by creating a roster of the civil servants to ensure that only bona fide workers—and no "ghost" or "phantom" workers—are on the payroll. An alternative is to release workers with a lump-sum benefit. This increases the short-run cost of reducing the size of the government, and may encourage the better workers to leave, but in some countries it has provided an impetus for the development of private entrepreneurship. A sweeping removal of subsidies may not be possible, but targeting them to the truly needy further reduces costs; many subsidies benefit urban dwellers who are relatively well-off. Ghana's program has kept adjustment on track while helping the poor. Subsidies to unprofitable state-owned enterprises are a big drain on budgets. Several African countries have experimented with privatization (Niger and Togo), liquidation (Benin, Ghana, and Mali), or rehabilitation under management contracts (Senegal). Not all of these efforts have been successful.

It is essential to correct overvalued exchange rates. This promotes a more sustainable pattern of consumption, encourages the export sector to diversify, and may yield faster export growth. Côte d'Ivoire and Mauritius show how quickly exporters can respond to improvement (and deterioration) in real export prices.

Adjustment also aims to reverse the bias against agriculture. Taxes in many poor countries (not only in Africa) discourage domestic food production and encourage food imports. Better incentives and agricultural modernization can raise the incomes of the rural poor, increase food security, and generate foreign exchange. Policies of this sort include price decontrol (Mali, Niger, Nigeria, Somalia, and Uganda) and the reform or abolition of agricultural marketing boards (Nigeria, Senegal, and Somalia). Higher farm output has also been achieved through broadly conceived extension services, which combine changes in farming methods with improvements in credit delivery, marketing, and the supply of inputs.

Regional integration has been a political aspiration since African independence. Cooperative arrangements have continued in Francophone Africa but have often broken down elsewhere. Small internal markets and low purchasing power are barriers to international competitiveness and the rationale for regional integration. As governments have moved to more market-oriented policies, at least one impediment to integration has been removed. But even if agreement on its political aspects could be reached, the benefits of integration will not be attained unless regional transport and communications systems are upgraded.

Even as economic performance improves, it will be offset by rapid population growth in much of Sub-Saharan Africa. In several countries (Kenya, Senegal, and Somalia), fairly strong economic growth in the 1980s has yielded low or negative growth in per capita GNP. Excessive population growth also exacerbates the problems of food security, education, urbanization, and environmental degradation.

Adjustment in the highly indebted countries

The shocks of the 1980s also hit the highly indebted middle-income countries, most of them in Latin America, extremely hard. High commodity prices and cheap external financing fueled public investment and social welfare programs during the 1970s. When the external environment deteriorated and commodity prices fell, many countries postponed adjustment and continued to rely on external borrowing. Sharply rising real interest rates and falling commodity prices raised the cost of external capital dramatically in the 1980s, which led to a halt in voluntary financing. Wrenching adjustments became necessary.

Per capita incomes in the middle-income debtors declined on average during the 1980s. Restrictive domestic policies and real devaluations reduced imports, which often led to trade and even current account surpluses. These policies, combined with the lack of external financing, meant that net investment in some countries, such as Argentina, fell to zero.

The task of adjustment encompasses trade reform, fiscal and public sector reform, and control of inflation and debt. Most of the countries have made substantial progress in at least one of these areas. But the macroeconomic situation remains unstable, and rates of investment are still low (Figure 1.6).

Primary budget deficits (that is, excluding debt service payments) have been reduced, but public sector borrowing requirements remain high. Consolidated, inflation-corrected deficits are still nearly double the average for the developing world as a share of GDP, and interest payments account for a big share of spending. Since domestic financial markets are in most cases too shallow to provide financing on the required scale, central banks have accommodated government spending by expanding the monetary base. Inflation is higher than elsewhere; several of the countries have seen triple- and even quadruple-digit inflation.

Heterodox anti-inflationary programs (based on wage and price controls and the fixing of the exchange rate) have been tried, sometimes repeatedly, in Argentina, Brazil, and Mexico. Most of these attempts have met with outright failure. Their chief defect has been a lack of fiscal improvement. Stabilization programs that leave the fundamentals inconsistent with low inflation are bound to fail. Where the fiscal deficit has been cut appropriately—as in Mexico—the programs have been more successful.

Some highly indebted countries (Costa Rica, Côte d'Ivoire, and the Philippines) have adopted fiscal programs with moderate success, although the programs have yet to be sustained. Often, several years of austerity have been followed by a burst of spending that reverses the earlier gains. Such instability retards saving, investment, exports, and growth. Nonetheless, some debtor countries have made good progress on fiscal reform. Chile, Colombia, Mexico, Morocco, and Uruguay have all reduced their budget deficits through tax reform, higher revenues, and lower spending.

Some countries, again including Chile, Mexico, and Morocco, have also pursued trade reform. For example, since 1985 Mexico has liberalized its trade regime and maintained its competitiveness. Costa Rica and the Philippines have focused on labor-intensive manufactured exports; in these countries the share of manufactured exports increased steadily between 1982 and 1987, and manufactures now account for about half of all exports.

Adjustment in the centrally planned economies

The centrally planned economies face a formidable challenge in moving toward decentralized decisionmaking and greater reliance on markets. The prices of many of their products have little to do with costs. The responsibilities of managers for production and investment are badly defined. Financial systems are rudimentary, and the tools of macroeconomic management are underdeveloped. Few mechanisms allow labor and capital to be reallocated as economic conditions change.

Governments in many of these economies have recognized the need for reform. The task is daunting, but the benefits could be immense. The experience of China during the past ten years demonstrates this. The reform of agriculture, the opening of the economy to foreign trade, technology, and investment, and the new reliance on incentives in the industrial sector have led to an average growth rate of more than 10 percent a year during the 1980s.

Although prices still play a relatively modest role

in the Chinese economy, the exchange rate adjustments of the early 1980s were essential in making Chinese enterprises more competitive. China has become a major exporter of manufactures in a very short time. The Chinese government also avoided relying too much on external borrowing. It postponed ambitious industrial investment programs in the late 1970s and again in the early 1980s. More recently it has faced difficulties in macroeconomic policy. Domestic credit has been allowed to expand too quickly, which has led to inflationary pressures and shortages.

Economic reforms in Eastern Europe, although similar to those in China, have had less spectacular results, and some countries are in considerable difficulty. Several factors explain this. One is that low costs of production, at present exchange rates, have enabled China to compete successfully against middle-income exporters of manufactures. In contrast, costs in Eastern Europe are generally higher; competing against the newly industrialized economies of East Asia and the lower-income members of the European Community (EC) has therefore been difficult. Moreover, some of the countries tried to modernize their industries with heavy investment financed by foreign borrowing and without reforming economic management. This proved costly when real interest rates rose in the 1980s.

Development issues

The slow pace of adjustment in many countries is a major concern. But the task is neither simple nor purely economic. It requires institutional capacity and political skill. It is inhibited by vested interests, for it affects acquired rights, income, benefits, rents, and costs. Where economic structures have been in place for some time, the pain of adjustment can be enormous. If reform is to last, it must not be rushed. The burden will have to be fairly shared. And support from the international community must be forthcoming.

Poverty, population growth, and the environment

In many countries poverty cannot be separated from rapid population growth. As per capita incomes rise, population growth rates eventually decline. That process has been at work in such countries as the Republic of Korea and Thailand, as it was earlier in the high-income economies. But the demographic transition is still at an early stage in some low-income Asian countries, such as India and Bangladesh. Africa's population is growing faster than has that of any other region of the world in this century. In some countries fertility rates are close to the biological limit. This strains the capacity of the economy to maintain the standard of living and reduces the ability of the government to provide social services, including education and health. Yet some societies remain unconvinced of the need to reduce population growth.

The links among poverty, environmental degradation, and population growth are often direct. As more and more people in poverty press upon limited natural resources in rural areas, they begin to deplete the stock of renewable resources. In South Asia the long-term deforestation of watersheds has caused severe erosion. Population pressure on the fragile land base in Africa and the Middle East has become serious. The arid and semiarid areas of the world are likely to face a crisis of water scarcity by 2000. Desertification and deforestation—often irreversible—have reduced the land available for agriculture, wildlife habitats, and recreation.

But not all environmental degradation results from the pressure of population growth. Intensive use of hydrocarbons by high-income countries and deforestation in sparsely populated tropical areas are starting to have global effects. The same is true of the growing amounts of hazardous materials that are generated mainly by industrial countries. Some developing countries are experiencing serious air and water pollution. Increasingly—although with differing degrees of urgency—developing country governments are attempting to curb the adverse externalities of growth.

Protectionism and trade

The acknowledged success of outward-oriented development is partly responsible for the move toward market-based policies. Moreover, the high-income countries recognize the role of trade in promoting growth and industrial development in the low- and middle-income countries—and thus have accorded them a variety of concessions and preferences. (These include the Generalized System of Preferences, the EC's Lomé Convention, and the U.S. Caribbean Basin Initiative.) Despite this, and despite the encouraging growth in world trade in recent years, the world's trading system has become markedly less liberal. Governments have reduced conventional tariff protection but have raised other barriers to trade instead.

Specific "safeguard actions" taken by industrial countries increasingly discriminate against the developing countries. Voluntary restraint agreements for steel, bilateral agreements for textiles, the tighter Multifibre Arrangement (MFA), and lower quotas on sugar and other agricultural products have their greatest effect on the exports of the developing countries. The share of developing country exports that face nontariff barriers (NTBs) is roughly 20 percent, about twice the share of industrial country exports. Much of the discussion of NTBs focuses on manufactured goods, but the proportion of agricultural exports from the developing countries facing NTBs is higher (26 percent, compared with 18 percent for manufactures).

Another disturbing departure from the principle of nondiscrimination embodied in the General Agreement on Tariffs and Trade (GATT) is the increase in bilateral trade agreements. Bilateral arrangements could—although they need not necessarily—discriminate against nonmembers (see Box 1.1). If they do, they might greatly harm the world trading system.

The rise of bilateralism and the increasing use of nontariff barriers underline the importance of the Uruguay Round of trade negotiations. These talks are tackling complicated issues such as trade in services, the protection of intellectual property rights, and the politically contentious matter of agricultural trade reform. Progress on agriculture would be particularly welcome for some of the highly indebted countries, such as Argentina and Brazil. Agreements on trade in financial services might prepare the way for greater integration of domestic financial systems and international capital markets, resulting in improvements in efficiency and resource allocation.

Many developing countries have significantly liberalized trade in the course of their broad structural adjustment programs. These steps have benefited the countries taking them. However, it is often believed that countries which liberalize unilaterally lose a bargaining chip that might have been used at the GATT negotiations to increase their access to export markets. In fact, credit is given in the GATT for the binding of (that is, acceptance of treaty limits on) tariffs. Such commitments can be negotiated and traded even after tariffs have been unilaterally reduced.

Developing countries can also improve their export prospects by following an appropriate exchange rate policy. Many developing countries have corrected their overvalued exchange rates in the 1980s; real effective exchange rates have declined for most developing countries (see Figure

Box 1.1 Project 1992 and the developing countries

The European Community (EC) plans to "complete the internal market" by 1992 by removing barriers to the free circulation of goods, services, and factors of production. The aim is to promote European specialization, strengthen competition, and increase efficiency. But Project 1992 is bound to have substantial implications for non-EC countries. The EC market accounts for about 30 percent of the export earnings of the developing countries.

To achieve the free movement of goods and services within the EC, three measures will be required, each of which has an impact on the developing countries. The first is the *abolition of border controls*. These are used to enforce national quantitative restrictions (QRs). They affect mainly imports of textiles and clothing covered by the Multifibre Arrangement, but other imports from developing economies, such as bananas from Latin America and toys from Asia, are also affected. The EC may convert national QRs into community-wide QRs. What happens will depend on the outcome of the Uruguay Round.

The second measure is the *elimination of technical barriers* to trade. This will proceed along two separate avenues: mutual recognition (most barriers) and harmonization (health, safety, and environmental regulations). The principle of mutual recognition implies that products legally marketed in one member state, whether manufactured in the EC or imported into the EC, can circulate freely throughout the EC. This should be especially welcome to relatively small suppliers in the developing countries, since the added costs of technical barriers are particularly onerous for them.

The third measure is the *opening up of public procurement*. This will extend to four key areas not covered by the relevant GATT code: energy, telecommunications, transport, and water supply. To the extent that public procurement concentrates on high-technology sectors, the change will matter more to the industrial than to the developing countries.

If Project 1992 promotes faster domestic growth without raising external trade barriers, Europe will import more, and the developing countries would benefit. The distribution of the new demand among exporters will depend on its composition and on existing trade preferences. The main focus of Project 1992 is on trade in manufactures. The effects of the single market on developing countries will depend on their competitiveness and on the EC's trade policy toward them. The nature of EC trade preferences toward different groups of developing countries may also change as a result of the introduction of a unified market.

1.7). Countries with an appropriate real exchange rate have usually experienced faster and more stable growth than the rest. As development proceeds, it becomes even more important to adopt and maintain an industrialization strategy that is neutral toward production for domestic or foreign markets.

In the Uruguay Round the developing countries are for the first time playing a significant role in multilateral trade negotiations. Thirteen developing and industrial countries have formed the Cairns Group to promote their common interests as agricultural producers. The developing countries have recognized their stake in the world trading system. This reinforces the need for a successful conclusion to the Uruguay Round and for adherence to the spirit as well as the letter of the principles of the GATT. The proposed strengthening of the GATT, including its surveillance of countries' trade policies, should help to bring this about. The failure of the Uruguay Round would not only hamper the growth of world trade but also represent a rejection of the development strategy that has been promoted by the international community and multilateral organizations, at the very time that developing countries are coming to accept it.

The debt problem

Although many developing countries have had difficulty in servicing their external debt, from the start of the debt crisis in 1982 the focus has been on the seventeen highly indebted middle-income countries whose debts are primarily to the commercial banks. This reflects the systemic risk that the failure of creditor banks might have posed to the international financial system in the early years of the crisis. Although some banks remain at risk, the debt strategy they have followed since 1982 has sought to remove this systemic risk by building up appropriate provisions for doubtful assets. In the past few years the debt problems of Sub-Saharan Africa have won official recognition. These problems differ from those of the other highly indebted countries in that the debt is owed mainly to governments. Nonetheless, virtually all the debtor countries have been adversely affected by the rise in real interest rates and the decline in commercial bank lending since 1982.

Systemic collapse has been avoided. But for most of the highly indebted countries the debt crisis has become a growth crisis as well. In 1988 they grew by less than 2 percent, failing to respond both to high export demand and to the rapid growth of the high-income countries. (Export volume increased by about 6 percent, and dollar unit values rose by more than 15 percent in a delayed reaction to the sharp depreciation of the dollar.) Their situation did show one sign of improvement during 1988, however. The ratio of debt stock to exports declined for the first time since 1982. Nevertheless, two major Latin American debtors (Argentina and Brazil) experienced significant economic instability during the year.

Korea has shown that it is possible to grow out of a heavy debt burden. But when commercial creditors are reluctant to increase their exposure in countries with debt problems and domestic savings are transferred abroad to service the debt, borrowers cannot finance the investment they need to generate growth. The resources for investment could come from higher domestic saving or from repatriated capital. Before 1982 the highly indebted countries received about 2 percent of GNP a year in resources from abroad; since then they have transferred roughly 3 percent of GNP a year in the opposite direction. Domestic saving would have had to rise by 5 percent of GNP—or in other words by about a quarter—to offset this change in net transfers. Despite strong fiscal contraction in some countries, none of the countries has succeeded in restoring adequate net investment (see Box 1.2).

The Baker initiative of 1985 stressed the need to maintain net flows of funds from official and private lenders. Although net flows of long-term capital from official creditors averaged nearly $6 billion a year over the past three years, net flows from commercial banks fell to an average of less than $2 billion a year.

During 1988 and 1989, governments and creditor banks alike concluded that debt reduction would have to be an element in resolving the debt crisis. Creditor governments agreed at the 1988 Toronto summit to grant debt relief to the poorest and most heavily indebted countries, such as the countries of Sub-Saharan Africa. The Paris Club subsequently agreed on the equivalence among the various types of debt relief granted by different creditor governments. For private creditors, the menu approach that has been developed since 1986 has created a variety of voluntary methods of debt re-

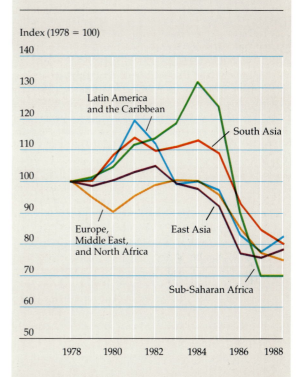

Figure 1.7 Real effective exchange rates in developing countries by region, 1978 to 1988

Index (1978 = 100)

Note: The real effective exchange rate is the trade-weighted exchange rate adjusted for relative inflation. An increase in the index indicates an appreciation of the currency. The regional index values, which are based on a total sample of eighty-three developing countries, are annual averages weighted by the dollar value of exports.
Source: IMF and World Bank data.

duction. These include debt buybacks (in which a debtor buys back part of its foreign debt with either international reserves or new foreign exchange), exit bonds, and debt-equity swaps. In all these cases the benefits for the debtor vary according to the discount at which it acquires its existing debt. In 1988 the commercial banks reached a major refinancing agreement with Brazil—at $82 billion, the largest on record—which contained financial innovations allowing for debt reduction. But for the highly indebted countries in general, the net reduction in external obligations achieved to date has been small.

The prolongation of the debt crisis, and particularly its manifestation in the low growth rates of heavily indebted countries, led the international community to reevaluate the debt strategy in 1989.

Box 1.2 Debt concepts

A variety of concepts are used to measure and assess the economic burden of external debt.

Debt stock, which is often reported as debt outstanding and disbursed, measures the total debt liabilities of the debtor. The payment obligation arising from this is *debt service* and comprises interest and principal payments. The debt stock does not necessarily predict the debt service because currency revaluations, interest rates, and the maturity structure of the debt all affect debt service.

Two concepts describe the net effect of borrowing and repayments on the flow of financial resources. *Net flows* refers to disbursements minus principal repayments. It measures whether new financing exceeds debt being retired. If debt levels remain prudent, net flows should be positive in all but the most advanced low- and middle-income countries because of continued external financing for domestic investment. *Net transfers* refers to disbursements minus interest and principal repayments. Negative net transfers imply that total debt service payments exceed gross inflows, that net real resources are being transferred from the economy, and that a trade surplus is thus required. When the real interest rate exceeds the growth rate, any borrower must expect eventually to make net transfers to its creditors. At that stage the borrower's income should have risen sufficiently for its saving to finance the transfer. The increase in the real interest

rate in the early 1980s forced many developing countries to make net transfers abroad much earlier than they had expected.

Moratoria (the suspension of contractual debt service payments), *arrears* (overdue service payments), *new money* (additional borrowing), *rescheduling* (changing the time profile of repayments without altering the total debt obligation), and *debt relief* are all ways of altering either the pattern or size of repayment flows. Forward-looking and sustainable changes in debt structure are more likely to create the environment needed for domestic investment and growth than are arrears or annual renegotiations.

Box table 1.2 shows how the burden of debt of the developing countries has changed during the 1980s. Debt stocks in Latin America and Sub-Saharan Africa have grown as a share of GNP during the 1980s, but private credit flows now represent a much smaller share of gross disbursements, especially to Latin America.

Net flows remain positive, except to middle-income East Asia; these countries are repaying debt out of efficiently invested borrowing. In most developing countries net transfers have turned sharply negative. Except in Sub-Saharan Africa and low-income Asia, resources are being transferred to creditors at rates significantly higher than those at which resources were received in 1981.

Box table 1.2 Long-term lending to developing countries, 1981 and 1987
(billions of dollars, unless otherwise noted)

Item	All developing countries 1981	1987	Sub-Saharan Africa 1981	1987	Middle-income East Asia 1981	1987	Low-income Asia 1981	1987	Europe, Middle East, and North Africa 1981	1987	Latin America and the Caribbean 1981	1987
Total long-term debt outstanding and disbursed	503	996	50	109	50	102	60	142	134	260	209	384
As a percentage of GNP	23	42	26	85	28	40	8	16	30	47	27	52
Gross disbursements of long-term lending	124	87	11	9	14	11	11	21	28	27	61	20
Private sources	92	49	6	3	10	8	5	10	17	18	53	10
As a percentage of total	74	56	58	32	75	73	45	48	62	68	88	49
Multilateral sources	12	22	2	4	2	2	3	6	2	5	3	6
Net flows[a]	77	16	8	5	10	−9	6	11	14	3	39	5
Private sources	53	−2	4	1	7	−8	2	4	7	7	34	1
Multilateral sources	10	12	2	3	1	0	2	5	2	2	2	3
Net transfers[b]	35	−38	6	2	6	−16	4	5	4	−12	16	−19

Note: Data are based on the sample of 111 countries participating in the Debtor Reporting System.
a. Gross disbursements minus principal repayments.
b. Gross disbursements minus the sum of interest and principal payments.

Although the details of the new strategy are still being worked out, the overall framework is clear. Debt reduction will receive official support and official funding from the IMF and the World Bank, provided it takes place in the context of strong, effective adjustment programs. The strategy will continue to treat each country separately and is likely to evolve as particular countries reach new agreements with their creditors and official agencies. It will aim to reward those countries that have tried hardest to restructure their economies. Very few creditor governments will be willing to contribute resources directly, but they are reviewing regulatory and accounting obstacles that might impede debt relief by private creditors. They will also encourage the creditor banks to waive the clauses in existing agreements that make debt reduction difficult to arrange.

The new strategy recognizes that debtor countries will continue to need new money from abroad. The question arises whether debt reduction is consistent with new lending from existing creditors. The stakes for banks in some of the larger countries are high enough for them to continue to provide new money, even as they simultaneously agree to reduce debt. But some banks will not want to reduce debt and provide new money at the same time. Official financing will continue. Increasingly, countries will have to look to new forms of external finance, such as direct and portfolio equity investment, and to the return of flight capital.

The most critical component of the debt strategy remains continued adjustment by the debtor countries. Without strong adjustment, no debt strategy can restore growth. It is the goal of the new strategy to ensure that countries that do pursue serious adjustment policies will be able to return to growth.

The debt crisis illustrates the fundamental tension between dependence on private markets on the one hand and government intervention on the other—a theme that recurs later in this Report. Because commercial banks were heavily exposed when the debt crisis began in 1982, creditor governments intervened to ensure the stability of the international financial system. Individual debtor governments, such as those of Argentina, Chile, and Yugoslavia, acquired large amounts of private debt in the belief that doing so would help them to preserve relations with the commercial banks. If the exposure of the banks had been small enough to pose no threat to their solvency, they might have reached agreements with the debtors on their own. And then the crisis would have taken a very different course.

Growth prospects

Uncertainty after the stock market crash of 1987 reduced expectations of growth early in 1988. Those expectations were confounded by a year of strong growth, which has bolstered the prospects for a gradual return to trend growth of about 3 percent for the high-income OECD countries. Expansion in Japan and Europe, especially in Germany and the United Kingdom, broadens the basis for sustained growth. Moreover, the high rate of investment in 1988 should increase capacity and productivity, which will help to ease inflationary pressures.

Lingering uncertainties, however, cloud the medium-term forecast. They concern the policy changes needed to reduce large domestic and international imbalances and to offset growing inflationary pressures in several of the large economies. The United States can continue to run a current account deficit only if foreign investors and governments are willing to purchase its assets. This, in turn, depends on their expectations with regard to economic stability in the United States, the U.S. fiscal deficit, and U.S. interest rates relative to those in other economies. Moreover, within Europe, major imbalances could strain the European Monetary System. The scale of these international imbalances, concern about inflation, and needed adjustments in monetary policy are likely to cause volatility in interest rates and exchange rates over the near term.

Accordingly, the World Bank has prepared two views of the next decade. One scenario is predicated on adjustment with growth. It assumes that credible policy actions are taken to reduce the macroeconomic imbalances within and among the industrial countries. Such measures include a program to reduce the U.S. budget deficit, followed by an easing in monetary policy (more so in the United States than elsewhere). Real and nominal interest rates therefore fall, as compared with the 1980–88 averages, and the dollar depreciates further against the currencies of the other big industrial countries. Structural adjustment policies of the kind discussed above enable the low- and middle-income countries to take advantage of growth; the lower interest rates ease their debt burden. This combination of plausible adjustments by both high-income and low- and middle-income governments yields, overall, good prospects for

Table 1.1 Selected economic indicators in the adjustment-with-growth and low scenarios
(average annual percentage change)

Indicator	Trend for 1965–87	Recent experience, 1980–88	Scenario for 1988–95	
			Adjustment with growth	Low
High-income OECD countries				
GDP growth	3.1	2.7	2.6	2.4
Inflation (local currency)	6.4	5.6	4.2	4.1
Nominal rate of interest[a]	8.8	10.2	8.6	9.5
Real rate of interest[a,b]	3.0	5.5	3.0	4.0
Low- and middle-income countries				
Merchandise export volume	3.8	5.4	5.1	4.1
Manufactures	12.0	10.0	7.4	5.7
Primary goods	1.3	2.5	2.8	2.7
Merchandise import volume	4.3	0.5	5.7	4.6

Note: The adjustment-with-growth scenario assumes the adoption of policies (by the major industrial and developing countries) that reduce structural rigidities and imbalances and allow for a gradual return to trend through the year 2000. The low scenario assumes that some needed policy changes are not made, interest rates remain high, growth falters, and there is increased protectionism.
a. Average six-month rate on Eurodollar deposits.
b. Nominal interest rate deflated by the GDP deflator for the United States.

world growth through the year 2000. Even so, many low- and middle-income countries would be unlikely to achieve the high growth rates they experienced in the 1960s and 1970s.

The alternative is the low scenario. It assumes that the appropriate policy actions are taken neither in the high-income countries nor in certain of the low- and middle-income countries. Crisis is averted through continued financing of the imbalances, but the low scenario entails great macroeconomic uncertainty, higher real and nominal interest rates, increased protectionism, and lower growth.

Key factors underlying these two scenarios are summarized in Table 1.1. With adjustment, real GDP growth in the high-income OECD countries averages 2.6 percent over the medium term (1988–95) and rises to trend growth of about 3 percent by the year 2000. Inflation measured in local currencies averages about 4 percent a year. Some adjustment by the United States as well as other increases in world saving lower real interest rates to 3.0 percent from their average of 5.5 percent in the 1980s. Merchandise exports of the low- and middle-income countries should grow by more than 5 percent a year, with the demand for manufactured exports rising at more than 7 percent a year. A bias toward investment helps to raise commodity prices in nominal terms, but in real terms (deflated by the unit value of manufactures) they are expected to continue to decline through 1995. This underlines the need for the developing countries that rely on primary commodity exports to diversify their economies.

Without appropriate policy changes, the low scenario shows growth in the high-income OECD countries slowing to 2.4 percent a year in the medium term and through 2000. That is significantly less than the average for the 1970s and 1980s. Growth in trade is correspondingly lower. More important, the failure to right macroeconomic imbalances keeps real and nominal interest rates high (about 4 and 10 percent respectively). Lower external demand and higher interest rates reduce the prospects for growth in the low- and middle-income countries to below the averages of the 1980s.

How does the adjustment-with-growth scenario in the high-income countries affect the growth prospects of the low- and middle-income countries? The answer largely depends on their own policy adjustments and on population growth. East and South Asian countries, which have stable macroeconomic environments and a substantial share of manufactures in exports, are expected to grow at about 6 percent a year (see Table 1.2). Some of them are likely to "graduate" to the high-income category. Moreover, because their population growth is expected to slow, per capita income in some countries rises by more than 5 percent a year. Per capita income in the region as a whole rises by 4.3 percent a year. Prospects for internal financing of investment in physical and human capital are good. Even in the low scenario, the Asian development effort is expected to continue to succeed.

As structural adjustment proceeds, real GDP growth in Sub-Saharan Africa is expected to average 3.2 percent a year through 1995, before accelerating in the second half of the decade. But with population growing at nearly the same rate, per capita real income for the region stagnates. Even with an optimistic view of adjustment, the region's per capita income will not return to the level of the mid-1960s over the projection horizon. More, and more effective use of, external financing will be needed to keep Sub-Saharan Africa from falling further behind. These prospects reinforce the view that policies—internal and external—require continued adjustment.

If certain countries in Latin America and in Europe, the Middle East, and North Africa make the necessary economic adjustments, and if these policies revive investment, these regions could do better over the next decade than they have in the 1980s. Per capita income is expected to grow again in Latin America, but at only about 1 percent a year; this rate is probably insufficient for the economic revitalization that is necessary for Latin America to keep pace with other parts of the world. Per capita income should grow more strongly than hitherto in the developing countries of Europe, the Middle East, and North Africa. But without internal reform, external stimulus, and lower interest rates, there is a real danger that the economic situation in much of the middle-income world could deteriorate further.

Debt reduction scenario

Recent discussions of debt relief suggest a third scenario. This combines a reduction in the debt burden of the highly indebted countries with the shift in the macroeconomic policy mix of the industrial countries that is part of the adjustment-with-growth scenario. Under this illustrative scenario, debt stocks are reduced by 20 percent over three years.

The reduction in net resource transfers in the form of interest payments associated with the reduction in debt stocks could be as much as $5 billion to $6 billion over three years. If the reduction in interest payments is used to import needed investment goods, investment rates would rise by several percentage points. As a result of the debt reduction, GDP for the highly indebted countries could be about 1 percent higher at the end of the three years.

Even though all countries are treated similarly in this scenario, some countries fare better than others because countries react differently to increases in imports and investment. For example, the potential increase in GDP for Argentina, Brazil, Mexico, and Nigeria could be as much as 2 percent each. Recent initiatives envisage different countries receiving different levels and kinds of debt reduction on the basis of their adjustment programs.

The models underlying this scenario tie investment directly to resource flows and thus omit two key unquantifiable elements in debt reduction. First, a reduction in the debt overhang is likely to increase the probability that the country can meet future interest obligations; this will significantly improve the investment climate and thereby both increase investment and at some stage encourage the return of flight capital. Second, if debt reduction leads to a sharp decline in new money, and

Table 1.2 Growth prospects in the adjustment-with-growth and low scenarios
(average annual percentage change)

Country group	GDP growth				GDP per capita growth			
	Trend for 1965–87	Recent experience, 1980–88	Scenario for 1988–95		Trend for 1965–87	Recent experience, 1980–88	Scenario for 1988–95	
			Adjustment with growth	Low			Adjustment with growth	Low
Low- and middle-income countries	5.0	4.0	4.6	3.7	2.7	2.0	2.7	1.8
Excluding China and India	4.8	2.6	3.8	3.0	2.2	0.2	1.5	0.7
Sub-Saharan Africa	3.4	0.5	3.2	3.1	0.6	−2.5	0.1	−0.1
Asia	6.2	7.3	6.0	4.9	4.0	5.5	4.3	3.2
Europe, Middle East, and North Africa	4.6	2.9	3.5	2.8	2.4	0.7	1.6	0.8
Latin America and the Caribbean	4.7	1.7	3.1	2.3	2.1	−0.6	1.2	0.4
Seventeen highly indebted countries	4.6	1.3	3.2	2.3	2.0	−1.2	1.0	0.2
High-income OECD countries	3.1	2.7	2.6	2.4	2.3	2.1	2.1	1.9

Figure 1.8 Domestic and external liabilities in selected developing countries, 1975, 1981, and 1987
(percentage of GNP)

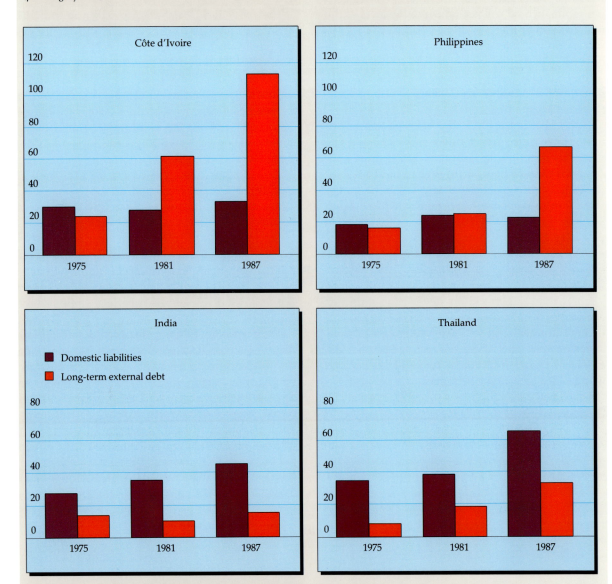

Note: Domestic liabilities are defined as total liquid liabilities of the financial system (*International Financial Statistics,* line 55l), expressed in local currency. External debt is total long-term debt outstanding and disbursed, expressed in U.S. dollars at current exchange rates.
Source: IMF and World Bank data.

possibly even to an increase in negative net transfers, investment will drop. These considerations reinforce the view that continued and powerful structural adjustment by the debtor countries remains the most important ingredient in dealing with the debt problem.

Beyond the debt crisis

All the evidence points to continued low capital flows to the developing countries in the coming decade. Official flows cannot fully offset the sharp reduction in private flows. This underlines the

Table 1.3 Selected capital flows to developing countries, 1981 and 1987
(billions of dollars)

	Official development assistance				Foreign direct investment	
	Total		Official grants			
Country group	1981	1987	1981	1987	1981	1987
All developing countries	24.5	30.4	14.5	20.0	10.2	9.5
Sub-Saharan Africa	7.1	11.1	4.9	7.3	1.3	0.8
Middle-income East Asia	1.8	2.2	0.9	1.5	1.8	2.5
Low-income Asia	5.3	7.2	2.7	3.5	0.2	1.3
Europe, Middle East, and North Africa	8.2	6.3	5.1	5.0	1.3	0.8
Latin America and the Caribbean	2.1	3.6	0.9	2.7	5.6	4.1

Note: Data are based on the sample of 111 countries participating in the Debtor Reporting System. Data exclude certain countries with significant flows associated with offshore banking activities.
Source: OECD and World Bank data.

need for developing countries to adopt economic policies that increase domestic saving and ensure that resources are used as efficiently as possible. In this, the financial sector can play a crucial role.

There is little doubt that over the past fifteen years many developing countries have relied too much on external borrowing and too little on domestic resources. In a sample of thirty-eight developing countries for which data on the liabilities of the domestic financial system were available, external debt at the end of 1986 exceeded domestic debt by more than 50 percent. For Latin America, external debt was on average two-and-a-half times greater than domestic bank liabilities. This shows how much these countries have come to depend on external financing. Figure 1.8 illustrates the range of experience. In countries with rapidly expanding external debt and shallow domestic financial systems, such as Côte d'Ivoire and the Philippines, external liabilities were two to five times greater than domestic bank liabilities. India and Thailand, in contrast, have relatively deep domestic financial systems; they have consciously limited their recourse to external financing.

One lesson of the debt crisis is that commercial bank lending at floating rates is not the ideal form of financing for long-term development. It exposes the borrower to interest rate and exchange rate fluctuations, and it does not tie the borrower's payments to the outcome of the investment. Alternative forms of finance—foreign direct and portfolio investment and commodity bonds, for example—distribute risk between creditor and debtor. Borrowing countries may also hedge their currency exposures by adjusting the currency composition of reserves and borrowings to reflect the likely impact of exchange rate and commodity price changes on their future cash flows.

Foreign direct investment has been an important

source of financing for economies at all levels of income (see Table 1.3). It frequently brings additional benefits: access to new technologies or to markets in which the foreign investing firm is active. It is also likely to bolster competition in domestic markets. During the 1980s foreign direct investment in developing countries has been stable, averaging $10 billion to $15 billion a year (about 10–15 percent of total capital inflows). The relative stability of the aggregate flow masks important changes in its size, sourcing, and composition in different low- and middle-income countries. The direction of foreign direct investment is strongly influenced by political and economic stability and by policies toward trade and capital flows. Restrictions on profit repatriation and access to foreign exchange are especially important (see Box 1.3). Foreign direct investment has to be serviced through profit remittances, and it may be a more expensive source of finance than borrowing. But as long as it provides access to international markets, better technology, and greater domestic competition, it should be welcomed by most developing economies.

Other forms of risk sharing between developing countries and the international capital markets have been very little developed to date. Some oil bonds have been sold, and some deals have been collateralized by commodity exports. The rapid financial innovation of the past decade can be expected to spread to developing countries in due course.

Foreign aid also remains an important source of external finance, particularly for low-income countries in Sub-Saharan Africa. Some industrial countries, notably Japan, have expanded their overseas development assistance in the 1980s. By early 1989 Japan had extended nearly 90 percent of the $30 billion program announced in 1987 to "recycle"

Box 1.3 Foreign equity investment

Economic policies that promote sustainable growth are also likely to attract foreign equity investment. Investor surveys show that growth and stability of the host economy are key factors in determining the attractiveness of a foreign investment. In part, this is because equity investment is relatively illiquid and sometimes requires a lengthy development phase before earning positive returns. When the foreign investment produces for the host market, as in Brazil and Korea, the investor's concern with the long-term macroeconomic environment is reinforced.

Industrial and trade policies also strongly influence foreign investment. Outward-oriented strategies supported by tax, foreign exchange, and other policies usually attract more foreign equity investment, especially to the export processing sectors. Transparent and consistent investment policies are important. Singapore, for example, treats foreign investments on essentially the same terms as domestic investments. It has attracted large flows which, along with domestic investment, have contributed to rapid growth.

Mauritius shows that policies to provide incentives for foreign investment can work, provided the macroeconomic environment is stable. To attract foreign investment and diversify from its traditional reliance on raw sugar, it adopted an Export Processing Zone program in 1970. Mauritius successfully expanded the share of manufactures from almost nothing to 24 percent of total exports by 1977. But growth slowed in the late 1970s and early 1980s, partly because of failures in macroeconomic policy (currency overvaluation, fiscal overexpansion, and a tax policy that discouraged domestic saving). Foreign investment plummeted. The country adopted a structural adjustment program in the early 1980s that called for better credit allocation, an expansion of term finance for the private sector, and investment policies aimed at further export diversification. Growth and foreign investment have revived.

---

funds to developing countries. Saudi Arabia continues to provide 3 percent of GDP in development aid, and Kuwait has recently provided 2 percent. In general, however, low oil prices in the 1980s have prevented the high-income oil-exporting countries from maintaining their aid programs.

Moving beyond the debt crisis calls for effort by debtor and creditor alike. Credible and sustainable structural adjustment is necessary to encourage the return of flight capital and to ensure that domestic and external resources are made available and are put to productive use. And creditors need to be more imaginative in their lending; they must tailor the form and maturity of financial flows to the characteristics of the projects being financed. The creativity of the international capital markets should be brought to bear on the problems of the debtor countries.

2

Why does finance matter?

Financial systems provide payment services. They mobilize savings and allocate credit. And they limit, price, pool, and trade the risks resulting from these activities. These diverse services are used in varying combinations by households, businesses, and governments and are rendered through an array of instruments (currency, checks, credit cards, bonds, and stocks) and institutions (banks, credit unions, insurance companies, pawnbrokers, and stockbrokers). A financial system's contribution to the economy depends upon the quantity and quality of its services and the efficiency with which it provides them.

Financial services make it cheaper and less risky to trade goods and services and to borrow and lend. Without them an economy would be confined to self-sufficiency or barter, which would inhibit the specialization in production upon which modern economies depend. Separating the timing of consumption from production would be possible only by first storing goods. The size of producing units would be limited by the producers' own capacity to save. Incomes would be lower, and complex industrial economies would not exist.

Finance is the key to investment and hence to growth. Providing saved resources to others with more productive uses for them raises the income of saver and borrower alike. Without an efficient financial system, however, lending can be both costly and risky. Self-financed investment is one

way to overcome these difficulties, but profitable investment opportunities may exceed the resources of the individual enterprise. Investment by the public sector is another answer; in this case additional savings are mobilized through the tax system. But excessive centralization brings its own difficulties, especially in gathering the information needed to make sound investments. Efficiency therefore requires a balance among internally generated resources, centrally organized saving and investment, and market-based financial arrangements.

Market-based arrangements are voluntary. As such they are driven by the desire for profit, tempered by concerns about risk. Competition ensures that transaction costs are held down, that risk is allocated to those most willing to bear it, and that investment is undertaken by those with the most promising opportunities.

Such arrangements may take many forms but tend to mirror an economy's complexity and political orientation. Informal finance, such as loans within families and between friends or from pawnbrokers and moneylenders, is still important in many countries. But as economies grow, these arrangements need to be augmented by the services that only formal institutions—commercial banks, collective investment institutions, and capital markets—can supply. For example, by transforming the size and maturity of financial assets, formal institutions can mediate between the many small depositors who prefer liquid assets and the few large borrowers who need long-term loans to finance investment. They can provide other useful services too: insurance, hedging (using options and futures contracts), and so on. In a diversified market-based system, governments retain a key role as prudential regulators, because experience has shown that financial markets—essential though they are—can be prone to instability and vulnerable to fraud.

Finance and growth

Malthus predicted that growing populations and fixed amounts of land and other natural resources would ultimately stifle economic growth. But natural resource endowments have declined in importance in most high-income countries. In Great Britain, for example, the value of land and minerals was 60 percent of the value of all tangible assets in 1688 but only 15 percent in 1977. In fact, natural resources have not determined wealth. In 1870, Australia, a country rich in natural resources, had twice the per capita income of Switzerland, which has few; today Switzerland's per capita income exceeds Australia's by more than half. During the

past three decades Hong Kong, Japan, the Republic of Korea, and Singapore have had among the world's highest per capita income growth rates despite their relatively poor resource endowments. Resource-rich Argentina has hardly grown at all.

The biggest difference between rich and poor is the efficiency with which they have used their resources. The financial system's contribution to growth lies precisely in its ability to increase efficiency.

Finance and trade

The financial system makes its biggest contribution to growth by providing a medium of exchange. In a barter economy, trade requires a "mutual coincidence of wants." It is therefore limited by the costly search for trading partners. Specialization is discouraged in economies with no medium of exchange, so their productivity is low. Money facilitates specialization by reducing trading costs and linking different markets. The adoption of a standard unit of account serves the same goal (see Box 2.1).

Historically, economies moved first from basic self-sufficiency to barter trade and then to trade against commonly accepted commodities such as

Table 2.1 Saving and growth in developing countries, 1965 to 1987

Country group by GDP growth rate	Gross national savings/GDP	Gross investment/GDP	Change in GDP/investment	M2/GDP
High growth (over 7 percent)				
Seven countries	28.0	28.6	26.3	43.0[a]
Excluding China	23.2	26.7	33.1	. .
Medium growth (3–7 percent)				
Fifty-one countries	18.5	22.6	23.6	31.2
Low growth (less than 3 percent)				
Twenty-two countries	19.0	19.0	10.1	23.8

Note: Data are weighted averages times 100 and are based on a sample of eighty developing countries. M2 is currency in circulation plus demand, time, and savings deposits at banks. Investment is gross domestic investment.
a. Because of lack of data, average is for 1977–87 only.
Source: IMF, *International Financial Statistics*, and World Bank data.

gold. Maintaining inventories of commodity money was costly, and the safekeepers of gold and other commodity monies soon learned the advantages of allowing the direct exchange of deposit certificates. Such economizing on the use of commodity money gave birth to deposit money and banking. The continuing search for cheaper means of payment led to paper money, credit cards, and electronic transfers.

Most developing countries have a widely accepted medium of exchange, although they will need more advanced payment systems as their economies become larger and more complex. But, some countries, particularly in Latin America, have failed to provide a currency with a stable value. In inflationary economies local currency becomes less acceptable as a medium of exchange. Inflation also undercuts money's use as a unit of account: it makes financial contracts riskier, reduces the information imparted by relative prices, and distorts the allocation of resources.

Finance and saving

Saving determines the rate at which productive capacity, and hence income, can grow. On average, the more rapidly growing developing countries have had higher saving rates than the slower-growing countries (see Table 2.1). These rates are influenced by many factors. In analyzing them it is useful to distinguish between the flow of "saving" and the stock of "savings." In this Report, "saving" will always refer to the flow of real resources that are not consumed in the period under study and that are therefore available for investment. "Savings" will refer to the stock of accumulated saving, or wealth. An increase in the stock of financial assets will be called "financial deepening."

Many factors affect the saving rate: the rate of income growth, the age composition of the popu-

lation, and attitudes toward thrift. The services provided by government, such as social security, can affect saving, as can taxes and government deficits. Macroeconomic and political stability affect expectations and thus affect saving. Whether financial variables affect the saving rate is still an open question.

Liquidity and ease of access may make financial instruments a more attractive home for savings. And financial services may encourage saving if they raise the net returns. Higher interest rates raise the return, but they can also enable savers to achieve a target stock of financial wealth with a lower saving rate. The effect of higher interest rates is therefore ambiguous. Empirical estimates range from a large positive effect to no effect at all.

Although interest rates have an uncertain effect on the amount people save, their effect on the form in which people save is clear. High interest rates favor financial over nonfinancial forms of saving. A recent study using 1985 data for eighty-one developing economies found that the ratio of liquid liabilities to GNP (a measure of financial depth) rose by 0.75 percentage point in response to a 1.0 percentage point increase in the nominal interest rate paid on deposits. However, the ratio fell by 1.70 percentage points in response to a 1.0 percentage point increase in the rate of inflation. (This asymmetry may reflect the fact that some liquid liabilities—currency, for example—pay no interest and thus cannot fully compensate savers for inflation. It may also reflect a risk premium that rises with the inflation rate.) Overall, higher real interest rates are likely to lead to financial deepening as savers switch some of their saving from real to financial assets and from foreign to domestic assets. Conversely, the negative real interest rates that many countries saw during the 1970s discouraged the holding of financial assets.

Governments can influence financial saving in

other ways too. By imposing direct taxes on banks, by requiring banks to hold noninterest-bearing reserves at the central bank, or by forcing banks to invest in low-interest government bonds, they reduce the return on bank deposits. Historically, governments raised finance by debasing commodity money. Today they do the same by granting themselves a monopoly in the creation of currency. The rent earned from this monopoly is called seigniorage (see Chapter 4). The more governments rely on it for revenue, the less savers are inclined to hold their wealth in financial form. As discussed

in the next section, the amount saved in financial form affects the productivity of investment.

Finance and investment

The financial system intermediates only part of a country's total investment, because firms and households finance much of their investment directly out of their own saving. Only when investment exceeds saving is it necessary to borrow, just as when saving exceeds investment it is necessary to lend. The financial system's task is to move ex-

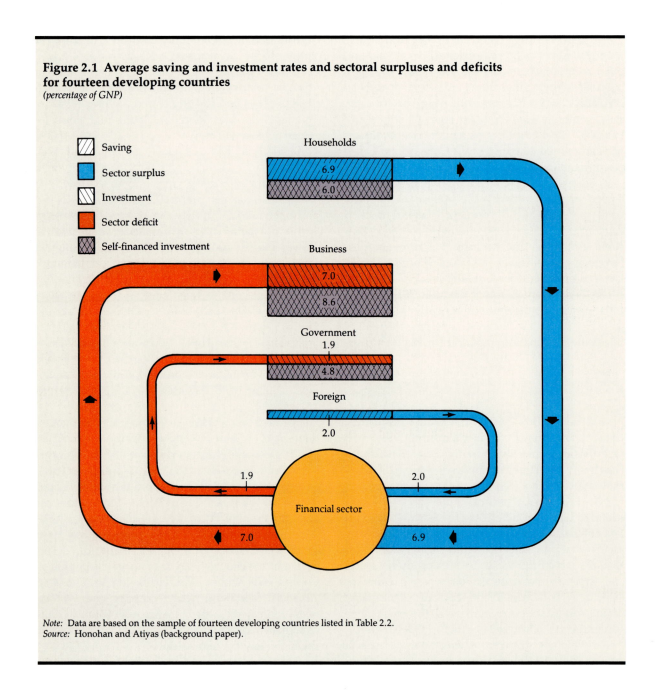

Figure 2.1 Average saving and investment rates and sectoral surpluses and deficits for fourteen developing countries
(percentage of GNP)

Note: Data are based on the sample of fourteen developing countries listed in Table 2.2.
Source: Honohan and Atiyas (background paper).

Table 2.2 Average sectoral surpluses in fourteen developing countries, selected years
(*percentage of GNP*)

Country and period	Households	Business	Government	Foreign
Cameroon, 1980–84	4.0	−9.4	2.7	2.8
China, 1982–86	7.0	−8.1	0.3	0.8
Colombia, 1970–86	3.5	−4.6	−0.2	1.3
Côte d'Ivoire, 1971–78	1.5	−7.7	1.3	4.4
Ecuador, 1980–85	5.1	−6.8	−2.5	5.0
India, 1970–82	5.5	−1.2	−5.5	1.1
Korea, Rep. of, 1980–85	7.0	−13.4	1.1	5.2
Malaysia, 1980, 1985–86	16.8	−7.2	−12.2	1.7
Philippines, 1983–85	9.1	−7.0	−3.6	2.9
Portugal, 1977–79, 1981	14.3	−16.1	−7.3	7.6
Thailand, 1981–83	6.8	−6.5	−4.3	5.7
Tunisia, 1977, 1980–84	2.1	−13.7	2.5	9.1
Turkey, 1971–81	7.7	−11.0	−0.9	3.2
Yugoslavia, 1970–85	7.0	−8.2	0.7	1.2
Average (weighted)	6.9	−7.0	−1.9	2.0
Self-financing ratio[a]	215	55	72	—

Note: Sectoral surpluses may not sum to zero where figures have been derived from independent sources.
a. A self-financing ratio is a sector's saving divided by its investment, expressed as a percentage. This ratio overstates true self-financing to the extent that there is intrasectoral borrowing or lending. Data are derived from the weighted sectoral saving and investment averages shown in Figure 2.1.
Source: Honahan and Atiyas (background paper).

cess saving from economic units in surplus to those in deficit.

Figure 2.1 shows the average saving and investment rates for fourteen developing countries. Households saved 12.9 percent of GNP and invested 6.0 percent; that left them with a surplus of 6.9 percent of GNP. Businesses saved 8.6 percent of GNP and invested 15.6 percent; that left them with a deficit of 7.0 percent of GNP. The foreign sector was a net lender and the government a net borrower. The financial sector is the channel for all these flows. Note that the country-by-country sectoral balances which underlie these averages vary widely. Table 2.2 shows the balances for each of the countries that are aggregated in Figure 2.1. The surplus of the household sector, for instance, ranges from Côte d'Ivoire's 1.5 percent (in 1971–78) to Malaysia's 16.8 percent (in 1980–86).

Taking the fourteen countries together, Table 2.2 shows that businesses financed 55 percent of their investment from their own saving (in the form of depreciation allowances and retained earnings). Governments financed 72 percent of their investment from their saving (that is, from the excess of taxes and other income over consumption spending plus transfers). And households as a group financed all of their investment from their saving. Altogether, roughly half of all investment was self-financed.

An advantage of self-finance is that, in combining the acts of saving and investing, it internalizes all the information, transaction, monitoring, and enforcement costs that would be involved if the resources were lent to someone else. No complex contracts, collateral, or other devices are required to reduce the risks inherent in lending. The shortcoming of self-finance is that an individual's investment opportunities may not match his or her resources or may be inefficiently limited by them.

Even though the financial system intermediates only part of total investable resources, it plays a vital role in allocating saving. In the early stages of development, relatives, friends, and moneylenders may be the only sources of external finance. As the financial system grows, local banks, then national financial institutions, and finally securities markets and foreign banks become sources of funds for investors. Smoothly functioning financial systems lower the cost of transferring resources from savers to borrowers, which raises the rate paid to savers and lowers the cost to borrowers (see Box 2.2). The ability of borrowers and lenders to compare interest rates across markets improves the allocation of resources.

Historically, the quality of investment has been at least as important for growth as the quantity. Although the fastest-growing countries had higher rates of investment than the others in Table 2.1, empirical studies generally find that less than half the growth in output is attributable to increases in labor and capital. Higher productivity explains the rest. Higher labor productivity reflects better

Box 2.2   Transaction costs and the supply of credit

The impact of financial intermediation and interest rate ceilings on credit can be demonstrated geometrically. In the diagrams in Box figure 2.2 the horizontal axis measures the quantity of borrowing or lending per unit of time (X), and the vertical axis measures the cost of borrowing (r) and the return for lending (i). The economy's demand for credit is depicted in the first diagram by the downward-sloping curve labeled D. Its negative slope reflects, in part, the increasing quantity (per unit of time) of profitable investment as the cost of borrowing declines. The upward-sloping curve labeled S depicts the economy's supply of credit, the amount of saving offered to others either directly or through intermediaries such as banks. Its positive slope reflects, in part, the increasing share of total saving provided for financial assets as their return rises relative to the return on real assets or investment abroad. If there were no transaction costs or interest rate regulations, the market-determined rate of interest would be $r = i$, and the amount of credit per period would be X.

It is costly, however, for lenders to locate credit-worthy borrowers directly. In the center diagram, the amount lenders must charge borrowers to cover that cost is reflected in the curve S_d. The vertical distance between this curve and the supply of funds curve (S) is the amount of these transaction costs (including the cost of covering the expected defaults). If lenders had to find borrowers on their own, they would be willing

to supply X_d in the expectation of earning (after deducting expected costs) i_d. For that amount of credit borrowers would be paying r_d. Transaction costs introduce a wedge between the cost to borrowers and the return to lenders, which reduces the amount lent.

Banks or other intermediaries exist, in part, because they are able to reduce the transaction costs of borrowing and lending. This is reflected in the curve S_b. The wedge between the cost to borrowers and the return to lenders is now the banks' spread. Assuming that bank spreads are less than the costs of direct lending, the amount lent increases from X_d to X_b, the return to lenders increases from i_d to i_b, and the cost to borrowers falls from r_d to r_b. The better banks are at reducing transaction costs, the greater these effects. Reducing taxes on banking (such as unremunerated reserve requirements, which are a part of these costs) has the same effect.

The third diagram shows the effect of an interest rate ceiling (the horizontal orange line at i_c). If the ceiling is applied to deposit rates, it will reduce the amount lent (to X_c) and raise the cost to borrowers (to r_c). If the ceiling applies instead to lending rates, banks will set deposit rates at i'_c, deducting transaction costs. The amount deposited (and lent, when abstracting from reserve requirements) will be X'_c. The excess demand for credit ($X_o - X'_c$) cannot be satisfied, and lenders will ration the available supply.

Box figure 2.2   The supply of and demand for credit

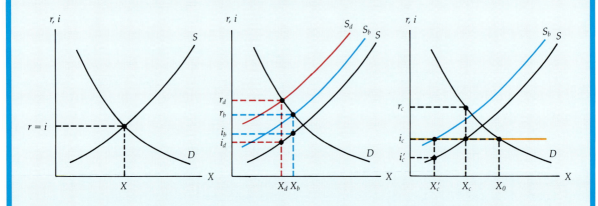

health, skills, education, and work effort; higher capital productivity reflects technical progress and the more efficient use of saving.

As more saving moves through the financial sys-

tem, financial depth increases. The financial systems of higher-income countries are usually deeper (as measured by the ratio of liquid liabilities to GNP) than those in poorer ones (see Figure 2.2).

They are also deeper in the most rapidly growing countries than in the slowest-growing countries (as shown by the ratio of M2 to GDP in Table 2.1).

Faster growth, more investment, and greater financial depth all come partly from higher saving. In its own right, however, greater financial depth also contributes to growth by improving the productivity of investment. Investment productivity, as measured by the ratio of the change in GDP to investment (the inverse of the incremental capital-output ratio—ICOR), is significantly higher in the faster-growing countries, which also have deeper financial systems (Table 2.1). This suggests a link between financial development and growth. How might this work? It was noted above that positive real interest rates favor financial saving over other forms of saving and therefore promote financial deepening. Provided that intermediaries are good at selecting viable projects, greater intermediation will ensure that the better investments are financed and will thereby increase the average productivity of investment. Table 2.3 groups the countries of Table 2.1 that had meaningful interest rate data according to their real interest rates: positive, moderately negative (0 to −5 percent), and strongly negative. The first group had lower inflation rates, deeper financial sectors, moderately higher investment rates, and significantly more productive investments than the others.

More important, the growth rates of the countries with positive real interest rates were considerably higher on average than those of the others. As the world economy adjusted to the first oil price shock of the early 1970s, productivity and growth fell nearly everywhere. But the fall was much

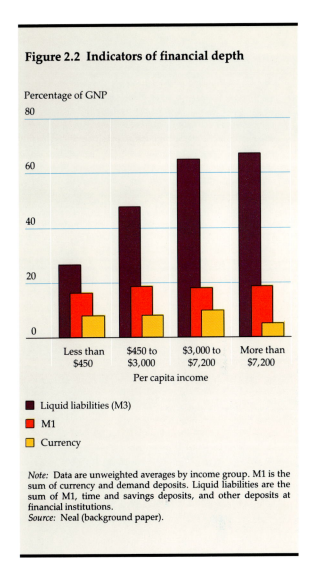

Figure 2.2 Indicators of financial depth

Percentage of GNP

- Liquid liabilities (M3)
- M1
- Currency

Note: Data are unweighted averages by income group. M1 is the sum of currency and demand deposits. Liquid liabilities are the sum of M1, time and savings deposits, and other deposits at financial institutions.
Source: Neal (background paper).

Table 2.3 Growth rates and other economic indicators for country groups with positive, moderately negative, and strongly negative real interest rates, 1965 to 1973 and 1974 to 1985
(average percent)

| | 1965–73 | | | 1974–85 | | |
| | | Negative | | | Negative | |
Indicator	Positive	Moderately	Strongly	Positive	Moderately	Strongly
Real interest rate	3.7	−1.7	−13.7	3.0	−2.4	−13.0
GDP growth rate	7.3	5.5	4.6	5.6	3.8	1.9
M3/GDP	28.9	27.0	29.1	40.3	34.0	30.5
Investment/GDP	21.4	19.7	21.4	26.9	23.2	23.0
Change in GDP/investment	36.7	31.1	21.7	22.7	17.3	6.2
Change in real M3/real saving	18.7	12.7	6.4	16.6	8.2	−0.9
Inflation rate	22.2	7.1	40.2	20.8	23.9	50.3
Volatility of inflation rate	17.1	5.3	27.2	12.2	9.1	23.5

Note: Real interest rates were calculated from nominal rates according to the following formula: $[(1 + r) / (1 + p) − 1] \times 100$, where r is the deposit rate and p is the inflation rate. Inflation is the percentage change in the consumer price index (CPI). M3 is currency plus the sum of nonbank deposits of the public at all identified deposit-taking institutions. Real saving is gross domestic savings deflated by the average annual CPI rate. Volatility of inflation is the absolute deviation of the inflation rate from its level the year before.
Source: Gelb (background paper).

Box 2.3 Real interest rates and growth

Most developing countries have periodically held their interest rates below market-clearing levels. These artificially low interest rates have "repressed" their financial systems, shrinking financial assets in real terms especially at times of high inflation. If financial depth promotes economic growth, artificially low real interest rates may be an obstacle to development.

A background study for this Report estimated the relationship between real interest rates and growth for the thirty-three developing countries with populations of more than 1 million and acceptable data for the period 1965–85 (the same countries that are grouped by interest rates in Table 2.3). When the data for these countries were averaged over each of two periods, 1965–73 and 1974–85 (to take into account the marked deterioration in growth of virtually all countries after the first oil shock), higher real rates of interest on short-term deposits were indeed associated with faster growth. In a simple regression where GY is the growth rate, R is the real interest rate, and $SHIFT$ is the dummy for the second period

$$GY = -0.12 + 0.20R + -0.02\ SHIFT \qquad \overline{R}^2 = 0.45$$
$$(-2.5) \quad (5.2) \qquad (-3.4)$$

However, assessing the impact of interest rates on economic performance is not straightforward. Causation could run in either direction. To analyze the association between interest rates and growth, this study decomposed the relationship into a chain of relationships more likely to run in one direction. The hypothesized chain ran from interest rates to financial depth and to saving and from financial depth to the productivity of investment.

The resulting estimates showed that higher real interest rates (obtained by raising repressed rates toward modestly positive levels) are associated with increased financial depth and with a modest increase in saving and investment. In the second link in the hypothesized chain, financial depth was strongly associated with more productive investment. When the estimates of each link are put together, they suggest that, although real interest rates have a smaller effect on growth than

indicated in the simple regression, the association is strong and appears to operate primarily through the effect of greater financial depth on the productivity of investment. (Note, however, that countries with repressed financial systems often suffer serious distortions in other sectors of the economy as well. The strong relationship between real interest rates and growth may therefore reflect the correlation between macroeconomic imbalances and price distortions, particularly the negative association between high inflation rates and growth, as well as financial repression.)

Box figure 2.3 plots some of the country data used in this study. The value of each country's average investment rate (horizontal axis) is plotted against its average growth rate (vertical axis) for the second period (1974–85). Although higher investment rates are associated on average with higher growth rates, the figure shows that the relationship is loose. The differences between growth rates and investment rates reflect differences in the productivity of investment. Any line drawn from the origin represents a given growth-investment ratio (the inverse of the incremental capital-output ratio); if all investments were equally productive, differences in growth rates would reflect differences in investment rates only, and all points would fall on a line that represents the average productivity of investment. In the figure that line—labeled "average productivity of investment"—corresponds to the sample average. Thus the position of points with respect to the line reflects differences in the productivity of investment among the sample countries, with those above the line being more productive than the average and those below it less.

The blue squares depict countries with positive real interest rates, the white squares those with moderately negative rates, and the red squares those with strongly negative rates. Investments in all the countries with positive real rates were more productive than average. Investments were generally less productive than average in the countries with strongly negative real rates, four of which actually had negative growth rates over the period.

greater in the countries with negative real interest rates. Overall, output grew almost three times faster, on average, in the countries with positive real interest rates than in the countries with strongly negative rates. Further analysis suggests that positive real interest rates helped growth mainly by improving the quality of investment and not just by increasing the quantity of investment (see Box 2.3). Although the rate of investment was only 17 percent higher in the countries with positive real rates, the average productivity of their

investment was almost four times higher. Note, however, that many of the countries with positive real interest rates also had more stable macroeconomic policies and more open trading systems, which should also raise growth rates.

Risks and costs of finance

Lending is risky. Intermediaries must cover the costs of devising contracts that limit risk, of monitoring and enforcing those contracts, and of losses.

Box figure 2.3 Real interest rates, investment, productivity, and growth in thirty-three developing countries in 1974–85

■ Positive real interest rates

□ Moderately negative real interest rates (0 to −5 percent)

■ Strongly negative real interest rates (less than −5 percent)

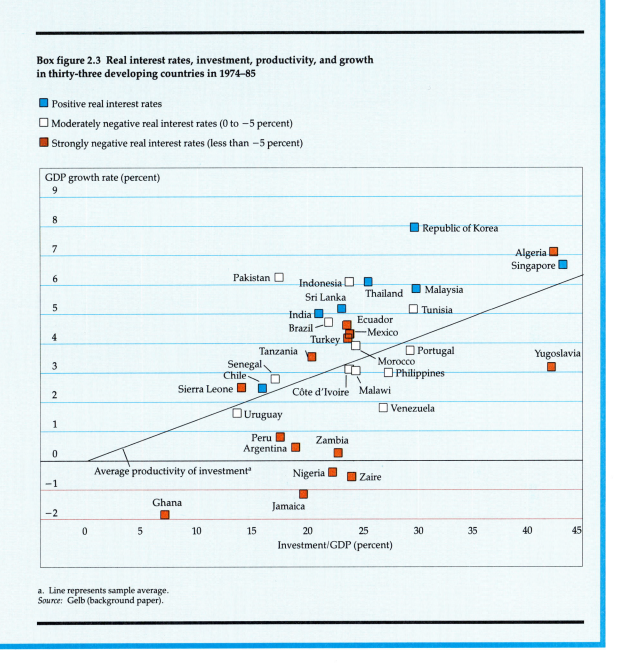

a. Line represents sample average.
Source: Gelb (background paper).

The extent of financial contracting depends on the extent to which cultural, legal, and institutional arrangements can reduce these costs. If they remain prohibitive, businesses will prefer to rely on self-finance.

Risks

Financial contracts involve credit risk, price risk, and liquidity risk. Credit risk is the danger that the borrower will default. Price risk is the risk of loss caused by unexpected changes in prices—in interest or exchange rates, for example. Liquidity risk is the risk of being unable to sell financial assets quickly, except at a steep discount. In addition, there is the risk that the default of one or a few large borrowers will endanger the whole financial system. This is called systemic risk.

Informational asymmetries are one source of credit risk. Entrepreneurs have "inside" information about their own projects and creditworthiness. Lenders can reduce credit risk either by de-

Box 2.4 Swapping risk

All economic activities are subject to a wide variety of technical, economic, and financial risks. Many risks are amenable to actuarial calculations and can be covered by straightforward insurance policies, but others are not. Financial systems can help to overcome some risks by redistributing them among market participants.

Some types of risk can be limited through portfolio diversification; other risks can be hedged by using an appropriate instrument, such as a forward contract or option. The key to any hedge is to find a counterparty willing and able to take the other side of the contract. Financial institutions have become adept at inventing hedging instruments and arranging hedging contracts between different parties.

One hedging instrument has become quite popular in the 1980s and has contributed greatly to the growing integration of national financial markets. It is the "swap." Swaps involve the exchange of future streams of payments between two or more parties and enable the participants to convert debt servicing obligations from one currency into another or from fixed to floating interest rates. Swaps exploit the segmentation of financial markets that causes differences in the markets' perception of different borrowers. Thus, although a triple-

A-rated firm may be able to borrow in both dollars and yen at a lower rate than a B-rated firm, it may have a comparative advantage in borrowing in yen because of its greater name recognition. Yet the second firm may desire yen debt, perhaps because it exports to Japan. A currency swap allows both firms to borrow where they have a comparative advantage (thus reducing market segmentation), swap loans and repayment streams to match their desired risk profiles, and end up with a lower cost of funds. The same principles are at work when a firm borrowing at fixed interest rates swaps payment streams with one borrowing at floating rates.

The importance of hedging devices is clearest when there are none. For example, in many developing countries firms—including those with foreign currency liabilities—are prohibited from holding foreign currency assets and cannot buy forward contracts; this limits their ability to hedge their foreign exchange risk. Similarly, developing country farmers, who cannot participate in world futures markets, are unable to hedge the substantial risks associated with fluctuations in the "world" prices of their crops. In these circumstances producers are likely to invest less and produce less.

---

veloping their own expertise in the selection of borrowers or by relying on information from institutions such as credit rating agencies. Measures that increase the information available to lenders, such as the strengthening of accounting and auditing requirements, improve lenders' ability to identify the borrowers with the best investment opportunities. When information is poor, lenders can discriminate between borrowers only in very broad terms.

To cover risk, lenders raise the interest rate they charge on loans. But this may be partially self-defeating, because the more creditworthy borrowers may choose not to borrow, which would leave the lender with less creditworthy clients. (This is the problem of adverse selection.) Furthermore, to cover the higher cost of borrowing, clients may take on riskier projects. (This is the problem of moral hazard.) Because of their limited ability to identify risks and monitor behavior, lenders tend to require collateral and to ration credit to the most creditworthy borrowers rather than to charge higher interest rates on riskier loans. Borrowers with little collateral are likely to be the most affected by credit rationing.

Financial risk can be reduced by improving the

availability and quality of information about borrowers (individuals, enterprises, or financial intermediaries), by improving the design and enforcement of loan contracts, and by enlarging the range of instruments so as to permit greater diversification of portfolios. Risk cannot usually be eliminated altogether, but the irreducible risk can often be transferred to those more willing to bear it. Loan maturities, the choice of adjustable or fixed interest rates, equity and venture capital arrangements, and collateral or cosigner requirements are all examples of different risk assignments. Much recent financial innovation has been driven by attempts to exploit comparative advantage in risk bearing (see Box 2.4).

Transaction costs

The services offered by financial institutions require the collection and processing of a great deal of information and the design, monitoring, and enforcing of contracts. Providing these services is expensive. Financial institutions must cover administrative costs (essentially payroll and rent), taxes, the cost of capital and of adhering to government regulations, and losses from default. They do so by charging fees for specific services and interest on loans.

The burden of costs will shift between the parties according to the arrangements adopted. Informal financial entrepreneurs rely on personal knowledge of borrowers; their information costs are low. In more advanced systems information and enforcement become more expensive. In the early stages of financial development, banks build the cost of gathering credit information into their spreads. Later, firms supply more information on their own behalf. A corporation issuing bonds or equities must provide investors with information about itself. Firms send audited accounts to their shareholders and to the tax authorities. They may pay a credit rating agency to grade their securities.

Transaction costs are also borne by depositors, investors, and government agencies. Depositors incur costs in visiting bank branches and waiting in line to cash checks. Investors devote resources to analyzing information. Government agencies usually bear some of the costs of monitoring and enforcement. A securities and exchange commission may be called upon to certify the accuracy of information provided in corporate prospectuses; deposit insurance corporations may assume responsibility for monitoring deposit institutions. Government agencies generally cover their costs by levying fees on issued securities or collecting premiums from insured institutions.

Spreads between borrowing and lending rates and between buying and selling prices reflect the intermediary's costs, expected loan and trading losses, reserve requirements, and taxation. Commercial banks' spreads vary with the size and risk of loans. The average spread between lending rates and the cost of funds in a high-income country is between 2 and 3 percentage points. In noninflationary developing countries, spreads are similar to those in industrial countries, but because the range of services offered may be more limited and operating procedures more cumbersome, depositors' and borrowers' combined transaction costs may be higher. Spreads in inflationary countries can be more than 10 percent, although that reflects the burden of high reserve requirements as well as transaction costs. Prime borrowers may be able to acquire funds through international markets for a fee as low as one-tenth of 1 percent of the amount raised. Although spreads tend to be narrower in direct transactions than in intermediated ones, the difference is partly offset by the additional costs borne by the principals.

High accounting standards and strong contract enforcement help to reduce the risk of loss. Competition, however, is the most effective way to keep transaction costs low. Access to a wide range of institutions and markets, including international markets, stimulates competition.

Government intervention

Governments intervene in the provision of financial services for many reasons. Historically, they have controlled the means of payment, both to guarantee its soundness and to collect seigniorage. More recently, governments have tried to use their control of money creation to influence the level of economic activity and their control of the allocation and pricing of credit to influence the composition of investment. (Chapter 4 discusses the recent experience of the developing countries with policies of this sort.) They have also intervened to ensure that financial intermediaries behave prudently.

Fractional reserve banking systems (in which banks hold only partial reserves against liabilities and lend out the rest of their deposits) have suffered from occasional instability, excessive risk taking, and fraud. The liabilities issued by banks in response to the demands of depositors are short-term, highly liquid, and supposedly low-risk. Loans, by contrast, are usually longer-term, less liquid, and riskier. This difference is one reason banks charge borrowers more than they pay depositors. But because banks are so highly leveraged, relatively small losses on loans can leave them unable to honor their liabilities. When the public suspects that a bank is insolvent, the result is often a run on the bank, which sometimes spreads to other, solvent, banks. The drain of bank reserves causes a multiple contraction in bank credit. When runs become widespread, as they occasionally did in the nineteenth and early twentieth centuries, financial panic can trigger a collapse of the credit-payment process and a sharp recession.

Governments have devised ways of dealing with bank runs. When they occurred, central banks—acting as lenders of last resort—provided liquidity by rediscounting sound loans. In several high-income countries the government provided deposit insurance. By guaranteeing the value and liquidity of deposits up to a certain size, deposit insurance was designed to prevent runs from starting (see Box 2.5). The lender-of-last-resort facility was designed to prevent them from spreading.

Although prudential regulation has a different rationale than economic regulation aimed at alter-

Box 2.5   Deposit insurance

Most high-income and a few developing countries have established deposit insurance schemes. Deposit insurance guarantees the nominal value and liquidity of deposits up to a certain size. The insurer is an institution, generally government-owned, established for that purpose, and funded with premiums paid by the institutions whose deposits are insured. Deposit insurance can help to establish confidence in the safety of saving with banks (or other covered institutions) in countries with limited banking habits. The principal targets of deposit insurance are small, unsophisticated depositors who are least able to assess the soundness of a particular depository. By assuring depositors that their money is safe even if the depository is not, deposit insurance supplements the central bank's lender-of-last-resort role in forestalling bank runs.

Like all insurance, deposit insurance suffers from the risk of moral hazard. Because insured depositors no longer need to be concerned about the quality of their depository's assets, market regulation of bank behavior is reduced. A considerable degree of market regulation can be retained if deposit insurance coverage is limited to relatively small deposits. The interbank deposit market, which has become an important source of short-term liquidity for all advanced banking systems, can impose a significant measure of discipline on banks

and should never be insured. This contrasts with the savings and loan associations in the United States, which, in addition to having insured deposits, do most of their short-term borrowing from the Federal Home Loan Bank System, which lends according to less demanding standards (see Box 5.4 in Chapter 5). An inescapable fact of deposit insurance is that it places greater responsibility on government to see to it that insured institutions behave prudently.

With or without insurance, depositors would be fully protected if banks were closed and liquidated the moment their capital fell to zero. This is not a practical possibility: the condition of a bank cannot be known to inspectors minute by minute and, because liquidation takes time, asset values can decline before liquidation can be completed. However, up-to-date market accounting, frequent inspection, and swift action by inspectors to close insolvent banks are clearly important in minimizing losses. In some countries the laws establishing deposit insurance provide the mechanisms for exactly such steps. Furthermore, the enhanced supervisory capability that sometimes accompanies the establishment of deposit insurance can and should be used to spot problems in bank management and in banks' portfolios well before insolvency occurs and to compel banks to take corrective action.

ing the allocation of resources, it too affects the structure and efficiency of the financial sector. For example, many governments have honored the liabilities of insolvent financial institutions even when there was no formal insurance. Government guarantees and lender-of-last-resort facilities, however, changed the behavior of both depositors and bankers. Depositors and other buyers of bank liabilities that were either explicitly or implicitly insured no longer had to monitor banks to protect the value of their deposits. Bankers no longer had to worry about runs, so they could make riskier loans. Governments therefore had to regulate and supervise the system.

Deposit insurance, coupled with regulation and supervision, has reduced the problem of bank runs but has been less successful in preventing fraud and excessive risk taking by banks, as the present widespread insolvency among the financial institutions of the developing countries makes clear (see Chapter 5). And high-income countries have not been exempt (see Box 5.4). It is often argued that government supervision is not an efficient substitute for market supervision—in the form, for exam-

ple, of monitoring and control of bank managers by stockholders and depositors. Innovative financial entrepreneurs have often been able to evade the rules; those intent on deceiving bank examiners have often succeeded in hiding losses for some time.

Many countries have therefore moved in recent years to strengthen the role of the private sector in monitoring and controlling financial enterprises. Some have set higher capital requirements for financial institutions. This ensures that the owners have an adequate stake in the efficiency with which depositors' resources are used. Similarly, stringent audit and reporting requirements make an institution's financial condition visible to depositors and investors. And yet some governments have also covered losses that in the past would have been borne by market participants. This runs counter to the principle of allowing market signals a greater role in supervising the system.

The task of balancing efficiency, which requires freedom to act, and stability, which evidently requires a degree of government regulation, is extremely difficult. Some theorists argue for an uncompromising market-based approach, but in practice all governments have chosen some form of supervision. If markets are to judge, price, and allocate risk correctly, governments must clearly define the areas in which they have taken responsibility—and allow losses to be incurred in those that are not insured. (Chapter 6 discusses prudential regulation in more detail.)

The structure of the financial system

The financial system consists of many institutions, instruments, and markets. Financial institutions range from pawnshops and moneylenders to banks, pension funds, insurance companies, brokerage houses, investment trusts, and stock exchanges. Financial instruments range from the common—coins, currency notes, and checks; mortgages, corporate bills, bonds, and stocks—to the more exotic—futures and swaps of high finance. Markets for these instruments may be organized formally (as in stock or bond exchanges with centralized trading floors) or informally (as in over-the-counter or curb markets). For analytical purposes, the system can be divided into users of financial services and providers.

Users of financial services

Financial institutions sell their services to households, businesses, and government. The boundaries between these sectors are not always clear-cut.

HOUSEHOLDS. The household sector includes small, mainly unregulated firms and individuals. Their main financial needs are for payment services, for liquid assets in which to save, and for relatively small amounts of credit. They seek convenience (nearby branches, for example), simplicity, liquidity, and security.

After making their own investments, households as a group have surplus resources to lend (Figure 2.1). Hence, they demand convenient assets to hold. This demand, as well as the demand for a medium of exchange, may be met by currency. To a lesser extent it may be met by bank deposits, although hoarding commodities or participating in informal saving arrangements are alternatives. Accumulated investment in housing is a large part of the nonliquid wealth of households at all but the poorest income levels. As incomes rise, insurance and contractual savings schemes (life insurance and pensions) also become important.

Households also need credit. Street vendors, for example, need short-term finance to purchase daily stocks. Small farmers need seasonal or medium-term credit to buy capital. Would-be homeowners need long-term mortgage financing. Households are often unable to convince financial institutions that they are creditworthy. So they turn to lenders who do not require formal business records or collateral—to family and friends or to local pawnbrokers and moneylenders. (Chapter 8 examines informal finance in greater detail.)

BUSINESSES. Wealthier households and corporations have more complicated financial needs. They require check and wire transfer payments; deposits in larger amounts and at longer maturities; letters of credit; guarantees; purchase and sale of foreign exchange; underwriting; advice on financial, accounting, and tax matters; and so forth. The business sector is invariably a net borrower; it needs short-term credit to finance inventories and long-term funds to finance capital expansion. Nevertheless, it also holds a substantial share of gross financial assets. For example, in 1984, businesses held 48, 49, and 64 percent of demand deposits in Korea, Malaysia, and Tunisia respectively.

The business sector includes public as well as private enterprises. Public enterprises are generally in capital-intensive industries such as utilities and transportation. In developing countries many of the larger manufacturing firms are publicly owned as well. Many public enterprises have been run not to generate profit but to provide employment and to supply goods and services at reasonable prices. Because many have incurred losses, they have been unable to finance their investment from retained earnings. Public enterprises have been heavy borrowers in both domestic and foreign markets. Their losses have been a drain on national saving.

Some of the largest corporations can meet most of their demand for financial services by themselves and may even be able to supply financial services to others: trade credits to their customers, for instance. They can also tap financial markets directly by issuing their own financial instruments (commercial paper, bonds, equity securities, and so on). Yet direct financing has been negligible in most developing countries and unimportant in most high-income ones. In France, Italy, Japan, and the United Kingdom, for example, stocks and bonds financed an average of less than 9 percent of corporate investment; 30 percent of it was financed with bank loans and the rest from internally generated funds.

GOVERNMENT. As well as being regulators of their financial systems, governments are among their clients. All governments use payment services. In most developing countries, governments, like businesses, are net borrowers, and they use the financial system as a source of funding for current and capital spending. In industrial countries, government deficits are financed mainly by selling securities to the public. In developing countries they are usually financed by borrowing from banks. In Sierra Leone, Zaire, and Zambia, for example, more than 70 percent of bank credit has gone to the government in recent years, and in Mexico 55 percent. Much of that credit was supplied by the central banks, which thereby increased the stocks of reserve money in these countries. The inflation caused by excessive monetary growth has greatly retarded the development of the financial sector in developing countries, especially since interest rates have often been held down.

Governments have also used the financial system to serve development or other goals. They have directed credit, often at subsidized interest rates, to priority sectors. Many developing country governments own banks or other financial institutions and thus play a direct role in allocating resources. Monetary policy is conducted through the financial sector (see Box 2.6). The influence of governments on the amount and pattern of investment has therefore been much greater than their own investment spending would suggest.

Providers of financial services

Financial systems differ from country to country, yet there are many similarities. In addition to the central bank, most countries have five main classes of financial institution: deposit and credit institutions, contractual savings institutions, collective investment institutions, securities markets, and informal financial enterprises. (Chapters 7 and 8 discuss the services provided by these parts of the financial system in more detail.) Casualty insur-

Box 2.6   Monetary policy

Governments intervene in finance partly to control the supply of money and credit. When the budget deficit is large, governments often cover it by creating money. Excessive creation of money to cover budget deficits is the most common cause of inflation. When the fiscal deficit is not a consideration, the objective of monetary and credit policy is usually to maintain stable prices.

Governments have various tools to control the monetary aggregates. Perhaps the most common technique in developing countries is for the central bank to specify credit ceilings for each commercial bank. Such ceilings have been criticized because they discourage competition and the mobilization of deposits.

Another approach is for the central bank to fix the amount of deposit liabilities that can be created by the banking sector by imposing reserve requirements and controlling the quantity of reserves available to banks. Central banks often control the level of reserves through the refinancing facilities they provide to commercial banks. But if refinancing is used to channel credit to preferred sectors, it cannot easily be used for monetary control as well. Other countries use the movement of government deposits between commercial banks and the central bank to control the level of reserves. In countries with more developed financial systems, central banks adjust bank reserves, and hence the money supply, through the purchase or sale of government securities. These transactions are called open

market operations. When the central bank buys a security, it pays with a check drawn on itself, thereby increasing its liabilities. Open market operations cannot be used in a system without an established government bill market. Monetary control with open market operations leaves the allocation of credit to market forces.

The degree of integration with world financial and capital markets also affects the execution of monetary policy. An open and fully integrated economy that chooses to maintain fixed exchange rates would have to maintain the money supply at the level demanded at the "world" price level and interest rate. Any other quantity of money would result in changes in the foreign exchange reserves of the central bank. The central bank's purchase or sale of foreign exchange would replace open market operations as the tool for determining bank reserves and, hence, the money supply.

A fixed exchange rate constrains the central bank's ability to create money and is thus a potential source of monetary discipline. A market-determined exchange rate restores a measure of domestic monetary independence. With either fixed or floating exchange rates, central banks will need to set reserve requirements at levels comparable to those in other countries if banking business is not to be driven abroad. Noninterest-earning reserve requirements are a tax on banks and as such will affect their competitiveness.

Table 2.4 The institutional structure of selected financial systems, 1985

| | Assets as a percentage of total gross assets of the financial system | | | | | | As a percentage of GNP | |
Country	Central banks	Deposit banks	Specialized lending institutions	Contractual savings institutions	Collective investment institutions	Long-term debt securities and equities[a]	Net financial assets	Total external debt
Developed markets								
Australia	5	31	14	17	1	33	..	—
Canada	1	33	2	26	8	30	165	—
France	6	56	10	7	5	16	109	—
Germany, Fed. Rep. of	4	41	14	9	2	30	158	—
Japan	2	45	9	6	7	30	300	—
Sweden	4	27	18	16	1	35	..	—
United Kingdom	1	35	1	26	3	34	188	—
United States	2	28	7	19	4	40	210	—
Average	3	37	9	16	4	31	188	—
Emerging markets								
Argentina	32	43	11	5	0	10	..	80
Brazil	27	32	12	2	4	23	59	50
Chile	14	44	1	11	1	28	75	145
India	10	47	6	12	1	24	65	19
Korea, Rep. of	9	53	14	4	10	10	66	57
Malaysia	7	34	12	13	3	32	247	52
Nigeria	23	46	2	3	7	19	49	26
Pakistan	21	65	1	2	1	11	45	39
Philippines	30	38	14	3	3	14	38	82
Portugal	20	72	1	2	1	4	124	85
Thailand	16	55	12	1	0	17	89	47
Turkey	33	54	4	6	0	3	27	50
Venezuela	20	46	25	1	0	8	65	74
Average	20	48	9	5	2	16	79	62

Note: Total financial system assets are the assets of all the institutions shown in this table plus the stock of outstanding securities and equities. To eliminate double-counting caused by the assets of one institution being the liabilities of another, net financial assets have been approximated by the sum of total liquid liabilities (IFS, line 55l) plus securities and equities. To deflate these stocks by the flow of GNP, five-quarter arithmetic averages are constructed from year-end data for 1984 and 1985, assuming constant exponential growth during the year.
a. The sum of government bonds, corporate bonds, and corporate equity.
Source: IMF, *International Financial Statistics*, and World Bank data.

ance companies are also generally considered part of the financial sector, but they are not discussed in this Report.

Table 2.4 compares the structure of the financial sector in high-income countries with its structure in some of the more advanced developing countries. Banks in developing countries hold a bigger share of all financial assets (48 percent) than they do in industrial countries (37 percent). The table understates this dominance, because the developing countries included are those with the most sophisticated financial systems. When central banks are included, the predominance of the banking sectors of most developing countries is even greater, for the central banks in the sample hold 20 percent of the financial sector's assets in developing countries compared with only 3 percent in developed markets. In addition to issuing currency and overseeing the operation of the payment system, the central bank acts as banker to the government and to other banks. In contrast, nonbank in-

termediaries and contractual savings institutions hold a much larger share of financial assets in high-income countries than they do in developing ones. The relatively small domestic financial sectors of the developing countries stand in sharp contrast to their relatively large reliance on foreign financing.

Different financial institutions provide services that are both complementary to and competitive with each other. Deposit institutions offer payment and liquid deposit facilities, and contractual savings institutions provide illiquid savings opportunities that cater to the longer-term needs of customers. Collective investment institutions offer small investors the benefits of professional management and low-cost risk diversification, encouraging them to diversify their savings into marketable securities. On the lending side, commercial banks have traditionally provided working capital and trade finance, but longer-term lending is gaining with the spread of universal banking. Factoring companies specialize in financing inventories and receivables, whereas development banks and leasing companies provide long-term investment finance.

Money and capital markets provide investment instruments appropriate for contractual savings and collective investment institutions, whose services to the saving public are thereby improved. The efficient functioning of financial markets also depends on institutions that lend and borrow little on their own account: investment banks, securities brokers, and credit rating agencies. Commercial banks also improve the working of financial markets by providing credit and payment facilities to market makers and other market participants.

Different financial institutions and markets compete for a limited pool of savings by offering different instruments. Money and capital markets increase competition between suppliers. Money markets give merchant banks, or commercial banks with limited branch networks, greater access to funds. Because such banks specialize in lending to larger corporations, the corporate loan market may be highly competitive, even though a few large domestic banks may continue to dominate the retail deposit market.

Money markets also provide large corporations and nonbank financial institutions with efficient short-term instruments for investing their liquid funds and thus compete directly with commercial banks' traditional deposit facilities. They also enable large corporations to issue short-term securities in the form of commercial paper and thus further reduce the market power that large banks may have in the domestic banking sector. Finally, capital markets enable contractual savings and collective investment institutions to play a more active role in the financial system.

The complementary and competitive interaction of financial institutions has policy implications. To promote an efficient financial system there must be competition, but the system must also offer an array of services. Rather than restrict the growth and diversification of the main banking groups, governments in the larger economies would be wise to promote greater competition by encouraging money and capital markets, specialized credit institutions (such as leasing and factoring companies), and contractual savings and collective investment institutions. Economies too small to support such specialized institutions can spur competition by allowing economic agents to buy financial services abroad.

The financial systems of many developing countries are inadequate, or less efficient than they could be, or both. Efficient financial systems help countries to grow, partly by mobilizing additional financial resources and partly by allocating those resources to the best uses. As economies develop, so must the financial systems that serve them. The next chapter illustrates the central role of finance in development by reviewing the evolution of financial systems since preindustrial times.

3

The evolution of financial systems

In preindustrial economies, finance was largely concerned with the development of a medium of exchange. Barter was inefficient, transaction costs were high, and the lack of a medium of exchange limited the extent of the market and the opportunities for specialization. With the growth of nonlocal trade, the development of payment media became linked to the financing of trade. Otherwise, apart from the financing of governments and seaborne trade, borrowing and lending were mostly informal and on a small scale.

The spread of urban society, and above all the advent of large-scale industrialization in the second half of the nineteenth century, altered the role that finance had to play. Finance was now concerned with mobilizing resources for large infrastructure projects and for investments with heavy capital requirements that exceeded the capabilities of small family firms.

The systems that emerged often suffered from fraud and mismanagement. They proved unstable and experienced frequent crises. Speculative manias, fueled by financial institutions, caused mounting concern, and after the Great Depression of the 1930s governments began to supervise their financial systems more closely. But government intervention was by no means entirely successful. It made the financial system less flexible, and although it reduced fraud it did not eliminate it. Moreover, economic agents proved adept at getting around the regulations. In recent years the focus has shifted back to deregulation, partly in response to financial innovation and partly to promote competition and efficiency.

The evolution of financial systems ought to cast light on two questions that are of interest to policymakers in developing countries. What role should financial systems play in promoting industrialization and development? And what role should governments play in creating such systems?

Development of payment systems

The search for an efficient medium of exchange gradually led to the monetization of precious metals. As a result the payment mechanism became simpler and safer. The new monies facilitated trade and provided a store of value and a unit of account. Governments played an important part in this change by owning and regulating mints and thus ensuring the quality and acceptability of coins. But they were also frequently responsible for debasing coins by lowering their weight or adulterating them with less precious metals, such as copper.

Metallic payment was a big step forward. Gradually, however, paper-based instruments, which were cheaper and more convenient, came to replace coins and bullion. Payment orders, letters of credit, and negotiable bills of exchange evolved with the expansion of nonlocal trade in Europe. These were particularly useful in triangular trade, because only net settlements had to be made in specie. Commercial bills known as *hundi* were developed in India. In Japan, the need for cash was reduced by the use of bills and rice warehouse warrants and by the development of clearing facilities.

The direct role of governments in creating paper-based credit instruments was limited—although they provided the legal framework that was necessary for their use. Governments played a greater part in the development of paper money. They were involved either directly (as in China) or indirectly (which was more common), through granting the right to issue paper money to private bankers. China invented paper money in the ninth century. The ruler, acutely aware of the problems of paper money, enforced acceptance with the threat of death and by strictly limiting issuance (see Box 3.1), although there were many later instances of overissue. Paper money was subsequently introduced in Japan. In Europe, bank notes (representing promises to pay on demand) were issued in the seventeenth century by goldsmiths, notaries, and merchants, who gradually developed into bankers. Banks created by special charter, such as the Bank of England, also issued notes. In the colonies of North America, a chronic shortage of bullion led to the issue of land-backed certificates, which circulated as paper money.

The overissue of bank notes often undermined the credibility of paper money and led to financial crises and the suspension of the notes' convertibility into bullion. This happened in the American Carolinas and France in the eighteenth century, and in several European and Latin American countries in the nineteenth century. Attempts in the nineteenth century to regulate the supply of gold-backed bank notes in England stimulated the use of checks drawn on bank deposits to make payments and thus promoted the spread of a more efficient and versatile instrument of payment. The growing use of bank notes issued by different bankers led to the creation of clearing facilities, which were later extended to cover the clearing of checks.

As central banks evolved to cope with the recurring financial crises of the latter part of the nineteenth century, they came to monopolize the note issue. This led to the eventual adoption of fiat money—that is, paper (and later credit) money not backed by bullion. Fiat money solved the problem of loss of confidence in bank notes issued by individual banks, but not the problem of overissue of paper money by the central bank. Many countries in Asia, Europe, and Latin America suffered episodes of hyperinflation after governments had used the central bank's printing presses to finance their deficits.

The twentieth century has seen further innovation in payment instruments, including plastic cards and electronic transfers. These were developed primarily to improve the efficiency of payments rather than to promote expansion of trade. In most countries, central banks now play an important role in the payment system: they provide clearing and settlement facilities to banks and to other institutions that offer payment services.

Development of trade finance

In preindustrial economies, governments borrowed to pay for wars, and seaborne trade was financed, as it had been since classical times, by so-called bottomry loans (a combination of loan and

---

Box 3.1 Marco Polo discovers paper money

''In this city of Kanbalu [Beijing] is the mint of the Great Khan, who may truly be said to possess the secret of the alchemists, as he has the art of producing money . . . He causes the bark to be stripped from . . . mulberry-trees . . . This . . . is made into paper, resembling, in substance, that which is manufactured from cotton, but quite black. When ready for use, he has it cut into pieces of money of different sizes, nearly square, but somewhat longer than they are wide . . . The coinage of this paper money is authenticated with as much form and ceremony as if it were actually of pure gold or silver; for to each note a number of officers, specially appointed, not only subscribe their names, but affix their seals also . . . The act of counterfeiting it is punished as a capital offence. When thus coined in large quantities, this paper currency is circulated in every part of the Great Khan's dominions; nor dares any person at the peril of his life, refuse to accept it in payment. All his subjects receive it without hesitation, because, wherever their business may call them, they can dispose of it again in the purchase of merchandise they may require; such as pearls, jewels, gold, or silver. With it, in short, every article may be procured.''

Marco Polo
The Travels of Marco Polo, Book II, Chapter 24
(Komroff 1926, pp. 156–57)

Box 3.2   Trade financing in Renaissance Italy

The businessmen and bankers of northern Italy's Renaissance city-states—particularly Genoa, Florence, and Venice—developed many of the fundamental practices of modern finance. Their innovations included double-entry bookkeeping and the provision of credit through discounted promissory notes. One of their most important innovations, however, was trade credit.

Suppose that a Florentine textile manufacturer received a potentially profitable order from Barcelona and had the means to fill it. Two things might keep him from accepting the business. First, the importer might not pay until he received the goods—perhaps not even until he had sold them. Meanwhile, the exporter would have to pay for materials, labor, storage, and shipment. Second, having produced and shipped his goods, the exporter would have to bear the risk that the importer might simply fail to pay. And there was no court to which the exporter could take the Barcelona merchant.

Commercial banks—that is, banks which specialize in financing commerce—came into being to solve such problems. By providing short-term finance (working capital), commercial banks enabled such merchants to pay for materials and labor in advance. They solved the second problem by having trusted agents in major cit-

ies. For a fee, the bank could pay the exporter as soon as the shipment embarked. The importer would then pay the bank's agent—adding a fee—when the shipment arrived. For an additional fee the same bank might even insure the shipment.

Over time, the Italian banks developed this vital trade-financing function. The leading Florentine banking family, the Medici, acquired agents or correspondents in Europe's trading cities and made itself indispensable in the continent's commerce. Probably in the thirteenth or fourteenth century, the bankers invented a variation that limited the degree to which their own capital was tied up over the course of the transaction. This was the ''acceptance,'' or ''four-name paper.'' The Barcelona agent (name 1) would sign a document ''accepting'' the liability of the importer (name 2) to the exporter (name 3), and the document would be conveyed to the banker in Florence (name 4). The banker would disburse (after subtracting a discount) to the exporter against this acceptance. The banker could then sell the acceptance at a discount in the Florentine financial market and thus replace most or all of the cash the bank had disbursed. After some weeks the importer would pay the agent, the agent would pay the bank, and the bank would repurchase the acceptance, concluding the operation.

insurance contract, which was repayable upon the safe completion of the voyage). Otherwise, borrowing and lending were mostly on a small scale and were limited to trade credit, short-term loans to farmers, and loans for nonbusiness purposes. The financial system comprised money changers and moneylenders and a few private bankers who dealt mostly with wealthy individuals, accepting deposits for safekeeping and providing loans. In addition, tax farmers helped to administer the tax system by collecting and transferring taxes, and various religious establishments offered their services as safekeepers.

The expansion of commerce was driven by the spread of trade fairs from medieval times and by advances in maritime technology in the fifteenth century. It led to the accumulation of large personal fortunes in Europe. Deposit banking and general and maritime insurance evolved to meet the growing needs of merchants and wealthy individuals. The creation of trading companies with special charters and limited liability gave rise to the issue and informal trading of company securities. The pace of financial development differed from country to country; the city–states of northern

Italy, for instance, made significant advances in trade finance (see Box 3.2).

Apart from granting charters to trading companies and note-issuing banks, governments promoted financial development indirectly, through the preservation of peace or the waging of wars and through their success or failure in maintaining macroeconomic stability. War finance was the spur for many of the innovations of this period—the creation of the Bank of England and other chartered banks, for example, and the issue of government bonds.

Urbanization and the capital requirements of infrastructure projects toward the end of the eighteenth century created a need to mobilize new financial resources. But the onset of the Industrial Revolution had relatively little impact on finance: the capital requirements of early industrial enterprises were small. Many owners came from prosperous trading or artisan families that were diversifying into manufacturing; such owners provided most of the capital from their own resources. Families, friends, and wealthy private investors provided the balance. Banks supplied mainly short-term working capital, which was routinely rolled over. Even so, bankers and industrialists (foundry owners, brewers, textile manufacturers, and so on) developed close relationships, mainly through cross partnerships.

The impact of large-scale industrialization

Financial development accelerated with the expansion of the railways and, especially, with the advent of large-scale industrialization in the second half of the nineteenth century. Advances in mechanical and electrical engineering and the increasing scale of production of electricity and chemicals meant that industrial enterprises needed more capital. This required a big change in industrial finance.

The possibility of incorporating joint-stock companies with limited liability made it easier for enterprises to attract the capital they needed to grow. Stock exchanges evolved to facilitate the issue and trading of debentures and shares. Banks and insurance companies expanded their operations. Several new types of institution were formed, including occupational pension funds and investment companies, although these were small to begin with. Savings banks, credit cooperatives, and farmer banks, mortgage banks, building societies, and savings and loan associations began to meet the financial needs of farmers, traders, savers, and homeowners, all of whom had been neglected by the commercial banks. Most of the financial institutions that we are familiar with today appeared before the end of the past century.

Different institutional structures and financial practices emerged among the industrializing countries. These have had a pervasive impact on the functioning of financial systems and have given rise to a persistent debate about the role of financial systems in promoting industrialization and economic development. But except in the United States, where chartering provisions prohibited interstate banking and prevented the emergence of nationwide banking, governments' involvement in shaping the organization of financial systems was limited to changing the legal framework to allow the creation of joint-stock banks and nonfinancial corporations and enacting subsequent regulatory changes to govern the operations of large corporations (see Chapter 6).

In Germany, several other continental European countries, and Japan, the banking sector became an important source of finance for industry. Banks operated as "universal" banks, engaging in both commercial and investment banking: they ac-cepted deposits, made long-term loans, issued and underwrote corporate securities, and took equity positions in industry. Universal banking first appeared in Belgium and France, but it was more successful in Germany and Switzerland, where its introduction coincided with the expansion of technologically advanced industries. In these countries, the leading commercial banks developed close links with industry and played a crucial role in raising long-term industrial finance and promoting industrial concentration and efficiency.

In Japan, major legal and regulatory reforms were implemented after the Meiji Restoration in 1868. The aim was to modernize Japan's economy and promote industrialization. Traditional trading houses, such as Mitsui and Sumitomo, were able to develop into large banks alongside newly established banking groups. The emergence of *zaibatsu* groups—family-based conglomerates with wide-ranging interests in industry, commerce, banking, and finance—speeded economic development. Initially, leading banks within zaibatsu groups provided long-term finance to their partner enterprises and only short-term credit to others. Later on, as the zaibatsu firms became more self-sufficient financially, their banks provided long-term finance to other enterprises and in effect became universal banks like those in Germany.

In Britain, the preference of the big joint-stock banks for short-term self-liquidating investments limited their provision of long-term finance for industry. A relatively high concentration of private wealth fueled equity and bond finance, initially through informal channels but later through organized securities markets. But weaknesses in the British securities markets (and especially the use of misleading prospectuses by undercapitalized and often unscrupulous company promoters) undermined investors' confidence in new industries such as electricity and chemicals. This delayed large-scale industrialization. Traditional industries that could finance their investment from internal funds continued to prosper, however.

As noted above, chartering restrictions prevented commercial banks from developing into nationwide institutions in the United States. As a result, the New York Stock Exchange became a substantial source of finance for industry. The repayment of the federal debt after the American Civil War and the accumulation of bank balances and trust funds in New York increased the supply of investment funds. Private banks, which were allowed to operate as universal banks, maintained considerable influence well into the twentieth century. They assisted in the formation of America's big industrial groups, as did the large New York joint-stock banks and the trust and life insurance companies. Until at least the turn of the century, leading American commercial banks operated more like German universal banks than British deposit banks, and their relations with industry were much closer than in Britain.

Stock exchanges developed from informal trading in the shares and debentures of chartered trading companies, which appeared in Britain, the Netherlands, and other countries in the sixteenth and seventeenth centuries. By the middle of the nineteenth century, stock exchanges were dominated by domestic and foreign government bonds and, to a lesser extent, by the bonds and shares of railway and other public utilities. The securities of industrial companies were relatively unimportant, except on the New York Stock Exchange. However, all the major countries had informal sources of equity and long-term debt finance for industry. Stock exchanges became a more important source of industrial finance as industry's capital requirements grew in the second half of the nineteenth century.

At the turn of the century, bond and equity markets were already well developed in Britain and the United States. But much like the present situation in most developing countries, the financial systems of the big industrial economies were dominated by commercial banks (see Figure 3.1). Insurance companies and other institutions accounted for only small shares of total financial assets.

Financial crises

In preindustrial economies financial crises were usually caused by war, natural disaster, or the debasement of the currency—although in the few centuries before the Industrial Revolution, the failure of private or state-chartered banks had sometimes precipitated wider financial instability. With the growth of banking and the expansion of securities markets in the nineteenth century, however, a system's stability began to depend on the soundness of its institutions. Ways therefore had to be found to provide liquidity to institutions in distress. Bigger and more complicated loans, extended over longer maturities, increased the risks of default and fraud on both sides. This underlined the need for prudential regulation and for laws to make financial contracts easily enforceable.

Financial crises often began as speculative manias, linked as a rule to foreign conquest; discov-

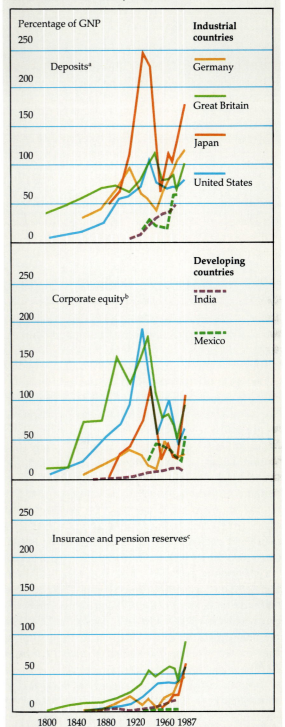

Figure 3.1 The evolution of financial assets in selected countries, 1800 to 1987

Note: There are some differences in definitions and coverage across countries.
a. Deposits with banks and other institutions.
b. Data refer to both listed and unlisted companies.
c. Accumulated reserves with insurance companies and pension funds.
Source: For 1800–1965: Goldsmith 1985; for 1965–87: central bank reports.

Box 3.3 Financial swindles

Swindles have taken many forms, from chain letters to wildcat banking, from penny stock scandals to insider trading. A typical swindle is the Ponzi scheme. It takes its name from Carlo Ponzi, a Bostonian of the 1920s. His idea was to lure investors by promising very high returns on the basis of a plausible but fictitious plan. He used the capital provided by latecomers to pay earlier investors. The scheme collapsed when the inflow of new money was inadequate to cover the outflow.

Few swindles are pure Ponzi schemes. Most mix genuine investment with insider trading. An early example of insider trading was the South Sea Bubble of 1720. John Bull and other managers of the South Sea Company borrowed from the company to buy its shares. As share prices rose, they made excellent profits. But to prevent the bubble from bursting, the company needed to raise capital at an accelerating rate and to see the price of its shares move continuously

upward. When the bubble burst and the share price collapsed, the directors of the South Sea Company were held in breach of trust and ordered to make good the losses of investors out of their own funds.

Penny stocks are stocks that sell for pennies but have great potential according to their promoters. Modern swindlers use telemarketing (thanks to cheap long-distance phone rates and computerized telephone dialing) to reach thousands of people. By manipulating stock prices and exaggerating the prospects of their companies, they induce greedy and gullible investors to part with their money. When investors want to sell, the promoters pressure them not to; if the investors insist, the promoters may refuse to accept their sell orders or to answer their calls. Today schemes of this kind are operated on an international scale. Swindlers are evidently part of the trend toward global finance.

---

eries of land, gold, and other natural resources; technological breakthroughs; or economic deregulation. Sometimes financial swindles were the cause, as in the first recorded insider-trading scandal, the South Sea Bubble of 1720 (see Box 3.3). Spectacular crises were common during the nineteenth and early twentieth centuries. In 1816 and again in 1825 banks failed in England when they were unable to redeem their notes or meet the withdrawals of their depositors. In 1857 many banks collapsed in the United States. In 1866 the failure of Overend, Guerney, one of the largest discount houses in the City of London, caused a crisis that had extensive repercussions throughout the world. In 1873 major banking crises occurred in both Germany and the United States. In 1890, Baring Brothers, a British private bank that suffered losses from underwriting a failed issue of Argentine securities, came close to collapse. In 1931–33 a massive crisis devastated the banking system of the United States. Banks in several European countries also failed.

To contain the damage caused by such crises, central banks (notably the Bank of England and the Bank of France) developed the lender-of-last-resort facility. Initially, they acted as bankers to the government but not to other banks. Gradually, prompted by the need to provide liquidity in times of trouble, they evolved during the nineteenth century into bankers' banks. The development of the lender-of-last-resort facility was bedeviled by

the conflicting requirements of providing support to the system without bailing out imprudent or fraudulent banks.

After the Great Depression, governments in several countries introduced new regulations. The toughest measures were taken in the United States. New rules prevented banks from holding equities in industrial and commercial companies on their own account, from engaging in investment banking, and from paying interest on demand deposits. The Federal Deposit Insurance Corporation was created to provide insurance for depositors' funds, and the Securities and Exchange Commission was set up to supervise the securities markets. Coupled with continuing restrictions on bank mergers and branching, these measures constrained the growth of commercial banks, which remained fragmented and were unable to meet the long-term financing requirements of American business. Instead, these were largely met by the securities markets.

Other countries (including Canada, France, and Italy) also separated investment from commercial banking and imposed maturity controls on the lending and deposits of commercial banks. In contrast, neither Germany nor Japan (prior to World War II) prohibited universal banking, and in Britain such measures were irrelevant because the big commercial banks had specialized in deposit banking of their own accord. Germany did enact detailed prudential controls, but universal banking continued. The big commercial banks substantially increased their involvement in industry during the 1920s and 1930s, when widespread company failures caused many debt claims to be converted into equity.

The American banking crisis of the 1930s and its impact on the Great Depression have been much debated. Some have argued that the crisis and its economic repercussions were exacerbated by the failure of the Federal Reserve System to provide adequate liquidity to stem the collapse of small banks. Others have stressed the banks' weak loan portfolios, which were concentrated in agriculture and real estate. The pattern of recent bank failures in the United States, which is quite similar to that of the 1930s, underlines the threat posed by poor loan diversification and excessive speculative financing of real estate—both of which can be attributed to restrictions on interstate banking and inadequate supervision of the banks. Recent studies have also shown that security underwriting and investment banking had little to do with the bank failures of the 1930s. The present worldwide trend toward universal banking argues for the abolition of the legal separation of commercial and investment banking. At the same time there is a growing recognition that effective prudential regulation and supervision are essential.

Financial systems in developing countries

The evolution of financial systems in developing countries reflected their diverse political and economic histories. Latin American and Mediterranean countries, politically independent since at least the first quarter of the nineteenth century, suffered frequent bouts of financial instability. These prevented the emergence of mature financial systems. In contrast, developing countries in Africa and Asia, under colonial rule until the end of World War II, enjoyed relative financial stability—but their financial systems suffered from colonial neglect and stagnation.

The financial systems of most developing countries were heavily oriented toward agricultural exports, other primary production, and foreign trade. In Africa and Asia, financial systems catered principally to expatriate communities. Financial services for the indigenous populations were limited. Foreign banks confined their operations to port towns and other centers of commerce where the expatriate communities were gathered. The domestic population, especially in Asia, hoarded precious metals and jewelry. Hoarding was insurance against financial emergencies caused by war, crop failure, natural disaster, and personal mishap—but it was saving denied to productive investment.

Sound banking promoted financial stability in Africa and Asia. Currency boards regulated the money supply and maintained reserves that were invested in London and Paris. The financial systems of most African countries, however, were underdeveloped until independence. They comprised a few foreign colonial banks, post office savings banks, cooperative societies, and moneylenders. Nigeria was the only African country with indigenous commercial banks before the late 1940s (see Box 3.4).

Financial development was more advanced in Asia. As in Africa, foreign banks confined their operations largely to the financing of foreign trade, but they also helped to finance internal trade. Most Asian countries also had a fairly well-developed indigenous banking system, with commercial banks, cooperative credit societies, and informal bankers and moneylenders. India, in particular, had a sophisticated indigenous banking structure. It had evolved over several centuries, developing the use of commercial bills known as *hundi* for financing nonlocal trade and relying on an elaborate system of personal relations to finance local, mostly small-scale activities (see Box 3.5).

Foreign banks operated in pre-1949 China, mostly in treaty ports, and some indigenous banks (*shansi*) remitted funds across regions and financed local trade. Foreign banks promoted foreign direct investment in railroad construction, mining, and manufacturing. They also made massive loans to the Chinese government and in the process gained control of its customs and salt revenues. Modern Chinese banks came into being in the 1930s. They had close links with the government and the ruling families and were able to seize the initiative from foreign banks and emerge as the dominant group. After 1949 China built a monobanking system typical of centrally planned economies.

Indigenous bankers and moneylenders were able to meet the borrowing needs of local traders and farmers by maintaining close personal contact with them and acquiring intimate knowledge of their operations. Their services were accessible but expensive. Informal financial institutions, such as rotating savings and credit associations (ROSCAs), also emerged in most countries (see Chapter 8). Indigenous bankers and informal financial institutions, however, could not mobilize the resources required for industrialization.

Box 3.4 Financial underdevelopment in Nigeria

In the late 1940s, Nigeria had a population of 30 million and no more than twenty-nine bank branches. Seventeen of these belonged to the Bank of British West Africa and eight to Barclays Bank (D.C.O.). The other four were branches of indigenous banks. In addition, Nigeria had a post office savings bank, a network of credit cooperatives, and later on some development corporations. Moneylenders operated in the informal market alongside other informal institutions known as *isusu*.

Nigeria was the only country in Africa to develop indigenous commercial banks (that is, banks incorporated within the territory and owned and managed by Africans) before the late 1940s. Three indigenous banks were created in the 1930s to serve the African population, but of these only the National Bank of Nigeria survived. In the early 1950s the number of indigenous banks increased, although most of them soon failed. Then in the years before and after independence, both colonial and local banks greatly expanded the number of branches so that by 1962 there were more than 200 commercial bank branches.

African traders believed that the colonial banks were mostly concerned with maintaining the dominance of expatriate trading houses. Understandably, colonial banks feared that loans to local traders and farmers could be risky, but their failure to mobilize savings deposits is harder to justify. Indigenous banks attracted funds from the public by offering attractive interest rates, advertising (with an appeal to nationalist sentiment), and opening branches. The expansion of banking facilities by both colonial and local banks and their success in mobilizing deposits before and after independence indicated the potential for changing the savings and financial habits of the local population—a potential that went untapped because of the colonial banks' orientation toward the expatriate communities.

Box 3.5 Indigenous banking in India

At independence, India had an indigenous banking system with a centuries-old tradition. This system had developed the *hundi*, a financial instrument still in use that is similar to the commercial bills of Western Europe. Hundis were used to finance local trade as well as trade between port towns and inland centers of production. They were often discounted by banks, especially if they were endorsed by indigenous bankers.

Indigenous bankers combined banking with other activities, much as the goldsmiths, merchants, and shippers of eighteenth- and nineteenth-century Europe had done. They usually belonged to certain castes or communities, such as the Multanis, Marwaris, and Chettiars, and they differed in the extent to which they relied on their own resources, rather than deposits and other funds, for their lending. Indigenous bankers often endorsed hundis issued by traders and sometimes provided personal guarantees for loans from commercial banks. Such bankers were collectively known as Shroffs, a term that probably originally referred to money changers but over time came to refer to the more sophisticated and influential indigenous bankers. The main moneylenders were the Sowkars (who lent to farmers from their own resources or funds borrowed from the Chettiars and other indigenous bankers) and the Pathans (who lent mainly to poor people and often resorted to intimidation to ensure repayment).

Indigenous banking was based on an elaborate and extensive network of personal relations that overcame the problems of dealing with large numbers of customers. Brokers were used for making introductions and vouching for the creditworthiness of individual borrowers but did not offer personal guarantees. Some brokers specialized in introducing indigenous bankers to commercial banks, while others brought together traders and indigenous bankers.

Throughout the nineteenth century, Latin American countries relied too much on foreign capital. Argentina and a few other countries developed active mortgage-bond markets and stock exchanges alongside thriving but fragile banking sectors. Unfortunately, however, recurring financial crises undermined attempts to develop the system adequately. Finance lagged behind the region's achievements in infrastructure, agriculture, and mining. Instability resulted from too much foreign borrowing; the overissue of currency; imprudent domestic banking; speculation in commodity, securities, and foreign exchange markets; excess capacity in industry and commerce; regional wars; and internal political unrest. Many of these were to figure in the debt crisis of the 1980s.

Latin American economies ran for long periods with inconvertible paper money, high inflation, and depreciating exchange rates. Producers and exporters of primary commodities welcomed this;

they stood to benefit and had a strong hold on government policies. Latin American countries occasionally suspended the servicing of their external debt. Foreign lenders, however, were usually lenient, probably because the region had immense potential for profitable investment. Major international houses arranged so-called funding loans, such as the Brazilian loan of 1898, which had many features in common with the multiyear rescheduling agreements of recent years. In contrast, foreign lenders imposed strict controls on the finances of many other countries, such as China, Egypt, Greece, and Turkey. Their governments were forced to cede revenues from stamp and customs duties and from state monopolies (on salt, matches, and tobacco) until the debts were fully repaid.

International banking crises seriously affected the financial markets of Latin America and the Mediterranean countries. At the first signs of trouble, foreign banks withdrew capital by calling their loans, reducing their advances, and pressing for remittances. The financial systems of Africa and Asia were better insulated, but their economies were hit just as hard by the effect of financial turmoil on international trade.

World War I and the depression of the 1930s played havoc with the world economy. Latin American countries were particularly affected by the development of man-made raw materials and the transformation of the British Commonwealth into a protectionist bloc. Most of them defaulted on their foreign debts, but the central and other state banks that had been created in the 1920s averted the panics of earlier periods.

Before World War II, developing country governments had a poor record on financial development. In Latin America and the Mediterranean countries, they failed to create sound legal and regulatory systems and to maintain macroeconomic stability. Borrowers relied excessively on foreign capital, and financial systems were undermined by imprudence. In Africa and Asia the restricted use of bank credit, the limited spread of the banking habit, and the persistence of the hoarding habit were all legacies of colonial banking systems that had failed to reach the indigenous population.

Financial regulation after World War II

After World War II, governments began to take a greater interest in the financing of high priority sectors such as industrial investment, exports, and housing. They created, or helped to create, credit institutions that specialized in long-term finance. National investment banks or institutions, such as Crédit National in France and the Industrial Bank of Japan, promoted industrial development through medium- and long-term lending and equity participations. They also encouraged the use of modern techniques of lending and credit appraisal.

Direct government intervention in the financial systems of several industrial countries increased with the nationalization of large commercial banks (for example, in France and Italy) in the aftermath of the crisis of the 1930s and World War II. Public sector banks—postal savings banks, postal giros, and savings banks linked with regional and local government, as in Germany and Switzerland—also extended their reach. Special export credit institutions, such as the U.S. Export-Import Bank, supplied export finance.

Domestic and international financial activities expanded, new institutions such as leasing and factoring companies came into being, and the contractual savings institutions continued to grow. Noncommercial financial institutions, such as mutual and municipal savings banks, urban and agricultural credit cooperatives, building societies and savings and loan associations, came to play a prominent part in financing small and medium-size enterprises, agriculture, and housing. Despite mergers, competition intensified because the demarcation lines between different types of institutions were eroding and because domestic markets were opening up to foreigners. In most countries the trend toward universal banking continued: the big commercial banks moved into a variety of ancillary services, such as insurance brokering, fund management, and securities transactions (see Box 3.6).

Regulation, taxation, and the organization of social security played a significant role in shaping the structure of different financial systems. In the United States, commercial banks continued to be prevented from becoming nationwide, universal banks—although the development of bank holding companies made the restrictions less binding. At the same time, the growth of funded occupational pension schemes increased the supply of long-term funds to the securities markets. Australia, Britain, and Canada saw similar developments, although none placed restrictions on nationwide banking.

In Germany and other continental European countries, securities markets played a much smaller role in the financial system. This was be-

Box 3.6   Universal banking

One of the most important trends in financial markets in recent years has been the spread of ''universal banking.'' This term has different meanings but usually refers to the combination of commercial banking (collecting deposits and making loans) and investment banking (issuing, underwriting, placing, and trading company securities). It also involves close links and extensive consultations between banks and industry. Universal banking has been criticized for threatening to concentrate excessive power among a few banks and for introducing potential conflicts of interest. Adequate regulation and supervision ought to overcome these difficulties, especially if securities markets and other financial institutions are able to compete effectively.

Universal banking began in Belgium with the Société Générale de Belgique in 1822. Its initial impact was rather small, but it attracted considerable attention following the creation of Crédit Mobilier in France in 1852. By the 1860s similar institutions had been formed in Italy and Spain, but most of these ran into trouble. Universal banking was put on a more solid basis in Germany when Deutsche Bank and Commerzbank were set up in 1870 to finance foreign trade. They were largely unaffected by the company failures in Germany before the international crisis of 1873, and after 1876 they gradually became universal banks with an extensive deposit business and close links to German industry.

The German universal banks helped to establish many large industrial companies and presided over the gradual concentration of industry in Germany. Their expanding role in industrial finance coincided with technological advances that greatly increased their clients' capital requirements. With seats on supervisory boards and proxy voting rights on behalf of individual shareholders (who deposited their shares with the banks), they began to exercise tremendous influence.

Universal banking in Japan dates from the 1870s, when traditional trading houses such as Mitsui were allowed to establish joint-stock banks. It increased in importance after the emergence of the zaibatsu conglomerates, which had extensive interests in industry, commerce, banking, and finance. The zaibatsu banks became more prominent after the 1920s—although some of the most important banks of that period, such as Yasuda (now Fuji) and Dai-Ichi, had close links with various zaibatsus without being formally incorporated with them.

In the United States, state-chartered commercial banks operated as universal institutions along the lines of German banks, underwriting and distributing corporate securities until the Great Depression. National banks were prevented from engaging in investment banking (although in 1927 they were allowed to underwrite corporate securities on the same basis as state-chartered banks). But by the turn of the century, the big New York banks had combined with private bankers and trust and insurance companies to create large industrial trusts. Britain and France, after the failures of the 1860s, were perhaps the only countries in which the leading commercial banks specialized in deposit banking and short-term, self-liquidating lending. After the Great Depression, commercial and investment banking were legally separated in the United States, Canada, and several European countries—but not in Germany, Japan, and Britain (where functional specialization continued to be based on tradition).

Universal banking began to spread again after the mid-1960s. In Germany the large commercial banks are actively involved in investment banking and in the German stock exchanges. They provide both short- and long-term debt finance to industry, hold equity in industry (although their equity holdings are concentrated in a few large companies), and exert a strong influence on corporate affairs. Swiss and Dutch banks are similar, except that they do not hold direct equity stakes in industrial companies. In Sweden, commercial banks are authorized to act as stockbrokers, but they are not allowed to hold equity except through holding companies. In Belgium, holding companies such as the Société Générale de Belgique have large equity stakes in both banks and industrial companies. Many industrial countries (for example, Belgium, Britain, Canada, France, and Greece) have reformed the membership regulations of their stock exchanges to allow banks and other financial institutions to act as stockbrokers. In recent years, universal banking practices have been adopted by the large commercial banks in Britain and France, which also have considerable interests in insurance business.

In Japan, the zaibatsu groups were dismantled after World War II, and commercial and investment banking were legally separated. Banks exert their influence through the new industrial groups, and relations between banks and industry are close. Equity holdings are limited, but Japanese financial practice gives debt an equity-like role.

The success of universal banking seems to reflect not only the economies of scale and scope enjoyed by large and diversified financial institutions but also the importance of universal banks in monitoring corporate performance and controlling the behavior of corporate managers. With the convergence of the world's financial systems, securities markets and institutional investors have a bigger role in Germany and Japan, and commercial banks are becoming more involved in investment banking in Britain, Canada, Japan, and the United States. Concerns about the concentration of power and conflicts of interest can be met by regulation and supervision—for example, by requiring that a separate subsidiary handle securities trading—and by the development of securities markets and other intermediaries.

cause savers sought safety and liquidity; generous social security systems organized on a pay-as-you-go basis worked to the same end. Universal banking forged closer relations between banks and industry. There were differences within Europe (in attitudes toward universal banking, for example, and in the extent of government intervention), but the common features were the secondary importance of securities markets and institutional investors and the greater influence of banks in corporate finance.

In Japan, the zaibatsu conglomerates were dismantled after World War II at the behest of the American authorities. Investment banking was separated from commercial banking, and the growth of securities markets was encouraged. However, industrial groups, although less significant than the earlier zaibatsus, grew up around the major banks and large general trading companies. They came to play a central role in the industrial reconstruction of postwar Japan and promoted close relations between industry and finance. The regulatory framework favored the provision of bank loans for industrial investment. As in Europe, the securities markets and institutional investors played relatively minor roles in the financial system.

Most developed countries used direct controls to regulate the overall expansion of credit and to influence the sectoral allocation of financial resources. Several countries put interest rate ceilings on deposits and loans and restricted the banks' branch networks. But the mix of controls and regulations varied widely. The authorities in the United States and Germany did not set credit ceilings, although they conducted selective credit policies through special institutions. Britain set credit ceilings for purposes of monetary control and used some selective credit devices, but for the most part it did not use interest rate controls or branching restrictions. France, Italy, Sweden, and other European countries all used detailed and comprehensive controls. France adopted medium-term refinancing schemes, levied special taxes on interest paid and received, and put caps on lending margins. Similar controls have been widely applied in the Francophone countries of North and Sub-Saharan Africa. Japan used interest rate and branching controls and influenced the allocation of credit to high priority sectors through the so-called "overloan" position of large commercial banks.

Many countries provided a fiscal bias in favor of long-term saving through life insurance policies and occupational pension schemes. Home ownership and housing finance benefited from generous fiscal incentives, and specialized housing finance institutions enjoyed considerable fiscal and regulatory advantages. Since bank deposits and credits often faced ceilings or other controls, housing finance and contractual savings assumed great importance in most industrial countries.

Financial innovation since the 1970s

In the late 1960s and early 1970s, high inflation and changes in financial markets undermined many of the credit and banking controls then in use. Several countries, including Britain, Canada, France, the Netherlands, and Sweden, enacted a series of wide-ranging banking reforms. These abolished the distinctions among different types of institution, relaxed both global and selective credit controls, removed branching restrictions, and liberalized interest rates on lending and wholesale deposits.

Financial deregulation was interrupted by the macroeconomic turmoil that followed the rise in oil prices in 1973. Many countries reimposed credit controls, hoping to contain monetary expansion without raising interest rates. But deregulation resumed in the late 1970s. It ranged from the elimination or relaxation of controls on credit, interest rates, and foreign exchange to the removal of restrictions on the activities of institutions and on new financial instruments. In most countries the changes were cautious and gradual. This contrasted sharply with the experience of some Latin American countries.

Deregulation was prompted by the growing realization that direct controls had become less effective over time. The growth of the Euromarkets, the development of new financial instruments, and the advent of electronic technology all made it easier to bypass the restrictions. Governments also recognized that the prolonged use of directed and subsidized credit programs would lead to the inefficient use of resources and hinder the development of better systems.

The Eurocurrency markets are markets in which assets and liabilities denominated in a particular currency are held outside the country of that currency (dollar-denominated assets held outside the United States, for example). These markets first appeared in the 1960s and have greatly contributed to the financial innovations of the past twenty years. They have regulatory and fiscal advantages—transactions are anonymous, exempt from reserve requirements, and exempt from the interest equalization tax that was imposed on foreign borrowings in the New York markets in the mid-

1960s. They speeded the international transfer of financial technology. However, one result of their growth was an excessive emphasis on the expansion of bank lending, which led in the end to the developing country debt crisis of the 1980s.

In the 1960s the main innovations of the Eurocurrency markets were revolving medium-term floating rate credit facilities and the syndication of large Eurocredits among several participating banks. Later innovations included changes in maturity patterns (very short-term Euronotes and Eurocommercial paper, and perpetual debt instruments), in pricing (floating rate notes and zero-coupon bonds), and in funding options (complex convertible bonds and bonds issued with warrants). These innovations blurred the traditional distinctions between equity and debt, short-term and long-term debt, and bank debt and marketable securities. The development of swaps brought about greater integration of markets through the international diffusion of new instruments and the opening up of national markets previously closed to Euromarket activity.

Most industrial countries have encouraged the development of government bond markets, so that they can finance their public sector deficits in a noninflationary way, and have established or revived their money markets, so that monetary and credit control can be achieved through open market operations. All this marks a considerable shift in the balance of power from governments to financial markets. In addition, equity markets have been reformed to allow commercial banks to play an active part as market makers and securities houses, and new markets with less demanding listing requirements have been created for smaller companies. Governments have used fiscal incentives to stimulate venture capital and personal investments in mutual funds and equities. Financial futures and traded options markets have been established to allow hedging against the greater volatility in exchange rates, interest rates, and equity prices that followed the move to floating exchange rates and the use of indirect methods to control money and credit.

Recent years have also witnessed a major expansion in international transactions fueled by the accumulation of insurance and pension reserves and the liberalization and modernization of stock exchanges. As in the nineteenth century, however, this expansion of capital flows has exerted a destabilizing influence on markets, because foreign investors tend to repatriate their funds in troubled times.

Effective competition in banking, especially for corporate business, has increased with the opening of domestic markets and the creation of specialized nonbank financial intermediaries. But retail banking has also become more competitive, because commercial banks are turning toward the household sector and offering new credit, deposit, and payment instruments.

Deregulation has eliminated many of the manmade barriers to global finance, and technology has lowered the barriers imposed by nature. Advances in computing, information processing, and telecommunications have boosted the volume of business by reducing transaction costs, expanding the scope of trading, and creating information systems that enable institutions to control their risk more efficiently.

Deregulation, technology, and other common trends have caused a growing convergence of national financial systems. Universal banks and specialized institutions as well as institutional investors and securities markets all now play important parts in the financial systems of most high-income countries. Nowhere is this convergence more evident than in Japan, which has successfully expanded the nonbanking segments of its financial system to the point that it now has the largest securities houses and stock market in the world, as well as the largest commercial banks, postal savings bank, and housing finance institution.

The trend of convergence has been reinforced by the vast accumulation of financial assets by both households and corporations in most high-income countries (Figure 3.1). This underscores the growing importance of the financial sector as a service industry and its shift from the mobilization and allocation of new financial savings to the management and reallocation of existing resources.

Current policy concerns in industrial countries

Since the late 1970s the focus of financial regulation has also shifted. There is now less emphasis on product and price controls and more on prudential regulation and supervision. Another goal has been to promote competition. Financial systems are undoubtedly more efficient as a result. But some of the changes have caused concern in developed countries. Financial institutions are exposed to greater risks, the potential for conflicts of interest between institutions and their customers has increased, and the implications for the long-term performance of industrial and commercial corporations are unclear. The widespread distress of deposit institutions in the United States and Norway in the 1980s underlines the growing risk exposure of financial institutions in a deregulated but inadequately supervised system (see Box 5.4 in Chapter 5).

International efforts to regulate the risk exposure of financial institutions yielded the recent agreement, under the aegis of the Bank for International Settlements, on new capital requirements for commercial banks, based on risk weights for different types of assets. In the Eurobond and Eurocredit markets, concern centers on the risks taken by banks in the pursuit of new business and on poor profitability due to fierce price competition.

Developments in the equity markets have raised different issues: insider trading, the growing number of hostile takeovers, and the methods used by corporate raiders and incumbent managements to take or retain control. Hostile takeovers may promote efficiency, but they also cause an accumulation of corporate debt and may worsen the conflicts of interest between managers, shareholders, and bondholders. There is also concern that institutional investors and corporate managers stress short-term performance at the expense of long-term efficiency. So far, however, the evidence has been inconclusive.

The next chapter will review the systems of finance in place in developing countries and assess the interventionist role played by government in the pricing and allocation of credit. Perhaps the most important lesson to be learned from the experience of the high-income countries is that the financial decisions of private agents are also imperfect—witness the savings and loan debacle in the United States and the excessive lending of commercial banks to developing countries in the 1970s. The future is uncertain. Under any system of finance mistakes will be made. Market-based financial systems, like public ones, are subject to fraud and instability. The goal is not perfection but a system which mobilizes resources efficiently, minimizes allocative mistakes, curbs fraud, and stops instability from turning into crisis.

Governments must certainly play their part. In most high-income countries, they continue to influence the pricing and allocation of credit, but only to a modest extent. Their main concern is to regulate and supervise financial institutions and markets while maintaining a stable macroeconomic environment. The need for prudential regulation increases as financial systems become deeper and more complex. From the development of the lender-of-last-resort facility during the nineteenth century and the introduction of deposit insurance after the Great Depression to the recent emphasis on risk-weighted capital requirements and the growing adoption of regulation by function rather than by institution, a main concern of financial regulation has been the achievement of stability without undermining efficiency. But finance remains a dynamic field, changing far too rapidly to achieve a perfect balance between the freedom needed to stimulate competition and growth and the control needed to prevent fraud and instability.

4 Financial sector issues in developing countries

Governments have made control over finance an important tool of their development strategies during the past few decades. Most believed that without intervention their financial systems would not be cooperative partners in the development effort. Dependent in the 1950s and 1960s on imports of manufactured goods and exports of agricultural products and raw materials, developing economies adopted a variety of strategies to promote rapid industrialization and the modernization of agriculture. A few, such as Hong Kong, the Republic of Korea, and Singapore, attempted from early on to integrate their economies with international markets. Most countries, however, pursued an industrialization strategy based on import substitution. Some provided only moderate and relatively uniform protection to domestic industries, primarily through tariffs, and others (Argentina, India, and Tanzania, for example) provided extensive protection through high tariffs and quantitative import restrictions.

Developing country governments also took an active role in economic decisionmaking. At the very least, governments owned and controlled capital-intensive infrastructure such as roads, ports, water and electric power utilities, and telecommunications. Many also controlled selected enterprises in heavy industry and natural resource extraction. Several countries went further, bringing other industrial and commercial enterprises under government control as well. In centrally planned economies, large-scale production was carried out by government entities to the virtual exclusion of independent organizations, decentralized decisionmaking, and market forces.

Although the extent of intervention varied among countries, nearly all governments considered it necessary to intervene in the financial sector in order to channel cheap credit toward the sectors that were to be at the forefront of development. The financial systems of most developing countries in the 1950s and 1960s could not adequately support a process of industrialization and agricultural modernization. Formal financial systems usually consisted of a few institutions, often foreign-owned, which had branches in the major cities only. These provided financing mainly to trading companies, mines, and plantations, which were often foreign-owned as well. Local businesses had difficulty borrowing from banks; local farmers had no access to them at all. An indigenous informal financial sector made up of moneylenders, traders, and pawnbrokers provided loans to farmers and small businesses (see Chapter 8). Informal lenders charged high rates, however, and the scale of lending was small. There were few sources of equity and long-term finance for industry, and what was available was expensive. In some countries the banks were owned by industrial groups. This reduced the access of outsiders to finance and concentrated a great deal of wealth and power in the hands of a few.

Chapter 2 stressed the roles of risk, information, and transaction costs in determining the supply of finance. In developing countries, investment was relatively risky. Production was in new sectors and used technologies unfamiliar to the work force, entrepreneurs and managers were inexperienced, and marketing channels had not been developed. Natural calamities and fluctuating commodity prices could drastically affect the incomes of farmers. Government policy was a constraint and a source of uncertainty: trade and pricing policies discriminated against exports and agriculture; devaluations and tariff changes could radically alter a firm's competitive position and the cost of servicing its foreign debt; trade and foreign exchange restrictions could reduce access to needed imports. Volatile inflation caused abrupt swings in relative prices, periodic recessions reduced product demand, and government borrowing crowded firms out of the financial markets.

Furthermore, the instruments and markets through which risks could be pooled or transferred were undeveloped. Financiers lacked the tools to evaluate, price, and monitor risks. The weakness of accounting, auditing, and disclosure regulations limited the information available to lenders about borrowers. Legal procedures for collateral and foreclosure were poorly specified. These factors, together with uncertainty about borrowers' prospects and the future inflation rate, deterred creditors from providing long-term funds; lack of information and collateral discouraged banks from lending to farmers and small businesses.

Governments could have tried to increase the willingness of creditors to provide long-term finance and equity capital by modernizing legal systems and making contracts more easily enforceable; by clarifying property rights and improving title transfer and loan security; by improving bank regulation and supervision; by training accountants and auditors; and by ensuring adequate disclosure of information. Chapter 6 discusses such changes in more detail. But institution building takes time. Understandably, many governments wanted faster results. Moreover, many wanted to use the financial system for such purposes as allocating resources to projects with high social returns, redistributing income, reducing costs in state-owned enterprises (SOEs), and offsetting the effects of an overvalued exchange rate and restrictive trade policies.

Rather than lay the foundations of a sound financial system, most governments concentrated on intervention designed to channel resources to activities that they felt were poorly served by exist-ing financial institutions. Toward this end, they nationalized the largest, and in some cases all, commercial banks; in Costa Rica, India, Indonesia, Mexico, and Pakistan, for example, the majority of banking system assets are government-owned. In addition, they created and supported development finance institutions (DFIs), which were specifically mandated to provide long-term finance to particular sectors. Governments applied interest rate and credit allocation controls to public and private institutions alike and ordered banks to open branches in rural areas. Bilateral and multilateral aid agencies participated in targeted credit programs by providing financial support and institutional assistance.

Governments in high-income countries also intervened in their financial systems. Although they exerted some influence over the flow of credit, interest rate and credit controls were less extensive than in developing countries. The principal emphasis was instead on measures designed to safeguard the stability of the financial system. In developing countries, however, governments paid inadequate attention to regulatory and prudential matters, to the detriment of their financial systems.

Government intervention in credit allocation

Developing country governments have played a large role in credit allocation. For example, in Pakistan in 1986, 70 percent of new lending by the national banks, which dominate the banking system, was targeted by government, although this proportion was reduced substantially by 1988. In India about one-half of bank assets had to be placed in reserve requirements or government bonds, and 40 percent of the remainder had to be lent to priority sectors at controlled interest rates. In Yugoslavia in 1986, 58 percent of short-term loans were directed credits. In Brazil in 1987, government credit programs accounted for more than 70 percent of the credit outstanding to the public and private sectors. In Turkey in the early 1980s, roughly three-quarters of all financial system advances were made at government directive or at preferential interest rates, or both, although the proportion has since fallen (see Box 4.1). In Malaysia directed credit has accounted for an estimated 30 percent of bank portfolios.

Many such regimes were immensely complicated. At one point Korea had 221 formal directed credit programs. In 1986 the Philippines had forty-nine schemes for agriculture and twelve for indus-

Box 4.1 Directed credit in Turkey

In the early 1980s roughly three-quarters of all advances from the Turkish financial system were made at government directive, at preferential interest rates, or both. The preferred borrowers were the public administration, state-owned enterprises, farmers, exporters, artisans and small firms, house buyers, industrial investors, backward regions, and so on. Within agriculture, there were programs for sales cooperatives, credit cooperatives, and the like. Programs in other sectors were also subdivided—for example, by loan maturity—with different interest rates and conditions for each. Banks were also required to place 20 percent of their deposits in medium- and long-term credits.

To help banks defray the cost of loans at low interest rates, the Interest Rate Rebate Fund subsidized preferential credits by levying a surcharge on nonpreferential credits. The central bank operated an extensive system of rediscounts for priority sectors. In addition to these basic systems, the State Investment Bank (which lent to state-owned enterprises and has since been abolished) received special loans from the Treasury and from the social security system at favorable interest

rates, the central bank provided low-interest loans directly to state-owned enterprises, and the government kept substantial noninterest-bearing deposits at the Agricultural Bank.

In the early 1980s these policies helped to push real interest rates on nonpreferential credit to between 30 and 50 percent. Rates remain high today, but the large public sector borrowing requirement is now the main cause. The government has recently liberalized the credit system. Direct credit and rediscounts made available by the central bank were reduced from 49 percent of total credit in 1980 to 18 percent in 1987. By 1986 there were only five categories of central bank rediscount rates; three years earlier there had been thirty. The proportion of credit extended on preferential terms (defined as credits bearing negative real interest rates) declined from 53 percent at the end of 1983 to 35 percent in September 1987. Preferential credit is now provided only for agriculture, industrial artisans, exports, and housing. Interest rates on short- and medium-term directed credit were raised substantially in early 1988.

try. Interest rates, maturities, and eligibility criteria were often different for each program.

Directed credit programs usually targeted industry, state-owned enterprises, agriculture, small and medium-scale firms, and (to a lesser extent) housing, exports, and underdeveloped regions. In the case of industry the aim was to provide cheaper long-term finance and foreign exchange and thus to promote investment and rapid industrialization. In the case of agriculture it was to raise output and speed the introduction of new technologies. Credit directed to small enterprises was intended to generate employment; in housing, the intent was to provide affordable homes for poor households. Export credit programs sought to bridge the period between production and payment and to compensate exporters for industrial and trade policies that were biased against them.

Interventions were of five main types: lending requirements imposed on banks, refinance schemes, loans at preferential interest rates, credit guarantees, and lending by DFIs. In Brazil commercial banks were required to allocate between 20 and 60 percent (depending on bank size) of their net sight deposits for agriculture. In Mexico banks were required until recently to use 31, 10, 6, and 1.6 percent of their deposit and other liabilities for

lending to the government, DFIs, housing, and exports, respectively. Forced lending has now been eliminated as part of a comprehensive financial liberalization program. Banks in Burundi, Turkey, and Tunisia had to use 8, 20, and 43 percent respectively of their deposits (or other categories of assets and liabilities) for medium- and long-term lending or investment in public sector bonds (although in Tunisia the requirement has recently been reduced). In Nigeria banks were required until recently to comply with a scheme in which credit was allocated among sixteen sectors; portfolio requirements now apply to only two sectors, agriculture (15 percent) and manufacturing (40 percent).

In many countries commercial banks, and sometimes also DFIs, could refinance loans to preferred sectors on attractive terms. Bangladesh has twelve refinancing schemes. Turkey in 1983 had about thirty categories of rediscount rates, although by 1986 it had only five. Indonesia's central bank operates thirty-two different schemes. In a sample of sixty-five developing countries more than half had export refinance schemes. Many of the banks initially attracted by the interest rate spreads in these programs later found them inadequate to cover the high default rates.

Governments often specified preferential interest rates for lending to priority sectors. These rates were substantially lower than those on regular loans, which themselves were often kept artificially low. In Peru in 1980–82 the average differential between general and preferential real rates was 32 percentage points; the corresponding figure in Turkey was 36 percentage points.

Some governments have also provided guarantees. In high-income countries credit guarantees are the main form of assistance to small businesses. At least seventeen developing countries—including Cameroon, Colombia, India, Korea, Malaysia, Morocco, Nepal, the Philippines, and Sri Lanka—have established formal guarantee schemes for small and medium-scale enterprises. Guarantees and crop insurance have also been used in support of agriculture in countries such as Brazil, India, Mexico, Panama, and Sri Lanka. At least ten developing countries have guarantee schemes for preshipment export credit; even more have export insurance schemes.

Development finance institutions have been perhaps the most common means of directing credit. They were actively encouraged and supported by bilateral and multilateral creditors. Virtually all developing and high-income countries have at least one, and many have a special institution for each priority sector. Kenya, for example, has five government DFIs and three others in which the government has a big stake: one each for agriculture, tourism, and housing; four for industry; and one that serves the former East African Community. Brazil and India both have complex systems of national and state DFIs. The importance of DFIs varies from country to country, however. Industrial DFIs accounted for less than 10 percent of credit outstanding to manufacturing in Malaysia and Thailand in 1987, whereas in Mexico and Turkey they accounted for around one-third. In Morocco, the three sectoral DFIs accounted for 79 percent of all long-term finance. In some countries virtually all formal credit for agriculture and housing is provided by public institutions.

The impact of directed credit programs
on credit and growth

It is impossible to be precise about the effect of directed credit on the allocation of resources. In some countries it is likely that the programs have had little impact, because they supported lending which would have happened anyway, because they offered only weak incentives, because direc-

tives were not enforced, or because the programs covered only a small share of total credit. In other countries, however, directed credit programs had a significant effect. In Korea, reflecting the bias of credit directives, industry's share of credit increased from 44 percent to 69 percent between 1965 and 1986. In Pakistan and Tunisia there was a sharp decline in the share of commerce in total credit; this too reflected the bias of directed credit in favor of other sectors.

State-owned enterprises in some countries have clearly benefited from directed credit, especially if foreign financing is taken into account. The share of SOEs in nongovernmental borrowing from domestic banks in 1983–85 was 56 percent in Guyana, 43 percent in Mexico, 25 percent in Nepal, and 18 percent in Brazil. The share of SOEs in value added was much lower—in Guyana and Mexico not more than 25 percent and in Brazil and Nepal less than 5 percent. The foreign obligations of SOEs now account for more than half the external debt of Brazil, the Philippines, and Zambia. By 1986 the outstanding stock of foreign loans to SOEs for a sample of ninety-nine developing countries was twice that to the private sector. Although SOEs are capital-intensive, and therefore might be expected to borrow heavily, the way in which the enterprises were managed is a large factor in their high indebtedness. Artificially low prices, excessive staffing, or activities that were inherently unviable have resulted in low profits and low retained earnings. Borrowing was necessary not just for investment but also to cover losses.

In some countries, such as Ecuador (see Box 4.2) and Sri Lanka, lending programs for small and medium-size enterprises are succeeding in attracting the participation of local banks. Small firms almost everywhere continue to have difficulty obtaining funds, however. Lenders have avoided participating in schemes or have concentrated their support on the wealthier enterprises. Banks have been reluctant to use guarantees because the procedures are slow and complicated.

Export credit programs have increased exporters' share of credit in several countries. But the schemes have sometimes been narrow in coverage. In many countries they have not applied to indirect exporters, and small and new exporters also have difficulty. Preshipment refinance is not always automatic and fluctuates with changes in monetary and credit policy.

Although individual sectors have benefited from directed credit, the overall effect on growth is hard to gauge. Fast- and slow-growing countries alike

Box 4.2   Lending program for small enterprises in Ecuador

In 1980, Ecuador's Corporación Financiera Nacional, the country's largest government-owned development finance institution, established a fund—Fondo de Fomento para la Pequeña Industria y la Artesanía (FOPINAR)—to refinance loans from local financial institutions to small enterprises. The fund is autonomous and operates from a head office in Quito as well as from regional branches. Its financing has come principally from multilateral institutions via the government, which bears the foreign exchange risk. At the end of 1988, FOPINAR had approved the refinancing of 7,467 loans averaging $14,000. Enterprises outside the main urban centers have received 48 percent of the loans (by value).

There are now some forty participating financial intermediaries. The government-owned Banco de Fomento Nacional (BFN), primarily an agricultural bank, accounts for 45 percent of the loans to about 75 percent of the borrowers. Private development finance institutions and commercial banks account for the rest. (The four most active banks account for around 23 percent of total lending, and other banks and finance institutions each account for between 1 and 3 percent.) To participate in the program, the institutions must meet criteria regarding the quality of their FOPINAR portfolio, their overall debt-to-equity ratio, and their standing with the central bank and the superintendency of banks. In or-

der to encourage the participating institutions to become more independent, the program requires them to provide 10 percent of project costs from their own resources. Terms and conditions have been designed to provide FOPINAR and the institutions with adequate spreads (currently 2.5 percent and 5.0–6.0 percent respectively) and to keep interest rates to borrowers positive in real terms. The latter goal has not been fully achieved, mainly because of the very high inflation of the past year and the lack of an automatic procedure for adjusting interest rates.

Collection has been quite good. Arrears on the FOPINAR portion of the discounted loans of the private development finance institutions and commercial banks have averaged less than 3 percent. In June 1988 arrears represented about 11 percent of their overall portfolios.

FOPINAR's independence has allowed it to respond flexibly to changing conditions. FOPINAR actively promoted the program and set terms that were sufficiently generous to attract the financial institutions. It has helped to train the institutions' staff, and they and FOPINAR have accorded a high priority to supervising the loans. Automatic debiting of the institutions for amounts due to FOPINAR gives them an incentive to judge their lending carefully.

have intervened extensively in credit allocation. What matters is whether those who thereby received directed credit used their resources more productively than those who were denied credit would have. This is almost impossible to ascertain, although in some countries well-designed credit programs undoubtedly did improve resource allocation. In countries with highly protectionist trade regimes and macroeconomic instability, directed credit reinforced existing distortions. When structural adjustment was finally undertaken, many of the firms that had been financed became unprofitable. In countries that minimized price and other distortions and maintained macroeconomic stability, directed credit appears to have been more successful.

Credit programs can be useful when used to tackle the inadequacies of financial markets. For example, in countries without venture capital or equity finance, new and risky firms have found it difficult to obtain outside financing. Rather than forgo these investments, governments have directed commercial banks and DFIs to provide the

necessary financing. Because of the high risk, interest earnings have not covered portfolio losses, and lenders (or their guarantors) have frequently lost money. It is possible, however, that some of the high-risk firms have been sufficiently successful to compensate for the poor performance of others and that the overall program produced a net gain for the economy. Yet few governments and DFIs have turned out to be successful venture capitalists. Equity finance is a more appropriate way to finance risky ventures than bank loans. If governments establish the conditions necessary for equity finance, intervention will not be necessary.

Even well-designed credit controls tend to lose effectiveness if maintained too long. Moreover, the potential for mistakes grows as economies become more complex. The Korean government, for example, exercised extensive control of credit allocation through a combination of moral suasion and explicit programs. The policy was successful: the economy grew rapidly. Nevertheless, the government made mistakes in the latter half of the 1970s, encouraging large investments in shipping and heavy industry that resulted in excess capacity and slower growth in the early 1980s. Recognizing the inefficiencies of excessive intervention, the government has begun to liberalize its financial policies (see Chapter 9).

Directed credit programs have often been used not to correct the inadequacies of financial markets but to channel funds to priority sectors regardless of whether these were the most productive investments. Policies aimed more directly at goods markets or at the distribution of income—price reform in agriculture, grants for the poor, and so on—might have been more successful and would have avoided many of the drawbacks of directed credit.

Problems of directed credit programs

The interest rates charged on directed credits often deviated substantially from rates on non-preferential credit. The large implicit subsidy had to be borne by someone. Subsidies have sometimes been covered by low-cost loans from international agencies, by a charge against public spending, or by cheap rediscounts from the central bank. Otherwise, they had to be covered by cross-subsidization: higher rates charged to other borrowers, lower rates paid to depositors, smaller profits (or greater losses) for financial institutions. Such subsidies were often substantial: in Brazil in 1987 they were estimated at between 4 and 8 percent of GDP. In Mexico subsidies relating to development finance institutions and official trust funds were estimated to average 3 percent of GDP during 1982–87. Subsidies of this magnitude, when financed by the central bank or charged to the government budget, have compromised efforts at monetary or fiscal restraint.

Subsidized credit often failed to reach its intended beneficiaries. Lenders misclassified loans in order to comply with central bank directives. Within priority sectors, larger and more influential borrowers benefited most. Much was at stake: acquiring subsidized credit could sometimes add more to profits than producing goods. A review of ten small and medium-scale industry projects showed that the distribution of loans was skewed in favor of larger firms. Studies of agricultural and housing programs show similar results. Directed credit programs do redistribute income, but not necessarily in favor of the poor (see Box 4.3). Furthermore, when rates of return in targeted activities were lower than elsewhere, borrowers did not use directed credit as intended. A study of an agricultural scheme in Colombia found that nearly half

> ## Box 4.3 Credit and income redistribution in Costa Rica
>
> In Costa Rica, subsidized agricultural credit has been extended by four commercial banks, all government-owned. They were well positioned to reach the small farmer. By the mid-1970s the three smaller banks had more than thirty regional offices and the largest (Banco Nacional) had more than a hundred, two-thirds of which were rural offices specializing in credit for small farmers.
>
> Data for Banco Nacional, which accounted for 60 percent of agricultural credit disbursed, reveal that in 1974 just 10 percent of its agricultural loans accounted for 80 percent of the total agricultural credit it extended. The distribution of agricultural credit (and hence subsidies) disbursed by Banco Nacional was actually more skewed than the distribution of income and land. Low interest rates on the loans implied subsidies equivalent to 4 percent of GDP and almost 20 percent of value added in agriculture. That suggests an average credit subsidy of $10,210 on each of the big loans that accounted for 80 percent of the credit. In 1974 a family with an income of $10,500 was in the top 10 percent of the income distribution.

the funds had been diverted to other uses. Korea had an active curb market in which those with access to subsidized credit at times lent to others without.

By limiting the availability of credit to nonpriority firms, directed credit programs have crowded such firms out of formal credit markets and forced them to rely on retained earnings or more expensive borrowing from informal sources. Enterprises (in India, for example) have sometimes become quasi-financial intermediaries themselves because formal markets did not serve them adequately.

Once directed credit programs are begun, they create a constituency of beneficiaries who do not want them stopped. This has made it extremely difficult for governments to reduce their support of such programs—regardless of how costly or inefficient governments perceive them to be.

The impact of directed credit programs on financial systems

Whatever conclusion is drawn concerning the impact of directed credit programs on growth and the distribution of income, it is clear that they have damaged financial systems. Many directed credits have become nonperforming loans. The ability to borrow at cheap rates encouraged less productive investment. Those who borrowed for projects with low financial returns could not repay their loans. In other cases borrowers willingly defaulted because they believed creditors would not take court action against those considered to be in priority sectors. The distorted allocation of resources and the erosion of financial discipline have left intermediaries unprofitable and, in many cases, insolvent. Extensive refinance schemes at low interest rates have reduced the need for intermediaries to mobilize resources on their own, leading to a lower level of financial intermediation. Moreover, by encouraging firms to borrow from banks, directed credit programs have impeded the development of capital markets.

The adverse impact of directed credit on financial institutions is clearest in the case of development finance institutions. Industrial DFIs were generally deemed a success in their early years. Some of them have been conservative lenders and have managed to avoid excessive political interference; especially in countries with sound trade, fiscal, and monetary policies, they have continued to perform reasonably well (see Box 4.4). But for most the assessment is now far less positive. Portfolios and financial performance have deteriorated mark-edly; many DFIs are insolvent, and some have had to be closed. In a sample of eighteen industrial DFIs worldwide, on average nearly 50 percent of their loans (by value) were in arrears, and accumulated arrears were equivalent to 17 percent of the portfolio value. For three of these institutions, loans accounting for between 70 and 90 percent of the portfolio value were in arrears. The situation may be worse than the numbers show, because the rescheduling of overdue loans and growing loan portfolios reduce arrears ratios. Industrial DFIs have continued to depend on governments and foreign official creditors for funding because poor performance left them unable to pay market rates of interest, because the term structure of interest rates often forbade the higher rates necessary to mobilize longer-term resources, and because markets for longer-term domestic instruments were poorly developed.

The economic shocks of the 1980s added to the arrears of many industrial DFIs, but the roots of the problem usually lay deeper. Most industrial DFIs specialized in medium- and long-term lending for investment. Such lending was vulnerable to business cycle fluctuations and provided insufficient diversification of risk. Because most industrial DFIs did not provide working capital finance, take deposits, or provide other current services, and because they invested in equities to only a limited extent, they also lacked up-to-date information on their borrowers. Furthermore, when weak DFIs diversified into deposit taking, they were unable to compete with commercial banks.

Multilateral lenders encouraged industrial DFIs to calculate economic as well as financial rates of return. This is undoubtedly useful in distorted environments, but it may have diverted attention from the borrower's overall prospects, management capabilities, and day-to-day operating decisions. Many DFIs have permitted clients to finance investments with too little equity. Moreover, because many DFIs relied heavily on foreign resources, they had to pass foreign exchange risk on to clients who could neither bear nor hedge it. When currencies were devalued, many firms could not repay the loans. Finally, like government-owned commercial banks, government DFIs have had trouble recruiting and retaining competent staff because of uncompetitive salaries. Managers appointed for political reasons have often been unqualified and open to outside pressure in making loans.

The performance of agricultural DFIs has also been poor. Studies show default rates ranging from 30 to 95 percent for subsidized agricultural credit programs. Agricultural DFIs have suffered from many of the same problems as industrial DFIs: too much government intervention, overreliance on governments and official creditors for funding, inappropriate lending criteria (such as crop and livestock models that hold little relevance for the farms under review). In addition, lending to small farmers is relatively risky and has high transaction costs, especially if combined with technical assistance. And governments have often been unwilling to foreclose on small farmers, which has seriously eroded financial discipline.

Housing finance institutions have had problems, and several have been closed, but on the whole they have fared better than industrial and agricultural DFIs. They have had more success in mobilizing resources, although funding in some cases has come from compulsory savings schemes. The better housing banks view themselves as household sector banks and offer a range of services. They also tend to be located in countries with legal systems that make it possible to enforce collateral arrangements. Some housing intermediaries, pressured to behave like social agencies rather than bankers, have lent on excessively high loan-to-income or loan-to-value ratios; this has caused losses and poor recovery from collateral. Where fixed interest rates were charged on mortgages but

inflation and short-term deposit rates were rising (as in several Latin American countries and in the United States in the 1970s), housing banks that depended on short-term deposits were badly hurt. Mortgage indexation has provided some protection, but in countries such as Argentina and Brazil indexation was tied to wages; when these declined in real terms, the banks were left short of income.

Macroeconomic policies and financial development

In some countries macroeconomic instability has compounded the difficulties that financial systems now face. Macroeconomic conditions in developing countries in the 1980s were the result not only of external shocks but also of the development strategies that had been pursued in the 1960s and 1970s.

Government borrowing and inflation

By the 1980s many developing countries had come to rely on foreign borrowing to help finance increasing public sector deficits. When the inflow of foreign capital dried up in the early 1980s, some countries were able to reduce their fiscal deficits. But many were not. They lacked adequate instruments of taxation; social and political considerations made it hard to cut spending; and most of their external debt had been contracted at floating rates, so that the rise in real interest rates sharply increased the cost of servicing that debt.

Central government deficits tell only part of the story. A more complete definition of the deficit is the public sector borrowing requirement (PSBR), which in principle consolidates the net borrowing needs of all public sector entities, including public enterprises and the central bank. In practice, it often excludes some entities for lack of data. In some countries the reported PSBR became quite large. For example, in 1984 the PSBR was 15 percent of GDP in Argentina, 11 percent in Chile, 8 percent in the Philippines, and 13 percent in Yugoslavia.

PSBR data are unavailable for many countries, but Figure 4.1 shows how central government deficits, the narrow measure of public borrowing, were financed in twenty-four developing and eleven high-income countries in 1975–85. The contrast between the two groups is striking. In the developing countries 47 percent of the deficit was financed by borrowing from the central bank, 15 percent by borrowing from domestic financial institutions and markets, and 38 percent by borrow-

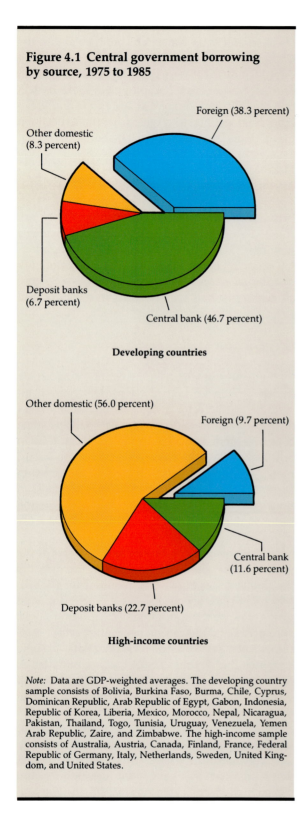

Figure 4.1 Central government borrowing by source, 1975 to 1985

Foreign (38.3 percent)

Other domestic (8.3 percent)

Deposit banks (6.7 percent)

Central bank (46.7 percent)

Developing countries

Other domestic (56.0 percent)

Foreign (9.7 percent)

Central bank (11.6 percent)

Deposit banks (22.7 percent)

High-income countries

Note: Data are GDP-weighted averages. The developing country sample consists of Bolivia, Burkina Faso, Burma, Chile, Cyprus, Dominican Republic, Arab Republic of Egypt, Gabon, Indonesia, Republic of Korea, Liberia, Mexico, Morocco, Nepal, Nicaragua, Pakistan, Thailand, Togo, Tunisia, Uruguay, Venezuela, Yemen Arab Republic, Zaire, and Zimbabwe. The high-income sample consists of Australia, Austria, Canada, Finland, France, Federal Republic of Germany, Italy, Netherlands, Sweden, United Kingdom, and United States.

ing from abroad (although foreign financing declined from 44 percent in 1975–82 to 26 percent in 1983–85). High-income countries, in contrast, relied mainly on nonbank financial institutions and

markets to finance their deficits, borrowing less than 12 percent of the total from central banks.

The governments of developing countries turned to their central banks because domestic financial markets were too shallow to meet their needs. To the extent that central banks financed such borrowing by issuing money, the result was higher inflation. The average inflation rate in developing countries increased from 10 percent a year in 1965–73 to 26 percent in 1974–82 and 51 percent in 1983–87. Inflation rates in high-income countries also rose in the 1970s but have been held to less than 5 percent a year in the 1980s. Half of all developing countries continue to enjoy single-digit inflation, but the number of countries with double- and triple-digit inflation has risen in recent years (see Table 4.1). During 1983–87, seven countries (Argentina, Bolivia, Brazil, Nicaragua, Peru, Sierra Leone, and Uganda) had average inflation rates of more than 100 percent, whereas in 1965–73 none did, and between 1974 and 1982 only Argentina did. Four of the seventeen highly indebted middle-income countries had triple-digit and eleven had double-digit inflation during 1983–87, which underscores the interrelation of external debt, fiscal deficits, and inflation. Other factors, such as repeated devaluations, have added to inflationary pressures, but deficit financing has provided the primary impetus.

One way or another, the domestic financing of large public sector deficits has taxed the financial process. Inflation is a tax on certain financial assets (see Box 4.5). Although some governments have sought to reduce the inflationary impact of public sector borrowing, the measures adopted are, in effect, alternative forms of taxation. Argentina, for example, set reserve requirements on demand deposits at more than 70 percent, Brazil at more than 40 percent, and Zaire at 51 percent. Reserve requirements constitute forced loans to the central bank, usually at below-market rates. Another approach has been to require banks, insurance companies, and other financial institutions to invest part of their funds in low-yielding government bonds. India and Pakistan, for example, have used this approach to finance large budget deficits at low cost while maintaining reasonable price stability (although Pakistan has curtailed the practice in recent years).

High reserve requirements and forced investments in low-interest government securities crowded out private sector borrowing and discouraged financial intermediation. The implicit tax reduced intermediaries' profits or was passed along to depositors and borrowers in the form of lower

Table 4.1 Average annual inflation rates, 1965 to 1987
(percent)

Item	1965–73	1974–82	1983–87
High-income countries	5	9	4
Developing countries	10	26	51
China and India	3	4	7
Other low-income	20	16	13
Highly indebted countries	14	45	120
Other middle-income	6	15	12
Number of developing countries with inflation rates in excess of			
20 percent	4	15	27
30 percent	2	9	17
100 percent	0	1	7

Note: The average annual rate of inflation is measured by the growth rate of the GDP implicit deflator. Aggregates for country groups are GDP-weighted averages. Data for developing countries are based on a sample of eighty-eight countries.

deposit rates or higher lending rates. Explicit taxes on financial intermediation, as in Turkey and the Philippines (see Box 4.6), exerted additional upward pressure on the spread between deposit and lending rates.

The impact of interest rate policies and inflation

Interest rate controls and inflation have set back financial development in many countries. Govern-ments kept interest rates low partly to encourage investment, partly to redistribute income, and partly because they themselves wished to borrow cheaply. Many governments also believed that low deposit rates (the corollary of low lending rates) would not discourage financial saving.

Experience has shown that some of these ideas were wrong. As Chapter 2 pointed out, there is strong evidence that real interest rates and infla-tion have a significant effect on financial savings,

---

Box 4.5 The inflation tax

An economy's willingness to hold money—that is, its demand for money—generally grows with its real GNP. Such demand may also change in response to yields on other assets and expectations. If the money issue exceeds the increase in the economy's willingness to hold money, the result is inflation, which operates like a tax. Asset holders "pay" the tax by losing purchasing power on their money holdings. Those who have issued money liabilities "collect" the tax in the form of a reduction in the real value of their liabilities. To the extent that the money issuer pays interest on these liabilities, it returns some of the tax to asset holders. Central banks typically do not pay interest sufficient to offset the tax on their money issue: they pay no interest on currency and usually a below-market interest rate on reserves. Box table 4.5 provides estimates of the inflation tax (as a share of GNP) flowing to the central bank on reserve money for ten countries in 1987.

It might seem that a high inflation rate implies a high inflation tax as a percentage of GNP, but this is not always so. High inflation rates (that is, high rates of inflation tax) discourage people from holding money. When the money stock held by the economy is a small percentage of GNP, the inflation tax will be corre-spondingly small. Hence, if inflation has been high and the money stock—the tax base—has declined as a per-centage of GNP, the central bank must issue a larger amount of money and generate a higher inflation rate to secure a given amount of revenue.

Box table 4.5 The inflation tax in selected countries, 1987

Country	Inflation tax (percentage of GNP)	Reserve money (percentage of GNP)	Inflation rate (percent)
Argentina	4.0	6.3	174.8
Côte d'Ivoire	0.5	14.4	3.4
Ecuador	2.0	8.1	32.5
Ghana	2.0	7.9	34.2
Mexico	3.7	6.0	159.2
Nigeria	0.9	9.6	9.7
Peru	4.8	9.1	114.5
Philippines	0.6	8.0	7.5
Turkey	2.8	7.9	55.1
Zaire	4.2	8.2	106.5

Note: The inflation tax is defined as the decline in the purchasing power of average reserve money (IFS, line 14) due to inflation. It is calculated as $M \times [i/(1 + i)]$, where M is the average reserve money at year-end and year-beginning and i is the decimal inflation rate measured by the change in the CPI from December to December. [Over any interval for which the prices rise by i, each money unit loses $i/(1 + i)$ of its purchasing power.]
Source: IMF, *International Financial Statistics*, and World Bank data.

Box 4.6 Taxation of financial intermediation in the Philippines

Like many countries, the Philippines collects special taxes from financial institutions. The most important of these are the gross receipts tax (GRT) and the implicit tax on reserve requirements.

The GRT is imposed on all receipts (income and capital gains) of a bank. Formerly applied at a uniform rate, it is now imposed on a sliding scale, with a rate of 5 percent for instruments with maturities of less than two years. Lower rates apply to longer maturities, with those of more than seven years free of tax. The implicit tax on reserve requirements arises because these are remunerated at 4 percent, which is much lower than market interest rates. Reserve requirements have varied but have for several years been more than 20 percent of bank deposit liabilities (except for long-term deposits of more than two years, which attract a much lower rate).

The impact of these taxes increased markedly during 1983–85. Major devaluations and an acceleration of inflation led to a sharp increase in interest rates as the authorities acted to restore stability. By the end of 1984, with money market rates at around 35 percent (compared with inflation of only 5 percent over the following twelve months), a bank would have had to earn more than 47 percent on a short-term loan simply to service money market borrowings, in view of the reserve requirements and the GRT. In other words, at the margin these taxes added more than 12 percentage points to the cost of intermediation. In fact, bank lending rates and spreads were held down by the weakness of demand for loans and the banks' continued access to funds from depositors at lower interest rates. Nevertheless, the combined burden of the GRT and the implicit tax on reserve requirements in 1984 exceeded 150 percent of value added in the banking system. The impact of the taxes has since come down with the decline in interest rates.

A withholding tax on deposit interest income, which is levied at the rate of 20 percent, also imposes some distortions. Although a credit against income tax, it is not refundable if the computed income tax liability falls below the amount of the tax already withheld. A further imposition is the lending requirement for agrarian reform—10 percent of banks' net loanable funds—which virtually all banks satisfy by investing in eligible government securities. Although these securities now carry market interest rates, this was not the case until recently.

and various studies have found that financial savings and the rate at which these are lent are positively related to economic growth.

Figure 4.2 compares real interest rates in thirty-five developing countries (as a group and by region) with the U.S. Treasury bill rate between 1967 and 1985. Except for a brief period after the first oil shock, real interest rates were much lower in the developing countries—and substantially negative for much of the period. Within the sample, average real rates were almost consistently negative in Africa, Europe, and Latin America. In Asia, however, average real rates were positive in most years.

Negative real interest rates were sometimes the result of deliberate policy, but sometimes they were inadvertent, a consequence of governments' failure to modify administered rates to compensate for rising inflation. Even in the absence of government regulation, the level of real interest rates has been highly sensitive to inflation because of lags in the adjustment of nominal rates. In Argentina, Israel, and Uruguay in the 1980s, volatile inflation caused sharp fluctuations in real rates.

Because of this link between inflation and real interest rates, macroeconomic stability is vital for financial sector development. In countries that have maintained low and stable inflation through prudent monetary and fiscal policies, financial sector growth has been rapid, even where interest rates were (moderately) regulated. The financial sectors of Japan and Malaysia have grown rapidly during the past three decades, thanks largely to price stability. Malaysia's financial depth, as measured by the ratio of M2 to GNP, rose from 31 percent in 1970 to 75 percent in 1987. Thailand's financial sector has grown rapidly since inflation was brought down; using the same measure, financial depth grew from 34 percent in 1980 to 60 percent in 1987, as real interest rates became positive. In contrast, Argentina has long suffered from high and variable inflation; its financial depth, which exceeded 50 percent of GNP in the late 1920s, had declined to around 30 percent of GNP by 1970 and to 18 percent by 1987 (see Figure 4.3). Other high-inflation countries, such as Bolivia and Yugoslavia, have also experienced slow or negative growth in financial depth.

In the 1970s the problem was low real interest rates. In the 1980s, however, some countries have experienced high real interest rates. Although most developing countries still place restrictions on interest rates, there has been a trend toward

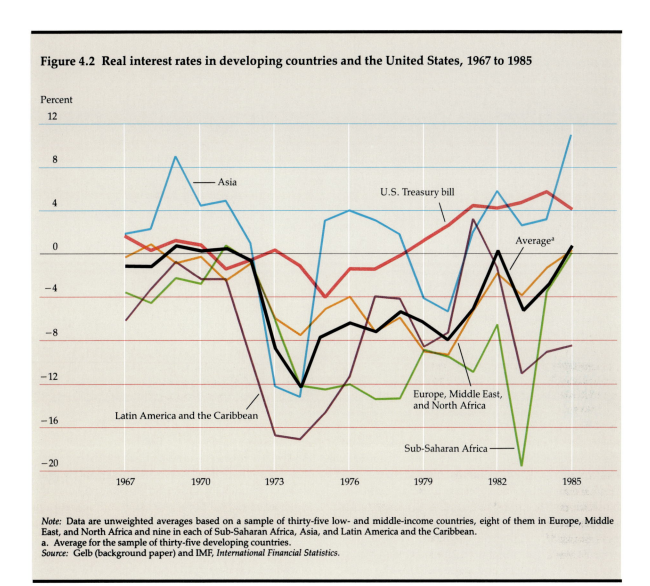

Figure 4.2 **Real interest rates in developing countries and the United States, 1967 to 1985**

Percent

Asia

U.S. Treasury bill

Average[a]

Europe, Middle East,
and North Africa

Latin America and the Caribbean

Sub-Saharan Africa

Note: Data are unweighted averages based on a sample of thirty-five low- and middle-income countries, eight of them in Europe, Middle East, and North Africa and nine in each of Sub-Saharan Africa, Asia, and Latin America and the Caribbean.
a. Average for the sample of thirty-five developing countries.
Source: Gelb (background paper) and IMF, *International Financial Statistics.*

deregulation. Some countries with unstable macroeconomic conditions and distressed banks and borrowers have seen real interest rates on nonpreferential credit rise to high levels (see Table 4.2). Real rates have also been high in some economically stable countries that administered rates, (for example, Korea and Thailand) because of a decline in inflation and strong loan demand. Although moderately positive real interest rates are desirable, extremely high real rates are not. They can cause distress among borrowers (see Chapter 5) and swell fiscal deficits. Chapter 9 returns to the difficulties confronting governments that intend to liberalize their financial systems.

Interest rate controls and inflation have had other adverse consequences as well. As noted above, artificially low interest rates cause excess demand for credit and force financial institutions to ration their lending—which may favor borrowers who need the money least. By preventing financial institutions from charging higher interest rates on longer-term and riskier loans, governments' interest rate policies have discouraged the very sort of lending they sought to foster. Together with directed credit programs, they have also discouraged competition. The combination of inflation and low deposit rates has led to capital outflows and thereby reduced the resources available for relending by financial intermediaries. The development of unofficial (curb) markets, however, has alleviated some of the adverse consequences of interest rate and other controls (see Box 4.7).

Inflation, by causing uncertainty and instability in relative prices, makes longer-term investments

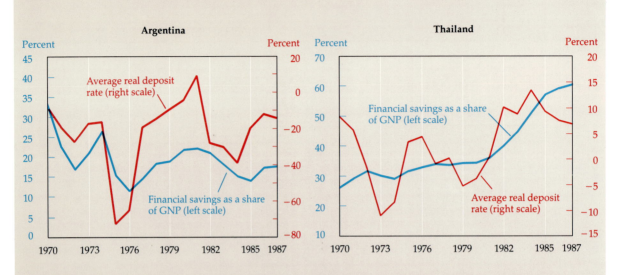

Figure 4.3 Financial savings and the real deposit rate in Argentina and Thailand, 1970 to 1987

Note: Financial savings are M2 (currency in circulation plus demand, time, and savings deposits at banks) and are five-quarter averages.
Source: Gelb (background paper); IMF, *International Financial Statistics*; Easterly 1989; central bank bulletins; and World Bank data.

riskier and more difficult to finance. It also makes the future purchasing power of financial contracts less certain. Even when interest rates are not regulated, uncertainty about future inflation makes it hard for lenders and borrowers to agree upon an appropriate fixed nominal interest rate. The lender risks inflation turning out higher than expected, the borrower risks inflation turning out lower than expected. The higher and more variable the inflation and the longer the time horizon, the greater the risks. In countries such as Argentina loans of more than thirty days became unusual.

Several countries that have had chronic inflation,

including Brazil, Chile, Colombia, and Israel, have authorized the use of indexed financial contracts. Indexation links the value of the financial contract to a price index. If indexation is complete, if the index accurately reflects prices, and if adjustment is immediate, indexation denominates the contract in terms of purchasing power rather than money. At high inflation rates, private sector borrowers often find it too risky to take on purchasing power obligations, because they fear their income will fail to keep pace. The public sector, in contrast, does not have this problem. It cannot go bankrupt in its domestic markets as long as it has the power to

Table 4.2 Real loan interest rates for selected countries, 1980 to 1986
(percent)

Country	1980	1981	1982	1983	1984	1985	1986
Argentina	5.1	31.2	−18.7	−22.9	−29.7	−6.3	3.9
Brazil	−2.5	4.9	26.2	0.2	7.5	−0.1	−0.1
Chile	12.1	38.8	35.7	15.9	11.5	11.1	7.5
Colombia	..	..	..	..	..	14.1	11.8
Indonesia	..	..	10.9	9.9	16.4	17.4	13.1
Korea, Rep. of	−12.3	5.1	6.6	7.9	7.4	6.6	8.6
Philippines	..	4.2	8.9	−5.4	−15.0	21.7	17.9
Thailand	1.4	5.9	16.0	13.3	19.2	15.2	15.1
Turkey	−0.6	50.2	37.7	28.0	28.7	42.0	51.0

Note: Real interest rates were calculated from nominal rates according to the following formula: $[(1 + r) / (1 + p) − 1] \times 100$, where r is the interest rate and p is the inflation rate.
Source: Easterly 1989.

Box 4.7   The curb market

In many developing countries, economic regulation (often in the form of interest rate controls) has led to the growth of an unregulated curb market, which can be an important source of funds for both business and households. In the Republic of Korea, it has been estimated that the outstanding obligations in the curb market in 1964 were roughly equal to 70 percent of the volume of loans outstanding from commercial banks. By 1972 the ratio had been reduced to about 30 percent, largely as a result of interest rate reforms in the formal sector in the mid-1960s. After the monetary authorities reduced interest rates in the late 1970s, there was a resurgence in the market. But the market has recently declined again. Business shifted from the curb market to nonbank institutions that were allowed to offer substantially higher returns.

According to one survey, about 26 percent of firms borrowed from the curb market, which supplied about 20 percent of their total borrowing. About 70 to 80 percent of credit from the curb market to small and medium-size firms was extended without collateral. But the curb market uses a sophisticated credit rating system, and prime companies pay an interest rate substantially lower than less creditworthy ones. The aver-

age annual interest rate on curb loans was 24.0 percent in 1985, when the general bank loan rate was 10.0–11.5 percent.

The curb market has been closely integrated with the formal market. According to one popular method of transaction, an informal lender makes a savings deposit at a bank branch, which then extends a loan to a borrower designated by the depositor. The informal lender thereby earns the savings deposit rate plus about 1 percent a month from the borrower, without any risk of default.

The curb market has been a significant part of the financial system in other countries as well. In Argentina, for example, the reimposition of interest rate controls and financial repression after 1982 led to the rapid expansion of the curb market. According to one estimate, informal credit from the curb market represented nearly a quarter of the total granted by commercial banks and finance companies in 1984.

Experience shows that the curb market becomes active when the formal financial sector is heavily regulated and interest rates are held below market levels. The curb market is effectively an unregulated bills market.

---

print money. Thus at high rates of inflation, most indexed contracts are issued or backed by the government or by public entities. Indexing financial instruments can be useful in inducing lenders and borrowers to make longer-term commitments at some middle range of inflation, say 10 to 40 percent a year, but it is no substitute for controlling inflation. If unaccompanied by adequate stabilization measures, indexation tends to make inflation worse (see Box 4.8).

As an alternative to indexing, some countries, including Turkey, Uruguay, and Yugoslavia, have adopted foreign currency deposit schemes. In effect, these index deposits to the exchange rate. Such schemes have increased the flow of savings into the financial system. But they can also complicate monetary management. Since the domestic value of the foreign exchange deposits rises automatically with currency devaluation, the monetary aggregates tend to accommodate inflationary pressures. To the extent that loans extended against foreign exchange deposits are denominated in domestic currency, the banks lose with each devaluation if the interest rate differential is insufficient to cover the change in currency values. This puts

pressure on the central bank to provide accommodation. In Yugoslavia, for example, central bank losses on the foreign currency deposit scheme have added to inflationary pressures.

Exchange rate policies and financial development

During the 1970s many developing countries allowed their exchange rates to appreciate in real terms. This was made possible by relatively favorable terms of trade and by the availability of foreign loans to finance the resulting current account deficits. The real appreciation of the exchange rate favored production of nontraded over traded goods and encouraged reliance on imported inputs. Financial institutions accordingly allocated a larger share of credit to firms in the nontraded goods sector, as Figure 4.4 illustrates in the case of Colombia.

Overvalued exchange rates and controlled interest rates combined to stimulate capital outflows. These flows were illegal in countries with foreign exchange controls, but such controls have rarely been effective. Although capital flight is hard to measure, the discrepancies between increases in

Box 4.8 Financial indexation in Brazil

By 1964 Brazil's inflation rate had risen to 100 percent a year. A new government took office in April 1964 determined to stabilize the economy. It felt unable to cut the deficit immediately, but wanted to finance it with noninflationary debt sales in domestic financial markets. This was impossible because exorbitant real interest rates would have been needed to compensate bondholders for bearing the inflation risk. In 1965, therefore, the government issued an indexed Treasury bond—a bond whose principal and interest would be adjusted periodically in line with the inflation rate. The government also encouraged the indexation of other financial instruments, including savings accounts and corporate debentures.

The experiment had mixed results. Indexation undoubtedly succeeded in increasing the flow of savings through the financial system and to the government (see Box table 4.8). Corporations, however, remained reluctant to issue indexed debentures because they were unsure whether the returns on their assets could keep pace with index-linked obligations. There was a similar problem in the housing market. Most mortgages could not be fully index-linked because wages generally lagged behind inflation. Borrowers' monthly payments were therefore linked to wages, which were usually adjusted once a year, and their outstanding mortgage balances were indexed to prices. The housing finance system grew rapidly through the late 1960s and 1970s. But when inflation once again reached the triple-digit level in the 1980s, the system faced severe liquidity problems because liabilities and assets rose much faster than wage-linked income cash flow. Moreover, when prices accelerated, asset holders tended to switch their portfolios from money-denominated instruments to indexed instruments. This created sharp liquidity pressures for commercial banks and short-term financial markets, from which asset holders withdrew resources, as well as for housing finance intermediaries, which had difficulty coping with large and often temporary resource inflows.

The government succeeded in financing more of its deficit with indexed bonds. In the 1980s, however, the real stock of indexed bonds increased—in part, because most bonds carried an exchange rate clause and in February 1983 there was a sharp real devaluation, but also because the public sector's borrowing needs rose markedly. Inflation accelerated and the debt servicing requirements on the indexed bonds added significantly to the public sector borrowing requirement. As part of its 1986 Cruzado Plan, the government suspended most forms of financial indexation, hoping to relieve the "inflation-feedback" spiral that indexation seemed to be causing. When the Cruzado Plan failed and inflation revived toward the end of 1986, nominal interest rates surged. The government found itself in the same position as in the mid-1960s. It again began to issue index-linked bonds.

Box table 4.8 Key financial instruments, selected years, 1965 to 1985
(percentage of GDP)

Year		Nonindexed				Indexed		
	M1	Exchange acceptances	Treasury bills	Total	Time and savings deposits	Treasury, state, and municipal bonds	Real estate bonds	Total
1965	17.2	1.3	—	18.5	0.6	0.9	0.0	1.5
1970	14.6	3.4	0.3	18.3	2.8	4.4	0.8	8.0
1975	13.5	4.2	2.8	20.5	8.3	5.5	0.7	14.5
1979	9.3	2.1	3.0	14.4	10.3	3.7	0.1	14.1
1985	3.9	1.3	0.3	5.5	13.6	9.1	0.0	22.7

Note: 1980 was an anomalous year because a limit was placed on financial indexation.
Source: For 1965–79, Goldsmith 1986; for 1985, based on central bank data.

external debt and the uses of finance recorded in the balance of payments accounts—especially for many Latin American countries in the early 1980s—point to massive capital flight. Capital outflows are not an exclusively Latin American phenomenon, of course. There have been capital outflows from member countries of the West African Monetary Union, which have few restrictions on capital transfers. Thailand, which also had relatively liberal policies toward capital movements, experienced capital outflows when U.S. interest rates increased sharply in the early 1980s; these outflows stopped when domestic interest rates were adjusted accordingly.

The task of financial reform

At the onset of industrialization in the developing countries, financial markets were inadequate to meet the demands placed upon them. This justified some form of government intervention. But extensive directed credit programs at subsidized interest rates proved an inefficient way to overcome market failures and redistribute income. Macroeconomic instability, combined with credit and interest rate controls, made matters worse. Most governments neglected to address the underlying weaknesses of their financial systems. This inattention to the conditions necessary for financial development did not significantly impede growth during the 1970s. Favorable terms of trade and cheap foreign funding enabled developing countries to finance growing investment expenditures despite the small size of their financial systems. But as events of the 1980s demonstrated, financial institutions were left weak and vulnerable to change.

In the early 1980s most developing countries confronted deteriorating terms of trade, falling export volumes, rising international interest rates, and a sudden curtailment of foreign lending. Many countries no longer had the foreign exchange to finance large current account deficits or the fiscal resources to continue subsidizing inefficient industries. In countries that were forced to devalue to discourage imports and stimulate exports, firms in the nontraded goods sector became less profitable, and the debt service obligations of enterprises that had borrowed in foreign currency increased. Fewer and more expensive imports hurt company profitability, as did the collapse in demand in the countries that adjusted to the shocks by tightening their monetary and fiscal policies. Many firms were unable to service their debts. Other aspects of trade adjustment, such as lower import restrictions or tariffs, had similar effects: they reduced the profitability of previously protected enterprises and added to the nonperforming assets of financial institutions. In turn, many financial intermediaries became insolvent.

Now, more than ever, developing countries need to rely on domestic resources to finance development. The importance of sound macroeconomic policies for building efficient financial systems cannot be overemphasized. Large public sector deficits that demand financing from shallow domestic financial systems invariably lead to inflation or crowd out private sector borrowing. The interaction of high and unstable inflation and rigidly ad-

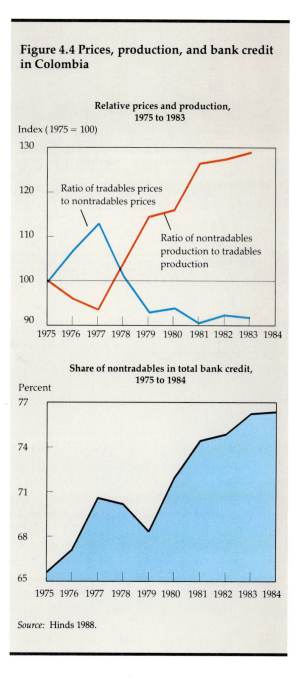

Figure 4.4 Prices, production, and bank credit in Colombia

Relative prices and production, 1975 to 1983

Index (1975 = 100)

Ratio of tradables prices to nontradables prices

Ratio of nontradables production to tradables production

Share of nontradables in total bank credit, 1975 to 1984

Percent

Source: Hinds 1988.

ministered interest rates is certain to cause financial disintermediation, and to do much other economic harm besides.

Granting that sound macroeconomic policy is essential, financial sector reform can make an important contribution to development. Chapters 5 through 9 will examine different aspects of the task of building better financial systems in developing countries. Chapter 5 begins by looking in more detail at the distress of financial institutions and the first steps to be taken in reshaping financial systems.

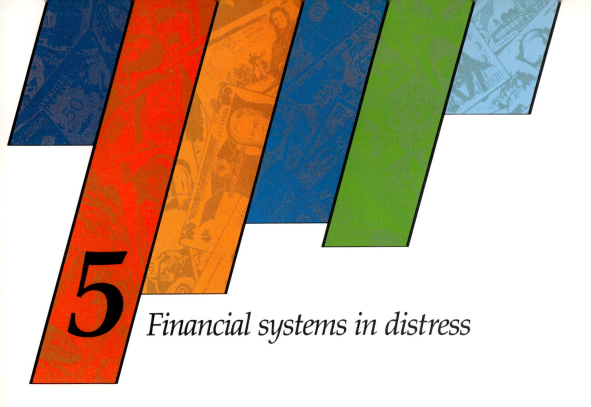

5 Financial systems in distress

Not since the 1930s have so many firms in developing countries been unable to service their debts. Their difficulties are rooted in the international shocks of the 1980s and their domestic aftermath and in the policies that governments have pursued over the past thirty years. The inability of firms to service debt has caused distress for many financial institutions. In some countries incipient financial crises forced the government to assist troubled banks. In others, although there has been no crisis, banks' losses are large enough to require government intervention. Failure to take action is costly. With delay, losses mount and so does the cost of restructuring. In all, more than twenty-five governments have helped distressed financial institutions during the past decade. Much has been learned from these measures.

In 1981 the Chilean government liquidated three commercial banks, four finance companies, and a development bank. Together these accounted for more than one-third of all loans made by the financial system. Fourteen months later the authorities intervened again. They placed eight institutions, which accounted for nearly half of all loans, under central bank management and extended financial support to all but one of the remaining commercial banks.

In the United States more than 1,000 savings and loan associations (S&Ls) were closed or merged with sounder institutions between 1980 and 1988.

By early 1989, 600 S&Ls, or one-fifth of all S&Ls, were still thought to be insolvent, and the loss to the S&L deposit insurance fund was expected to total at least $120 billion. Among commercial banks the failure rate rose from ten a year during the 1970s to more than 150 a year in the late 1980s. In early 1989 about 10 percent of commercial banks were on the regulators' "watch list."

Cases like these are spectacular, but much financial distress remains hidden. Because intermediaries have rolled over unpaid loans and have capitalized unpaid interest, their insolvency is not apparent from their accounts. Accounting information may be kept confidential, and what is available is often unreliable. Where audits have been made using generally accepted accounting principles, nonperforming loans have proved to be substantial. In nearly all instances of government intervention, intermediaries' actual losses have proved to be far larger than reported. The number of bad and doubtful loans in the portfolios of many institutions is such that expected losses exceed the sum of capital, reserves, and loss provisions; these institutions are technically insolvent.

If reliable information were available, countries could be ranked according to the share of nonperforming loans in banks' total assets. At one end of the range would be countries in which nearly all intermediaries are profitable and solvent and nonperforming loans amount to only 1 or 2 percent of assets. At the other would be countries in which 20 percent or more of all loans are nonperforming and many, if not most, banks are insolvent (some having losses equal to many times their capital). Although lack of data makes it impossible to measure financial distress precisely, it is clear that distress is widespread. Box 5.1 presents information for a select group of countries. This information may overstate the severity of distress in some countries and understate it for others.

In most cases banks are not illiquid (that is, they can still meet payment demands), but so many of their debtors are unable or unwilling to service their loans that the banks are making losses. The failure of some borrowers to service loans is common; even healthy banks expect to have some nonperforming loans. But losses large enough to impair the profitability and solvency of so many institutions in so many countries are unprecedented. Even during the depression of the 1930s, very few large banks in developing countries failed.

That banks remain open and continue to accept deposits and make loans does not mean that they

---

Box 5.1 Examples of financial distress

Argentina. The failure of a large private bank sparked the 1980–82 banking crisis. By 1983, 71 of 470 financial institutions had been liquidated. The restructuring process is not yet complete.

Bangladesh. Four banks that accounted for 70 percent of total credit had an estimated 20 percent of nonperforming assets in 1987. Loans to two loss-making public enterprises amounted to fourteen times the banks' total capital.

Bolivia. In late 1987 the central bank liquidated two of twelve private commercial banks; seven more reported large losses. In mid-1988 reported arrears stood at 92 percent of commercial banks' net worth.

Chile. In 1981 the government liquidated eight insolvent institutions that together held 35 percent of total financial system assets. In 1983 another eight institutions (45 percent of system assets) were taken over: three were liquidated, five restructured and recapitalized. In September 1988, central bank holdings of bad commercial bank loans amounted to nearly 19 percent of GNP.

Colombia. The 1985 losses of the banking system as a whole amounted to 140 percent of capital plus reserves. Between 1982 and 1987 the central bank intervened in six banks (24 percent of system assets), five of which in 1985 alone had losses equal to 202 percent of their capital plus reserves.

Costa Rica. Public banks, which do 90 percent of all lending, considered 32 percent of loans "uncollectible" in early 1987. This implied losses of at least twice capital plus reserves. Losses of private banks were an estimated 21 percent of capital plus reserves.

Egypt. In early 1980 the government felt compelled to close several large Islamic investment companies.

Ghana. By mid-1988 the net worth of the banking system was negative, having been completely eroded by large foreign exchange losses and a high proportion of nonperforming loans. The estimated cost of restructuring is $300 million, or nearly 6 percent of GNP.

Greece. Nonperforming loans to ailing industrial companies amount to several times the capital of the largest commercial banks, which hold more than 80 percent of total bank assets.

Guinea. The government that assumed power in 1984 inherited a virtually defunct banking system: 99 percent of loans proved irrecoverable. All six state-owned banks were liquidated, and three new commercial banks were established, each with foreign participation.

Kenya. Many of the nonbank financial institutions that have sprung up since 1978 are insolvent, and in 1986 several of the larger ones collapsed.

Korea. Seventy-eight insolvent firms, whose combined debts exceeded assets by $5.9 billion, were dissolved or merged during 1986 and 1987. In addition, the central bank lowered interest rates on its rediscounts to commercial banks on loans to troubled industries.

Kuwait. Because of large losses sustained by speculators in stock and real estate markets, an estimated 40 percent of bank loans were nonperforming by 1986. The government has supported banks by providing highly concessional loans.

Madagascar. In early 1988, 25 percent of all loans were irrecoverable, and 21 percent more were deemed "difficult to collect." Given the low level of reserves (less than 5 percent of assets), the banking system as a whole was insolvent.

Malaysia. The 1986 failure of a deposit-taking cooperative (DTC) that held only 0.2 percent of the banking system's total deposits led to runs on other DTCs. Twenty-four DTCs (2.1 percent of total deposits) were judged insolvent, and all twenty-four were rescued. Three ailing commercial banks, with 5.2 percent of total deposits, were recapitalized during 1985–86.

Nepal. In early 1988 the reported arrears of three banks (95 percent of the financial system) averaged 29 percent of all assets.

Norway. Commercial and savings banks suffered heavy losses in 1987 and 1988 owing to the collapse of the price of oil and to imprudent lending. The authorities replaced the management and board of a leading bank and forced banks to write off bad loans, restructure their operations, raise new capital, and merge with other institutions.

Pakistan. Under old regulations, which allowed indefinite accrual of income regardless of loan classification, the capital-to-assets ratios of five large banks (90 percent of the banking system) averaged 3 percent. Under new regulations the banks must make a major recapitalization effort to reach a similar ratio.

Philippines. Between 1981 and 1987, 161 smaller institutions holding 3.5 percent of total financial system assets were closed. In addition, the authorities intervened in two large public and five private banks. The public banks were liquidated in 1986, and their largest bad assets (equal to 30 percent of the banking system's assets) were transferred to a separate agency. The five private banks are still under central bank supervision.

Spain. Between 1978 and 1983 fifty-one institutions holding nearly a fifth of all deposits were rescued; two were eventually liquidated, and the rest were sold to sound banks.

Sri Lanka. Two state-owned banks comprising 70 percent of the banking system have estimated nonperforming assets of at least 35 percent of their total portfolios.

Tanzania. In early 1987 the main financial institutions had long-standing arrears amounting to half their portfolio, and implied losses were nearly 10 percent of GNP.

Thailand. The resolution of a 1983 crisis involving

forty-four finance companies that held 12 percent of financial system assets cost $190 million, or 0.5 percent of GNP. Between 1984 and 1987 the government intervened in five banks that held one-quarter of bank assets.

Turkey. A financial crisis erupted in 1982 with the collapse of several brokers, and five banks were rescued at a cost equal to 2.5 percent of GNP. Since 1985 two large banks have been restructured, but more may need to be done. Banks' reported losses are 6 percent. According to some estimates, losses exceed 10 percent.

UMOA countries.[1] More than 25 percent of bank credits in the UMOA countries are nonperforming. At least twenty primary banks are bankrupt: nonperforming credits are almost six times the sum of their capital, reserves, and provisions.

United States. Between 1980 and 1988 nearly 1,100 savings and loan associations (S&Ls) were closed or merged. In early 1989, more than 600 (one-fifth of all S&Ls) were insolvent, and the cost of restructuring was estimated to be roughly $80 billion in terms of present value. By 1989, 10 percent of commercial banks were on the regulators' "watch list."

Uruguay. After several banks failed in 1981–82, the central bank began to aid banks by purchasing their worst assets; by 1983 it had acquired $830 million in bad loans. The potential cost of recapitalizing the banks has been estimated at $350 million, or 7 percent of GNP.

1. The Union Monétaire Ouest Africaine (UMOA), or West African Monetary Union, comprises Benin, Burkina Faso, Côte d'Ivoire, Mali, Niger, Senegal, and Togo.

are solvent or that their insolvency has no economic cost—only that they remain liquid (see Box 5.2). It is possible for banks in one country to have larger losses than banks in another and still be more liquid. Thus waiting for banks to become illiquid before taking action can be costly. Indeed, in countries where government help has enabled insolvent banks to stay open, the cumulative costs of distress may well be higher than in countries where the authorities have closed or restructured insolvent banks.

Bank restructuring is not an end in itself. Banks' losses reflect the difficulties of firms in other sectors, and these difficulties are a result not only of external shocks and subsequent policy changes but also of the development strategies pursued by many countries. Resolving firms' problems and changing the policies that gave rise to them may prove more difficult than restructuring loss-

making banks, partly because of employment considerations. Although it is recognized that insolvency among financial institutions has deeper causes elsewhere, this chapter focuses mainly on banks' portfolio problems—their consequences, causes, and cures.

Economic consequences of financial distress

Weakened by large losses, many financial institutions in developing countries have become less able to provide the services described in Chapter 2. Their diminished capacity to improve the allocation of resources has contributed to slow growth and has undermined some countries' attempts at structural adjustment. Where governments have chosen to delay the restructuring of troubled firms and intermediaries, the high recurrent costs of assistance have compromised efforts to tighten monetary and fiscal policy and in some cases have led to further macroeconomic instability.

Resource misallocation

The rising proportion of nonperforming loans has limited the volume of credit that banks can extend to new clients. Moreover, credit allocation has often become perverse, with banks extending more rather than fewer loans to their least solvent clients, especially to large borrowers. New loans to troubled firms might have been justified if the loans had been used to restructure the ailing enterprises or if the firms had not been insolvent but merely illiquid. But much new lending has simply financed the servicing of prior loans or prolonged the lives of nonviable firms. By channeling additional funds to borrowers unable to make profitable use of the resources already at their disposal, lenders have delayed the process of adjustment.

Credit misallocation caused by financial distress has been more pronounced in some countries than in others. In some countries losses built up gradually as banks, complying with government directives, continued to lend to unprofitable sectors. In other countries, however, loan portfolios deteriorated rapidly, especially in the highly indebted countries following the shocks of the early 1980s. With a large proportion of their clients suddenly in difficulty, bankers had to extend additional credit to their most troubled borrowers to stave off their own bankruptcy. Thus borrowers took on new debt to service old debt, domestic as well as foreign. In countries that experienced acute financial distress, a growing share of credit has gone toward debt service instead of investment. Figure 5.1 shows that, in a select group of countries, the ratio of new credit to investment rose after 1980.

Widespread distress increases the demand for credit and therefore exerts upward pressure on real interest rates. During the 1980s real interest rates in several developing countries have often been extremely high, far exceeding the return on investment. Although various explanations for high real interest rates have been offered (including expected devaluation, unexpectedly low inflation, tight monetary policies, heavy public sector borrowing, and the reduced availability of foreign savings), the main reason firms were willing to borrow at real interest rates much higher than their return on capital was to avoid bankruptcy. The countries in which real lending rates have been highest (Argentina, Chile, Colombia, Costa Rica, Turkey, and Uruguay) are all countries in which

---

Box 5.2 Bank solvency and liquidity

A bank is solvent if the value of its assets is greater than the value of its liabilities to depositors and other creditors; "net worth" is the amount by which assets exceed liabilities. The larger a bank's net worth, the larger its cushion against insolvency—that is, the larger the fall in asset values that the bank can sustain and still be solvent. Bank supervisors try to ensure that banks have adequate capital, which is often defined as some minimum fraction of total or risk assets. If the required capital-to-assets ratio is 5 percent, for example, a bank with $100 million in assets and $98 million in liabilities (hence a net worth of $2 million) would be instructed to find $3 million of additional capital to bring net worth up to $5 million. Many banks in developing countries are insolvent and unable to earn the large sums needed to regain solvency; the negative net worth of some of these banks is many times their capital.

A bank is liquid as long as it can meet day-to-day operating expenses and withdrawals. Because it is highly leveraged, a bank can remain liquid long after becoming insolvent. That some countries have not experienced runs does not signify that their banks are sounder than banks in countries where runs did occur but merely that they are more liquid. Public ownership of banks, implicit or explicit deposit guarantees, periodic provision of liquidity to weak banks, and macroeconomic stability make depositors less likely to withdraw funds from insolvent banks and thereby help those banks to remain liquid.

---

firms and intermediaries have been under great financial stress.

The use of new lending to cover interest payments, together with the high real interest rates in some countries, has inhibited investment and thus production. Gross investment in developing countries fell from an average of 25.1 percent of GNP in 1978 to 21.7 percent in 1986. The decline has been particularly steep in the seventeen highly indebted countries, where gross investment fell during the same period from 25.0 percent of GNP to 17.5 percent, a level barely adequate to maintain the existing stock of capital. Although reduced aggregate demand and increased macroeconomic instability are the principal causes of the decline in investment, domestic financial distress has been a contributing factor.

The financial system's reduced ability to direct credit toward profitable borrowers has under-

Figure 5.1 Ratio of new credit to investment in selected developing countries, 1973 to 1979 and 1980 to 1986

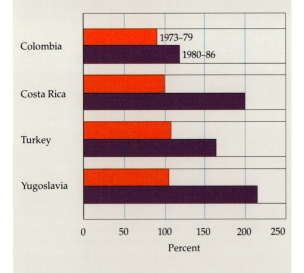

Note: New credit is the change in the stock of outstanding credit to the nonfinancial sector. Investment is gross fixed capital formation.
Source: IMF, *International Financial Statistics,* and World Bank data.

mined some countries' efforts at structural reform. Successful adjustment largely depends on the release of resources from less productive uses and their redeployment to more productive firms. Continued lending to unprofitable firms has impeded this flow. As a result the resources needed to finance investments made profitable by policy changes, such as devaluations and tariff reductions, have not been available. This has delayed recovery from recession in the short run and, by misdirecting resources that could be used for investment, has slowed future growth.

Macroeconomic consequences of financial distress

In the nineteenth century, before the advent of deposit insurance and official lenders of last resort, financial distress was usually deflationary. Rumors of bank insolvency precipitated bank runs, which forced even solvent banks to call in loans. This resulted in a contraction of the money supply and a corresponding fall in economic activity. Today central banks in developing countries are well versed in providing liquidity to the financial sys-

tem. They have succeeded in stemming incipient runs on banks, as in Chile in 1983 and Malaysia in 1986. Occasionally deposits have shifted suddenly from one class of intermediary to another perceived as safer. In Argentina in 1980 depositors moved their holdings from domestic private banks, several of which had failed, to state- or foreign-owned banks. Such shifts created difficulties for the deposit-losing institutions, but the monetary authorities had the means to avoid sharp declines in total liquidity.

The existence of a lender of last resort has enabled countries to avert banking panics, but the financial distress of recent years has nevertheless contributed to macroeconomic instability, particularly in the highly indebted countries. Unlike in the nineteenth century, however, falls in output have typically been associated with expansions rather than contractions of the money supply. The weakness of firms and financial institutions has made it difficult for many governments to tighten monetary or fiscal policy without making matters worse for ailing banks. Thus, even as many countries were attempting to redress macroeconomic imbalances through fiscal and monetary restraint, the need to assist troubled banks and their borrowers compromised the governments' efforts. Subsidies to state-owned financial institutions in the Philippines, for example, were equivalent to 3.4 percent of GNP in 1986, which made it difficult for the government to reduce its budget deficit.

Many governments have aided banks by transferring to the central bank the foreign exchange risk on banks' foreign currency liabilities. The central bank exchanged liabilities denominated in domestic currency for liabilities denominated in foreign currency. Later, depreciations of the domestic currency resulted in valuation losses for the central bank. These losses had an indirect expansionary effect because banks were required to pay the central bank less than the amount needed to buy the foreign exchange to cover their obligations. To buy the necessary foreign exchange, the central bank then had to print money. In some countries the difference between what the central bank paid on foreign obligations and what it received from banks and governments has accounted for a large share of monetary expansion. The central banks of Costa Rica, Ecuador, and Yugoslavia had losses that sometimes exceeded the amount of new credit extended by the domestic banking system (see Figure 5.2).

A handful of countries (Argentina, Bolivia, and Yugoslavia among them) tried to alleviate financial distress by lowering interest rates. Lower deposit rates, however, contributed to inflation and capital flight by encouraging holders of wealth to turn away from domestic financial assets toward goods or foreign financial assets. The process of disintermediation and the declining demand for domestic financial assets compounded banks' difficulties, and the declining demand for money also amplified the inflationary effects of excessive money creation.

Financial distress may not be the principal cause of inflation, but the complex interaction between financial weakness and macroeconomic policy is certainly important. Distress and inflation are mutually reinforcing. Measures to assist banks have frequently added to inflation and thereby aggravated the distress they were meant to relieve. Resolving the banks' portfolio problems and preventing their recurrence calls for a clearer understanding of why so many firms are unable or unwilling to service their loans.

Roots of financial distress

Explanations of firms' financial difficulties can be grouped under three headings: macroeconomic conditions, industrial and financial policy, and debtor and creditor behavior. The importance of macroeconomic factors is clearest for the countries with large external debt burdens. The countries with the most acute domestic financial distress have generally been those with the most severe foreign debt difficulties. The external shocks that led to the international debt crisis and the policy adjustments that came after it left many domestic firms unprofitable and unable to service their debts, domestic or foreign.

The macroeconomic shocks of the early 1980s are only a proximate cause of financial distress, however. The financial and industrial policies pursued by many countries during the 1960s and 1970s left their financial systems weak and vulnerable to change. Banks were often directed to provide subsidized credit to firms in favored regions or sectors. In some countries firms in priority sectors have been consistently unprofitable. In others they were profitable only as long as they were protected; today such firms account for a large proportion of nonperforming loans.

In most cases macroeconomic conditions, directed credit programs, and interest rate controls are the principal factors underlying the current difficulties of firms and their creditors (as discussed in Chapter 4). But they are not the only factors. Many

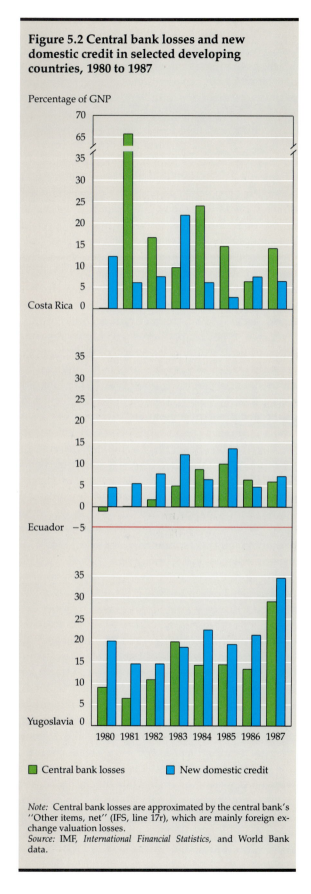

Figure 5.2 Central bank losses and new domestic credit in selected developing countries, 1980 to 1987

Percentage of GNP

Central bank losses

New domestic credit

Note: Central bank losses are approximated by the central bank's "Other items, net" (IFS, line 17r), which are mainly foreign exchange valuation losses.
Source: IMF, *International Financial Statistics*, and World Bank data.

governments gave too little thought to the ways in which concentration of risk, the quality of information flows, the adequacy of legal codes, and the nature of the regulatory environment can affect financial efficiency. Inattention to these issues has permitted borrowers and lenders to behave in ways that have contributed to banks' losses.

An important aspect of borrower behavior has been the tendency of certain groups of firms in developing countries to become highly leveraged. Chapter 4 concluded that the high leverage of these firms is partly a result of their governments' directed credit programs. The availability of credit at low or negative real interest rates discouraged the expansion of domestic deposits and gave borrowers a strong incentive to take on debt—an incentive reinforced in most countries by tax codes and by the lack of developed equity markets. Because credit was rationed, only firms with privileged access to lenders could become highly leveraged. One group of privileged borrowers consisted of firms in priority sectors, including public enterprises, another of firms belonging to industrial-financial conglomerates. Where banks were privately owned, the rationing of subsidized credit encouraged companies to buy their own banks in order to secure the advantages of cheap credit by lending generously to themselves.

A drawback to higher leverage was that firms became more vulnerable to a decline in earnings or a rise in interest rates. The firms most embarrassed by the decline in their profits and cash flows in the early 1980s were already highly leveraged at the beginning of the economic downturn. Many of these made matters worse when they reacted to declining sales and cash shortages by borrowing more rather than by cutting costs (laying off workers and closing plants, for example). Some expected the economic downturn to be short-lived and so considered borrowing to be their best strategy. Some on the brink of bankruptcy saw additional borrowing as their only course. Others, in countries with a history of government bailouts, gambled that the government would intervene to assist overindebted firms. This assumption often proved well founded. For example, the Korean monetary authorities, in 1972 and again in 1982, lowered lending rates because the prevailing rates were endangering too many borrowers. In Turkey public enterprises in financial straits have regularly received large budgetary transfers. In Chile the central bank granted generous terms to banks refinancing the debt of distressed but viable borrowers.

Firms could borrow more only if their bankers let them. Bankers often did cooperate when a financial institution belonged to the same conglomerate as its clients. In Chile, Colombia, Spain, and Thailand, for example, most bad loans were to related companies. Government-owned banks were often told to continue lending to public enterprises and priority sectors—another example of at-less-than-arm's-length credit negotiations. Other bankers continued to lend to unprofitable firms, particularly large ones, to prevent them from going bankrupt and in turn bankrupting the banks. Examination of failed and troubled banks has almost invariably revealed this type of mismanagement (see Box 5.3).

Bankers have been influenced by the authorities in other ways. Although only a few developing countries (Colombia, India, Kenya, the Philippines, Trinidad and Tobago, Turkey, and Venezuela) have explicit deposit insurance schemes, it became clear that governments would at least protect deposits in government-owned banks and the bigger private banks. Despite the difficulties of the 1980s, in only a handful of countries have depositors lost money. Implicit deposit insurance averted bank runs, but in doing so it removed the discipline associated with that threat. Depositors' lack of concern about the riskiness of bank portfolios has allowed undercapitalized banks to stay in business and encouraged bankers to take bigger risks. The smaller the amount of shareholder capital at stake, the more willing bankers will be to ''bet the bank'' by financing risky projects.

Mismanagement and speculative behavior persist because prudential regulation and supervision are inadequate in many countries. Prudential regulation has two purposes: to prevent excessively risky behavior by lenders in the first instance and, should portfolio problems develop, to force lenders to address them promptly. In most countries, however, inadequate regulation has permitted risky lending, and ineffective supervision has permitted banks to ignore their losses. For want of timely and reliable accounting information, the authorities lack a clear picture of the health of the intermediaries under their supervision. Effective supervision is particularly important in financial liberalization because newly deregulated intermediaries are likely to engage in less familiar, and therefore more risky, types of lending. Box 5.4 argues that the combination of deregulation and inadequate supervision has proved costly in the case of the U.S. savings and loan industry. Chapter 9 contains further discussion of the experience of

Box 5.3   How good bankers become bad bankers

The quality of management is an important difference between sound and unsound banks, and in most countries the better-managed financial institutions have succeeded in remaining solvent. Four types of mismanagement commonly occur in the absence of effective regulation and supervision.

• *Technical mismanagement.* Poor lending policies are the most common form of technical mismanagement and are usually a consequence of deficient internal controls, inadequate credit analysis, or political pressures. Poor lending policies often lead to excessive risk concentration, the result of making a high proportion of loans to a single borrower or to a specific region or industry. Banks sometimes lend excessively to related companies or to their own managers. Mismatching assets and liabilities in terms of currencies, interest rates, or maturities is another common form of technical mismanagement.

• *Cosmetic mismanagement.* A crossroads for management is reached when a bank experiences losses. Strong supervision or a good board of directors would ensure that the losses are reported and corrective measures taken. Without these, bankers may engage in "cosmetic" mismanagement and try to hide past and current losses. There are many ways to do this. To avoid alerting shareholders to the difficulties, bankers often keep dividends constant despite poorer earnings. And to keep dividends up, bankers may retain a smaller share of income for provisions against loss, thereby sacrificing capital adequacy. If a dividend target exceeds profits, bankers may resort to accounting measures that increase net profits on paper, even if more taxes must be paid as a result. By rescheduling loans, a banker can classify bad loans as good and so avoid making provisions. The capitalization of unpaid interest raises profits by increasing apparent income. The reporting of income can be advanced and the recording of expenditure postponed.

• *Desperate management.* When losses are too large to be concealed by accounting gimmicks, bankers may adopt more desperate strategies. The most common of these include lending to risky projects at higher loan rates and speculating in stock and real estate markets. Such strategies, however, involve greater risk and may well lead to further losses. The problem then becomes one of cash flow: it gets harder to pay dividends, cover operating costs, and meet depositors' withdrawal demands with the income earned on the remaining good assets. To avoid a liquidity crisis a bank may offer high deposit rates to attract new deposits, but the higher cost of funds eventually compounds the problems.

• *Fraud.* Fraudulent behavior sometimes causes the initial losses, but once illiquidity appears inevitable, fraud becomes common. As the end approaches, bankers are tempted to grant themselves loans that they are unlikely to repay. Another common fraud is the "swinging ownership" of companies partly owned by the bank or banker: if a company is profitable, the banker will arrange to buy it from the bank at a low price, and if the company is unprofitable, the banker will sell it to the bank at a high price.

---

several developing countries that liberalized their financial sectors.

The lack of clear legal procedures for dealing with insolvent banks has been another obstacle to prompt action. In Argentina, for example, the Central Banking Act did not empower the central bank to take over banks, replace managers and directors, or order owners to provide new capital. As a result, intervention led to numerous lawsuits.

The difficulty of foreclosing on defaulting borrowers has caused losses for many banks. In some countries willful default is encouraged by the fact that bankruptcy and foreclosure procedures are slow and cumbersome. In Egypt, Pakistan, Portugal, and Turkey, for example, loan recovery proceedings frequently drag on for several years (see Box 6.4 in Chapter 6). In others, willful default has a more political cause: borrowers in priority sectors such as agriculture realize that governments are reluctant to let lenders foreclose. The default rate among small farmers in Ghana and India, for example, has been particularly high.

In sum, poor prudential regulation and supervision, together with inadequate legal systems, let lenders and borrowers in many countries behave in ways that have added to banks' losses.

Lessons of financial restructuring

As the 1980s proceeded, the distress of financial institutions in some countries precipitated crises and so forced the authorities to take action. As Box 5.1 indicates, intervention ranged from the closing of a few intermediaries with a small fraction of total assets, as in Malaysia, to the closing and replacement of nearly every bank, as in Guinea. During the next few years many more countries—especially those contemplating broader programs

Box 5.4 The U.S. savings and loan crisis: the lessons of moral hazard

More than 500 of the 3,000 savings and loan associations in the United States were insolvent at the beginning of 1989. The cost to the Federal Savings and Loan Insurance Corporation (FSLIC) of restructuring the S&L industry through liquidations, consolidations, and assisted mergers was, as of early 1989, estimated to be roughly $80 billion in terms of present value. Because its own assets were insufficient to meet the potential obligations, FSLIC had been unable to close or otherwise dispose of many insolvent institutions, and so loss-making S&Ls were allowed to remain in operation. In early 1989 the U.S. government announced its intention to cover the FSLIC shortfall through a combination of government funding and higher deposit insurance premiums to be paid by S&Ls.

The difficulties of the S&L industry began in the late 1970s. S&Ls had traditionally lent funds on twenty-to-thirty-year mortgages at fixed rates and funded themselves with short-term deposits. Higher inflation rates in the late 1970s and early 1980s and the correspondingly higher interest rates that S&Ls had to pay on deposits sharply depressed earnings.

The response of the U.S. Congress and several state legislatures was to authorize S&Ls to take on a wider range of lending and borrowing. Ceilings on deposit rates were phased out, and the maximum size of an insured deposit went up from $40,000 to $100,000. Unfortunately, lawmakers paid less attention to strengthening the system of prudential regulation and supervision. Increased lending and borrowing powers gave S&Ls new opportunities for loss as well as profit. They were required to risk little of their own capital; any losses beyond those amounts would be absorbed by FSLIC. This gave them strong incentives to take greater risks, since they would enjoy all the gains but suffer only some of the losses. In addition, deposit insurance premiums were levied at a flat rate per dollar of deposit, so the premium structure did not discourage risk taking. Insurance experts and economists use the term "moral hazard" to describe this situation of distorted incentives.

Although only a minority of S&Ls fell prey to moral hazard, they did so with gusto. Their losses were compounded by changes in the tax law that made real estate (in which many of these S&Ls had invested) a less attractive investment; by a severe economic downturn in oil-producing areas, particularly Texas; by delays in the imposition of remedial prudential regulations; by delays in the closure of insolvent S&Ls; and by an accounting system that used historical cost-based values rather than current market values to determine income and solvency.

Valuable (albeit costly) lessons have been learned from this experience. Appropriate prudential regulation must accompany the economic deregulation of deposit-taking institutions that are explicitly or implicitly insured by the government. Adequate capital levels, preferably related to risks undertaken, are vital. Risk-related insurance premiums can help. Strong supervisory and examination powers, enforced by well-trained and well-paid personnel, are important. Market value accounting systems are indispensable. Finally, if an institution falters toward insolvency, early regulatory intervention is necessary to prevent small problems from exploding into costly horrors.

---

of structural reform—will face difficult choices concerning the restructuring of their domestic financial institutions and the reshaping of their financial systems. Even some countries that have already taken steps may find further intervention necessary because many institutions still in operation are insolvent.

Restructuring a financial system is both a challenge and an opportunity. Not all institutions are worth recapitalizing; some need to be closed or merged with healthier ones. Restructuring gives countries a chance to build financial systems that can better provide the services their changing economies need.

Rationale for intervention

During the 1980s more than twenty-five developing countries have undertaken extensive reorganizations of their financial institutions. In most cases financial crises had occurred or were imminent, and governments could not stand aside. Other countries, such as Pakistan and Sri Lanka, have not experienced crises but have nonetheless taken steps to strengthen their financial systems. Several of the centrally planned economies have decided to reorganize their financial systems to make them more efficient and competitive. Many governments, however, have been reluctant to take action, and their delay has led to continued losses at the institutional level and slower recovery at the macroeconomic level.

The authorities in some countries may be unaware of the seriousness of the situation, since a bank's poor health is not always apparent from its audited financial statements. Even when governments understand the problem, they are often unwilling to act. Some may hope that intervention will not be necessary because defaulting borrowers will start to repay or because banks will make adequate provisions for their bad loans. But, as Box 5.5 argues, the likelihood of spontaneous recovery is low. Other considerations—the budgetary costs of restructuring, issues of fairness in allocating the losses, the embarrassment of bad loans made to public enterprises or political allies, or fear of bank runs—also lead governments to ignore the problem as long as they can.

If there is no crisis, should governments intervene merely to relieve financial distress? One reason most may have to is that earlier interventions have made a market solution unlikely. By providing implicit or explicit deposit guarantees and by regularly granting assistance to troubled banks and firms, governments have suppressed the market forces that otherwise would have eliminated or reorganized unprofitable firms and allocated the associated losses. Until governments take the further step of performing the market's loss-allocating function, losses will continue. As losses mount, so do the costs of supporting the loss-making institutions. The continuing costs of periodic support will eventually outweigh the one-time cost of restructuring.

Governments can either take the next step, by performing the market's loss-allocating function,

---

Box 5.5   Can banks "muddle through"?

Governments have often refrained from intervening in the financial sector in the hope that ailing banks will recover spontaneously. Rather than obliging the banks to make provisions for their losses (which might force those with losses larger than capital into bankruptcy), many governments have permitted them to operate with impaired capital positions. For banks to recover unaided, at least one of two things must happen: enough defaulting borrowers must resume servicing their debts or banks must earn enough to restore capital adequacy.

Simply waiting for economic upturn is risky. In the meantime, only banks whose remaining good assets can generate more than enough income to cover costs will be able to begin recapitalizing themselves. In recent years the earnings of many large U.S. banks, for example, have been sufficient to enable them to make substantial provisions against nonperforming international loans. The larger a bank's nonperforming loans, however, the smaller its income and the longer it will need to recapitalize itself. If a bank is losing money, spontaneous recovery is impossible.

To increase income, banks may increase the spread between deposit and loan rates. Box figure 5.5 shows the spread necessary for a "typical" bank (as defined in the note to the figure) to recapitalize itself through retained earnings over a period of five years. A bank with initial losses equaling 20 percent of assets, for example, would need a spread of 7.1 percent to recapitalize itself in five years. In practice, competition will limit the amount by which spreads can be enlarged. Banks that set lending rates too high or deposit rates too low eventually lose business to competitors. Similarly, government efforts to assist the entire financial sector by mandating larger spreads are likely to aggravate banks' difficulties: too large a gap between deposit and loan rates causes lenders and borrowers alike to seek cheaper intermediation.

A "wait and see" approach is likely to prove costly. To recapitalize themselves, banks with large losses (losses greater than their capital) must increase earnings substantially. If efforts to increase earnings lead bankers to engage in overly risky behavior, however, new losses will make spontaneous recovery even less feasible.

Box figure 5.5 Lending margins needed to recover in five years from given levels of loss

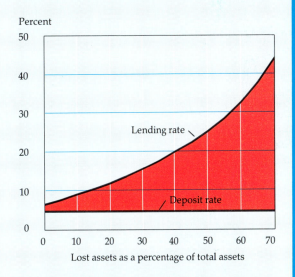

Note: This example assumes administration costs of 2 percent of assets, a required capital-to-assets ratio of 5 percent, a reserve requirement of 10 percent of assets, a deposit rate of 5 percent, and no defaults among new borrowers.

or take a step in the other direction, by withdrawing deposit guarantees and ending financial assistance to unprofitable intermediaries, so that the problems have to be resolved by the private sector. Once losses have become substantial, a market-imposed solution is likely to be costlier than government action because it could lead to bank runs and the loss of foreign credit lines. Events in Argentina, Chile, Colombia, Thailand, and Turkey illustrate the difficulty. After initially allowing creditors of failed institutions to lose money, the authorities in each country were forced to extend assistance to prevent widespread bank runs. Prompt government action is thus the less costly route, in terms of both the economic costs of continued resource misallocation and the accumulated financial losses that the government is likely to end up bearing.

Aspects of intervention

The central aim of intervention to relieve financial distress has not been to protect the interests of bank managers or bank owners or even to preserve particular banks as institutions but rather to keep the financial system as a whole in operation. Rehabilitating insolvent financial institutions has been the first step in that process. Most governments chose to close only small banks; larger ones, particularly those that were critical elements of the financial system, were merged or recapitalized.

Intervention has consisted of across-the-board relief, case-by-case restructuring, or a combination of the two. Case-by-case restructuring requires manpower, skill, and time, as the authorities must make management-level decisions concerning the fate of individual institutions. If, in addition, the costs of information and of bargaining with creditors are high, an across-the-board approach may look attractive. It seems faster, and it may be politically more palatable because it is less obvious who gains and who loses.

One across-the-board solution is to generate inflation deliberately to reduce real debt burdens. This happened in Argentina between 1981 and 1983. Another is for the authorities to absorb the banks' foreign exchange losses, as in Costa Rica, the Dominican Republic, Ecuador, and Yugoslavia. Across-the-board intervention, however, has usually proved wasteful. Since financial distress has seldom been evenly distributed among lenders or borrowers, much of the relief has gone to firms and intermediaries that did not need it. More important, troubled borrowers and banks usually

need restructuring, not just financial assistance. Restructuring is feasible only as part of a case-by-case approach.

INFORMATION FLOWS. Most countries have discovered that the information needed to judge the intermediaries' financial condition is either unavailable or unreliable. In only a few developing countries is bank supervision sophisticated enough to indicate the quality of an institution's earnings and portfolios. Even banks' audited statements are often misleading: interest is accrued whether it is received or not, nonperforming loans are rolled over, and new loans are provided to cover unpaid interest. Even banks with very few performing loans may report profits and pay taxes and dividends. One large state-owned bank in Latin America, for example, showed positive earnings for 1987, but three months after publishing its accounts its managers admitted that 60 percent of all loans were nonperforming. Insolvent, illiquid, and unprofitable, the bank lost approximately $100 million during 1987 alone.

Despite the poor quality of financial statements, in countries with serious financial distress there were usually warning signals. Some institutions offered deposit rates higher than those offered by other intermediaries, a sign that they were short of cash. At the macroeconomic level, real interest rates well above the average return on investment suggested that many firms were short of funds and were borrowing to remain in business. In some countries the failure of smaller institutions such as finance companies and new banks provided further evidence of widespread distress. Normally, governments tax banks through various mechanisms, including reserve requirements. Where loan portfolios deteriorated, however, the authorities were forced to cut the rate of taxation. As the amount of assistance to troubled banks increased, central bank profits declined, and some central banks even sustained large losses.

In short, acute distress has generated signals ranging from high real interest rates, widening interest rate spreads, a decline in the ability of banks to satisfy reserve requirements, and complaints from established borrowers about the scarcity of credit to the more obvious sign of failures among smaller intermediaries. Even if a central bank lacks the precise information that a good system of supervision would provide, it can hardly be unaware of widespread distress.

Better information about banks' portfolios gives the authorities a clearer idea of the intervention that may be necessary. The authorities in several countries, among them Bolivia and Ghana, commissioned external auditors to conduct independent audits of domestic banks. But lack of precise information is not a reason to refrain from taking action. The government of the Philippines relied upon the management of the two largest banks (the Development Bank of the Philippines and the Philippine National Bank, which are publicly owned and together hold about half of the banking system's assets) to identify nonperforming assets. It then assumed responsibility for all nonperforming loans above a certain value, along with a corresponding amount of liabilities.

At the heart of any review of a bank's financial condition is the issue of accrual of unpaid interest and the provisioning of loans. Because loan rollovers and interest capitalization have been common, the quality of loan portfolios can be judged only if loans are classified by the probability of their being serviced rather than simply by whether they are current or in arrears. In practice, adjusting for accrued but unpaid interest has been the single largest correction to banks' accounts following intervention. This underlines the importance of forcing banks to stop accruing interest and to make provisions for bad loans as soon as debt service is interrupted.

ALLOCATING LOSSES. Once governments intervened, they had to decide how to allocate losses in excess of capital and provisions. Regardless of formal obligation, most governments protected depositors against loss to avoid bank runs. Foreign creditors were also protected, even where they had lent to domestic banks without the benefit of government guarantees, as in Chile. Taxpayers had to absorb the losses instead.

Most governments have decided that the private owners of insolvent institutions should be replaced or at least have their ownership diluted. The techniques for doing this vary. In the United States the courts appoint the deposit insurance agency as receiver, and that agency arranges for the sale of institutions. In Colombia and Spain the law allows the government to write off the value of shares and to issue new shares to other than former shareholders. In Thailand existing shareholders were allowed to keep their shares, but the issuance of many new shares greatly reduced their value. After restructuring insolvent banks, the Chilean government provided cheap credit and generous tax incentives to those willing to buy shares in the two biggest banks.

Most governments have decided to replace management as well, in the hope that new managers, distanced from the mistakes of the past, will be able to make the changes necessary to restore the banks to profitability. In addition to loan foreclosure and recapitalization, measures to lower operating costs and improve profitability were needed—for example, closing branches and reducing staffing levels, establishing new interest rate structures, and eliminating loss-making activities. The Development Bank of the Philippines cut its staff by 50 percent, closed thirteen of its seventy branches, and plans to privatize all but thirteen of its remaining branches. In Guinea the number of people employed in the financial sector fell from 2,350 to 530, and lending to the public sector (including state-owned enterprises) has virtually ceased.

Failure to hold bank owners and managers responsible for past problems may encourage excessive risk taking in the future and thereby cause further financial instability. In large markets such as the United States, finding new owners and managers willing to take over weak institutions is usually straightforward, but in smaller markets there may be few potential buyers and few managers with the necessary expertise. Moreover, arranging the transfer to new management may take some time. So governments have sometimes found themselves responsible for the institutions in which they intervened. Both the Spanish and Chilean governments, for example, became the owners and operators of several restructured banks until suitable buyers were found.

COST CONSIDERATIONS. At the time of intervention the economic costs of financial distress have already been incurred in the form of poor past investments and slower growth in output. Restructuring has no economic cost. On the contrary, it brings an economic gain in that the economy may once again enjoy the benefits of a well-functioning financial system. The budgetary cost of restructuring consists of the government's cash outlays, which are a transfer from taxpayers to the creditors of insolvent banks.

This cost has depended on the extent to which the banks' losses exceeded their capital. In the United States, for example, the expected cost of dealing with the remaining insolvent S&Ls is equivalent to approximately 2 percent of GNP, and in Spain the estimated losses of banks were equivalent to 16.8 percent of GNP. In some developing countries banks' losses as a percentage of GNP

have been even larger. The cost of paying off depositors has been one reason most governments
have chosen to close small banks and rehabilitate
the bigger ones.

To make insolvent intermediaries solvent again,
governments took over bad assets. In some cases
they acquired bank liabilities at the same time; in
others they replaced the bad assets with good
ones. The authorities in the Philippines chose the
first approach; they drastically shrank the balance
sheets of the two largest banks by assuming 76
percent of their assets and a corresponding share
of their liabilities. The second solution was more
common, however; governments bought bad assets in exchange for long-term government securities, and the interest on the securities was then
used by banks to pay interest on deposits. This
method was used, for example, in Chile. Buying
the bad assets for cash would have been too large a
fiscal outlay and might have added to inflation by
expanding the money supply.

Over time, restructuring costs are bearable, even
for a country in which the bad assets acquired by
the authorities amount to as much as 20 percent of
GNP. In such a case, if the real interest rate paid on
government bonds is 5 percent, the annual real
cost to taxpayers will be 1 percent of GNP. And
that figure may exaggerate the additional cost to
the taxpayer. In most cases the government has
already been paying some form of subsidy to help
banks cover their losses. Furthermore, it may be
able to realize something on the nonperforming
assets.

Once the authorities have acquired the bad assets, they must decide what to do with them. A
mechanism is needed to pursue bad debtors and
dispose of physical assets taken over in foreclosure
proceedings. Central banks have generally proved
ineffective at recovery and liquidation. One possibility is to commission the banks that made the
original loans to handle them on behalf of the central bank, but this has worked only when the
banks were under new management and freed
from the obligations of previous relationships. Another course, followed by the Philippines, is to establish an independent recovery agency with its
own funding and staff.

Over the longer run, many countries have decided that their central banks should not be responsible for intervening in banks, ordering recapitalization, changing management and directors,
or handling the disposition of nonperforming
loans and the liquidation or merger of insolvent
banks. Some countries have set up specialized in-

stitutions to handle these tasks. In the United
States they are carried out by the deposit insurance
agencies, which collect premiums to cover the
losses of insolvent intermediaries. In keeping with
their obligation to cover those losses, the insurance
agencies have the power to inspect insured banks.
The advantage of an insurance arrangement is
that, in principle, it shifts the cost of monitoring
intermediaries and covering their losses from the
government to the financial system and codifies
the procedure for dealing with troubled institutions. This is likely to produce quicker action than
the ad hoc approach of most developing countries.

RESTRUCTURING BORROWERS. The portfolio problems of financial institutions reflect the difficulties
of their clients. If loss-making firms are not restructured, the newly recapitalized banks that lend to
them will eventually become insolvent again. Restructuring indebted borrowers is harder than restructuring financial institutions. Bank restructuring may involve closing branches and laying off
personnel, but it mostly entails rewriting paper
claims. Restructuring companies raises the same
difficult issues of management, ownership, and
fairness that have to be addressed in the case of
banks, but it also calls for decisions about the
viability of firms, the restructuring of physical
assets, and the disposition of large numbers of
employees.

Because recapitalized banks are in a new position of strength with regard to their former clients,
they can refuse to lend money to those they think
nonviable. Thus, in principle, restructured financial institutions have an important role to play in
the restructuring of loss-making firms. But if the
private sector's restructuring skills are undeveloped, if the borrowers in need of restructuring are
large, or if the legal system is weak, governments
may have to play a more active role, perhaps with
the help of outside experts. Box 5.6 provides an
example of the complexities that can be involved in
restructuring a large, overindebted firm.

Reforming the financial system

The present frailty of financial institutions in many
developing countries is the visible expression of a
complex set of problems. Financial distress in
many cases was precipitated by the macroeconomic shocks of the 1980s, but its roots lie in the
development strategies followed since the 1960s.
Banks in many countries were directed to provide
subsidized credit to priority sectors and public en-

The Valores Industriales S.A. (VISA) group, an integrated beverage and consumer goods conglomerate with more than 40,000 employees, is one of Mexico's largest industrial concerns. During the late 1970s VISA borrowed heavily to finance ambitious expansion and diversification plans, but by 1987 it could no longer service its debt. Like other Mexican companies that had borrowed abroad, VISA was hurt by devaluation, high interest rates, and the recession that began in 1982. As debt service began to consume most of its severely depressed cash flow, investment plans had to be postponed and basic maintenance expenditure reduced to a minimum. The consequent decline in efficiency and productivity made matters worse, and in early 1987 VISA engaged the International Finance Corporation (IFC) to help it formulate a restructuring proposal that would restore the conglomerate's viability and reduce its $1.7 billion debt to a sustainable level.

Eighteen months of negotiations among the existing shareholders and creditors, Mexican government agencies, and new investors and creditors produced a complex restructuring agreement. VISA was to merge two large companies—fully integrating their manufacturing facilities—redeploy some of its other installations, and reorganize its administration. In addition, several noncore businesses would be sold.

VISA offered its creditors a variety of options, including debt buybacks at a discount, debt-for-debt swaps (including exchange of VISA debt for sovereign debt), and debt-to-equity conversions. The array of options made it easier for VISA to meet the needs of its sixty-seven creditors, who held varying views of VISA's future profitability, had different liquidity preferences, and faced different accounting and loss provision regimes. Creditors were also permitted to trade claims among themselves. Some creditors chose to receive cash for their claims, at a substantial discount from face value. Others rescheduled $153 million at floating market rates and $75 million at lower fixed rates and also received an equity stake in the restructured company.

To finance its restructuring and debt reduction program, VISA raised $334 million in cash from new and existing shareholders and investors. Of this, $135 million came from new long-term loans, $36 million from bond sales to the Mexican public, and $5 million from public share offerings in the Mexico City Stock Exchange; the sale of assets (including automotive parts firms and hotels) brought $108 million, and a foreign institutional investor bought a $50 million equity stake.

The restructuring restored VISA's competitiveness and reduced its debt from $1.7 billion to $0.4 billion, leaving it a viable concern. The success of its negotiated debt reduction program was based on the sharing of losses between lenders and shareholders. Many more firms in developing countries will have to go through similar reorganizations to become viable.

terprises and often were not permitted to foreclose on defaulting borrowers; occasionally the process was more political than developmental, with loans being made to friends of the government. Many loans went to industries in which countries had no comparative advantage and which were profitable only as long as they were protected. By the 1980s many firms became unable to service their debts. This is not to suggest that all directed loans were mistakes; many were successful. Financial institutions are highly leveraged, however, and so can be bankrupted if even a small fraction of their loans go bad. The inadequacy of prudential regulation and supervision meant that most institutions were not made to take adequate provisions or write off bad loans, and their books gradually became a catalogue of past mistakes.

Problems at the microeconomic level were exacerbated by macroeconomic policy in many countries. Interest rate ceilings hindered the growth of financial systems and encouraged capital flight.

Overly expansionary fiscal policies led governments to borrow heavily at home and abroad. Financial distress has been most serious in countries with large external debts. Domestic borrowing in those same countries crowded out private sector borrowing and produced inflation. In countries with greater macroeconomic stability, financial distress tends to be chronic rather than acute.

Economic recovery requires the restructuring of financial intermediaries and insolvent firms. It also requires a policy environment in which finance can become less a tool for implementing interventionist development strategies and more a voluntary market process for mobilizing and allocating resources. The success of that transition depends partly on increasing lenders' confidence that future financial contracts will be honored, which in turn calls for an improvement in the ability of lenders to assess risk and to enforce contracts. This is the subject of the next chapter.

6

Foundations of financial systems

If financial systems are to be efficient and robust, they must be set within a suitable legal and regulatory framework. The difficulties of financial institutions in developing countries, discussed in Chapters 4 and 5, have much to do with weak legal systems, a lack of reliable financial information, and inadequate prudential regulation. A system of laws and regulations is needed to promote the use of contracts that are clear about the rights and obligations of contracting parties, to encourage discipline and the timely enforcement of contracts, and to foster responsible and prudent behavior on both sides of the financial transaction. Prudent and efficient financial intermediation calls for reliable information on borrowers, so adequate accounting standards and auditing arrangements are essential. Governments must also ensure that financial institutions (especially if they take deposits from the general public) are acting honestly. These are the objectives. This chapter examines the measures that can help to achieve them.

Financial contracts and debt recovery

Since ancient times, lenders have insisted upon appropriate assurances of repayment. Their difficulty has been that although they have considerable bargaining power before they enter into a loan agreement, the borrower is in the stronger position once the money is handed over. The borrower may waste or misuse the funds or simply refuse to repay.

Under early Roman law, if the debtor did not pay within a specified time after judgment had been passed, creditors were at liberty to dispose of the matter by selling him into slavery or executing him. Later Roman law viewed this as rather harsh and introduced a procedure whereby the whole of the debtor's property could be seized and sold, but the debtor was still not discharged from his liabilities. Eventually, voluntary bankruptcy proceedings with full discharge were introduced for the unfortunate borrower who could prove that his embarrassment was due to forces beyond his control.

By the fourteenth century, after the rediscovery of the Justinian codes of Roman law, debt recovery in Italy and Spain was based on Roman proceedings. These later influenced most of the countries of continental Europe. Under English common law, remedies were harsher. Defaulting debtors were usually imprisoned during the Middle Ages, and no distinction was made between honest but unfortunate debtors and dishonest ones. More lenient treatment of honest debtors was first introduced by statutory law in the sixteenth century. Debtor prisons remained common almost everywhere well into the nineteenth century, but have since been abolished (or at least used only in cases of fraud).

Industrial countries introduced far more complex bankruptcy statutes during the nineteenth century to deal with a larger number of different creditors. And in the twentieth century, with the emergence of large corporations, reorganization rather than liquidation became an important objective of bankruptcy statutes—first in the United States and more recently in other countries as well.

Apart from these ultimate remedies, creditors have traditionally made extensive use of collateral (mortgages, floating charges, liens, and so forth) and personal guarantees to reduce the probability and cost of default. Consequently, annual loan losses of commercial banks in industrial countries have typically been less than 1 percent of outstanding balances (which has helped to keep total intermediation costs at less than 4 percent). Nonperforming loans in many developing countries are now 20 percent of total loans and in some cases more. Profitable lending becomes almost impossible at these default rates, because few investments will yield returns high enough to cover the interest that must be charged (see Box 5.5 in Chapter 5). Only optimistic speculators or borrowers who intend to defraud the lender would be willing to borrow large sums at real rates of interest in excess of 10 or 15 percent.

The ultimate security of the lender is the commercial success of the borrower. This should be the primary basis for the decision to lend. But it is often difficult for lenders to assess the probability that a project will succeed. People who write eloquent loan and project proposals are not necessarily good managers or entrepreneurs, and vice versa. Bankers have thus traditionally been very conservative in their lending decisions and have relied largely on the track record of loan applicants. This inevitably meant that people with substantial wealth could borrow more than others. Since wealth can be acquired by inheritance as well as by entrepreneurial gifts, the governments of many developing countries viewed lending on the security of personal property as in conflict with their development objectives. For example, the Tandon study group appointed by the Reserve Bank of India pointed out in the early 1970s that "nationalization of the major commercial banks . . . called for a new policy with respect to deposit mobilization . . . and equitable disbursal of credit. The banking system was asked to adopt a new approach as a credit agency, based on development and potential rather than on security only, to assist the weaker sections of society . . . the security-oriented system tended to favor borrowers with strong financial resources, irrespective of their economic function'' (Banking Laws Committee 1978, p. 77). This approach overlooks the fact that credit decisions are rarely the best way to deal with social inequities.

Developing the legal foundations

The development of clear legal rules concerning the economic rights and obligations of different agents should go hand in hand with economic and financial development. In rural societies local sanctions have played an important part in limiting dishonesty by contracting parties (see Chapter 8), but urbanization has made local sanctions less effective. More complex rules and regulations are required to govern the impersonal relations of modern commercial life. And the emergence of large corporations has called for a continuously evolving set of rules to resolve the shifting conflicts of interest among shareholders, managers, bondholders, employees, and consumers.

Most developing countries have legal systems that were imposed during colonial rule. These were often at odds with local custom. Indonesia's sophisticated system of customary *adat* law uses legal concepts (for example, with respect to land tenure) that are quite different from those in the civil and commercial codes imported by the Dutch. Under the Dutch, adat law applied to Indonesians and Dutch law to Europeans and modern institutions such as companies and banks (since adat law does not cover loan contracts or similar transactions). These parallel systems are still in use today. Inevitably, they cause conflict and uncertainty, and weak judicial administration has compounded the problems. As a result the legal system has a diminished role in the settlement of disputes. Even in countries with only one legal system, the difficulties can be severe. A report of the Indian Banking Laws Committee (1978, p. 76) observed that "the present chaotic state of our credit-security law, particularly of our personal property security law, is primarily due to the application of archaic principles and concepts of Common Law developed a century ago.''

In contrast to other developing countries, Korea and Thailand have imported and adapted foreign legal systems on their own initiative. Korea enacted new codes based on German law in 1958 and 1962 (see Box 6.1). Thailand adopted a civil and commercial code based on the French and German codes in 1923. Japan had done the same in 1898 and 1899. In all three cases local customs and polit-

(an issue closely related to the assignment and transferability of property rights), to rationalize company legislation (especially with regard to disclosure of information and bankruptcy and reorganization proceedings), and to strengthen law enforcement. Contract performance can be improved by making breach of contract more costly. Provision of security, such as pledged or mortgaged assets and third-party guarantees, is one approach. Lenders can ensure repayment in other ways too: by attaching covenants to the loan contract, by appointing a representative to the board of directors, through contingent ownership of assets (by means of convertible debt securities, for example), and by closely monitoring the borrower.

Property rights and collateral

The legal recognition of property rights—that is, rights of exclusive use and control over particular resources—gives owners incentives to use resources efficiently. Without the right to exclude others from their land, farmers do not have an incentive to plow, sow, weed, and harvest. Without land tenure, they have no incentive to invest in irrigation or other improvements that would repay the investment over time. Efficiency can be further served by making property rights transferable. A farmer might then sell his land to a more productive farmer and take up another occupation for which he is better suited. Together, these rights to use, benefit from, and freely dispose of an asset constitute ownership.

China's rural economic reforms consisted mainly of restoring land tenure to households. Farmers in China do not own their land, but tenure is now fairly long term; it amounts to the leasehold concept of common law. Farmers can use this leasehold as collateral. The success of the reforms dramatically illustrates the benefits that can spring from changes in an economy's legal infrastructure.

Property rights are not usually absolute. The state claims a share of the benefits from the use of resources in taxes—to pay for, among other things, the protection of property rights from external and internal threats. Societies recognize many other restrictions on property rights for the common good, including the right of eminent domain to build roads, harbors, power lines, and other infrastructure. Property rights may also be limited in time—for example, through leasehold of land rather than absolute ownership or (less directly) through inheritance taxes applied to a broad range of assets.

Changes in the value of resources as a result of

ical conditions when the new codes were introduced were quite different from those prevailing in the countries whose legal systems were used as models. But the need to furnish their economies with a legal infrastructure that would facilitate exchange and financial intermediation was pressing. All three governments adapted the foreign codes to local customs (particularly with respect to family law) and to economic circumstances.

In some countries inherited legal systems have not been updated to meet the changing needs of the economy. In addition, commercial laws may be weakly enforced because of cumbersome procedures or because inadequate resources are devoted to the task. But just as too few rules can create uncertainty, so can too many—especially if they keep changing.

To make their legal systems more effective, governments need to provide for acceptable collateral economic development may require an expansion and redefinition of property rights from time to time, especially since conflicts between rights over different resources cannot be fully avoided. As resources become scarcer and more valuable, property rights become more important. Gradually, they have been extended to formerly "free" goods such as pastures, water, coastal fishing zones, broadcast frequencies, geostationary satellite orbits, technical inventions, and other intellectual property. Property rights are becoming universal.

MORTGAGES. The assignment and transferability of property rights promote economic efficiency directly by creating new incentives, but also indirectly by making financial intermediation possible. They do this by allowing borrowers to offer security in the form of mortgages over real estate or other collateral. Some assets are better collateral than others. Immobile, general purpose assets, such as real estate, have very desirable properties: they cannot be easily misappropriated, and they can be quickly resold for an amount close to the purchase price. A copper smelter, in contrast, retains its value only if it can compete with other plants and the price of copper does not fall. Extensive debt financing of copper smelters is therefore risky.

When taking collateral, the lender is mainly interested in the efficient transfer of property rights,

because the security is invoked only in the case of default and may deteriorate or disappear if too much time elapses before he can take possession. Mortgages over land and other real estate are therefore one of the best forms of collateral. In most countries real estate accounts for between half and three-quarters of national wealth. If ownership is widely dispersed, tenure is secure, and title transfer is easy, real estate can be good collateral for nearly any type of lending (see Box 6.2). Unfortunately, these conditions are not always met in developing countries. Land distribution is often skewed, tenure (if any) insecure, and title transfer cumbersome. One key to a smoothly functioning system of land tenure is land registers supported by cadastral surveys. In many developing countries these are still woefully inadequate or missing altogether.

Often, a loan secured with real estate will finance not the acquisition of real estate but something entirely different, perhaps a new entrepreneurial venture. The risk for the lender remains low because the borrower is bearing the entrepreneurial risk. But if the entrepreneur has no suitable collateral, the risks to the lender increase dramatically. The lender will then need far more information and perhaps a share in the proceeds if the venture proves a success. Venture capital, equity participation (with or without parallel loans), debt securities convertible into equity, and profit sharing ac-

---

Box 6.2   Financial and economic effects of land tenure in Thailand

Thailand has a relatively efficient system of land tenure, title transfer, and use of collateral. In 1901 the government introduced the Torrens system in which land titles are based on cadastral land surveys and registered with central land record offices. The use of land as collateral increased significantly, but land registration was concentrated in the more heavily populated areas. In the early 1960s half of the land area of Thailand was designated as national forest reserve, including land that was already being farmed. Most farmers in the forest reserve have no transferable title to their land, but the government has enforced the forest reserve policy flexibly and has not evicted farmers. About one-fifth of the farmed land does not have secure and transferable title.

Although uncertainty about continued possession does not seem to worry untitled farmers, lack of titled ownership affects their access to institutional credit. Untitled farmers cannot provide collateral and are lim-

ited to borrowing on the basis of personal or group guarantees or from moneylenders. (Moneylenders charge interest rates of 40–50 percent, compared with about 15 percent for loans from financial institutions.) In a sample study of matched groups of titled and untitled farmers, titled farmers were able to borrow on average three times more per acre of land. Secure land title not only affected the ability to obtain mortgage credit (which accounted for half of all credit among titled farmers) but also doubled access to unsecured credit.

Thanks to easier access to credit, titled farmers made significantly more land improvements and used significantly more machinery and other inputs. As a result they enjoyed 12–20 percent higher farm revenues and 12–27 percent higher productivity than untitled farmers in similar regions. The government has recently taken steps to improve land tenure for untitled farmers.

several centuries. The spread of such facilities in various countries has increased the use of inventories as collateral.

For goods in transit, the bill of lading can serve as security. Documentary export-import credit is an important application of this sort of collateral. Korea and some other countries have further developed this idea by creating a domestic letter of credit based on an irrevocable export letter of credit. In this way the primary exporter can extend his creditworthiness to suppliers of intermediate inputs.

DEBT RECOVERY. Legal systems in developing countries often favor the borrower by making it hard for the lender to foreclose on collateral. Originally, such provisions were intended to protect small borrowers against unscrupulous moneylenders, but today they may adversely affect the ability of state-owned commercial banks to collect on loans. This raises the costs of intermediation and weakens banks' portfolios; as a result the ability of lenders to extend loans to new and creditworthy borrowers is undermined. Creditors often have to sue the defaulting debtor for payment, which in many countries in South Asia, for example, may take several years. Once a judgment has been obtained, the creditor may then have to sue for execution of his claim. Five to eight years may pass from the date of nonpayment to the final recovery of the collateral. Pakistan is among the countries that have recently taken legal and procedural steps to speed this process (see Box 6.4).

Cumbersome recovery procedures have led to new lending arrangements that redress the balance in favor of the creditor. Hire purchase and leasing may have become popular partly because the lender retains title to the asset being financed and can take possession without any legal formalities if the borrower is late in paying. Leasing also owes its popularity to its role in circumventing interest rate controls and taxes. It has often restored access to financing that excessive bank regulation and weak legal systems had blocked.

Company law

Large enterprises have become an important part of modern economic activity in most industrial and developing countries. Today, the largest 100 corporations typically account for between 30 and 50 percent of total manufacturing production in industrial countries. Industrial concentration is often even more pronounced in developing countries.

cording to Islamic principles (see Box 6.3) are all examples of such arrangements.

In some countries other assets can serve as collateral. Inventories and other movable goods are inherently poor collateral because they have comparatively little value, are destructible, and can be sold privately and informally. They are difficult to use as collateral when left in the possession of the borrower. A partial solution is to make some goods legally "immovable" by creating special title registers. This is feasible only for a few large and high-value movables, such as ships, aircraft, motor vehicles, or industrial machines. Another solution is to store commodities of a standardized quality in certified warehouses and issue warrants. Rice warehouse warrants have been used in Japan for

Box 6.4   Commercial law enforcement in Pakistan

Pakistan's financial institutions have suffered badly from excessive arrears. Matters did not improve when the major commercial banks were nationalized in the 1970s. Enforcement of loan contracts in default was too slow to have much disciplinary effect on borrowers. Often it took five years or longer before the bank could foreclose on mortgaged property.

Recognizing the problem, the government established a system of special banking courts in 1979. In 1984 a corresponding system was established to deal with loan recovery for the newly introduced Islamic financing instruments. Problems remain, however. Debtors can still challenge court rulings at every step, and five-year delays can still occur. More special courts are to be established over the next two years, and their jurisdiction will be narrowed to exclude very small claims. Once a bank has obtained judgment from a special court, it will no longer have to apply separately for execution of the decree.

An institutional innovation of the nineteenth century made this possible: the general incorporation of joint-stock companies with limited liability. Until the 1850s free incorporation and limited liability were viewed with considerable skepticism. General incorporation was prompted by the large capital requirements of railway construction, which could not be met by the small private banking houses.

The new companies called for rules and regulations to protect the interests of shareholders, creditors, and other interested parties, including employees. The resulting structure of control features agents (directors or independent auditors) who monitor management on behalf of the owners; elaborate accounting, information, and disclosure procedures; disciplinary systems that align the interests of managers and owners; and a clear assignment of responsibilities. With hundreds and sometimes millions of shareholders, limited liability became essential. Individual shareholders had little influence over the affairs of the company. They had become "investors," in some ways creditors more than owner-managers. Limited liability shifted more of the risk to other creditors. As a result better bankruptcy and reorganization rules

were needed too, so that creditors could take control if the company ran into difficulty. And most countries have enacted labor laws to offer employees some protection against unscrupulous owners and managers.

State or private ownership—does it matter?

An alternative to the joint-stock structure for managing large enterprises is state ownership. Some of the first big industrial enterprises and financial institutions were publicly owned. State ownership is the predominant form of industrial organization in centrally planned economies, and state-owned enterprises account for a substantial part of the economy in many other countries. In a sample of nineteen developing countries in 1984 and 1985, state enterprises accounted for an average of 13 percent of GNP and 31 percent of domestic investment; they were concentrated in capital-intensive heavy industry and utilities such as steel, chemicals, electricity, oil, and gas. Intermediate forms of "ownership" such as cooperatives, mutuals, foundations, and franchises have also become common. State enterprises in some countries are legally constituted as joint-stock corporations; some of these (but not all) seem to operate like private enterprises.

Successful public enterprises such as British Steel, Renault (before its recent difficulties), and Brazil's Empresa Brasileira de Aeronáutica (EMBRAER) are often cited as proof that public enterprises can be as efficient and innovative as private enterprises. Indeed, it is often argued that ownership does not matter as much as the independence and accountability of management and the extent of competition.

In practice, however, the form of ownership goes a long way to determine the environment within which management operates. Lines of authority and responsibility are often blurred in state enterprises. Their chief executives usually take orders from various government agencies, their freedom to reward and discipline employees is circumscribed by rules of seniority and guaranteed employment, and their own compensation is rarely linked directly to profits. Understanding these drawbacks, some governments have tried to create a self-regulating regime for their state enterprises. But the boundary between the government's domain and the market's is ambiguous. Economies of scale, externalities, and scarcity of information cause complications that may prompt governments to intervene.

For centuries bankruptcy procedures have enabled creditors to recover their resources from debtors who defaulted. The emergence of large corporations, however, called for a new approach. When a company is having difficulty in servicing its debt, reorganizing the enterprise might yield higher returns to its creditors than closing it down and selling its assets. Reorganization might mean rescheduling its interest and principal payments, reducing its interest charges, downgrading the quality of claims against it (for example, by releasing mortgage liens or by swapping debt for equity), or reducing or canceling its debts.

Such a far-reaching modification of the rights of creditors cannot be taken lightly and can be justified only if it is in their best interests—that is, if it will make them (or society) better off than debt recovery through liquidation. Reorganization may also weaken the incentives for good performance, particularly if the present management is left in place. Reorganization becomes more difficult as the number of creditors grows. Rules are needed, for example, to ensure that a few small creditors cannot jeopardize a reorganization plan that is in the interests of the majority.

Few developing countries have well-developed laws and procedures for reorganization. Often the task is delayed and takes place only through ad hoc government intervention. Indonesia's bankruptcy code, for instance, has rarely been used. China and Hungary have recently reintroduced bankruptcy regulations because state enterprises are becoming more independent and the private and cooperative sectors are expanding. Because many developing countries are now trying to rely more on decentralized decisionmaking, market forces, the private sector, and financial intermediation, they too will need to introduce procedures for corporate restructuring that go beyond liquidation and bankruptcy. To ensure that such procedures do not encourage managers to take excessive risks, governments could devise penalties for recklessness and fraud and for concealing the insolvency of a corporation.

Timely and accurate accounts

Because financial claims cannot be fully secured, monitoring and information are essential. In informal financial markets, information is usually obtained as a by-product of other activities of the lender—for example, through his trading with the borrower. For larger organizations, more formal monitoring techniques are necessary, both for internal use to monitor the performance of subunits and for use by outsiders with a legitimate interest in the performance of the corporation. These techniques are management accounting and financial accounting, respectively.

Standardized accounting concepts and principles were developed only after the financial crises of the 1920s and 1930s. Before then, there was no urgent need to standardize the conventions of management accounting: owners and managers set their own rules. But with the emergence of general incorporation and limited liability, standardized information became essential—a point brought home forcefully during the 1930s, when many small investors lost their savings because they trusted inaccurate financial statements.

Governments responded by tightening accounting and auditing requirements in a number of ways. In the United States, for example, the Securities and Exchange Commission (SEC) was created to regulate securities markets and to make the financial process more transparent. The SEC turned to the professional association of accountants to develop accounting concepts (such as fair market value, consistency, accrual, going concern) and detailed rules, or "generally accepted accounting principles," that became binding on the profession. A similar approach was adopted in the United Kingdom and in many Commonwealth countries.

Continental Europe and Japan and several other countries adopted a somewhat different approach. They placed greater emphasis on detailed rules laid down in company laws, usually with particular stress on prudence (historical cost accounting) as opposed to fair value, and on a larger role for the tax authorities in defining accounting rules. In many of these countries, tax accounts and financial accounts must be drawn up on a fully consistent basis.

Because of these and other differences in approach, company accounts cannot be easily compared across countries. For example, companies in Germany, Japan, Korea, and Thailand usually appear highly leveraged (that is, with high levels of debt relative to net worth) when compared with companies in Argentina, Brazil, Canada, or the United States. Most of the difference, however, is due to different accounting conventions. The first group relies more on historical cost accounting, with many assets (especially land) valued at less than their market value, whereas the second group regularly revalues some or all assets. In many countries with high inflation, full revaluation has become the rule because historical cost accounting becomes virtually meaningless under such conditions. Market valuation can be equally troublesome for assets with drastic, cyclical changes in value (for example, some types of securities, raw materials, and commercial real estate).

Efforts have recently been made to harmonize accounting and auditing practices internationally through the International Accounting Standards Committee and, in a more far-reaching way, within the European Community. The result is a convergence of the Anglo-Saxon and continental approaches, with greater standardization of financial statement formats on the one hand and a greater use of the concept of fair market value on the other.

In developing countries accounting and auditing practices are sometimes weak, and financial laws and regulations do not demand accurate and timely financial reports. Developing an effective accounting and auditing profession is essential for building efficient financial markets, and projects to do this have recently been introduced in Indonesia and Madagascar, for example. Training and education are the main requirements, but appropriate regulation and regulatory bodies are also needed.

Timely accounts are very important for financial institutions. Annual or quarterly accounting might be sufficient for most nonfinancial firms, but financial institutions can lose their risk capital virtually overnight if, say, they hold large open positions in foreign exchange or futures and options contracts. Internal and external financial reporting therefore needs to be much more frequent, with certain kinds of information available to management daily.

Prudential regulation of financial institutions and markets

Procedures for settling private disputes are set forth in most company laws, commercial codes, and special banking acts, but the development of a sound financial system requires additional measures. Prudential supervision by government authorities is warranted for banks and some other financial institutions and markets. Banks hold an important part of the money supply, create money, are the main means of implementing monetary policy, administer the payments system, and intermediate between savings and investments. Problems in one bank can quickly spread through the entire financial system. Bank failures have monetary and macroeconomic consequences, disrupt the payments system, and lead to disintermedia-

tion (which decreases the mobilization of resources and the availability of finance for investment).

As financial systems develop, different institutions evolve to take over some activities formerly performed by banks and to provide new services. All these institutions, old and new, are integrated in an increasingly complex financial system. This complexity limits the ability of creditors to exercise effective control and calls for prudential regulation and supervision.

Regulation of banks

Bank supervisors in many developing countries focus on compliance with monetary policy regulations, foreign exchange controls, and economic policy regulations such as those for allocating credit. They pay relatively little attention to the prudential aspects of financial monitoring. For example, in many countries supervisors make no independent assessment of the quality of assets and give scant regard to accounting procedures and management controls. Together with macroeconomic instability and the lack of adequate legislation, this is one of the main causes of bank insolvency.

Governments in developing countries are preoccupied with faster economic growth; they see banks as an instrument for promoting the desired investments. Often, however, these investments are the most risky from a bank's point of view, so the volume of credit extended to them remains less than the governments would like. The government reaction is often to force the banks to extend credit to priority sectors. This policy has been pursued without adequate attention to the risks involved. With the benefit of prudential regulation and supervision, however, governments can obtain information about the consequences of their policies while there is still time to modify them.

The goal of bank supervision, then, is to promote a safe, stable, and efficient financial system. The main task is to prevent bank failures, but this does not mean that financial institutions should not be allowed to fail. Bank supervisors must try to identify problems at an early stage and intervene before the situation gets out of hand. For this reason they have to be organized in such a way that they are constantly aware of developments.

ORGANIZATION. In many developing countries supervision tends to rely predominantly on analysis of bank reports or on bank inspections. Off-site supervision cannot assess risk adequately, and inspections tend to be too infrequent. Effective su-

An adequate system of bank supervision should allow for both off-site supervision and on-site inspection. The task of the off-site supervisors is to analyze reports of the banks, identify possible problems, and propose remedies. Banks in most countries have to submit monthly balance sheet information for purposes of monetary control. It would make sense to combine the two reporting requirements.

After receiving the reports, the *off-site* supervisors should:

- Check their completeness, accuracy, and consistency
- Check their compliance with prudential ratios and regulations
- Analyze the financial situation of the bank and identify the main changes in financial ratios
- Identify other risks such as foreign exchange risks, interest rate risks, and concentration risks
- Prepare a summary for the management of the supervisory agency and recommend action.

The *on-site* inspectors should check the accuracy of the periodic reports to the supervisor and analyze those aspects of a bank that cannot be adequately monitored by off-site supervision. Inspections, however, should not become audits. They should focus on the bank's main activities and on the potential problems that were identified by off-site supervision. Inspections should assess the quality of assets, management and control procedures, and accounting systems. The inspectors should:

- Study the main credit files (and a sample of smaller files) to assess the lending procedures and the quality of the loans
- Evaluate lending procedures and review minutes of meetings of the credit committee and the board of directors
- Check management information systems and internal controls, especially with regard to the activities of branches and subsidiaries
- Evaluate accounting procedures, especially those for provisioning and interest accrual.

pervision calls for both. Off-site supervisors should analyze reports periodically submitted by the banks, and on-site inspectors should verify their accuracy, obtain detailed information about potential problem areas, and review the elements that off-site supervisors cannot properly assess. Box 6.5 goes into this in more detail.

LICENSING. The purpose of licensing should be to ensure adequate capitalization and sound management, not to limit entry or restrict competition. Bank supervisors should have the authority to screen potential owners and managers to prevent those lacking adequate professional qualifications, financial backing, and moral standing from obtaining a banking license. In many countries restrictions on entry into banking are so severe that they cause oligopolistic practices and suppress competition.

Sometimes entry restrictions are defended by citing the poor quality of the existing banks' portfolios. The supervisors fear that these banks could not withstand competition from new institutions with "clean" portfolios. If portfolios are weak because of government lending directives or drastic adjustment programs, a good case can be made for cleaning up the balance sheets of the existing banks before liberalizing entry. More generally,

however, managers and shareholders should be held responsible for past mistakes. If that means losing market share to leaner and more efficient competitors and, in extreme cases, bankruptcy or reorganization, so be it. But liberal entry into financial services should not mean unqualified entry. Several countries with easy entry (Egypt, Thailand, and Turkey, for instance) have experienced problems with unregulated, undercapitalized, and poorly managed banks and other financial institutions.

CAPITAL ADEQUACY. Banks need capital to absorb unusual losses. The need to maintain an adequate capital-to-assets ratio exerts discipline on lending. Regulations should set minimum guidelines for capital adequacy that cover both assets and items not listed on the balance sheet (such as guarantees and lines of credit). Standards of capital adequacy can take account of different degrees of risk by requiring, for example, 100 percent capital for high-risk items such as industrial shares, 10 percent for unsecured loans, 5 percent for secured loans, and so on. The recent agreement among major industrial countries on standards of capital adequacy uses risk weights and might serve as a starting point for others. In many countries financial institutions were significantly undercapitalized even before portfolio and other losses were recognized. Government-owned banks, in particular, often operate with little capital. When government officials and the public at large believe that state ownership is a guarantee against failure, the management is not subject to the discipline that capital adequacy requirements would provide for a private institution.

ASSET CLASSIFICATION AND PROVISIONING. Banks in developing countries rarely make realistic provisions for potential losses or problem assets. Often they fail to write off or provide for actual losses or to suspend interest on nonperforming loans. As a result their balance sheets and income statements are misleading. Bank supervisors should be able to require banks to make appropriate provisions for loan losses, to write off uncollectible assets, and to suspend interest on nonperforming loans.

LIQUIDITY. In many developing countries banks have to comply with a short-term liquidity ratio. This ratio is often used more as a reserve requirement for purposes of monetary policy than as a prudential measure to guard against lack of liquidity. Liquidity risk arises because banks borrow money at short maturities and lend it at long. The risk is not just that a bank will not be able to repay depositors' money when called, but also that interest rates on short-term liabilities will rise faster than those on longer-term assets. Ratios therefore need to be set and monitored for long-term as well as short-term liquidity.

PORTFOLIO CONCENTRATION. Limits on lending as a percentage of a bank's capital are necessary to prevent the concentration of risk in a single borrower, a group of related borrowers, or a particular industry. Some developing countries set no lending limits at all. In others the limits are set at imprudent levels, in some cases exceeding 100 percent of bank capital. Ghana's central bank had legal authority to set lending limits but until recently did not do so. The resulting concentration of risk eventually led to the technical insolvency of several major banks.

ENFORCEMENT POWERS. In many countries supervisors can impose fines and penalties for criminal acts and violations of specific banking statutes. There may, however, be little they can do to address unsafe and unsound banking practices. Their options are either to cancel the banking license or to do nothing—neither of which is accep-

table. Supervisors could be empowered to take certain intermediate steps: impose fines for unsound practices, suspend dividends, deny requests to expand the number of branches or undertake new corporate activities, issue cease and desist orders, remove managers or directors, and hold directors legally accountable for losses incurred through illegal actions and willful contraventions of prudential regulations. The lack of such powers often causes inaction.

RESTRUCTURING. Bank supervisors try to minimize losses by intervening at or near the point of a bank's technical insolvency. Poor information, an inadequate legal framework, and lack of political will often permit banks to stay open, multiplying their losses, even after they have lost their book capital many times over. In many developing countries banks are subject to the same bankruptcy and restructuring procedures as nonfinancial corporations. While bank restructuring is under way, depositors may not have access to their funds. In addition, shareholders may retain an equity interest which they use to obstruct plans to recapitalize and transfer ownership. If supervisors are to dispose of insolvent banks quickly, they must be granted authority to close a bank; to replace its management and directors; to dissolve existing shareholder interests; to purchase, sell, or transfer bad assets; and to merge, restructure, or liquidate as necessary.

AUDITS. In some developing countries the authorities require no external audits of banks. In others audits are performed, but there are no clear guidelines on the standards to be used or on the scope, content, and frequency of the audit program. As a result audits are often inadequate and misleading. Indeed, it is not uncommon for banks that are known to be insolvent to be given clean audit reports. The prudential framework therefore needs to set minimum audit standards and to prescribe the form and content of the related financial disclosures.

POLICY PRIORITIES AND POLITICAL WILL. To be effective, prudential regulation must be backed by a political commitment to supervision and enforcement. The supervisory body must be given clear policy goals, and it must be independent. Too often in developing countries, supervisors are undercut by political interference. Such interference was blatant in the Philippines in the 1970s and early 1980s, when supervisors feared reprisals if they attempted to discipline bank managers; it happens in a subtler form in many countries. Once aware of the scale of a banking problem, governments often postpone the day of reckoning. When they finally act, the cost of putting matters straight may be far greater.

One sign of political commitment is the amount of resources given to the supervisory agency. If the government means business, it must give the supervisory agency clearly defined responsibilities and then support that mandate with adequate funds for staffing and training. Bank supervisors must be offered good compensation and career prospects if they are to resist corruption and command the respect of the institutions they supervise. If the civil service cannot attract personnel of the required quality, it might be sensible to have banks examined by private auditing firms and to recover the costs through a general levy on banks (with due care to avoid conflicts of interest).

Regulation of other financial institutions

Many of the principles of bank supervision and regulation also apply to other financial institutions, such as finance companies, insurance companies, pension funds, and mutual funds. A vital test in deciding on the extent of regulation is the number and type of creditors. Financial institutions that do not have deposit-like liabilities to the general public need not be regulated as closely as those that do, because their deposits are not part of the payments mechanism and their insolvency is not as costly to the economy. The general provisions of commercial and company laws may therefore be adequate. Conversely, those financial institutions that are like banks in all but name (for example, some investment funds) should be just as closely regulated and supervised (see Box 6.6).

INSURANCE. Insurance companies are usually heavily regulated in both industrial and developing countries. These regulations have often been introduced in response to failures or fraud. Regulations typically provide for compulsory disclosure of information, government supervision with implicit or explicit guarantees of solvency, oversight of contract terms and conditions, controls on entry, restrictions on investment portfolios, and rules concerning prices or profits. Regulation to promote transparency is desirable, but many of these measures limit competition and efficiency. For example, instead of insisting that a large share of insurance assets be placed in low-interest govern-

Box 6.6 Investment funds in Egypt

The recent experience of Egypt illustrates the need for adequate regulation and supervision of non-bank financial intermediaries that take deposits from the general public. Investment funds were organized in the mid-1970s to handle remittances from Egyptian workers abroad and the savings of small investors. These Islamic investment companies paid profit-related returns, sometimes as high as 30 percent a year. They were not required to conform to banking regulations and did not come under the supervision of the central bank.

Some of these institutions have faced increasing difficulties in the past two years, and their financial condition has deteriorated. Many had made large initial profits through trade finance not otherwise available to importers or through foreign exchange transactions in the parallel market. Some paid high dividends to earlier depositors out of funds paid in by new depositors. When deposit growth slowed, some could no longer pay the promised high returns. To prevent further deterioration, the government had to step in.

A law regulating the investment funds was passed in 1988. It restricts deposit taking to joint-stock companies, imposes minimum capital standards, and vests regulatory oversight with the Capital Markets Authority.

ment bonds, portfolio restrictions should require that risks be adequately diversified. Life insurance and other contractual savings schemes would then be more attractive to savers. Investments in shares and corporate bonds have often been severely restricted, eliminating a potentially important source of long-term capital.

SECURITIES MARKETS. An appropriate regulatory framework for securities is needed to increase investor confidence. Regulation is unlikely to be satisfactory if left entirely to the market. The experience of many countries shows that some government guidance is desirable. In Hong Kong, for example, the stock market collapsed in 1973 partly because of insider abuses. A new securities commission helped to restore confidence. It was able to persuade brokers and underwriters that an orderly market which protected investors was in their own long-term interests.

The regulations need to provide for adequate disclosure of information about companies so that investors can make informed decisions; they need to license securities intermediaries and to curtail improper activities in the market, especially the use of privileged information by corporate officers and directors for their personal gain (insider trading). These regulations are usually embodied in the company laws that form the legal framework for joint-stock companies.

If securities firms and the securities market as a whole are to perform efficiently, the firms must be profitable and well capitalized and have professionally trained staff. This does not happen automatically in an emerging securities market. The government has a crucial role. If minimum capital requirements are set too high in relation to the size of the market, new securities firms will not appear. But if firms have insufficient capital, they will not be able to take on the risks of underwriting new issues; nor will they be able to work as market makers (that is, to buy and sell shares for their own account) and thus provide liquidity for the secondary market. Brokerage rates, underwriting fees, and so on must be high enough for firms to attract and train staff and still leave their shareholders with an adequate return on capital.

The regulation of companies and securities markets is linked to important social issues. Promoting widespread ownership of productive assets may be one way to forestall greater concentration of wealth and economic power. At the same time, it can provide an income for the elderly at a time when industrialization and urbanization are breaking down the extended family and the traditional transfer of income between generations.

7

Developing financial systems

What sort of financial systems will the developing countries possess in twenty years? During the past twenty years, internationalization of markets and a common set of forces have pushed the financial systems of high-income countries into rough alignment. The financial systems of developing countries, however, remain quite heterogeneous. Most developing countries have begun to place greater emphasis on market signals, but some governments will continue to intervene extensively in credit allocation and pricing, and some will continue to rely on inflationary financing. As a result their financial systems will remain shallow, with little long-term finance. Economic structures will continue to differ as well, with some countries remaining primarily agrarian, others industrialized, some oriented toward domestic markets and imposing tight controls on capital movements, and others more oriented toward external markets and having fewer controls. Because of these differences in developing countries' economic structures and approaches to development, their financial systems are likely to remain quite diverse over the next two decades.

There are nevertheless pressures that are leading most developing countries to rethink the shape of their financial systems. One is the effort to apply some of the lessons learned from past intervention in financial markets, and another is the need to adapt to the decline in foreign capital inflows. A third is the rapid changes that have occurred in financial technology and banking practice. This chapter considers the evolution of formal financial institutions and markets in response to these pressures. Chapter 8 will turn to the informal markets.

Financing investment

Certainly in the next decade, and perhaps in the next two, the net flow of foreign capital to most developing countries is likely to be relatively small, regardless of how the present debt crisis is resolved. This has important implications for financial sector development. Developing countries will be forced to rely primarily on domestic saving to cover the cost of investment. In the past, most relied heavily on foreign financing, and in many countries external debt exceeds domestic debt. Moreover, practically all long-term credit was provided by foreign loans. The decline in funding from abroad will make living with a shallow domestic financial system and little long-term finance difficult. Unless countries develop their financial systems, would-be investors will have to rely primarily upon retained earnings, and the funding of large projects, particularly ones that require longer-term finance, will be difficult.

Despite considerable differences in level of development and in investment rates, countries are quite similar in the composition of their capital

Box 7.1 The structure of investment and the capital stock

Surprisingly, in relation to national income or GNP, the level and composition of investment (that is, the change in capital stock) and the capital stock itself are quite similar among both low- and high-income countries. Economies with very high rates of investment and rapid growth (such as China, Korea, and Japan) have similar assets-to-GNP ratios, because rapid growth of the capital stock is balanced by rapid growth of output. In the centrally planned economies, assets-to-GNP ratios tend to be somewhat higher, owing to lower productivity and a large volume of inventories. Box table 7.1 presents capital stock estimates for a few countries for which such data are available.

On average, gross investment is about 20 percent of GNP. Among developing countries, however, investment rates vary considerably, ranging from less than 15 percent of GNP in Sub-Saharan Africa to well over 30 percent in China. Machinery and equipment typically account for two-fifths of gross investment, and housing, other buildings, and civil works for one-fifth each. Perhaps one-half of the total is thus invested in assets with a life of fifty years or more, with the rest ranging mostly between ten and twenty years.

Because of substantial differences in asset life, the structure of the capital stock is quite different from the pattern of investment flows: long-lived assets (primarily structures) account for about two-thirds of total reproducible fixed assets, medium-lived machinery and equipment for about one-fifth, and short-lived inventories, livestock, and consumer durables for the remainder. The value of total reproducible assets is typically equivalent to 200 to 300 percent of GNP.

Box table 7.1 Estimates of the net capital stock in selected countries
(percentage of GNP)

Item	United States, 1978	Federal Republic of Germany, 1977	Mexico, 1978	India, 1975	Hungary, 1977
Total reproducible assets	295	325	209	239[a]	405
Housing	87	106	64	67	73
Other structures	93	117	64	58[a]	135
Machinery and equipment	45	47	43	43	69
Inventories	33	21	20	34	70
Livestock	2	2	4	10	8
Consumer durables	35	33	13	27	51
Land	89	108	50	131	150

a. Adjusted from Goldsmith 1985 to make estimate consistent with those for other countries and with national accounts estimates.
Source: Goldsmith 1985.

stock and of gross investment flows. The reproducible capital stock is usually equivalent to two to four years of gross national product (see Box 7.1). Long-lived assets, such as housing, commercial buildings, schools, roads, and water supply systems, account for the bulk of physical wealth in all countries. The capital stock of the business sector is surprisingly small in the aggregate. Fixed assets in manufacturing and utilities are each equivalent to about 40 percent of GNP, fixed assets in commerce are equivalent to 10 to 15 percent of GNP, and inventories are equivalent to 20 to 30 percent of GNP. In terms of gross investment flows and the demand for financial services the business sector looms larger than its share of the capital stock might suggest. Its capital stock is constantly being remolded as new machinery replaces old, produc-

tion and distribution facilities are upgraded, and new plants are built.

Business finance

Many of the financial policies pursued by developing countries during the past several decades were intended to redress perceived shortcomings of domestic financial markets. Two issues have been of particular concern: first, the supply of equity capital and long-term finance and, second, the lack of access to finance for certain classes of borrowers. In formulating policies to address these two concerns, however, countries have paid too little attention to the balance between risk and reward.

PATTERNS OF FINANCE. In the past, developing country governments relied on directed credit, ad-

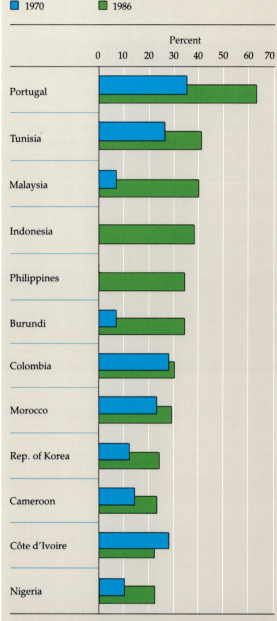

Figure 7.1 Shares of medium- and long-term credit in total credit outstanding from commercial banks and other financial institutions in selected developing countries, 1970 and 1986

◼ 1970   ◼ 1986

Percent

Note: Data are end-of-year shares. Data for Cameroon, Colombia, Korea, Malaysia, Nigeria, and the Philippines refer to commercial banks only. "Credit for equipment" has been used as a proxy for medium- and long-term credit in Korea. Data for 1970 refer to 1974 for Cameroon, average of monthly shares for Nigeria, and 1975 for Portugal; data for 1986 refer to 1985 for Cameroon and Morocco, 1987 for Indonesia, and June 1986 for Nigeria. Data were not available for Indonesia and the Philippines for 1970.
Source: Central bank bulletins and World Bank data.

ministered interest rates, and foreign borrowing to ensure that certain sectors received enough long-term financing. As Figure 7.1 indicates, however, in some countries commercial banks and other financial institutions have begun in recent years to extend more medium- and long-term credit. In other countries, although banks provide little formal long-term finance, they do offer lines of credit and short-term loans that they roll over regularly as long as the borrower is in good standing. This type of financing, acceptable to many firms, is used extensively as an alternative to long-term finance in high-income as well as developing countries. From the viewpoint of some borrowers, however, short-term credit lines are imperfect substitutes for longer-term loans. They entail the risk of nonrenewal, a risk that may lead investors to forgo certain projects.

Neither in theory nor in practice are there simple norms of corporate financial structure. Financial theorists have argued that the debt-to-equity ratios of corporations are irrelevant if capital markets are perfect (see Box 7.2). More realistic theories, which take into account the costs of taxation, information, and monitoring and control, point to a variety of tradeoffs between equity and debt. In practice, no single pattern of corporate finance and control has been found to be best.

It is nonetheless useful to distinguish among firms according to the variability of their earnings. Higher leveraging becomes riskier the more earnings fluctuate. The firms that can best afford to be highly leveraged are large and capital-intensive and have highly predictable earnings—utilities, for example. In fact, modern finance got its start with infrastructure projects such as canals, railways, and (later) public utilities. Today, much of the capital for investment by public utilities in industrial countries is provided by retained earnings, because the basic infrastructure investments have already been made. Thanks to the stability of their income and the long life of their assets, public utilities are usually able to raise what external financing they do need by issuing bonds or other long-term debt.

In most developing countries, utilities and large transport companies have borrowed heavily from domestic banks and from abroad and are now among the borrowers that are unable to service their debts. This does not necessarily mean that they overborrowed, however. Most such companies are publicly owned, and their products are frequently priced too low to yield an adequate return on their huge investments. If prices were set

Box 7.2 Corporate finance in theory and practice

Much attention has been paid in academic circles to identifying the factors that influence corporate financial structure and dividend policies. The seminal article by Modigliani and Miller in 1958 demonstrated that in a world with perfect capital markets a corporation's debt-to-equity ratio is irrelevant to the firm's market value. In such a world the value of the firm is determined entirely by its investment decisions, which can therefore be completely separated from financing decisions. But markets are never perfect, and in practice financing decisions are not irrelevant. Subsequent developments in corporate finance theory relaxed some of the explicit or implicit conditions underpinning the assumption of perfect capital markets.

Corporate taxes and the worldwide practice of tax deductibility of interest payments provide an incentive for debt finance. This incentive is weakened, however, by the direct and indirect costs of financial distress and bankruptcy, which are more likely to be encountered in a highly leveraged company. Information flows are not perfect, and this has an important influence on financing decisions. In particular, managers have better information on a firm's performance and prospects than do outside creditors and shareholders. By maintaining sta-

ble dividends, firms help to signal their confidence about future prospects. This may explain why firms continue to pay dividends even if they need additional external finance or if taxes on capital gains are lower than those on dividend income.

Furthermore, since the interests of managers may differ from those of creditors and shareholders, the latter group must incur costs in trying to monitor and affect the way the company is run. Decisions on capital structure will be influenced by the ability of creditors and shareholders to get the information they need in order to exercise control over managers.

Recent theories have provided some plausible explanations for the differences in corporate financing patterns between the bank-based systems of Germany and Japan, on the one hand, and the market-based systems of the United States and United Kingdom, on the other. The two bank-based systems involve greater corporate indebtedness (although the difference is not as large as suggested by reported accounting data). This may be explained by the close relations between banks and industry—that is, by the ability of bankers to influence the decisions of managers.

to yield a higher return, retained earnings could provide most of the investment funds required.

Some large, capital-intensive firms—in steel, cement, or petrochemicals, for example—have a less predictable income stream. These firms cannot afford to be as highly leveraged as utilities and should rely more on equity financing, much of which can come from retained earnings if the firms are profitable. If they are private and large enough to be known to the public, these firms can obtain funding by issuing equities or by finding foreign partners. Where a particular industry accounts for a large part of a country's output, it would be desirable for the country to diversify its risk. It could do so by seeking equity funding abroad or by issuing debt instruments whose payments are linked to the price of the commodity. Foreign lenders would thus bear some of the risk of price fluctuations.

Many industries in this second group borrowed heavily during the 1970s to finance large investment programs. Too heavily as it turned out: substantial overinvestment left many of them unable to service their debts. As a result there has been little investment in these sectors during the 1980s. Care must be taken that firms in these indus-

tries do not once again overinvest and become overindebted when additions to capacity become necessary.

To foster sounder corporate financial structures, governments need to reconsider the policies that gave certain classes of firms an incentive to become highly leveraged. Low prices and high costs left many state-owned enterprises dependent on external finance for investment. Subsidized credit, tax biases against equity finance, the limited size of capital markets, and lax or ineffective bankruptcy laws encouraged firms to finance themselves by borrowing rather than by retaining earnings or issuing equity. In some countries the knowledge that the government was likely to help troubled firms made it safer to rely on borrowing. In others the existence of financial-industrial conglomerates in conjunction with weak supervision and regulation of banks worked to the same end.

Increasing the supply of long-term finance—both debt and equity—remains a priority, particularly in inflationary countries and in countries that have depended on foreign borrowing for most of their long-term funding. Macroeconomic stability is essential. Indexation can help to maintain some long-term finance in inflationary economies, but it

Box 7.3 The financial history of a Pakistani firm

Ajmal Hosiery, a family-owned business in Lahore, Pakistan, was established by Malik Ahmad Din in 1947. He began with an abandoned hosiery mill and two obsolete knitting machines. By the late 1950s the firm was well-known across the country.

Malik's original scheme was to let his business grow at a pace that would require no external financing, because he was uncomfortable with the paperwork involved in getting a loan. Moreover, he feared that information given to financial institutions could be used by the tax authorities. The company grew modestly during its first twenty years by plowing profits back into the business. Sales increased from around 50,000 rupees (Rs) in 1947 to Rs1.3 million in 1969.

The company obtained its first bank financing—an Rs50,000 line of credit—in 1969 when it executed its first export order. This venture into the international market was not successful; it cost the company Rs100,000. The company reentered the export market in 1972 but could obtain a line of credit of only Rs200,000 from a local bank. Although there was clear potential for exports, the firm needed working capital finance. In 1973 the State Bank of Pakistan introduced its Export Refinance Scheme, which provided cheap financing to eligible exporters through the commercial banking system. The firm could not exploit the scheme fully because banks thought its collateral inadequate. Nevertheless, the scheme helped the company to reach sales of Rs5.0 million in 1979, by which time its bank credit line amounted to Rs1.3 million.

The firm had always relied solely on internally generated funds to finance investment. Consequently, investment in plant and equipment had not kept pace with sales. In 1976, however, it obtained a long-term loan of Rs1.0 million to expand its capacity; the lender was the Industrial Development Bank of Pakistan.

The company has grown dramatically during the 1980s. It has used the government's enlarged export financing scheme and has also obtained term financing (in 1980, 1984, and 1988) for modernizing its plant and equipment. Sales grew fivefold between 1980 and 1988. In 1989–90 the firm plans to reach sales of Rs90.0 million, a figure three times higher than its 1988 sales of Rs30.0 million and 1,800 times its sales of Rs50,000 at inception in 1947.

---

is a poor substitute for price stability. Allowing institutions to charge interest rates that reflect the higher risks of longer-term lending will increase its supply, as will improvements in legal and accounting systems that increase lenders' ability to monitor and control their clients. Relatively risky projects should be financed with equity capital, where repayment is linked to profits; long-term loans with fixed returns are unsuitable for such projects.

ACCESS TO FINANCE. Many governments have sought to improve the access of smaller firms to finance, partly for social reasons and partly because such firms are often thought to be the most dynamic part of the economy. Although small-scale manufacturing, service, and commercial firms are generally less capital-intensive than heavy industry or housing and thus have considerably smaller investment needs, they should have access to credit if they can use it more productively than larger borrowers. As Box 7.3 illustrates, credit can allow a small firm to invest and grow.

Because small firms have little name recognition, they can neither borrow abroad nor issue equity. They depend for external funding on trade credits from other firms or on loans from financial intermediaries. Bankers everywhere, however, are reluctant to lend to small borrowers. First, they may find it uneconomical to lend the small sums required. Second, it is difficult to judge the risk, particularly when an investment project is a new venture. Small firms often lack a track record and rarely keep reliable accounts. Third, small borrowers often lack adequate collateral.

In developing countries, bankers' reluctance to lend to small firms has been compounded by other factors. Financial policies have left small firms unable to compete for credit on the same terms as larger firms. Most directed credit programs have discriminated against small borrowers. Interest rate ceilings have prevented lenders from raising interest rates to compensate for additional risk and higher costs. And small firms have less political influence: lenders know that governments are unlikely to intervene on behalf of a failing small firm.

In short, the policies that led to overleveraging by many large firms have also limited access to credit for small borrowers. Changing those policies will improve the flow of finance to small firms. In addition, measures that improve the links between formal and informal financial markets (discussed in Chapter 8) would serve the same purpose.

Financial innovations that secure loans by means

other than collateral are of particular benefit to small firms. By renting buildings and leasing equipment, small firms can acquire the use of assets without borrowing. With the development of securities markets, venture capital is more likely to appear as a source of finance for risky new projects. In the past, governments have relied upon development finance institutions for venture capital, but the risks for them were at least as great as for commercial banks.

MONITORING AND CONTROL. In their efforts to increase the supply of equity capital and long-term finance, governments have paid little attention to the possibility of reducing risk by enabling lenders to monitor and control the use of financial resources. Monitoring can be done by banks where they are the dominant lenders (as in Germany and Japan) or by specialized institutions, such as credit rating agencies and stockbroking firms, where financial markets are more important (as in the United States and the United Kingdom).

The experience of Germany and Japan suggests that high leverage can be compatible with successful industrialization. For such an approach to be effective, lenders must have the confidence of, and a strong commitment to, their borrowers. This in turn calls for the banks to maintain long-term relationships with firms. The banks' involvement may take different forms, such as holding equity positions or having seats on boards of directors, but extensive consultations with managers are crucial. Banks must also have the means to take swift corrective action when necessary—to replace managers, restructure operations, or foreclose on loans if need be.

Close ties between industry and finance have worked well in some countries, but in others, especially in Latin America, they have not. In several developing countries, small groups of businessmen have used the funds of banks under their control to create industrial conglomerates. By eliminating information and control problems, the existence of such groups permitted the financing of some profitable, although more risky, ventures. However, groups have used their control of finance to exclude potential competition. They have captured economic rents for their owners by passing on cheap credits to related firms. And they have rescued and supported fundamentally unviable businesses. When speculative ventures backfired or industrial companies suffered losses, group banks continued to provide funding long after the ailing firms had become insolvent. For close ties between industry and finance to work, regulators must prevent banks from lending imprudently to related firms.

Household finance

Demographic trends will affect the financial systems of developing countries. As the share of the population living in urban areas increases, and as incomes rise, more people will live apart from the rest of their family, and more will live past retirement age unsupported by their children. These changes will increase the demand for credit to finance housing and for certain types of financial assets.

Housing is a major investment in all countries: it accounts for between 20 and 30 percent of a country's capital stock (Box 7.1). In rural areas much housing is built by the owner out of locally available materials; the cash expenditure may be relatively small and spread out over a long period. In urban areas and particularly for middle-class housing, the expense of building or buying a house is large relative to income and incurred all at once. The rapid growth of the urban population of most developing countries will almost certainly lead to a greater demand for mortgage finance. Most families require a loan to buy or build a middle-class house. The need for mortgage finance in many developing countries is demonstrated by the common sight of abandoned, half-completed structures—a significant waste of resources in view of the share of housing in total investment.

Some governments provide concessional finance for housing to preferred borrowers, often civil servants, but others discourage mortgage lending in order to free resources for investment in industry. As urbanization proceeds, it will be important for governments to recognize the scale of housing investment, to improve laws concerning the use of housing as collateral, and to integrate housing finance on a nonpreferential basis with the remainder of the financial system (see Box 7.4).

As more of the population will want and be able to make provision for retirement, there will be an opportunity to develop contractual savings institutions, such as life insurance companies and pension funds. Individuals with greater wealth will wish to hold more diversified portfolios. Investment in housing and contractual savings both provide some diversification, but in a stable macroeconomic environment households are also likely to demand securities with greater yields (and correspondingly greater risk) than bank deposits. In

Box 7.4 Housing finance

The formal financial sector in most developing countries finances only a small share of housing investment. Mortgage credit from the formal sector was 28 percent of all housing investment in a sample of eleven developing countries, compared with more than 60 percent in OECD countries. The difference partly reflects the shallowness of financial systems in developing countries. Years of financial repression not only have minimized the role of the formal sector in housing finance, but have raised housing prices because negative real interest rates favored investments in real assets. In another sample of eleven developing countries the average ratio of house value to annual household income was 5.5, compared with 3.0 in five high-income countries.

Several other factors explain the lack of smoothly functioning markets for housing finance in developing countries. Countries have often given little priority to housing finance. Because housing is a large investment, it requires long-term finance, and in many countries inflation, interest rate controls, and the instability of financial markets have deterred long-term lending of any kind. Inadequate legal systems diminish the value of housing as collateral and hence also diminish lenders' willingness to provide mortgage finance. And policymakers have been concerned that increased finance for housing might drive the cost of housing even higher.

Shelter is a basic human need. Secure ownership of a house can raise the welfare of the household that lives in it. Moreover, when a house is purchased through a mortgage, the buyer becomes, in effect, a contractual saver: the buyer is paying the lender for the right to live in the house while saving for its purchase. And when the title to a house can be easily transferred, the household gains a relatively riskless form of collateral. Furthermore, a housing loan, which is fungible with other household resources, may provide the funds that would permit the household to undertake a productive investment.

---

a growing number of developing countries, sales to individuals of corporate securities and shares in mutual funds have begun to increase. As macroeconomic stability is restored in other countries, investors' interest in securities will continue to grow.

Building financial institutions and markets

In planning for the future it is important to have a clear and consistent objective for finance. The key objective of the financial system is the provision of financial services at prices that reflect their cost. The financial system can also be used in moderation for other objectives. In the past, however, developing country governments have tried to do too much—using the financial system to finance the government budget deficit, redistribute income, and serve as a tool in implementing their development strategies. Multiple and often conflicting objectives have impaired the financial system in many developing countries.

Financial markets are never perfect. In allocating credit they can make two sorts of mistakes: funding low-yielding projects and failing to fund high-yielding ones. In the early stages of development, developing country governments, fearing that the costs of failing to fund good projects were likely to be high, intervened to direct credit. Perhaps that assessment was sound at the time, but experience has since revealed too many errors of the first kind—funding low-yielding projects. With time, economies have become more complex, information flows have improved, and financial managers have become more skilled. In most countries both sorts of error can be minimized by leaving more decisions to a diverse and competitive financial system that responds to market signals. The primary role of government then shifts to making market signals more meaningful and, in particular, to preventing its own actions from distorting them.

On occasion the government may have a role to play as a promoter of financial institutions and markets in order to create a diversified and competitive financial system. Many high-income and developing countries have used fiscal incentives to favor particular institutions and markets. Such incentives may be justified to encourage financial diversity, particularly if the existing markets are dominated by large banks and are uncompetitive. Fiscal incentives, however, should be used only moderately, should have clear objectives, and should be withdrawn once those objectives are achieved. In the long term, countries should opt for regimes that do not favor one type of instrument or institution over others.

Countries must also choose the range of permissible activities for financial institutions. Banks in many high-income countries are operating increasingly as universal banks, engaging in commercial as well as investment banking activities. Arguments in favor of universal banking include savings in overhead costs, better information about clients, and greater diversification of risks. The arguments against are mostly prudential: universal banking could lead to undue exposure to risk and a concentration of economic power. As discussed in Chapter 6, however, prudential regulation can deal with these drawbacks.

The banking sector

The banking sector in developing countries must confront several difficult issues. The most pressing is that many banks are insolvent and must be restructured. This problem was discussed in Chapter 5. Another is that wide-ranging intervention in the financial sector must gradually give way to systems that provide services in response to market signals. This, in turn, calls for more competition and better management.

INCREASING COMPETITION. Commercial (or deposit) banks hold between 50 and 90 percent of the assets of all financial intermediaries in most developing countries and will continue to be at the heart of their financial markets for the foreseeable future. In many countries these markets are dominated by a few large banks. The lack of effective competition is not so much due to monopolies based on economies of scale as to restrictions on interest rates, on product innovation, on branching, and on the entry of new institutions. Greater freedom for banks to respond to market signals, to choose their own customers, to set interest rates, and to determine the location of branches would stimulate greater competition. The creation of new banks and other institutions should be constrained only by the prudential regulations discussed in Chapter 6. Competition also means allowing failed institutions to go out of business. Allowing foreign institutions to open branches, start joint ventures with a local institution, or provide specialized services from abroad can be another source of competition.

Although economies of scale are not great in finance, it may not be possible in small economies to ensure a competitive market for every financial product. A few commercial banks supplemented by a postal savings bank may be all a small economy can support. Even in larger economies, financial markets are often uncompetitive. In these it should at least be possible to promote competition

in big product markets, such as wholesale banking (loans to larger borrowers) and deposit taking in cities. This can be done, even when the creation of another big commercial bank would not be justified, by encouraging the development of specialized intermediaries. A postal savings bank, for instance, would extend financial services to new clients and foster competition for deposits; finance and leasing companies would spur competition in the market for loans.

To improve competition and efficiency, some small countries have opened their markets to foreign banks or have encouraged joint ventures between foreign and domestic institutions. Many small and medium-size countries could buy the specialized financial services they need (such as reinsurance, swaps, and forward contracts) from abroad. Small, specialized institutions and foreign competition can force even big oligopolistic banks to behave competitively—although not necessarily across the full range of financial services.

As the demand for financial services grows, countries will need to encourage the development of nonbank financial intermediaries and securities markets in order to broaden the range of services and to stimulate competition and efficiency. Some countries have already made considerable progress toward more diversified financial systems. In Malaysia, for example, a wide variety of institutions and markets are operating in an environment of macroeconomic stability. Brazil and other Latin American countries have had some success in institution building, although high and volatile inflation continues to undermine financial development. In recent years several developing countries have broadened their money and capital markets and created new intermediaries, such as leasing companies and contractual savings institutions. Most countries, however, are still at an early stage of financial development.

IMPROVING MANAGEMENT. Poor management has contributed to banks' difficulties in many countries. A 1988 study of bank failure in the United States concluded that management weaknesses, especially among smaller banks, were an important factor in 90 percent of the cases analyzed. Improvements must be made in the skills of management and in the banks' internal systems, particularly if the banks are to survive in the more competitive markets of the future (see Box 7.5). Many management tasks are similar to those of bank regulators and supervisors, as discussed in Chapter 6. Indeed, banks with large branch net-

Box 7.5   Bank modernization: Indonesia's experience

Indonesia began to deregulate its financial sector in 1983 and enacted a second set of measures in 1988. These signaled—at least potentially—a fundamental shift from a highly protected state banking oligopoly to a broadly competitive financial market. In a competitive environment, state banks would need to improve service, productivity, product innovation, and marketing skills. They would also need to introduce better risk management, because competitive pressures would narrow lending spreads and increase balance sheet volatility.

Bank Negara Indonesia 1946 (or BNI) is the largest of Indonesia's five state commercial banks, which together accounted for 71 percent of commercial bank assets in 1987. BNI's board of managing directors reacted to the changing environment by adopting an ambitious modernization program with the support of an international consulting firm. This program was given top priority from its inception in 1983 to the end of 1988.

The program had an institutional component and a technology component. The institutional component included an attempt to identify business opportunities following deregulation; a reorganization to refocus the bank on its marketplace priorities, reinforce risk management, and speed management decisions; manpower management programs to improve the evaluation, deployment, development, and motivation of staff; and a comprehensive revamping of the bank's procedures for managing its assets and liabilities. The project was accompanied by a massive effort to train staff.

The technology component was the full-scale automation of the bank's retail and wholesale functions. In preparation for automation, BNI greatly simplified its procedures. To attract and retain the necessary technical expertise, it paid higher salaries.

It is too soon to judge the overall success of BNI's reforms. BNI's competitors have begun or announced similar programs of their own.

---

works internalize a considerable part of the supervisory function.

The internal systems of banks in developing countries have some common problems. Many banks are operated without the benefit of a formal planning process. Financial plans and budgets may not exist, and little is done to control costs. As a result institutions react to, rather than anticipate, changes in the external environment. This makes them vulnerable to sudden change.

The information available to management is neither timely nor complete. At one bank in Nepal, unreconciled differences in interbranch accounts have existed for years and are equal to the whole of the bank's capital. Without good information, it is difficult to take corrective action on credit extensions, problem loans, or off-balance-sheet risks. Commercial banks in many countries have lax accounting and auditing procedures and continue to accrue income long after loans are nonperforming and recovery has become doubtful. Sometimes new lending is used to conceal debt servicing problems; overdraft facilities are particularly vulnerable to such abuse.

Poor management is most often reflected in improper lending. A lack of written lending policies makes it more difficult to manage risk; without written policies, senior managers find it hard to control the lending of their middle managers. Ex-

cessive concentration of risk is common. Too many loans to one borrower, an affiliated group, or borrowers in one industry means that the quality of those loans could be jointly damaged by a single factor. Banks in Texas are an example of excessive risk concentration. When the price of oil was high, Texas banks were among the nation's most profitable; when the price fell after 1982, they sustained large losses, and several of the leading banks failed.

Excessive lending to related firms has proved a serious problem in Chile, Kenya, Turkey, and other developing countries. In Spain, the Rumasa group contained twenty banks and more than 700 companies and used the twenty banks to finance the related firms. When the firms experienced difficulties, the banks became insolvent. In the aftermath of the crisis, it was discovered that 400 of the firms were phantom companies created to borrow money, conceal the use of funds, and maintain the appearance of financial health.

Poor risk selection is the source of many problem loans. This includes advancing an excessive proportion of the required capital without demanding an adequate infusion of the borrower's own funds. Speculative loans based on the appreciation of asset prices can also be dangerous. In Malaysia, a fall in property prices and a rise in the debt servicing costs in the early 1980s adversely affected loans to those speculating in real estate. In Kuwait, a collapse in the securities markets, together with the system of settlement by postdated checks, created serious problems for banks that had extended credit against securities and real estate.

One of the most important tasks of management is to train and motivate staff. The most successful international commercial banks appear to be those with the best in-house training programs, where top managers train and assess future managers. Commercial banks in developing countries should draw on the experience of banks in other countries in devising training programs for their own staff. Countries such as Guinea, Hungary, and Korea have established joint venture banks with foreign commercial banks in order to transfer skills more rapidly (see Box 7.6).

Accountability is a problem for many banks in developing countries because organizational structures are overly complicated and responsibilities are poorly defined. To improve accountability, commercial banks in high-income countries are making greater use of independent profit centers. Each branch is managed as a profit center, as are other units supplying services such as leasing and consumer credit. Profit centers are judged and rewarded on the basis of the profits they generate. Separately managed cost centers (for example, check processing) have to be judged on the basis of unit costs because there is no way for the market to

evaluate their services. Only the head office or certain major subsidiaries qualify to be investment centers and thereby have a say in the use of profits. Credit ceilings are used to limit the authority of branch managers and to prevent undue loan concentration on the books of a branch. Large loans require approval at higher levels and are carried on the books of the head office. Internal prices permit the efficient transfer of resources without undermining the profit incentive of each branch. The profit center approach has much to recommend it. In practice, however, it is complicated and requires skill and experience to work well.

Nonbank financial institutions

In most developing countries, nonbank financial institutions (finance companies, development finance institutions, investment banks, mutual funds, leasing and factoring companies, insurance companies, pension funds, and so on) are a relatively small part of the financial system. Countries such as Brazil, India, Jordan, Korea, and Malaysia, however, do have a large nonbank financial sector. Sometimes, stringent bank regulation or favorable tax treatment gives nonbank intermediaries a strong competitive edge. In Korea, for example, finance companies have grown rapidly since 1982 largely because they have greater freedom than banks in setting interest rates.

Box 7.6   Banks in Guinea

Like most African countries at independence, Guinea had a commercial banking sector that was dominated by a few foreign banks. In 1960 it established the Bank of the Republic of Guinea as a socialist monobank. This was later divided into four specialized banks, each dealing with one function or a single category of customer. The management of the banking system was centralized, and the four specialized banks were, in practice, departments of the central bank—that is, the government. Credit was allocated in accordance with five-year plans. (Credit to the private sector was prohibited during 1965–79.) The banks confined themselves to providing working capital for state enterprises, which in most cases meant financing their recurring losses. By 1985, 80 percent of the banks' loans were irrecoverable. The banks were grossly overstaffed with badly trained employees and managers. Discrepancies in interbank claims amounted to 10 percent of their combined balance sheet.

A change of government and a new development strategy in 1984 gave a larger role to market forces and private sector initiative. The central bank was strengthened with foreign technical advisers, the specialized banks were liquidated, and a currency reform and a large devaluation were implemented. Three new commercial banks started business, with foreign participation. Foreign workers now account for about 7 percent of staff, but their number will be gradually reduced as nationals finish their training. The total personnel of the new system is a quarter of the old. Intermediation margins have initially been high, because there has been little competition among the banks, and the demand for credit has expanded rapidly as the economy has recovered. The banks also say that their nonperforming assets are substantial (one-third of their portfolio), so further improvements in the legal framework for loan recovery may be needed.

DEVELOPMENT FINANCE INSTITUTIONS. The most common type of nonbank intermediary in developing countries is the development finance institution (DFI). Most are public or quasi-public institutions that derive much of their funding from the government or from foreign assistance. Originally, they were intended to provide small and medium-size enterprises with the long-term finance that the commercial banks would not supply. During the 1970s that mandate was broadened to include the promotion of priority sectors. Using government funds, DFIs extended subsidized credit to activities judged unprofitable or too risky by other lenders. In practice, the DFIs found it difficult to finance projects with high economic but low financial rates of return and remain financially viable at the same time. The DFIs' difficulties have been discussed in Chapter 4. Today many of them are insolvent. If they are to remain in operation, they will have to be restructured.

DFIs face competition from commercial banks, leasing companies, and other sources of long-term and equity finance. The procedures of other institutions are often speedier and less bureaucratic. Moreover, commercial banks offer much more than just long-term loans. If DFIs were to charge market rates for their services, many would soon lose their customers. Where other institutions offer competing services and the existing DFIs are financially and institutionally weak, the best course is to close the DFIs or merge them with sounder institutions. There is no reason to close DFIs that can mobilize their own funds and are profitable at market interest rates—although it might be sensible to merge them with commercial banks, which thereby would gain expertise in long-term financing.

Monitoring and control of borrowers has posed particular problems for DFIs. Because they provide mostly long-term loans, they do not have the same day-to-day contact with customers as commercial banks. And the narrow specialization of DFIs has made it difficult for them to diversify their risks; they have been particularly vulnerable to fluctuations in the business cycle. Merger with commercial banks would help to solve both problems. Alternatively, DFIs might expand their range of services within the constraints of their institutional capabilities and professional skills. Activities potentially suitable for DFIs include consulting and leasing; the skills involved are similar to those required by DFIs' existing activities.

The operations of DFIs need to be strengthened in the ways already outlined for commercial banks. The DFIs that are to remain in the public sector need professional boards of directors, trained management, and competitive salaries. They also need to place greater emphasis on loan appraisal and recovery.

To attract more funds from the public, DFIs need to charge market rates on their loans. Borrowing long-term funds will be feasible only if there is a market for long-term finance (this is discussed further below). Some DFIs have acquired equity holdings. Selling the shares of firms that have become profitable could free resources to finance new ventures and increase the supply of securities in local capital markets. To the extent that DFIs continue to lend foreign resources, better management of foreign exchange risk will be necessary. In many countries clients of DFIs and, in turn, the institutions themselves were badly affected by sharp currency devaluations. If foreign exchange risk is to be passed on to borrowers, loans should go only to those with foreign exchange revenues or hedging opportunities.

Past experience has shown that DFIs cannot achieve all of their objectives and remain financially viable. If they are to lend for socially attractive but financially dubious purposes, they should do so as agents of the government with no risk to themselves. In some countries they have used managed funds to this end.

LEASING COMPANIES. Smaller and less well-established enterprises find leasing companies an attractive source of long-term finance. By leasing plant and equipment, small firms can avoid the requirements for collateral that often prevent them from obtaining long-term finance for a direct purchase. Of course, leasing depends on the ability to repossess leased assets (in fact, as well as in principle) and on the existence of markets for used equipment. The share of leasing in capital formation (excluding building and construction) in selected developing countries ranges from 0.5 percent in Thailand (1986) to 8 percent in Korea (1985) to 14 percent in Malaysia (1985). This compares with shares of 8 percent in Germany, 9 percent in Japan, and 20–28 percent in five other industrial countries.

Governments can encourage leasing by ensuring that tax systems do not discriminate against this type of financing and by amending laws that are unclear or unfavorable (as they are in Thailand). The more successful leasing companies in developing countries have been joint ventures between national institutions (commercial as well as financial) on one side and overseas leasing companies or bank groups with experience in leasing on the other.

VENTURE CAPITAL COMPANIES. Venture capital is temporary start-up financing in the form of equity capital or loans, with returns linked to profits and with some measure of managerial control. Venture capitalists expect losses on some ventures to be greater than with traditional financing, but they invest because they think that greater than normal returns on others will more than make up for those losses. Venture capital is ideally suited to projects involving uncertainty, poor information, and lack of collateral. It is therefore an alternative to finance from DFIs. It is clearly not suitable for every country, however. It requires an entrepreneurial class and an environment conducive to private sector initiatives. A source of long-term investable resources is also necessary. And an active secondary market—either a secondary stock exchange with less demanding listing requirements or an adequate network of business contacts—is essential so that investments can be sold.

CONTRACTUAL SAVINGS INSTITUTIONS. Contractual savings institutions (life insurance companies, occupational pension schemes, national provident funds, and funded social security systems) have long-term and generally predictable liabilities. They are potentially good sources of finance for investment in corporate bonds and equities. In high-income countries these institutions are the main suppliers of long-term finance. They provide savers with opportunities to diversify risk and with the benefits of investing in a portfolio selected by professional investors.

A major impediment to the development of contractual savings as a source of long-term corporate finance has been the preemptive use of these funds by government. In many countries—Brazil, Colombia, Ecuador, India, Kenya, and Malaysia, for instance—governments require contractual savings institutions to invest a significant part of their

---

Box 7.7   Pension funds as a source of term finance

Compulsory pension funds have contributed significantly to the supply of long-term investment funds in Singapore and Chile. In Singapore the Central Provident Fund receives exceptionally high mandatory contributions from employers and employees. Such contributions rose to 50 percent of salaries in 1984, before being temporarily reduced to 35 percent in 1986. Funds are mostly invested in government bonds, but employees are now allowed to use their provident fund savings to buy housing. At retirement, employees receive either a lump-sum payment equivalent to their contributions plus the accumulated return on the assets of the fund or an annuity determined by their life expectancy at retirement. The accumulated resources of the provident fund are now equivalent to about 65 percent of GNP—a substantial amount of very long-term savings (with average maturity between twenty-five and thirty years), which will continue to grow.

Chile restructured its pension system in 1981. Contributions are compulsory but are privately managed by competitive firms. Employees can choose among plans and switch at their discretion. Thus managers who perform better can expect to gain accounts. Compulsory contributions are set at 10 percent of salaries. Benefits based on life expectancy are determined at retirement; the minimum pension is 85 percent of the legal minimum wage, or about 40 percent of the average wage.

In the first eight years of the new system, the total value of assets grew to about 18 percent of GDP. Two-thirds of the funds are invested in government securities, one-quarter in mortgage bonds, and the rest in shares and other investments. Initially the earnings on assets were very high (owing to high real interest rates), but they are now about 4–5 percent in real terms.

The fraction of the portfolio invested in equity shares was negligible until 1985, because companies that had a dominant shareholder did not qualify for pension fund investment. Only with the denationalization of a number of large state enterprises (mainly utilities) and some further relaxation of prudential standards has it become possible for the pension managers to invest in corporate equities. Investment in corporate equities is likely to remain a small part of assets, not because of regulation, but because securities are in short supply. Even after the denationalization program, the value of all corporate stock is only about 25 percent of GNP; the value of pension assets will grow to about 100 percent of GNP as the system matures.

The main issue for both funded and pay-as-you-go social security systems is the rapid increase in life expectancy. This will require adjustments in the contribution rates, retirement benefits, or the retirement age.

resources in government securities or programs with low returns in the social sectors. (Sometimes contractual savings institutions hold government securities because they lack alternative investment opportunities.)

Although a government with a deficit needs funds from a source other than the banking system, it does not necessarily need long-term finance. Furthermore, the government's legitimate concern with the soundness of the assets in which pension funds invest need not preclude investment of those funds in the private sector. Governments in high-income countries have enacted prudential rules for pension and insurance investments, and these rules allow pension funds to invest in private sector activities. Chile and Singapore have moved in recent years to allow the pension authorities to invest in other than government securities (see Box 7.7).

Because pension and insurance institutions are likely to be relatively large and therefore able to afford professional management, these managers are able to play a role in the monitoring and control of the firms in which they invest. Governments can encourage the industry to develop by creating a regulatory framework that seeks a proper balance between safety and real returns and by fostering greater competition.

Securities markets

Well-developed securities markets enlarge the range of financial services. Short-term money markets provide competition to the banks in supplying credit to larger corporations, and under appropriate conditions capital markets can provide long-term finance to government and large firms.

MONEY MARKETS. The development of securities markets usually starts with trading in a short-term money market instrument, often a government security. Other money market instruments are interbank deposits, bankers' acceptances, certificates of deposit, and commercial paper issued by nonfinancial corporations. Money markets provide a noninflationary way to finance government deficits. They also allow governments to implement monetary policy through open market operations and provide a market-based reference point for setting other interest rates. Furthermore, money markets are a source of funds for commercial banks and other institutions with limited branch

Box 7.8   Capital markets in India

In the 1950s India's capital markets helped to mobilize financial resources for the corporate sector. The importance of these markets then diminished, because subsidized credits were available from commercial and development banks, equities had to be issued at a discount substantially below market value, the capital market lacked liquidity, and investor safeguards were inadequate.

A reform of the Foreign Exchange Regulations Act in the early 1970s limited the expansion of foreign-owned and foreign-controlled companies. In response, many companies decided to become Indian companies. This led to the issue of substantial quantities of company shares at low prices. The market's revival continued in the 1980s, as various measures were introduced to stimulate both demand and supply. Incentives for equity and debenture issues included reducing the corporate rate of tax for listed companies and fixing the permitted interest rate for debentures above that for fixed deposits but below that for bank loans. The government also authorized the use of cumulative, convertible preference shares and equity-linked debentures and gave generous fiscal incentives to investors.

The growth of the Indian capital markets has been impressive. Equity market capitalization on the Bombay exchange increased from $11.8 billion to $19.4 billion between the end of 1980 and 1987; average capitalization ratios remained roughly equal to 6.5 percent of GNP. The number of listed companies on all exchanges increased from 2,114 in 1981 to 6,017 in 1987. New issues of debentures also multiplied. However, there were also abuses, such as the use of misleading prospectuses and insider trading. In addition, the processing of new issues, which were heavily oversubscribed because of their low prices, was plagued by delays in share allocation.

In April 1988 the Securities and Exchange Board of India was established to oversee and regulate the markets. In August 1988 a credit rating agency was established to grade capital issues. In January 1989 proposals were published regarding the appointment of market makers offering bid-and-asked quotations, the responsibility of stockbrokers for vetting companies before listing, the opening of stockbroking to banks and other financial institutions, and the creation of a second-tier market for smaller enterprises, with less onerous listing requirements. The measures were intended to improve market liquidity and transparency and to provide adequate protection to investors.

Table 7.1 Equity market indicators, 1987

Country	Average market capitalization[a] (percentage of GNP)	Turnover ratio[b] (percentage of average capitalization)	Number of companies listed
High-income countries			
Japan	92	93	1,912
United Kingdom	80	72	2,135
United States	58	93	7,181
Germany, Fed. Rep. of	21	161	507
France	18	56	650
Developing countries			
Jordan	60	15	101
Malaysia	58	23	232
Chile	27	11	209
Korea, Rep. of	19	111	389
Portugal	10	44	143
Zimbabwe	10	4	53
Thailand	9	114	125
Mexico	8	159	233
Brazil	7	43	590
Philippines	7	62	138
Venezuela	7	8	110
India	6[c]	19[c]	6,017
Greece	5	18	116
Pakistan	5	9	379
Nigeria	4	1	100
Colombia	3	8	96
Turkey	3	6	50
Argentina	2	16	206

a. Average market capitalization is a five-quarter average of the total value of listed stock, based on year-end data, assuming constant exponential growth during the year.
b. Turnover ratio is the value of stocks actually traded as a percentage of the average total value of listed stock.
c. Bombay exchange.
Source: IFC.

networks, including foreign banks and leasing and factoring companies. By enabling large corporations to issue short-term securities in the form of commercial paper, money markets make the corporate loan market more competitive and reduce the market power of large commercial banks. Measures to promote the growth of money markets have been among the most successful financial reforms in high-income and developing countries alike in the 1980s.

One such measure is to issue government securities at market interest rates. The reluctance of finance ministries to pay market rates on their debt is usually the biggest obstacle to the development of money markets. Governments also need to remove regulatory obstacles, such as the rules that prevent banks from issuing certificates of deposit or corporations from issuing commercial paper. The publication of clear rules of conduct for market participants is essential.

CAPITAL MARKETS. Capital markets provide long-term debt and equity finance for the government and the corporate sector. By making long-term investments liquid, capital markets mediate between the conflicting maturity preferences of lenders and borrowers. Capital markets also facilitate the dispersion of business ownership and the reallocation of financial resources among corporations and industries.

In mature economies, new share issues have been overshadowed in recent years by the retirement of existing equity. In the United States and the United Kingdom, as a result of mergers and takeovers and the spread of share repurchase programs, net new equity finance has been negative for several years. In earlier periods, however, securities markets were far more important as a source of finance. From 1901 to 1912, for example, new stock issues provided 14 percent of corporate financing in the United States. In several developing countries, including India and Korea, the securities markets have raised impressive amounts of new equity and bond finance in recent years (see Box 7.8).

Several developing countries have made great

strides in recent years in establishing and invigorating equity markets. Such markets now exist in more than forty countries. Indeed, the market capitalization of stock exchanges (that is, the total value of listed shares) is a greater proportion of GNP in Jordan and Malaysia than in France and Germany, and India's stock exchanges list more companies than the stock markets of any other country except the United States (see Table 7.1). In many countries, however, equity markets remain small. Only a few countries have active corporate bond markets; they include Canada, India, Korea, and the United States.

The supply of equities has been limited by the reluctance of owners of private companies to dilute their ownership and control by issuing stock or to comply with requirements to disclose information about their operations. The availability of less expensive debt finance has also discouraged equity issues. Some countries—for example, Korea—have provided considerable tax incentives to encourage corporations to go public. In Jordan, any firm seeking limited liability must offer a substantial percentage of its shares to the general public. Chile

requires all limited liability companies of a certain size to make the same financial disclosures as publicly listed firms. In the past, demand for securities has been inhibited by the lack of investor confidence. In the future, much of the demand is likely to come from institutional investors.

A primary reason for the underdeveloped state of capital markets in many developing countries is the absence of an appropriate legal, regulatory, and tax framework. In some countries new shares have to be issued at par value, which makes them unattractive to companies if the market value of their shares has appreciated significantly. In other countries the tax-free status of time deposits or government and public enterprise bonds lessens the appeal of private corporate instruments. Far more important in developing countries, however, is lax enforcement of corporate income taxes. This makes it possible for closely held corporations to avoid taxes by showing very low accounting profits; publicly traded corporations cannot hide their profits without hurting investor confidence.

A common problem in securities markets, especially early in their development, is the danger of a speculative boom followed by a sharp decline. Such crises have affected markets in Brazil, Hong Kong, Korea, Mexico, the Philippines, Singapore, and Thailand. Large increases and declines in prices also affect securities markets in high-income countries, but they can be much more pronounced in young markets. The Wall Street collapse of October 1987 was far less abrupt than the collapse of many smaller markets (see Figure 7.2).

Countries with a relatively large business sector and middle class should encourage the development of securities markets. Fiscal policies that discriminate against equities should be changed. Governments also need to define the operational scope of underwriters, brokers, dealers, merchant banks, and mutual funds and to encourage the establishment of credit rating agencies. Privatization of state-owned enterprises can be another stimulus to securities markets. Privatization has been one of the forces revitalizing Chile's equity market in recent years. In France, 167 state enterprises and subsidiaries were divested from late 1986 through early 1988, and their shares were taken up by more than 13 million individuals. As a result the capitalization of the Paris stock market increased by an amount equivalent to 6 percent of GDP.

Encouraging foreign portfolio investment is another way to raise demand for securities in developing countries. The increasing role of institutional investors means that foreign portfolio

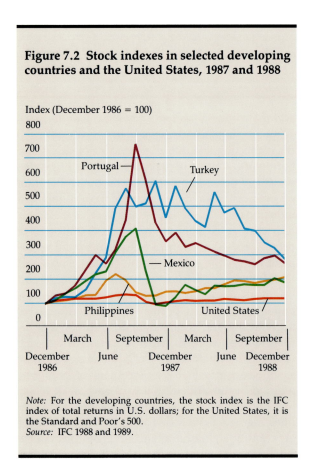

Figure 7.2 Stock indexes in selected developing countries and the United States, 1987 and 1988

Index (December 1986 = 100)

Note: For the developing countries, the stock index is the IFC index of total returns in U.S. dollars; for the United States, it is the Standard and Poor's 500.
Source: IFC 1988 and 1989.

investment might grow substantially. Prices in several emerging markets have shown a low or negative correlation with price movements in the United States and Japan and thus offer foreign investors an opportunity to reduce risk. During 1975–87, equity markets in six developing countries outperformed the market in the United States, and two of them (Chile and Korea) outperformed Japan.

In capital-exporting countries, regulations on foreign portfolio investment limit the extent to which contractual savings institutions can invest abroad. In developing countries, concern over volatile flows of money and increasing control by foreigners has prompted a variety of restrictions and disincentives. Foreign portfolio investment is usually passive, but the concerns of developing countries can in any case be met by such means as the closed-end country fund, whose shares can be traded but not redeemed. More than thirty developing country funds, most of them closed-end, have been floated in emerging markets since 1980. Since issue, the market value of twenty-five of them has increased by 86 percent (as of August 1988).

Priorities for reform

Building a financial system more responsive to the needs of lenders and borrowers will require substantial improvements in the macroeconomic, legal, and regulatory environments. Developing countries also need to broaden the range and improve the efficiency of their financial institutions and markets. Much can be achieved by removing obstacles to the development of different instruments, by adopting a system of regulation by function rather than by institution, and by strengthening the management capabilities of individual institutions.

To operate efficiently, financial institutions and markets have to be guided primarily by market forces rather than government directives. Competition needs to be strengthened by encouraging the entry of new and innovative providers of financial services, by phasing out interest rate controls and high levies on financial transactions, and by stimulating the development of money and capital markets.

8 Issues in informal finance

Small-scale producers and enterprises have long been known to account for a large share of economic activity in developing countries. Most of these enterprises are noncorporate: small farmers, producers, tradespeople, and independent traders. They do not maintain income statements and balance sheets, are not registered with any government office, and often are not licensed as businesses. Recent studies that have attempted to quantify their importance conclude that the noncorporate sector accounts for 30–70 percent of the labor force in some developing countries.

Noncorporate businesses differ greatly in their demand for financial services. Street vendors need short-term finance to buy stock, and they need a depository for temporary surpluses. Small-scale producers need somewhat larger and longer-term loans to buy equipment or to hire nonfamily labor. Small farmers need to cope with an uncertain and fluctuating income stream, which they do by accumulating liquid assets and sometimes rolling loans over to subsequent cropping seasons. As farming becomes more capital-intensive, farmers may also demand longer-term credit to buy equipment. This chapter examines the ability of informal and formal institutions to satisfy the financial needs of households, agriculture, and noncorporate enterprises.

Formal financial arrangements are often not well suited to the needs of the noncorporate sector. The sums involved can be too small for a formal institu-

tion because many of the costs of advancing a loan or accepting a deposit are independent of the size of the transaction. Often the cost to formal institutions of opening branches in villages and small towns is not justified by the business that can be generated. In one African country it was estimated that an institution serving a largely noncorporate clientele would require a minimum of 2,500 deposit accounts to cover the cost of a single employee for a year. Noncorporate borrowers rarely have collateral acceptable to banks. Their creditworthiness resides in their human capital, which is difficult for formal intermediaries to gauge. The interest rates that banks are allowed to pay for deposits or to charge on loans often fail to reflect these factors. All this makes supplying financial services to the informal sector unprofitable for formal institutions.

The popular view of informal finance is of powerful moneylenders who exploit the poor through usurious interest and unfair seizure of collateral. In fact, informal finance is both extensive and diverse. The informal sector accounts for most of the financial services provided to the noncorporate sector. In addition to family and friends, who provide a large percentage of the loans, informal finance consists of professional moneylenders, pawnbrokers, tradespeople, and associations of acquaintances. In separate studies of five Asian countries, professional moneylenders provided less than 20 percent of informal rural credit; on average they accounted for only 6 percent.

Informal financial arrangements reduce transaction costs and risk in ways denied to formal institutions. Moneylenders, for example, can operate out of their own homes or on the street, maintain only the simplest accounts, and mix finance with other business. The services they provide are outside the review and control of the monetary authorities. The remaining costs can be fully reflected in implicit or explicit interest rates.

Freedom from regulation allows informal agents greater flexibility. But it also denies them many of the legal sanctions available to formal intermediaries. In place of formal legal mechanisms, informal agents rely on their knowledge of one another and on local sanction to reduce the risk of lending. Social standing and the ability to obtain future financial services are often at stake in the market for informal financial services. These sanctions are effective. That is why informal financial arrangements are so widespread (see Box 8.1).

Informal financial arrangements

Without trying to be exhaustive, this section offers examples of informal financial arrangements. The examples cover three main sorts of transactions: short-term finance for daily stocks or emergencies; finance to smooth a fluctuating income stream; and finance for larger, long-term investments. The limitations of informal arrangements are then examined.

Short-term credit

Noncorporate enterprises commonly require small amounts of short-term funds to cover immediate expenditures, such as a business opportunity, a social obligation, or an emergency. Such funding might come from moneylenders or pawnbrokers but is more likely to be borrowed from relatives or friends. The choice of arrangement will depend on cost and convenience.

But informal short-term credit may entail hidden costs. For instance, lending between friends and relatives often carries low interest or no explicit interest charge. In societies with strong traditions of mutual assistance and reciprocity, individuals who need funds can call on friends and relatives for help. Acceptance of such help obligates the borrower to reciprocate by providing nonfinancial services or by supplying funds in turn when the lender needs to borrow. These traditional obligations of mutual support can be a problem for those who wish to accumulate capital. The desire to protect personal savings from family and friends creates a strong demand for less accessible savings instruments when these become available.

Market vendors and other small businesses often turn to moneylenders for their short-term credit needs. The so-called five-six arrangement under which the borrower receives $5 in the morning and repays $6 to the lender in the evening is common. The interest rate of 20 percent a day seems extremely usurious. But the moneylender does not perform the transaction every day of the year, and

Box 8.1 Informal finance in Niger

A sample of 398 village households in rural Niger in 1986 indicated that informal credit accounted for 84 percent of total loans and was equal to 17 percent of agricultural income. Informal *tontines* (rotating savings and credit associations), money guards, and merchant finance predominate. The first two supply a variety of services in the local market, and merchant finance bridges formal and informal markets. Large wholesalers borrow from formal banks, purchase a range of consumer goods, and then consign these goods through a network of small village retailers. These retailers, in turn, may sell the items to villagers on credit.

Out of a sample of fifty-six tontines in twenty-two villages, some had only four members, others more than forty. The average member contribution ranged from 100 CFA francs (25 cents) to CFAF25,000 ($70).

The total size of all fifty-six tontines, as measured by member contributions per meeting, was the equivalent of $72,000. This suggests a promising base for deposit mobilization in rural Niger.

Many of the money guards are traders who have storage facilities, offer deposit and pawnbroking services, and market goods in other regions. Fifty-six money guards were surveyed in 1986 in the twenty-two villages in the tontine sample. Their deposit base ranged from several depositors to as many as 150, and (in the immediate postharvest season) from CFAF10,000 ($30) to CFAF5 million ($13,000). They neither paid interest on their deposits nor charged fees for safekeeping. Money guards also provided loans, the average size of which was CFAF55,000 ($144).

loan losses and transaction costs reduce the realized rate of return. To keep collection rates high and transaction costs low and to minimize the cost of idle funds, the moneylender maintains relations with the same borrowers. Conversely, borrowers are paying not only for that day's loan but also for continuing access to immediate credit.

Loans from moneylenders are typically short-term and are extended to clients of long standing; they are rarely tied to collateral. Most moneylenders use their own funds for lending. Interest rates are high. Where entry is restricted and alternative financial services are lacking, high interest rates may be partly a result of imbalances in economic and social power, but the cost and risk of small loans are also high. To meet the demand for timely and convenient loans, the moneylender must maintain adequate liquidity, some of which will be idle during slack periods. The opportunity cost of this reserve is part of the moneylender's costs. Many noncorporate agents with access to formal credit may also borrow from moneylenders if formal lenders take too long to process an application. Two to three weeks is quick for many formal intermediaries, and two to three months is not uncommon. Often, loans from moneylenders are used to make a transaction at short notice, and funds from formal lenders are used to repay the moneylenders.

Borrowers who own marketable assets may turn to pawnbrokers for short-term credit. Pawnbrokers take possession of assets for a fixed term and lend against them at an agreed rate of interest. During the term of the loan the borrower is free to repay and thereby to redeem his asset. Once the term expires, the pawnbroker can sell the asset and keep the proceeds. Because the loan has collateral, the pawnbroker needs no further information about risk. But the pawnbroker must know the resale market well if he is to sell such assets profitably—especially since the borrower has the option of avoiding the pawnbroker altogether by selling and then repurchasing the asset on his own.

Pawnbroking is an example of how collateral is used in some informal arrangements to reduce risk and fill the gaps in information that characterize the noncorporate sector. Other, slightly more sophisticated solutions include sale and repurchase arrangements (in which the borrower retains physical possession of the asset while the moneylender has legal title) and the use of overdraft checks for loan surety. In these cases commercial law makes repayment enforceable, and recourse to banking law continues to be avoided.

Seasonal credit and short-term savings

Another common need is to smooth fluctuations in income. This can be done with liquid savings or seasonal credit. In rural areas marketing intermediaries are often an important source of credit for farmers. In urban areas retailers may offer credit for the goods they sell. Marketing agents often provide lines of credit to farmers in return for a commitment to sell produce through the agents. The farmer may be charged explicit interest, or he may pay indirectly through the price received for his crop. The agent knows the farmer, and this reduces his risk and transaction costs.

It is sometimes difficult for analysts to determine the implicit interest charges when loans or repayments are made in kind. In the Sudan, for example, a merchant might provide a farmer with two sacks of millet in return for three sacks at harvesttime two months later. The apparent monthly interest rate is 25 percent. But the true rate is much lower because the price of millet is typically higher between harvests than at harvesttime.

Philippine corn traders provide credit to many farmers. Transaction costs are low for lender and borrower alike, and interest rates range from 2 to 3 percent a month. (Interest rates on bank loans to corn traders are 1.5–2.0 percent a month.) The terms of the loans are flexible—most range from four to five months—but because borrowers are vulnerable to the climate, it is common for traders to carry loans over to a second or even a third harvest. Although the interest costs of trader credit are higher than for loans from formal institutions, transaction costs are lower, and so the total cost of borrowing is roughly the same. The difference is that formal, targeted credit is simply not available to most corn producers when it is needed.

Noncorporate agents can smooth their consumption by saving. Formal intermediaries have been slow to develop deposit services for this sector, but a variety of informal arrangements allow farmers, small businesses, and households to pool their savings. The simplest such arrangement is the use of money guards—local people who safeguard cash for those who have no secure means of doing so. Most such deposits earn no interest and are secured only by the word of the money guard. The guards maintain enough liquidity to return deposits at short notice. Some deposits may be used by the guards for business transactions or for lending, but if so the practice is seldom made public.

Informal deposit services are also provided by group savings associations. Deposits can be made at regular or irregular intervals. Funds are sometimes lent temporarily and then returned to the depositor at the end of an agreed period, or they can be applied to the cost of providing a public good. A popular arrangement is the rotating savings and credit association (ROSCA), which is described in detail in Box 8.2. Members pool money by making periodic payments into a fund, which then rotates among members as a lump-sum payout. This allows at least some members to finance large expenditures sooner than if they had relied on their own savings. Some ROSCAs even meet the demand for the larger and longer-term loans that are needed to finance the cost of housing.

The popularity of such arrangements shows the potential for pooling individual savings among small farmers or microentrepreneurs. In England and elsewhere building societies—which later became an important part of the formal financial system—often began as ROSCAs.

Long-term finance

Because informal lenders and their customers are small and isolated, the risks of long-term lending are greater. Not much term finance is provided by the informal sector, but some informal arrangements have developed, mainly for housing finance. One example is key money, as in Bolivia and Korea. A home buyer can lease his house in exchange for a large cash payment. After an agreed period the house and the money are reexchanged. The interest that could have been earned on the money is the rental value of the house. The recipient of key money may use it to finance a business venture or the purchase of the house, thus circumventing the lack of conventional mortgage finance. He must then save enough to return the original amount to the renter by the end of the rental period.

Limitations of informal financial arrangements

Despite their success in providing financial services to small businesses that would otherwise lack them, informal financial arrangements do not meet all the needs of the sector. For example, such arrangements do not allow savings to be collected from more than a small group of individuals well known to one another, and they do not move funds over large distances. Especially in rural areas local markets may be segmented from national markets, which limits the supply of credit. Most loans are from family and friends or group associations and are at low interest rates. The higher rates that moneylenders and pawnbrokers charge are in large part due to the higher costs and risks associated with informal loans. But some loans from moneylenders are at very high interest rates because of the power imbalance that exists between borrower and lender. In fact, much of the traditional criticism of moneylenders has derived from the high interest charges and intimidating practices of loan sharks—lenders who often finance illegal activities. Except in housing finance, informal arrangements generally do not provide term finance. These shortcomings may inhibit the long-term planning and investment that are necessary if productivity is to rise.

The limitations of informal financial arrangements do not call for completely new institutions. Indeed, formal intermediaries have often failed where informal arrangements have prospered. Formal institutions, and the policymakers who set their rules, might learn much about these markets by studying informal arrangements more closely. Their essential features are these. Transactions are undertaken by mutual consent, so the arrangements must meet the needs of both the buyer and the seller of the service. Transaction costs are kept to a minimum. And lenders are able to reduce the risk of default by using knowledge that they have already gathered from other social or business dealings. Sometimes informal arrangements provide a basis for establishing links with formal institutions so as to provide a fuller range of services.

Semiformal finance

Several approaches have been tried to overcome the limitations of informal finance for the noncorporate sector. As discussed in Chapter 4, many government programs of directed, low-cost lending have experienced serious difficulties. Two types of lending arrangements, which fall in the gray area between informal and formal finance, offer some promise. These are group lending schemes and cooperative financial institutions, which can be found the world over.

Group lending schemes

The funds for group lending schemes can come from a commercial bank, a government development bank, or private institutions. The role of the group varies. In some cases the funds are lent to the group as a whole, which then allocates them among members. Or loans may be made directly to individual members of the group. In either case the group provides a guarantee; it is answerable to the outside lender for the repayment of loans.

The idea is that by joining together, small borrowers can reduce the costs of borrowing and improve their access to credit. The outside lender's costs are reduced because lending to a group lowers the risk of dealing with small businesses and circumvents the problems involved in selecting borrowers. The groups themselves must be selective in accepting new members. In this way, groups act as a substitute for information about borrowers and thereby reduce the costs of processing loans. Group members encourage each other to repay on time so that the rest can qualify for loans in the future. This directly reduces the lender's commercial risks.

The two most common means of providing group accountability are (a) joint and several liability and (b) limited liability. Joint and several liability encourages extremely careful selection of members because any member can be held liable for the defaults of others. It may, however, deter the comparatively wealthy from joining the group, since they have more to lose. In rural Zimbabwe, schemes based on joint and several liability worked well in times of average production but fared worse than other schemes in the same area in times of drought and low production. The threat of default led farmers to withhold repayment and hope for a general amnesty, since they would be, in any event, accountable for other members' debts.

Group lending schemes based on limited liability are more common. In Malawi and Nepal borrowers are required to put part of their loans in a fund that would be forfeited if any member defaulted. If all members repay their loans, these deposits are

Box 8.3   The Grameen Bank: an alternative approach to noncorporate finance in Bangladesh

While the government struggled to create a viable rural banking system in Bangladesh, a small private initiative was started in 1976 to help the landless without normal bank collateral to obtain credit. This program has become the Grameen (Rural) Bank. The unique operating procedures of the Grameen Bank grew out of several earlier attempts to reach the rural poor and were a sharp departure from traditional banking. The bank's customers, who are restricted to the very poor, are organized into five-person groups, and each group member must establish a regular pattern of weekly saving before seeking a loan. The first two borrowers in a group must make several regular weekly payments on their loans before other group members can borrow. Most loans are to finance trading and the purchase of livestock.

By February 1987 the Grameen Bank was operating 300 branches covering 5,400 villages. Nearly 250,000 persons were participating, among them an increasing number of women, who accounted for about 75 percent of the total. The membership included about 13 percent of households with less than half an acre of land in the areas in which the bank was operating. Loans are small—on average, about 3,000 taka ($100) in 1985. By the end of 1986 about Tk1.5 billion had been

disbursed, of which almost Tk1.2 billion had been recovered. Outstanding loans were thus about Tk300 million, with almost 70 percent held by women borrowers.

In sharp contrast to the Bangladesh commercial banking system, the Grameen Bank has experienced excellent loan recovery. As of February 1987 about 97 percent of loans had been recovered within one year after disbursement and almost 99 percent within two years. This good performance is reportedly attributable to a combination of factors: close supervision of field operations, dedicated service by bank staff, borrowing for purposes that generate regular income, solidarity within groups, and repayment in weekly installments. Another factor which encourages repayment is the borrower's knowledge that the availability of future loans depends on the repayment of borrowed funds.

Bank staff meet weekly with groups to disburse loans, collect savings deposits and loan payments, and provide training in financial responsibility. This means high operating costs. The ratio of expenses to loans rose from 9 percent in 1984 to 18 percent in 1986. These high costs have been partially offset by low-cost funds from international agencies.

---

returned. This practice has resulted in a good record of repayment. In Malawi, where 10 percent of loans was held as security, 97 percent of seasonal credit disbursed between 1969 and 1985 was recovered. In Nepal's Small Farmer Development Program, which required security deposits of 5 percent, the repayment rate in 1984 was 88 percent. These repayment rates compare favorably with other small-borrower credit programs. Another way of imposing limited liability is to link continued access to credit with prompt repayment of existing loans (as is done in Ghana, Malawi, and Zimbabwe).

Group lending schemes have improved access to credit in many countries, but they too have drawbacks. Groups have often been created at the initiative of governments or private development agencies. This top-down approach means that a scheme can be extended rapidly, but it may undercut the force of local sanction. In one Latin American scheme, bank employees formed groups from lines of borrowers at their windows. Such arbitrary selection is unlikely to achieve group accountability. A second shortcoming is that the schemes rely

on external funds. Few collect deposits, partly because the supply of cheap external funds reduces the intermediary's incentive to provide this service, but also because deposit taking is viewed as too complex a task for unpaid group leaders. Despite these drawbacks, some group lenders, such as the Grameen Bank of Bangladesh, have an impressive record (see Box 8.3).

Cooperative finance

In group lending, borrowers and intermediaries are separate entities. In a cooperative arrangement, borrowers and depositors own the intermediary. In some countries such cooperatives fall outside the regulations that govern banks and similar institutions. This can give financial cooperatives flexibility, but it can also cut them off from the rediscounting and other facilities that are generally available to other institutions.

In many developing countries cooperatives operate under a government department that supports them with funds, technical assistance, and policy guidance. Government support is attractive to the cooperatives' managers because it allows lending to expand quickly, but it weakens the incentive of cooperative members to provide their own finance. When loans are made according to government directive, lenders may find it difficult to collect. Such loans are often seen as grants and hence as resources that can be spent on consumption. Often, cooperatives have been promoted as a counter to usurious moneylenders and marketing agents. This has sometimes led the advocates of cooperatives and credit unions to think that financial services can be supplied to small producers for less than the real cost.

Moreover, the goals of government and cooperatives can differ greatly: governments often view cooperatives as instruments for the conduct of broader policy. In Africa, for example, a ministry wished to use the cooperative credit system to channel low-interest funds from foreign donors to targeted programs. When the ministry's plan was presented to the cooperative, the director declined because he felt that the funds would never be recouped by his institution. The director was told to reconsider or resign. The plan went into effect, repayment rates were extremely low, and other cooperative lending programs were undermined. The cooperative managed to refuse liability for nonrepayment, but the defaults affected repayments of the institution's other loans.

Similarly, the support of foreign donors can be a mixed blessing. Cooperatives may seem a suitable channel for development funds, but they often end up with heavy liabilities and a bad collection record. This mirrors the experience of development banks discussed in Chapter 4. Cooperatives that lend internally generated funds with an eye on the rate of return do better than those that are told what to do by outsiders. Even those loans that involve no liability for the cooperative incur staff costs which may overburden a small institution.

Despite the difficulties, cooperatives are a good way of increasing access to financial services. Their costs are often low because they use volunteer labor and because they can reduce risk through group accountability and local sanction. Where governments have been more concerned with the viability of cooperatives than with social objectives—and where interest rate restrictions have been relatively modest—cooperatives have flourished and the supply of financial services has broadened. In Togo, for example, savings in the credit union system grew by 25 percent a year and loans by 33 percent a year during 1977–86. Members elect a board of directors, which decides on interest rates, dividends on shares, and lending policies. The credit unions are federated, and they jointly manage a central fund, invest in low-risk financial instruments, and mediate transfers between member unions with surplus funds and those with deficits. Loans from the central fund to unions lacking liquidity amounted to only 13 percent of its assets; deposits with financial institutions accounted for 81 percent. Togo's credit unions, like informal suppliers of financial services, live or die in the marketplace. But unlike informal intermediaries, they have access to broader financial markets through their federated structure. As a result, they can intermediate between regions and diversify their assets.

Improving finance for the noncorporate sector

Although informal financial arrangements do serve the needs of the noncorporate sector, they cannot be regarded as adequate. Many of the attempts by governments and international donors to increase the supply of finance to the noncorporate sector have focused on providing access to affordable credit. They have foundered because they did not take into account the true costs and risks of lending to the sector. Lowering the costs and risks would help to put the sector within reach of formal institutions. Greater competition between formal and informal lenders would improve the allocation of resources.

Improving the legal environment

Legal reforms could make it easier for small enterprises with relatively large financial needs to use formal services. Such reforms include better definition and enforcement of property rights. Squatters and small farmers with clear land titles would then have an acceptable form of collateral. Property laws that limit inheritance by women or prohibit married women from holding property in their own names limit their access to credit. In many countries banking laws require women to obtain permission from their husbands or fathers to borrow. In much of Africa such laws reduce agricultural investment by placing an economically irrelevant barrier between the farmer and her source of finance.

Laws meant to protect borrowers have often made loan contracts harder to enforce and have thereby raised the risk of lending. Licensing and registration formalities and taxation of businesses need to be kept in check. Small businesses in Peru, for example, are forced to operate clandestinely because legal status costs too much. So regulation fails even in its narrow objective. Meanwhile, the economic welfare of suppliers and customers is reduced because businesses would have better access to formal credit if they were properly registered and licensed.

Links between informal and formal finance

Improvements in the provision of financial services might be gained by upgrading informal arrangements and linking them to formal institutions. This implies building upon, not supplanting, the existing arrangements. The linking of informal arrangements with cooperatives is becoming increasingly common in Africa. In Kinkala, a small rural town in the People's Republic of the Congo, a savings and credit cooperative, Coopérative d'Epargne et de Crédit (COOPEC), has 268 members. Informal arrangements operate in the local market. Among them is a ROSCA with twenty-four members. Each member contributes 2,000 CFA francs a month (about $4.50 in 1985) and receives the total collection of CFAF48,000 every two years. This scheme has been linked with COOPEC so that ROSCA members (who are also enrolled in the cooperative) make their monthly contribution to the COOPEC manager, who deposits the total CFAF48,000 in a savings account. ROSCA members are considered a good risk; their loan applications are looked upon favorably by the COOPEC loan committee. In this way, COOPEC has mobilized funds from its members and has satisfied credit demand.

An example of an apparently successful conversion of borrowing groups into a cooperative bank is the Working Women's Forum of Madras. In 1978 thirty women engaged in petty trade organized as a group to borrow from a commercial bank. Despite the success of this and other affiliated groups of Indian women, dissatisfaction with delays and inflexible disbursement and repayment schedules led them to form and staff their own bank in 1981.

An example of upgrading that produced mixed results is the conversion of indigenous savings and credit associations (*isusu*) into cooperatives in eastern Nigeria. Cooperatives based on isusu performed better in most respects than the rest. Members of these cooperatives, however, not only remained members of indigenous savings and credit associations but also held most of their savings there. This was partly because the government gave the cooperatives easy access to funds, which reduced their incentive to collect deposits and undercut their independence. Many cooperative members, seeing that this new source of finance was risky, continued to rely on the informal arrangements. If the advantages of formality are visible and worthwhile, clients will participate and the institution will prosper. If not, they will return to the informal arrangements.

Formal intermediation for the noncorporate sector

Governments in many developing countries have encouraged formal institutions to serve the noncorporate sector. The means have included low-cost rediscount facilities for targeted lending through commercial banks, mandatory lending targets, and state-supported lending institutions. As Chapter 4 pointed out, these policies have created weak institutions and have thereby retarded the development of an efficient financial sector. They have been particularly damaging to the farm sector. These failures have come to be widely recognized, and a search for better solutions is under way.

Government-supported credit programs for the noncorporate sector can work. This is shown by the Badan Kredit Kecamatan (BKK) program in Indonesia (see Box 8.4). The program provides loans to rural enterprises and other small borrowers. Its viability has been maintained through interest rates that reflect lending costs and through the use of local sanction to enforce repayment. Shared profits encourage careful lending by BKK staff. Funds for the program have come from a government-mandated rediscounting facility, but the scheme was designed to maintain its independence.

Most of the successful formal institutions that serve the noncorporate sector, however, take deposits. Some institutions have greatly improved their position by doing so. The Banco Agricola in the Dominican Republic began to offer passbook savings services in 1984 because it was in serious financial difficulty and urgently needed funds. By 1987 deposits had increased more than twentyfold. Although 60 percent of the depositors were previous borrowers from the institution, the rest were a new clientele who demanded only a safe and convenient store for liquidity.

Mobilization of voluntary deposits is desirable for several reasons. First, resource allocation can be improved if noncorporate agents have good deposit opportunities with positive real rates of interest and low transaction costs. Second, the flow of

Box 8.4 The Badan Kredit Kecamatan: financial innovation for the noncorporate sector in Indonesia

A government project in central Java, the Badan Kredit Kecamatan (BKK), lends tiny sums without collateral, largely to middle-aged peasant women. The BKK takes no longer than a week to process the one-page loan application form and does not supervise the loans.

It sounds like a recipe for disaster, yet the BKK is one of the most successful banking operations of its kind in the world. More than 35 percent of central Java's 8,500 villages are serviced by almost 500 subdistrict BKK units and 3,000 village posts. As of December 31, 1987, the BKK had 516,000 outstanding loans, 90 percent of which were for less than $60. The BKK earned $1.4 million in profits in 1987—a 14 percent return on the consolidated average outstanding portfolio for that year. Although the delinquency rate appears to be high—about 20 percent of outstanding loans—a closer look reveals that about three-quarters of arrears are several years old and should be written off. If these loans were subtracted, the actual repayment rate would be around 95 percent. (The BKK resists writing off bad debts because it feels that this sends the wrong message to borrowers.)

Starting in 1970, at the initiative of the governor of central Java, a BKK unit was created in each of the subdistricts (kecamatan) with an initial loan of 1 million rupiah. The loan was provided by the provincial government through the regional development bank at 1 percent interest per month. Additional funds are borrowed from the regional development bank, also at 1 percent interest per month. To bypass restrictions and paperwork, these BKK units were classified as nonbanks. This enabled the BKK to charge interest rates high enough to cover its costs, to avoid credit allocation, and to ignore traditional collateral requirements.

BKK loans are relatively cheap. Daily credit from moneylenders costs 20 percent a day. Monthly loans through the organization of retired military officers cost 47.5 percent a month. The BKK's effective monthly rate is about 7.5 percent. A maximum of one week elapses between loan application and disbursement or rejection. If the first loan is repaid on time, new loans may be disbursed on the same day as the application. To get a loan, borrowers must fill out a simple one-page form and receive the approval of their village leader. No collateral is required. The system relies upon character references from local officials and peer pressure to encourage repayment.

The BKK reduces risk by making initial, short-term loans of about $5. The administrative costs would seem prohibitive. But these loans introduce villagers to the financial system and enable them to graduate to larger loans. Most clients agreed that the greatest incentive for repaying on time was the expectation of getting another loan.

Each local BKK is an independent unit, not a bank branch. The staff of the regional development bank supervises the local units carefully. Salaries of BKK staff are low, but motivation to expand the portfolio and maintain a good collection rate is high, since 10 percent of a BKK's profits are divided among its staff. If a BKK goes bankrupt, staff members are no longer paid.

The main source of BKK funds has been loans from the regional development bank. Each loan to borrowers, however, has a mandatory savings component that earns interest and can be withdrawn when the loan is fully repaid. Recently the BKK began a voluntary savings program in nine units. More than $30,000 was raised within seven months, with an average savings account of only $9. Most of these voluntary savers were not BKK borrowers. The program will be duplicated at 400 of the healthiest units in 1988–89.

---

resources is typically from small savers to high-yield activities in the corporate sector. Inadequate deposit facilities can block the most important channel for this flow. Third, financial institutions require the independence and discipline that only voluntary deposits can provide. Institutions gain from extra information on potential borrowers, from the relationships that bind intermediary and client, and from the borrowers' knowledge that loans come from neighbors and not distant government or international agencies.

A strengthening of formal financial institutions (as discussed in Chapter 7) will be needed if they are to provide sustainable financial services to the noncorporate sector. This means better management and improved incentives for employees. Innovation will be needed to contain the added risks of providing finance to the noncorporate sector. Group lending is one example. Another is the ratcheting of loans—making small loans initially and bigger ones after the borrower has proved creditworthy. This has been the practice of many group schemes and of both the Grameen Bank and the BKK.

Formal institutions could extend more of their services to the noncorporate sector if it was profitable to do so. This means improving the ability of banks to reduce loan losses and establishing clear property rights for borrowers. Above all, profitability requires reducing directed credit programs with interest rate restrictions, since these fail to reflect the costs and risks involved in lending to the noncorporate sector.

Most of the financial needs of the noncorporate sector are met quite well by a wide variety of informal arrangements. Providers of informal services rely on their knowledge of their customers and on local sanction to contain credit risk. But some informal financial arrangements are costly, and they offer limited alternatives in instruments and suppliers.

Governments, in their efforts to overcome these shortcomings, have underestimated the difficulties of supplying services to the sector. Government programs have benefited the few people fortunate enough to receive cheap credit, but in general they have failed to reduce costs or to facilitate the transfer of resources from those with surplus funds to those who can make use of them or to promote viable financial institutions. Financial services to rural areas and to the urban poor would benefit from better legal systems, more clearly defined property rights, and better links between informal and formal financial institutions.

9

Toward more liberal and open financial systems

A number of countries, both developed and developing, have taken steps to liberalize their financial systems during the past decade. Interest rates have been liberalized in Argentina, Australia, Chile, France, Ghana, Indonesia, Japan, the Republic of Korea, Malaysia, New Zealand, Nigeria, the Philippines, Sri Lanka, Turkey, the United States, and Uruguay. In other countries, such as Thailand and Yugoslavia, interest ceilings have been managed more flexibly than before. Several countries, such as Chile and Korea, privatized their commercial banks. Argentina, Chile, Pakistan, and Turkey reduced their directed credit programs, and interest rate subsidies were reduced or abolished in Korea and the Philippines.

Several factors prompted these shifts in policy. During the past decade many developing countries began to place greater emphasis on the private sector and on market-determined pricing. In higher-income countries, the inflationary shocks of the 1970s and early 1980s underscored the limitations of regulations on interest rates and credit. Rapid advances in telecommunications and information processing have spurred the development of new financial instruments and have promoted greater financial integration both domestically and internationally. This has made it harder for governments to control financial markets.

The lessons of reform are obscured by difficulties in interpretation. The starting point and the pace and breadth of financial reform varied among countries, and it is difficult to disentangle the effects of financial reform from those of other reforms that were taking place at the same time. Overall, though, it seems clear that financial liberalization has helped to mobilize resources through the formal financial system and to improve the efficiency with which they are used.

The task of reform is not straightforward. This chapter discusses the pitfalls to be avoided in the transition from a regulated financial sector to one that is more market-oriented. It also discusses the issues raised by the integration of a country's financial system with international financial markets.

Recent experiences with financial reform

The pace and scope of reform have differed substantially from country to country. Financial sectors in most of the high-income countries were already mature and market-based, and reform focused on eliminating controls and thereby promoting competition. In some developing countries, however, financial systems were heavily repressed before reform. Three countries in Latin America—Argentina, Chile, and Uruguay—shifted within a few years from highly controlled to largely uncontrolled finance. The Philippines and Turkey also eliminated most of their interest rate controls within a very short period, but they did not undertake major financial reforms in other areas. Elsewhere, reforms were even more limited and were introduced more gradually. Some developing countries—Malaysia, for instance—already had market-oriented systems, but in others, such as China, the overall economy remained controlled. The process of reform was frequently interrupted when political resistance or deteriorating economic conditions forced governments to slow or even to reverse liberalization.

With few exceptions developing countries introduced financial reforms in periods of economic stress as part of stabilization and structural adjustment programs. But the degree of stress also varied among countries. For example, Argentina, Chile, Turkey, and Uruguay had large fiscal deficits and suffered from inflation of between 50 and 200 percent in the five years before financial reform. In contrast, Indonesia, Korea, Malaysia, and New Zealand had relatively low levels of inflation both before and after financial reform. Although these countries were also attempting to stabilize their economies and restructure their trade and industrial sectors, their reforms were quite different because they were conducted against a more stable background.

Southern Cone countries

Three of the most dramatic and far-reaching programs of financial reform were carried out by Argentina, Chile, and Uruguay in the mid-1970s. The measures included the lifting of controls on interest rates and capital movements (local banks were allowed to offer dollar-denominated loans and deposits), the elimination of directed credit programs, the privatization of nationalized banks, and the lowering of barriers to entry for both domestic and foreign banks. These reforms were implemented relatively quickly, during periods of high and volatile inflation, and as part of broader programs of stabilization and liberalization. Each program encountered serious difficulties, partly because of the way in which financial deregulation was handled and partly because of problems in the real sector.

Following the reforms in Chile, inflation declined from 600 percent in 1974 to 20 percent in 1981. In the face of decelerating inflation, the real interest rate rose to extremely high levels: lending rates were more than 30 percent in real terms in the years between 1975 and 1982. In Argentina and Uruguay, in contrast, inflation remained high and

volatile. As it surged from time to time, real interest rates fell, but even so they were often very high in both countries.

All three governments tried to change deep-seated inflationary expectations by publishing a schedule of preannounced changes in the exchange rate. These schedules (*tablita*) allowed for a slowing rate of devaluation and were intended to convince the public that the domestic rate of inflation would gradually converge with the international rate. Similarly, the countries liberalized their capital accounts to bring domestic and foreign interest rates into line. It was hoped that these measures would hasten the return to low inflation and at the same time bring down the countries' high domestic interest rates. Inflation, however, stayed higher than the rate implied by the tablita, and as a result the real exchange rate appreciated considerably and exports and output suffered. The wide differentials between high domestic and lower foreign interest rates, together with preannounced changes in exchange rates, promised very high returns and attracted large inflows of capital. These in turn caused rapid monetary expansion and made it difficult to control domestic demand. The lack of effective regulation and supervision allowed speculation and reckless lending to go unchecked.

To restore external balance in the early 1980s, all three countries had to devalue their currencies substantially. These and other measures were necessary, but, together with persistently high interest rates, they added to the financial distress of the corporate sector, and many financial institutions failed. By one estimate, the nonperforming assets of Chile's banks amounted to 79 percent of capital and reserves in 1982 and to more than 150 percent in 1983. The monetary authorities in all three countries were forced to rescue failing banks. Monetary expansion, partly caused by these efforts to assist the banks, undermined the governments' broader adjustment programs and jeopardized financial liberalization. Argentina and Chile were both forced to reintroduce direct controls on their financial sectors. But after nationalizing its failed banks, Chile resumed its liberal policies. It began a long-term program to rehabilitate and reprivatize the banks and to put in place a sound system of prudential regulation and supervision. Argentina, too, has been gradually liberalizing since it reimposed direct controls.

The financial crises in the Southern Cone countries were caused by macro- and microeconomic problems at home and shocks from abroad. Within a brief period firms faced rapid changes in relative prices, a fall in domestic sales, sharp increases in interest rates, a major devaluation of the currency, and a sudden termination of external credit. The biggest problems began in the real sectors of the economy, but efforts to liberalize the financial sector undoubtedly contributed to the resulting instability.

The Philippines and Turkey

The Philippines and Turkey have also reformed their financial systems, which were once heavily repressed. Their reforms, however, centered on freeing interest rates. In the early 1980s the Philippines liberalized interest rates and allowed commercial banks to provide a much broader range of financial services. In the first years after the reforms, interest rates rose to about 10 percent in real terms, and the financial sector grew rapidly. But when the country suffered serious macroeconomic instability during 1983–85, a widespread financial crisis developed.

Beginning in the late 1970s the Philippines pursued expansionary policies to sustain high economic growth despite a world recession. The fiscal deficit increased from 0.2 percent of GNP in 1978 to 4 percent in 1982, and the current account deficit rose from 5 percent of GNP to 8 percent over the same period. Political uncertainty reinforced a gradual loss of confidence in the domestic economy; capital began to flow abroad just as the supply of foreign finance began to dry up. A smaller external deficit in later years was made possible only by sharp cuts in imports and domestic absorption. The peso devaluation of 1983–84 and the large fiscal deficit caused inflation to rise to 50 percent in 1984. In that year the government implemented a stringent stabilization program that included the sale of new high-yield instruments by the central bank, with the aim of slowing monetary growth. To keep their deposit base in the face of this new competition, banks and financial companies also increased their interest rates, which at times rose to more than 20 percent in real terms. The highly leveraged corporate sector thus faced mounting financial strain.

Financial distress in the corporate sector, bad management in the banks, political corruption, and inadequate regulation and supervision all led to a rapid deterioration in the balance sheets of financial institutions. Eventually the crisis forced the government to intervene. A number of smaller banks were taken into the public sector, and the two largest banks, both government-owned, were

radically reorganized. Between 1980 and 1986 the banking system's assets shrank 44 percent in real terms.

Until 1980 the Turkish government maintained strict control of nominal interest rates. Inflation was high, and real interest rates were negative. In 1980 the government removed the controls and allowed banks to issue negotiable certificates of deposit (CDs). At the same time it embarked upon a stabilization and structural adjustment program. The financial reforms were short-lived, however. Two years later, after financial difficulties, the central bank reimposed ceilings on deposit interest rates.

Turkey's liberalization program differs from the others in several respects. The government's budget deficit declined between 1980 and 1982, which took some pressure off the financial markets. The government did not liberalize capital flows between 1980 and 1982 and thus avoided some of the complications that plagued the Southern Cone countries. The annual inflation rate, as measured by changes in the wholesale price index, declined from more than 100 percent in 1980 to 25 percent in 1982. Real interest rates increased sharply during the stabilization period. The domestic currency depreciated in real terms, GNP growth became positive after two years of contraction, and the composition of demand shifted from domestic absorption toward exports. Turkey appeared to be on the right path.

These macroeconomic changes, however, hit corporate profits and left businesses struggling to adjust. Financial problems in the corporate sector then caused distress in the banking system. Nonperforming loans, especially among smaller banks, prompted intense competition for financial resources. Banks that needed liquidity increased their deposit rates. Bigger banks tried to limit this competition with a gentlemen's agreement on interest rates, but they failed and the competition continued. Banks also issued large volumes of CDs through brokerage houses (which offered higher interest rates), even though this practice was prohibited after 1981. Additional financial resources were used to meet immediate obligations and to refinance nonperforming loans: in other words, many insolvent borrowers continued to borrow. Indicators of financial depth improved during this period, but a large part of the additional intermediation went to finance interest payments on nonperforming loans.

The government finally intervened in mid-1982. It found that some banks had failed to meet their reserve requirements because of liquidity prob-

New Zealand is an example of a developed country that has made the transition from a heavily regulated financial system to one more reliant on market forces. By 1984 government intervention in finance had become widespread. Most intermediaries were subject to interest rate controls, credit was directed toward preferred sectors such as housing and farming, and intermediaries were obliged to buy government securities at below-market interest rates. Although these policies stimulated investment in housing and agriculture and provided the government with a cheap source of deficit financing, they contributed to slow growth by reducing the credit available for other, potentially more profitable activities. They also undermined financial stability and the effectiveness of monetary policy as financial intermediation shifted to firms less amenable to regulation and to institutions less constrained by prudential standards.

Following the 1984 election the government introduced a new market-oriented strategy. The comprehensive package of structural reforms sought to spur growth and to redress external imbalance by increasing the role of market forces in the economy. Included were trade liberalization, labor market reforms, measures to restore fiscal discipline, and reform of state-owned enterprises (including privatization). In the financial sector the government abolished all interest rate controls and credit directives, floated the exchange rate, introduced market-based tenders for sales of government securities, and established a new system of monetary control. To promote competition among financial institutions, the government encouraged the entry of new banks irrespective of domicile and extended the right to deal in foreign exchange to institutions outside the banking sector. External capital controls were removed to deepen the foreign exchange market. Liberalization was accompanied by strengthened supervisory capabilities. Prudential regulation emphasized the prevention of system-wide failure rather than failures of individual institutions, and the government chose not to introduce a deposit insurance scheme.

It is too early to make definitive judgments on the success of the financial reforms, but the evidence thus far is reassuring. The removal of capital controls did not lead to capital flight—an outcome attributed to the credibility and the comprehensive nature of New Zealand's program of reform. The number of banks operating in New Zealand has risen from four to fifteen. Financial activity appears to have gravitated back toward the banking sector, and the narrowing of some banking margins, especially on foreign exchange transactions and consumer loans, indicates that competition has increased. New Zealand's apparent success suggests the importance of incorporating financial reforms into a broader program of structural reform.

lems. The government merged five insolvent banks with bigger ones, imposed ceilings on deposit interest rates, and increased its monitoring. In the meantime several brokerage houses, including some of the largest, went bankrupt.

While Turkey reregulated interest rates, the Philippines—after substantially restructuring its financial intermediaries—continued its liberal policy. The financial problems of both countries reflected past economic policies and bad bank management. External shocks, structural adjustment, and abnormally high interest rates turned these problems into a financial crisis. The liberalization of interest rates left the corporate sector vulnerable to macroeconomic shocks. In both countries weak prudential regulation and supervision allowed the capitalization of interest and a rapid deterioration of bank portfolios.

Reforms in other countries

Australia, Japan, Malaysia, New Zealand (see Box 9.1), and the United States have all liberalized their interest rates during the past decade. Restrictions on the services that could be offered by different institutions were also reduced or eliminated. Financial systems in these countries were already market-oriented, and the reforms were designed to stimulate further competition and efficiency. With modestly rising inflation in the 1970s and early 1980s, interest rate controls on deposits prevented institutions from competing effectively with unregulated suppliers in the securities markets and Euromarkets. Although the reforms generally improved the efficiency of financial systems, they caused stress for certain institutions such as the savings and loan system in the United States and finance companies in Malaysia. Interest rates in general were affected more by macroeconomic developments than by the financial reforms. Bank deposit and loan rates rose modestly in real terms. Financial depth increased substantially. Interest rate spreads and the dispersion of rates in different market segments narrowed—all signs of greater competition and efficiency.

Other countries that had more repressed systems have also undertaken financial reforms. The scope and pace of reforms, however, have been

Box 9.2   Financial reform in Korea

Korea's heavily regulated financial system was a key instrument in the government's industrial policy of the 1960s and 1970s. Interest rates were controlled and were kept low during most of this period. A substantial proportion of bank credit—well above one-third—was directed by the government to designated sectors. By the late 1970s, however, a growing consensus had emerged that this approach was retarding the growth of the financial sector and preventing the efficient allocation of resources. Confronted with a significant macroeconomic imbalance and slower economic growth, the government changed directions.

Stabilization, structural adjustment, and financial reform programs were all introduced in the early 1980s. The government adopted several measures to encourage competition in the financial market. Nonbank institutions, which were relatively new and lightly regulated, were further deregulated, and barriers to entry were greatly relaxed. Additional foreign financial institutions, including banks and life insurance companies, were allowed to open branches. Commercial banks, most of which had been owned by the government, were privatized. The government eliminated its preferential lending rates and did not introduce any new directed credit programs. At the same time, the authorities fostered greater competition among different sorts of financial institutions by allowing them to offer a wider range of services.

The loans of commercial banks, even after privatization, continued to be closely monitored and supervised. The authorities continued to regulate the interest rates of banks and nonbank institutions, but they partially deregulated interest rates in the money and securities markets. Controls on capital flows were maintained. When inflation started to decline, real interest rates rose, and growing numbers of highly indebted firms found it difficult to service their debts. The government swiftly reduced nominal interest rates, but because inflation declined, real lending rates stayed between 5 and 10 percent throughout the 1980s. By the mid-1980s Korea had established macroeconomic stability: the annual inflation rate fell to 2–3 percent, and the fiscal and current account deficits were eliminated. Industry undertook a major restructuring. The financial sector has grown rapidly in the 1980s, largely owing to the explosive expansion of nonbank institutions and securities markets and, to a lesser extent, to growth in the banking sector. The ratio of M3 to GNP almost doubled between 1980 and 1987 (see Box table 9.2). Building on this progress, the government began the full liberalization of bank interest rates in late 1988. Most lending rates were freed at that time, although deposit rates are still controlled. The government also announced plans to open Korea's financial markets to further foreign participation.

Box table 9.2   Korea's financial sector, 1980, 1984, and 1987
(percentage of GNP)

Indicator	1980	1984	1987
M2	34.2	37.2	41.3
M3	48.6	68.1	94.4
Corporate bonds	4.5	8.0	10.2
Stock market capitalization	6.9	7.8	26.8

Note: M2 is currency in circulation plus demand, time, and savings deposits and residents' foreign currency deposits at the central bank and deposit money banks. M3 is the sum of M2, deposits at nonbank financial institutions, debentures, commercial bills, and certificates of deposit.
Source: Bank of Korea and Ministry of Finance, Republic of Korea.

---

limited and gradual. In Indonesia the major banks are still publicly owned, but the government has liberalized the credit ceilings and interest rates of public banks and shifted control to the banks' managements. Certain categories of deposit and loan rates, however, remain controlled. Korea also changed its financial policy in the 1980s, moving away from heavy regulation to a more market-oriented approach. These reforms have led to rapid growth in the financial sector (see Box 9.2). Financial reforms in Greece, Morocco, Portugal, and Tunisia have included a substantial reduction in directed credit programs, an extensive—although far from complete—liberalization of interest rates, and efforts to develop money and capital markets.

Latin American countries, other than those of the Southern Cone, have proceeded much more cautiously. Several countries, particularly Brazil and Mexico, were more successful in building balanced and diversified institutional structures. But financial reform there and elsewhere in Latin America was hindered by the failure to reduce inflation.

In Sub-Saharan Africa financial reforms are in place or under way in several countries, including Côte d'Ivoire, Ghana, Guinea, Madagascar, Mozambique, Nigeria, and Tanzania. The objectives are to restructure institutions, improve regulatory procedures, and prepare the way for a greater reliance on markets. The centrally planned economies have also undertaken some financial reforms that involve higher interest rates and somewhat greater competition in the provision of services.

Lessons of reform

These attempts at financial sector reform point to certain pitfalls, although the longer-term benefits are considerable. The clearest lesson is that reforms carried out against an unstable macroeconomic background can make that instability worse. Complete liberalization of interest rates in countries with high and unstable rates of inflation can lead to high real interest rates and wide spreads between lending and deposit rates. Furthermore, it did not prove possible in unstable economies to prevent the real exchange rate from appreciating or to keep interest rates in line with the productivity of the real sector. As a result, the removal of capital controls allowed volatile capital flows and undermined monetary control.

In contrast, countries with reasonable macroeconomic stability were able to avoid the pitfalls of high real interest rates, fluctuations in the real exchange rate, and insolvency among firms and banks. Some countries with considerable macroeconomic instability chose to liberalize gradually; they retained certain controls on interest rates and capital flows while encouraging greater competition and adjusting interest rates to reflect market conditions. These countries also avoided serious disruption and achieved rapid growth in their financial sectors.

A second lesson is that where prices are distorted owing to protection or price controls, financial liberalization may not improve the allocation of resources, which is one of its key objectives. In fact, deregulation may make matters worse by causing the financial system to respond more flexibly to bad signals. For example, Chile's overvalued exchange rate in the early 1980s greatly favored the nontradables sector, which led to excessive investment in real estate. Financial reform allowed more resources to flow to that sector. In the subsequent crisis, real estate was one of the sectors that were hardest hit. Exchange rate realignments and reforms in trade and public enterprise policy should precede, or at least happen along with, financial liberalization.

A third lesson is that direct intervention in finance must be replaced by an adequate, if less invasive, system of laws and regulations. Failure to provide adequate prudential regulation and banking supervision contributed to financial insolvency in the Southern Cone, the Philippines, and Turkey. In freeing the financial system from heavy economic regulation, these countries failed to establish an adequate system of prudential regulation. In Chile, for example, privatizing banks without an adequate framework of prudential regulation allowed them to be acquired by industrial groups, which used them to make excessive loans to group firms. Effective regulation and supervision by bank management, by market forces, and by public authorities are all necessary to reduce recklessness and fraud.

Financial liberalization, like other reforms, involves transfers of wealth and income. Creditors gain from higher interest rates, and debtors lose. Financial institutions with long-term loans and short-term deposits can be adversely affected by interest rate deregulation that results in higher rates. Firms with foreign exchange debt can suffer huge losses when the currency is devalued. In the long run the change in relative prices is necessary to bring about economic adjustment; in the short run the losses can be a political and economic obstacle to needed reforms. So a fourth lesson is that the authorities must anticipate how reforms will change relative prices and how these changes will affect different groups. Considerations of equity and political feasibility alike may make it necessary to provide transitional compensation to those most adversely affected.

All this suggests that in the initial stages of reform many developing countries will be unable to liberalize as extensively as some of the high-income countries. Although generalization is hazardous, experience to date suggests the following steps in moving from a regulated to a more liberal financial system. Reform should start by getting the fiscal deficit under control and establishing macroeconomic stability. The government should then scale down its directed credit programs and adjust the level and pattern of interest rates to bring them into line with inflation and other market forces. In the initial stage of reform the government should also try to improve the foundations of finance—that is, the accounting and legal systems, procedures for the enforcement of contracts, disclosure requirements, and the structure of prudential regulation and supervision. It should encourage managerial autonomy in financial institutions. If institutional insolvency is widespread, the government may need to restructure some financial institutions in the early stages of reform. Measures to improve efficiency in the real sector—that is, more liberal policies toward trade and industry—also ought to be taken at an early stage.

In the next stage, financial reform should seek to promote the development of a greater variety of markets and institutions and to foster competition. Broader ranges for deposit and lending rates should be introduced. On the external side, foreign entry into domestic financial markets should be encouraged to increase competition and efficiency—but perhaps with restrictions, until domestic institutions are able to compete fully. Until such reforms are well under way, it will probably be necessary to maintain controls on the movement of capital. If, however, a country already has an open capital account, the government should give priority to maintaining macroeconomic stability to avoid destabilizing capital flows. After substantial progress has been made toward reform, the government can move to the final stage: full liberalization of interest rates, the elimination of the remaining directed credit programs, the relaxation of capital controls, and the removal of restrictions on foreign institutions.

In sequencing the removal of exchange controls, trade transactions should be liberalized first and capital movements later. Latin America's experience suggests that liberalizing them simultaneously is undesirable. The speed of adjustment in the capital market is faster than in the goods market. An inflow of capital can lead to an appreciation of the exchange rate, which undermines trade liberalization. In the end, internal and external liberalization will be complementary, but external reform should wait until internal reform and the recovery of domestic markets are under way. When macroeconomic stability has been established and the domestic financial system has been liberalized and deepened, it will be safe to allow greater freedom for foreign institutions and capital flows, to link the domestic and international financial markets.

If the reform process as a whole is too quick, firms that entered into contracts and arrangements under the old rules and that would otherwise be viable may face heavy losses. A gradual liberalization will also impose losses, but it will allow firms time to adjust and financial institutions time to develop the new skills they will need. Undue delay, however, carries the cost of perpetuating the inefficiencies of financial repression. The appropriate balance must be judged in each case. Here, at any rate, generalization is not helpful.

Components of financial reform

Many countries have taken the first steps toward reforming their financial systems. The elements necessary to take the process further will vary, depending both on economic circumstances and on political possibilities. This section reviews the main components of a broadly conceived program of financial reform.

Financing fiscal deficits

Macroeconomic stability depends on reducing public deficits to a level that can be financed by means other than inflation or other taxes on the financial sector. Central government deficits have in recent years been equivalent to about one-fifth of total government spending for a large sample of developing countries. About half of this total was financed by borrowing from central banks. The resulting monetary expansion caused high inflation in many countries. Government borrowing from the domestic banking system through high reserve and liquidity requirements is less inflationary than borrowing from the central bank, but it reduces bank profitability, distorts interest rates, and crowds out private sector borrowers. To the extent that a government finances its deficit domestically, borrowing from a securities market is therefore preferable to forced borrowing from financial institutions, which in turn is preferable to borrowing from the central bank.

In most countries it is possible to start a market for government bills, provided the government is willing to pay the market interest rate. Indeed, several developing countries, including Indonesia, the Philippines, and Sri Lanka, have established short-term government securities markets. This is desirable not only because borrowing from such a market is less inflationary than borrowing from banks but also because a bills market makes it possible for the government to engage in open market operations. These can be used to manage the monetary and credit aggregates without the distortions entailed by direct controls. A government bills market is also a first step toward building a broader market for corporate securities. Once market participants have become familiar with owning and trading government instruments and the infrastructure of brokers and traders is in place, it is relatively easy for the private sector to issue its own securities. And by borrowing from a bills market instead of from the insurance and pension systems, governments free long-term funds for investment in private sector assets.

Interest rate policy

Studies suggest that rigid ceilings on interest rates have hindered the growth of financial savings and reduced the efficiency of investment. High and volatile inflation worsens their impact. In most countries this overall rigidity has been compounded by a pattern of interest rates that failed to discriminate between borrowers on the basis of loan maturity, risk, or administrative cost. Governments have often told banks to charge lower interest rates on loans to small borrowers and on loans of longer maturity. Growing recognition of the harm that administered interest rates can cause has recently led many governments to give market forces a bigger say. Governments in developing and developed countries alike have deregulated interest rates during the past decade.

If the initial conditions are wrong, however, liberalization may fail to bring about the correct pattern of interest rates. In countries that have not yet been restored to macroeconomic stability, governments may need to continue managing interest rates. In such cases the aim should be to adjust interest rates to reflect changes in inflation and exchange rates. Countries with open economies need to pay close attention to the differentials between domestic and international rates. Beyond that, governments should phase out preferential interest rates. When good progress has been made toward establishing macroeconomic stability, liberalizing industry, and restructuring the financial system, the government might then move toward a more thoroughgoing liberalization of interest rates. Some countries began by setting ranges and allowing banks to fix their rates within them. As liberalization moved to later stages, the ranges were widened and then removed.

Directed credit

In most developing countries government intervention in the allocation of credit has been extensive. Although a degree of intervention may have been useful during the early stages of development, many countries have come to recognize that this policy has had an adverse effect on industrial and financial development. The evidence suggests that directed credit programs have been an inefficient way of redistributing income and of dealing with imperfections in the goods market. Some programs that were well designed and narrowly focused, however, have been reasonably successful in dealing with specific imperfections in the financial markets, such as a lack of risk capital. In the future, governments should attack the conditions that made directed credit appear desirable—imperfections in markets or extreme inequalities in income—instead of using directed credit programs and interest rate subsidies.

Many governments are unwilling to eliminate directed credits entirely but are nonetheless increasing the flow of credit to the private sector and reducing their own role in credit allocation. Two principles should guide the design of any remaining programs. First, there can be only a limited number of priority sectors: a wide variety of directed credit programs means that nothing is being given priority. Second, governments should be conscious of how little information they have in relation to the information they would need to price credit for different sectors appropriately.

With regard to interest rates, the aim should be to eliminate the difference between the subsidized rate and the market rate. The lowest interest rate should not be less than the rate charged by the commercial banks to prime borrowers. Increasing the availability of credit to priority sectors should be the main focus of the remaining directed credit programs, since experience has shown that generous subsidies badly distort the allocation of resources.

Charging nonprime borrowers the prime rate implies a subsidy to the extent of the added risk and administrative costs. Instead of forcing the banks to cover these costs by charging other borrowers more or paying depositors less, the authorities would be better advised to bear the costs themselves. Directed credit administered through central bank rediscounts rather than through quantitative allocations forced on the banks promotes voluntary lending. Governments should not, however, let central bank rediscounts become a significant source of monetary expansion. Sectors that require large subsidies should be dealt with in the budget, not through credit allocation.

Finally, it seems more defensible to provide directed credits for certain activities (for example, exports or research and development) or for specific sorts of financing such as long-term loans than to target specific subsectors such as textiles or wheat. Targeting specific sectors is too risky in a world of shifting comparative advantage.

Institutional restructuring and development

Many financial institutions today are insolvent, and successful financial reform requires that they be restructured. Insolvent institutions allocate new resources inefficiently because their aim is to avoid immediate bankruptcy rather than to seek out customers with the best investment opportunities. Because financial institutions often become insolvent as a result of ill-advised policies toward trade and industry, policy reforms and the restructuring of industrial companies may also be necessary. Governments should not simply recapitalize the insolvent financial institutions but should seize the opportunity to restructure the financial system in line with the country's future needs.

Liberalization should not be limited to the reform of the banking system but should seek to develop a more broadly based financial system that will include money and capital markets and nonbank intermediaries. A balanced and competitive system of finance contributes to macroeconomic stability by making the system more robust in the face of external and internal shocks. Active securities markets increase the supply of equity capital and long-term credit, which are vital to industrial investment. Experience in countries such as Malaysia and the Philippines suggests that the liberalization of commercial banking will not add much by itself to the availability of long-term credit and equity capital. In Korea, by contrast, the rapid growth of the securities market and the development of new nonbank institutions substantially improved the supply of long-term credit even though only limited liberalization of the banking system took place.

In many developing countries today the financial institutions in the most distress are part of the public sector. Privatization of government banks is one way of improving their efficiency. But this course should be followed only after the quality of bank portfolios and the regulatory framework have improved. In some countries thin capital markets mean that selling bank shares to a large number of individuals is hardly feasible. Hence privatization of public banks may simply shift the ownership of the bank from the government to large industrial groups. That would increase economic concentration and undermine sound banking—as Chile discovered in the late 1970s. In small countries with few banks and weak regulation and supervision, greater foreign participation in bank ownership and management (as in Guinea of late) is well worth considering.

Where public institutions are not privatized, other steps should be taken to improve efficiency. It is important that managers of public banks be professionals with autonomy and accountability; clear procedures will be needed that keep government interference in individual loan decisions, asset management, and personnel policy to a minimum. It is equally important that public banks not be shielded from prudential regulation.

External financial policy

Financial reforms have been undertaken in international as well as domestic markets. Many high-income countries have eased their capital controls and cut restrictions on the entry of foreign intermediaries. The result has been an increase in cross-border financial flows and in foreign participation in domestic markets. Conversely, the development of offshore markets has reinforced the trend toward deregulation in domestic markets. Offshore financial markets have grown much more quickly than domestic markets in recent years—a sign of the pace at which finance is becoming an integrated global industry. International bank lending and net issues of international bonds grew two and a half times faster than GNP in the high-income countries during 1976–86.

The growing importance of international finance is also reflected in the rise in the share of foreign loans, or of purchases of foreign securities, in banks' transactions. For example, the ratio of external assets to total assets for banks in the high-income countries rose from 14 percent at the end of 1975 to 19 percent at the end of 1985. External finance went mainly to firms in high-income countries, but some of the growth represents commercial bank lending to the now overly indebted developing countries. Similarly, the greater participation of foreign financial institutions has been evident in most major markets. The number of foreign banking firms in the high-income countries has increased sharply. The ratio of the assets of foreign banks to the assets of all banks increased in Belgium from 8 percent at the end of 1960 to 51 percent at the end of June 1985, in France from 7 to 18 percent, in the United Kingdom from 7 to 63 percent, and in Luxembourg from 8 to 85 percent. In the United States the ratio increased from 6 percent at the end of 1976 to 12 percent in mid-1985.

Advances in telecommunications and data processing have driven these changes, which are likely to prove irreversible. The greater international mobility of capital, the globalization of financial markets, and the development of new financial instruments have rendered a closed financial policy costly and largely ineffective. To varying degrees, developing countries have participated in the trend toward more open and integrated financial markets, partly in response to the growing economic integration brought about by trade, tourism, and migrant labor. Some countries have adopted foreign currency deposit schemes to induce a greater flow of remittances from migrant workers. To encourage remittances and to discourage and, if possible, reverse capital flight, countries will need to make domestic financial assets competitive in yield with foreign assets. Achieving macroeconomic stability with positive real rates of interest and a realistic exchange rate will also encourage foreign investors to increase direct and portfolio investments.

The merging of domestic and international finance has certain advantages for any country. Foreign competition forces domestic institutions to be more efficient and to broaden the range of services they offer. It can also accelerate the transfer of financial technology, which is especially important for developing countries. The countries that succeed in integrating their markets with the rest of the world will gain greater access to capital and to financial services such as swaps, which will permit them to diversify their risks. But opening financial markets also poses problems. If it is done prematurely, it can lead to volatile financial flows that can magnify domestic instability. Free entry of foreign institutions can lead to the disintermediation of high-cost domestic banks. Furthermore, internationalization means giving up a large degree of autonomy in domestic monetary and financial policy. Domestic deposit and lending rates can be kept in line with world rates only if reserve requirements and banks' costs of intermediation are in line with those in other countries.

ENTRY OF FOREIGN FINANCIAL INSTITUTIONS. Attitudes toward licensing foreign banks and other financial institutions vary widely among developing countries. A few exclude foreign financial institutions; others permit representative offices but not branches. At the other extreme, the Bahamas, Bahrain, Hong Kong, Panama, and Singapore view exports of financial services as a source of employment and foreign exchange. They either allow foreign institutions to operate under the same rules as domestic banks or provide liberal rules for offshore financial institutions.

Maximizing the benefits of foreign entry requires the deregulation of domestic financial institutions and the establishment of a competitive environment. Artificially low interest rates, directed credit, barriers to entry, and other impediments to competition make it likely that foreign intermediaries will simply capture monopoly rents rather than promote competition and efficiency. Where markets are not fully liberalized and domestic

banks have not been restructured, foreign participation may be beneficial, but some restrictions will remain necessary to prevent excessive disintermediation by local banks.

CAPITAL FLOWS. The integration of domestic and world financial markets requires freer trade not only in financial services but also in financial assets. Restrictions on capital flows have been relaxed in many developing countries, generally as part of broader programs of reform. Capital flows are already quite free in Argentina, Chile, Malaysia, Mexico, the Philippines, Thailand, Uruguay, and Francophone Africa. A growing number of developing countries are encouraging foreign participation in their domestic securities markets. Since 1980 more than thirty closed-end funds have been established as a means for foreigners to invest in developing country equities.

Capital movements to and from the developing countries are already substantial. In 1982, for example, more than a quarter of cross-border bank lending went to developing countries. (In more recent years the flows have, of course, been much smaller.) The developing countries' stock of outstanding foreign debt is very large—$1,176 billion at the end of 1988, of which more than half was lent by commercial sources. In 1987 the recorded amount of foreign bank deposits held by residents of developing countries was $290 billion; this is undoubtedly an understatement of capital held abroad. Economic agents in many developing countries have been borrowing and depositing more abroad than in their own banks. This partly reflects the natural international diversification of portfolios, but to a greater extent it reflects efforts to avoid the repressed yields of domestic financial systems.

The scale of capital flows to and from developing countries does not mean that their financial markets have been substantially open. On the contrary, many developing countries continue to restrict outward capital flows in an attempt to direct more domestic funds to domestic investment. Furthermore, fears that foreigners would gain control of domestic corporations have led to restrictions on inward portfolio investment in new ventures.

Although the capital market should not be opened prematurely, freer capital movements will promote better alignment of domestic interest rates with international rates, increase the availability of funds from abroad, and provide more opportunities for risk diversification.

Conclusions of the Report

This Report has tried to capture the essentials of the complex field of finance. In at least two respects it fails to do justice to the subject. First, too often the developing countries have been discussed as though they were all alike, when in fact policies and experience vary widely among countries. Second, the Report has treated in a perfunctory way the human and political dimensions of the subject, both in discussing the origins of the financial problem and in offering prescriptions for change.

Unlike the problems of industry, those of finance are not frozen in bricks and mortar, plant and machinery. Financial claims, together with the all-important "rules of the game," could be rewritten overnight by government decree. But this is not to imply that reforming a country's financial system can be accomplished quickly or easily. Time is needed for people to acquire the necessary skills in accounting, management, and bank supervision. Training staff, building new institutions, and—perhaps hardest of all—getting people to revise their expectations have proved among the greatest challenges to development. Moreover, change is certain to encounter political opposition: people benefiting from the present arrangements will resist reform. Others—although they stand to benefit in the long run—will be hurt in the short run and may not choose to make the sacrifices demanded today for uncertain gains in the future. Change may be most resisted in the very countries where it is most necessary.

Once reform is under way, the response will not be immediate; indeed, it may be painfully slow. After prolonged periods of inflation and many failed attempts to control it, the public will expect inflation to continue and will behave accordingly. Entrepreneurs unpersuaded of the permanence of new policy will be slow to change their ways.

This Report has tried to specify the prerequisites for building an efficient financial system capable of mobilizing and allocating resources on a voluntary basis. Such a system would continue to make mistakes and waste resources. But it would probably make fewer mistakes and waste fewer resources than the interventionist approach followed in many developing countries today.

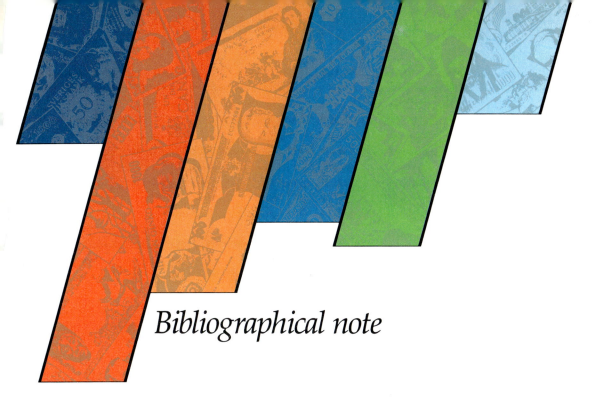

Bibliographical note

This Report has drawn on a wide range of World Bank reports and on numerous outside sources. World Bank sources include ongoing research, as well as country economic, sector, and project work. The principal sources for each chapter are noted below. These and other sources are then listed alphabetically by author or organization in two groups: background papers commissioned for this Report and a selected bibliography. The background papers, some of which will be available through the Policy, Planning, and Research (PPR) Working Paper series, synthesize relevant literature and Bank work. The views they express are not necessarily those of the World Bank or of this Report.

In addition to the principal sources listed, many persons, both inside and outside the World Bank, helped with the Report. In particular, the core team wishes to thank Paul Beckerman, Gerard Caprio, Alan Gelb, and Patrick Honohan for their extensive support. Others who provided notes or detailed comments include Robert Aliber, Jean Baneth, Charles Blitzer, Robert Buckley, Anthony Churchill, Mansoor Dailami, William Easterly, Mark Gertler, Manuel Hinds, Thomas Hutcheson, Melanie Johnson, Deena Khatkhate, Johannes Linn, Linda Lowenstein, Carlos Massad, Diane McNaughton, John Odling-Smee, Guy Pfeffermann, Vincent Polizatto, Paul Popiel, Sarath Rajapatirana, Bertrand Renaud, and Alain Soulard.

Chapter 1

Data in this chapter were drawn mainly from IMF, OECD, and World Bank sources. Background sources for the analysis of the international economic environment include Fardoust 1989 and work by the International Commodity Markets and International Economic Analysis and Prospects divisions of the International Economics Department of the World Bank. The analysis of structural adjustment relies on World Bank 1988a. Shahrokh Fardoust was particularly helpful on the section concerning prospects for growth. Ahmad Jamshidi, Robert Lynn, and Christian Petersen created the debt reduction scenarios. Box 1.1 was drafted by André Sapir. Box 1.3 benefited from comments by Oey Meesook. Desmond McCarthy provided useful comments on the chapter.

Chapter 2

The section "Finance and growth" draws particularly on the background papers by Balassa, Bhatt, Gelb, Honohan and Atiyas, and Neal; the seminal classics McKinnon 1973 and Shaw 1973; the work of Khatkhate (particularly 1972); and Fry 1988. In addition, it benefited from Asian Development Bank 1985, Fischer 1987, Haque 1988, Jung 1986, Lanyi and Saracoglu 1983, Modigliani 1986, Rossi 1988, Sundararajan 1987, and White 1988. The section "Risks and costs of finance" draws primarily on the background paper by Mayer and on Baltensperger and Devinney 1985, North 1987, Tobin 1984, and Williamson 1985. The section "Government intervention" draws primarily on Bernanke 1983 and Kaufman 1988. Box 2.1 is based on material supplied by Alan Gelb and Gerard Caprio. Jacques Polak provided useful comments on the chapter.

Chapter 3

The discussion of the historical evolution of financial systems in high-income countries draws extensively on Born 1983; Cameron 1967 and 1972; Goldsmith 1969, 1985, and 1987; and Kindleberger 1978 and 1984. For developing countries prior to the 1940s, the discussion is based mainly on Sayers 1952, Crick 1965, Newlyn and Rowan 1954, Okigbo 1981, Diaz-Alejandro 1982 and 1985, Joslin 1963, Young 1925, and Fetter 1931. The discussion of postwar developments in high-income countries is based mainly on Vittas 1978, Bank for International Settlements 1986, Watson and others 1988, and Suzuki and Yomo 1986. Box 3.2 was drafted by Paul Beckerman. Charles Kindleberger provided detailed comments on the chapter.

Chapter 4

This chapter draws heavily on World Bank and IMF sources. The section "Government intervention in credit allocation" also benefited from Virmani 1982; Diamond 1957 and 1968; Levitsky and Prasad 1987; Levitsky 1986; Hanson and Neal 1987; Nair and Filippides 1988; Von Pischke, Adams, and Donald 1983; Adams, Graham, and Von Pischke 1984; and Gordon 1983. The section "Macroeconomic policies and financial development" draws on Hanson and Neal 1987, Easterly 1989, Fischer 1986, Jud 1978, Hinds 1988, and Polak 1989. Box 4.3 is based on Vogel 1984a. Box 4.4 was drafted by Vincent Rague and Moina Varkie, Boxes 4.5 and 4.8 by Paul Beckerman, and Box 4.6 by Patrick Honohan. Box 4.7 is based on Cole and Park 1983 and unpublished material by Jia-Dong Shea and Ya-Hwei Yang and by Juro Teranishi. Alberto Musalem provided useful comments on the chapter.

Chapter 5

The information in this chapter comes primarily from World Bank databases, financial sector re-

ports, and contributions from operational staff. Atiyas 1989 and the background papers by Al-Sultan, Antoniades and Kouzionis, Larrain, Montes-Negret, Sheng, Silverberg, Sundaravej and Trairatvorakul, and Tenconi provided information on specific countries. The discussion of financial distress and its consequences draws heavily on Hinds 1988. The discussion of financial restructuring draws on the background paper by de Juan and an unpublished paper by Alfredo Thorne. Veneroso 1986 and de Juan 1987 were also helpful. Box 5.3 is based on de Juan 1987, and Box 5.6 is based on material prepared by Jorge Martins.

Chapter 6

This chapter draws extensively on the Bank's operational experience with financial institutions and systems in developing countries. The discussion of property rights, contracts, economic institutions, and legal systems draws on Williamson 1985, North 1981, Furubotn and Pejovich 1974, Posner 1977, von Mehren and Gordley 1977, and the *International Encyclopedia of Comparative Law* (International Association of Legal Science). The discussion of company law and corporate governance draws on Grossfeld and Ebke 1978 and Bacon and Brown 1977. Dalhuisen 1986 is the main source on bankruptcy laws. The section on accounting draws on Nobes and Parker 1985 and a background note by Maurice Mould. The discussion of banking legislation, regulation, and supervision draws on the background papers by Effros and Polizatto. Box 6.1 draws on Song 1983, Box 6.2 on Feder and others 1988, and Box 6.3 on Iqbal and Mirakhor 1987. Box 6.4 was drafted by Akhtar Hamid, Box 6.5 by Harry Snoek, and Box 6.6 by the Bank's Legal Department. Ibrahim Shihata, Ahmed Jehani, Hans Jurgen Gruss, and other staff of the Bank's Legal Department and Robert C. Effros and Harry Snoek of the IMF provided valuable comments on the chapter.

Chapter 7

This chapter draws on a wide range of sources, including those cited for earlier chapters. The discussion of business finance draws on the background paper by Mayer and on Aoki 1984, Cable 1985, Corbett 1987, Edwards 1987, and others. The household finance discussion draws on the background papers by Buckley and Renaud. The discussion of institution building draws on the operational experience of the Bank and on the background papers by the Capital Markets Department of the IFC, de Juan, Ibanez, Polizatto, Reilly, and Skully. Other useful sources are Davis 1985, Hector 1988, Sprague 1986, and van Agtmael 1984. Box 7.1 is based on Goldsmith 1985 and national accounts data; Box 7.2 on the background paper by Mayer and on Mayer 1987, Modigliani and Miller 1958, and others; Box 7.4 on the background paper by Buckley; and Box 7.8 on the background paper by Kar. Box 7.3 was drafted by Salman Shah and Box 7.5 by Brian Dickie. Tarsicio Castaneda and Roland Tenconi provided material for the other boxes.

Chapter 8

The discussion of microenterprises draws on papers presented at the 1988 World Conference on "Support for Microenterprises" and particularly on Chandavarkar 1988, Meyer 1988, and Seibel 1988. Liedholm 1985 also provided background material for this section. The discussion of the financial needs of small farmers and of the financial arrangements available to them is based on the work of Dale Adams and The Ohio State University Rural Finance Group. The discussion of the financial needs of and services to the noncorporate sector draws on an unpublished manuscript by J. D. Von Pischke. The material on trader financing draws on Larson 1988. The discussion of group lending and cooperative finance is based on Wieland 1988 and Vogel 1988. Hans Dieter Seibel provided material for the section on the links between informal and formal finance. Box 8.1 is based on a background note by Douglas Graham, Box 8.2 on a background note by Dale Adams, Box 8.3 on a background note by Richard Meyer, and Box 8.5 on background notes by Susan Goldmark. Background material was also provided by John Gadway, Bruce Gardner, Claudio Gonzalez-Vega, Mario Massini, H. J. Mittendorf, and Glenn Pederson.

Chapter 9

The data used in this chapter were drawn mainly from IMF publications and World Bank sources. The discussion of recent experiences with financial reform and the lessons of reform benefited from Atiyas 1989, Corbo and de Melo 1985, Edwards 1984, Fry 1988, McKinnon 1988a and 1988b, McKinnon and Mathieson 1981, Velasco 1988, and the background papers by Balassa, and Cho and Khatkhate. The discussion of interest rate policy

benefited from McKinnon 1988a and 1988b and Leite and Sundararajan 1988. The discussion of institutional restructuring and development benefited from a background note by Alan Gelb. The section on external financial policy uses data and material from Watson and others 1988. Box 9.1 was drafted by Murray Sherwin and Gerald Halliday.

Background papers

These papers are available from the World Development Report office, World Bank, Washington, D.C.

Al-Sultan, Fawzi H. "Averting Financial Crisis: The Case of Kuwait."

Antoniades, Dimitris, and Dimitris Kouzionis. "Financial Distress of Industrial Firms in Greece and Their Impact on the Greek Banking System."

Balassa, Bela. "The Effects of Interest Rates on Savings in Developing Countries."

———. "Financial Liberalization in Developing Countries."

Bhatt, V. V. "On Financial Innovations and Credit Market Evolution."

———. "On Participating in the International Capital Market."

Buckley, Robert. "Housing Finance in Developing Countries: A Transaction Cost Approach."

Capital Markets Department, International Finance Corporation. "Attractiveness of Emerging Markets for Portfolio Investment."

———. "Debt to Equity Conversion."

———. "Leasing."

Cho, Yoon Je, and Deena Khatkhate. "Lessons from Financial Liberalization in Asia and Latin America—A Comparative Study."

de Juan, Aristobulo. "Does Bank Insolvency Matter?"

Effros, Robert C. "Financial Sector Study: The Relationship between Law and Development."

Gelb, Alan. "Financial Policies, Efficiency, and Growth: An Analysis of Broad Cross-Section Relationships."

Honohan, Patrick, and Izak Atiyas. "Intersectoral Financial Flows in Developing Countries."

Ibanez, F. "Venture Capital and Entrepreneurial Development."

Kar, Pratip. "Capital Markets in India."

Larrain, Mauricio. "How the 1981–83 Chilean Banking Crisis Was Handled."

Mayer, Colin. "Myths of the West: Lessons from Developed Countries for Development Finance."

Montes-Negret, Fernando. "The Decline and Recovery of Colombia's Banking System: 1982–1987."

Neal, Craig R. "An Analysis of Macro-Financial Data for Eighty-Five Developing Countries."

Polizatto, Vincent P. "Prudential Regulation and Banking Supervision: Building an Institution."

Ranganathan, Ashok. "Sources of Finance—An Analysis of Four Companies."

Reilly, T. C. "Purposes, Issues, and Approaches in Capital Market Development."

Renaud, Bertrand. "Understanding the Collateral Qualities of Housing for Financial Development: The Korean 'Chonse' as Effective Response to Financial Sector Shortcomings."

Sheng, Andrew. "Financial Adjustment in a Period of Disinflation: The Case of Malaysia."

Silverberg, Stanley. "U.S. Banking Problems in the 1980s."

Skully, Michael T. "Contractual Savings Institutions: An Examination of Life Insurance Companies, Private Pension Funds, and National Provident/Social Security Pension Funds in Developing Countries."

Sundaravej, Tipsuda, and Prasarn Trairatvorakul. "Experiences of Financial Distress in Thailand."

Tenconi, Roland. "Restructuring of the Banking System in Guinea."

Selected bibliography

The word "processed" describes works that are reproduced from typescript by mimeograph, xerography, or similar means; such works may not be cataloged or commonly available through libraries, or may be subject to restricted circulation.

Adams, Dale, and Jerry R. Ladman. 1979. "Lending to the Rural Poor through Informal Groups: A Promising Financial Market Innovation?" *Savings and Development* 2.

Adams, Dale, and Robert C. Vogel. 1986. "Rural Financial Markets in Low-Income Countries: Recent Controversies and Lessons." *World Development* 14, 4: 447–87.

Adams, Dale, Douglas Graham, and J. D. Von Pischke, eds. 1984. *Undermining Rural Development with Cheap Credit.* Boulder, Colo.: Westview Press.

Adera, Abebe. 1987. "Agricultural Credit and the Mobilization of Resources in Rural Africa." *Savings and Development* 11, 1: 29–73.

Agarwala, Ramgopal. 1983. *Price Distortions and Growth in Developing Countries.* World Bank Staff Working Paper 575. Washington, D.C.

Akyuz, Yilmaz. 1988. "Financial System and Policies in Turkey in the 1980s." Geneva: United Nations Conference on Trade and Development (UNCTAD), Money, Finance and Development Division. Processed.

Allan, David E., Mary E. Hiscock, and Derek Roebuck. 1974. *Credit and Security: The Legal Problems of Development Financing.* New York: Crane, Russak.

Aoki, Masahiko, ed. 1984. *The Economic Analysis of the Japanese Firm.* New York: North-Holland.

Asian Development Bank. 1985. *Improving Domestic Resource Mobilization through Financial Development.* Manila.

Atiyas, Izak. 1989. "The Private Sector's Response to Financial Liberalization in Turkey: 1980–82." Policy, Planning, and Research Working Paper 147. Washington, D.C.: World Bank, Country Economics Department. Processed.

Bacon, Jeremy, and James K. Brown. 1977. *The Board of Directors: Perspectives and Practices in Nine Countries.* New York: Conference Board.

Bagehot, Walter. 1873. *Lombard Street: A Description of the Money Market.* London: Kegan, Paul.

Balino, Tomas J. T. 1987. "The Argentine Banking Crisis of 1980." IMF Working Paper 87/77. Washington, D.C.: International Monetary Fund. Processed.

Baltensperger, Ernst, and Timothy M. Devinney. 1985. "Credit Rationing Theory: A Survey and Synthesis." *Journal of Institutional and Theoretical Economics* 141, 4: 475–502.

Bank for International Settlements. 1986. *Recent Innovations in International Banking.* Basle.

Banking Laws Committee, Government of India. 1978. *Report on Personal Property Security Law, 1977.* Delhi: Government of India Press.

Beckerman, Paul. 1988. "Consequences of Upward Financial Repression." *International Review of Applied Economics* 2 (June): 233–49.

Benston, George J., and George G. Kaufman. 1988. *Risk and Solvency Regulation of Depository Institutions: Past Policies and Current Options.* Staff Memorandum 88-1. Chicago: Federal Reserve Bank of Chicago, Research Department.

Bernanke, Ben. 1983. "Non-Monetary Effects of the Financial Crisis in the Propagation of the Great Depression." *American Economic Review* 73, 3 (June): 257–76.

Bhatt, V. V. 1986. "Improving the Financial Structure in Developing Countries." *Finance & Development* 23, 2: 20–22.

———. 1987. "Financial Innovations and Credit Market Evolution." *Economic and Political Weekly* 22, 22: 45–54.

Blejer, Mario I. 1983. "Liberalization and Stabilization Policies in the Southern Cone Countries: An Introduction." *Journal of Interamerican Studies and World Affairs* 25, 4 (November).

Blejer, Mario I., and Silvia B. Sagari. 1988. "Sequencing the Liberalization of Financial Markets." *Finance & Development* (March): 18–27.

Born, Karl Erich. 1983. *International Banking in the 19th and 20th Centuries.* New York: St. Martin's Press.

Bosworth, Barry P., Andrew S. Carron, and Elisabeth H. Rhyne. 1987. *The Economics of Federal Credit Programs.* Washington, D.C.: Brookings Institution.

Bratton, Michael. 1986. "Financing Smallholder Production: A Comparison of Individual and Group Credit Schemes in Zimbabwe." *Public Administration and Development* 6: 115–32.

Braverman, Avishay, and J. Luis Guasch. 1989. "Rural Credit Reforms in LDCs: Issues and Evidence." *Journal of Economic Development* (June).

Brothers, Dwight S., and Leopoldo Solis M. 1966. *Mexican Financial Development.* Austin: University of Texas Press.

Cable, John. 1985. "Capital Market Information and Industrial Performance: The Role of West German Banks." *Economic Journal* 95 (March): 118–32.

Cameron, Rondo E. 1953. "The Crédit Mobilier and the Economic Development of Europe." *Journal of Political Economy* 61, 6 (December): 461–88.

———. 1967. *Banking in the Early Stages of Industrialization: A Study in Comparative Economic History.* New York: Oxford University Press.

Cameron, Rondo E., ed. 1972. *Banking and Economic Development: Some Lessons of History.* New York: Oxford University Press.

Campbell, John Y., and Robert J. Shiller. 1988. "Stock Prices, Earnings and Expected Dividends." NBER Working Paper 2511. Cambridge, Mass.: National Bureau of Economic Research. Processed.

Chandavarkar, Anand G. 1988. "The Role of Informal Credit Markets in Support of Microbusinesses in Developing Countries." Paper prepared for the World Conference on "Support for Microenterprises," sponsored by the Inter-American Development Bank, the U.S. Agency for International Development, and the World Bank, Washington, D.C., June 6–9. Processed.

Chen, Marty. 1983. "The Working Women's Forum: Organizing for Credit and Change." *Seeds* 6.

Cheng, Hang-Sheng, ed. 1986. *Financial Policy and Reform in Pacific Basin Countries.* New York: Lexington Books.

Cho, Yoon Je. 1984. "On the Liberalization of the Financial System and Efficiency of Capital Allocation under Uncertainty." Ph.D. diss., Stanford University.

———. 1986. "Inefficiencies from Financial Liberalization in the Absence of Well-Functioning Equity Markets." *Journal of Money, Credit and Banking* 18, 2 (May): 191–99.

———. 1988a. "The Effect of Financial Liberalization on the Efficiency of Credit Allocation: Some Evidence from Korea." *Journal of Development Economics* 29: 101–10.

———. 1988b. "Some Policy Lessons from the Opening of the Korean Insurance Market." *World Bank Economic Review* 2, 2: 239–54.

Christen, Robert Peck. n.d. "What Microenterprise Credit Programs Can Learn from the Moneylenders." Cambridge, Mass.: ACCION International. Processed.

Coats, Warren L., Jr. 1976. "A Review and Correction of the Case for Inflationary Finance." Departmental Memorandum 76/36. Washington, D.C.: International Monetary Fund. Processed.

———. 1988. "Capital Mobility and Monetary Policy: Australia, Japan, and New Zealand." In Hang-Sheng Cheng, ed. *Monetary Policy in Pacific Basin Countries.* Boston: Kluwer Academic Publishers.

Coats, Warren L., Jr., and D. R. Khatkhate, eds. 1980. *Money and Monetary Policy in Less Developed Countries: A Survey of Issues and Evidence.* Oxford: Pergamon Press.

———. 1984. "Monetary Policy in Less Developed Countries: Main Issues." *Developing Economies* 22, 4: 329–48.

Cole, David C., and Yung Chul Park. 1983. *Financial Development in Korea, 1945–1978.* Cambridge, Mass.: Harvard University Press.

Corbett, Jenny. 1987. "International Perspectives on Financing: Evidence from Japan." *Oxford Review of Economic Policy* 3, 4 (Winter): 30–55.

Corbo, Vittorio, and Jaime de Melo, eds. 1985. *Liberalization with Stabilization in the Southern Cone of Latin America.* Special issue of *World Development* 13, 8 (August).

Corbo, Vittorio, Jaime de Melo, and James Tybout. 1986. "What Went Wrong with the Recent Reforms in the Southern Cone." *Economic Development and Cultural Change* 34: 607–40.

Corbo, Vittorio, Morris Goldstein, and Mohsin S. Khan, eds. 1987. *Growth-Oriented Adjustment Programs: Proceedings of a Symposium Held in Washington, D.C., February 25–27, 1987.* Washington,

D.C.: International Monetary Fund and the World Bank.

Corrigan, E. Gerald. 1987. *Financial Market Structure: A Longer View.* Seventy-second Annual Report. New York: Federal Reserve Bank of New York.

Cortes, Mariluz, Albert Berry, and Ashfaq Ishaq. 1987. *Success in Small and Medium-Scale Enterprises: The Evidence from Colombia.* New York: Oxford University Press.

Crick, W. F., ed. 1965. *Commonwealth Banking Systems.* Oxford: Clarendon Press.

Dalhuisen, J. H. 1986. *Dalhuisen on International Solvency and Bankruptcy.* New York: Matthew Bender.

Darmawi, H. 1972. "Land Transactions under Indonesian *Adat* Law." *Journal of The Law Association for Asia and the Western Pacific* 3: 283–316.

Davis, Steven I. 1985. *Excellence in Banking.* London: Macmillan.

de Juan, Aristobulo. 1987. "From Good Bankers to Bad Bankers: Ineffective Supervision and Management Deterioration as Major Elements in Banking Crises." Washington, D.C.: World Bank, Financial Policy and Systems Division, Country Economics Department.

de Melo, Jaime, and James Tybout. 1985. "The Effects of Financial Liberalization on Savings and Investment in Uruguay." *Economic Development and Cultural Change* (July): 561–87.

Desai, B. M. 1980. *Group Lending Experiences in Reaching Small Farmers.* Economics and Sociology Occasional Paper 761. Columbus: Ohio State University.

Diamond, William. 1957. *Development Banks.* Baltimore, Md.: Johns Hopkins University Press.

Diamond, William, ed. 1968. *Development Finance Companies: Aspects of Policy and Operation.* Baltimore, Md.: Johns Hopkins Press.

Diamond, William, and V. S. Raghavan, eds. 1982. *Aspects of Development Bank Management.* Baltimore, Md.: Johns Hopkins University Press.

Diaz-Alejandro, Carlos. 1982. "No Less Than One Hundred Years of Argentine Economic History, Plus Some Comparisons." Center Discussion Paper 392. New Haven, Conn.: Economic Growth Center, Yale University. Processed.

———. 1985. "Good-bye Financial Repression, Hello Financial Crash." *Journal of Development Economics* 19, 112: 1–24.

Donaldson, T. H. 1986. *How to Handle Problem Loans: A Guide for Bankers.* Basingstock, England: Macmillan.

Dornbusch, Rudiger, and F. Leslie Helmers, eds. 1988. *The Open Economy: Tools for Policymakers in Developing Countries.* New York: Oxford University Press.

Dornbusch, Rudiger, and Mario Henrique Simonsen, eds. 1983. *Inflation, Debt, and Indexation.* Cambridge, Mass.: MIT Press.

Easterly, William R. 1989. "Fiscal Adjustment and Deficit Financing during the Debt Crisis." Policy, Planning, and Research Working Paper 138. Washington, D.C.: World Bank, Country Economics Department. Processed.

Edwards, Jeremy. 1987. "Recent Developments in the Theory of Corporate Finance." *Oxford Review of Economic Policy* 3, 4 (Winter): 1–12.

Edwards, Jeremy, John Kay, and Colin Mayer. 1987. *The Economic Analysis of Accounting Profitability.* New York: Clarendon Press.

Edwards, Sebastian. 1984. *The Order of Liberalization of the External Sector in Developing Countries.* Essays in International Finance 156. Princeton, N.J.: International Finance Section, Department of Economics, Princeton University.

———. 1985. "The Behavior of Interest Rates and Real Exchange Rates during a Liberalization Episode: The Case of Chile 1973–83." NBER Working Paper 1702. Cambridge, Mass.: National Bureau of Economic Research. Processed.

Edwards, Sebastian and Alejandra. 1987. *Monetarism and Liberalization: The Chilean Experiment.* Cambridge, Mass.: Ballinger.

Emery, Robert F. 1970. *The Financial Institutions of Southeast Asia: A Country-by-Country Study.* New York: Praeger.

Fama, Eugene. 1985. "What's Different about Banks?" *Journal of Monetary Economics* 15, 1 (January): 29–39.

Fardoust, Shahrokh. 1989. "Long-Term Outlook for the World Economy." Washington, D.C.: World Bank, International Economic Analysis and Prospects Division, International Economics Department. Processed.

Feder, Gershon, and others. 1988. *Land Policies and Farm Productivity in Thailand.* Baltimore, Md.: Johns Hopkins University Press.

Felix, David. 1987. "Alternative Outcomes of the Latin American Debt Crisis: Lessons from the Past." *Latin American Research Review* 22, 2: 3–46.

Ferguson, E. James. 1961. *The Power of the Purse: A History of American Public Finance, 1776–1790.* Chapel Hill: University of North Carolina Press.

Fetter, Frank Whitson. 1931. *Monetary Inflation in Chile.* Princeton, N.J.: Princeton University Press.

Fischer, Stanley. 1986. *Indexing, Inflation and Economic Policy.* Cambridge, Mass.: MIT Press.

———. 1987. "Economic Growth and Economic

Policy." In Vittorio Corbo, Morris Goldstein, and Mohsin S. Khan, eds. *Growth-Oriented Adjustment Programs: Proceedings of a Symposium Held in Washington, D.C., February 25–27, 1987.* Washington, D.C.: International Monetary Fund and the World Bank.

———. 1988. "Economic Development and the Debt Crisis." Policy, Planning, and Research Working Paper 17. Washington, D.C.: World Bank, Country Economics Department. Processed.

Fisher, Irving. 1933. "The Debt-Inflation Theory of Great Depressions." *Econometrica* 1:337–57.

Freris, A. F. 1986. *The Greek Economy in the Twentieth Century.* New York: St. Martin's Press.

Friedman, Benjamin M., ed. 1985. *Corporate Capital Structures in the United States.* Chicago: University of Chicago Press.

Fry, Maxwell J. 1980. "Savings, Investment, Growth and the Cost of Financial Repression." *World Development* 8: 317–27.

———. 1988. *Money, Interest, and Banking in Economic Development.* Baltimore, Md.: Johns Hopkins University Press.

Furubotn, Eirik G., and Svetozar Pejovich, eds. 1974. *The Economics of Property Rights.* Cambridge, Mass.: Ballinger.

Galbis, Vicente. 1977. "Financial Intermediation and Economic Growth in Less Developed Countries: A Theoretical Approach." *Journal of Development Studies* 13, 2 (January).

———. 1979. "Inflation and Interest Rate Policies in Latin America, 1967–76." *IMF Staff Papers* 26, 2 (June): 334–66.

———. 1981. "Interest Rate Management: The Latin American Experience." *Savings and Development* 5, 1.

———. 1982. "Analytical Aspects of Interest Rate Policies in Less Developed Countries." *Savings and Development* 6, 2.

———. 1986. "Financial Sector Liberalization under Oligopolistic Conditions and a Bank Holding Company Structure." *Savings and Development* 10, 2: 117–40.

Galvez, Julio, and James Tybout. 1985. "Microeconomic Adjustments in Chile during 1977–81: The Importance of Being a *Grupo.*" *World Development* 13, 8: 969–94.

Gautama, Sudargo, and others. 1973. *Credit and Security in Indonesia: The Legal Problems of Development Finance.* New York: Crane, Russak.

Gelb, Alan, and Patrick Honohan. 1989. *Financial Sector Reforms in Adjustment Programs.* Policy, Planning, and Research Working Paper 169.

Washington, D.C.: World Bank, Country Economics Department. Processed.

Gertler, Mark. 1988. "Financial Structure and Aggregate Economic Activity: An Overview." *Journal of Money, Credit and Banking* 20, 3 (August): 559–88.

Goldsmith, Raymond William. 1969. *Financial Structure and Development.* New Haven, Conn.: Yale University Press.

———. 1971. "The Development of Financial Institutions during the Post-War Period." *Banca Nazionale del Lavoro Quarterly Review* 97 (June): 129–92.

———. 1983. *The Financial Development of India: 1860–1977.* New Haven, Conn.: Yale University Press.

———. 1985. *Comparative National Balance Sheets: A Study of Twenty Countries, 1688–1978.* Chicago: University of Chicago Press.

———. 1986. *Brasil 1850–1984: Desenvolvimento Financeiro sob um Seculo de Inflação* (Brazil 1850–1984: Financial development under a century of inflation). São Paulo: Harper & Row de Brasil.

———. 1987. *Premodern Financial Systems.* Cambridge: Cambridge University Press.

Goode, R. M. 1988. *Legal Problems of Credit and Security.* London: Sweet & Maxwell.

Gordon, David L. 1983. *Development Finance Companies, State and Privately Owned: A Review.* World Bank Staff Working Paper 578. Washington, D.C.

Grossfeld, Bernhard, and Werner Ebke. 1978. "Controlling the Modern Corporation: A Comparative View of Corporate Power in the United States and Europe." *American Journal of Comparative Law* 26 (Summer): 397–433.

Hammond, Bray. 1957. *Banks and Politics in America from the Revolution to the Civil War.* Princeton, N.J.: Princeton University Press.

Hanson, James A., and Roberto de Rezende Rocha. 1986. *High Interest Rates, Spreads, and the Costs of Intermediation: Two Studies.* World Bank Industry and Finance Paper 18. Washington, D.C.

Hanson, James A., and Craig R. Neal. 1986. *Interest Rate Policies in Selected Developing Countries, 1970–82.* World Bank Industry and Finance Paper 14. Washington, D.C.

———. 1987. "The Demand for Liquid Financial Assets: Evidence from 36 Developing Countries." Washington, D.C.: World Bank, Industry Department. Processed.

Haque, Nadeem. 1988. "Fiscal Policy and Private Sector Saving Behavior in Developing Economies." *IMF Staff Papers* 35, 2: 316–35.

Harberger, Arnold C. 1985. "Lessons for Debtor Country Managers and Policymakers." In Gordon W. Smith and John T. Cuddington, eds. *International Debt and the Developing Countries.* Washington, D.C.: World Bank.

Hector, Gary. 1988. *Breaking the Bank: the Decline of BankAmerica.* Boston: Little, Brown.

Hinds, Manuel. 1988. "Economic Effects of Financial Crisis." Policy, Planning, and Research Working Paper 104. Washington, D.C.: World Bank, Country Economics Department. Processed.

Horioka, Charles Y. 1986. "Why Is Japan's Private Savings Rate So High?" *Finance & Development* 23 (December): 22–25.

Horiuchi, Akiyoshi. 1984. "The 'Low Interest Rate Policy' and Economic Growth in Postwar Japan." *Developing Economies* 22 (December): 349–71.

Hossain, Mahabub. 1988. *Credit for Alleviation of Rural Poverty: The Grameen Bank in Bangladesh.* Research Report 65. Washington, D.C.: International Food Policy Research Institute.

Hu, Yao-Su. 1984. *Industrial Banking and Special Credit Institutions: A Comparative Study.* No. 632. London: Policy Studies Institute.

Huppi, Monika, and Gershon Feder. 1989. "The Role of Groups and Credit Cooperatives in Rural Lending." Washington, D.C.: World Bank, Agriculture and Rural Development Department. Processed.

International Association of Legal Science. 1973. *International Encyclopedia of Comparative Law.* Tübingen: J. C. B. Mohr.

International Finance Corporation. 1988. *Emerging Stock Markets Factbook, 1988.* Washington, D.C.

———. 1989. *Emerging Stock Markets Factbook, 1989.* Washington, D.C.

International Monetary Fund. Various years. *International Financial Statistics.* Washington, D.C.

———. 1987. *World Economic Outlook: Revised Projections by the Staff of the International Monetary Fund.* Washington, D.C.

———. 1988. *World Economic Outlook: A Survey by the Staff of the International Monetary Fund.* Washington, D.C.

———. 1989. *World Economic Outlook: A Survey by the Staff of the International Monetary Fund.* Washington, D.C.

Iqbal, Zubair, and Abbas Mirakhor. 1987. *Islamic Banking.* Occasional Paper 49. Washington, D.C.: International Monetary Fund.

Jayawardena, Lal. 1988. "Structural Change in the World Economy and New Policy Issues in Developing Countries." Helsinki: World Institute for Development Economics Research. Processed.

Jevons, William S. 1898. *Money and the Mechanism of Exchange.* New York: Appleton.

Joslin, David. 1963. *A Century of Banking in Latin America.* New York: Oxford University Press.

Jucker-Fleetwood, E. E. 1964. *Money and Finance in Africa.* New York: Frederick A. Praeger.

Jud, Gustav Donald. 1978. *Inflation and the Use of Indexing in Developing Countries.* New York: Praeger.

Jung, Woo S. 1986. "Financial Development and Economic Growth: International Evidence." *Economic Development and Cultural Change* 34, 2: 333–46.

Kane, Edward J. 1988. "Tension between Competition and Coordination in International Financial Regulation." Working Paper 88-61. Columbus: Ohio State University, College of Business. Processed.

Kaufman, George G. 1985. *Implications of Large Bank Problems and Insolvencies for the Banking System and Economic Policy.* Staff Memorandum 85-3. Chicago: Federal Reserve Bank of Chicago, Research Department.

———. 1988. "A Framework for the Future." Paper presented at the Fourteenth Annual Conference of the Federal Home Loan Bank of San Francisco, December 8–9, 1988. Processed.

Kennedy, William P. 1987. *Industrial Structure, Capital Markets, and the Origins of British Economic Decline.* Cambridge: Cambridge University Press.

Khan, Mohsin S., and Malcolm D. Knight. 1985. *Fund-Supported Adjustment Programs and Economic Growth.* Occasional Paper 41. Washington, D.C.: International Monetary Fund.

Khan, Mohsin S., and Roberto Zahler. 1985. "Trade and Financial Liberalization in the Context of External Shocks and Inconsistent Domestic Policies." *IMF Staff Papers* 32, 1 (March): 22–55.

Khatkhate, D. R. 1972. "Analytic Basis of the Working of Monetary Policy in Less Developed Countries." *IMF Staff Papers* 19, 3 (November).

———. 1980. "False Issues in the Debate on Interest Rate Policies in Less Developed Countries." *Banca Nazional del Lavoro Quarterly Review* 133 (June).

———. 1988. "Assessing the Impact of Interest Rates in Less Developed Countries." *World Development* 16, 5: 577–88.

Khatkhate, D. R., and Klaus-Walter Riechel. 1980. "Multipurpose Banking: Its Nature, Scope, and

Relevance for Less Developed Countries." *IMF Staff Papers* 27 (September): 479–516.

Khatkhate, D. R., and D. P. Villanueva. 1978. "Operation of Selective Credit Controls in the LDCs: Some Critical Issues." *World Development* (July).

Kindleberger, Charles Poor. 1978. *Manias, Panics, and Crashes: A History of Financial Crises*. New York: Basic Books.

———. 1984. *A Financial History of Western Europe*. London: Allen & Unwin.

———. 1988. "The Financial Crises of the 1930s and the 1980s: Similarities and Differences." *KYKLOS* 41, 2: 171–86.

King, Mervyn A. 1977. *Public Policy and the Corporation*. London: Chapman and Hall.

Kirkpatrick, C. H., Norman Lee, and F. I. Nixson. 1984. *Industrial Structure and Policy in Less Developed Countries*. London: Allen & Unwin.

Komroff, Manuel, ed. 1926. *The Travels of Marco Polo*. New York: Random House.

Krooss, Herman E., and Martin R. Blyn. 1971. *A History of Financial Intermediaries*. New York: Random House.

Kwack, Yoon Chick, and others. 1973. *Credit and Security in Korea: The Legal Problems of Development Finance*. New York: Crane, Russak.

Laird, Sam, and Julio Nogues. 1988. "Trade Policies and the Debt Crisis." Policy, Planning, and Research Working Paper 99. Washington, D.C.: World Bank, International Trade Division, International Economics Department. Processed.

Landes, David S. 1979. *Bankers and Pashas: International Finance and Economic Imperialism in Egypt*. Cambridge, Mass.: Harvard University Press.

Lanyi, Anthony, and Rüşdü Saracoglu. 1983. *Interest Rate Policies in Developing Countries*. IMF Occasional Paper 22. Washington, D.C.: International Monetary Fund.

Larson, Donald W. 1988. "Marketing and Credit Linkages: The Case of Corn Traders in the Southern Philippines." Paper presented at the workshop on "Financial Intermediation in the Rural Sector: Research Results and Policy Issues," sponsored by the U.S. Agency for International Development, Manila, September 26–27. Processed.

Leite, Sérgio Pereira, and V. Sundararajan. 1988. "Issues on Interest Rate Management and Liberalization." Washington, D.C.: International Monetary Fund, Central Banking Department. Processed.

Levitsky, Jacob. 1986. *World Bank Lending to Small Enterprises: A Review*. World Bank Industry and Finance Paper 16. Washington, D.C.

Levitsky, Jacob, and Ranga N. Prasad. 1987. *Credit Guarantee Schemes for Small and Medium Enterprises*. World Bank Technical Paper 58. Washington, D.C.

Liedholm, Carl. 1985. "Small-Scale Enterprise Credit Schemes: Administrative Costs and the Role of Inventory Norms." MSU International Development Working Paper 25. East Lansing: Department of Agricultural Economics, Michigan State University. Processed.

Liedholm, Carl, and Donald Mead. 1987. "Small Scale Industries in Developing Countries: Empirical Evidence and Policy Implications." MSU International Development Working Paper 9. East Lansing: Department of Agricultural Economics, Michigan State University. Processed.

Long, Millard F. 1968. "Why Peasant Farmers Borrow." *American Journal of Agricultural Economics* (November): 991–1,008.

———. 1983. "Review of Financial Sector Work." Washington, D.C.: World Bank, Financial Development Division, Industry Department. Processed.

———. 1987. "Crisis in the Financial Sector." *State Bank of India Monthly Review* (June): 289–97.

Maharjan, Krishna H., Chesada Loohawenchit, and Richard L. Meyer. 1983. "Small Farmer Loan Repayment Performance in Nepal." ADC Research Paper 20. Rosslyn, Va.: Agricultural Development Council. Processed.

Matthews, R. C. O., C. H. Feinstein, and J. C. Odling-Smee. 1982. *British Economic Growth 1856–1973*. Stanford, Calif.: Stanford University Press.

Mayer, Colin. 1987. "The Assessment: Financial Systems and Corporate Investment." *Oxford Review of Economic Policy* 3, 4 (Winter): i–xvi.

McKinnon, Ronald I. 1973. *Money and Capital in Economic Development*. Washington, D.C.: Brookings Institution.

———. 1988a. *Financial Liberalization and Economic Development: A Reassessment of Interest-Rate Policies in Asia and Latin America*. San Francisco: International Center for Economic Growth.

———. 1988b. "Financial Liberalization in Retrospect: Interest Rate Policies in LDCs." In G. Ranis and T. R. Schultz, eds. *The State of Development Economics*. New York: Basil Blackwell.

McKinnon, Ronald I., and Donald Mathieson. 1981. *How to Manage a Repressed Economy*. Essays in International Finance 145. Princeton, N.J.: International Finance Section, Department of Economics, Princeton University.

Meyer, Richard. 1988. "Financial Services for Microenterprises: Programs or Markets." Paper prepared for the World Conference on "Support for Microenterprises," sponsored by the Inter-American Development Bank, the U.S. Agency for International Development, and the World Bank, Washington, D.C., June 6–9. Processed.

Michie, R. C. 1987. *The London and New York Stock Exchanges, 1850–1914.* London: Allen & Unwin.

Minsky, Hyman P. 1982. "The Financial-Instability Hypothesis: Capitalist Processes and the Behavior of the Economy." In Charles Poor Kindleberger and Jean-Pierre Laffargue, eds. *Financial Crises: Theory, History, and Policy.* Cambridge: Cambridge University Press.

Mires, Ralph E., and Kenneth Spong. 1988. "The Death of a Bank: Assuring an Orderly Transition." In *Banking Studies: Problem Banks.* Special issue. Kansas City, Mo.: Division of Bank Supervision and Structure, Federal Reserve Bank of Kansas City.

Modigliani, Franco. 1986. "Life Cycle, Individual Thrift, and the Wealth of Nations." *American Economic Review* 76, 3 (June): 297–313.

Modigliani, Franco, and M. H. Miller. 1958. "The Cost of Capital, Corporation Finance and the Theory of Investment." *American Economic Review* 48: 261–97.

Mosley, Paul, and Rudra Prasad Dahal. 1987. "Credit for the Rural Poor: A Comparison of Policy Experiments in Nepal and Bangladesh." *Manchester Papers on Development* 3, 2 (July): 45–59.

Nair, Govindan, and Anastasios Filippides. 1988. "How Much Do State-Owned Enterprises Contribute to Public Sector Deficits in Developing Countries—and Why?" Policy, Planning, and Research Working Paper 45. Background paper for *World Development Report 1988.* Washington, D.C.: World Bank, World Development Report office. Processed.

Nevin, Edward. 1961. *Capital Funds in Underdeveloped Countries: The Role of Financial Institutions.* New York: St. Martin's Press.

Newlyn, W. T., and D. C. Rowan. 1954. *Money and Banking in British Colonial Africa: A Study of the Monetary and Banking Systems of Eight British African Territories.* Oxford: Clarendon Press.

Nobes, Christopher, and R. H. Parker, eds. 1985. *Comparative International Accounting.* Oxford: P. Allan.

North, Douglass C. 1981. *Structure and Change in Economic History.* New York: Norton.

———. 1987. "Institutions, Transaction Costs and Economic Growth." *Economic Inquiry* 25 (July): 419–28.

Office of the Comptroller of the Currency. 1988. *Bank Failure: An Evaluation of the Factors Contributing to the Failure of National Banks.* Washington, D.C.: Office of the Comptroller of the Currency, Administrator of National Banks.

Okigbo, P. N. C. 1981. *Nigeria's Financial System.* Harlow, Essex: Longman.

Organisation for Economic Co-operation and Development. 1987. *Bank Profitability: Statistical Supplement.* Paris.

———. 1988. *Economic Outlook* 44 (December).

Platt, D. C. M. 1960. "British Bondholders in Nineteenth Century Latin America: Injury and Remedy." *Inter-American Economic Affairs* 14, 3: 3–43.

Pohl, Manfred, and Deutsche Bank, A.G. 1988. *Studies on Economic and Monetary Problems and on Banking History.* Mainz: Hase & Koehler.

Polak, Jacques J. 1989. *Financial Policies and Development.* Paris: Development Centre of the Organisation for Economic Co-operation and Development.

Popiel, Paul A. 1987. "Financial Institutions in Distress: Causes and Remedies." *International Journal of Development Banking* 5, 2 (July).

———. 1988. *Development of Money and Capital Markets.* EDI Working Papers. Washington, D.C.: World Bank, Economic Development Institute.

Portes, Richard, and Alexander Swoboda, eds. 1987. *Threats to International Financial Stability.* New York: Cambridge University Press.

Posner, Richard A. 1977. *Economic Analysis of Law.* Boston: Little, Brown.

Roe, Alan. 1988. "The Financial Sector in Stabilisation Programmes." Discussion Paper 77. Coventry: Development Economics Research Centre, University of Warwick. Processed.

Roe, Alan, and Paul A. Popiel. 1988. *Managing Financial Adjustment in Middle-Income Countries.* EDI Policy Seminar Report 11. Washington, D.C.: World Bank.

Rossi, Nicola. 1988. "Government Spending: The Real Interest Rate and the Behavior of Liquidity-Constrained Consumers in Developing Countries." *IMF Staff Papers* 35, 1: 104–40.

Sayers, R. S., ed. 1952. *Banking in the British Commonwealth.* Oxford: Clarendon Press.

———. 1962. *Banking in Western Europe.* Oxford: Clarendon Press.

Schmidt, R. H., and Erhard Kropp, eds. 1987. *Rural Finance: Guiding Principles.* Rural Development Series. Eschborn: Bundesministerium für wirtschaftliche Zusammenarbeit and Deutsche Gesellschaft für Technische Zusammenarbeit GmbH, and Deutsche Stiftung für Internationale Entwicklung.

Scott, John. 1986. *Capitalist Property and Financial Power: A Comparative Study of Britain, the United States, and Japan.* New York: New York University Press.

Seibel, Hans Dieter. 1988. "Financial Innovations for Microenterprises: Linking Informal and Formal Financial Institutions: Asia and Africa." Paper prepared for the World Conference on "Support for Microenterprises," sponsored by the Inter-American Development Bank, the U.S. Agency for International Development, and the World Bank, Washington, D.C., June 6–9. Processed.

Shaw, Edward S. 1973. *Financial Deepening in Economic Development.* New York: Oxford University Press.

Shiller, Robert J. 1980. "Do Stock Prices Move Too Much to Be Justified by Subsequent Changes in Dividends?" NBER Working Paper Series 456. Cambridge, Mass.: National Bureau of Economic Research. Processed.

———. 1984. "Stock Prices and Social Dynamics." Cowles Foundation Discussion Paper 719. New Haven, Conn.: Cowles Foundation for Research in Economics, Yale University. Processed.

Snoek, Harry. 1988. "Problems of Bank Supervision in Developing Countries." Washington, D.C.: International Monetary Fund, Central Banking Department. Processed.

Song, Sang Hyun, ed. 1983. *Introduction to the Law and Legal System of Korea.* Seoul: Kyung Mun Sa.

Sprague, Irvine H. 1986. *Bail-out: An Insider's Account of Bank Failures and Rescues.* New York: Basic Books.

Stiglitz, Joseph E., and Andrew Weiss. 1981. "Credit Rationing in Markets with Imperfect Information." *American Economic Review* 71 (June): 393–410.

Subercaseaux, Guillermo. 1922. *Monetary and Banking Policy of Chile.* Oxford: Clarendon Press.

Sundararajan, V. 1987. "The Debt-Equity Ratio of Firms and the Effectiveness of Interest Rate Policy: Analysis with a Dynamic Model of Saving, Investment, and Growth in Korea." *IMF Staff Papers* 34, 2: 260–310.

———. 1988. "Banking Crisis and Adjustment: Recent Experience." Paper presented at the Seminar on Central Banking, sponsored by the

International Monetary Fund, Washington, D.C., November 28–December 9. Processed.

Suzuki, Yoshio. 1980. *Money and Banking in Contemporary Japan: The Theoretical Setting and Its Application.* New Haven, Conn.: Yale University Press.

Suzuki, Yoshio, and Hiroshi Yomo, eds. 1986. *Financial Innovation and Monetary Policy: Asia and the West.* Tokyo: University of Tokyo Press.

Swanson, Daniel, and Teferra Wolde-Semait. 1988. *Africa's Public Enterprise Sector and Evidence of Reforms.* World Bank Technical Paper 95. Washington, D.C.

Timberg, T. A., and C. V. Aiyar. 1980. *Informal Credit Markets in India.* Domestic Finance Studies 62. Washington, D.C.: World Bank.

Tobin, James. 1984. "On the Efficiency of the Financial System." *Lloyds Bank Review* 153 (July): 1–15.

Tybout, James R. 1983. "Credit Rationing and Investment Behavior in a Developing Country." *Review of Economics and Statistics* 65, 4 (November): 598–607.

van Agtmael, Antoine. 1984. *Emerging Securities Markets: Investment Banking Opportunities in the Developing World.* London: Euromoney.

van Wijnbergen, Sweder. 1983. "Interest Rate Management in LDCs." *Journal of Monetary Economics* 12, 3 (September): 433–52.

Velasco, Andrés. 1987. "Financial Crises and Balance of Payments Crises: A Simple Model of the Southern Cone Experience." *Journal of Development Economics* 27: 263–83.

———. 1988. "Liberalization, Crisis, Intervention: The Chilean Financial System, 1975–85." IMF Working Paper. Washington, D.C.: International Monetary Fund, Central Banking Department. Processed.

Veneroso, Frank. 1986. "New Patterns of Financial Instability." Washington, D.C: World Bank, Industry Department. Processed.

Virmani, Arvind. 1982. *The Nature of Credit Markets in Developing Countries: A Framework for Policy Analysis.* World Bank Staff Working Paper 524. Washington, D.C.

Vittas, Dimitri, ed. 1978. *Banking Systems Abroad.* London: Inter-Bank Research Organization.

Vogel, Robert C. 1984a. "The Effect of Subsidized Agricultural Credit on Income Distribution in Costa Rica." In Dale Adams, Douglas Graham, and J. D. Von Pischke, eds. *Undermining Rural Development with Cheap Credit.* Boulder, Colo.: Westview Press.

———. 1984b. "Savings Mobilization: The Forgotten Half of Rural Finance." In Dale Adams,

Douglas Graham, and J. D. Von Pischke, eds. *Undermining Rural Development with Cheap Credit.* Boulder, Colo.: Westview Press.

————. 1988. "The Role of Groups, Credit Unions and Other Cooperatives in Rural Lending." Washington, D.C.: World Bank, Agricultural Policies Division, Agriculture and Rural Development Department. Processed.

Vogel, Robert C., and Paul Burkett. 1986. *Mobilizing Small-Scale Savings: Approaches, Costs, and Benefit.* World Bank Industry and Finance Paper 15. Washington, D.C.

von Mehren, Arthur Taylor, and James Russell Gordley. 1977. *The Civil Law System.* Boston: Little, Brown.

Von Pischke, J. D., Dale W Adams, and Gordon Donald. 1983. *Rural Financial Markets in Developing Countries.* Baltimore, Md.: Johns Hopkins University Press.

Watson, Maxwell, and others. 1988. *International Capital Markets: Developments and Prospects.* Washington, D.C.: International Monetary Fund.

White, Lawrence H. 1988. "Money and Capital in Economic Development: A Retrospective Assessment." Title Markets Development Policy Paper. Washington, D.C.: U.S. Agency for International Development.

Wieland, Robert. 1988. "A Summary of Case Studies of Group Lending and Cooperative Finance in LDCs." Washington, D.C.: World Bank, Agricultural Policies Division, Agriculture and Rural Development Department. Processed.

Williamson, Oliver E. 1985. *The Economic Institutions of Capitalism: Firms, Markets, Relational Contracting.* New York: Free Press.

Wilson, Stuart. 1952. "The Business of Banking in India." In R. S. Sayers, ed. *Banking in the British Commonwealth.* Oxford: Clarendon Press.

World Bank. 1988a. *Adjustment Lending: An Evaluation of Ten Years of Experience.* Policy and Research Series 1, Country Economics Department. Washington, D.C.

————. 1988b. *Recent Developments in Developing Country Debt.* Debt and International Finance Division, International Economics Department. Washington, D.C.

————. 1988c. *World Debt Tables, 1988–89 Edition: External Debt of Developing Countries.* Washington, D.C.

Young, John Parke. 1925. *Central American Currency and Finance.* Princeton, N.J.: Princeton University Press.

Youngjohns, B. J. 1982. "Cooperatives and Credit: A Re-examination." *Development Digest* 20, 1: 3–9.

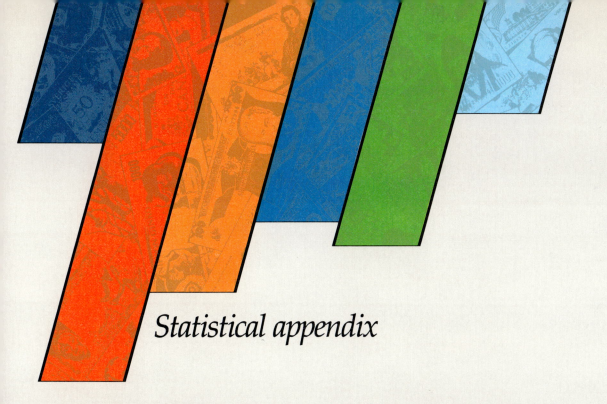

Statistical appendix

The tables in this statistical appendix present summary data on the population, national accounts, trade, and external debt of the low- and middle-income economies, the high-income economies, and all reporting economies as a group. Readers should refer to the "Definitions and data notes" for an explanation of the country groupings and to the technical notes to the World Development Indicators for definitions of the concepts used.

Table A.1 Population growth, 1965 to 1987, and projected to 2000

Country group	1987 population (millions)	Average annual growth (percent)				
		1965–73	1973–80	1980–87	1987–90	1990–2000
Low- and middle-income economies	3,859	2.5	2.1	2.0	2.1	1.9
Low-income economies	2,820	2.5	2.1	2.0	2.1	1.9
Middle-income economies	1,039	2.4	2.3	2.2	2.1	1.9
Sub-Saharan Africa	442	2.6	2.8	3.1	3.3	3.1
East Asia	1,511	2.7	1.7	1.5	1.6	1.5
South Asia	1,079	2.4	2.4	2.3	2.2	1.9
Europe, Middle East, and North Africa	390	2.0	2.1	2.1	2.0	2.0
Latin America and the Caribbean	404	2.6	2.4	2.2	2.1	1.9
17 highly indebted countries	582	2.6	2.4	2.4	2.3	2.2
High-income economies	776	1.0	0.8	0.7	0.6	0.5
OECD members	746	1.0	0.7	0.6	0.5	0.4
Total reporting economies	4,635	2.2	1.9	1.8	1.8	1.7
Oil exporters	578	2.7	2.8	2.7	2.6	2.5

Table A.2 Population and GNP per capita, 1980, and growth rates, 1965 to 1988

Country group	1980 GNP (billions of dollars)	1980 population (millions)	1980 GNP per capita (dollars)	Average annual growth of GNP per capita (percent)					
				1965–73	1973–80	1980–85	1986	1987	1988[a]
Low- and middle-income economies	2,347	3,354	700	4.1	2.7	1.2	2.7	2.5	3.5
Low-income economies	765	2,459	310	3.3	2.6	3.9	3.6	3.0	6.5
Middle-income economies	1,582	894	1,770	4.6	2.6	−0.3	2.1	2.1	2.5
Sub-Saharan Africa	200	356	560	3.1	0.5	−3.7	0.8	−4.4	−0.2
East Asia	566	1,362	420	5.1	4.6	6.4	5.8	6.8	9.3
South Asia	221	923	240	1.4	2.0	2.9	2.2	0.9	5.6
Europe, Middle East, and North Africa[b]	591	338	1,730	6.0	2.4	0.0	1.0	−0.2	0.1
Latin America and the Caribbean	698	347	2,010	4.1	2.5	−2.2	1.8	1.9	−0.9
17 highly indebted countries	892	494	1,810	4.2	2.6	−2.6	1.7	0.5	−1.0
High-income economies	7,961	741	10,740	3.5	2.2	1.5	2.0	2.8	3.0
OECD members	7,698	716	10,750	3.5	2.1	1.7	2.1	2.7	3.3
Total reporting economies	10,308	4,095	2,520	2.7	1.5	0.6	1.3	1.8	2.6
Oil exporters	951	479	1,980	4.7	2.7	−2.3	−2.7	−1.3	..

a. Preliminary.   b. Figures after 1980 exclude Iran and Iraq.

Table A.3 Population and composition of GDP, selected years, 1965 to 1988
(billions of dollars, unless otherwise specified)

Country group and indicator	1965	1973	1980	1984	1985	1986	1987	1988[a]
Low- and middle-income economies								
GDP	373	841	2,387	2,469	2,496	2,565	2,798	3,053
Domestic absorption[b]	374	838	2,423	2,452	2,489	2,567	2,800	..
Net exports[c]	−2	2	−36	17	7	−2	−2	..
Population (millions)	2,375	2,895	3,354	3,635	3,705	3,782	3,859	3,918
Low-income economies								
GDP	162	305	771	799	815	775	793	893
Domestic absorption[b]	164	304	777	808	843	800	807	..
Net exports[c]	−2	1	−5	−10	−28	−26	−14	..
Population (millions)	1,745	2,131	2,459	2,660	2,709	2,764	2,820	2,878
Middle-income economies								
GDP	208	534	1,616	1,670	1,681	1,800	2,024	2,172
Domestic absorption[b]	208	532	1,646	1,644	1,645	1,778	2,022	..
Net exports[c]	0	2	−30	27	35	22	2	..
Population (millions)	630	764	894	975	996	1,017	1,039	1,040
Sub-Saharan Africa								
GDP	28	63	207	184	185	154	137	146
Domestic absorption[b]	28	62	205	184	185	160	140	..
Net exports[c]	0	1	2	−0	1	−5	−4	..
Population (millions)	239	294	356	403	415	428	442	456
East Asia								
GDP	91	212	573	640	629	630	709	852
Domestic absorption[b]	91	210	576	631	630	613	673	..
Net exports[c]	0	2	−4	9	−1	17	35	..
Population (millions)	980	1,207	1,362	1,446	1,465	1,487	1,511	1,515
South Asia								
GDP	65	93	221	253	277	296	320	316
Domestic absorption[b]	67	94	232	264	291	307	330	..
Net exports[c]	−2	−1	−12	−11	−14	−11	−10	..
Population (millions)	647	783	923	1,010	1,033	1,056	1,079	1,103
Europe, Middle East, and North Africa[d]								
GDP	74	186	473	458	470	525	561	567
Domestic absorption[b]	74	185	487	473	487	556	607	..
Net exports[c]	−0	1	−15	−15	−17	−31	−45	..
Population (millions)	250	292	338	367	374	382	390	398

Table A.3 (continued)

Country group and indicator	1965	1973	1980	1984	1985	1986	1987	1988[a]
Latin America and the Caribbean								
GDP	99	253	716	673	682	700	773	837
Domestic absorption[b]	98	254	726	639	651	683	762	..
Net exports[c]	1	−0	−10	34	31	17	11	..
Population (millions)	239	294	347	379	387	395	404	412
17 highly indebted countries								
GDP	121	300	915	816	826	825	877	934
Domestic absorption[b]	119	299	921	778	789	805	861	..
Net exports[c]	1	1	−6	38	38	20	16	..
Population (millions)	341	419	494	543	556	569	582	596
High-income economies								
GDP	1,412	3,340	7,914	8,543	8,933	10,860	12,570	13,963
Domestic absorption[b]	1,403	3,309	7,859	8,517	8,906	10,805	12,536	..
Net exports[c]	9	31	55	26	27	55	34	..
Population (millions)	646	700	741	762	767	772	776	781
OECD members								
GDP	1,397	3,293	7,654	8,284	8,693	10,633	12,329	13,695
Domestic absorption[b]	1,389	3,267	7,662	8,263	8,669	10,570	12,286	..
Net exports[c]	8	26	−8	21	24	62	43	..
Population (millions)	632	681	716	734	738	742	746	749
Total reporting economies								
GDP	1,786	4,186	10,300	11,011	11,431	13,465	15,428	17,125
Domestic absorption[b]	1,779	4,154	10,279	10,969	11,398	13,418	15,410	..
Net exports[c]	7	31	20	42	33	47	18	..
Population (millions)	3,021	3,595	4,095	4,397	4,472	4,554	4,635	4,699
Oil exporters								
GDP	78	226	966	993	1,011	855	855	..
Domestic absorption[b]	76	211	863	957	985	877	863	..
Net exports[c]	3	15	102	36	26	−21	−7	..
Population (millions)	321	396	479	534	548	563	578	593

Note: Components may not sum to totals because of rounding.
a. Preliminary.
b. Private consumption plus government consumption plus gross domestic investment.
c. Includes goods and nonfactor services.
d. Figures after 1980 exclude Iran and Iraq.

Table A.4 GDP, 1980, and growth rates, 1965 to 1988

Country group	1980 GDP (billions of dollars)	Average annual growth of GDP (percent)					
		1965–73	1973–80	1980–85	1986	1987	1988[a]
Low- and middle-income economies	2,387	6.6	4.9	3.4	4.7	4.2	5.0
Low-income economies	771	6.0	4.7	5.9	5.8	5.4	8.6
Middle-income economies	1,616	6.9	5.1	2.2	3.9	3.4	2.6
Sub-Saharan Africa	207	6.1	3.2	−0.5	3.2	−1.3	3.1
East Asia	573	7.9	6.5	7.8	7.3	8.6	9.4
South Asia	221	3.8	4.4	5.4	4.6	3.1	7.6
Europe, Middle East, and North Africa[b]	591	7.6	4.3	2.3	3.1	1.9	2.6
Latin America and the Caribbean	716	6.4	5.2	0.5	3.6	2.7	1.0
17 highly indebted countries	915	6.6	5.2	0.2	3.5	1.7	1.5
High-income economies	7,913	4.6	2.9	2.3	2.6	3.4	3.7
OECD members	7,655	4.5	2.8	2.4	2.7	3.3	3.7
Total reporting economies	10,302	4.9	3.3	2.6	3.1	3.6	4.0
Oil exporters	964	7.4	5.0	0.8	−0.9	1.3	..

a. Preliminary.
b. Figures after 1980 exclude Iran and Iraq.

Table A.5 GDP structure of production, selected years, 1965 to 1987

(percentage of GDP)

	1965		1973		1980		1984		1985		1986		1987[a]	
Country group	Agri-cul-ture	Indus-try	Agri-cul-ture	Indus-try	Agri-cul-ture	Indus-try	Agri-cul-ture	Indus-try	Agri-cul-ture	Indus-try	Agri-cul-ture	Indus-try	Agri-cul-ture	Indus-try
Low- and middle-income economies	29	30	23	34	19	38	19	35	19	36	18	35	17	..
Low-income economies	41	26	37	31	32	36	33	33	31	33	31	32	30	35
Middle-income economies	19	32	15	35	12	38	12	37	12	37	13	36	..	..
Sub-Saharan Africa	40	18	33	24	28	32	33	26	33	26	33	23	31	26
East Asia	37	34	31	40	26	44	25	41	23	42	23	43	21	45
South Asia	42	19	45	18	35	22	31	24	30	24	29	25	28	25
Europe, Middle East, and North Africa[b]	22	32	16	38	14	41	13	39	13	..	14	..	15	..
Latin America and the Caribbean	15	32	12	33	9	36	10	35	10	35	11	35	..	..
17 highly indebted countries	18	31	15	33	12	36	14	35	14	35	13	34	..	..
High-income economies	5	40	5	38	3	37	3	35	3	35	3	34	3	34
OECD members	5	40	5	38	3	37	3	35	3	34	3	34	3	34
Total reporting economies	10	38	8	37	7	37	6	35	6	35	6	34	6	34
Oil exporters	19	32	14	38	11	47	13	40	13	38	13	35	..	..

a. Preliminary.
b. Figures after 1980 exclude Iran and Iraq.

Table A.6 Sector growth rates, 1965 to 1987

(average annual percentage change)

	Agriculture			Industry			Services		
Country group	1965–73	1973–80	1980–87	1965–73	1973–80	1980–87	1965–73	1973–80	1980–87
Low- and middle-income economies	3.1	2.6	3.4	8.8	4.9	5.1	7.1	6.4	3.4
Low-income economies	3.0	2.1	4.0	10.6	6.9	8.6	5.9	4.9	5.2
Middle-income economies	3.3	3.3	2.5	8.0	4.0	2.9	7.5	6.9	2.8
Sub-Saharan Africa	2.4	0.3	1.2	13.5	4.7	−1.2	4.1	3.6	1.5
East Asia	3.2	3.0	5.9	12.7	9.3	10.1	9.2	6.4	6.4
South Asia	3.4	2.4	1.4	3.7	5.4	7.2	3.9	5.7	6.1
Europe, Middle East, and North Africa[a]	3.5	3.1	2.4	8.7	1.6	1.9	8.3	8.5	3.2
Latin America and the Caribbean	2.9	3.7	2.2	6.9	4.8	0.8	7.1	6.3	1.3
17 highly indebted countries	3.0	2.2	1.8	8.0	5.2	0.2	7.2	6.2	1.2
High-income economies	1.4	0.5	2.5	3.9	2.2	*1.9*	4.5	3.4	*3.0*
OECD members	1.4	0.5	2.4	3.7	2.0	2.3	4.5	3.3	*3.0*
Total reporting economies	2.5	1.8	*3.2*	4.8	2.8	*2.5*	4.9	3.9	*3.1*
Oil exporters	3.3	2.2	2.4	9.4	3.3	−1.5	6.4	8.0	2.7

Note: Figures in italics are for years other than those specified.
a. Figures after 1980 exclude Iran and Iraq.

Table A.7 Consumption, investment, and saving, selected years, 1965 to 1987
(percentage of GDP)

Country group and indicator	1965	1973	1980	1984	1985	1986	1987[a]
Low- and middle-income economies							
Consumption	79.7	76.3	74.7	75.9	75.6	76.1	75.8
Investment	20.8	23.4	26.8	23.4	24.1	24.0	24.3
Saving	18.6	22.1	23.6	21.3	21.6	21.3	23.1
Low-income economies							
Consumption	81.3	76.5	75.5	77.4	76.6	76.3	74.1
Investment	19.8	23.3	25.2	23.8	26.9	27.1	27.7
Saving	18.3	22.7	23.6	21.5	22.3	22.5	25.4
Middle-income economies							
Consumption	78.5	76.2	74.3	75.2	75.2	76.1	76.8
Investment	21.4	23.4	27.6	23.2	22.7	22.6	23.1
Saving	18.7	21.7	23.6	21.1	21.2	20.8	21.9
Sub-Saharan Africa							
Consumption	85.2	80.4	78.5	88.7	87.3	88.9	86.2
Investment	14.4	18.6	20.8	11.5	12.4	14.5	16.4
Saving	12.6	15.5	18.3	7.8	9.0	7.2	9.4
East Asia							
Consumption	77.0	71.4	71.1	69.6	69.2	67.4	65.1
Investment	22.8	27.7	29.5	28.9	31.0	29.8	29.9
Saving	23.0	28.3	27.8	29.0	29.3	31.3	33.7
South Asia							
Consumption	85.0	82.9	82.2	82.2	81.0	81.1	80.8
Investment	17.9	17.7	23.1	22.0	23.9	22.6	22.4
Saving	14.4	16.6	17.9	17.2	18.4	18.1	20.3
Europe, Middle East, and North Africa[b]							
Consumption	78.2	74.2	72.6	75.4	75.5	77.2	80.6
Investment	22.3	25.1	30.5	27.9	28.1	28.6	27.5
Saving	17.6	26.0	26.0	22.0	21.8	20.3	..
Latin America and the Caribbean							
Consumption	78.5	78.8	77.2	78.2	77.9	80.2	80.4
Investment	20.3	21.2	24.2	16.7	17.5	17.4	18.2
Saving	19.1	19.0	20.3	16.3	16.9	15.2	16.2
17 highly indebted countries							
Consumption	77.9	78.3	75.4	78.7	77.8	79.0	78.7
Investment	21.0	21.4	25.3	16.6	17.6	18.6	19.4
Saving	19.9	19.5	22.1	16.3	17.5	16.8	..
High-income economies							
Consumption	79.5	75.0	77.1	78.9	79.8	79.3	78.9
Investment	19.9	24.0	22.2	20.8	19.9	20.2	20.8
Saving	20.8	25.4	23.5	21.4	20.4	20.9	21.2
OECD members							
Consumption	79.6	75.2	77.9	79.2	80.0	79.3	79.0
Investment	19.8	24.0	22.2	20.6	19.7	20.1	20.7
Saving	20.8	25.4	22.6	21.2	20.3	20.9	21.1
Total reporting economies							
Consumption	79.6	75.3	76.5	78.2	78.9	78.7	78.4
Investment	20.1	24.0	23.3	21.4	20.8	20.9	21.5
Saving	20.4	24.8	23.5	21.3	20.7	21.0	21.5
Oil exporters							
Consumption	76.6	70.9	63.8	72.0	73.5	77.8	76.8
Investment	19.9	22.4	25.7	24.3	24.0	24.7	24.1
Saving	18.2	24.3	34.7	24.6	23.7	19.8	22.2

a. Preliminary.
b. Figures after 1980 exclude Iran and Iraq.

Table A.8 Growth of export volume, 1965 to 1988

	Average annual change in export volume (percent)					
Country group and commodity	1965–73	1973–80	1980–85	1986	1987[a]	1988[b]
By commodity						
Low- and middle-income economies	5.2	3.8	4.4	5.6	6.6	7.1
Manufactures	11.6	12.8	9.7	8.5	16.3	9.7
Food	2.4	4.2	3.6	0.0	5.2	1.3
Nonfood	2.1	0.4	1.2	5.6	−1.5	4.9
Metals and minerals	4.8	6.5	0.1	7.0	9.2	−2.1
Fuels	5.5	−0.4	1.0	5.4	−5.4	10.7
Total reporting economies	8.7	4.6	2.4	4.9	5.9	8.5
Manufactures	10.7	6.1	4.5	2.3	7.2	8.1
Food	4.6	6.8	1.9	11.6	12.3	6.2
Nonfood	3.1	0.9	2.1	0.6	14.5	6.4
Metals and minerals	6.8	8.6	0.4	6.1	0.7	3.5
Fuels	8.6	0.5	−3.9	12.5	−4.3	6.2
By country group						
Low- and middle-income economies	5.2	3.8	4.4	5.6	6.6	7.1
Manufactures	11.6	12.8	9.7	8.5	16.3	9.7
Primary goods	4.3	1.2	1.5	3.6	−0.3	5.7
Low-income economies	9.6	2.3	1.5	7.0	4.3	6.8
Manufactures	1.8	8.5	10.0	15.9	23.3	10.8
Primary goods	11.2	1.1	−1.1	3.4	−4.0	4.6
Middle-income economies	3.9	4.4	5.3	5.2	7.3	7.2
Manufactures	16.8	13.8	9.7	7.1	14.8	9.5
Primary goods	2.4	1.2	2.5	3.7	1.2	6.1
Sub-Saharan Africa	15.1	0.2	−3.3	1.1	−3.3	4.3
Manufactures	7.6	5.6	4.4	1.3	4.8	5.1
Primary goods	15.4	−0.0	−3.7	1.1	−3.5	3.5
East Asia	9.7	8.7	9.1	14.4	13.4	9.3
Manufactures	17.5	15.5	13.2	19.3	23.8	11.2
Primary goods	7.3	4.7	4.8	8.1	−1.0	5.9
South Asia	−0.7	5.8	3.6	8.9	10.2	7.1
Manufactures	0.6	8.2	2.6	10.4	15.7	13.2
Primary goods	−1.8	3.1	4.9	7.3	3.9	−0.7
Europe, Middle East, and North Africa	..	..	..	..	..	..
Manufactures	..	..	..	..	..	..
Primary goods	..	..	..	..	..	..
Latin America and the Caribbean	−1.0	0.9	4.5	−4.2	4.0	8.3
Manufactures	16.6	10.1	10.2	−10.6	5.5	14.5
Primary goods	−1.8	−0.5	3.0	−2.3	3.6	6.5
17 highly indebted countries	3.0	1.2	2.4	−3.7	2.0	7.3
Manufactures	13.4	10.2	7.8	−8.6	5.5	13.5
Primary goods	2.3	−0.3	0.9	−1.9	0.8	5.2
High-income economies	9.9	4.8	1.8	4.8	5.9	8.8
Manufactures	10.6	5.5	3.8	1.3	5.7	7.1
Primary goods	8.9	3.5	−2.5	13.6	6.3	13.6
OECD members	9.4	5.4	3.3	3.6	6.4	7.8
Manufactures	10.6	5.2	3.7	1.4	4.9	6.1
Primary goods	6.7	5.9	2.2	10.2	10.6	13.6
Oil exporters	8.7	0.0	−7.0	13.5	−5.2	10.5
Manufactures	11.7	3.9	9.9	8.8	15.1	11.0
Primary goods	8.6	−0.1	−8.2	14.0	−7.4	10.0

a. Estimated.
b. Projected.

Table A.9 Change in export prices and terms of trade, 1965 to 1988
(average annual percentage change)

Country group	1965–73	1973–80	1980–85	1986	1987[a]	1988[b]
Export prices						
Low- and middle-income economies	6.1	14.8	−4.3	−8.3	11.5	4.8
Manufactures	6.4	8.2	−3.7	9.4	10.3	8.7
Food	5.9	8.6	−4.1	7.2	−7.4	16.1
Nonfood	4.6	10.2	−4.9	0.0	21.1	2.5
Metals and minerals	2.5	4.7	−4.5	−4.8	13.3	22.7
Fuels	8.0	26.2	−4.1	−46.7	22.9	−17.4
High-income OECD members						
Total	4.8	10.3	−3.1	12.0	10.9	6.8
Manufactures	4.6	10.8	−2.8	19.6	13.4	8.4
Terms of trade						
Low- and middle-income economies	0.1	2.6	−2.0	−9.3	1.3	1.0
Low-income economies	−4.8	4.0	−1.1	−16.8	4.2	−1.6
Middle-income economies	1.7	2.1	−2.4	−6.7	0.3	1.7
Sub-Saharan Africa	−8.5	5.0	−2.3	−23.2	3.3	−5.3
East Asia	−0.6	1.2	−0.6	−7.0	1.4	1.8
South Asia	3.7	−3.4	1.7	2.8	−2.1	5.2
Europe, Middle East, and North Africa	..	..	..	..	..	..
Latin America and the Caribbean	3.9	2.4	−1.9	−14.0	−2.1	−0.4
17 highly indebted countries	1.4	3.5	−1.3	−13.7	−0.7	−0.8
High-income economies	−1.2	−2.0	−0.4	8.7	−0.1	0.2
OECD members	−1.0	−3.3	−0.2	12.4	−0.2	0.7
Oil exporters	0.3	9.6	−2.2	−47.5	16.7	−17.3

a. Estimated.
b. Projected.

Table A.10 Growth of long-term debt of low- and middle-income economies, 1970 to 1988
(average annual percentage change, nominal)

Country group	1970–73	1973–80	1980–85	1986	1987	1988
Low- and middle-income economies						
Debt outstanding and disbursed	17.9	22.0	14.5	12.8	11.6	1.5
Official	15.1	17.9	14.6	20.1	20.4	6.2
Private	20.7	25.2	14.4	8.3	5.7	−2.3
Low-income economies						
Debt outstanding and disbursed	16.9	17.1	13.0	21.8	21.7	6.2
Official	15.0	14.8	11.5	23.6	23.1	8.3
Private	26.1	24.9	16.9	18.1	18.8	1.4
Middle-income economies						
Debt outstanding and disbursed	18.4	23.7	14.9	10.6	8.9	0.1
Official	15.3	20.5	16.7	18.2	18.9	5.0
Private	20.0	25.2	14.1	7.2	4.0	−2.8
Sub-Saharan Africa						
Debt outstanding and disbursed	20.9	25.3	12.6	22.5	20.5	4.7
Official	17.2	22.9	13.7	29.7	27.7	4.4
Private	25.5	29.0	10.5	11.6	7.9	5.3
East Asia						
Debt outstanding and disbursed	23.6	22.4	17.7	17.7	11.2	0.2
Official	27.1	18.5	15.8	21.7	24.1	7.4
Private	20.7	25.5	19.0	15.3	3.1	−5.2
South Asia						
Debt outstanding and disbursed	11.7	11.2	10.8	14.3	16.7	4.9
Official	12.4	11.2	8.3	16.4	15.3	7.6
Private	1.8	11.6	36.1	4.4	24.6	−8.3
Europe, Middle East, and North Africa						
Debt outstanding and disbursed	21.6	28.5	15.9	12.3	13.5	1.9
Official	15.2	25.2	18.3	13.6	14.3	7.5
Private	30.0	31.7	13.9	11.0	12.8	−3.9
Latin America and the Caribbean						
Debt outstanding and disbursed	16.8	21.2	14.2	8.8	7.5	0.2
Official	11.8	15.0	15.5	24.2	23.9	4.4
Private	18.8	23.1	13.9	5.1	3.0	−1.4
17 highly indebted countries						
Debt outstanding and disbursed	17.4	21.8	13.6	11.4	8.8	1.0
Official	13.3	15.4	14.5	30.1	28.3	4.9
Private	19.1	23.8	13.4	6.7	2.8	−0.7

Table A.11 Investment, saving, and financing requirement, 1965 to 1987
(percentage of GNP)

Country	Gross domestic investment			Gross national saving			Balance of payments: total to be financed		
	1965–73	1973–80	1980–87	1965–73	1973–80	1980–87	1965–73	1973–80	1980–87
Latin America and the Caribbean									
*Argentina	19.7	23.4	14.4	20.4	22.6	9.5	0.7	−0.8	−4.9
*Bolivia	25.4	24.7	8.3	21.3	18.3	−1.6	−4.1	−6.4	−9.9
*Brazil	21.3	23.9	19.7	19.1	19.3	17.0	−2.1	−4.6	−2.8
*Chile	14.3	17.3	17.4	11.9	12.1	7.7	−2.4	−5.2	−9.8
*Colombia	18.9	18.8	19.9	15.8	19.0	16.0	−3.2	0.2	−3.8
*Costa Rica	21.8	25.5	25.4	13.0	13.8	15.0	−8.8	−11.7	−10.4
*Ecuador	19.0	26.7	23.3	12.7	21.2	17.5	−6.2	−5.6	−5.8
Guatemala	13.3	18.7	13.4	11.6	16.4	9.5	−1.7	−2.3	−3.9
*Jamaica	32.0	20.2	22.8	23.7	13.6	11.2	−8.4	−6.6	−11.6
*Mexico	20.6	24.2	23.4	14.9	20.5	22.1	−5.7	−3.7	−1.3
*Peru	24.1	23.9	27.0	20.9	19.7	23.0	−3.2	−4.2	−4.1
*Uruguay	12.0	15.7	12.8	12.0	11.3	9.7	−0.0	−4.4	−3.1
*Venezuela	31.1	34.2	21.4	31.9	35.8	24.2	0.8	1.6	2.8
Sub-Saharan Africa									
Cameroon	16.6	21.8	22.4	..	16.9	18.2	..	−4.9	−4.1
*Côte d'Ivoire	22.8	29.1	19.9	..	16.8	9.9	..	−12.3	−10.0
Ethiopia	12.8	9.5	11.7	11.0	6.9	4.9	−1.8	−2.6	−6.8
Ghana	12.3	8.7	7.1	8.7	..	2.0	−3.5	−1.8	−5.1
Kenya	22.6	26.2	25.1	17.2	16.4	18.3	−5.5	−9.8	−6.8
Liberia	19.1	28.7	15.0	..	27.5	7.7	..	−1.2	−7.3
Malawi	20.0	29.7	19.0	..	10.7	7.0	..	−19.0	−12.0
Niger	9.7	23.8	17.2	..	9.7	2.7	..	−14.1	−14.6
*Nigeria	16.3	22.8	14.5	11.8	24.4	12.8	−4.5	1.6	−1.8
Senegal	14.7	17.5	15.5	..	4.2	−2.8	..	−13.3	−18.3
Sierra Leone	13.8	14.1	13.7	9.8	−1.0	5.3	−4.0	−15.1	−8.4
Sudan	11.9	16.2	16.0	11.0	9.6	4.2	−0.9	−6.6	−11.9
Tanzania	19.9	23.9	18.7	17.1	13.6	9.0	−2.8	−10.3	−9.7
Zaire	13.7	15.0	14.3	16.9	8.6	4.9	3.2	−6.4	−9.4
Zambia	31.9	28.5	18.4	34.3	19.9	4.9	2.4	−8.6	−13.5
East Asia									
Indonesia	15.8	24.5	28.0	13.7	24.6	24.9	−2.1	0.1	−3.2
Korea, Republic of	23.9	31.0	30.4	17.6	25.7	30.0	−6.3	−5.3	−0.4
Malaysia	22.3	28.7	32.9	22.6	29.4	28.1	0.2	0.6	−4.7
Papua New Guinea	27.8	22.0	27.6	..	11.1	3.5	..	−11.0	−24.0
*Philippines	20.6	29.1	22.7	19.7	24.3	18.2	−1.0	−4.8	−4.5
Thailand	24.3	26.9	25.2	22.1	21.9	20.7	−2.1	−5.0	−4.4
South Asia									
India	18.4	22.5	24.5	16.9	22.2	22.8	−1.5	−0.3	−1.7
Pakistan	16.1	17.5	17.5	..	11.6	13.7	..	−5.9	−3.8
Sri Lanka	15.8	20.6	27.3	11.2	13.4	16.2	−4.6	−7.2	−11.0
Europe, Middle East, and North Africa									
Algeria	32.1	44.5	35.8	31.7	38.9	35.4	−0.4	−5.6	−0.4
Egypt, Arab Republic of	14.0	29.3	28.4	9.3	18.1	16.2	−4.7	−11.2	−12.2
*Morocco	15.0	25.6	22.7	13.6	16.4	14.7	−1.4	−9.1	−7.9
Portugal	26.6	29.7	29.4	..	..	25.8	..	..	−3.6
Tunisia	23.3	29.9	29.1	17.8	23.6	22.1	−5.5	−6.3	−7.1
Turkey	18.5	21.8	22.7	16.0	18.1	19.3	−2.5	−3.7	−3.3
*Yugoslavia	29.9	35.6	38.9	27.2	32.9	38.9	−2.6	−2.7	−0.1

Note: An asterisk indicates a highly indebted country.

Table A.12 Composition of debt outstanding, 1970 to 1987
(percentage of total long-term debt)

Country	Debt from official sources			Debt from private sources			Debt at floating rate		
	1970–72	1980–82	1987	1970–72	1980–82	1987	1973–75	1980–82	1987
Latin America and the Caribbean									
*Argentina	12.6	9.0	14.2	87.4	91.0	85.8	6.6	29.2	79.3
*Bolivia	58.2	50.3	73.3	41.8	49.7	26.7	7.4	28.0	27.9
*Brazil	30.7	12.6	24.1	69.3	88.3	76.2	26.1	46.1	58.3
*Chile	47.0	11.0	22.0	53.0	89.0	78.0	8.3	23.4	68.2
*Colombia	68.2	46.1	53.8	31.8	53.9	46.2	5.4	33.7	36.8
*Costa Rica	39.8	36.8	51.0	60.2	63.2	49.0	15.6	42.4	49.8
*Ecuador	51.8	30.6	34.9	48.2	69.4	65.1	8.2	36.5	68.6
Guatemala	47.5	71.0	66.0	52.5	29.0	34.0	3.5	5.6	29.4
*Jamaica	7.4	68.3	82.3	92.6	31.7	17.7	4.6	17.4	24.9
*Mexico	19.5	10.9	16.4	80.5	89.1	83.6	32.0	61.7	67.6
*Peru	15.5	39.3	46.0	84.5	60.7	54.0	16.1	23.0	29.9
*Uruguay	44.2	21.1	20.3	55.8	78.9	79.7	10.1	28.5	65.0
*Venezuela	29.9	3.0	3.4	70.1	97.0	96.6	17.1	60.3	68.7
Sub-Saharan Africa									
Cameroon	82.2	57.2	67.5	17.7	42.8	32.5	1.8	11.1	5.0
*Côte d'Ivoire	51.4	23.8	40.4	48.6	76.2	59.6	19.3	37.1	37.1
Ethiopia	87.3	91.2	83.3	12.7	8.8	16.7	1.5	2.1	5.8
Ghana	56.6	88.5	86.5	43.4	11.5	13.5	0.0	0.0	5.6
Kenya	58.3	55.9	74.4	41.7	44.1	25.6	2.1	10.0	3.6
Liberia	81.1	75.3	82.9	18.9	24.7	17.1	0.0	15.6	10.7
Malawi	85.9	73.0	95.8	14.1	27.0	4.2	2.3	21.1	2.7
Niger	96.9	42.3	67.9	3.0	57.7	32.1	0.0	13.1	9.2
*Nigeria	68.8	14.6	44.6	31.2	85.4	55.4	0.7	48.6	48.8
Senegal	59.2	69.5	90.3	40.8	30.5	9.7	24.7	8.5	4.1
Sierra Leone	60.6	68.2	83.0	39.4	31.8	17.0	3.8	0.1	0.6
Sudan	86.1	74.4	75.2	13.9	25.6	24.8	2.2	9.7	1.0
Tanzania	63.6	75.9	89.2	36.4	24.1	10.8	0.4	0.3	2.5
Zaire	42.5	66.9	84.7	57.5	33.1	15.3	32.8	11.5	5.3
Zambia	21.8	70.2	86.0	78.2	29.8	14.0	20.7	10.0	14.7
East Asia									
Indonesia	72.1	51.8	54.9	27.9	48.2	45.1	4.9	15.0	23.9
Korea, Republic of	35.2	34.3	38.1	64.8	65.7	61.9	11.9	29.0	24.4
Malaysia	51.0	22.1	21.0	49.0	77.9	79.0	17.4	36.1	43.7
Papua New Guinea	6.2	25.6	31.4	93.8	74.4	68.6	0.0	23.5	18.0
*Philippines	22.6	32.6	43.8	77.4	67.4	56.2	7.2	23.4	45.2
Thailand	40.1	40.4	50.4	59.9	59.6	49.6	0.4	21.9	26.1
South Asia									
India	95.1	91.1	75.5	4.9	8.9	24.5	0.0	3.3	12.0
Pakistan	90.6	92.8	94.6	9.4	7.2	5.4	0.0	3.1	5.4
Sri Lanka	81.6	80.9	80.2	18.4	19.1	19.8	0.0	12.1	6.0
Europe, Middle East, and North Africa									
Algeria	45.9	18.9	17.0	54.1	81.1	83.0	34.0	24.2	33.0
Egypt, Arab Republic of	66.9	82.1	79.7	33.1	17.9	20.3	3.1	2.5	1.9
*Morocco	79.2	56.5	71.9	20.8	43.5	28.1	2.7	26.8	30.5
Portugal	29.3	24.7	17.9	70.7	75.3	82.1	0.0	33.9	41.1
Tunisia	71.8	60.7	68.9	28.2	39.3	31.1	0.0	13.4	16.2
Turkey	92.4	63.1	58.0	7.6	36.9	42.0	0.8	23.1	30.9
*Yugoslavia	37.5	23.6	35.1	62.5	76.4	64.9	3.2	10.1	39.2

Note: An asterisk indicates a highly indebted country.

World Development Indicators

Contents

Key

In each table, economies are listed in their group in ascending order of GNP per capita except for those for which no GNP per capita can be calculated. These are italicized, in alphabetical order, at the end of their group. The reference numbers below reflect the order in the tables.

Figures in the colored bands are summary measures for groups of economies. The letter *w* after a summary measure indicates that it is a weighted average; *m*, a median value; *t*, a total.

All growth rates are in real terms.

Data cutoff date is April 30, 1989.

. . = not available.
0 and 0.0 = zero or less than half the unit shown.
Blank means not applicable.

Figures in italics are for years or periods other than those specified.

Afghanistan	38	Honduras	53	Panama	81
Algeria	84	Hong Kong	102	Papua New Guinea	50
Argentina	82	Hungary	80	Paraguay	61
Australia	105	India	21	Peru	68
Austria	108	Indonesia	36	Philippines	46
Bangladesh	5	*Iran, Islamic Republic of*	93	Poland	76
Belgium	106	*Iraq*	94	Portugal	87
Benin	24	Ireland	97	*Romania*	95
Bhutan	2	Israel	99	Rwanda	22
Bolivia	44	Italy	103	Saudi Arabia	98
Botswana	63	Jamaica	58	Senegal	43
Brazil	78	Japan	116	Sierra Leone	23
Burkina Faso	11	Jordan	70	Singapore	101
Burma	39	*Kampuchea, Democratic*	41	Somalia	19
Burundi	14	Kenya	26	South Africa	75
Cameroon	60	Korea, Republic of	85	Spain	96
Canada	114	Kuwait	112	Sri Lanka	33
Central African Republic	25	Lao People's Democratic Republic	8	Sudan	27
Chad	3	*Lebanon*	77	Sweden	115
Chile	67	Lesotho	30	Switzerland	120
China	18	Liberia	37	Syrian Arab Republic	72
Colombia	66	Libya	91	Tanzania	10
Congo, People's Republic of the	57	Madagascar	12	Thailand	55
Costa Rica	71	Malawi	6	Togo	20
Côte d'Ivoire	52	Malaysia	73	Trinidad and Tobago	90
Denmark	113	Mali	13	Tunisia	64
Dominican Republic	51	Mauritania	35	Turkey	65
Ecuador	62	Mauritius	69	Uganda	17
Egypt, Arab Republic of	49	Mexico	74	United Arab Emirates	117
El Salvador	56	Morocco	48	United Kingdom	104
Ethiopia	1	Mozambique	9	United States	119
Finland	111	Nepal	7	Uruguay	79
France	109	Netherlands	107	Venezuela	88
Gabon	86	New Zealand	100	*Viet Nam*	42
Germany, Federal Republic of	110	Nicaragua	54	Yemen Arab Republic	47
Ghana	32	Niger	16	Yemen, People's Democratic Republic of	34
Greece	89	Nigeria	31	Yugoslavia	83
Guatemala	59	Norway	118	Zaire	4
Guinea	40	Oman	92	Zambia	15
Haiti	29	Pakistan	28	Zimbabwe	45

Note: For economies with populations of less than 1 million, see Box A.1; for nonreporting nonmember economies, see Box A.2.

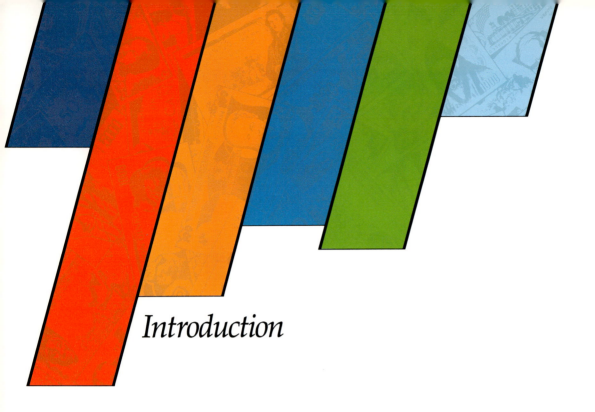

Introduction

The World Development Indicators provide information on the main features of social and economic development. Most of the data collected by the World Bank are on the low- and middle-income economies. Because comparable data for high-income economies are readily available, these are also included here. Additional information on some of these and other countries may be found in other World Bank publications, notably the *Atlas*, *World Tables*, *World Debt Tables*, and *Social Indicators of Development*. Data available for nonreporting nonmembers are summarized in the main tables and shown by country in Box A.2 of the technical notes.

This edition presents revised country classifications and new regional groupings. In these notes the term "country" does not imply political independence, but may refer to any territory whose authorities present for it separate social or economic statistics. As in the past, the Bank classifies economies for certain operational and analytical purposes according to GNP per capita, and in this edition some new groups are shown, others have been dropped, and some have been renamed. See the definitions and data notes at the beginning of the main report for a detailed description of the country groupings.

Every effort has been made to standardize the data. However, full comparability cannot be en-

sured, and care must be taken in interpreting the indicators. The statistics are drawn from sources thought to be most authoritative, but many of them are subject to considerable margins of error. Variations in national statistical practices also reduce the comparability of data which should thus be construed only as indicating trends and characterizing major differences among economies, rather than taken as precise quantitative indications of those differences.

The indicators in Table 1 give a summary profile of economies. Data in the other tables, rearranged this year, fall into the following broad areas: production, domestic absorption, fiscal and monetary accounts, trade and balance of payments, external finance, and human resources.

Two tables have been suspended from this edition, one added, and two more modified. The table on labor force has been dropped since updates depend on population census data that are usually collected only every five or ten years. The trade table on origin and destination of manufactured exports has now been replaced with Table 17, OECD imports of manufactured goods: origin and composition. Table 18, Balance of payments and reserves, now shows receipts of workers' remittances on a net basis rather than credits only, which was the practice in the past. Table 30, Income distribution and ICP estimates of GDP, as the name indicates, now includes International Comparison Program (ICP) data on GDP comparisons. See the technical notes for details on these changes.

Data on external debt are compiled directly by the Bank on the basis of reports from developing member countries through the Debtor Reporting System. Other data are drawn mainly from the United Nations and its specialized agencies and the International Monetary Fund (IMF); country reports to the World Bank and Bank staff estimates are also used to improve currentness or consistency. For most countries, national accounts estimates are obtained from member governments by World Bank staff on economic missions and are, in some instances, adjusted by Bank staff to conform to international definitions and concepts to provide better consistency.

For ease of reference, ratios and rates of growth are shown; absolute values are reported in only a few instances in the World Development Indicators but are usually available from other World Bank publications, notably the recently released 1988–89 edition of the *World Tables*. Most growth rates are calculated for two periods, 1965–80 and 1980–87, and are computed, unless noted otherwise, by using the least-squares regression method. Because this method takes all observations in a period into account, the resulting growth rates reflect general trends that are not unduly influenced by exceptional values, particularly at the end points. To exclude the effects of inflation, constant price economic indicators are used in calculating growth rates. Details of this methodology are given at the beginning of the technical notes. Data in italics indicate that they are for years or periods other than those specified—up to two

years earlier for economic indicators and up to three years on either side for social indicators, since the latter tend to be collected less regularly but change less dramatically over short periods of time. All dollar figures are U.S. dollars. The various methods used for converting from national currency figures are described, where appropriate, in the technical notes.

Differences between figures in this year's and last year's edition reflect not only updating revisions to the countries themselves, but also revisions to historical series and changes in methodology. In addition, the Bank also reviews methodologies in an effort to improve the international comparability and analytical significance of the indicators, as explained in the technical notes.

As in the *World Development Report* itself, the main criterion used to classify economies in the World Development Indicators is GNP per capita. These income groupings are analytically useful for distinguishing economies at different stages of development. Many of the economies are further classified by geographical location. Other classifications include 17 highly indebted countries and all oil exporters. The major classifications used in the tables this year are 42 low-income economies with per capita incomes of $480 or less in 1987, 53 middle-income economies with per capita incomes of $481–$5,999, and 25 high-income economies. For a final group of 10 nonreporting nonmember economies, paucity of data, differences in method for computing national income, and difficulties of conversion are such that only aggregates, where available, are shown in the main tables. Country-specific data for selected indicators for these countries, however, are included in Box A.2 in the technical notes.

Economies with populations of less than 1 million are not shown separately in the main tables, but basic indicators for these countries and territories are in a separate table in Box A.1.

The summary measures are overall estimates: countries for which individual estimates are not shown, because of size, nonreporting, or insufficient history, have been included by assuming they follow the trend of reporting countries during such periods. This gives a more consistent aggregate measure by standardizing country coverage for each period shown. Group aggregates include countries with less than 1 million population, even though country-specific data for these countries do not appear in the tables. Where missing information accounts for a significant share of the overall estimate, however, the group measure is reported as not available.

Throughout the World Development Indicators, the data for China do not include Taiwan, China. However, footnotes to Tables 14–18 provide estimates of the international transactions for Taiwan, China.

The table format of this edition follows that used in previous years. In each group, economies are listed in ascending order of GNP per capita, except those for which no such figure can be calculated. These are italicized and in alphabetical order at the end of the group deemed to be appropriate. This order is used in all tables except Table 19, which covers only OPEC and high-income OECD countries. The alphabetical list in the key shows the reference number for each economy; here, too, italics indicate economies with no estimates of GNP per capita. Economies in the high-income group marked by the symbol † are those classified

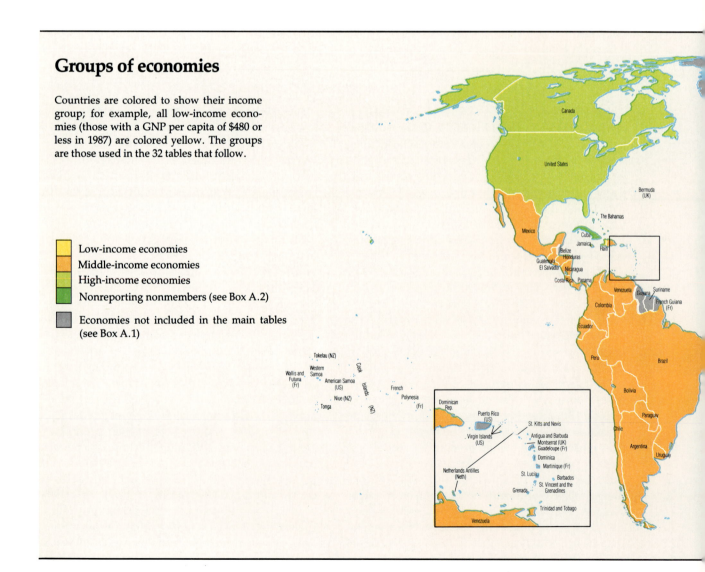

Groups of economies

Countries are colored to show their income group; for example, all low-income economies (those with a GNP per capita of $480 or less in 1987) are colored yellow. The groups are those used in the 32 tables that follow.

Low-income economies
Middle-income economies
High-income economies
Nonreporting nonmembers (see Box A.2)
Economies not included in the main tables (see Box A.1)

by the United Nations or otherwise regarded by their authorities as developing. In the colored bands are summary measures—totals, weighted averages, or median values—calculated for groups of economies if data are adequate.

The methodology used for computing the summary measures is described in the technical notes. For these numbers, w indicates that the summary measures are weighted averages; m, median values; and t, totals. The coverage of economies is not uniform for all indicators, and the variation from measures of central tendency can be large; therefore readers should exercise caution in comparing the summary measures for different indicators, groups, and years or periods.

The technical notes and footnotes to tables should be referred to in any use of the data. These notes outline the methods, concepts, definitions, and data sources used in compiling the tables. The bibliography gives details of the data sources, which contain comprehensive definitions and descriptions of concepts used. It should also be noted that country notes to the *World Tables* provide additional explanations of sources used, breaks in comparability, and other exceptions to standard statistical practices that have been identified by Bank staff on national accounts and international transactions.

Comments and questions relating to the World Development Indicators should be addressed to:

Socio-Economic Data Division
International Economics Department
The World Bank
1818 H Street, N.W.
Washington, D.C. 20433.

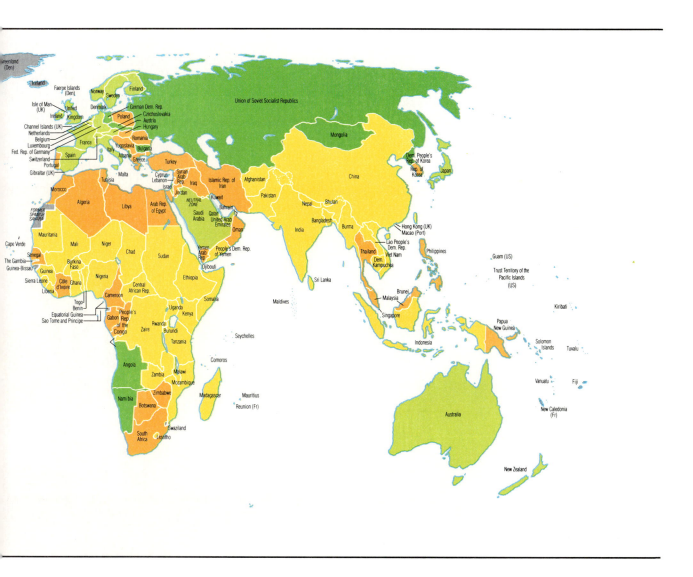

Population

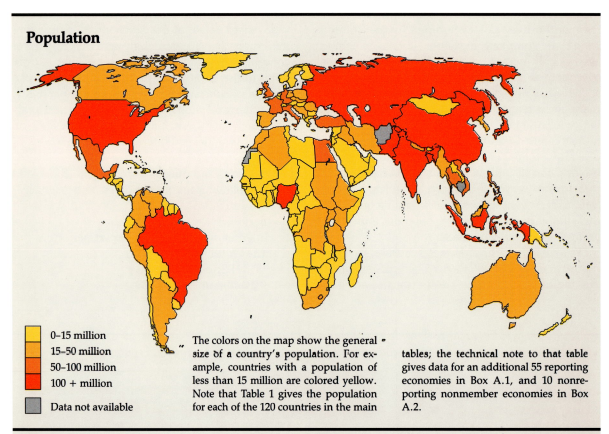

0–15 million
15–50 million
50–100 million
100 + million

Data not available

The colors on the map show the general size of a country's population. For example, countries with a population of less than 15 million are colored yellow. Note that Table 1 gives the population for each of the 120 countries in the main tables; the technical note to that table gives data for an additional 55 reporting economies in Box A.1, and 10 nonreporting nonmember economies in Box A.2.

Fertility and mortality

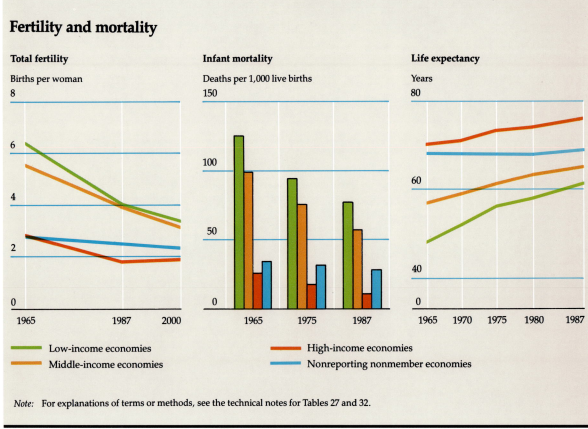

Total fertility

Births per woman

Infant mortality

Deaths per 1,000 live births

Life expectancy

Years

Low-income economies

Middle-income economies

High-income economies

Nonreporting nonmember economies

Note: For explanations of terms or methods, see the technical notes for Tables 27 and 32.

Share of agriculture in GDP

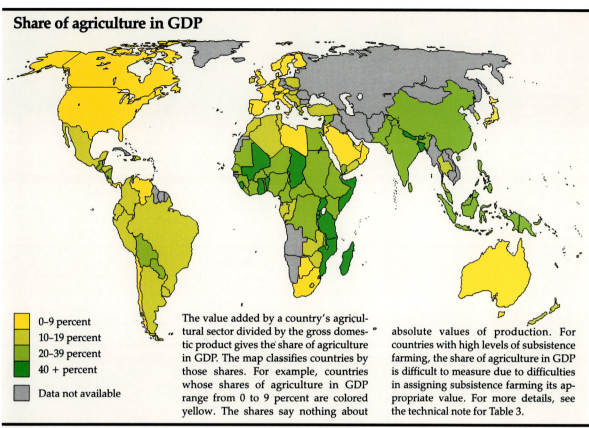

- ☐ 0–9 percent
- ☐ 10–19 percent
- ☐ 20–39 percent
- ☐ 40 + percent
- ☐ Data not available

The value added by a country's agricultural sector divided by the gross domestic product gives the share of agriculture in GDP. The map classifies countries by those shares. For example, countries whose shares of agriculture in GDP range from 0 to 9 percent are colored yellow. The shares say nothing about absolute values of production. For countries with high levels of subsistence farming, the share of agriculture in GDP is difficult to measure due to difficulties in assigning subsistence farming its appropriate value. For more details, see the technical note for Table 3.

External balances of low- and middle-income countries

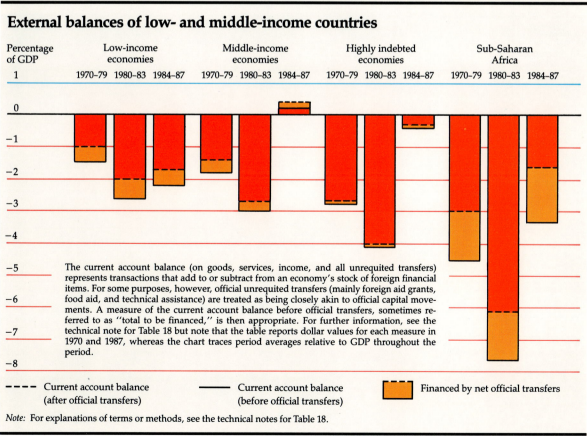

The current account balance (on goods, services, income, and all unrequited transfers) represents transactions that add to or subtract from an economy's stock of foreign financial items. For some purposes, however, official unrequited transfers (mainly foreign aid grants, food aid, and technical assistance) are treated as being closely akin to official capital movements. A measure of the current account balance before official transfers, sometimes referred to as "total to be financed," is then appropriate. For further information, see the technical note for Table 18 but note that the table reports dollar values for each measure in 1970 and 1987, whereas the chart traces period averages relative to GDP throughout the period.

- - - - Current account balance (after official transfers)
- —— Current account balance (before official transfers)
- ☐ Financed by net official transfers

Note: For explanations of terms or methods, see the technical notes for Table 18.

Table 1. Basic indicators

		Population (millions) mid-1987	Area (thousands of square kilometers)	GNP per capita[a] Dollars 1987	GNP per capita[a] Average annual growth rate (percent) 1965-87	Average annual rate of inflation[a] (percent) 1965-80	Average annual rate of inflation[a] (percent) 1980-87	Life expectancy at birth (years) 1987
	Low-income economies	**2,822.9 t**	**37,015 t**	**290 w**	**3.1 w**	**8.9 w**	**8.6 w**	**61 w**
	China and India	**1,866.1 t**	**12,849 t**	**300 w**	**3.9 w**	**2.9 w**	**5.5 w**	**65 w**
	Other low-income	**956.9 t**	**24,166 t**	**280 w**	**1.5 w**	**18.2 w**	**13.3 w**	**54 w**
1	Ethiopia	44.8	1,222	130	0.1	3.4	2.6	47
2	Bhutan	1.3	47	150	..	..	..	48
3	Chad	5.3	1,284	150	−2.0	6.3	5.3	46
4	Zaire	32.6	2,345	150	−2.4	24.7	53.5	52
5	Bangladesh	106.1	144	160	0.3	14.9	11.1	51
6	Malawi	7.9	118	160	1.4	7.0	12.4	46
7	Nepal	17.6	141	160	0.5	7.8	8.8	51
8	Lao PDR	3.8	237	170	..	..	46.5	48
9	Mozambique	14.6	802	170	..	..	26.9	48
10	Tanzania	23.9	945	180	−0.4	9.9	24.9	53
11	Burkina Faso	8.3	274	190	1.6	6.2	4.4	47
12	Madagascar	10.9	587	210	−1.8	7.9	17.4	54
13	Mali	7.8	1,240	210	..	..	4.2	47
14	Burundi	5.0	28	250	1.6	8.5	7.5	49
15	Zambia	7.2	753	250	−2.1	6.4	28.7	53
16	Niger	6.8	1,267	260	−2.2	7.5	4.1	45
17	Uganda	15.7	236	260	−2.7	21.2	95.2	48
18	China	1,068.5	9,561	290	5.2	0.0	4.2	69
19	Somalia	5.7	638	290	0.3	10.5	37.8	47
20	Togo	3.2	57	290	0.0	6.9	6.6	53
21	India	797.5	3,288	300	1.8	7.6	7.7	58
22	Rwanda	6.4	26	300	1.6	12.4	4.5	49
23	Sierra Leone	3.8	72	300	0.2	8.0	50.0	41
24	Benin	4.3	113	310	0.2	7.4	8.2	50
25	Central African Rep.	2.7	623	330	−0.3	8.5	7.9	50
26	Kenya	22.1	583	330	1.9	7.3	10.3	58
27	Sudan	23.1	2,506	330	−0.5	11.5	31.7	50
28	Pakistan	102.5	796	350	2.5	10.3	7.3	55
29	Haiti	6.1	28	360	0.5	7.3	7.9	55
30	Lesotho	1.6	30	370	4.7	8.0	12.3	56
31	Nigeria	106.6	924	370	1.1	13.7	10.1	51
32	Ghana	13.6	239	390	−1.6	22.8	48.3	54
33	Sri Lanka	16.4	66	400	3.0	9.4	11.8	70
34	Yemen, PDR	2.3	333	420	..	..	5.0	51
35	Mauritania	1.9	1,031	440	−0.4	7.7	9.8	46
36	Indonesia	171.4	1,905	450	4.5	34.2	8.5	60
37	Liberia	2.3	111	450	−1.6	6.3	1.5	54
38	*Afghanistan*	..	648	..	..	4.9	..	..
39	*Burma*	39.3	677	..	..	..	..	60
40	*Guinea*	6.5	246	..	..	2.9	..	42
41	*Kampuchea, Dem.*	..	181	..	..	..	..	..
42	*Viet Nam*	65.0	330	..	..	..	..	66
	Middle-income economies	**1,038.5 t**	**36,118 t**	**1,810 w**	**2.5 w**	**20.4 w**	**62.3 w**	**65 w**
	Lower-middle-income	**609.6 t**	**16,781 t**	**1,200 w**	**2.2 w**	**16.9 w**	**36.7 w**	**64 w**
43	Senegal	7.0	196	520	−0.6	6.5	9.1	48
44	Bolivia	6.7	1,099	580	−0.5	15.7	601.8	53
45	Zimbabwe	9.0	391	580	0.9	6.4	12.4	58
46	Philippines	58.4	300	590	1.7	11.7	16.7	63
47	Yemen Arab Rep.	8.5	195	590	..	..	11.4	51
48	Morocco	23.3	447	610	1.8	6.1	7.3	61
49	Egypt, Arab Rep.	50.1	1,002	680	3.5	7.3	9.2	61
50	Papua New Guinea	3.7	462	700	0.8	7.5	4.4	54
51	Dominican Rep.	6.7	49	730	2.3	6.8	16.3	66
52	Côte d'Ivoire	11.1	322	740	1.0	9.5	4.4	52
53	Honduras	4.7	112	810	0.7	5.6	4.9	64
54	Nicaragua	3.5	130	830	−2.5	8.9	86.6	63
55	Thailand	53.6	514	850	3.9	6.3	2.8	64
56	El Salvador	4.9	21	860	−0.4	7.0	16.5	62
57	Congo, People's Rep.	2.0	342	870	4.2	6.6	1.8	59
58	Jamaica	2.4	11	940	−1.5	12.8	19.4	74
59	Guatemala	8.4	109	950	1.2	7.1	12.7	62
60	Cameroon	10.9	475	970	3.8	8.9	8.1	56
61	Paraguay	3.9	407	990	3.4	9.4	21.0	67
62	Ecuador	9.9	284	1,040	3.2	10.9	29.5	65
63	Botswana	1.1	582	1,050	8.9	8.1	8.4	59
64	Tunisia	7.6	164	1,180	3.6	6.7	8.2	65
65	Turkey	52.6	781	1,210	2.6	20.7	37.4	64
66	Colombia	29.5	1,139	1,240	2.7	17.4	23.7	66
67	Chile	12.5	757	1,310	0.2	129.9	20.6	72

Note: For data comparability and coverage, see the technical notes. Figures in italics are for years other than those specified.

		Population (millions) mid-1987	Area (thousands of square kilometers)	GNP per capita[a] Dollars 1987	GNP per capita[a] Average annual growth rate (percent) 1965–87	Average annual rate of inflation[a] (percent) 1965–80	Average annual rate of inflation[a] (percent) 1980–87	Life expectancy at birth (years) 1987
68	Peru	20.2	1,285	1,470	0.2	20.5	101.5	61
69	Mauritius	1.0	2	1,490	3.2	11.4	8.1	67
70	Jordan	3.8	98	1,560	. .	. .	2.8	66
71	Costa Rica	2.6	51	1,610	1.5	11.3	28.6	74
72	Syrian Arab Rep.	11.2	185	1,640	3.3	8.3	11.0	65
73	Malaysia	16.5	330	1,810	4.1	4.9	1.1	70
74	Mexico	81.9	1,973	1,830	2.5	13.0	68.9	69
75	South Africa	33.1	1,221	1,890	0.6	10.0	13.8	60
76	Poland	37.7	313	1,930	. .	. .	29.2	71
77	*Lebanon*	. .	10	. .	. .	9.3	. .	. .
	Upper-middle-income	**432.5** *t*	**20,272** *t*	**2,710** *w*	**2.9** *w*	**23.2** *w*	**86.8** *w*	**67** *w*
78	Brazil	141.4	8,512	2,020	4.1	31.3	166.3	65
79	Uruguay	3.0	176	2,190	1.4	57.8	54.5	71
80	Hungary	10.6	93	2,240	3.8	2.6	5.7	70
81	Panama	2.3	77	2,240	2.4	5.4	3.3	72
82	Argentina	31.1	2,767	2,390	0.1	78.2	298.7	71
83	Yugoslavia	23.4	256	2,480	3.7	15.3	57.2	71
84	Algeria	23.1	2,382	2,680	3.2	9.8	5.6	63
85	Korea, Rep.	42.1	98	2,690	6.4	18.8	5.0	69
86	Gabon	1.1	268	2,700	1.1	12.7	2.6	52
87	Portugal	10.2	92	2,830	3.2	11.5	20.8	73
88	Venezuela	18.3	912	3,230	−0.9	10.4	11.4	70
89	Greece	10.0	132	4,020	3.1	10.5	19.7	76
90	Trinidad and Tobago	1.2	5	4,210	1.3	14.0	6.2	70
91	Libya	4.1	1,760	5,460	−2.3	15.4	0.1	61
92	Oman	1.3	212	5,810	8.0	17.6	−6.5	55
93	*Iran, Islamic Rep.*	47.0	1,648	. .	. .	15.6	. .	63
94	*Iraq*	17.1	435	. .	. .	. .	. .	64
95	*Romania*	22.9	238	. .	. .	. .	. .	70
	Low- and middle-income	**3,861.4** *t*	**73,133** *t*	**700** *w*	**2.7** *w*	**16.5** *w*	**43.9** *w*	**62** *w*
	Sub-Saharan Africa	441.7 *t*	20,999 *t*	330 *w*	0.6 *w*	12.3 *w*	15.2 *w*	51 *w*
	East Asia	1,512.7 *t*	14,019 *t*	470 *w*	5.1 *w*	8.8 *w*	5.4 *w*	68 *w*
	South Asia	1,080.9 *t*	5,158 *t*	290 *w*	1.8 *w*	8.4 *w*	7.8 *w*	57 *w*
	Europe, M.East, & N.Africa	389.6 *t*	11,430 *t*	1,940 *w*	2.5 *w*	13.1 *w*	23.7 *w*	64 *w*
	Latin America & Caribbean	403.5 *t*	20,306 *t*	1,790 *w*	2.1 *w*	29.3 *w*	109.1 *w*	66 *w*
	17 highly indebted	**582.5** *t*	**21,213** *t*	**1,430** *w*	**2.0** *w*	**26.0** *w*	**91.2** *w*	**63** *w*
	High-income economies	**777.2** *t*	**33,757** *t*	**14,430** *w*	**2.3** *w*	**7.9** *w*	**5.2** *w*	**76** *w*
	OECD members	746.6 *t*	31,085 *t*	14,670 *w*	2.3 *w*	7.6 *w*	5.0 *w*	76 *w*
	†Other	30.6 *t*	2,673 *t*	7,880 *w*	3.5 *w*	15.9 *w*	13.3 *w*	70 *w*
96	Spain	38.8	505	6,010	2.3	12.3	10.7	77
97	Ireland	3.6	70	6,120	2.0	12.0	10.2	74
98	†Saudi Arabia	12.6	2,150	6,200	4.0	17.2	−2.8	63
99	†Israel	4.4	21	6,800	2.5	25.2	159.0	75
100	New Zealand	3.3	269	7,750	0.9	10.2	11.5	75
101	†Singapore	2.6	1	7,940	7.2	4.9	1.3	73
102	†Hong Kong	5.6	1	8,070[b]	6.2[b]	8.1	6.7	76
103	Italy	57.4	301	10,350	2.7	11.2	11.5	77
104	United Kingdom	56.9	245	10,420	1.7	11.2	5.7	75
105	Australia	16.2	7,687	11,100	1.8	9.2	7.8	76
106	Belgium	9.9	31	11,480	2.6	6.7	5.1	75
107	Netherlands	14.7	37	11,860	2.1	7.3	2.3	77
108	Austria	7.6	84	11,980	3.1	5.8	4.3	74
109	France	55.6	547	12,790	2.7	8.0	7.7	77
110	Germany, Fed. Rep.	61.2	249	14,400	2.5	5.2	2.9	75
111	Finland	4.9	337	14,470	3.2	10.5	7.2	76
112	†Kuwait	1.9	18	14,610	−4.0	16.3	−4.6	73
113	Denmark	5.1	43	14,930	1.9	9.3	6.8	75
114	Canada	25.9	9,976	15,160	2.7	7.1	5.0	77
115	Sweden	8.4	450	15,550	1.8	8.0	7.9	77
116	Japan	122.1	378	15,760	4.2	7.8	1.4	78
117	†United Arab Emirates	1.5	84	15,830	. .	. .	−0.3	71
118	Norway	4.2	324	17,190	3.5	7.7	6.1	77
119	United States	243.8	9,373	18,530	1.5	6.5	4.3	75
120	Switzerland	6.5	41	21,330	1.4	5.3	3.9	77
	Total reporting economies	**4,638.6** *t*	**106,890** *t*	**3,010** *w*	**1.5** *w*	**9.8** *w*	**13.7** *w*	**65** *w*
	Oil exporters	578.4 *t*	17,303 *t*	1,520 *w*	2.1 *w*	15.0 *w*	20.1 *w*	61 *w*
	Nonreporting nonmembers	**371.5** *t*	**26,645** *t*	. .	. .	. .	. .	**69** *w*

Note: For countries with populations of less than 1 million, see Box A.1. † Economies classified by the United Nations or otherwise regarded by their authorities as developing. a. See the technical notes. b. GNP data refer to GDP.

Table 2. Growth of production

	GDP		Agriculture		Industry		(Manufacturing)[a]		Services, etc.	
	1965–80	1980–87	1965–80	1980–87	1965–80	1980–87	1965–80	1980–87	1965–80	1980–87
Low-income economies	5.4 w	6.1 w	2.7 w	4.0 w	8.7 w	8.6 w	8.1 w	10.3 w	5.7 w	5.1 w
China and India	5.3 w	8.5 w	2.9 w	5.1 w	8.0 w	12.0 w	7.9 w	11.7 w	5.7 w	6.9 w
Other low-income	5.5 w	1.7 w	2.3 w	1.9 w	10.0 w	0.2 w	9.0 w	3.9 w	5.7 w	2.9 w
1 Ethiopia	2.7	0.9	1.2	−2.1	3.5	3.8	5.1	3.8	5.2	3.5
2 Bhutan	..	..	..	..	..	..	..	..	..	..
3 Chad[b]	0.1	5.1	..	2.6	..	10.0	..	8.5	..	6.3
4 Zaire[b]	1.3	1.6	..	3.2	..	3.6	..	0.6	..	−1.2
5 Bangladesh[b]	2.4	3.8	1.5	2.4	3.8	4.7	6.8	2.4	3.4	5.2
6 Malawi	5.8	2.6	..	2.5	..	1.9	..	..	..	3.0
7 Nepal	1.9	4.7	1.1	4.2	..	..	..	..	..	..
8 Lao PDR	..	5.3	..	..	..	..	..	..	..	..
9 Mozambique	..	−2.6	..	−11.1	..	−8.4	..	..	..	6.2
10 Tanzania	3.7	1.7	1.6	3.8	4.2	−2.4	5.6	−3.5	6.7	0.8
11 Burkina Faso	..	5.6	..	6.1	..	3.9	..	..	..	5.8
12 Madagascar[b]	1.6	0.3	..	2.2	..	−2.0	..	..	..	−0.5
13 Mali[b]	3.9	3.4	2.8	0.3	1.8	9.8	..	..	7.6	5.9
14 Burundi	3.5	2.6	3.3	1.7	7.8	4.9	6.0	6.6	2.7	3.5
15 Zambia[b]	1.9	−0.1	2.2	3.2	2.1	−0.7	5.3	0.8	1.5	−0.6
16 Niger[b]	0.3	−1.9	−3.4	2.8	11.4	−4.3	..	−0.9	3.4	−8.0
17 Uganda	0.8	0.4	1.2	−0.5	−4.1	1.4	−3.7	..	1.1	3.0
18 China	6.4	10.4	3.0	7.4	10.0	13.2	9.5[c]	12.6[c]	7.0	7.6
19 Somalia	3.3	2.2	..	2.8	..	1.0	..	−0.5	..	0.9
20 Togo[b]	4.5	−0.5	1.9	0.8	6.8	−1.6	..	..	5.4	−0.7
21 India	3.7	4.6	2.8	0.8	4.0	7.2	4.3	8.3	4.6	6.1
22 Rwanda[b]	5.0	2.4	..	1.1	..	4.8	..	2.5	..	3.9
23 Sierra Leone	2.6	0.7	2.3	1.6	−1.0	−2.3	4.3	0.6	5.8	1.3
24 Benin	2.1	2.8	..	2.5	..	8.3	..	4.6	..	1.3
25 Central African Rep.	2.6	2.0	2.1	2.4	5.3	2.2	..	0.3	2.0	1.6
26 Kenya	6.4	3.8	4.9	3.4	9.8	3.0	10.5	4.3	6.4	4.4
27 Sudan	3.8	−0.1	2.9	0.8	3.1	2.1	..	1.6	4.9	−1.3
28 Pakistan	5.1	6.6	3.3	3.4	6.4	9.1	5.7	8.9	5.9	7.1
29 Haiti[b]	2.9	−0.4	..	..	..	..	..	..	..	..
30 Lesotho	5.9	2.3	..	0.4	..	0.4	..	12.9	..	4.0
31 Nigeria	6.9	−1.7	1.7	0.6	13.1	−4.4	14.6	−2.1	7.6	−0.3
32 Ghana[b]	1.4	1.4	1.6	0.0	1.4	0.1	2.5	1.3	1.1	4.2
33 Sri Lanka	4.0	4.6	2.7	3.1	4.7	4.2	3.2	6.2	4.6	5.7
34 Yemen, PDR[b]	..	..	..	..	..	..	..	..	..	..
35 Mauritania	2.0	1.4	−2.0	1.5	2.2	5.1	..	..	6.5	−1.3
36 Indonesia[b]	8.0	3.6	4.3	3.0	11.9	2.1	12.0	7.8	7.3	5.6
37 Liberia	3.3	−1.3	5.5	1.2	2.2	−6.0	10.0	−5.0	2.4	−0.8
38 Afghanistan	2.9	..	..	..	..	..	..	..	..	..
39 Burma	..	..	..	..	..	..	..	..	..	..
40 Guinea[b]	3.8	..	..	..	..	..	..	..	..	..
41 Kampuchea, Dem.	..	..	..	..	..	..	..	..	..	..
42 Viet Nam	..	..	..	..	..	..	..	..	..	..
Middle-income economies	6.2 w	2.8 w	3.4 w	2.5 w	6.0 w	2.9 w	8.1 w	3.0 w	7.3 w	3.1 w
Lower-middle-income	5.7 w	2.1 w	3.5 w	2.3 w	6.0 w	1.8 w	6.9 w	2.1 w	6.3 w	2.3 w
43 Senegal[b]	2.1	3.3	1.4	4.2	4.8	4.3	3.4	4.3	1.3	2.4
44 Bolivia[b]	4.5	−2.1	3.8	2.5	3.7	−6.6	5.4	−6.9	5.6	−1.1
45 Zimbabwe	4.4	2.4	..	2.3	..	1.4	..	1.8	..	3.3
46 Philippines[b]	5.9	−0.5	4.6	1.8	8.0	−2.8	7.5	−1.1	5.2	0.0
47 Yemen Arab Rep.[b]	..	5.6	..	2.3	..	8.7	..	14.2	..	6.0
48 Morocco[b]	5.4	3.2	2.2	3.6	6.1	1.2	5.9	1.5	6.5	4.3
49 Egypt, Arab Rep.	6.8	6.3	2.7	2.7	6.9	5.5	..	6.1	9.4	8.1
50 Papua New Guinea[b]	4.6	3.0	3.2	2.2	..	5.3	..	1.0	..	2.0
51 Dominican Rep.[b]	7.3	1.6	4.6	1.0	10.9	1.0	8.9	0.4	6.7	1.3
52 Côte d'Ivoire	6.8	2.2	3.3	1.6	10.4	−2.4	9.1	8.2	8.6	4.2
53 Honduras	5.0	1.3	2.0	1.7	6.8	1.2	7.5	1.9	6.2	1.1
54 Nicaragua[b]	2.6	−0.3	3.3	−0.2	4.2	0.4	5.2	0.6	1.4	−0.9
55 Thailand[b]	7.2	5.6	4.6	3.7	9.5	5.9	11.2	6.0	7.6	6.4
56 El Salvador[b]	4.3	−0.4	3.6	−1.6	5.3	0.0	4.6	−0.3	4.3	0.2
57 Congo, People's Rep.[b]	6.4	5.5	3.1	1.5	10.3	10.9	..	9.7	4.7	−1.9
58 Jamaica[b]	1.3	0.4	0.5	1.4	−0.1	−0.4	0.4	1.7	2.7	0.8
59 Guatemala[b]	5.9	−0.7	..	..	..	..	..	..	..	..
60 Cameroon[b]	5.1	7.0	4.2	2.4	7.8	11.0	7.0	8.5	4.8	6.9
61 Paraguay[b]	6.9	1.3	4.9	2.0	9.1	−0.3	7.0	0.8	7.5	1.9
62 Ecuador[b]	8.7	1.5	3.4	3.6	13.7	1.4	11.5	0.2	7.6	0.9
63 Botswana[b]	14.2	13.0	9.7	−7.8	24.0	19.2	13.5	4.5	11.5	9.5
64 Tunisia	6.6	3.6	5.5	4.2	7.4	2.7	9.9	6.1	6.5	4.1
65 Turkey	6.3	5.2	3.2	3.3	7.2	6.7	7.5	8.2	7.6	5.0
66 Colombia	5.6	2.9	4.3	2.1	5.5	5.2	6.2	3.2	6.4	2.0
67 Chile[b]	1.9	1.0	1.6	3.6	0.8	1.5	0.6	0.9	2.7	0.3

Note: For data comparability and coverage, see the technical notes. Figures in italics are for years other than those specified.

		GDP		Agriculture		Industry		(Manufacturing)[a]		Services, etc.	
		1965–80	*1980–87*	*1965–80*	*1980–87*	*1965–80*	*1980–87*	*1965–80*	*1980–87*	*1965–80*	*1980–87*
68	Peru[b]	3.9	1.2	1.0	3.0	4.4	0.5	3.8	1.5	4.3	1.4
69	Mauritius	5.6	5.5	..	5.2	..	8.7	..	10.9	..	4.1
70	Jordan	..	4.3	..	4.1	..	4.5	..	3.1	..	4.3
71	Costa Rica[b]	6.2	1.8	4.2	1.7	8.7	2.0	..	..	6.0	1.7
72	Syrian Arab Rep.[b]	8.7	0.3	4.8	−1.1	11.8	1.5	..	..	9.0	0.3
73	Malaysia[b]	7.4	4.5	..	3.4	..	5.8	..	6.3	..	3.8
74	Mexico[b]	6.5	0.5	3.2	1.4	7.6	−0.3	7.4	0.0	6.6	0.8
75	South Africa	4.1	1.0	..	0.3	..	−0.1	..	−0.5	..	2.3
76	Poland[b]	..	..	..	..	..	..	..	..	..	..
77	*Lebanon*[b]	−1.2	..	..	..	..	..	..	..	..	..
	Upper-middle-income	**6.7** *w*	**3.4** *w*	**3.4** *w*	**2.6** *w*	**5.8** *w*	**3.7** *w*	**9.2** *w*	**4.1** *w*	**8.2** *w*	**3.8** *w*
78	Brazil	9.0	3.3	3.8	2.6	9.8	2.4	9.6	*1.2*	10.0	4.1
79	Uruguay	2.4	−1.3	1.0	0.2	3.1	−3.2	..	−1.6	2.3	−0.6
80	Hungary[b]	5.6	1.7	2.7	2.5	6.4	1.3	..	..	6.2	1.8
81	Panama[b]	5.5	2.6	2.4	2.5	5.9	−0.8	4.7	0.7	6.0	3.5
82	Argentina[b]	3.5	−0.3	1.4	1.6	3.3	−0.9	2.7	0.0	4.0	−0.3
83	Yugoslavia	6.0	1.5	3.1	1.4	7.8	1.4	..	..	5.5	1.6
84	Algeria[b]	7.5	3.8	5.6	6.0	8.1	4.3	9.5	8.5	7.2	2.6
85	Korea, Rep.[b]	9.5	8.6	3.0	4.4	16.5	10.8	18.7	10.6	9.3	7.7
86	Gabon[b]	9.5	0.6	..	..	..	..	..	..	..	..
87	Portugal	..	1.4	..	−0.9	..	*1.0*	..	..	..	*1.4*
88	Venezuela[b]	3.7	0.2	3.9	3.5	1.5	−0.9	5.8	3.0	6.3	0.8
89	Greece	5.6	1.4	2.3	−0.1	7.1	0.4	8.4	0.0	6.2	2.5
90	Trinidad and Tobago	*5.1*	−6.1	*0.0*	4.5	*5.0*	−8.6	*2.6*	−9.5	*5.8*	−3.4
91	Libya	4.2	..	10.7	..	1.2	..	13.7	..	15.5	..
92	Oman[b]	15.2	12.7	..	9.4	..	*15.1*	..	*37.9*	..	*12.2*
93	*Iran, Islamic Rep.*	6.2	..	4.5	..	2.4	..	10.0	..	13.6	..
94	*Iraq*	..	..	..	..	..	..	..	..	..	..
95	*Romania*	..	..	..	..	..	..	..	..	..	..
	Low- and middle-income	**5.9** *w*	**4.0** *w*	**3.0** *w*	**3.4** *w*	**6.7** *w*	**5.1** *w*	**8.1** *w*	**6.0** *w*	**6.9** *w*	**3.6** *w*
	Sub-Saharan Africa	**5.1** *w*	**0.4** *w*	**1.7** *w*	**1.2** *w*	**9.5** *w*	**-1.2** *w*	**8.8** *w*	**0.6** *w*	**5.5** *w*	**1.2** *w*
	East Asia	**7.2** *w*	**8.0** *w*	**3.3** *w*	**5.9** *w*	**10.8** *w*	**10.1** *w*	**10.7** *w*	**10.4** *w*	**7.6** *w*	**6.4** *w*
	South Asia	**3.8** *w*	**4.8** *w*	**2.7** *w*	**1.4** *w*	**4.3** *w*	**7.2** *w*	**4.5** *w*	**8.0** *w*	**4.7** *w*	**6.1** *w*
	Europe, M.East, & N.Africa	**6.2** *w*	**..**	**3.5** *w*	**..**	**5.0** *w*	**..**	**..**	**..**	**8.6** *w*	**..**
	Latin America & Caribbean	**6.0** *w*	**1.4** *w*	**3.2** *w*	**2.2** *w*	**6.0** *w*	**0.8** *w*	**6.9** *w*	**0.6** *w*	**6.7** *w*	**1.8** *w*
	17 highly indebted	**6.1** *w*	**1.1** *w*	**2.8** *w*	**1.8** *w*	**6.9** *w*	**0.2** *w*	**7.2** *w*	**0.4** *w*	**6.7** *w*	**1.7** *w*
	High-income economies	**3.7** *w*	**2.6** *w*	**0.8** *w*	**2.8** *w*	**3.2** *w*	**2.3** *w*	**3.6** *w*	**3.3** *w*	**3.7** *w*	**2.7** *w*
	OECD members	**3.6** *w*	**2.7** *w*	**0.8** *w*	**2.6** *w*	**3.1** *w*	**2.5** *w*	**3.6** *w*	**3.2** *w*	**3.7** *w*	**2.7** *w*
	†Other	**8.1**	**−2.6** *w*	**..**	**10.1** *w*	**..**	**−8.1** *w*	**..**	**4.8** *w*	**..**	**4.1** *w*
96	Spain[b]	4.6	2.1	2.6	*0.9*	5.1	*0.4*	5.9	*0.4*	4.1	*2.1*
97	Ireland	5.3	*0.9*	..	2.2	..	*1.7*	..	..	..	−0.0
98	†Saudi Arabia[b]	11.3	−5.3	4.1	*10.3*	11.6	−*10.4*	8.1	*6.1*	10.5	*4.4*
99	†Israel[b]	6.8	2.2	..	..	..	..	..	..	..	..
100	New Zealand[b]	2.5	2.9	..	*3.1*	..	*4.0*	..	*3.3*	..	*2.1*
101	†Singapore[b]	10.1	5.4	2.8	−3.9	11.9	4.0	13.2	3.3	9.4	6.4
102	†Hong Kong	8.6	*5.8*	..	..	..	..	..	..	..	..
103	Italy[b]	3.8	2.1	0.8	*0.8*	4.0	0.5	5.1	0.9	4.1	2.9
104	United Kingdom	2.4	2.6	*1.6*[d]	*3.2*	−0.5[d]	*1.8*	−*1.2*[d]	*1.3*	2.2[d]	2.6
105	Australia[b]	4.2	3.2	2.7	*5.0*	3.0	*1.9*	1.3	0.4	5.7	*3.1*
106	Belgium[b]	3.9	1.3	0.5	2.6	4.4	1.1	4.7	2.3	3.8	1.2
107	Netherlands[b]	4.1	1.5	*4.7*	5.4	*4.0*	..	*4.8*	..	*4.4*	..
108	Austria[b]	4.3	1.6	2.2	0.8	4.5	1.1	4.7	1.6	4.4	1.9
109	France[b]	4.3	1.6	1.0	2.6	4.3	−*0.1*	5.2	−*0.5*	4.6	2.3
110	Germany, Fed. Rep.[b]	3.3	1.6	1.4	1.9	2.8	0.4	3.3	1.0	3.7	2.1
111	Finland	4.0	2.8	0.0	−1.1	4.4	2.7	4.9	3.1	4.7	3.9
112	†Kuwait[b]	1.3	−1.1	..	23.6	..	−2.3	..	*1.4*	..	−0.9
113	Denmark	2.9	2.5	*0.8*	4.3	*1.8*	3.1	*3.1*	2.2	*3.5*	2.2
114	Canada	5.0	2.9	0.7	2.6	3.5	3.0	3.8	3.6	6.7	2.1
115	Sweden	2.9	1.3	−0.2	1.5	2.3	2.6	2.4	2.5	3.4	1.8
116	Japan[b]	6.3	3.8	0.8	0.8	8.5	4.9	9.4	6.7	5.2	3.1
117	†United Arab Emirates	..	−4.3	..	*11.6*	..	−*8.4*	..	*9.6*	..	*4.8*
118	Norway	4.4	3.7	−0.4	*2.0*	5.6	*4.4*	2.6	*1.8*	4.2	*3.5*
119	United States[b]	2.7	3.1	1.0	*3.5*	1.7	*2.9*	2.5	*3.9*	3.4	*3.0*
120	Switzerland[b]	2.0	1.7	..	..	..	..	..	..	..	..
	Total reporting economies	**4.1** *w*	**2.9** *w*	**2.2** *w*	**3.2** *w*	**3.9** *w*	**2.5** *w*	**4.3** *w*	**3.7** *w*	**4.2** *w*	**2.9** *w*
	Oil exporters	**6.5** *w*	**0.7** *w*	**3.1** *w*	**2.4** *w*	**6.3** *w*	**−1.5** *w*	**7.7** *w*	**2.8** *w*	**7.7** *w*	**2.7** *w*
	Nonreporting nonmembers	**..**	**..**	**..**	**..**	**..**	**..**	**..**	**..**	**..**	**..**

Average annual growth rate (percent)

a. Because manufacturing is generally the most dynamic part of the industrial sector, its growth rate is shown separately.   b. GDP and its components are at purchaser values.   c. World Bank estimate.   d. Data refer to the period 1973–80.

Table 3. Structure of production

	GDP[a] (millions of dollars)		Agriculture		Industry		(Manufacturing)[b]		Services, etc.	
	1965	1987	1965	1987	1965	1987	1965	1987	1965	1987
Low-income economies	155,450 *t*	756,130 *t*	43 *w*	31 *w*	27 *w*	37 *w*	20 *w*	..	30 *w*	32 *w*
China and India	111,850 *t*	514,210 *t*	42 *w*	30 *w*	31 *w*	41 *w*	24 *w*	..	27 *w*	29 *w*
Other low-income	42,880 *t*	239,390 *t*	45 *w*	33 *w*	17 *w*	27 *w*	9 *w*	12 *w*	38 *w*	40 *w*
1 Ethiopia	1,180	4,800	58	42	14	18	7	12	28	40
2 Bhutan[c]	..	250	..	*51*	..	*16*	..	*4*	..	*32*
3 Chad[c]	290	980	42	43	15	18	12	15	43	39
4 Zaire[c]	3,140	5,770	21	32	26	33	16	..	53	35
5 Bangladesh[c]	4,380	17,600	53	47	11	13	5	7	36	39
6 Malawi	220	1,110	50	37	13	18	..	..	37	45
7 Nepal	730	2,560	65	57	11	*14*	3	5	23	29
8 Lao PDR	..	700	..	..	..	..	..	..	..	..
9 Mozambique	..	1,490	..	50	..	12	..	..	..	38
10 Tanzania	790	3,080	46	61	14	8	8	5	40	31
11 Burkina Faso	260	1,650	53	38	20	25	..	15	27	38
12 Madagascar[c]	670	2,070	*31*	43	*16*	16	*11*	..	*53*	42
13 Mali[c]	260	1,960	65	54	9	12	5	6	25	35
14 Burundi	150	1,150	..	59	..	14	..	9	..	27
15 Zambia[c]	1,060	2,030	14	12	54	36	6	23	32	52
16 Niger[c]	670	2,160	68	34	3	24	2	9	29	42
17 Uganda	1,100	3,560	52	76	13	5	8	5	35	19
18 China	65,590	293,380	39	31	38	49	30[d]	34[d]	23	20
19 Somalia	220	1,890	71	65	6	9	3	5	24	26
20 Togo[c]	190	1,230	45	29	21	18	10	7	34	54
21 India	46,260	220,830	47	30	22	30	15	20	31	40
22 Rwanda[c]	150	2,100	75	37	7	23	2	*16*	18	40
23 Sierra Leone	320	900	34	45	28	19	6	4	38	36
24 Benin	220	1,570	59	46	8	14	..	4	33	39
25 Central African Rep.	140	1,010	46	41	16	13	4	8	38	46
26 Kenya	920	6,930	35	31	18	19	11	11	47	50
27 Sudan	1,330	8,210	54	37	9	15	4	8	37	48
28 Pakistan	5,450	31,650	40	23	20	28	14	17	40	49
29 Haiti[c]	350	2,250	..	..	..	..	..	..	..	..
30 Lesotho	50	270	65	21	5	28	1	15	30	51
31 Nigeria	5,850	24,390	54	30	13	43	6	8	33	27
32 Ghana[c]	2,050	5,080	44	51	19	16	10	10	38	33
33 Sri Lanka	1,770	6,040	28	27	21	27	17	16	51	46
34 Yemen, PDR[c]	..	840	..	16	..	23	..	..	..	61
35 Mauritania	160	840	32	37	36	22	4	..	32	41
36 Indonesia[c]	3,840	69,670	56	26	13	33	8	14	31	41
37 Liberia	270	*990*	27	*37*	40	28	3	5	34	*35*
38 *Afghanistan*	600	..	..	..	..	..	..	..	..	..
39 *Burma[c]*	..	..	..	..	..	..	..	..	..	..
40 *Guinea[c]*	520	..	..	..	..	..	..	..	..	..
41 *Kampuchea, Dem.*	..	..	..	..	..	..	..	..	..	..
42 *Viet Nam*	..	..	..	..	..	..	..	..	..	..
Middle-income economies	198,180 *t*	1,959,680 *t*	20 *w*	..	34 *w*	..	19 *w*	..	46 *w*	..
Lower-middle-income	102,382 *t*	737,643 *t*	21 *w*	..	29 *w*	..	18 *w*	..	50 *w*	..
43 Senegal[c]	810	4,720	25	22	18	27	14	17	56	52
44 Bolivia[c]	710	4,470	23	24	31	24	15	13	46	53
45 Zimbabwe	960	5,240	18	11	35	43	20	31	47	46
46 Philippines[c]	6,010	34,580	26	24	28	33	20	25	46	43
47 Yemen Arab Rep.[c]	..	4,270	..	28	..	17	..	12	..	55
48 Morocco[c]	2,950	16,750	23	19	28	31	16	18	49	50
49 Egypt, Arab Rep.	4,550	34,470	29	21	27	25	..	14	45	54
50 Papua New Guinea[c]	340	3,030	42	*34*	18	*26*	..	*9*	41	*40*
51 Dominican Rep.[c]	890	4,910	23	*17*	22	*30*	16	*16*	55	*53*
52 Côte d'Ivoire	760	7,650	47	36	19	25	11	*16*	33	39
53 Honduras	460	3,530	40	22	19	24	12	15	41	55
54 Nicaragua[c]	570	3,200	25	*21*	24	*34*	18	*28*	51	*46*
55 Thailand[c]	4,390	48,200	32	16	23	35	14	24	45	49
56 El Salvador[c]	800	4,750	29	14	22	22	18	17	49	64
57 Congo, People's Rep.[c]	200	2,150	19	12	19	33	..	8	62	55
58 Jamaica[c]	970	2,860	10	6	37	41	17	22	53	53
59 Guatemala[c]	1,330	7,040	..	..	..	..	..	..	..	..
60 Cameroon[c]	810	12,660	33	24	20	31	10	13	47	45
61 Paraguay[c]	440	4,570	37	27	19	26	16	16	45	47
62 Ecuador[c]	1,150	10,610	27	16	22	31	18	19	50	53
63 Botswana[c]	50	1,520	34	3	19	57	12	6	47	40
64 Tunisia	880	8,450	22	18	24	32	9	15	54	50
65 Turkey	7,660	60,820	34	17	25	36	16	26	41	46
66 Colombia	5,570	31,940	30	19	25	35	18	19	46	46
67 Chile[c]	5,940	18,950	9	..	40	..	24	..	52	..

Note: For data comparability and coverage, see the technical notes.   Figures in italics are for years other than those specified.

| | | GDP[a] (millions of dollars) | | Distribution of gross domestic product (percent) | | | | | | | |
| | | | | Agriculture | | Industry | | (Manufacturing)[b] | | Services, etc. | |
		1965	1987	1965	1987	1965	1987	1965	1987	1965	1987
68	Peru^c	5,020	45,150	18	11	30	33	17	23	53	56
69	Mauritius	190	1,480	16	15	23	32	14	24	61	53
70	Jordan	..	4,270	..	9	..	28	..	13	..	64
71	Costa Rica^c	590	4,310	24	18	23	29	..	..	53	53
72	Syrian Arab Rep.^c	1,470	23,990	29	27	22	19	..	..	49	54
73	Malaysia^c	3,130	31,230	28	..	25	..	9	..	47	..
74	Mexico^c	21,640	141,940	14	9	27	34	20	25	59	57
75	South Africa	10,540	74,260	10	6	42	44	23	23	48	50
76	Poland^c	..	..	..	..	..	..	..	..	..	..
77	*Lebanon*^c	1,150	..	12	..	21	..	..	..	67	..
	Upper-middle-income	96,080 t	1,240,630 t	19 w	..	38 w	..	20 w	..	43 w	..
78	Brazil	19,450	299,230	19	*11*	33	*38*	26	*28*	48	*51*
79	Uruguay	930	6,420	15	13	32	32	..	27	53	55
80	Hungary^ce	..	26,060	..	15	..	40	..	..	..	44
81	Panama^c	660	5,490	18	9	19	*18*	12	*8*	63	*73*
82	Argentina^c	16,500	71,530	17	13	42	43	33	31	42	44
83	Yugoslavia	11,190	59,960	23	11	42	43	..	..	35	45
84	Algeria^c	3,170	64,600	15	12	34	42	11	12	51	45
85	Korea, Rep.^c	3,000	121,310	38	11	25	43	18	30	37	46
86	Gabon^c	230	3,500	26	11	34	41	..	..	40	48
87	Portugal	..	34,290	..	9	..	40	..	..	..	51
88	Venezuela^c	9,820	49,610	6	6	40	38	..	22	55	56
89	Greece	5,270	40,900	24	16	26	29	16	18	49	56
90	Trinidad and Tobago	690	4,260	8	4	48	39	..	10	44	57
91	Libya	1,500	..	5	..	63	..	3	..	33	..
92	Oman^c	60	8,150	61	*3*	23	*43*	0	6	16	*54*
93	*Iran, Islamic Rep.*	6,170	..	26	..	36	..	12	..	38	..
94	*Iraq*	2,430	..	18	..	46	..	8	..	36	..
95	*Romania*	..	..	..	..	..	..	..	..	..	..
	Low- and middle-income	356,860 t	2,687,970 t	30 w	..	31 w	..	20 w	..	39 w	..
	Sub-Saharan Africa	26,770 t	128,840 t	43 w	33 w	19 w	28 w	9 w	11 w	39 w	40 w
	East Asia	90,670 t	708,540 t	38 w	21 w	34 w	45 w	26 w	..	28 w	35 w
	South Asia	60,260 t	288,260 t	46 w	31 w	21 w	28 w	14 w	18 w	34 w	41 w
	Europe, M.East, & N.Africa	68,330 t	..	24 w	..	35 w	..	..	..	40 w	..
	Latin America & Caribbean	95,000 t	730,300 t	16 w	..	33 w	..	23 w	..	51 w	..
	17 highly indebted	115,050 t	830,320 t	19 w	..	33 w	..	21 w	..	48 w	..
	High-income economies	1,391,660 t	12,370,800 t	5 w	..	41 w	..	30 w	..	55 w	..
	OECD members	1,373,380 t	12,130,500 t	5 w	..	41 w	..	30 w	..	55 w	..
	†Other	10,980 t	209,050 t	5 w	..	54 w	..	11 w	..	41 w	..
96	Spain^c	23,750	287,970	15	*6*	36	*37*	..	27	49	*57*
97	Ireland	2,340	*21,910*	..	*10*	..	*37*	..	..	..	*53*
98	†Saudi Arabia^c	2,300	71,470	8	*4*	60	50	9	9	31	46
99	†Israel^c	3,590	35,000	..	..	..	..	..	..	..	..
100	New Zealand^c	5,410	31,850	..	*8*	..	*31*	..	21	..	*61*
101	†Singapore^c	970	19,900	3	1	24	38	15	29	74	62
102	†Hong Kong	2,150	*36,530*	2	*0*	40	29	24	22	58	70
103	Italy^c	72,150	748,620	10	*4*	37	34	25	23	53	61
104	United Kingdom	89,100	575,740	3	*2*	46	38	34	25	51	60
105	Australia^c	22,920	183,280	9	*4*	39	33	26	17	52	63
106	Belgium^c	16,840	142,300	5	*2*	41	31	30	22	53	67
107	Netherlands^c	19,640	214,420	..	*4*	..	30	..	19	..	66
108	Austria^c	9,480	117,660	9	*3*	46	37	33	26	45	60
109	France^c	99,660	873,370	8	*4*	38	*31*	27	22	54	66
110	Germany, Fed. Rep.^c	114,790	1,117,780	4	*2*	53	38	40	*33*	43	60
111	Finland	7,540	77,900	16	*7*	37	35	23	24	47	58
112	†Kuwait^c	2,100	17,940	0	*1*	70	*51*	3	*11*	29	48
113	Denmark	8,940	85,480	*9*	*5*	*36*	29	*23*	20	*55*	66
114	Canada	46,730	373,690	6	*3*	41	35	27	*19*	53	62
115	Sweden	19,880	137,660	6	*3*	40	35	28	24	53	62
116	Japan^c	91,110	2,376,420	9	*3*	43	41	32	29	48	57
117	†United Arab Emirates	..	23,720	..	*2*	..	*57*	..	*10*	..	*41*
118	Norway^c	7,080	83,080	8	*4*	33	35	21	15	59	62
119	United States^c	700,970	4,497,220	3	*2*	38	*30*	28	20	59	*68*
120	Switzerland^c	13,920	170,880	..	..	..	..	..	..	..	..
	Total reporting economies	1,749,600 t	15,139,800 t	10 w	..	39 w	..	28 w	..	52 w	..
	Oil exporters	78,020 t	845,520 t	19 w	..	32 w	..	14 w	..	48 w	..
	Nonreporting nonmembers	..	..	..	..	..	..	..	..	..	..

a. See the technical notes.   b. Because manufacturing is generally the most dynamic part of the industrial sector, its share of GDP is shown separately.   c. GDP and its components are shown at purchaser values.   d. World Bank estimate.   e. *Services, etc.* includes the unallocated share of GDP.

Table 4. Agriculture and food

		Value added in agriculture (millions of current dollars)		Cereal imports (thousands of metric tons)		Food aid in cereals (thousands of metric tons)		Fertilizer consumption (hundreds of grams of plant nutrient per hectare of arable land)		Average index of food production per capita (1979-81=100)
		1970	1987	1974	1987	1974/75	1986/87	1970[a]	1986	1985-87
	Low-income economies	**83,666 t**	**236,213 t**	**22,767 t**	**27,750 t**	**6,002 t**	**6,677 t**	**161 w**	**706 w**	**115 w**
	China and India	**55,045 t**	**155,356 t**	**11,295 t**	**15,943 t**	**1,582 t**	**791 t**	**224 w**	**997 w**	**119 w**
	Other low-income	**28,413 t**	**80,006 t**	**11,472 t**	**11,807 t**	**4,420 t**	**5,886 t**	**72 w**	**318 w**	**106 w**
1	Ethiopia	931	2,031	118	609	54	570	4	66	89
2	Bhutan[b]	..	109	3	18	0	3	..	10	112
3	Chad[b]	142	418	37	71	20	29	7	13	104
4	Zaire[b]	585	1,857	343	415	1	56	8	15	99
5	Bangladesh[b]	3,636	8,327	1,866	1,781	2,076	1,589	157	673	95
6	Malawi	119	411	17	11	0	10	52	131	87
7	Nepal	579	1,411	18	61	0	22	27	205	99
8	Lao PDR	..	..	53	37	8	0	2	0	123
9	Mozambique	..	747	62	406	34	344	22	19	84
10	Tanzania	473	1,882	431	188	148	55	31	77	90
11	Burkina Faso	126	626	99	164	28	22	3	61	118
12	Madagascar[b]	266	879	114	140	7	115	61	23	97
13	Mali[b]	207	1,051	281	86	107	77	31	166	101
14	Burundi	159	681	7	13	6	2	5	23	100
15	Zambia[b]	191	222	93	150	5	116	73	148	97
16	Niger[b]	420	729	155	83	73	11	1	7	87
17	Uganda	929	2,710	36	26	0	15	14	..	123
18	China	31,818	90,102	6,033	15,897	0	583	410	1,740	124
19	Somalia	167	1,224	42	343	111	156	25	16	102
20	Togo[b]	85	354	6	86	11	6	3	78	89
21	India	23,227	65,254	5,261	46	1,582	208	110	571	109
22	Rwanda[b]	136	784	3	11	19	16	3	20	86
23	Sierra Leone	108	402	72	152	10	43	17	22	98
24	Benin	121	726	7	77	9	8	36	63	114
25	Central African Rep.	60	415	7	37	1	6	12	1	94
26	Kenya	484	2,139	15	274	2	107	238	518	93
27	Sudan	757	3,044	125	707	46	890	28	67	100
28	Pakistan	3,352	7,430	1,274	378	584	456	146	862	105
29	Haiti[b]	..	..	83	178	25	89	4	23	96
30	Lesotho	23	57	48	94	14	32	10	130	83
31	Nigeria	5,080	7,379	389	677	7	0	2	94	105
32	Ghana[b]	1,030	2,568	177	223	33	64	13	27	106
33	Sri Lanka	545	1,628	951	533	271	284	531	1,015	83
34	Yemen, PDR[b]	..	132	148	212	0	10	..	66	87
35	Mauritania	58	310	115	206	48	30	11	50	90
36	Indonesia[b]	4,340	17,769	1,919	2,001	301	379	133	980	117
37	Liberia	91	368	42	117	3	2	63	46	96
38	Afghanistan	..	..	5	64	10	103	24	106	..
39	Burma	819	4,707	26	..	9	0	21	206	127
40	Guinea	..	..	63	203	49	92	19	4	93
41	Kampuchea, Dem.	..	..	223	80	226	2	11	0	..
42	Viet Nam	..	..	1,854	653	64	76	513	620	114
	Middle-income economies	**49,192 t**	..	**40,543 t**	**71,827 t**	**1,925 t**	**5,361 t**	**327 w**	**653 w**	**101 w**
	Lower-middle-income	**28,500 t**	..	**22,000 t**	**36,535 t**	**1,600 t**	**5,338 t**	**355 w**	**661 w**	**101 w**
43	Senegal[b]	208	1,024	341	431	27	80	17	40	105
44	Bolivia[b]	202	1,056	209	258	22	219	7	20	94
45	Zimbabwe	214	570	56	71	0	38	446	571	91
46	Philippines[b]	1,996	8,371	817	910	89	349	287	425	93
47	Yemen Arab Rep.[b]	118	1,192	158	835	33	83	1	111	115
48	Morocco[b]	789	3,110	891	2,251	75	611	117	382	109
49	Egypt, Arab Rep.	1,942	7,291	3,877	9,326	610	1,977	1,312	3,193	106
50	Papua New Guinea[b]	240	858	71	184	0	0	58	314	98
51	Dominican Rep.[b]	282	910	252	683	16	117	334	414	99
52	Côte d'Ivoire	462	2,728	172	675	4	0	74	83	105
53	Honduras	212	765	52	178	31	137	156	220	88
54	Nicaragua[b]	193	570	44	129	3	35	215	535	74
55	Thailand[b]	1,837	7,745	97	255	0	18	59	236	107
56	El Salvador[b]	292	656	75	182	4	227	1,043	906	89
57	Congo, People's Rep.[b]	49	262	34	97	2	0	114	59	92
58	Jamaica[b]	93	174	340	412	1	333	873	509	102
59	Guatemala	..	..	138	284	9	193	298	621	94
60	Cameroon[b]	364	3,009	81	290	4	6	34	75	94
61	Paraguay[b]	191	1,240	71	2	10	2	98	57	107
62	Ecuador[b]	401	1,707	152	347	13	53	133	409	101
63	Botswana[b]	28	48	21	137	5	44	15	5	75
64	Tunisia	245	1,504	307	1,170	59	396	76	226	114
65	Turkey	3,383	10,610	1,276	624	16	3	157	604	101
66	Colombia	1,817	6,198	503	863	28	0	286	770	97
67	Chile[b]	558	..	1,737	249	323	18	313	400	104

Note: For data comparability and coverage, see the technical notes. Figures in italics are for years other than those specified.

		Value added in agriculture (millions of current dollars)		Cereal imports (thousands of metric tons)		Food aid in cereals (thousands of metric tons)		Fertilizer consumption (hundreds of grams of plant nutrient per hectare of arable land)		Average index of food production per capita (1979–81=100)
		1970	1987	1974	1987	1974/75	1986/87	1970[a]	1986	1985–87
68	Peru[b]	1,351	4,773	637	1,894	37	237	300	313	98
69	Mauritius	30	220	160	197	22	15	2,095	2,364	103
70	Jordan	44	375	171	950	79	20	74	300	108
71	Costa Rica[b]	222	793	110	195	1	54	1,001	1,616	92
72	Syrian Arab Rep.[b]	435	6,528	339	1,374	47	31	68	435	96
73	Malaysia[b]	1,198	. .	1,023	2,130	1	. .	489	1,570	126
74	Mexico[b]	4,462	12,205	2,881	4,797	. .	4	232	737	97
75	South Africa	1,362	4,194	127	266	. .	. .	422	621	84
76	Poland[b]	. .	. .	4,185	2,962	. .	. .	1,678	2,342	108
77	*Lebanon*[b]	136	. .	354	479	26	37	1,354	577	. .
	Upper-middle-income	**21,519** *t*	. .	**18,589** *t*	**35,414** *t*	**328** *t*	**25** *t*	**295** *w*	**645** *w*	**101** *w*
78	Brazil	4,392	27,965	2,485	3,871	31	7	186	514	107
79	Uruguay	268	847	70	166	6	0	485	471	100
80	Hungary[b]	1,010	4,022	408	660	. .	. .	1,497	2,615	110
81	Panama[b]	149	*479*	63	116	3	1	387	616	96
82	Argentina[b]	2,250	9,053	0	1	. .	. .	26	43	98
83	Yugoslavia	2,212	6,815	992	782	770	1,315	97		103
84	Algeria[b]	492	8,021	1,816	3,823	54	4	163	361	100
85	Korea, Rep.[b]	2,311	13,817	2,679	8,758	234	. .	2,450	3,853	
86	Gabon[b]	60	379	24	56	. .	22	97		
87	Portugal	. .	3,180	1,861	1,344	. .	. .	428	978	103
88	Venezuela[b]	826	2,938	1,270	2,003			170	1,404	93
89	Greece	1,569	6,461	1,341	1,074			861	1,707	103
90	Trinidad and Tobago	40	178	208	282			880	432	95
91	Libya	93	. .	612	1,426			62	184	76
92	Oman[b]	40	*232*	52	287			. .	936	. .
93	*Iran, Islamic Rep.*	2,120	. .	2,076	5,621	. .	13	60	614	99
94	*Iraq*	579	. .	870	4,212			34	351	105
95	*Romania*	. .	. .	1,381	197			565	1,301	112
	Low- and middle-income	**134,381** *t*	**476,848** *t*	**63,309** *t*	**99,577** *t*	**7,928** *t*	**12,039** *t*	**230** *w*	**683** *w*	**111** *w*
	Sub-Saharan Africa	**14,988** *t*	**42,714** *t*	**3,959** *t*	**7,805** *t*	**910** *t*	**3,056** *t*	**33** *w*	**86** *w*	**100** *w*
	East Asia	**45,446** *t*	**152,121** *t*	**14,877** *t*	**31,086** *t*	**923** *t*	**1,407** *t*	**367** *w*	**1,326** *w*	**121** *w*
	South Asia	**32,198** *t*	**88,877** *t*	**9,404** *t*	**2,833** *t*	**4,522** *t*	**2,562** *t*	**114** *w*	**586** *w*	**109** *w*
	Europe, M.East, & N.Africa	**19,526** *t*	. .	**23,405** *t*	**40,252** *t*	**1,010** *t*	**3,289** *t*	**475** *w*	**960** *w*	**105** *w*
	Latin America & Caribbean	**18,567** *t*	. .	**11,537** *t*	**17,334** *t*	**563** *t*	**1,725** *t*	**176** *w*	**451** *w*	**98** *w*
	17 highly indebted	**27,380** *t*	. .	**13,657** *t*	**20,351** *t*	**637** *t*	**1,886** *t*	**169** *w*	**425** *w*	**101** *w*
	High-income economies	**89,077** *t*	**303,305** *t*	**68,943** *t*	**73,740** *t*	**53** *t*	. .	**993** *w*	**1,172** *w*	**104** *w*
	OECD members	**88,273** *t*	**298,987** *t*	**65,535** *t*	**60,255** *t*	. .	. .	**995** *w*	**1,163** *w*	**103** *w*
	†Other	**714** *t*	**4,318** *t*	**3,409** *t*	**13,485** *t*	**53** *t*	. .	**514** *w*	**3,131** *w*	**134** *w*
96	Spain[b]	. .	*12,557*	4,675	1,943			593	909	104
97	Ireland	559	2,785	640	461			3,690	8,661	98
98	†Saudi Arabia[b]	219	*3,446*	482	8,627			54	3,496	209
99	†Israel c	295	. .	1,176	1,905	53	. .	1,401	2,198	104
100	New Zealand[b]	869	*3,210*	92	57			7,745	6,219	110
101	†Singapore[b]	44	105	682	810			2,500	13,000	94
102	†Hong Kong	62	*171*	657	826			. .	0	56
103	Italy[b]	8,465	25,962	8,101	7,329			896	1,692	101
104	United Kingdom	2,995	*8,567*	7,540	3,722			2,631	3,798	108
105	Australia[b]	2,178	*7,115*	2	27			232	258	97
106	Belgium[b]	920	2,964	4,585[d]	4,747[d]			5,686[d]	5,283[d]	. .
107	Netherlands[b]	1,827	8,456	7,199	4,593			7,493	7,695	110
108	Austria[b]	992	3,844	164	99			2,426	2,062	109
109	France[b]	9,366	*26,979*	654	1,130			2,435	3,091	106
110	Germany, Fed. Rep.[b]	5,951	16,541	7,164	4,462			4,263	4,279	112
111	Finland	1,205	5,155	222	126			1,930	2,184	105
112	†Kuwait[b]	8	*176*	101	364			. .	1,000	. .
113	Denmark	882	4,134	462	351			2,234	2,445	121
114	Canada	3,280	*10,449*	1,513	447			191	474	110
115	Sweden	1,394	4,531	300	265			1,646	1,365	103
116	Japan[b]	12,467	65,384	19,557	27,795			3,882	4,271	109
117	†United Arab Emirates	. .	*420*	132	642			. .	737	. .
118	Norway	624	2,872	713	460			2,443	2,720	108
119	United States[b]	27,829	87,482	460	1,306			816	918	97
120	Switzerland	. .	. .	1,458	911			3,831	4,204	106
	Total reporting economies	**221,239** *t*	. .	**132,252** *t*	**173,316** *t*	**7,981** *t*	**12,039** *t*	**473** *w*	**834** *w*	**110** *w*
	Oil exporters	**22,452** *t*	. .	**18,105** *t*	**46,905** *t*	**1,038** *t*	**2,466** *t*	**143** *w*	**607** *w*	**108** *w*
	Nonreporting nonmembers	. .	. .	**15,475** *t*	**37,330** *t*	. .	**67** *t*	**566** *w*	**1,251** *w*	**111** *w*

a. Average for 1969–71.   b. *Value added in agriculture* data are at purchaser values.   c. *Value added in agriculture* data refer to net domestic product at factor cost.   d. Includes Luxembourg.

Table 5. Commercial energy

		Average annual energy growth rate (percent)			Energy consumption per capita (kilograms of oil equivalent)		Energy imports as a percentage of merchandise exports	
		Energy production		Energy consumption				
		1965-80	1980-87	1965-80	1980-87	1965	1987	1965	1987
	Low-income economies	**10.0 w**	**4.4 w**	**8.2 w**	**4.6 w**	**126 w**	**297 w**	**6 w**	**10 w**
	China and India	**9.1 w**	**6.0 w**	**8.8 w**	**4.8 w**	**146 w**	**390 w**	**4 w**	**5 w**
	Other low-income	**12.4 w**	**-0.4 w**	**5.0 w**	**3.9 w**	**73 w**	**116 w**	**8 w**	**16 w**
1	Ethiopia	7.5	5.9	4.1	2.2	10	21	8	55
2	Bhutan	..	..	..	..	..	..	..	..
3	Chad	..	..	..	..	..	..	..	..
4	Zaire	9.4	3.6	3.6	1.2	74	73	6	2
5	Bangladesh	..	15.4	..	8.1	..	47	..	21
6	Malawi	18.2	4.6	8.0	-0.2	25	40	7	10
7	Nepal	18.4	12.9	6.2	10.3	6	23	10	31
8	Lao PDR	..	-0.3	4.2	1.9	24	37	..	..
9	Mozambique	19.8	-44.1	2.2	1.9	81	86	13	..
10	Tanzania	7.3	3.0	3.7	2.2	37	35	10	56
11	Burkina Faso	..	..	10.5	..	7	..	11	7
12	Madagascar	3.9	10.0	3.5	1.4	34	39	8	36
13	Mali	38.6	9.4	7.0	2.6	14	24	16	32
14	Burundi	..	13.3	6.0	9.2	5	20	11	8
15	Zambia	25.7	1.2	4.0	0.1	464	380	6	11
16	Niger	..	16.5	12.5	3.2	8	42	9	9
17	Uganda	-0.5	3.5	-0.5	4.2	36	26	1	17
18	China	10.0	5.5	9.8	4.4	178	525	0	2
19	Somalia	..	..	16.7	1.8	14	81	8	9
20	Togo	2.9	9.7	10.7	-2.2	27	52	4	8
21	India	5.6	8.1	5.8	6.0	100	208	8	17
22	Rwanda	8.8	6.6	15.2	4.6	8	42	10	53
23	Sierra Leone	..	..	0.8	-1.3	109	77	11	10
24	Benin	..	9.3	9.9	5.0	21	46	10	97
25	Central African Rep.	6.7	0.9	2.2	4.1	22	30	9	1
26	Kenya	13.1	9.2	4.5	-0.2	110	99	13	39
27	Sudan	17.8	1.2	2.0	0.6	67	58	5	38
28	Pakistan	6.5	6.9	3.5	6.5	135	207	7	26
29	Haiti	..	4.7	8.4	1.6	24	50	6	16
30	Lesotho	..	..	..	..	..	10	1	
31	Nigeria	17.3	-3.3	12.9	5.9	34	133	7	3
32	Ghana	17.7	-8.1	7.8	-4.1	76	129	6	14
33	Sri Lanka	10.4	9.5	2.2	3.9	106	160	6	25
34	Yemen, PDR	..	..	-6.4	2.6	..	707	..	..
35	Mauritania	..	..	9.5	0.1	48	113	2	8
36	Indonesia	9.9	1.0	8.4	3.9	91	216	3	13
37	Liberia	14.6	-1.9	7.9	-10.1	182	169	6	11
38	*Afghanistan*	15.7	1.5	5.6	12.6	30	71	8	..
39	*Burma*	8.4	5.0	4.9	5.4	39	73	4	5
40	*Guinea*	16.5	1.5	2.3	0.9	56	59	..	..
41	*Kampuchea, Dem.*	..	5.7	7.6	2.1	19	59	7	..
42	*Viet Nam*	5.3	0.5	-2.6	1.6	106	88	..	..
	Middle-income economies	**3.7 w**	**3.3 w**	**6.6 w**	**2.8 w**	**585 w**	**1,077 w**	**8 w**	**11 w**
	Lower-middle-income	**6.6 w**	**4.7 w**	**5.9 w**	**2.4 w**	**531 w**	**863 w**	**8 w**	**10 w**
43	Senegal	..	..	7.4	-1.7	79	155	8	24
44	Bolivia	9.5	-0.4	7.7	-1.7	156	258	1	2
45	Zimbabwe	-0.7	-0.4	5.2	0.4	441	512	7	6
46	Philippines	9.0	10.1	5.8	-1.4	160	241	12	21
47	Yemen Arab Rep.	..	..	21.0	12.0	7	100	..	..
48	Morocco	2.5	-1.1	7.9	2.5	124	242	5	27
49	Egypt, Arab Rep.	10.7	7.5	6.2	6.6	313	588	11	5
50	Papua New Guinea	13.7	6.5	13.0	2.5	56	229	11	10
51	Dominican Rep.	10.9	6.2	11.5	2.5	127	335	8	37
52	Côte d'Ivoire	11.1	..	8.6	..	101	..	5	11
53	Honduras	14.0	4.5	7.6	2.5	111	192	5	15
54	Nicaragua	2.6	1.0	6.5	1.7	172	256	6	33
55	Thailand	9.0	40.2	10.1	7.3	82	330	11	15
56	El Salvador	9.0	3.5	7.0	1.6	140	218	5	14
57	Congo, People's Rep.	41.1	8.6	7.8	4.7	90	223	10	5
58	Jamaica	-0.9	4.7	6.1	-3.6	703	853	12	31
59	Guatemala	12.5	7.1	6.8	-0.7	150	169	9	16
60	Cameroon	13.0	17.1	6.3	6.4	67	144	6	1
61	Paraguay	..	13.6	9.7	4.8	84	224	16	10
62	Ecuador	35.0	1.1	11.9	1.4	162	625	11	3
63	Botswana	8.8	2.6	9.5	2.3	191	429	16	6
64	Tunisia	20.4	-1.2	8.5	6.0	170	496	12	15
65	Turkey	4.3	9.1	8.5	7.3	258	763	12	31
66	Colombia	1.0	10.4	6.0	2.1	413	757	1	2
67	Chile	1.8	3.2	3.0	1.5	652	822	5	9

Note: For data comparability and coverage, see the technical notes.   Figures in italics are for years other than those specified.

| | | Average annual energy growth rate (percent) | | | | Energy consumption per capita (kilograms of oil equivalent) | | Energy imports as a percentage of merchandise exports | |
| | | Energy production | | Energy consumption | | | | | |
		1965–80	1980–87	1965–80	1980–87	1965	1987	1965	1987
68	Peru	6.6	−0.7	5.0	0.2	395	485	3	1
69	Mauritius	2.1	6.7	7.2	2.9	160	382	6	7
70	Jordan	. .	. .	9.3	7.9	226	750	33	53
71	Costa Rica	8.2	6.9	8.8	2.6	267	580	8	12
72	Syrian Arab Rep.	56.3	2.7	12.4	4.4	212	900	13	40
73	Malaysia	36.9	17.0	6.7	6.2	313	771	11	4
74	Mexico	9.7	2.7	7.9	0.6	605	1,299	4	1
75	South Africa	5.1	5.9	4.3	3.7	1,744	2,465	5	0
76	Poland	4.0	1.9	4.8	0.9	2,027	3,386	. .	15
77	*Lebanon*	2.0	−5.4	2.0	3.5	713	871	51	. .
	Upper-middle-income	**2.7** *w*	**2.4** *w*	**7.3** *w*	**3.0** *w*	**653** *w*	**1,392** *w*	**8** *w*	**12** *w*
78	Brazil	8.6	10.4	9.9	4.0	286	825	14	17
79	Uruguay	4.7	11.9	1.3	−2.0	765	760	13	15
80	Hungary	0.8	1.8	3.8	1.1	1,825	3,062	12	18
81	Panama	6.9	11.1	5.8	4.5	576	1,627	61	29
82	Argentina	4.5	1.9	4.3	1.5	975	1,472	8	10
83	Yugoslavia	3.5	3.0	6.0	3.2	898	2,115	7	19
84	Algeria	5.3	4.7	11.9	5.3	226	1,003	0	2
85	Korea, Rep.	4.1	9.9	12.1	5.9	238	1,475	18	13
86	Gabon	13.7	0.2	14.7	3.0	153	1,121	3	1
87	Portugal	3.6	5.8	6.5	2.7	506	1,322	13	17
88	Venezuela	−3.1	−2.0	4.6	2.3	2,319	2,394	0	0
89	Greece	10.5	9.3	8.5	2.7	615	1,971	29	28
90	Trinidad and Tobago	3.8	−3.3	6.6	−0.3	2,776	5,182	60	4
91	Libya	0.6	−6.0	18.2	4.7	222	2,674	2	. .
92	Oman	23.0	11.0	30.5	9.4	14	2,130	. .	2
93	*Iran, Islamic Rep.*	3.6	7.2	8.9	2.6	537	955	0	. .
94	*Iraq*	6.2	3.0	7.4	4.9	399	732	0	. .
95	*Romania*	4.3	0.7	6.6	0.9	1,536	3,464	. .	. .
	Low- and middle-income	**5.5** *w*	**3.7** *w*	**7.2** *w*	**3.5** *w*	**253** *w*	**503** *w*	**7** *w*	**11** *w*
	Sub-Saharan Africa	**15.3** *w*	**−1.3** *w*	**5.6** *w*	**2.3** *w*	**71** *w*	**82** *w*	**7** *w*	**10** *w*
	East Asia	**9.8** *w*	**5.5** *w*	**9.4** *w*	**4.4** *w*	**168** *w*	**477** *w*	**6** *w*	**9** *w*
	South Asia	**5.8** *w*	**5.7** *w*	**5.7** *w*	**5.2** *w*	**99** *w*	**183** *w*	**7** *w*	**20** *w*
	Europe, M.East, & N.Africa	**4.4** *w*	**2.8** *w*	**6.2** *w*	**2.7** *w*	**746** *w*	**1,204** *w*	**9** *w*	**19** *w*
	Latin America & Caribbean	**1.9** *w*	**2.5** *w*	**6.9** *w*	**1.9** *w*	**515** *w*	**1,071** *w*	**8** *w*	**9** *w*
	17 highly indebted	**3.6** *w*	**1.7** *w*	**6.9** *w*	**2.1** *w*	**420** *w*	**776** *w*	**6** *w*	**10** *w*
	High-income economies	**3.1** *w*	**−0.1** *w*	**3.1** *w*	**0.6** *w*	**3,707** *w*	**4,953** *w*	**11** *w*	**11** *w*
	OECD members	**2.1** *w*	**1.8** *w*	**3.0** *w*	**0.5** *w*	**3,748** *w*	**6,573** *w*	**11** *w*	**12** *w*
	†Other	**7.7** *w*	**−9.8** *w*	**5.7** *w*	**2.8** *w*	**1,943** *w*	**3,030** *w*	**7** *w*	**7** *w*
96	Spain	3.6	7.8	6.5	1.9	901	1,939	31	23
97	Ireland	0.1	5.8	3.9	1.2	1,504	2,503	14	6
98	†Saudi Arabia	11.5	−14.4	7.2	5.0	1,759	3,292	0	1
99	†Israel	−15.2	−16.3	4.4	1.3	1,574	1,965	14	12
100	New Zealand	4.7	7.6	3.6	3.8	2,622	4,211	7	7
101	†Singapore	. .	. .	10.8	−1.0	670	4,436	17	21
102	†Hong Kong	. .	. .	8.4	4.1	413	1,525	4	3
103	Italy	1.3	1.2	3.7	0.0	1,568	2,676	16	14
104	United Kingdom	3.6	2.6	0.9	1.1	3,481	3,805	13	8
105	Australia	10.5	6.6	5.0	0.6	3,287	4,821	11	6
106	Belgium	−3.9	10.6	2.9	0.1	3,402	4,844	9[a]	9[a]
107	Netherlands	15.4	−1.2	5.0	1.3	3,134	5,198	12	11
108	Austria	0.8	−0.8	4.0	0.9	2,060	3,465	10	9
109	France	−0.9	8.0	3.7	0.6	2,468	3,729	16	12
110	Germany, Fed. Rep.	−0.1	0.3	3.0	0.2	3,197	4,531	8	7
111	Finland	3.8	8.7	5.1	3.1	2,233	5,581	11	13
112	†Kuwait	−1.6	−1.3	2.1	3.8	. .	4,715	0	0
113	Denmark	2.6	56.8	2.4	1.0	2,911	3,887	13	8
114	Canada	5.7	3.7	4.5	0.9	6,007	9,156	8	5
115	Sweden	4.9	6.6	2.5	2.3	4,162	6,453	12	8
116	Japan	−0.4	5.1	6.1	1.7	1,474	3,232	19	17
117	†United Arab Emirates	14.7	−1.7	36.6	5.4	105	5,094	4	2
118	Norway	12.4	5.7	4.1	2.7	4,650	8,932	11	6
119	United States	1.1	0.4	2.3	0.1	6,535	7,265	8	19
120	Switzerland	3.7	1.8	3.1	2.0	2,501	4,105	8	5
	Total reporting economies	**4.0** *w*	**1.3** *w*	**4.0** *w*	**1.4** *w*	**1,007** *w*	**1,253** *w*	**10** *w*	**11** *w*
	Oil exporters	**5.8** *w*	**−2.2** *w*	**7.4** *w*	**3.0** *w*	**325** *w*	**766** *w*	**5** *w*	**4** *w*
	Nonreporting nonmembers	**4.6** *w*	**2.8** *w*	**4.4** *w*	**2.8** *w*	**2,509** *w*	**4,777** *w*	. .	. .

a. Includes Luxembourg.

Table 6. Structure of manufacturing

		Value added in manufacturing (millions of current dollars)		Food and agriculture		Textiles and clothing		Machinery and transport equipment		Chemicals		Other[a]	
		1970	1986	1970	1986	1970	1986	1970	1986	1970	1986	1970	1986
	Low-income economies	**42,814** t	**163,354** t										
	China and India	**35,754** t	**129,774** t										
	Other low-income	**6,244** t	**31,119** t										
1	Ethiopia	149	518	46	51	31	23	0	0	2	3	21	22
2	Bhutan[b]	..	8	..	..	..	..	..	..	..	..	..	..
3	Chad[b]	51	132	..	45	..	40	..	0	..	0	..	15
4	Zaire[b]	286	..	*38*	40	*16*	16	7	8	*10*	8	29	29
5	Bangladesh[b]	387	1,249	30	26	47	36	3	6	11	17	10	15
6	Malawi	..	..	51	..	17	..	3	..	10	..	20	..
7	Nepal	32	113	..	..	..	..	..	..	..	..	..	..
8	Lao PDR	..	..	..	..	..	..	..	..	..	..	..	..
9	Mozambique	..	..	51	..	13	..	5	..	3	..	28	..
10	Tanzania	116	227	36	28	28	26	5	8	4	7	26	31
11	Burkina Faso	..	174	69	62	9	18	2	2	1	1	19	17
12	Madagascar[b]	118	..	36	*35*	28	*47*	6	*3*	7	..	23	15
13	Mali[b]	25	100	36	..	40	..	4	..	5	..	14	..
14	Burundi	16	102	*53*	..	*25*	..	*0*	..	*6*	..	*16*	..
15	Zambia[b]	181	461	49	44	9	13	5	9	10	9	27	25
16	Niger[b]	30	142	..	..	..	..	..	..	..	..	..	..
17	Uganda	158	152	40	..	20	..	2	..	4	..	34	..
18	China	28,794[c]	91,463[c]	..	*13*	..	*13*	..	26	..	*10*	..	*38*
19	Somalia	26	72	88	46	6	21	0	0	1	2	6	31
20	Togo[b]	25	*49*	..	..	..	..	..	..	..	..	..	..
21	India	6,960	38,311	13	11	21	16	20	26	14	15	32	32
22	Rwanda[b]	8	310	86	77	0	*1*	3	0	2	12	8	9
23	Sierra Leone	22	47	..	65	..	1	..	0	..	4	..	30
24	Benin	19	48	..	58	..	16	..	0	..	5	..	21
25	Central African Rep.	12	59	..	..	..	..	..	..	..	..	..	..
26	Kenya	174	709	31	35	9	12	18	14	7	9	35	29
27	Sudan	140	537	39	22	34	25	3	1	5	21	19	31
28	Pakistan	1,462	5,073	24	34	38	21	6	8	9	12	23	25
29	Haiti[b]	..	..	..	..	..	..	..	..	..	..	..	..
30	Lesotho	3	26	*11*	12	*26*	20	*0*	0	*0*	0	*63*	68
31	Nigeria	543	5,196	..	..	..	..	..	..	..	..	..	..
32	Ghana[b]	252	639	34	..	16	..	4	..	4	..	41	..
33	Sri Lanka	321	888	26	..	19	..	10	..	11	..	33	..
34	Yemen, PDR	..	..	..	..	..	..	..	..	..	..	..	..
35	Mauritania	10	..	..	..	..	..	..	..	..	..	..	..
36	Indonesia[b]	994	10,592	..	23	..	11	..	10	..	10	..	47
37	Liberia	15	47	..	..	..	..	..	..	..	..	..	..
38	Afghanistan	..	..	..	..	..	..	..	..	..	..	..	..
39	Burma	..	..	..	..	..	..	..	..	..	..	..	..
40	Guinea	..	..	..	..	..	..	..	..	..	..	..	..
41	Kampuchea, Dem.	..	..	..	..	..	..	..	..	..	..	..	..
42	Viet Nam	..	..	..	..	..	..	..	..	..	..	..	..
	Middle-income economies	**63,310** t	**388,586** t										
	Lower-middle-income	**30,215** t	**137,170** t										
43	Senegal[b]	141	626	51	48	19	15	2	6	6	7	22	24
44	Bolivia[b]	135	529	33	*37*	34	*16*	0	*2*	3	*4*	29	*41*
45	Zimbabwe	293	1,444	24	28	16	16	9	10	11	9	40	36
46	Philippines[b]	1,622	7,584	39	40	8	7	8	7	13	10	32	35
47	Yemen Arab Rep.[b]	10	491	*20*	..	*50*	..	*0*	..	*1*	..	*28*	..
48	Morocco[b]	641	2,582	..	26	..	16	..	10	..	11	..	37
49	Egypt, Arab Rep.	..	4,388	17	20	35	27	9	13	12	10	27	31
50	Papua New Guinea[b]	35	228	25	52	1	1	37	10	5	3	33	35
51	Dominican Rep.[b]	275	841	74	63	5	7	1	1	6	5	14	24
52	Côte d'Ivoire	149	1,191	27	..	16	..	10	..	5	..	42	..
53	Honduras	91	482	58	56	10	10	1	1	4	4	28	29
54	Nicaragua[b]	159	759	53	54	14	12	2	2	8	10	23	22
55	Thailand[b]	1,130	9,700	43	30	13	17	9	14	6	6	29	33
56	El Salvador[b]	194	612	40	*37*	30	*14*	3	*5*	8	*16*	18	*28*
57	Congo, People's Rep.[b]	..	177	65	*47*	4	*13*	1	*3*	7	*9*	23	*29*
58	Jamaica[b]	221	553	46	*50*	7	*6*	..	..	10	*13*	36	*31*
59	Guatemala	..	..	*42*	41	*14*	11	*4*	3	*12*	17	*27*	28
60	Cameroon[b]	119	1,321	47	50	16	13	5	7	4	6	28	23
61	Paraguay[b]	99	572	56	..	16	..	1	..	5	..	21	..
62	Ecuador[b]	305	2,230	43	33	14	13	3	7	8	10	32	38
63	Botswana[b]	5	67	..	52	..	12	..	0	..	4	..	32
64	Tunisia	121	1,161	29	17	18	19	4	7	13	13	36	44
65	Turkey	1,930	13,340	26	20	15	14	8	15	7	8	45	43
66	Colombia	1,154	5,817	31	34	20	14	8	8	11	13	29	31
67	Chile[b]	2,092	..	17	27	12	7	11	4	5	8	55	55

Note: For data comparability and coverage, see the technical notes. Figures in italics are for years other than those specified.

		Value added in manufacturing (millions of current dollars)		Distribution of manufacturing value added (percent; current prices)									
				Food and agriculture		Textiles and clothing		Machinery and transport equipment		Chemicals		Other[a]	
		1970	1986	1970	1986	1970	1986	1970	1986	1970	1986	1970	1986
68	Peru[b]	1,430	6,746	25	24	14	11	7	10	7	11	47	44
69	Mauritius	26	284	75	35	6	39	5	3	3	4	12	19
70	Jordan	32	508	21	28	14	5	7	2	6	7	52	58
71	Costa Rica	..	..	48	47	12	10	6	6	7	10	28	27
72	Syrian Arab Rep.	..	..	37	28	40	19	3	10	2	6	19	38
73	Malaysia[b]	500	..	26	21	3	5	8	23	9	14	54	37
74	Mexico[b]	8,449	31,968	28	24	15	12	13	14	11	12	34	39
75	South Africa	3,914	12,270	15	14	13	8	17	17	10	11	45	49
76	Poland[b]	..	..	20	15	19	16	24	30	8	6	28	33
77	Lebanon[b]	..	..	27	..	19	..	1	..	3	..	49	..
	Upper-middle-income	**33,064 t**	**254,917 t**										
78	Brazil	10,429	69,406	16	15	13	12	22	24	10	9	39	40
79	Uruguay	..	1,433	34	29	21	18	7	8	6	10	32	35
80	Hungary[b]	..	..	12	6	13	11	28	37	8	11	39	35
81	Panama[b]	127	422	41	48	9	7	1	3	5	8	44	34
82	Argentina[b]	5,750	21,496	24	24	14	10	18	16	9	12	35	37
83	Yugoslavia	..	..	10	13	15	17	23	25	7	6	45	39
84	Algeria[b]	682	7,401	32	26	20	20	9	11	4	1	35	41
85	Korea, Rep.[b]	1,880	29,397	26	15	17	17	11	24	11	9	36	35
86	Gabon[b]	..	..	37	..	7	..	6	..	6	..	44	..
87	Portugal	..	..	18	17	19	22	13	16	10	8	39	38
88	Venezuela[b]	2,140	14,072	30	23	13	8	9	9	8	11	39	49
89	Greece	1,642	6,482	20	20	20	22	13	14	7	7	40	38
90	Trinidad and Tobago	198	396	18	41	3	5	7	15	2	7	70	32
91	Libya	81	..	..	..	..	..	..	..	..	..	..	..
92	Oman[b]	..	464	..	29	..	0	..	0	..	0	..	71
93	Iran, Islamic Rep.	1,501	..	30	13	20	22	18	22	6	7	26	36
94	Iraq	325	..	26	..	14	..	7	..	3	..	50	..
95	Romania	..	..	..	..	..	..	..	..	..	..	..	..
	Low- and middle-income	**107,564 t**	**547,989 t**										
	Sub-Saharan Africa	**3,270 t**	**16,113 t**										
	East Asia	**37,490 t**	**189,131 t**										
	South Asia	**9,398 t**	**46,406 t**										
	Europe, M.East, & N.Africa	..	..										
	Latin America & Caribbean	**34,359 t**	**166,895 t**										
	17 highly indebted	**38,995 t**	**193,428 t**										
	High-income economies	**603,419 t**	**2,524,574 t**										
	OECD members	**598,731 t**	**2,488,845 t**										
	†Other	**2,350 t**	**29,216 t**										
96	Spain[b]	..	44,822	13	17	15	9	16	22	11	9	45	43
97	Ireland	785	..	31	28	19	7	13	20	7	15	30	28
98	†Saudi Arabia[b]	372	7,173	..	..	..	..	..	..	..	..	..	..
99	†Israel[b]	..	..	15	13	14	10	23	28	7	8	41	42
100	New Zealand[b]	1,721	5,037	24	26	13	10	15	16	4	6	43	43
101	†Singapore[b]	379	4,678	12	6	5	5	28	46	4	8	51	36
102	†Hong Kong	1,013	7,978	4	6	41	40	16	20	2	2	36	33
103	Italy[b]	30,942	140,078	10	7	13	13	24	32	13	10	40	38
104	United Kingdom	36,044	118,048	13	14	9	6	31	32	10	11	37	36
105	Australia[b]	9,058	29,296	16	18	9	7	24	21	7	8	43	45
106	Belgium[b]	8,226	26,055	17	19	12	8	22	23	9	13	40	36
107	Netherlands[b]	8,545	34,690	17	19	8	4	27	28	13	11	36	38
108	Austria[b]	4,873	25,461	17	17	12	8	19	25	6	6	45	43
109	France[b]	38,861	160,556	14	18	10	7	29	33	8	9	39	33
110	Germany, Fed. Rep.[b]	70,888	294,808	13	12	8	5	32	38	9	10	38	36
111	Finland	2,588	14,847	13	13	10	6	20	24	6	7	51	50
112	†Kuwait[b]	120	1,902	5	10	4	7	1	7	4	9	86	67
113	Denmark	2,929	13,887	20	22	8	6	24	23	8	10	40	39
114	Canada	17,002	59,617	16	15	8	7	23	25	7	9	46	44
115	Sweden	8,477	28,385	10	10	6	2	30	35	5	8	49	44
116	Japan[b]	73,339	573,536	8	10	8	6	33	38	11	10	40	37
117	†United Arab Emirates	..	2,290	..	..	..	..	..	..	..	..	..	..
118	Norway	2,416	10,698	15	21	7	3	23	26	7	7	49	44
119	United States[b]	253,864	835,793	12	12	8	5	31	35	10	10	39	38
120	Switzerland[b]	..	..	10	..	7	..	31	..	9	..	42	..
	Total reporting economies	**715,256 t**	**3,087,882 t**										
	Oil exporters	**19,676 t**	**123,904 t**										
	Nonreporting nonmembers	..	..										

a. Includes unallocable data; see the technical notes.   b. *Value added in manufacturing* data are at purchasers values.   c. World Bank estimate.

Table 7. Manufacturing earnings and output

		Earnings per employee					Total earnings as percentage of value added				Gross output per employee (1980=100)			
		Growth rates		Index (1980=100)										
		1970–80	1980–86	1984	1985	1986	1970	1984	1985	1986	1970	1984	1985	1986
Low-income economies														
China and India														
Other low-income														
1	Ethiopia	−4.6	−3.1	94	77	87	24	19	19	19	61	109	110	111
2	Bhutan	..	..	..	..	..	..	..	..	..	..	..	..	..
3	Chad	..	..	..	..	..	..	..	..	..	..	..	..	..
4	Zaire	..	..	..	..	..	..	..	..	..	..	..	..	..
5	Bangladesh	−2.9	−3.7	86	84	79	26	32	32	32	116	98	98	96
6	Malawi	..	..	..	..	..	36	..	..	..	121	..	..	..
7	Nepal	..	..	..	..	..	..	..	..	..	..	..	..	..
8	Lao PDR	..	..	..	..	..	..	..	..	..	..	..	..	..
9	Mozambique	..	..	..	..	..	29	..	..	..	..	..	..	..
10	Tanzania	..	−11.4	57	52	47	42	34	34	34	122	84	87	90
11	Burkina Faso	..	2.6	105	107	118	..	20	20	20	..	115	117	120
12	Madagascar	−0.9	−12.9	62	..	..	36	36	..	..	91	57	..	..
13	Mali	−8.4	..	..	..	..	46	..	..	..	..	..	..	..
14	Burundi	−7.8	..	..	..	..	..	..	..	..	..	..	..	..
15	Zambia	−3.3	0.2	100	100	114	34	26	26	26	109	102	109	78
16	Niger	..	..	..	..	..	..	..	..	..	..	..	..	..
17	Uganda	..	..	..	..	..	..	..	..	..	..	..	..	..
18	China	..	..	..	..	..	..	..	..	..	..	..	..	..
19	Somalia	−6.4	−8.6	71	69	61	28	30	30	30	..	71	69	61
20	Togo	..	..	..	..	..	..	..	..	..	..	..	..	..
21	India	−0.2	5.6	120	130	132	47	48	48	48	95	142	153	164
22	Rwanda	..	..	..	..	..	22	19	..	..	..	..	..	..
23	Sierra Leone	..	..	..	..	..	..	..	..	..	..	..	..	..
24	Benin	..	..	..	..	..	..	25	25	25	..	..	..	..
25	Central African Rep.	..	..	..	..	..	..	..	..	..	..	..	..	..
26	Kenya	−3.4	−3.7	82	79	81	53	46	46	46	38	93	94	96
27	Sudan	..	..	..	..	..	31	..	..	..	..	..	..	..
28	Pakistan	3.4	8.8	140	146	154	21	20	20	20	51	150	164	179
29	Haiti	−3.3	−0.5	107	102	105	..	..	..	..	..	..	..	..
30	Lesotho	..	..	..	..	..	..	48	48	48	..	..	..	..
31	Nigeria	0.0	..	..	..	..	18	..	..	..	105	..	..	..
32	Ghana	..	..	..	..	..	23	..	..	..	193	..	..	..
33	Sri Lanka	..	−1.0	83	101	..	..	..	..	..	70	111	135	..
34	Yemen, PDR	..	..	..	..	..	..	..	..	..	..	..	..	..
35	Mauritania	..	..	..	..	..	..	..	..	..	..	..	..	..
36	Indonesia	4.7	9.2	132	153	176	26	18	21	24	42	138	157	186
37	Liberia	..	1.6	111	107	99	..	..	..	..	..	..	..	..
38	*Afghanistan*	..	..	..	..	..	..	..	..	..	..	..	..	..
39	*Burma*	..	..	..	..	..	..	..	..	..	..	..	..	..
40	*Guinea*	..	..	..	..	..	..	..	..	..	..	..	..	..
41	*Kampuchea, Dem.*	..	..	..	..	..	..	..	..	..	..	..	..	..
42	*Viet Nam*	..	..	..	..	..	..	..	..	..	..	..	..	..
Middle-income economies														
Lower-middle-income														
43	Senegal	−4.8	−0.2	97	101	93	..	43	44	44	..	96	102	103
44	Bolivia	2.5	4.4	122	..	..	44	35	..	..	68	62	..	..
45	Zimbabwe	1.6	6.1	114	143	145	43	44	44	44	98	108	118	120
46	Philippines	−3.0	..	..	..	..	21	18	22	20	102	115	105	112
47	Yemen Arab Rep.	..	..	..	..	..	..	..	..	..	..	..	..	..
48	Morocco	..	..	..	..	..	..	51	51	51	..	..	..	..
49	Egypt, Arab Rep.	4.0	1.6	116	121	117	54	57	57	57	76	133	141	155
50	Papua New Guinea	2.9	0.1	89	96	94	42	36	36	36	..	96	103	101
51	Dominican Rep.	−1.0	−4.8	87	79	79	35	19	22	22	63	102	98	98
52	Côte d'Ivoire	−0.9	..	..	..	..	27	..	..	..	52	..	..	..
53	Honduras	−0.4	..	..	..	..	..	38	38	38	..	..	..	..
54	Nicaragua	..	−15.8	71	63	29	16	20	22	22	206	107	104	99
55	Thailand	1.0	7.2	137	143	148	25	24	24	24	68	133	138	140
56	El Salvador	2.4	..	..	..	..	28	21	20	..	71	89	87	..
57	Congo, People's Rep.	..	..	..	..	..	34	57	..	..	..	..	..	..
58	Jamaica	−0.2	..	..	..	..	43	..	..	..	..	..	..	..
59	Guatemala	−3.2	−0.1	110	98	105	..	24	23	23	..	..	..	..
60	Cameroon	..	..	..	..	..	29	37	37	37	..	..	..	..
61	Paraguay	..	..	..	..	..	..	..	..	..	..	..	..	..
62	Ecuador	2.9	−1.1	104	103	94	27	38	44	39	83	106	104	90
63	Botswana	*10.4*	−4.2	81	85	..	..	40	..	..	..	69	..	..
64	Tunisia	4.2	−4.9	83	78	76	44	47	47	47	95	91	87	83
65	Turkey	3.7	−2.3	84	89	94	26	24	24	24	108	131	125	139
66	Colombia	−0.2	6.2	117	116	154	25	20	18	20	84	110	126	140
67	Chile	..	−1.5	105	97	107	19	15	14	15	60	..	..	..

Note: For data comparability and coverage, see the technical notes.   Figures in italics are for years other than those specified.

		Earnings per employee					Total earnings as percentage of value added				Gross output per employee (1980=100)			
		Growth rates		Index (1980=100)										
		1970-80	1980-86	1984	1985	1986	1970	1984	1985	1986	1970	1984	1985	1986
68	Peru	..	1.2	92	111	115	..	19	19	19	82	70	66	75
69	Mauritius	1.7	−3.1	94	84	84	34	48	46	48	139	96	80	74
70	Jordan	..	−1.1	101	98	97	37	30	32	31	..	174	155	144
71	Costa Rica	..	..	..	..	..	41				..	..	..	..
72	Syrian Arab Rep.	2.2	−1.8	95	82	102	33	31	30	30	72	129	129	196
73	Malaysia	2.0	5.4	125	135	131	28	29	30	30	96	..	..	..
74	Mexico	1.2	−4.0	73	88	85	44	21	26	26	77	111	109	104
75	South Africa	2.7	0.4	109	106	102	46	50	50	49	45	97	98	101
76	Poland	..	..	..	..	..	..	..	..	..	..	..	..	..
77	*Lebanon*	..	..	..	..	..	..	..	..	..	..	..	..	..

Upper-middle-income

78	Brazil	4.0	−1.1	91	93	95	22	20	20	20	71	68	70	78
79	Uruguay	..	−1.2	84	96	109	..	21	22	25	..	112	108	107
80	Hungary	3.7	1.5	106	108	111	28	33	34	35	41	116	111	111
81	Panama	0.2	4.4	127	130	125	32	33	34	33	67	92	91	94
82	Argentina	1.7	4.4	126	104	118	30	23	19	21	83	115	108	127
83	Yugoslavia	1.3	−1.9	87	91	97	39	30	29	33	59	109	100	98
84	Algeria	0.1	−3.9	88	84	73	45	53	53	53	101	93	92	81
85	Korea, Rep.	10.0	5.8	119	125	138	25	26	27	27	40	139	141	158
86	Gabon	..	..	..	..	..	..	..	..	..	..	..	..	..
87	Portugal	2.5	1.3	87	104	115	34	38	43	43	..	117	127	..
88	Venezuela	3.8	−0.4	109	110	106	31	26	26	27	118	111	109	106
89	Greece	5.0	−0.3	99	102	94	32	39	39	39	57	99	104	98
90	Trinidad and Tobago	..	2.4	..	..	..	..	65	79	..	..	..	..	..
91	Libya	..	..	..	..	..	37	..	..	..	45	..	..	..
92	Oman	..	..	..	..	..	..	61	61	61	..	..	..	..
93	*Iran, Islamic Rep.*	..	..	..	..	..	25	..	..	..	85	..	..	..
94	*Iraq*	..	..	..	..	..	36	..	..	..	..	..	..	..
95	*Romania*	..	..	..	..	..	..	..	..	..	..	..	..	..

Low- and middle-income
  Sub-Saharan Africa
  East Asia
  South Asia
  Europe, M.East, & N.Africa
  Latin America & Caribbean

17 highly indebted

High-income economies
  OECD members
  †Other

96	Spain	4.5	1.9	99	110	113	52	40	41	41	..	122	126	..
97	Ireland	4.1	8.0	120	142	146	49	39	39	39	..	..	..	..
98	†Saudi Arabia	..	..	..	..	..	..	..	..	..	..	..	..	..
99	†Israel	8.8	−10.0	65	60	63	36	54	45	47	..	..	..	..
100	New Zealand	1.2	−1.6	92	95	..	62	..	59	..	..	114	121	..
101	†Singapore	3.6	8.8	142	152	165	36	36	38	37	73	114	114	126
102	†Hong Kong	6.1	2.6	105	111	115	..	59	63	61	..	..	..	..
103	Italy	4.1	0.4	103	99	104	41	46	43	43	57	122	116	122
104	United Kingdom	1.7	3.0	109	111	121	52	44	43	44	62	133	135	138
105	Australia	2.9	1.7	107	106	113	53	51	48	52	70	107	115	..
106	Belgium	4.3	−0.1	96	95	104	46	47	46	47	51	124	125	130
107	Netherlands	2.5	3.6	112	111	124	52	57	57	57	..	..	..	..
108	Austria	3.4	1.3	103	105	111	47	55	54	55	64	116	118	120
109	France	..	..	..	..	..	..	..	..	..	64	113	113	117
110	Germany, Fed. Rep.	3.5	1.0	101	102	107	46	48	46	45	60	114	117	105
111	Finland	2.6	2.1	107	110	114	47	43	43	49	73	116	122	134
112	†Kuwait	..	4.1	112	102	142	12	44	41	41	..	169	140	134
113	Denmark	2.5	−0.1	98	97	100	56	52	52	53	65	113	110	106
114	Canada	4.2	2.8	102	116	116	53	46	49	49	68	117	..	..
115	Sweden	0.4	0.1	97	98	100	52	37	37	37	73	121	124	116
116	Japan	3.2	1.8	107	109	111	32	35	35	37	45	120	123	115
117	†United Arab Emirates	..	..	..	..	..	..	..	..	..	..	..	..	..
118	Norway	2.6	1.4	101	105	107	50	55	57	59	75	112	121	113
119	United States	0.1	1.4	104	106	108	47	39	40	39	63	112	115	117
120	Switzerland	..	..	..	..	..	..	..	..	..	..	..	..	..

Total reporting economies
  Oil exporters

Nonreporting nonmembers

Table 8. Growth of consumption and investment

		General government consumption		Private consumption, etc.		Gross domestic investment	
		Average annual growth rate (percent)					
		1965–80	*1980–87*	*1965–80*	*1980–87*	*1965–80*	*1980–87*
	Low-income economies	**6.8** *w*	**4.4** *w*	**4.1** *w*	**4.4** *w*	**8.7** *w*	**10.2** *w*
	China and India	**6.1** *w*	**6.0** *w*	**4.0** *w*	**5.6** *w*	**8.3** *w*	**14.9** *w*
	Other low-income	**8.3** *w*	**0.7** *w*	**4.4** *w*	**2.4** *w*	**9.6** *w*	**−1.9** *w*
1	Ethiopia	6.4	*5.6*	3.0	*1.3*	−0.1	*2.0*
2	Bhutan	..	..	..	..	..	..
3	Chad	..	..	..	..	..	..
4	Zaire	0.7	−10.9	1.5	0.4	6.7	1.3
5	Bangladesh	a	a	2.7	3.7	0.0	2.9
6	Malawi	5.6	4.5	4.4	2.6	9.0	−10.5
7	Nepal	..	..	..	..	..	..
8	Lao PDR	..	..	..	..	..	..
9	Mozambique	..	−10.8	..	0.9	..	−23.1
10	Tanzania	a	−7.1	4.1	5.0	6.1	−5.6
11	Burkina Faso	8.7	3.4	2.0	2.5	8.8	2.0
12	Madagascar	2.0	−1.0	0.6	−0.1	1.5	−4.5
13	Mali	1.9	4.3	4.9	4.1	1.8	4.2
14	Burundi	7.3	2.9	3.7	*2.1*	9.0	*5.4*
15	Zambia	5.1	−2.5	−0.9	1.4	−3.6	−9.3
16	Niger	2.9	1.2	−2.4	2.3	6.3	−15.0
17	Uganda	a	..	1.0	..	−5.7	..
18	China	6.0	4.9	5.3	6.1	10.5	19.0
19	Somalia	11.1	1.1	3.5	1.1	10.7	2.7
20	Togo	9.5	1.9	5.0	−0.3	9.0	−6.4
21	India	6.3	8.8	2.7	4.9	5.0	3.7
22	Rwanda	6.2	3.2	5.1	2.0	9.0	9.2
23	Sierra Leone	a	a	3.1	−2.5	−1.0	−7.1
24	Benin	0.7	3.0	2.6	1.4	10.4	−12.7
25	Central African Rep.	−1.1	−3.1	4.2	1.6	−5.4	14.6
26	Kenya	10.6	0.8	5.7	3.1	7.2	−2.3
27	Sudan	0.2	−1.6	4.3	−1.4	6.4	−4.0
28	Pakistan	4.7	8.6	4.8	4.9	2.4	7.4
29	Haiti	1.9	−0.7	2.3	−0.2	14.8	−3.6
30	Lesotho	12.3	..	8.6	..	17.3	..
31	Nigeria	13.9	−3.6	5.0	0.0	14.7	−14.8
32	Ghana	3.8	−1.6	1.4	1.7	−1.3	3.2
33	Sri Lanka	1.1	8.4	4.0	6.3	11.5	−5.1
34	Yemen, PDR	..	..	..	..	..	..
35	Mauritania	10.0	−6.2	1.9	4.7	19.2	−5.5
36	Indonesia	11.4	4.1	5.9	4.9	16.1	4.1
37	Liberia	3.4	*1.3*	3.2	*0.8*	6.4	*−16.7*
38	*Afghanistan*	..	..	..	..	..	..
39	*Burma*	..	..	..	..	..	..
40	*Guinea*	..	..	..	..	..	..
41	*Kampuchea, Dem.*	..	..	..	..	..	..
42	*Viet Nam*	..	..	..	..	..	..
	Middle-income economies	**7.7** *w*	**2.5** *w*	**6.7** *w*	**2.4** *w*	**8.6** *w*	**−1.6** *w*
	Lower-middle-income	**7.4** *w*	**3.0** *w*	**5.2** *w*	**1.7** *w*	**7.1** *w*	**−3.7** *w*
43	Senegal	2.9	1.5	1.8	2.2	3.9	1.1
44	Bolivia	8.2	−5.2	4.1	0.6	4.4	−19.5
45	Zimbabwe	10.6	7.1	5.1	−2.7	0.9	−1.4
46	Philippines	7.7	−0.2	5.0	1.7	8.5	−14.6
47	Yemen Arab Rep.	..	3.7	..	3.8	..	−10.0
48	Morocco	11.0	4.3	4.5	2.7	11.1	−2.2
49	Egypt, Arab Rep.	a	5.3	5.5	5.0	11.3	2.7
50	Papua New Guinea	0.1	−0.9	4.1	1.8	1.4	−3.4
51	Dominican Rep.	0.3	..	7.1	..	13.5	..
52	Côte d'Ivoire	13.2	−5.7	7.5	3.5	10.7	−14.2
53	Honduras	6.9	2.8	4.9	1.1	6.8	−0.1
54	Nicaragua	6.6	*16.0*	2.0	*−8.1*	..	*4.0*
55	Thailand	9.5	5.6	6.2	4.0	8.0	3.9
56	El Salvador	7.0	3.2	4.1	−0.7	6.6	0.1
57	Congo, People's Rep.	5.5	*7.1*	1.4	*6.7*	4.5	−3.8
58	Jamaica	9.8	−1.5	2.0	2.4	−3.3	−1.2
59	Guatemala	6.2	1.5	5.1	−0.5	7.4	−5.4
60	Cameroon	5.0	10.0	4.2	5.7	9.9	3.3
61	Paraguay	5.1	2.6	6.4	2.1	13.9	−4.3
62	Ecuador	12.2	−2.5	6.8	1.7	9.5	−4.7
63	Botswana	12.0	*13.8*	9.2	*4.4*	21.0	*−1.5*
64	Tunisia	7.2	4.7	8.3	3.7	4.6	−3.8
65	Turkey	6.1	3.8	5.7	5.6	8.8	4.8
66	Colombia	6.7	3.0	5.9	2.4	5.8	−0.4
67	Chile	4.0	−0.8	0.9	−0.4	0.5	−3.6

Note: For data comparability and coverage, see the technical notes. Figures in italics are for years other than those specified.

		Average annual growth rate (percent)					
		General government consumption		Private consumption, etc.		Gross domestic investment	
		1965–80	*1980–87*	*1965–80*	*1980–87*	*1965–80*	*1980–87*
68	Peru	6.3	0.5	4.9	2.0	0.3	−5.2
69	Mauritius	7.1	2.2	4.4	3.2	8.3	10.8
70	Jordan	. .	5.3	. .	7.3	. .	−4.3
71	Costa Rica	6.8	−0.8	5.2	3.3	9.4	2.1
72	Syrian Arab Rep.	15.1	−0.6	11.9	−0.8	13.9	−0.4
73	Malaysia	8.5	2.3	5.9	0.1	10.4	−1.0
74	Mexico	8.5	3.2	5.8	−0.1	8.5	−7.9
75	South Africa	5.3	3.7	3.3	1.5	4.1	−7.3
76	Poland	. .	. .	. .	. .	. .	. .
77	*Lebanon*	. .	. .	. .	. .	. .	. .
	Upper-middle-income	**8.0** *w*	**2.1** *w*	**8.3** *w*	**3.1** *w*	**9.9** *w*	**0.1** *w*
78	Brazil	6.9	3.1	9.0	3.1	11.3	−0.9
79	Uruguay	3.2	1.1	2.4	−1.9	8.0	−12.5
80	Hungary	a	0.9	3.6	1.7	7.0	−1.8
81	Panama	7.4	*3.5*	4.6	*4.3*	5.9	−3.2
82	Argentina	3.2	1.3	3.0	0.4	4.6	−9.5
83	Yugoslavia	3.6	0.6	7.9	0.4	6.5	−0.2
84	Algeria	8.6	2.8	11.4	4.4	15.9	0.6
85	Korea, Rep.	7.7	5.5	7.8	5.5	15.9	10.0
86	Gabon	10.7	4.7	6.2	−2.2	14.1	−3.0
87	Portugal	8.1	2.3	7.1	1.2	4.6	−3.8
88	Venezuela	. .	0.4	. .	0.3	. .	−4.7
89	Greece	6.6	2.6	4.9	3.2	5.3	−4.5
90	Trinidad and Tobago	8.9	−3.5	6.7	−8.8	12.1	−15.8
91	Libya	19.7	. .	19.1	. .	7.3	. .
92	Oman	. .	a	. .	*13.6*	. .	*18.4*
93	*Iran, Islamic Rep.*	14.6	. .	10.1	. .	11.5	. .
94	*Iraq*	. .	. .	. .	. .	. .	. .
95	*Romania*	. .	. .	. .	. .	. .	. .
	Low- and middle-income	**7.4** *w*	**3.1** *w*	**5.7** *w*	**3.0** *w*	**8.6** *w*	**3.0** *w*
	Sub-Saharan Africa	**8.3** *w*	**−1.0** *w*	**3.9** *w*	**1.1** *w*	**9.3** *w*	**−8.3** *w*
	East Asia	**6.9** *w*	**4.6** *w*	**5.9** *w*	**5.2** *w*	**11.3** *w*	**12.1** *w*
	South Asia	**5.8** *w*	**8.6** *w*	**3.0** *w*	**4.9** *w*	**4.6** *w*	**3.7** *w*
	Europe, M.East, & N.Africa	**9.4** *w*	. .	. .	. .	**9.0** *w*	. .
	Latin America & Caribbean	**6.5** *w*	**2.1** *w*	**6.4** *w*	**1.3** *w*	**8.3** *w*	**−4.5** *w*
	17 highly indebted	**6.9** *w*	**1.3** *w*	**6.3** *w*	**1.3** *w*	**8.6** *w*	**−5.1** *w*
	High-income economies	**2.7** *w*	**2.7** *w*	**3.9** *w*	**3.0** *w*	**3.4** *w*	**3.1** *w*
	OECD members	**2.7** *w*	**2.7** *w*	**3.8** *w*	**3.0** *w*	**3.3** *w*	**3.1** *w*
	†Other	. .	. .	. .	. .	**14.3** *w*	. .
96	Spain	5.1	4.4	4.8	1.3	3.7	1.7
97	Ireland	6.1	0.7	4.3	−0.8	6.3	−2.1
98	†Saudi Arabia	a	. .	20.0	. .	27.5	. .
99	†Israel	8.8	−1.2	6.0	*3.8*	5.9	*0.2*
100	New Zealand	3.4	1.7	2.3	1.5	2.2	5.5
101	†Singapore	10.2	9.1	8.0	3.9	13.3	3.2
102	†Hong Kong	7.7	5.6	9.0	6.9	8.6	1.3
103	Italy	3.4	3.0	4.1	2.2	3.4	1.3
104	United Kingdom	2.3	0.9	2.2	3.2	0.6	5.3
105	Australia	5.0	3.7	4.1	3.2	2.8	0.8
106	Belgium	4.6	0.3	4.3	1.2	2.9	−0.8
107	Netherlands	2.9	0.9	4.8	1.0	1.8	2.6
108	Austria	3.7	1.8	4.4	2.0	4.5	1.8
109	France	3.6	2.5	4.7	2.1	3.9	−0.4
110	Germany, Fed. Rep.	3.5	1.4	4.0	1.2	1.7	0.5
111	Finland	5.3	3.7	3.8	4.5	2.9	0.8
112	†Kuwait	a	*3.9*	11.1	*0.8*	11.9	*−2.3*
113	Denmark	4.8	1.3	2.3	2.5	1.2	6.2
114	Canada	4.8	1.9	4.9	2.9	5.1	3.3
115	Sweden	4.0	1.5	2.5	1.5	0.9	1.8
116	Japan	5.1	2.9	6.0	2.9	6.7	3.9
117	†United Arab Emirates	. .	. .	. .	. .	. .	. .
118	Norway	5.5	3.6	3.9	3.6	4.2	2.6
119	United States	1.2	3.6	3.1	4.1	2.6	5.0
120	Switzerland	2.7	2.4	2.5	1.3	0.8	4.2
	Total reporting economies	**3.3** *w*	**2.7** *w*	**4.2** *w*	**3.0** *w*	**4.4** *w*	**3.1** *w*
	Oil exporters	**11.1** *w*	. .	**7.2** *w*	**1.9** *w*	**11.5** *w*	**−1.0** *w*
	Nonreporting nonmembers	. .	. .	. .	. .	. .	. .

a. General government consumption figures are not available separately; they are included in *private consumption, etc.*

Table 9. Structure of demand

	General government consumption		Private consumption, etc.		Gross domestic investment		Gross domestic savings		Exports of goods and nonfactor services		Resource balance	
Distribution of gross domestic product (percent)												
	1965	1987	1965	1987	1965	1987	1965	1987	1965	1987	1965	1987
Low-income economies	**12** *w*	**13** *w*	**69** *w*	**61** *w*	**20** *w*	**28** *w*	**19** *w*	**26** *w*	**8** *w*	**13** *w*	**−1** *w*	**−2** *w*
China and India	13 *w*	13 *w*	66 *w*	56 *w*	22 *w*	31 *w*	21 *w*	31 *w*	4 *w*	10 *w*	−1 *w*	−1 *w*
Other low-income	9 *w*	12 *w*	77 *w*	73 *w*	15 *w*	19 *w*	12 *w*	15 *w*	17 *w*	20 *w*	−3 *w*	−5 *w*
1 Ethiopia	11	19	77	77	13	14	12	3	12	11	−1	−11
2 Bhutan	..	..	..	..	..	..	..	..	..	..	..	..
3 Chad	20	8	74	104	12	18	6	−12	19	17	−6	−31
4 Zaire	9	17	61	73	14	13	30	10	36	33	15	−3
5 Bangladesh	9	8	83	90	11	11	8	2	10	6	−4	−9
6 Malawi	16	18	84	70	14	14	0	12	19	24	−14	−2
7 Nepal	a	11	100	78	6	21	0	11	8	13	−6	−10
8 Lao PDR	..	..	..	..	..	..	..	..	..	..	..	..
9 Mozambique	..	20	..	90	..	22	..	−10	..	11	..	−32
10 Tanzania	10	8	74	98	15	17	16	−6	26	13	1	−23
11 Burkina Faso	9	25	87	74	12	24	4	1	9	17	−8	−23
12 Madagascar	23	14	74	79	10	14	4	7	16	20	−6	−7
13 Mali	*10*	10	*84*	90	*18*	16	*5*	0	*12*	17	*−13*	−17
14 Burundi	7	17	89	76	6	20	4	8	10	9	−2	−12
15 Zambia	15	25	45	55	25	15	40	20	49	47	15	5
16 Niger	6	12	90	84	8	9	3	5	9	19	−5	−5
17 Uganda	10	7	78	88	11	12	12	5	26	10	1	−7
18 China	15	13	59	49	25	38	25	38	4	13	1	0
19 Somalia	8	11	84	89	11	35	8	1	17	11	−3	−34
20 Togo	8	21	76	74	22	17	17	6	20	31	−6	−12
21 India	10	13	74	65	18	24	16	22	4	7	−2	−2
22 Rwanda	14	12	81	83	10	17	5	5	12	8	−5	−12
23 Sierra Leone	8	7	83	83	12	9	9	10	30	9	−3	1
24 Benin	11	10	87	86	11	14	3	4	13	15	−8	−10
25 Central African Rep.	22	13	67	89	21	14	11	−2	27	17	−11	−16
26 Kenya	15	19	70	61	14	25	15	20	31	21	1	−5
27 Sudan	12	15	79	79	10	11	9	6	15	8	−1	−5
28 Pakistan	11	13	76	77	21	17	13	11	8	13	−8	−6
29 Haiti	8	10	90	85	7	12	2	5	13	12	−5	−8
30 Lesotho	18	16	109	158	11	25	−26	−73	16	10	−38	−99
31 Nigeria	5	11	83	69	14	16	12	20	13	31	−2	4
32 Ghana	14	9	77	87	18	11	8	4	17	20	−10	−6
33 Sri Lanka	13	10	74	77	12	23	13	13	38	25	1	−11
34 Yemen, PDR	..	..	..	..	..	..	..	..	..	..	..	..
35 Mauritania	19	13	54	73	14	20	27	14	42	50	13	−7
36 Indonesia	5	10	87	61	8	26	8	29	5	26	0	3
37 Liberia	12	*17*	61	*65*	17	*10*	27	*18*	50	*43*	10	9
38 *Afghanistan*	a	..	99	..	11	..	1	..	11	..	−10	..
39 *Burma*	..	..	..	..	..	..	..	..	..	..	..	..
40 *Guinea*	..	..	..	..	..	..	..	..	..	..	..	..
41 *Kampuchea, Dem.*	16	..	71	..	13	..	12	..	12	..	−1	..
42 *Viet Nam*	..	..	..	..	..	..	..	..	..	..	..	..
Middle-income economies	**11** *w*	**14** *w*	**67** *w*	**62** *w*	**21** *w*	**23** *w*	**21** *w*	**25** *w*	**17** *w*	**22** *w*	**0** *w*	**3** *w*
Lower-middle-income	10 *w*	13 *w*	71 *w*	68 *w*	20 *w*	21 *w*	18 *w*	21 *w*	17 *w*	22 *w*	−2 *w*	0 *w*
43 Senegal	17	17	75	77	12	13	8	6	24	28	−4	−7
44 Bolivia	9	14	74	84	22	9	17	2	21	14	−5	−8
45 Zimbabwe	12	20	65	59	15	18	23	22	..	27	8	3
46 Philippines	9	8	70	76	21	15	21	16	17	23	0	1
47 Yemen Arab Rep.	..	18	..	94	..	15	..	−12	..	4	..	−26
48 Morocco	12	18	76	68	10	19	12	14	18	25	1	−5
49 Egypt, Arab Rep.	19	14	67	77	18	19	14	8	18	15	−4	−11
50 Papua New Guinea	34	22	64	62	22	22	2	17	18	44	−20	−5
51 Dominican Rep.	19	..	75	..	10	..	6	..	16	..	−4	..
52 Côte d'Ivoire	11	17	61	65	22	13	29	19	37	34	7	6
53 Honduras	10	16	75	71	15	15	15	13	27	24	0	−3
54 Nicaragua	8	..	74	..	21	..	18	..	29	..	−3	..
55 Thailand	10	12	72	62	20	26	19	26	16	30	−1	0
56 El Salvador	9	11	79	81	15	14	12	8	27	19	−2	−6
57 Congo, People's Rep.	14	21	80	58	22	24	5	21	36	43	−17	−2
58 Jamaica	8	15	69	62	27	23	23	23	33	55	−4	0
59 Guatemala	7	8	82	85	13	14	10	7	17	16	−3	−6
60 Cameroon	13	11	75	74	13	18	12	15	24	16	−1	−4
61 Paraguay	7	6	79	76	15	25	14	18	15	22	−1	−7
62 Ecuador	9	12	80	71	14	23	11	17	16	23	−3	−7
63 Botswana	24	..	89	..	6	..	−13	..	32	..	−19	..
64 Tunisia	15	16	71	64	28	21	14	20	19	35	−13	−1
65 Turkey	12	9	74	67	15	26	13	23	6	21	−1	−2
66 Colombia	8	10	75	65	16	19	17	26	11	19	1	7
67 Chile	11	11	73	68	15	17	16	21	14	34	1	4

Note: For data comparability and coverage, see the technical notes. Figures in italics are for years other than those specified.

		General government consumption		Private consumption, etc.		Gross domestic investment		Gross domestic savings		Exports of goods and nonfactor services		Resource balance	
	Distribution of gross domestic product (percent)	1965	1987	1965	1987	1965	1987	1965	1987	1965	1987	1965	1987
68	Peru	10	11	59	67	34	25	31	23	16	9	−3	−2
69	Mauritius	13	11	74	60	17	26	13	29	36	69	−4	3
70	Jordan	..	27	..	76	..	26	..	−3	..	45	..	−30
71	Costa Rica	13	15	78	67	20	21	9	18	23	34	−10	−3
72	Syrian Arab Rep.	14	18	76	72	10	19	10	10	17	15	0	−9
73	Malaysia	15	16	61	47	20	23	24	37	42	64	4	14
74	Mexico	6	10	75	73	20	15	19	17	8	7	−2	2
75	South Africa	11	19	62	53	28	20	27	28	26	29	0	8
76	Poland	..	a	..	70	..	29	..	30	..	18	..	2
77	*Lebanon*	10	..	81	..	22	..	9	..	36	..	−13	..
	Upper-middle-income	**12** *w*	**14** *w*	**63** *w*	**60** *w*	**23** *w*	**25** *w*	**24** *w*	**27** *w*	**17** *w*	**22** *w*	**2** *w*	**2** *w*
78	Brazil	11	12	67	65	20	20	22	23	8	9	2	3
79	Uruguay	15	13	68	76	11	9	18	11	19	21	7	2
80	Hungary	a	10	75	63	26	27	25	26	..	38	−1	0
81	Panama	11	..	73	..	18	..	16	..	36	..	−2	..
82	Argentina	8	6	69	84	19	10	22	10	8	10	3	0
83	Yugoslavia	18	14	52	47	30	39	30	40	22	24	0	1
84	Algeria	15	16	66	55	22	29	19	29	22	14	−3	0
85	Korea, Rep.	9	11	83	52	15	29	8	38	9	45	−7	8
86	Gabon	11	23	52	43	31	31	37	34	43	41	6	3
87	Portugal	12	14	68	68	25	24	20	18	27	34	−5	−6
88	Venezuela	10	10	56	65	25	24	34	25	26	22	9	1
89	Greece	12	20	73	72	26	17	15	8	9	21	−11	−9
90	Trinidad and Tobago	12	19	67	62	26	22	21	18	65	33	−5	−4
91	Libya	14	..	36	..	29	..	50	..	53	..	21	..
92	Oman	..	..	..	..	..	..	..	..	..	..	..	..
93	*Iran, Islamic Rep.*	13	..	63	..	17	..	24	..	20	..	6	..
94	*Iraq*	20	..	50	..	16	..	31	..	38	..	15	..
95	*Romania*	..	..	..	..	..	..	..	..	..	..	..	..
	Low- and middle-income	**11** *w*	**13** *w*	**68** *w*	**63** *w*	**21** *w*	**24** *w*	**20** *w*	**25** *w*	**13** *w*	**20** *w*	**−1** *w*	**1** *w*
	Sub-Saharan Africa	**10** *w*	**15** *w*	**73** *w*	**72** *w*	**14** *w*	**16** *w*	**14** *w*	**13** *w*	**23** *w*	**25** *w*	**1** *w*	**−4** *w*
	East Asia	**14** *w*	**13** *w*	**63** *w*	**53** *w*	**23** *w*	**30** *w*	**23** *w*	**35** *w*	**8** *w*	**31** *w*	**0** *w*	**5** *w*
	South Asia	**9** *w*	**12** *w*	**76** *w*	**68** *w*	**18** *w*	**22** *w*	**15** *w*	**19** *w*	**6** *w*	**8** *w*	**−3** *w*	**−3** *w*
	Europe, M.East, & N.Africa	**13** *w*	**..**	**64** *w*	**..**	**22** *w*	**..**	**20** *w*	**..**	**20** *w*	**..**	**..**	**..**
	Latin America & Caribbean	**9** *w*	**11** *w*	**69** *w*	**69** *w*	**20** *w*	**18** *w*	**21** *w*	**20** *w*	**13** *w*	**12** *w*	**1** *w*	**1** *w*
	17 highly indebted	**10** *w*	**11** *w*	**68** *w*	**68** *w*	**21** *w*	**19** *w*	**22** *w*	**21** *w*	**13** *w*	**14** *w*	**1** *w*	**2** *w*
	High-income economies	**17** *w*	**18** *w*	**63** *w*	**61** *w*	**20** *w*	**21** *w*	**21** *w*	**21** *w*	**12** *w*	**19** *w*	**1** *w*	**0** *w*
	OECD members	**17** *w*	**18** *w*	**63** *w*	**61** *w*	**20** *w*	**21** *w*	**20** *w*	**21** *w*	**12** *w*	**18** *w*	**1** *w*	**0** *w*
	†Other	**14** *w*	**27** *w*	**49** *w*	**49** *w*	**24** *w*	**25** *w*	**34** *w*	**24** *w*	**52** *w*	**57** *w*	**10** *w*	**0** *w*
96	Spain	8	14	68	64	28	22	24	22	10	20	−3	0
97	Ireland	15	18	68	55	26	23	17	27	35	59	−9	6
98	†Saudi Arabia	18	38	34	44	14	27	48	17	60	32	34	−10
99	†Israel	20	31	65	58	29	17	15	11	19	38	−13	−6
100	New Zealand	13	15	62	56	26	29	26	29	22	26	−1	0
101	†Singapore	10	12	80	48	22	39	10	40	123	..	−12	0
102	†Hong Kong	7	7	64	62	36	25	29	31	71	124	−7	5
103	Italy	14	17	63	62	23	21	24	21	13	18	1	−0
104	United Kingdom	16	21	63	62	21	18	20	18	18	26	−1	−1
105	Australia	13	18	69	60	20	23	18	22	15	16	−2	−1
106	Belgium	13	16	64	65	23	16	23	19	36	63	0	3
107	Netherlands	15	16	70	61	16	21	15	23	43	52	−1	3
108	Austria	13	19	57	56	30	24	30	25	25	35	−1	1
109	France	16	19	57	61	26	20	27	20	13	21	1	0
110	Germany, Fed. Rep.	15	20	67	55	18	20	18	25	19	32	0	6
111	Finland	14	21	58	57	30	22	29	22	20	25	−2	0
112	†Kuwait	13	..	26	..	16	..	60	..	68	..	45	..
113	Denmark	16	25	72	53	13	19	12	21	29	32	−2	2
114	Canada	14	20	60	58	26	21	26	22	19	26	0	1
115	Sweden	18	27	72	52	11	18	10	21	22	33	−1	3
116	Japan	8	10	64	57	27	30	28	34	11	13	1	4
117	†United Arab Emirates	..	23	..	36	..	27	..	41	..	55	..	14
118	Norway	15	21	56	53	30	29	29	27	41	36	−1	−2
119	United States	19	21	63	66	17	16	18	13	6	10	1	−3
120	Switzerland	11	11	60	59	30	30	30	31	29	35	−1	0
	Total reporting economies	**15** *w*	**17** *w*	**64** *w*	**61** *w*	**20** *w*	**21** *w*	**20** *w*	**22** *w*	**12** *w*	**19** *w*	**0** *w*	**0** *w*
	Oil exporters	**11** *w*	**18** *w*	**66** *w*	**59** *w*	**20** *w*	**24** *w*	**24** *w*	**23** *w*	**23** *w*	**21** *w*	**5** *w*	**0** *w*
	Nonreporting nonmembers	..	..	..	..	..	..	..	..	..	..	..	..

a. General government consumption figures are not available separately; they are included in *private consumption, etc.*

Table 10. Structure of consumption

<table>
<tr><th colspan="14">Percentage share of total household consumption (range of years, 1980–85)</th></tr>
<tr>
<th colspan="2">Food</th>
<th rowspan="3">Clothing
and
footwear</th>
<th colspan="2">Gross rents, fuel
and power</th>
<th rowspan="3">Medical
care</th>
<th rowspan="3">Education</th>
<th colspan="2">Transport and
communication</th>
<th colspan="2">Other consumption</th>
</tr>
<tr>
<th rowspan="2">Total</th>
<th rowspan="2">Cereals
and
tubers</th>
<th rowspan="2">Total</th>
<th rowspan="2">Fuel and
power</th>
<th rowspan="2">Total</th>
<th rowspan="2">Motor cars</th>
<th rowspan="2">Total</th>
<th rowspan="2">Other
consumer
durables</th>
</tr>
<tr></tr>
<tr><td colspan="13">Low-income economies
China and India
Other low-income</td></tr>
<tr><td>1 Ethiopia</td><td>32</td><td>12</td><td>8</td><td>17</td><td>5</td><td>3</td><td>2</td><td>12</td><td>4</td><td>27</td><td>8</td></tr>
<tr><td>2 Bhutan</td><td>..</td><td>..</td><td>..</td><td>..</td><td>..</td><td>..</td><td>..</td><td>..</td><td>..</td><td>..</td><td>..</td></tr>
<tr><td>3 Chad</td><td>..</td><td>..</td><td>..</td><td>..</td><td>..</td><td>..</td><td>..</td><td>..</td><td>..</td><td>..</td><td>..</td></tr>
<tr><td>4 Zaire</td><td>55</td><td>15</td><td>10</td><td>11</td><td>3</td><td>3</td><td>1</td><td>6</td><td>0</td><td>14</td><td>3</td></tr>
<tr><td>5 Bangladesh</td><td>59</td><td>36</td><td>8</td><td>17</td><td>7</td><td>2</td><td>1</td><td>3</td><td>0</td><td>10</td><td>3</td></tr>
<tr><td>6 Malawi</td><td>55</td><td>28</td><td>5</td><td>12</td><td>2</td><td>3</td><td>4</td><td>7</td><td>2</td><td>15</td><td>3</td></tr>
<tr><td>7 Nepal</td><td>57</td><td>38</td><td>12</td><td>14</td><td>6</td><td>3</td><td>1</td><td>1</td><td>0</td><td>13</td><td>2</td></tr>
<tr><td>8 Lao PDR</td><td>..</td><td>..</td><td>..</td><td>..</td><td>..</td><td>..</td><td>..</td><td>..</td><td>..</td><td>..</td><td>..</td></tr>
<tr><td>9 Mozambique</td><td>..</td><td>..</td><td>..</td><td>..</td><td>..</td><td>..</td><td>..</td><td>..</td><td>..</td><td>..</td><td>..</td></tr>
<tr><td>10 Tanzania</td><td>62</td><td>30</td><td>12</td><td>8</td><td>3</td><td>1</td><td>5</td><td>2</td><td>0</td><td>10</td><td>3</td></tr>
<tr><td>11 Burkina Faso</td><td>..</td><td>..</td><td>..</td><td>..</td><td>..</td><td>..</td><td>..</td><td>..</td><td>..</td><td>..</td><td>..</td></tr>
<tr><td>12 Madagascar</td><td>58</td><td>22</td><td>6</td><td>12</td><td>7</td><td>1</td><td>6</td><td>4</td><td>1</td><td>14</td><td>2</td></tr>
<tr><td>13 Mali</td><td>57</td><td>22</td><td>5</td><td>6</td><td>5</td><td>1</td><td>2</td><td>20</td><td>2</td><td>10</td><td>3</td></tr>
<tr><td>14 Burundi</td><td>..</td><td>..</td><td>..</td><td>..</td><td>..</td><td>..</td><td>..</td><td>..</td><td>..</td><td>..</td><td>..</td></tr>
<tr><td>15 Zambia</td><td>43</td><td>9</td><td>11</td><td>13</td><td>5</td><td>0</td><td>8</td><td>6</td><td>1</td><td>18</td><td>1</td></tr>
<tr><td>16 Niger</td><td>..</td><td>..</td><td>..</td><td>..</td><td>..</td><td>..</td><td>..</td><td>..</td><td>..</td><td>..</td><td>..</td></tr>
<tr><td>17 Uganda</td><td>..</td><td>..</td><td>..</td><td>..</td><td>..</td><td>..</td><td>..</td><td>..</td><td>..</td><td>..</td><td>..</td></tr>
<tr><td>18 China</td><td>61[a]</td><td>..</td><td>12</td><td>8</td><td>3</td><td>1</td><td>1</td><td>1</td><td>..</td><td>16</td><td>..</td></tr>
<tr><td>19 Somalia</td><td>..</td><td>..</td><td>..</td><td>..</td><td>..</td><td>..</td><td>..</td><td>..</td><td>..</td><td>..</td><td>..</td></tr>
<tr><td>20 Togo</td><td>..</td><td>..</td><td>..</td><td>..</td><td>..</td><td>..</td><td>..</td><td>..</td><td>..</td><td>..</td><td>..</td></tr>
<tr><td>21 India</td><td>52</td><td>18</td><td>11</td><td>10</td><td>3</td><td>3</td><td>4</td><td>7</td><td>0</td><td>13</td><td>3</td></tr>
<tr><td>22 Rwanda</td><td>29</td><td>10</td><td>11</td><td>15</td><td>6</td><td>4</td><td>4</td><td>9</td><td>4</td><td>28</td><td>9</td></tr>
<tr><td>23 Sierra Leone</td><td>47</td><td>18</td><td>4</td><td>12</td><td>4</td><td>2</td><td>1</td><td>10</td><td>0</td><td>24</td><td>1</td></tr>
<tr><td>24 Benin</td><td>37</td><td>12</td><td>14</td><td>11</td><td>2</td><td>5</td><td>4</td><td>14</td><td>2</td><td>15</td><td>5</td></tr>
<tr><td>24 Central African Rep.</td><td>..</td><td>..</td><td>..</td><td>..</td><td>..</td><td>..</td><td>..</td><td>..</td><td>..</td><td>..</td><td>..</td></tr>
<tr><td>26 Kenya</td><td>42</td><td>18</td><td>8</td><td>13</td><td>3</td><td>0</td><td>2</td><td>9</td><td>1</td><td>26</td><td>6</td></tr>
<tr><td>27 Sudan</td><td>60</td><td>..</td><td>5</td><td>15</td><td>4</td><td>5</td><td>3</td><td>2</td><td>..</td><td>11</td><td>..</td></tr>
<tr><td>28 Pakistan</td><td>54</td><td>17</td><td>9</td><td>15</td><td>6</td><td>3</td><td>3</td><td>1</td><td>0</td><td>15</td><td>5</td></tr>
<tr><td>29 Haiti</td><td>..</td><td>..</td><td>..</td><td>..</td><td>..</td><td>..</td><td>..</td><td>..</td><td>..</td><td>..</td><td>..</td></tr>
<tr><td>30 Lesotho</td><td>..</td><td>..</td><td>..</td><td>..</td><td>..</td><td>..</td><td>..</td><td>..</td><td>..</td><td>..</td><td>..</td></tr>
<tr><td>31 Nigeria</td><td>52</td><td>18</td><td>7</td><td>10</td><td>2</td><td>3</td><td>4</td><td>4</td><td>1</td><td>20</td><td>6</td></tr>
<tr><td>32 Ghana</td><td>50</td><td>..</td><td>13</td><td>11</td><td>..</td><td>3</td><td>5[b]</td><td>3</td><td>..</td><td>15</td><td>..</td></tr>
<tr><td>33 Sri Lanka</td><td>43</td><td>18</td><td>7</td><td>6</td><td>3</td><td>2</td><td>3</td><td>15</td><td>1</td><td>25</td><td>5</td></tr>
<tr><td>34 Yemen, PDR</td><td>..</td><td>..</td><td>..</td><td>..</td><td>..</td><td>..</td><td>..</td><td>..</td><td>..</td><td>..</td><td>..</td></tr>
<tr><td>35 Mauritania</td><td>..</td><td>..</td><td>..</td><td>..</td><td>..</td><td>..</td><td>..</td><td>..</td><td>..</td><td>..</td><td>..</td></tr>
<tr><td>36 Indonesia</td><td>48</td><td>21</td><td>7</td><td>13</td><td>7</td><td>2</td><td>4</td><td>4</td><td>0</td><td>22</td><td>5</td></tr>
<tr><td>37 Liberia</td><td>..</td><td>..</td><td>..</td><td>..</td><td>..</td><td>..</td><td>..</td><td>..</td><td>..</td><td>..</td><td>..</td></tr>
<tr><td>38 Afghanistan</td><td>..</td><td>..</td><td>..</td><td>..</td><td>..</td><td>..</td><td>..</td><td>..</td><td>..</td><td>..</td><td>..</td></tr>
<tr><td>39 Burma</td><td>..</td><td>..</td><td>..</td><td>..</td><td>..</td><td>..</td><td>..</td><td>..</td><td>..</td><td>..</td><td>..</td></tr>
<tr><td>40 Guinea</td><td>..</td><td>..</td><td>..</td><td>..</td><td>..</td><td>..</td><td>..</td><td>..</td><td>..</td><td>..</td><td>..</td></tr>
<tr><td>41 Kampuchea, Dem.</td><td>..</td><td>..</td><td>..</td><td>..</td><td>..</td><td>..</td><td>..</td><td>..</td><td>..</td><td>..</td><td>..</td></tr>
<tr><td>42 Viet Nam</td><td>..</td><td>..</td><td>..</td><td>..</td><td>..</td><td>..</td><td>..</td><td>..</td><td>..</td><td>..</td><td>..</td></tr>
<tr><td colspan="13">Middle-income economies
Lower-middle-income</td></tr>
<tr><td>43 Senegal</td><td>55</td><td>17</td><td>12</td><td>15</td><td>6</td><td>2</td><td>0</td><td>6</td><td>0</td><td>10</td><td>2</td></tr>
<tr><td>44 Bolivia</td><td>33</td><td>..</td><td>9</td><td>12</td><td>1</td><td>5</td><td>7</td><td>12</td><td>..</td><td>22</td><td>..</td></tr>
<tr><td>45 Zimbabwe</td><td>43</td><td>9</td><td>11</td><td>13</td><td>5</td><td>0</td><td>8</td><td>6</td><td>1</td><td>19</td><td>..</td></tr>
<tr><td>46 Philippines</td><td>51</td><td>21</td><td>4</td><td>19</td><td>5</td><td>2</td><td>4</td><td>4</td><td>2</td><td>16</td><td>2</td></tr>
<tr><td>47 Yemen Arab Rep.</td><td>..</td><td>..</td><td>..</td><td>..</td><td>..</td><td>..</td><td>..</td><td>..</td><td>..</td><td>..</td><td>..</td></tr>
<tr><td>48 Morocco</td><td>44</td><td>15</td><td>9</td><td>6</td><td>1</td><td>7</td><td>5</td><td>10</td><td>1</td><td>18</td><td>4</td></tr>
<tr><td>49 Egypt, Arab Rep. of</td><td>36</td><td>7</td><td>4</td><td>5</td><td>1</td><td>14</td><td>11</td><td>3</td><td>1</td><td>26</td><td>2</td></tr>
<tr><td>50 Papua New Guinea</td><td>..</td><td>..</td><td>..</td><td>..</td><td>..</td><td>..</td><td>..</td><td>..</td><td>..</td><td>..</td><td>..</td></tr>
<tr><td>51 Dominican Rep.</td><td>46</td><td>13</td><td>3</td><td>15</td><td>5</td><td>8</td><td>3</td><td>4</td><td>0</td><td>21</td><td>8</td></tr>
<tr><td>52 Côte d'Ivoire</td><td>40</td><td>14</td><td>10</td><td>5</td><td>1</td><td>9</td><td>4</td><td>10</td><td>3</td><td>23</td><td>3</td></tr>
<tr><td>53 Honduras</td><td>36</td><td>..</td><td>8</td><td>20</td><td>..</td><td>8</td><td>5</td><td>3</td><td>..</td><td>20</td><td>..</td></tr>
<tr><td>54 Nicaragua</td><td>..</td><td>..</td><td>..</td><td>..</td><td>..</td><td>..</td><td>..</td><td>..</td><td>..</td><td>..</td><td>..</td></tr>
<tr><td>55 Thailand</td><td>30</td><td>7</td><td>16</td><td>7</td><td>3</td><td>5</td><td>5</td><td>13</td><td>0</td><td>24</td><td>5</td></tr>
<tr><td>56 El Salvador</td><td>33</td><td>12</td><td>9</td><td>7</td><td>2</td><td>8</td><td>5</td><td>10</td><td>1</td><td>28</td><td>7</td></tr>
<tr><td>57 Congo, People's Rep.</td><td>..</td><td>..</td><td>..</td><td>..</td><td>..</td><td>..</td><td>..</td><td>..</td><td>..</td><td>..</td><td>..</td></tr>
<tr><td>58 Jamaica</td><td>38</td><td>..</td><td>4</td><td>16</td><td>7</td><td>3</td><td>..</td><td>17</td><td>..</td><td>22</td><td>..</td></tr>
<tr><td>59 Guatemala</td><td>36</td><td>10</td><td>10</td><td>14</td><td>5</td><td>13</td><td>4</td><td>3</td><td>0</td><td>20</td><td>5</td></tr>
<tr><td>60 Cameroon</td><td>24</td><td>8</td><td>7</td><td>17</td><td>3</td><td>11</td><td>9</td><td>12</td><td>1</td><td>21</td><td>3</td></tr>
<tr><td>61 Paraguay</td><td>30</td><td>6</td><td>12</td><td>21</td><td>4</td><td>2</td><td>3</td><td>10</td><td>1</td><td>22</td><td>3</td></tr>
<tr><td>62 Ecuador</td><td>31</td><td>..</td><td>11</td><td>6[c]</td><td>1[c]</td><td>5</td><td>5[b]</td><td>11[d]</td><td>..</td><td>31</td><td>..</td></tr>
<tr><td>63 Botswana</td><td>35</td><td>13</td><td>8</td><td>15</td><td>5</td><td>4</td><td>9</td><td>8</td><td>2</td><td>22</td><td>7</td></tr>
<tr><td>64 Tunisia</td><td>42</td><td>10</td><td>9</td><td>20</td><td>3</td><td>3</td><td>7</td><td>6</td><td>1</td><td>14</td><td>5</td></tr>
<tr><td>65 Turkey</td><td>40</td><td>8</td><td>15</td><td>13</td><td>7</td><td>4</td><td>1</td><td>5</td><td>..</td><td>22</td><td>..</td></tr>
<tr><td>66 Colombia</td><td>29</td><td>..</td><td>6</td><td>13</td><td>2</td><td>7</td><td>5</td><td>13</td><td>..</td><td>27</td><td>..</td></tr>
<tr><td>67 Chile</td><td>29</td><td>7</td><td>8</td><td>13</td><td>2</td><td>5</td><td>6</td><td>11</td><td>0</td><td>29</td><td>5</td></tr>
</table>

Note: For data comparability and coverage, see the technical notes. Figures in italics are for years other than those specified.

		Food		Clothing and footwear	Gross rents, fuel and power		Medical care	Education	Transport and communication		Other consumption	Other consumer durables
		Total	*Cereals and tubers*		*Total*	*Fuel and power*			*Total*	*Motor cars*	*Total*	
68	Peru	35	8	7	15	3	4	6	10	0	24	7
69	Mauritius	20	4	8	10	3	13	5	12	1	33	5
70	Jordan	35	..	5	6	..	5	8	6	..	35	..
71	Costa Rica	33	8	8	9	1	7	8	8	0	28	9
72	Syrian Arab Rep.	..	..	..	..	..	..	..	..	..	..	..
73	Malaysia	*30*	..	*5*	*9*	..	*5*	*8*	*16*	..	*27*	..
74	Mexico	35ᵃ	..	10	8	..	5	5	12	..	25	..
75	South Africa	26	..	7	12	..	4	..	17	4	34	..
76	Poland	29	..	9	7	2	6	7	8	2	34	9
77	*Lebanon*	..	..	..	..	..	..	..	..	..	..	..

Upper-middle-income

		Total	*Cereals and tubers*		*Total*	*Fuel and power*			*Total*	*Motor cars*	*Total*	
78	Brazil	35	9	10	11	2	6	5	8	1	27	8
79	Uruguay	31	7	7	12	2	6	4	13	0	27	5
80	Hungary	25	..	9	10	5	5	7	9	2	35	8
81	Panama	38	7	3	11	3	8	9	7	0	24	6
82	Argentina	35	4	6	9	2	4	6	13	0	26	6
83	Yugoslavia	27	..	10	9	4	6	5	11	2	32	9
84	Algeria	..	..	..	..	..	..	..	..	..	..	..
85	Korea, Rep.	35	14	6	11	5	5	9	9	..	25	5
86	Gabon	..	..	..	..	..	..	..	..	..	..	..
87	Portugal	34	..	10	8	3	6	5	13	3	24	7
88	Venezuela	38	..	4	8	..	8	7	10	..	25	..
89	Greece	30	..	8	12	3	6	5	13	2	26	5
90	Trinidad and Tobago	..	..	..	..	..	..	..	..	..	..	..
91	Libya	..	..	..	..	..	..	..	..	..	..	..
92	Oman	..	..	..	..	..	..	..	..	..	..	..
93	*Iran, Islamic Rep.*	37	10	9	23	2	6	5	6	1	14	5
94	*Iraq*	..	..	..	..	..	..	..	..	..	..	..
95	*Romania*	..	..	..	..	..	..	..	..	..	..	..

Low- and middle-income
  Sub-Saharan Africa
  East Asia
  South Asia
  Europe, M.East, & N.Africa
  Latin America & Caribbean

17 highly indebted countries

High-income economies
  OECD members
  †Other

		Total	*Cereals and tubers*		*Total*	*Fuel and power*			*Total*	*Motor cars*	*Total*	
96	Spain	24	3	7	16	3	7	5	13	3	28	6
97	Ireland	22	4	5	11	5	10	7	11	3	33	5
98	†Saudi Arabia	..	..	..	..	..	..	..	..	..	..	..
99	†Israel	26	..	4	20	2	6	9	10	..	25	..
100	New Zealand	12	2	6	14	2	9	6	19	6	34	9
101	†Singapore	19	..	8	11	..	7	12	13	..	30	..
102	†Hong Kong	12	1	9	15	2	6	5	9	1	44	15
103	Italy	19	2	8	14	4	10	7	11	3	31	7
104	United Kingdom	12	2	6	17	4	8	6	14	4	36	7
105	Australia	13	2	5	21	2	10	8	13	4	31	7
106	Belgium	15	2	6	17	7	10	9	11	3	31	7
107	Netherlands	13	2	6	18	6	11	8	10	3	33	8
108	Austria	16	2	9	17	5	10	8	15	3	26	7
109	France	16	2	6	17	5	13	7	13	3	29	7
110	Germany, Fed. Rep.	12	2	7	18	5	13	6	13	4	31	9
111	Finland	16	3	4	15	4	9	8	14	4	34	6
112	†Kuwait	..	..	..	..	..	..	..	..	..	..	..
113	Denmark	13	2	5	19	5	8	9	13	5	33	7
114	Canada	11	2	6	21	4	5	12	14	5	32	8
115	Sweden	13	2	5	19	4	11	8	11	2	32	7
116	Japan	16	4	6	17	3	10	8	9	1	34	6
117	†United Arab Emirates	..	..	..	..	..	..	..	..	..	..	..
118	Norway	15	2	6	14	5	10	8	14	6	32	7
119	United States	13	2	6	18	4	14	8	14	5	27	7
120	Switzerland	17	..	4	17	6	15	..	9	..	38	..

Total reporting economies
  Oil exporters

Nonreporting nonmembers

a. Includes beverages and tobacco. b. Refers to government expenditure. c. Excludes fuel. d. Includes fuel.

Table 11. Central government expenditure

	Percentage of total expenditure												Total expenditure (percentage of GNP)		Overall surplus/deficit (percentage of GNP)	
	Defense		Education		Health		Housing, amenities; social security and welfare[a]		Economic services		Other[a]					
	1972	1987	1972	1987	1972	1987	1972	1987	1972	1987	1972	1987	1972	1987	1972	1987
Low-income economies	..	..	..	..	..	..	..	..	..	..	..	..	..	..	..	..
China and India	..	..	..	..	..	..	..	..	..	..	..	..	..	..	..	..
Other low-income	..	13.4 w	20.2 w	..	5.4 w	3.4 w	..	5.4 w	..	30.0 w	..	..	14.7 w	21.6 w	−3.2 w	−2.7 w
1 Ethiopia	14.3	..	14.4	..	5.7	..	4.4	..	22.9	..	38.3	..	13.7	..	−1.4	..
2 Bhutan	..	..	..	..	..	..	..	..	..	..	..	..	..	..	..	..
3 Chad	24.6	..	14.8	..	4.4	..	1.7	..	21.8	..	32.7	..	14.9	9.0	−2.7	−1.3
4 Zaire	11.1	..	15.2	..	2.3	..	2.0	..	13.3	..	56.1	..	19.8	..	−3.8	..
5 Bangladesh[b]	5.1	10.0	14.8	10.6	5.0	5.0	9.8	9.8	39.3	27.9	25.9	36.7	9.4	12.2	−1.9	−1.4
6 Malawi[b]	3.1	6.6	15.8	10.8	5.5	7.1	5.8	2.3	33.1	33.7	36.7	39.6	22.1	35.1	−6.2	−10.3
7 Nepal	7.2	6.2	7.2	12.1	4.7	5.0	0.7	6.8	57.2	48.5	23.0	21.5	8.5	18.3	−1.2	−7.5
8 Lao PDR	..	..	..	..	..	..	..	..	..	..	..	..	..	..	..	..
9 Mozambique	..	..	..	..	..	..	..	..	..	..	..	..	..	..	..	..
10 Tanzania	11.9	15.8	17.3	8.3	7.2	5.7	2.1	1.7	39.0	27.5	22.6	41.2	19.7	20.9	−5.0	−4.9
11 Burkina Faso	11.5	17.3	20.6	19.0	8.2	5.8	6.6	3.4	15.5	7.7	37.6	46.8	11.1	16.3	0.3	1.6
12 Madagascar	3.6	..	9.1	..	4.2	..	9.9	..	40.5	..	32.7	..	20.8	..	−2.5	..
13 Mali	..	..	..	..	..	..	..	..	..	..	..	..	..	35.5	..	−10.0
14 Burundi	10.3	..	23.4	..	6.0	..	2.7	..	33.9	..	23.8	..	19.9	..	0.0	..
15 Zambia[b]	0.0	0.0	19.0	8.3	7.4	4.7	1.3	2.3	26.7	21.0	45.7	63.7	34.0	40.3	−13.8	−15.8
16 Niger	..	..	..	..	..	..	..	..	..	..	..	..	..	..	..	..
17 Uganda	23.1	26.3	15.3	15.0	5.3	2.4	7.3	2.9	12.4	14.8	36.6	38.6	21.8	15.0	−8.1	−4.4
18 China	..	..	..	..	..	..	..	..	..	..	..	..	..	..	..	..
19 Somalia[b]	23.3	..	5.5	..	7.2	..	1.9	..	21.6	..	40.5	..	13.5	..	0.6	..
20 Togo	..	7.6	..	13.1	..	3.8	..	9.9	..	31.8	..	33.8	..	41.5	..	−5.0
21 India	26.2	21.5	2.3	2.7	1.5	1.9	3.2	5.7	19.9	21.5	46.9	46.8	11.1	18.1	−3.4	−8.1
22 Rwanda	25.6	..	22.2	..	5.7	..	2.6	..	22.0	..	21.9	..	12.5	..	−2.7	..
23 Sierra Leone[b]	3.6	..	15.5	..	5.3	..	2.7	..	24.6	..	48.3	..	23.9	13.7	−4.4	−8.9
24 Benin	..	..	..	..	..	..	..	..	..	..	..	..	..	..	..	..
25 Central African Rep.	..	..	..	..	..	..	..	..	..	..	..	..	..	..	..	..
26 Kenya[b]	6.0	9.1	21.9	23.1	7.9	6.6	3.9	1.7	30.1	22.8	30.2	36.8	21.0	25.0	−3.9	−4.6
27 Sudan[b]	24.1	..	9.3	..	5.4	..	1.4	..	15.8	..	44.1	..	19.2	..	−0.8	..
28 Pakistan	39.9	29.5	1.2	2.6	1.1	0.9	3.2	8.7	21.4	34.5	33.2	23.8	16.9	21.4	−6.9	−8.2
29 Haiti	..	..	..	..	..	..	..	..	..	..	..	..	14.5	..	..	..
30 Lesotho	0.0	9.6	22.4	15.5	7.4	6.9	6.0	1.5	21.6	25.5	42.7	41.1	14.5	24.3	3.5	−2.6
31 Nigeria[b]	40.2	2.8	4.5	2.8	3.6	0.8	0.8	1.5	19.6	35.9	31.4	56.2	8.3	27.7	−0.7	−10.3
32 Ghana[b]	7.9	6.5	20.1	23.9	6.3	8.3	4.1	7.3	15.1	15.7	46.6	38.3	19.5	14.1	−5.8	0.6
33 Sri Lanka	3.1	9.6	13.0	7.8	6.4	5.4	19.5	11.7	20.2	29.2	37.7	36.3	25.4	32.4	−5.3	−8.9
34 Yemen, PDR	..	..	..	..	..	..	..	..	..	..	..	..	..	..	..	..
35 Mauritania	..	..	..	..	..	..	..	..	..	..	..	..	..	..	..	..
36 Indonesia	18.6	8.6	7.4	8.8	1.4	1.5	0.9	1.7	30.5	23.5	41.3	55.9	15.1	24.0	−2.5	−0.9
37 Liberia	5.3	8.9	15.2	16.2	9.8	7.1	3.5	1.9	25.8	27.6	40.5	38.2	16.7	24.8	1.1	−7.9
38 Afghanistan	..	..	..	..	..	..	..	..	..	..	..	..	..	..	..	..
39 Burma	31.6	18.8	15.0	11.7	6.1	7.7	7.5	8.4	20.1	35.1	19.7	18.2	20.0	16.3	−7.3	−0.8
40 Guinea	..	..	..	..	..	..	..	..	..	..	..	..	..	..	..	..
41 Kampuchea, Dem.	..	..	..	..	..	..	..	..	..	..	..	..	..	..	..	..
42 Viet Nam	..	..	..	..	..	..	..	..	..	..	..	..	..	..	..	..
Middle-income economies	11.6 w	11.8 w	12.0 w	11.6 w	6.3 w	5.1 w	20.7 w	18.9 w	27.4 w	21.0 w	22.6 w	..	21.4 w	24.7 w	−3.2 w	−7.7 w
Lower-middle-income	11.5 w	..	17.7 w	13.1 w	5.8 w	3.5 w	15.9 w	10.6 w	23.1 w	19.5 w	26.1 w	47.6 w	20.5 w	25.5 w	−4.6 w	−6.4 w
43 Senegal	..	..	..	..	..	..	..	..	..	..	..	..	18.8	..	−2.8	..
44 Bolivia	18.8	..	31.3	..	6.3	..	0.0	..	12.5	..	31.3	..	9.6	..	−1.8	..
45 Zimbabwe	..	14.2	..	20.3	..	6.1	..	4.6	..	41.4	..	13.3	..	40.3	..	−10.8
46 Philippines[b]	10.9	9.2	16.3	18.0	3.2	5.5	4.3	3.8	17.6	50.5	47.7	12.9	13.4	13.5	−2.0	−5.0
47 Yemen Arab Rep.	33.8	22.2	4.0	16.5	2.9	3.6	0.0	0.0	2.7	6.3	56.6	51.4	13.4	31.9	−2.2	−19.9
48 Morocco	12.3	14.5	19.2	16.9	4.8	2.9	8.4	6.9	25.6	26.2	29.7	32.6	22.8	35.0	−3.9	−9.3
49 Egypt, Arab Rep.	..	19.5	..	12.0	..	2.5	..	16.0	..	10.0	..	40.1	..	45.5	..	−6.6
50 Papua New Guinea[b]	..	4.5	..	16.4	..	9.7	..	1.5	..	21.3	..	46.7	..	34.6	..	−3.3
51 Dominican Rep.	8.5	..	14.2	..	11.7	..	11.8	..	35.4	..	18.3	..	20.0	15.3	−0.2	−2.0
52 Côte d'Ivoire	..	..	..	..	..	..	..	..	..	..	..	..	..	..	..	..
53 Honduras	12.4	..	22.3	..	10.2	..	8.7	..	28.3	..	18.1	..	16.1	..	−2.9	..
54 Nicaragua	12.3	..	16.6	..	4.0	..	16.4	..	27.2	..	23.4	..	15.5	58.0	3.9	−16.3
55 Thailand	20.2	18.7	19.9	19.3	3.7	6.1	7.0	5.2	25.6	21.1	23.5	29.6	16.7	18.7	−4.2	−2.3
56 El Salvador	6.6	26.8	21.4	17.1	10.9	7.4	7.6	4.7	14.4	13.8	39.0	30.2	12.8	12.4	−1.0	0.6
57 Congo, People's Rep.	..	..	..	..	..	..	..	..	..	..	..	..	..	..	..	..
58 Jamaica	..	..	..	..	..	..	..	..	..	..	..	..	..	..	..	..
59 Guatemala	11.0	..	19.4	..	9.5	..	10.4	..	23.8	..	25.8	..	9.9	..	−2.2	..
60 Cameroon	..	8.1	..	12.7	..	3.5	..	11.9	..	35.7	..	28.0	..	23.4	..	−3.5
61 Paraguay	13.8	12.1	12.1	12.2	3.5	3.1	18.3	32.3	19.6	10.1	32.7	30.2	13.1	7.9	−1.7	1.5
62 Ecuador[b]	15.7	11.8	27.5	24.5	4.5	7.3	0.8	0.9	28.9	19.8	22.6	35.8	13.4	16.3	0.2	2.1
63 Botswana[b]	0.0	7.9	10.0	18.4	6.0	5.9	21.7	10.1	28.0	28.4	34.5	29.2	33.7	47.5	−23.8	28.2
64 Tunisia	4.9	..	30.5	..	7.4	..	8.8	..	23.3	..	25.1	..	23.1	..	−0.9	..
65 Turkey	15.5	11.4	18.1	12.6	3.2	2.4	3.1	3.5	42.0	23.6	18.1	46.6	22.7	22.8	−2.2	−4.2
66 Colombia	..	..	..	..	..	..	..	..	..	..	..	..	13.1	14.7	−2.5	−0.7
67 Chile	6.1	10.7	14.3	12.5	8.2	6.0	39.8	42.6	15.3	9.2	16.3	19.0	43.2	31.9	−13.0	0.1

Note: For data comparability and coverage, see the technical notes. Figures in italics are for years other than those specified.

		Percentage of total expenditure												Total expenditure (percentage of GNP)		Overall surplus/deficit (percentage of GNP)	
		Defense		Education		Health		Housing, amenities; social security and welfare[a]		Economic services		Other[a]					
		1972	1987	1972	1987	1972	1987	1972	1987	1972	1987	1972	1987	1972	1987	1972	1987
68	Peru[b]	14.5	..	23.6	..	5.5	..	1.8	..	30.9	..	23.6	..	16.1	14.7	−0.9	0.2
69	Mauritius	0.8	0.8	13.5	12.4	10.3	7.6	18.0	17.4	13.9	21.6	43.4	40.3	16.3	23.0	−1.2	0.2
70	Jordan	33.5	30.3	9.4	13.8	3.8	4.2	10.5	10.1	26.6	18.1	16.2	23.6	52.3	44.6	−7.6	−8.4
71	Costa Rica	2.8	2.2	28.3	16.2	3.8	19.3	26.7	26.7	21.8	12.3	16.7	23.3	18.9	28.3	−4.5	−4.8
72	Syrian Arab Rep.	37.2	38.9	11.3	9.4	1.4	1.4	3.6	6.7	39.9	22.6	6.7	21.0	28.8	37.1	−3.5	−10.9
73	Malaysia	18.5	..	23.4	..	6.8	..	4.4	..	14.2	..	32.7	..	26.5	31.9	−9.4	−8.2
74	Mexico	4.2	1.4	16.4	8.7	5.1	1.3	25.0	8.5	34.2	12.0	15.2	68.2	11.5	22.7	−2.9	−9.5
75	South Africa	..	..	..	..	..	..	..	..	..	..	..	..	21.8	32.7	−4.2	−4.4
76	Poland	..	..	..	..	..	..	..	..	..	..	..	..	..	40.1	..	−1.7
77	*Lebanon*	..	..	..	..	..	..	..	..	..	..	..	..	..	..	..	..
	Upper-middle-income	11.9 w	..	7.7 w	..	6.7 w	..	24.5 w	..	28.2 w	..	21.0 w	..	22.3 w	..	−1.8 w	−8.7 w
78	Brazil	8.3	..	8.3	..	6.7	..	35.0	..	23.3	..	18.3	..	17.4	26.1	−0.3	−13.3
79	Uruguay	5.6	10.2	9.5	7.1	1.6	4.8	52.3	49.5	9.8	8.3	21.2	20.1	25.0	23.9	−2.5	−0.7
80	Hungary	..	4.0	..	2.3	..	3.6	..	26.2	..	37.7	..	26.1	..	59.6	..	−3.6
81	Panama	0.0	0.0	20.7	15.9	15.1	15.5	10.8	14.0	24.2	8.1	29.1	46.5	27.6	34.6	−6.5	−4.2
82	Argentina	10.0	6.0	20.0	6.0	..	1.9	20.0	32.7	30.0	18.1	20.0	35.3	19.6	..	−4.9	..
83	Yugoslavia	20.5	55.1	0.0	0.0	24.8	0.0	35.6	11.2	12.0	16.3	7.0	17.3	21.1	8.0	−0.4	0.0
84	Algeria	..	..	..	..	..	..	..	..	..	..	..	..	..	..	..	..
85	Korea, Rep.	25.8	27.3	15.8	18.3	1.2	2.3	5.9	7.2	25.6	16.6	25.7	28.2	18.0	17.4	−3.9	0.5
86	Gabon	..	..	..	..	..	..	..	..	..	..	..	..	40.1	45.9	−12.9	0.1
87	Portugal	..	..	..	..	..	..	..	..	..	..	..	..	..	..	..	..
88	Venezuela	10.3	5.8	18.6	19.6	11.7	10.0	9.2	11.7	25.4	17.3	24.8	35.6	18.1	22.0	−0.2	−2.1
89	Greece	14.9	..	9.1	..	7.4	..	30.6	..	26.4	..	11.7	..	27.5	50.9	−1.7	−14.4
90	Trinidad and Tobago	..	..	..	..	..	..	..	..	..	..	..	..	..	..	..	..
91	Libya	..	..	..	..	..	..	..	..	..	..	..	..	..	..	..	..
92	Oman	39.3	43.9	3.7	11.3	5.9	4.8	3.0	1.2	24.4	17.1	23.6	21.8	62.1	47.4	−15.3	−5.2
93	*Iran, Islamic Rep.*	24.1	14.2	10.4	19.6	3.6	6.0	6.1	17.4	30.6	15.7	25.2	27.1	30.8	23.5	−4.6	−3.9
94	*Iraq*	..	..	..	..	..	..	..	..	..	..	..	..	..	..	..	..
95	*Romania*	5.4	4.7	2.9	1.8	0.5	0.8	16.2	21.9	61.8	55.5	13.1	15.4	..	..	..	..
	Low- and middle-income	13.2 w	12.6 w	12.2 w	10.4 w	5.9 w	4.6 w	18.1 w	16.6 w	..	21.8 w	..	..	18.0 w	24.5 w	−3.5 w	−7.7 w
	Sub-Saharan Africa	..	..	..	..	..	..	..	..	..	..	..	..	..	..	..	..
	East Asia	..	..	..	..	..	..	..	..	..	..	..	..	..	..	..	..
	South Asia	..	19.9 w	..	3.0 w	..	2.1 w	..	6.8 w	..	25.6 w	..	42.6 w	..	18.5 w	..	−8.5 w
	Europe, M.East, & N.Africa	..	14.9 w	..	12.3 w	..	..	..	..	..	..	..	26.6 w	..	30.1 w	−4.3 w	−7.0 w
	Latin America & Caribbean	7.3 w	..	13.5 w	..	6.8 w	..	29.1 w	..	23.4 w	..	20.0 w	..	16.9 w	..	−2.6 w	−10.2 w
	17 highly indebted	10.2 w	7.0 w	14.4 w	9.6 w	8.4 w	5.9 w	29.6 w	23.8 w	22.7 w	21.2 w	..	..	17.0 w	20.1 w	−2.7 w	−9.2 w
	High-income economies	21.8 w	14.9 w	..	4.6 w	11.1 w	12.5 w	41.9 w	..	13.0 w	9.9 w	..	25.7 w	22.6 w	28.7 w	−1.9 w	−4.3 w
	OECD members	21.7 w	14.7 w	..	4.5 w	11.2 w	12.6 w	42.3 w	..	13.0 w	9.9 w	..	25.6 w	22.2 w	28.4 w	−1.8 w	−4.4 w
	†Other	..	..	..	..	..	..	..	..	..	..	..	..	..	..	..	..
96	Spain	6.5	5.6	8.3	5.5	0.9	12.7	49.8	40.4	17.5	11.8	17.0	24.0	19.6	34.8	−0.5	−5.2
97	Ireland	..	3.1	..	11.4	..	13.0	..	30.3	..	13.9	..	28.3	32.7	60.4	−5.5	−13.0
98	†Saudi Arabia	..	..	..	..	..	..	..	..	..	..	..	..	..	..	..	..
99	†Israel	42.9	30.1	7.1	7.6	3.6	3.2	7.1	17.0	7.1	10.5	32.2	31.5	43.9	63.8	−15.7	0.8
100	New Zealand[b]	5.8	4.7	16.9	11.1	14.8	12.4	25.6	29.7	16.5	9.2	20.4	32.9	30.3	47.1	−4.0	0.6
101	†Singapore	35.3	19.0	15.7	18.2	7.8	4.1	3.9	15.9	9.9	19.9	27.3	23.0	16.7	28.9	1.3	1.4
102	†Hong Kong	..	..	..	..	..	..	..	..	..	..	..	..	..	..	..	..
103	Italy	6.3	3.2	16.1	7.4	13.5	9.6	44.8	36.3	18.4	12.1	0.9	31.4	27.6	52.0	−8.1	−16.5
104	United Kingdom	16.7	12.9	2.6	2.2	12.2	13.1	26.5	31.6	11.1	7.5	30.8	32.7	31.8	38.9	−2.7	−1.8
105	Australia	14.2	9.3	4.2	7.0	7.0	9.5	20.3	28.6	14.4	7.2	39.9	38.4	20.2	28.8	0.3	−1.2
106	Belgium	6.7	5.3	15.5	13.2	1.5	1.7	41.0	42.0	18.9	12.1	16.4	25.7	39.2	52.9	−4.3	−10.6
107	Netherlands	6.8	5.0	15.2	11.9	12.1	11.0	38.1	38.8	9.1	11.0	18.7	22.3	41.0	57.7	0.0	−3.2
108	Austria	3.3	2.8	10.2	9.7	10.1	12.5	53.8	46.7	11.2	12.0	11.4	16.4	29.6	40.3	−0.2	−5.3
109	France	..	6.3	..	7.8	..	20.8	..	38.5	..	..	..	26.6	32.3	45.1	0.7	−0.8
110	Germany, Fed. Rep.	12.4	..	1.5	..	17.5	..	46.9	..	11.3	..	10.4	..	24.2	30.1	0.7	−1.1
111	Finland	6.1	5.3	15.3	13.6	10.6	10.5	28.4	36.7	27.9	20.6	11.6	13.3	24.3	31.9	1.2	−1.0
112	†Kuwait	8.4	14.0	15.0	14.2	5.5	7.6	14.2	21.9	16.6	21.2	40.1	21.0	34.4	36.9	17.4	23.5
113	Denmark	7.3	5.2	16.0	8.6	10.0	1.3	41.6	40.3	11.3	7.7	13.7	37.0	32.6	39.8	2.7	−0.6
114	Canada	7.6	8.1	3.5	3.5	7.6	6.3	35.3	36.3	19.5	12.6	26.5	33.2	20.1	24.2	−1.3	−4.1
115	Sweden	12.5	6.6	14.8	8.9	3.6	1.2	44.3	50.8	10.6	9.2	14.3	23.3	27.9	42.9	−1.2	1.9
116	Japan[b]	..	..	..	..	4.3	..	6.1	..	18.3	..	30.5	..	12.7	17.4	−1.9	−4.9
117	†United Arab Emirates[b]	24.4	..	16.5	..	..	..	..	..	..	..	..	..	4.0	..	0.3	..
118	Norway	9.7	8.3	9.9	8.7	12.3	10.5	39.9	36.0	20.2	19.9	8.0	16.6	35.0	40.6	−1.5	3.9
119	United States	32.2	25.6	3.2	1.7	8.6	12.2	35.3	31.3	10.6	7.7	10.1	21.6	19.1	23.3	−1.5	−3.3
120	Switzerland	15.1	..	4.2	..	10.0	..	39.5	..	18.4	..	12.8	..	13.3	..	0.9	..
	Total reporting economies	20.6 w	14.4 w	..	5.3 w	10.3 w	..	38.3 w	..	14.7 w	11.4 w	16.1 w	27.3 w	22.1 w	28.5 w	−2.1 w	−4.8 w
	Oil exporters	14.9 w	11.4 w	14.5 w	12.4 w	..	4.9 w	..	15.1 w	30.5 w	17.2 w	25.0 w	35.0 w	22.0 w	33.1 w	−0.4 w	−5.4 w
	Nonreporting nonmembers	..	..	..	..	..	..	..	..	..	..	..	..	..	..	..	..

a. See the technical notes. b. Refers to budgetary data.

Table 12. Central government current revenue

<!-- Percentage of total current revenue / Tax revenue spanning headers -->

	Taxes on income profit, and capital gain		Social security contributions		Domestic taxes on goods and services		Taxes on international trade and transactions		Other taxes[a]		Nontax revenue		Total current revenue (percentage of GNP)	
	1972	1987	1972	1987	1972	1987	1972	1987	1972	1987	1972	1987	1972	1987
Low-income economies	..	..	..	..	..	..	..	..	..	..	..	..	..	..
China and India	..	..	..	..	..	..	..	..	..	..	..	..	..	..
Other low-income	..	29.0 w	..	..	..	31.9 w	..	20.7 w	..	..	..	19.3 w	..	17.8 w
1 Ethiopia	23.0	..	0.0	..	29.8	..	30.4	..	5.6	..	11.1	..	10.5	..
2 Bhutan	..	..	..	..	..	..	..	..	..	..	..	..	..	..
3 Chad	16.7	20.8	0.0	0.0	12.3	8.6	45.2	46.2	20.5	12.7	5.3	11.6	10.8	5.7
4 Zaire	22.2	29.9	2.2	0.9	12.7	15.1	57.9	33.4	1.4	5.6	3.7	15.2	14.3	16.3
5 Bangladesh[b]	3.7	9.8	0.0	0.0	22.4	28.4	18.0	42.6	3.8	2.7	52.2	16.6	8.6	9.5
6 Malawi[b]	31.4	35.5	0.0	0.0	24.2	28.9	20.0	16.8	0.5	0.6	23.8	18.2	16.0	22.6
7 Nepal	4.1	8.0	0.0	0.0	26.5	40.7	36.7	27.7	19.0	6.2	13.7	17.4	5.2	8.6
8 Lao PDR	..	..	..	..	..	..	..	..	..	..	..	..	..	..
9 Mozambique	..	..	..	..	..	..	..	..	..	..	..	..	..	..
10 Tanzania	29.9	25.8	0.0	0.0	29.1	57.4	21.7	8.6	0.5	3.1	18.8	5.1	15.8	16.3
11 Burkina Faso	16.8	20.6	0.0	4.5	18.0	22.7	51.8	39.4	3.2	6.8	10.2	10.5	11.4	15.3
12 Madagascar	13.1	..	7.2	..	29.9	..	33.6	..	5.5	..	10.8	..	18.3	..
13 Mali	..	8.2	..	4.6	..	22.2	..	28.1	..	26.9	..	10.1	..	15.1
14 Burundi	18.1	..	1.2	..	18.3	..	40.3	..	15.6	..	6.5	..	11.5	..
15 Zambia[b]	49.7	23.5	0.0	0.0	20.2	40.2	14.3	32.9	0.1	0.5	15.6	3.0	23.2	24.4
16 Niger	..	..	..	..	..	..	..	..	..	..	..	..	..	..
17 Uganda	22.1	5.5	0.0	0.0	32.8	19.1	36.3	75.3	0.3	0.0	8.5	0.0	13.7	9.3
18 China	..	..	..	..	..	..	..	..	..	..	..	..	..	..
19 Somalia[b]	10.7	..	0.0	..	24.7	..	45.3	..	5.2	..	14.0	..	13.7	..
20 Togo	..	35.7	..	6.3	..	9.6	..	32.3	..	1.1	..	22.2	..	31.8
21 India	21.3	13.7	0.0	0.0	44.5	37.8	20.1	28.2	0.9	0.4	13.2	19.9	10.8	14.5
22 Rwanda	17.9	..	4.4	..	14.1	..	41.7	..	13.8	..	8.1	..	9.8	..
23 Sierra Leone[b]	32.7	28.0	0.0	0.0	14.6	10.3	42.4	24.7	0.3	1.0	9.9	5.6	19.5	6.5
24 Benin	..	..	..	..	..	..	..	..	..	..	..	..	..	..
25 Central African Rep.	..	..	..	..	..	..	..	..	..	..	..	..	..	..
26 Kenya[b]	35.6	30.4	0.0	0.0	19.9	38.0	24.3	19.2	1.4	1.5	18.8	10.9	18.0	20.8
27 Sudan[b]	11.8	..	0.0	..	30.4	..	40.5	..	1.5	..	15.7	..	18.0	..
28 Pakistan	13.6	10.8	0.0	0.0	35.9	33.4	34.2	32.9	0.5	0.2	15.8	22.7	12.5	16.7
29 Haiti	..	11.8	..	0.0	..	42.2	..	21.4	..	10.3	..	14.3	..	10.4
30 Lesotho	10.2	11.1	0.0	0.0	2.3	10.3	73.7	67.8	5.9	0.2	7.8	10.5	15.4	22.0
31 Nigeria[b]	43.0	39.9	0.0	0.0	26.3	5.1	17.5	6.6	0.2	-14.5	13.0	62.9	9.4	18.5
32 Ghana[b]	18.4	21.5	0.0	0.0	29.4	25.3	40.6	42.5	0.2	0.1	11.5	10.6	15.1	14.5
33 Sri Lanka	19.1	11.7	0.0	0.0	34.7	37.2	35.4	30.8	2.1	3.7	8.7	16.6	20.0	21.5
34 Yemen, PDR	..	..	..	..	..	..	..	..	..	..	..	..	..	..
35 Mauritania	..	..	..	..	..	..	..	..	..	..	..	..	..	..
36 Indonesia	45.5	47.6	0.0	0.0	22.8	18.2	17.6	8.3	3.5	2.0	10.6	23.9	13.4	23.1
37 Liberia	40.4	34.1	0.0	0.0	20.3	32.0	31.6	26.9	3.1	2.5	4.6	4.4	17.0	17.0
38 Afghanistan	..	..	..	..	..	..	..	..	..	..	..	..	..	..
39 Burma	28.7	4.8	0.0	0.0	34.2	40.0	13.4	15.9	0.0	0.0	23.8	39.3	..	..
40 Guinea	..	..	..	..	..	..	..	..	..	..	..	..	..	..
41 Kampuchea, Dem.	..	..	..	..	..	..	..	..	..	..	..	..	..	..
42 Viet Nam	..	..	..	..	..	..	..	..	..	..	..	..	..	..
Middle-income economies	20.6 w	23.6 w	..	..	22.7 w	27.5 w	14.1 w	10.0 w	..	..	22.9 w	20.1 w	19.6 w	20.4 w
Lower-middle-income	26.8 w	29.4 w	..	..	26.9 w	33.6 w	17.3 w	12.2 w	..	..	15.0 w	18.2 w	16.9 w	20.1 w
43 Senegal	17.5	..	0.0	..	24.5	..	30.9	..	23.9	..	3.2	..	16.9	..
44 Bolivia	15.4	..	0.0	..	30.8	..	46.2	..	7.7	..	0.0	..	7.8	..
45 Zimbabwe	..	42.8	..	0.0	..	30.6	..	15.6	..	1.1	..	10.0	..	28.9
46 Philippines[b]	13.8	24.3	0.0	0.0	24.3	39.6	23.0	16.9	29.7	2.5	9.3	16.6	12.4	12.9
47 Yemen Arab Rep.	6.1	13.4	0.0	0.0	10.3	13.3	56.5	29.4	9.6	15.1	17.5	28.8	8.0	16.1
48 Morocco	16.4	18.9	5.9	5.2	45.7	46.2	13.2	14.3	6.1	7.2	12.6	8.2	18.5	25.6
49 Egypt, Arab Rep.[b]	..	15.2	..	14.6	..	12.0	..	13.4	..	7.9	..	37.0	..	39.0
50 Papua New Guinea[b]	..	41.7	..	0.0	..	13.4	..	25.2	..	2.0	..	17.8	..	23.5
51 Dominican Rep.	17.9	18.2	3.9	3.4	19.0	37.4	40.4	32.3	1.7	1.7	17.0	7.1	19.4	15.5
52 Côte d'Ivoire	..	..	..	..	..	..	..	..	..	..	..	..	..	..
53 Honduras	19.2	..	3.0	..	33.8	..	28.2	..	2.3	..	13.5	..	13.2	..
54 Nicaragua	9.5	14.4	14.0	10.5	37.3	48.5	24.4	7.1	9.0	10.6	5.8	8.9	12.6	36.8
55 Thailand	12.1	18.2	0.0	0.0	46.3	50.0	28.7	20.0	1.8	2.2	11.2	9.7	12.5	16.2
56 El Salvador	15.2	21.4	0.0	0.0	25.6	41.1	36.1	26.1	17.2	5.6	6.0	5.8	11.6	11.6
57 Congo, People's Rep.	19.4	..	0.0	..	40.3	..	26.5	..	6.3	..	7.5	..	18.4	..
58 Jamaica	..	..	..	..	..	..	..	..	..	..	..	..	..	..
59 Guatemala	12.7	..	0.0	..	36.1	..	26.2	..	15.6	..	9.4	..	8.9	..
60 Cameroon	..	31.3	..	5.4	..	14.9	..	18.7	..	4.0	..	25.8	..	18.8
61 Paraguay	8.8	12.2	10.4	12.7	26.1	26.1	24.8	11.4	17.0	22.5	12.9	15.1	11.5	9.6
62 Ecuador[b]	19.6	65.0	0.0	0.0	19.1	13.7	52.4	17.3	5.1	2.0	3.8	2.0	13.6	18.5
63 Botswana[b]	19.9	38.1	0.0	0.0	2.4	1.2	47.2	13.4	0.4	0.1	30.0	47.2	30.7	75.2
64 Tunisia	15.9	..	7.1	..	31.6	..	21.8	..	7.8	..	15.7	..	23.6	..
65 Turkey	30.8	42.6	0.0	0.0	31.0	33.2	14.6	7.4	6.1	4.1	17.5	12.7	20.6	18.5
66 Colombia	37.1	27.0	13.7	8.6	15.2	27.7	19.8	19.1	7.1	6.2	7.1	11.5	10.6	13.8
67 Chile	14.3	14.0	28.6	6.7	28.6	42.5	14.3	10.1	0.0	6.7	14.3	20.0	30.2	30.9

Note: For data comparability and coverage, see the technical notes. Figures in italics are for years other than those specified.

		Percentage of total current revenue												
		Tax revenue												Total current revenue (percentage of GNP)
		Taxes on income profit, and capital gain		Social security contributions		Domestic taxes on goods and services		Taxes on international trade and transactions		Other taxes[a]		Nontax revenue		
		1972	1987	1972	1987	1972	1987	1972	1987	1972	1987	1972	1987	1972	1987
68	Peru[b]	17.3	24.3	0.0	0.0	32.7	56.7	15.4	22.6	21.2	1.2	13.5	4.3	15.2	11.9
69	Mauritius	22.7	10.0	0.0	4.3	23.3	18.3	40.2	50.5	5.5	4.2	8.2	12.8	15.6	23.3
70	Jordan	9.0	10.2	0.0	0.0	14.9	13.5	34.7	27.8	7.1	10.7	34.2	37.9	26.6	30.7
71	Costa Rica	17.7	10.8	13.4	24.7	38.1	28.2	18.1	21.1	1.6	-0.2	11.0	15.5	15.7	23.7
72	Syrian Arab Rep.	6.8	24.7	0.0	0.0	10.4	8.9	17.3	7.2	12.1	12.2	53.4	47.0	25.1	24.2
73	Malaysia	25.2	33.7	0.1	0.8	24.2	18.6	27.9	17.6	1.4	2.1	21.2	27.2	20.3	24.8
74	Mexico	36.4	26.8	19.4	9.3	32.1	64.7	13.2	6.2	-9.8	-16.3	8.6	9.3	9.9	13.3
75	South Africa	54.8	52.7	1.2	1.2	21.5	31.8	4.6	2.9	5.0	2.8	12.8	8.6	21.2	29.2
76	Poland	..	27.5	..	25.8	..	29.9	..	6.7	..	4.0	..	6.2	..	38.7
77	Lebanon	..	..	..	..	..	..	..	..	..	..	..	..	..	..
	Upper-middle-income	16.0 w	20.1 w	..	..	19.6 w	24.8 w	11.2 w	8.3 w	..	..	28.4 w	21.2 w	22.2 w	20.2 w
78	Brazil	20.0	20.8	27.7	27.7	35.4	20.5	7.7	2.3	3.1	5.3	6.2	23.4	18.9	22.1
79	Uruguay	4.7	8.2	30.0	27.3	24.5	43.6	6.1	13.7	22.0	2.5	12.6	4.7	22.7	23.6
80	Hungary	..	18.0	..	24.2	..	31.5	..	6.5	..	11.1	..	8.8	..	55.3
81	Panama	23.3	23.7	22.4	16.2	13.2	16.0	16.0	12.1	7.7	3.4	17.3	28.6	21.8	29.7
82	Argentina	0.0	6.2	33.3	25.2	0.0	37.4	33.3	12.0	0.0	19.2	33.3	9.4	14.7	21.6
83	Yugoslavia	0.0	0.0	52.3	0.0	24.5	60.1	19.5	38.4	0.0	0.0	3.7	1.5	20.7	8.1
84	Algeria	..	..	..	..	..	..	..	..	..	..	..	..	..	..
85	Korea, Rep.	28.6	28.6	0.7	1.7	41.3	39.1	10.6	17.3	6.3	3.4	12.4	9.8	13.3	19.0
86	Gabon	18.2	44.2	6.0	0.0	9.5	6.5	44.9	16.2	4.2	1.9	17.2	31.2	28.3	47.1
87	Portugal	..	..	..	..	..	..	..	..	..	..	..	..	..	..
88	Venezuela	54.2	43.0	6.0	4.2	6.7	8.8	6.1	23.4	1.1	2.3	25.9	18.2	18.5	22.7
89	Greece	12.2	17.9	24.5	34.9	35.5	36.3	6.7	0.5	12.0	0.2	9.2	10.2	25.4	35.8
90	Trinidad and Tobago	..	..	..	..	..	..	..	..	..	..	..	..	..	..
91	Libya	..	..	..	..	..	..	..	..	..	..	..	..	..	..
92	Oman	71.1	20.9	0.0	0.0	0.0	0.8	3.0	2.3	2.3	0.6	23.6	75.4	47.4	42.2
93	Iran, Islamic Rep.	7.9	21.4	2.7	14.3	6.4	11.1	14.6	12.4	4.9	8.1	63.6	32.7	26.2	..
94	Iraq	..	..	..	..	..	..	..	..	..	..	..	..	..	..
95	Romania	6.0	0.0	8.2	16.5	0.0	0.0	0.0	0.0	0.0	12.3	85.8	71.2	..	..
	Low- and middle-income	20.2 w	22.3 w	..	..	25.6 w	28.6 w	15.7 w	12.6 w	..	..	21.7 w	20.4 w	16.1 w	20.2 w
	Sub-Saharan Africa	..	..	..	..	..	..	..	..	..	..	..	..	..	..
	East Asia	..	..	..	..	..	..	..	..	..	..	..	..	..	..
	South Asia	..	13.4 w	..	..	..	34.9 w	..	29.1 w	..	..	..	22.2 w	..	14.7 w
	Europe, M.East, & N.Africa	..	..	..	..	..	..	..	..	..	..	..	..	..	..
	Latin America & Caribbean	23.3 w	23.2 w	..	..	25.2 w	29.4 w	14.4 w	8.7 w	..	..	13.6 w	17.5 w	16.1 w	19.6 w
	17 highly indebted	18.3 w	20.0 w	..	..	28.1 w	32.1 w	13.9 w	9.8 w	..	..	12.4 w	17.0 w	16.1 w	18.7 w
	High-income economies	44.0 w	38.9 w	..	..	23.3 w	19.8 w	2.3 w	1.2 w	..	..	6.5 w	9.3 w	21.9 w	24.4 w
	OECD members	44.3 w	39.2 w	..	..	23.5 w	19.9 w	2.2 w	1.2 w	..	..	6.2 w	8.6 w	21.6 w	24.1 w
	†Other	..	..	..	..	..	..	..	..	..	..	..	..	..	..
96	Spain	15.9	22.6	38.9	38.2	23.4	27.7	10.0	2.7	0.7	1.3	11.1	7.5	19.7	29.5
97	Ireland	28.3	34.2	9.0	13.3	32.1	31.7	16.7	7.6	3.2	3.0	10.6	10.2	30.1	48.3
98	†Saudi Arabia	..	..	..	..	..	..	..	..	..	..	..	..	..	..
99	†Israel	40.0	34.6	0.0	6.0	20.0	29.5	20.0	4.6	10.0	6.4	10.0	18.9	31.3	55.2
100	New Zealand[b]	61.4	51.4	0.0	0.0	19.9	26.3	4.1	2.8	4.5	2.0	10.0	17.5	29.1	44.7
101	Singapore	24.4	20.9	0.0	0.0	17.6	13.9	11.1	3.1	15.5	12.2	31.4	50.0	21.5	26.3
102	Hong Kong	..	..	..	..	..	..	..	..	..	..	..	..	..	..
103	Italy	16.6	37.7	39.2	40.5	31.7	23.4	0.4	0.0	4.3	-4.1	7.7	2.4	23.3	36.1
104	United Kingdom	39.4	45.1	15.6	22.2	27.1	30.4	1.7	0.1	5.4	2.2	10.8	9.9	32.5	37.3
105	Australia	58.3	61.6	0.0	0.0	21.9	22.1	5.2	4.6	2.1	0.5	12.5	11.2	22.1	27.7
106	Belgium	31.3	38.1	32.4	35.0	28.9	21.0	1.0	0.0	3.3	2.3	3.1	3.6	35.0	43.5
107	Netherlands	32.5	25.7	36.7	39.9	22.3	21.9	0.5	0.0	3.4	2.5	4.7	10.1	43.4	51.5
108	Austria	20.7	18.4	30.0	37.1	28.3	26.8	5.4	1.5	10.2	7.5	5.5	8.7	29.7	34.8
109	France	16.9	17.8	37.1	45.6	37.9	27.6	0.3	0.0	2.9	0.9	4.9	8.1	33.4	42.5
110	Germany, Fed. Rep.	19.7	17.4	46.6	53.8	28.1	22.5	0.8	0.0	0.8	0.2	4.0	6.1	25.3	29.2
111	Finland	30.0	32.5	7.8	10.4	47.7	43.5	3.1	0.8	5.8	3.8	5.5	9.1	26.5	31.6
112	†Kuwait	68.8	0.4	0.0	0.0	19.7	0.0	1.5	1.3	0.2	0.0	9.9	97.7	55.2	66.1
113	Denmark	40.0	37.8	5.1	4.4	42.1	41.2	3.1	0.1	2.8	4.1	6.8	12.4	35.5	43.5
114	Canada	41.2	51.1	6.2	14.6	14.5	17.9	5.2	4.2	-0.6	0.0	10.9	12.2	21.1	20.1
115	Sweden	27.0	17.6	21.6	28.5	34.0	27.9	1.5	0.5	4.7	11.0	11.3	14.5	32.4	44.2
116	Japan[b]	..	..	..	..	..	..	..	..	..	..	..	..	11.2	12.6
117	†United Arab Emirates[b]	0.0	..	0.0	..	0.0	..	0.0	..	0.0	..	100.0	..	0.2	..
118	Norway	22.6	20.2	20.6	21.8	48.0	39.7	1.6	0.5	1.0	1.0	6.2	16.7	36.8	48.4
119	United States	59.4	52.4	23.6	32.8	7.1	3.5	1.6	1.7	2.5	0.8	5.7	8.8	17.6	20.1
120	Switzerland	13.9	..	37.3	..	21.5	..	16.7	..	2.6	..	8.0	..	14.5	..
	Total reporting economies	40.3 w	36.2 w	..	..	23.4 w	20.9 w	4.0 w	2.8 w	..	..	8.1 w	10.8 w	21.2 w	24.0 w
	Oil exporters	26.3 w	23.4 w	..	..	24.2 w	23.8 w	10.8 w	8.1 w	..	..	..	32.0 w	20.1 w	27.1 w
	Nonreporting nonmembers	..	..	..	..	..	..	..	..	..	..	..	..	..	..

a. See the technical notes.   b. Refers to budgetary data.

Table 13. Money and interest rates

| | | Monetary holdings, broadly defined | | | | | Average annual inflation (GDP deflator) | Nominal interest rates of banks (average annual percentage) | | | |
| | | Average annual nominal growth rate (percent) | | Average outstanding (percentage of GDP) | | | | Deposit rate | | Lending rate | |
		1965-80	1980-87	1965	1980	1987	1980-87	1980	1987	1980	1987
	Low-income economies										
	China and India										
	Other low-income										
1	Ethiopia	12.7	12.2	12.5	25.3	41.4	2.6	..	1.00	..	6.00
2	Bhutan	..	26.5	..	..	8.4	..	..	..	..	..
3	Chad	12.5	17.4	9.3	20.0	25.3	5.3	5.50	5.33	11.00	10.50
4	Zaire	28.2	53.9	11.1	8.9	8.8	53.5	..	..	..	..
5	Bangladesh	..	21.6	..	18.6	25.2	11.1	8.25	..	11.33	..
6	Malawi	15.4	17.7	17.6	20.3	25.0	12.4	7.92	14.25	16.67	19.50
7	Nepal	17.9	18.9	8.4	21.9	29.5	..	4.00	8.50	14.00	15.00
8	Lao PDR	..	..	..	..	8.1	46.5	..	..	..	..
9	Mozambique	..	..	..	..	..	26.9	..	..	..	..
10	Tanzania	*19.7*	19.8	..	37.2	25.9	24.9	4.00	15.75	11.50	27.50
11	Burkina Faso	17.1	12.6	9.3	18.5	23.1	4.4	6.19	5.25	9.38	8.00
12	Madagascar	11.9	15.4	19.6	27.6	25.7	17.4	5.63	*11.50*	9.50	*14.50*
13	Mali	14.4	13.7	..	17.9	22.5	4.2	6.19	5.25	9.38	8.00
14	Burundi	15.7	10.3	10.1	13.3	15.6	7.5	2.50	5.33	12.00	12.00
15	Zambia	12.7	28.9	..	32.6	30.6	28.7	7.00	13.23	9.50	21.20
16	Niger	18.3	6.1	3.8	13.3	18.1	4.1	6.19	5.25	9.38	8.00
17	Uganda	*23.1*	77.8	..	12.7	7.8	95.2	6.80	*30.00*	10.80	34.67
18	China	..	25.9	..	34.9	65.5	4.2	5.40	..	..	..
19	Somalia	20.4	37.2	12.7	17.9	16.1	37.8	4.50	*15.31*	7.50	22.00
20	Togo	20.3	11.2	10.9	29.0	44.5	6.6	6.19	5.25	9.38	8.00
21	India	15.3	17.0	25.7	36.2	45.4	7.7	..	..	16.50	16.50
22	Rwanda	19.0	10.4	15.8	13.6	16.7	4.5	6.25	6.25	13.50	13.00
23	Sierra Leone	15.9	47.8	11.7	20.6	10.3	50.0	9.17	12.67	11.00	28.54
24	Benin	17.3	6.8	10.6	21.1	20.4	8.2	6.19	5.25	9.38	8.00
25	Central African Rep.	12.7	6.9	13.5	18.9	18.3	7.9	5.50	7.19	10.50	11.42
26	Kenya	*18.6*	15.3	..	37.7	39.9	10.3	5.75	10.31	10.58	14.00
27	Sudan	21.0	34.8	14.1	28.2	35.5	31.7	6.00	..	..	..
28	Pakistan	14.7	14.8	40.8	38.7	39.6	7.3	..	..	..	..
29	Haiti	20.3	..	9.9	26.1	16.4	7.9	10.00	..	..	..
30	Lesotho	..	18.9	..	..	49.3	12.3	*9.60*	7.00	11.00	11.13
31	Nigeria	28.5	10.2	9.9	21.5	26.3	10.1	5.27	13.09	8.43	13.96
32	Ghana	25.9	44.2	20.3	16.2	11.7	48.3	11.50	17.58	19.00	25.50
33	Sri Lanka	15.4	16.7	32.3	35.3	36.7	12.4	14.50	11.50	19.00	9.80
34	Yemen, PDR	15.2	12.0	..	114.8	175.2	5.0	..	..	..	..
35	Mauritania	20.7	12.5	5.7	20.5	23.5	9.8	..	6.00	..	12.00
36	Indonesia	54.4	23.9	..	13.2	26.9	8.5	6.00	16.78	..	21.67
37	Liberia	..	..	..	..	..	1.5	10.30	5.88	18.40	13.63
38	*Afghanistan*	14.0	16.2	14.4	26.8	..	..	9.00	*9.00*	13.00	*13.00*
39	*Burma*	11.5	*14.3*	..	..	..	..	1.50	*1.50*	8.00	*8.00*
40	*Guinea*	..	..	..	..	..	..	..	..	..	..
41	*Kampuchea, Dem.*	..	..	..	..	..	..	..	..	..	..
42	*Viet Nam*	..	..	..	..	..	..	..	..	..	..
	Middle-income economies										
	Lower-middle-income										
43	Senegal	15.6	8.7	15.3	27.0	23.5	9.1	6.19	5.25	9.38	8.00
44	Bolivia	24.3	589.2	10.9	16.2	21.7	601.8	18.00	..	28.00	..
45	Zimbabwe	..	18.1	..	54.6	61.6	12.4	3.52	9.58	17.54	13.00
46	Philippines	17.7	15.9	19.9	19.0	20.7	16.7	12.25	8.20	14.00	13.34
47	Yemen Arab Rep.	..	22.0	..	61.8	73.9	11.4	9.33	9.50	..	..
48	Morocco	15.8	14.4	29.4	45.4	58.0	7.3	4.88	8.50	7.00	9.00
49	Egypt, Arab Rep.	17.7	22.6	35.3	52.2	93.8	9.2	7.04	..	..	..
50	Papua New Guinea	..	9.4	..	32.9	34.1	4.4	6.90	9.60	11.15	11.94
51	Dominican Rep.	18.5	22.4	18.0	23.4	29.5	16.3	..	..	..	..
52	Côte d'Ivoire	20.4	8.1	21.8	25.8	31.0	4.4	6.19	5.25	9.38	8.00
53	Honduras	14.6	11.3	15.4	22.8	30.5	4.9	7.00	9.62	18.50	15.54
54	Nicaragua	15.0	..	15.4	21.0	..	86.6	7.50	..	..	..
55	Thailand	17.8	18.4	23.6	37.3	64.9	2.8	12.00	9.50	18.00	15.00
56	El Salvador	14.3	18.3	21.6	28.1	31.5	16.5	..	..	..	..
57	Congo, People's Rep.	14.2	10.3	16.5	14.7	20.8	1.8	6.50	7.79	11.00	11.13
58	Jamaica	17.2	25.6	24.3	35.6	52.7	19.4	10.29	17.50	13.00	23.00
59	Guatemala	16.3	14.1	15.2	20.5	22.9	12.7	9.00	11.00	..	..
60	Cameroon	19.1	13.8	11.7	18.3	18.7	8.1	7.50	7.15	13.00	13.00
61	Paraguay	21.3	18.9	12.1	19.8	16.3	21.0	..	..	..	..
62	Ecuador	22.6	30.0	15.6	20.2	18.8	29.5	..	..	..	..
63	Botswana	..	23.5	..	30.7	29.5	8.4	5.00	7.50	8.48	10.00
64	Tunisia	17.4	*15.5*	29.2	41.1	..	8.2	2.50	5.50	7.25	10.00
65	Turkey	27.4	49.8	23.0	16.7	24.5	37.4	10.95	35.40	25.67	50.00
66	Colombia	26.5	..	19.8	23.7	..	23.7	..	..	19.00	..
67	Chile	137.5	..	16.3	17.6	..	20.6	37.46	26.60	47.14	38.28

Note: For data comparability and coverage, see the technical notes. Figures in italics are for years other than those specified.

		Monetary holdings, broadly defined					Average annual inflation (GDP deflator)	Nominal interest rates of banks (average annual percentage)			
		Average annual nominal growth rate (percent)		Average outstanding (percentage of GDP)				Deposit rate		Lending rate	
		1965–80	1980–87	1965	1980	1987	1980–87	1980	1987	1980	1987
68	Peru	25.9	*100.8*	18.7	16.3	..	101.5	..	..	..	..
69	Mauritius	21.8	18.3	27.3	41.1	50.0	8.1	9.25	9.38	*12.19*	14.13
70	Jordan	19.1	12.7	..	88.8	132.9	2.8	..	..	..	..
71	Costa Rica	24.6	27.0	19.3	38.8	36.9	28.6	..	14.06	..	23.82
72	Syrian Arab Rep.	21.9	*21.1*	24.6	40.9	..	11.0	5.00	..	..	..
73	Malaysia	21.5	13.5	26.3	69.8	124.3	1.1	6.23	*7.17*	7.75	8.19
74	Mexico	21.9	66.2	25.1	27.5	21.0	68.9	20.63	97.24	28.10	..
75	South Africa	14.0	15.0	56.6	49.5	51.0	13.8	5.54	8.70	9.50	12.50
76	Poland	..	24.0	..	58.3	38.1	29.2	3.00	6.00	8.00	12.00
77	*Lebanon*	16.2	*42.3*	83.4	..	..	..	..	..	..	..
	Upper-middle-income										
78	Brazil	43.4	..	20.6	18.0	..	166.3	115.00	517.40	..	..
79	Uruguay	65.5	53.8	28.0	30.5	34.7	54.5	50.30	60.83	66.62	95.80
80	Hungary	..	7.5	..	46.5	46.8	5.7	3.00	4.00	9.00	11.50
81	Panama	..	..	..	..	..	3.3	..	..	..	..
82	Argentina	86.0	283.8	..	22.2	19.1	298.7	87.97	*61.23*	..	..
83	Yugoslavia	25.7	54.4	43.6	59.1	46.0	57.2	5.88	79.25	11.50	111.25
84	Algeria	22.1	*17.5*	32.1	58.5	..	5.6	..	..	..	..
85	Korea, Rep.	35.5	18.7	11.1	31.8	44.1	5.0	19.50	10.00	18.00	10.00
86	Gabon	25.2	8.4	16.2	15.2	24.4	2.6	7.50	7.94	12.50	11.13
87	Portugal	19.5	22.8	77.7	96.3	104.7	20.8	18.20	..	18.50	..
88	Venezuela	22.3	16.0	17.3	36.3	45.8	11.4	..	8.94	..	8.48
89	Greece	21.4	25.1	35.0	61.6	80.0	19.7	14.50	*15.50*	21.25	21.82
90	Trinidad and Tobago	23.1	*12.4*	21.3	32.0	..	6.2	*6.57*	6.03	10.00	11.50
91	Libya	29.2	2.2	14.2	34.7	..	0.1	5.13	*5.50*	7.00	*7.00*
92	Oman	..	19.8	..	12.3	28.6	−6.5	..	7.48	..	9.10
93	*Iran, Islamic Rep.*	28.6	..	21.6	..	..	..	..	..	..	..
94	*Iraq*	..	..	19.7	..	..	..	..	..	..	..
95	*Romania*	..	7.5	..	..	..	..	..	..	..	..

Low- and middle-income
Sub-Saharan Africa
East Asia
South Asia
Europe, M.East, & N.Africa
Latin America & Caribbean

17 highly indebted

High-income economies
OECD members
†Other

96	Spain	19.7	9.1	59.2	75.2	64.8	10.7	13.05	8.97	16.85	16.36
97	Ireland	16.1	6.4	..	58.1	*47.6*	*10.2*	12.00	6.21	15.96	11.15
98	†Saudi Arabia	32.1	*11.6*	16.4	18.6	*52.6*	−2.8	..	..	..	..
99	†Israel	52.8	163.4	15.0	56.9	67.3	159.0	..	19.39	176.93	61.43
100	New Zealand	12.8	*16.4*	57.2	53.2	*55.3*	11.5	*11.00*	*16.32*	12.63	..
101	†Singapore	17.8	11.6	58.4	74.4	104.8	1.3	9.37	2.89	11.72	6.10
102	†Hong Kong	..	..	..	69.3	..	6.7	..	..	..	..
103	Italy	17.8	*12.2*	60.0	76.0	*66.5*	11.5	12.70	6.98	19.03	13.57
104	United Kingdom	13.8	13.2	47.8	46.2	65.0	5.7	14.13	5.35	16.17	9.63
105	Australia	13.1	*12.7*	51.7	46.9	*47.7*	7.8	8.58	13.77	10.58	19.83
106	Belgium[a]	10.4	*6.5*	59.2	57.0	*56.2*	5.7	7.69	5.00	..	9.33
107	Netherlands	14.7	*5.8*	55.2	79.0	*87.7*	2.3	5.96	3.55	13.50	8.15
108	Austria	13.3	7.5	48.9	72.6	84.1	4.3	5.00	3.03	..	..
109	France	15.3	9.1	53.5	72.5	72.1	7.7	6.25	5.31	18.73	15.82
110	Germany, Fed. Rep.	10.1	5.7	46.1	60.4	64.7	2.9	7.95	3.20	12.04	8.36
111	Finland	14.7	13.9	39.1	39.5	48.9	7.2	*9.00*	7.00	9.77	8.91
112	†Kuwait	17.8	5.6	28.1	33.1	93.1	−4.6	4.50	4.50	6.80	6.80
113	Denmark	11.5	15.6	45.8	42.6	58.7	6.8	10.80	7.07	17.20	13.62
114	Canada	15.3	7.3	40.2	64.5	62.7	5.0	12.86	7.66	14.27	9.52
115	Sweden	10.8	*5.2*	39.3	40.6	..	7.9	11.25	8.94	15.12	12.99
116	Japan	17.2	8.6	106.9	134.0	170.3	1.4	5.50	1.76	8.32	5.09
117	†United Arab Emirates	..	13.0	..	19.0	63.0	−0.3	9.47	..	12.13	..
118	Norway	12.6	12.7	51.9	51.6	59.1	6.1	5.08	*5.35*	12.63	*13.46*
119	United States	9.2	9.9	63.9	58.8	68.0	4.3	13.07	8.21	15.27	8.21
120	Switzerland	7.1	8.4	101.1	107.4	121.5	3.9	*7.75*	3.19	*5.56*	5.24

Total reporting economies
Oil exporters

Nonreporting nonmembers

a. Includes Luxembourg.

Table 14. Growth of merchandise trade

		Merchandise trade (millions of dollars)		Average annual growth rate [a] (percent)				Terms of trade (1980=100)	
		Exports 1987	Imports 1987	Exports 1965-80	1980-87	Imports 1965-80	1980-87	1985	1987
	Low-income economies	**95,802** t	**116,254** t	**5.6** w	**3.4** w	**4.5** w	**2.3** w	**92** m	**84** m
	China and India	**52,090** t	**62,377** t	**4.8** w	**9.6** w	**4.5** w	**10.6** w	**104** m	**101** m
	Other low-income	**43,712** t	**153,877** t	**5.9** w	**−0.1** w	**4.5** w	**−3.9** w	**91** m	**84** m
1	Ethiopia	402	1,150	−0.5	−0.6	−0.9	7.6	99	84
2	Bhutan	25	88	..	..	..	..	..	..
3	Chad	..	..	..	..	..	..	..	..
4	Zaire	1,594	1,149	4.7	−3.4	−2.9	−0.4	82	74
5	Bangladesh	1,074	2,620	..	6.2	..	2.3	124	91
6	Malawi	264	281	4.1	3.4	3.3	−6.1	73	67
7	Nepal	151	569	−2.3	5.1	3.0	6.4	91	93
8	Lao PDR	30	70	..	..	..	..	..	..
9	Mozambique	89	486	..	..	..	..	..	..
10	Tanzania	348	1,165	−4.0	−7.4	1.6	−0.4	90	90
11	Burkina Faso	202	540	6.8	4.9	5.8	2.0	80	74
12	Madagascar	310	386	0.7	−3.1	−0.4	−2.9	104	105
13	Mali	216	447	11.0	6.6	6.2	3.4	82	86
14	Burundi	84	206	3.0	8.3	2.0	2.4	100	75
15	Zambia	869	745	1.7	−3.3	−5.5	−6.2	72	79
16	Niger	361	417	12.8	−4.8	6.6	−6.2	108	86
17	Uganda	320	477	−3.9	2.7	−5.3	3.0	96	67
18	China*	39,542	43,392	5.5	11.7	7.9	14.2	95	87
19	Somalia	94	452	3.8	−7.7	5.8	−1.3	91	84
20	Togo	297	417	4.6	−3.0	8.6	−4.6	90	86
21	India	12,548	18,985	3.7	3.6	1.6	4.7	114	114
22	Rwanda	121	352	7.7	2.5	8.7	5.4	102	87
23	Sierra Leone	120	132	−3.8	−2.1	−2.7	−15.1	100	93
24	Benin	168	418	5.2	−0.1	6.7	0.4	90	88
25	Central African Rep.	130	186	−0.4	1.0	−1.1	−1.8	88	84
26	Kenya	961	1,755	0.3	−0.6	1.7	−3.0	92	80
27	Sudan	482	694	−0.3	4.2	2.3	−8.7	90	84
28	Pakistan	4,172	5,822	4.3	8.4	0.4	3.4	88	99
29	Haiti	261	378	7.0	−2.0	8.4	−2.5	97	109
30	Lesotho[b]	..	..	..	..	..	..	..	..
31	Nigeria	7,365	7,816	11.4	−5.1	15.2	−14.0	90	54
32	Ghana	1,056	836	−1.8	−1.6	−1.4	−2.9	91	85
33	Sri Lanka	1,393	2,085	0.5	6.5	−1.2	3.2	99	96
34	Yemen, PDR	409	1,450	−13.7	1.7	−7.5	3.3	99	73
35	Mauritania	428	474	2.7	11.2	5.4	1.7	112	98
36	Indonesia	17,206	14,453	9.6	2.7	14.2	−2.2	94	69
37	Liberia	385	208	4.5	−2.6	1.5	−10.2	91	93
38	*Afghanistan*	552	1,404	..	..	..	..	..	..
39	*Burma*	219	628	−2.1	−4.7	−1.7	−8.7	70	65
40	*Guinea*	..	..	..	..	..	..	..	..
41	*Kampuchea, Dem.*	..	..	..	..	..	..	..	..
42	*Viet Nam*	1,054	1,874	..	..	..	..	..	..
	Middle-income economies	**369,978** t	**353,481** t	**2.4** w	**5.5** w	**5.9** w	**−0.5** w	**92** m	**79** m
	Lower-middle-income	**144,178** t	**146,317** t	**5.3** w	**5.3** w	**4.1** w	**−1.7** w	**92** m	**78** m
43	Senegal	645	1,174	2.4	6.7	4.1	2.7	100	96
44	Bolivia	566	776	2.8	−0.8	5.0	−1.6	84	51
45	Zimbabwe	1,358	1,055	3.4	0.9	−1.8	−6.8	84	84
46	Philippines	5,649	7,144	4.7	−0.4	2.9	−4.0	92	98
47	Yemen Arab Rep.	19	1,311	2.8	−4.0	23.3	−11.0	93	93
48	Morocco	2,807	4,229	3.7	3.7	6.5	1.6	89	106
49	Egypt, Arab Rep.	4,040	8,453	2.7	8.4	6.0	2.8	84	64
50	Papua New Guinea	1,172	1,222	12.8	4.9	1.3	0.3	95	84
51	Dominican Rep.	711	1,783	1.7	−0.1	5.5	1.4	66	60
52	Côte d'Ivoire	2,982	2,168	5.6	3.4	8.0	−3.1	96	86
53	Honduras	827	895	3.1	3.1	2.5	−0.2	93	83
54	Nicaragua	300	923	2.3	−5.2	1.3	0.8	85	77
55	Thailand	11,659	12,955	8.5	10.2	4.1	3.4	74	81
56	El Salvador	634	975	2.4	−4.6	2.7	−0.7	96	75
57	Congo, People's Rep.	884	570	12.5	3.9	1.0	−0.7	94	64
58	Jamaica	649	1,207	−0.3	−6.2	−1.9	−1.5	95	100
59	Guatemala	1,084	1,479	4.8	−1.6	4.6	−4.6	87	80
60	Cameroon	1,714	2,168	5.2	9.7	5.6	3.4	92	66
61	Paraguay	952	1,202	7.9	13.8	4.6	2.2	82	76
62	Ecuador	2,021	2,250	15.1	5.5	6.8	−1.4	94	61
63	Botswana[b]	..	..	..	..	..	..	..	..
64	Tunisia	2,152	3,022	10.8	2.2	10.4	−2.5	83	79
65	Turkey	10,190	14,163	5.5	17.1	7.7	11.1	91	110
66	Colombia	5,024	4,230	1.4	7.5	5.3	−4.2	98	70
67	Chile	5,091	4,023	7.9	4.3	2.6	−8.3	79	77
*	Data for Taiwan, China are:	50,835	34,341	19.0	13.5	15.1	6.5	104	103

Note: For data comparability and coverage, see the technical notes.   Figures in italics are for years other than those specified.

		Merchandise trade (millions of dollars)		Average annual growth rate [a] (percent)				Terms of trade (1980=100)	
				Exports		Imports			
		Exports 1987	Imports 1987	1965-80	1980-87	1965-80	1980-87	1985	1987
68	Peru	2,605	4,060	2.3	−0.8	−0.2	−2.5	81	69
69	Mauritius	918	1,010	3.1	11.1	6.4	6.7	90	108
70	Jordan	930	2,691	13.7	5.9	9.7	0.6	93	106
71	Costa Rica	1,155	1,377	7.0	2.6	5.7	−1.5	95	84
72	Syrian Arab Rep.	1,357	2,546	11.4	−1.3	8.5	−5.3	95	78
73	Malaysia	17,865	12,506	4.4	9.7	2.9	−0.7	86	72
74	Mexico	20,887	12,731	7.6	6.6	5.7	−8.1	98	73
75	South Africa[b]	20,066	14,629	6.1	−0.1	0.1	−8.8	75	71
76	Poland	12,205	10,844	. .	4.3	. .	1.2	106	112
77	Lebanon	591	1,880	. .	. .	. .	. .	. .	. .
	Upper-middle-income	225,853 t	207,164 t	1.0 w	5.6 w	7.6 w	0.5 w	92 m	88 m
78	Brazil	26,225	16,581	9.3	5.6	8.2	−4.2	89	97
79	Uruguay	1,190	1,140	4.6	1.4	1.2	−6.5	87	97
80	Hungary	9,571	9,855	. .	3.9	. .	1.5	92	89
81	Panama	357	1,248	. .	3.8	. .	−3.3	94	71
82	Argentina	6,360	5,818	4.7	−0.3	1.8	−9.4	90	81
83	Yugoslavia	11,397	12,549	5.6	1.1	6.6	−2.0	111	116
84	Algeria	9,029	7,028	1.5	3.2	13.0	−4.6	97	56
85	Korea, Rep.	47,172	40,934	27.2	14.3	15.2	9.6	106	105
86	Gabon	1,285	836	8.1	−1.9	10.5	3.0	90	64
87	Portugal	9,167	13,438	3.4	12.2	3.7	3.8	85	99
88	Venezuela	10,567	8,725	−9.5	−0.4	8.7	−7.0	93	54
89	Greece	6,489	12,908	11.9	6.6	5.2	4.8	88	93
90	Trinidad and Tobago	1,462	1,219	−5.5	−7.1	−5.8	−15.1	96	61
91	Libya	6,061	4,877	3.3	−5.9	15.3	−15.3	92	47
92	Oman	3,941	1,882	. .	. .	. .	. .	. .	. .
93	Iran, Islamic Rep.	. .	10,359	. .	. .	. .	. .	. .	. .
94	Iraq	9,014	7,415	. .	. .	. .	. .	. .	. .
95	Romania	12,543	11,437	. .	. .	. .	. .	. .	. .
	Low- and middle-income	465,780 t	469,736 t	3.1 w	5.0 w	5.5 w	0.1 w	92 m	83 m
	Sub-Saharan Africa	28,471 t	32,516 t	6.6 w	−1.0 w	5.0 w	−5.8 w	91 m	84 m
	East Asia	193,993 t	170,740 t	9.7 w	10.1 w	8.6 w	6.1 w	94 m	84 m
	South Asia	19,616 t	30,871 t	1.7 w	4.8 w	0.6 w	3.7 w	95 m	94 m
	Europe, M.East, & N.Africa	113,691 t	146,301 t	. .	. .	. .	0.4 w	92 m	93 m
	Latin America & Caribbean	89,943 t	74,679 t	−2.1 w	3.0 w	4.4 w	−5.6 w	90 m	76 m
	17 highly indebted	112,628 t	95,193 t	0.4 w	2.1 w	6.3 w	−6.0 w	92 m	84 m
	High-income economies	1,924,470 t	2,007,404 t	7.0 w	3.3 w	4.4 w	4.8 w	94 m	97 m
	OECD members	1,784,793 t	1,871,384 t	7.2 w	4.2 w	4.2 w	5.2 w	94 m	98 m
	†Other	139,677 t	136,020 t	6.0 w	−4.2 w	10.6 w	0.4 w	95 m	54 m
96	Spain	34,099	49,009	12.4	6.9	4.4	5.6	90	111
97	Ireland	15,970	13,614	9.8	8.1	4.8	2.6	107	107
98	†Saudi Arabia	23,138	20,465	8.8	−16.3	25.9	−9.3	95	54
99	†Israel	8,475	14,300	8.9	7.3	6.3	3.8	94	89
100	New Zealand	7,179	7,255	4.2	4.5	1.1	4.2	97	98
101	†Singapore	28,592	32,480	4.7	6.1	7.0	3.7	101	102
102	†Hong Kong	48,475	48,462	9.5	11.4	8.3	9.1	103	106
103	Italy	116,582	122,211	7.7	3.8	3.5	4.3	95	114
104	United Kingdom	131,128	154,388	4.8	3.0	1.4	4.8	96	99
105	Australia	25,283	29,318	5.5	6.0	0.9	2.9	89	72
106	Belgium[c]	82,951	82,598	7.8	4.5	5.2	3.2	87	98
107	Netherlands	92,882	91,317	8.0	4.6	4.4	3.0	91	93
108	Austria	27,163	32,638	8.2	5.3	6.1	4.7	90	108
109	France	143,077	157,524	8.5	3.5	4.3	2.2	94	104
110	Germany, Fed. Rep.	293,790	227,334	7.2	4.7	5.3	4.6	88	120
111	Finland	20,039	19,860	5.9	3.8	3.1	3.5	96	109
112	†Kuwait	8,355	5,297	−1.9	−3.2	11.8	−5.5	92	54
113	Denmark	24,697	25,334	5.4	5.7	1.7	5.7	96	106
114	Canada	92,886	92,594	5.4	6.3	2.6	7.3	122	101
115	Sweden	44,313	40,621	4.9	5.7	1.8	2.8	88	96
116	Japan	229,055	146,048	11.4	5.8	4.9	3.6	112	153
117	†United Arab Emirates	12,000	7,226	10.9	0.1	20.5	−7.1	91	54
118	Norway	21,449	22,578	8.2	6.2	3.0	3.5	97	72
119	United States	252,567	422,407	6.4	−0.5	5.5	9.7	114	116
120	Switzerland	45,357	50,557	6.2	4.6	4.5	5.3	88	113
	Total reporting economies	2,390,197 t	2,477,661 t	6.1 w	3.4 w	4.6 w	3.9 w	93 m	84 m
	Oil exporters	168,325 t	153,727 t	3.0 w	−3.7 w	9.3 w	−5.7 w	94 m	61 m
	Nonreporting nonmembers	. .	. .	. .	. .	. .	. .	. .	. .

a. See the technical notes.   b. Figures are for the South African Customs Union comprising South Africa, Namibia, Lesotho, Botswana, and Swaziland; trade between the component territories is excluded.   c. Includes Luxembourg.

Table 15. Structure of merchandise imports

Percentage share of merchandise imports

	Food		Fuels		Other primary commodities		Machinery and transport equipment		Other manufactures	
	1965	1987	1965	1987	1965	1987	1965	1987	1965	1987
Low-income economies	**22** *w*	**7** *w*	**5** *w*	**9** *w*	**10** *w*	**7** *w*	**28** *w*	**34** *w*	**34** *w*	**43** *w*
China and India	**28** *w*	**5** *w*	**3** *w*	**5** *w*	**19** *w*	**10** *w*	**26** *w*	**34** *w*	**24** *w*	**47** *w*
Other low-income	**17** *w*	**9** *w*	**7** *w*	**14** *w*	**4** *w*	**4** *w*	**29** *w*	**33** *w*	**42** *w*	**39** *w*
1 Ethiopia	6	4	6	18	6	3	37	37	44	38
2 Bhutan	..	..	..	..	..	..	..	..	..	..
3 Chad	13	..	19	..	3	..	23	..	42	..
4 Zaire	18	13	7	3	5	5	33	37	37	42
5 Bangladesh	..	16	..	9	..	6	..	28	..	42
6 Malawi	15	5	5	9	3	3	21	33	57	49
7 Nepal	22	6	5	8	14	7	37	22	22	57
8 Lao PDR	27	..	15	..	6	..	18	..	33	..
9 Mozambique	17	..	8	..	7	..	24	..	45	..
10 Tanzania	10	6	9	17	2	2	34	44	45	31
11 Burkina Faso	23	16	4	3	14	5	19	34	40	42
12 Madagascar	19	9	5	29	2	2	25	30	48	30
13 Mali	20	12	6	16	5	2	23	44	47	27
14 Burundi	16	12	6	5	9	5	15	23	55	55
15 Zambia	9	7	10	12	3	1	33	39	45	41
16 Niger	12	18	6	6	6	11	21	31	55	33
17 Uganda	7	5	1	9	3	2	38	46	51	38
18 China*	36	3	0	2	25	11	12	39	27	46
19 Somalia	31	13	5	3	8	6	24	47	33	32
20 Togo	15	20	3	6	5	6	31	28	45	40
21 India	22	8	5	11	14	8	37	24	22	48
22 Rwanda	12	12	7	15	5	7	28	30	50	35
23 Sierra Leone	17	17	9	9	3	4	30	20	41	49
24 Benin	18	11	6	34	7	2	17	16	53	37
25 Central African Rep.	13	13	7	1	2	4	29	39	49	43
26 Kenya	10	9	11	21	3	4	34	34	42	33
27 Sudan	23	17	5	22	4	3	21	26	47	32
28 Pakistan	20	16	3	19	5	7	38	31	34	27
29 Haiti	25	27	6	11	6	5	14	19	48	38
30 Lesotho[a]	..	..	..	..	..	..	..	..	..	..
31 Nigeria	9	8	6	3	3	3	34	36	48	50
32 Ghana	12	6	4	17	3	3	33	36	48	37
33 Sri Lanka	41	17	8	17	4	3	12	27	34	37
34 Yemen, PDR	19	16	40	36	5	2	10	24	26	22
35 Mauritania	9	26	4	10	1	2	56	35	30	27
36 Indonesia	6	3	3	16	2	3	39	39	50	39
37 Liberia	16	19	8	21	3	3	34	29	39	29
38 *Afghanistan*	17	..	4	..	1	..	8	..	69	..
39 *Burma*	15	5	4	2	5	2	18	43	58	48
40 *Guinea*	..	..	..	..	..	..	..	..	..	..
41 *Kampuchea, Dem.*	6	..	7	..	2	..	26	..	58	..
42 *Viet Nam*	..	..	..	..	..	..	..	..	..	..
Middle-income economies	**15** *w*	**10** *w*	**8** *w*	**12** *w*	**11** *w*	**10** *w*	**31** *w*	**35** *w*	**36** *w*	**35** *w*
Lower-middle-income	**15** *w*	**10** *w*	**7** *w*	**10** *w*	**9** *w*	**7** *w*	**33** *w*	**35** *w*	**36** *w*	**38** *w*
43 Senegal	36	32	6	16	4	2	15	16	38	33
44 Bolivia	19	15	1	2	3	3	35	45	42	36
45 Zimbabwe	13	10	8	8	3	3	31	36	46	43
46 Philippines	20	8	10	17	7	7	33	28	30	40
47 Yemen Arab Rep.	40	27	6	0	6	2	26	32	21	39
48 Morocco	36	14	5	18	10	15	18	24	31	28
49 Egypt, Arab Rep.	26	24	7	2	12	7	23	28	31	39
50 Papua New Guinea	23	20	5	10	3	1	25	34	45	35
51 Dominican Rep.	23	13	10	15	4	5	24	27	40	40
52 Côte d'Ivoire	18	19	6	15	3	4	28	28	46	35
53 Honduras	11	5	6	14	1	1	26	31	56	48
54 Nicaragua	12	15	5	11	2	2	30	20	51	53
55 Thailand	6	5	9	13	6	9	31	32	49	40
56 El Salvador	15	12	5	8	4	4	28	20	48	56
57 Congo, People's Rep.	15	16	6	7	1	3	34	27	44	46
58 Jamaica	20	16	9	17	5	4	23	20	43	43
59 Guatemala	11	6	7	12	2	4	29	28	50	51
60 Cameroon	11	13	5	1	4	3	28	36	51	46
61 Paraguay	24	14	14	8	4	8	31	41	28	29
62 Ecuador	10	5	9	3	4	3	33	52	44	38
63 Botswana[a]	..	..	..	..	..	..	..	..	..	..
64 Tunisia	16	11	6	11	7	12	31	22	41	44
65 Turkey	6	4	10	22	10	13	37	29	37	32
66 Colombia	8	8	1	3	10	8	45	39	35	43
67 Chile	20	12	6	10	10	4	35	39	30	36
* Data for Taiwan, China are:	13	7	5	9	25	17	29	33	29	34

Note: For data comparability and coverage, see the technical notes.   Figures in italics are for years other than those specified.

		Percentage share of merchandise imports									
		Food		Fuels		Other primary commodities		Machinery and transport equipment		Other manufactures	
		1965	1987	1965	1987	1965	1987	1965	1987	1965	1987
68	Peru	17	13	3	1	5	3	41	47	34	36
69	Mauritius	34	19	5	7	3	5	16	20	43	48
70	Jordan	28	18	6	17	6	5	18	21	42	39
71	Costa Rica	9	4	5	10	2	2	29	30	54	54
72	Syrian Arab Rep.	22	12	10	26	9	4	16	24	43	33
73	Malaysia	25	10	12	6	10	4	22	50	32	30
74	Mexico	5	11	2	1	10	8	50	46	33	34
75	South Africa[a]	5	2	5	0	11	4	42	43	37	50
76	Poland	..	11	..	17	..	11	..	32	..	30
77	*Lebanon*	28	..	9	..	9	..	17	..	36	..
	Upper-middle-income	**14** *w*	**11** *w*	**9** *w*	**14** *w*	**13** *w*	**12** *w*	**27** *w*	**34** *w*	**35** *w*	**31** *w*
78	Brazil	20	9	21	27	9	8	22	28	28	28
79	Uruguay	7	8	17	16	16	7	24	30	36	39
80	Hungary	12	7	12	17	22	10	27	31	28	36
81	Panama	11	3	21	8	2	0	21	32	45	57
82	Argentina	6	5	10	11	21	9	25	37	38	37
83	Yugoslavia	16	6	6	17	19	10	28	30	32	35
84	Algeria	26	27	0	2	6	7	15	29	52	35
85	Korea, Rep.	15	6	7	15	26	17	13	34	38	28
86	Gabon	16	18	5	1	2	3	38	38	40	39
87	Portugal	16	13	8	12	19	8	27	33	30	34
88	Venezuela	12	14	1	0	5	4	44	45	39	36
89	Greece	15	18	8	14	11	7	35	24	30	36
90	Trinidad and Tobago	11	22	50	4	2	5	16	30	22	39
91	Libya	13	15	4	1	3	2	36	33	43	49
92	Oman	..	19	..	3	..	3	..	49	..	26
93	*Iran, Islamic Rep.*	16	..	0	..	6	..	36	..	42	..
94	*Iraq*	24	..	0	..	7	..	25	..	44	..
95	*Romania*	..	..	..	..	..	..	..	..	..	..
	Low- and middle-income	**17** *w*	**9** *w*	**7** *w*	**11** *w*	**11** *w*	**9** *w*	**30** *w*	**35** *w*	**36** *w*	**38** *w*
	Sub-Saharan Africa	**14** *w*	**12** *w*	**6** *w*	**10** *w*	**4** *w*	**4** *w*	**30** *w*	**33** *w*	**44** *w*	**41** *w*
	East Asia	**21** *w*	**6** *w*	**6** *w*	**10** *w*	**15** *w*	**12** *w*	**23** *w*	**36** *w*	**34** *w*	**36** *w*
	South Asia	**29** *w*	**10** *w*	**4** *w*	**13** *w*	**11** *w*	**7** *w*	**32** *w*	**26** *w*	**26** *w*	**43** *w*
	Europe, M.East, & N.Africa	..	**14** *w*	..	**15** *w*	..	**10** *w*	..	**32** *w*	..	**31** *w*
	Latin America & Caribbean	**12** *w*	**10** *w*	**9** *w*	**10** *w*	**8** *w*	**6** *w*	**34** *w*	**37** *w*	**36** *w*	**36** *w*
	17 highly indebted	**14** *w*	**10** *w*	**7** *w*	**12** *w*	**10** *w*	**7** *w*	**34** *w*	**36** *w*	**35** *w*	**36** *w*
	High-income economies	**19** *w*	**10** *w*	**11** *w*	**11** *w*	**19** *w*	**7** *w*	**20** *w*	**33** *w*	**31** *w*	**39** *w*
	OECD members	**19** *w*	**10** *w*	**11** *w*	**11** *w*	**20** *w*	**7** *w*	**20** *w*	**33** *w*	**31** *w*	**38** *w*
	†Other	**22** *w*	**9** *w*	**8** *w*	**7** *w*	**13** *w*	**5** *w*	**20** *w*	**33** *w*	**39** *w*	**46** *w*
96	Spain	19	11	10	16	16	8	27	35	28	29
97	Ireland	18	12	8	7	10	4	25	33	39	42
98	†Saudi Arabia	29	17	1	1	5	2	27	34	38	46
99	†Israel	16	6	6	7	12	6	28	39	38	41
100	New Zealand	7	7	7	7	10	4	33	39	43	44
101	†Singapore	23	8	13	18	19	5	14	39	30	30
102	†Hong Kong	25	8	3	3	13	6	13	25	46	59
103	Italy	24	15	16	14	24	11	15	28	21	33
104	United Kingdom	30	12	11	6	25	7	11	35	23	40
105	Australia	5	5	8	5	10	4	37	39	41	47
106	Belgium[b]	14	11	9	9	21	8	24	29	32	42
107	Netherlands	15	15	10	11	13	5	25	28	37	41
108	Austria	14	6	7	7	13	7	31	35	35	45
109	France	19	11	15	11	18	7	20	31	27	40
110	Germany, Fed. Rep.	22	12	8	10	21	8	13	28	35	43
111	Finland	10	6	10	13	12	7	35	37	34	37
112	†Kuwait	21	16	1	0	7	3	33	39	39	42
113	Denmark	14	12	11	8	11	6	25	30	39	44
114	Canada	10	6	7	5	9	5	40	55	34	30
115	Sweden	12	7	11	9	12	6	30	38	36	40
116	Japan	22	17	20	27	38	18	9	12	11	27
117	†United Arab Emirates	15	4	3	3	7	1	34	43	41	49
118	Norway	10	6	7	5	12	6	38	39	32	43
119	United States	19	6	10	11	20	5	14	42	36	36
120	Switzerland	16	7	6	4	11	6	24	32	43	51
	Total reporting economies	**18** *w*	**10** *w*	**10** *w*	**11** *w*	**18** *w*	**8** *w*	**22** *w*	**34** *w*	**32** *w*	**39** *w*
	Oil exporters	**14** *w*	**12** *w*	**7** *w*	**5** *w*	**8** *w*	**4** *w*	**34** *w*	**38** *w*	**39** *w*	**42** *w*
	Nonreporting nonmembers	..	..	..	..	..	..	..	..	..	..

a. Figures are for the South African Customs Union comprising South Africa, Namibia, Lesotho, Botswana, and Swaziland; trade between the component territories is excluded.   b. Includes Luxembourg.

Table 16. Structure of merchandise exports

	Fuels, minerals, and metals		Other primary commodities		Machinery and transport equipment		Other manufactures		(Textiles and clothing)[a]	
Percentage share of merchandise exports										
	1965	1987	1965	1987	1965	1987	1965	1987	1965	1987
Low-income economies	22 w	29 w	53 w	22 w	1 w	4 w	23 w	45 w	11 w	7 w
China and India	8 w	13 w	45 w	17 w	2 w	6 w	45 w	64 w	..	..
Other low-income	30 w	48 w	60 w	27 w	1 w	3 w	8 w	21 w	4 w	9 w
1 Ethiopia	1	3	98	96	1	0	0	1	0	*0*
2 Bhutan	..	..	..	..	..	..	..	..	..	..
3 Chad	4	..	93	..	0	..	4	..	0	..
4 Zaire	72	63	20	31	0	1	8	5	0	..
5 Bangladesh	..	16	..	33	..	17	..	33	..	..
6 Malawi	0	0	99	84	0	5	1	11	0	..
7 Nepal	0	2	78	26	0	2	22	70	..	*37*
8 Lao PDR	..	..	..	..	..	..	..	..	..	..
9 Mozambique	14	..	83	..	0	..	2	..	1	..
10 Tanzania	4	7	83	75	0	3	13	15	0	..
11 Burkina Faso	1	0	94	98	1	1	4	1	2	..
12 Madagascar	4	11	90	78	1	2	4	9	1	*3*
13 Mali	1	0	96	71	1	1	2	28	1	..
14 Burundi	1	1	94	85	0	0	6	15	0	..
15 Zambia	97	93	3	4	0	1	0	2	0	..
16 Niger	0	86	95	13	1	0	4	1	1	..
17 Uganda	14	4	86	96	0	0	1	0	0	..
18 China*	6	14	48	16	3	4	43	66	..	..
19 Somalia	6	1	80	98	4	0	10	1	*0*	..
20 Togo	49	66	48	26	1	1	3	7	0	..
21 India	10	9	41	22	1	10	48	59	36	*16*
22 Rwanda	40	9	60	90	0	0	1	1	*0*	..
23 Sierra Leone	25	22	14	19	0	1	60	58	0	..
24 Benin	1	42	94	38	2	6	3	15	0	..
25 Central African Rep.	1	0	45	66	0	0	54	33	0	..
26 Kenya	13	21	81	62	0	2	6	15	0	..
27 Sudan	1	14	98	79	1	3	0	4	0	..
28 Pakistan	2	1	62	32	1	3	35	64	29	*41*
29 Haiti	14	0	61	19	2	9	23	73	*3*	..
30 Lesotho[b]	..	..	..	..	..	..	..	..	..	..
31 Nigeria	32	91	65	8	0	0	2	1	0	..
32 Ghana	13	37	85	60	1	0	2	2	0	..
33 Sri Lanka	2	8	97	52	0	2	1	38	0	*25*
34 Yemen, PDR	80	92	14	8	2	0	4	0	2	..
35 Mauritania	94	31	5	66	1	0	0	2	0	..
36 Indonesia	43	54	53	18	3	3	1	24	0	*5*
37 Liberia	72	57	25	41	1	0	3	1	0	..
38 *Afghanistan*	0	..	86	..	0	..	13	..	13	..
39 *Burma*	5	4	94	85	0	8	0	3	0	..
40 *Guinea*	..	..	..	..	..	..	..	..	..	..
41 *Kampuchea, Dem.*	..	..	..	..	..	..	..	..	..	..
42 *Viet Nam*	..	..	..	..	..	..	..	..	..	..
Middle-income economies	35 w	23 w	53 w	20 w	0 w	16 w	13 w	43 w	3 w	12 w
Lower-middle-income	27 w	26 w	59 w	27 w	0 w	13 w	12 w	34 w	2 w	7 w
43 Senegal	9	25	88	60	1	4	2	11	1	..
44 Bolivia	92	93	3	5	0	0	4	2	0	*0*
45 Zimbabwe	45	17	40	43	1	3	15	37	6	..
46 Philippines	11	14	84	24	0	6	6	56	1	*6*
47 Yemen Arab Rep.	9	1	91	21	0	63	0	15	..	..
48 Morocco	40	20	55	32	0	1	5	48	1	*16*
49 Egypt, Arab Rep.	8	69	72	12	0	0	20	19	15	*12*
50 Papua New Guinea	1	59	89	35	0	1	10	5	..	..
51 Dominican Rep.	10	17	88	61	0	5	2	17	0	..
52 Côte d'Ivoire	2	4	93	86	1	2	4	7	1	*1*
53 Honduras	7	10	89	78	0	0	4	12	1	*0*
54 Nicaragua	4	2	90	88	0	0	6	10	0	..
55 Thailand	11	2	84	45	0	12	4	41	0	*18*
56 El Salvador	2	3	81	66	1	3	16	28	6	..
57 Congo, People's Rep.	5	67	32	17	2	1	61	15	0	*0*
58 Jamaica	28	14	41	21	0	4	31	62	4	..
59 Guatemala	0	3	86	62	1	3	13	33	4	..
60 Cameroon	17	51	77	40	3	5	2	4	0	*1*
61 Paraguay	0	1	92	87	0	0	8	12	0	*0*
62 Ecuador	2	41	96	55	0	1	2	3	1	..
63 Botswana[b]	..	..	..	..	..	..	..	..	..	..
64 Tunisia	31	26	51	13	0	6	19	55	2	*29*
65 Turkey	9	6	89	27	0	7	2	60	1	*33*
66 Colombia	18	33	75	46	0	1	6	20	2	*4*
67 Chile	89	69	7	23	1	3	4	6	0	*0*
* Data for Taiwan, China are:	2	1	56	6	4	30	37	63	5	17

Note: For data comparability and coverage, see the technical notes.   Figures in italics are for years other than those specified.

		Fuels, minerals, and metals		Other primary commodities		Machinery and transport equipment		Other manufactures		(Textiles and clothing)[a]	
		1965	*1987*	*1965*	*1987*	*1965*	*1987*	*1965*	*1987*	*1965*	*1987*
68	Peru	45	71	54	11	0	3	1	16	0	..
69	Mauritius	0	0	100	59	0	2	0	38	0	..
70	Jordan	27	30	54	14	11	14	7	41	1	4
71	Costa Rica	0	1	84	59	1	7	15	33	2	..
72	Syrian Arab Rep.	7	46	83	28	1	3	9	24	7	..
73	Malaysia	35	25	59	36	2	27	4	13	0	*3*
74	Mexico	22	44	62	9	1	28	15	19	3	*2*
75	South Africa[b]	24	12	44	9	3	3	29	75	1	..
76	Poland	..	19	..	14	..	33	..	34	..	*5*
77	*Lebanon*	13	..	53	..	14	..	20	..	2	..
	Upper-middle-income	**40** *w*	**22** *w*	**46** *w*	**15** *w*	**3** *w*	**25** *w*	**13** *w*	**40** *w*	**4** *w*	**15** *w*
78	Brazil	9	22	83	33	2	17	7	28	1	*3*
79	Uruguay	0	0	95	55	0	3	5	41	2	*17*
80	Hungary	..	7	..	22	..	34	..	37	..	*7*
81	Panama	35	13	63	73	0	0	2	13	1	*3*
82	Argentina	1	4	93	65	1	6	5	25	0	*3*
83	Yugoslavia	11	9	33	13	24	30	33	48	8	9
84	Algeria	58	98	38	0	2	0	2	1	0	0
85	Korea, Rep.	15	2	25	5	3	33	56	59	27	25
86	Gabon	50	63	39	26	1	2	10	8	0	..
87	Portugal	4	3	34	16	3	16	58	64	24	32
88	Venezuela	97	91	1	1	0	2	2	6	0	..
89	Greece	8	13	78	33	2	3	11	51	3	32
90	Trinidad and Tobago	84	72	9	5	0	1	7	22	0	0
91	Libya	99	99	1	*1*	1	*0*	0	*0*	0	..
92	Oman	..	*91*	..	2	..	5	..	2	..	*0*
93	*Iran, Islamic Rep.*	87	..	8	..	0	..	4	..	4	..
94	*Iraq*	95	..	4	..	0	..	1	..	0	..
95	*Romania*	..	..	..	..	..	..	..	..	..	..
	Low- and middle-income	**30** *w*	**25** *w*	**53** *w*	**20** *w*	**2** *w*	**16** *w*	**17** *w*	**41** *w*	**5** *w*	**11** *w*
	Sub-Saharan Africa	**34** *w*	**48** *w*	**58** *w*	**40** *w*	**1** *w*	**2** *w*	**6** *w*	**10** *w*	**0** *w*	..
	East Asia	**17** *w*	**12** *w*	**58** *w*	**15** *w*	**2** *w*	**21** *w*	**21** *w*	**52** *w*	**2** *w*	**14** *w*
	South Asia	**6** *w*	**8** *w*	**57** *w*	**28** *w*	**1** *w*	**8** *w*	**36** *w*	**56** *w*	**27** *w*	**23** *w*
	Europe, M.East, & N.Africa	..	..	..	..	..	..	..	..	..	..
	Latin America & Caribbean	**43** *w*	**39** *w*	**50** *w*	**28** *w*	**1** *w*	**13** *w*	**6** *w*	**20** *w*	**1** *w*	**3** *w*
	17 highly indebted	**38** *w*	**38** *w*	**51** *w*	**25** *w*	**3** *w*	**14** *w*	**8** *w*	**24** *w*	**1** *w*	**3** *w*
	High-income economies	**11** *w*	**9** *w*	**20** *w*	**12** *w*	**30** *w*	**39** *w*	**39** *w*	**39** *w*	**7** *w*	**5** *w*
	OECD members	**9** *w*	**7** *w*	**21** *w*	**12** *w*	**31** *w*	**41** *w*	**39** *w*	**39** *w*	**7** *w*	**5** *w*
	†Other	**57** *w*	**36** *w*	**14** *w*	**6** *w*	**4** *w*	**19** *w*	**26** *w*	**38** *w*	**11** *w*	**14** *w*
96	Spain	9	8	51	20	10	31	29	40	6	4
97	Ireland	3	2	63	29	5	32	29	36	7	5
98	†Saudi Arabia	98	90	1	1	1	4	1	5	0	..
99	†Israel	6	2	28	13	2	18	63	67	9	7
100	New Zealand	1	6	94	69	0	6	5	19	0	3
101	†Singapore	21	17	44	11	11	43	24	29	6	6
102	†Hong Kong	2	2	11	6	6	22	81	70	44	34
103	Italy	8	4	14	8	30	35	47	53	15	14
104	United Kingdom	7	14	10	9	41	37	41	40	7	4
105	Australia	13	37	73	38	5	8	10	17	1	1
106	Belgium[c]	13	8	11	12	20	27	55	54	12	7
107	Netherlands	12	14	32	26	21	20	35	40	9	5
108	Austria	8	5	16	8	20	33	55	54	12	9
109	France	8	5	21	19	26	36	45	41	10	5
110	Germany, Fed. Rep.	7	4	5	6	46	49	42	41	5	5
111	Finland	3	5	40	15	12	27	45	53	2	4
112	†Kuwait	84	85	9	2	4	4	3	7	0	..
113	Denmark	2	4	55	35	22	25	21	36	4	5
114	Canada	28	19	35	20	15	38	22	23	1	1
115	Sweden	9	6	23	10	35	44	33	40	2	2
116	Japan	2	1	7	1	31	65	60	32	17	3
117	†United Arab Emirates	99	79	1	4	0	0	0	16	..	..
118	Norway	21	51	28	11	17	17	34	21	2	1
119	United States	8	6	27	16	37	47	28	31	3	2
120	Switzerland	3	3	7	4	30	35	60	58	10	6
	Total reporting economies	**15** *w*	**12** *w*	**27** *w*	**14** *w*	**25** *w*	**35** *w*	**35** *w*	**40** *w*	**7** *w*	**6** *w*
	Oil exporters	**67** *w*	**69** *w*	**25** *w*	**7** *w*	**3** *w*	**10** *w*	**7** *w*	**12** *w*	**1** *w*	..
	Nonreporting nonmembers	..	..	..	..	..	..	..	..	..	..

a. Textiles and clothing is a subgroup of other manufactures.   b. Figures are for the South African Customs Union comprising South Africa, Namibia, Lesotho, Botswana, and Swaziland; trade between the component territories is excluded.   c. Includes Luxembourg.

Table 17. OECD imports of manufactured goods: origin and composition

		Value of imports of manufactures, by origin (millions of dollars)		Composition of 1987 imports of manufactures by high-income OECD countries (percent)				
		1967	1987	Textiles and clothing	Chemicals	Electrical machinery and electronics	Transport equipment	Others
	Low-income economies	**1,168** *t*	**28,141** *t*	**48** *w*	**7** *w*	**3** *w*	**2** *w*	**40** *w*
	China and India	**694** *t*	**19,843** *t*	**49** *w*	**7** *w*	**4** *w*	**1** *w*	**40** *w*
	Other low-income	**473** *t*	**8,298** *t*	**48** *w*	**7** *w*	**2** *w*	**3** *w*	**40** *w*
1	Ethiopia	1	39	17	8	12	1	62
2	Bhutan	0	0	24	3	22	0	51
3	Chad	0	1	4	0	2	78	15
4	Zaire	32	294	0	5	0	0	95
5	Bangladesh	..	696	84	0	0	0	16
6	Malawi	0	13	87	0	2	2	9
7	Nepal	2	118	88	0	1	0	11
8	Lao PDR	0	2	49	8	1	0	42
9	Mozambique	3	6	6	5	7	8	74
10	Tanzania	0	4	3	0	31	2	65
11	Burkina Faso	6	33	60	17	2	1	20
12	Madagascar	0	12	2	3	10	1	85
13	Mali	36	34	57	1	4	37	
14	Burundi	3	2	2	1	3	0	94
15	Zambia	2	27	22	0	4	0	74
16	Niger	0	376	0	98	0	0	2
17	Uganda	1	3	17	7	38	9	29
18	China	193	14,306	49	9	5	1	36
19	Somalia	1	4	1	0	14	3	82
20	Togo	0	14	3	0	0	2	95
21	India	501	5,537	46	3	1	0	49
22	Rwanda	0	1	6	4	34	3	53
23	Sierra Leone	72	64	0	0	0	0	99
24	Benin	0	3	24	2	1	0	72
25	Central African Rep.	9	46	0	0	0	0	100
26	Kenya	16	90	6	4	13	2	74
27	Sudan	1	17	26	8	7	15	44
28	Pakistan	123	1,884	79	0	0	0	21
29	Haiti	9	405	45	2	18	0	35
30	Lesotho[a]	..	..	..	..	..	..	..
31	Nigeria	15	93	9	20	5	2	64
32	Ghana	13	33	1	1	4	3	91
33	Sri Lanka	7	775	76	1	0	4	20
34	Yemen, PDR	5	3	8	1	8	11	73
35	Mauritania	0	3	31	14	6	1	48
36	Indonesia	18	2,599	33	4	1	2	60
37	Liberia	33	345	0	0	0	48	51
38	*Afghanistan*	9	57	91	0	0	1	8
39	*Burma*	2	18	29	3	1	1	66
40	*Guinea*	27	107	0	45	0	0	55
41	*Kampuchea, Dem.*	1	1	38	0	14	0	48
42	*Viet Nam*	2	0	..	..	..	..	..
	Middle-income economies	**2,816** *t*	**152,017** *t*	**25** *w*	**5** *w*	**17** *w*	**6** *w*	**48** *w*
	Lower-middle-income	**1,269** *t*	**42,398** *t*	**26** *w*	**6** *w*	**23** *w*	**7** *w*	**38** *w*
43	Senegal	6	31	9	24	7	28	32
44	Bolivia	2	15	44	8	0	5	42
45	Zimbabwe	13	440	9	0	0	0	91
46	Philippines	97	3,119	34	3	30	0	32
47	Yemen Arab Rep.	0	7	1	1	28	5	64
48	Morocco	16	1,191	67	15	6	1	11
49	Egypt, Arab Rep.	19	520	68	3	2	1	27
50	Papua New Guinea	3	28	3	0	4	31	62
51	Dominican Rep.	6	846	47	1	7	0	45
52	Côte d'Ivoire	4	186	24	3	1	2	70
53	Honduras	2	86	53	2	0	1	44
54	Nicaragua	1	3	2	14	7	2	74
55	Thailand	20	3,919	33	2	14	0	50
56	El Salvador	1	89	49	1	31	0	19
57	Congo, People's Rep.	8	79	0	0	2	12	86
58	Jamaica	48	474	40	54	1	0	4
59	Guatemala	4	86	67	9	0	3	20
60	Cameroon	2	58	28	1	3	2	65
61	Paraguay	4	38	14	19	0	0	66
62	Ecuador	3	40	14	6	5	1	74
63	Botswana[a]	..	..	..	..	..	..	..
64	Tunisia	12	1,208	64	15	7	1	13
65	Turkey	18	3,743	77	5	1	1	16
66	Colombia	23	573	26	5	0	1	68
67	Chile	11	228	9	33	2	3	53

Note: For data comparability and coverage, see the technical notes.

		Value of imports of manufactures, by origin (millions of dollars)		Composition of 1987 imports of manufactures by high-income OECD countries (percent)				
		1967	1987	Textiles and clothing	Chemicals	Electrical machinery and electronics	Transport equipment	Others
68	Peru	7	297	56	6	3	0	35
69	Mauritius	0	526	85	0	1	0	14
70	Jordan	1	138	2	40	9	3	46
71	Costa Rica	1	303	66	2	11	1	20
72	Syrian Arab Rep.	2	26	19	1	7	4	69
73	Malaysia	24	4,553	16	3	60	0	20
74	Mexico	232	14,708	5	4	33	16	42
75	South Africa[a]	453	2,444	5	18	2	2	73
76	Poland	214	2,140	23	15	5	13	44
77	*Lebanon*	12	131	12	3	2	3	80
	Upper-middle-income	**1,547 t**	**109,619 t**	**24 w**	**4 w**	**14 w**	**6 w**	**51 w**
78	Brazil	102	8,610	9	8	9	15	58
79	Uruguay	11	301	57	2	0	0	41
80	Hungary	112	2,030	26	20	9	3	42
81	Panama	24	479	10	4	1	35	50
82	Argentina	59	1,083	12	18	1	2	67
83	Yugoslavia	235	5,711	28	8	9	13	42
84	Algeria	14	176	0	42	2	5	51
85	Korea, Rep.	150	33,247	27	2	18	8	45
86	Gabon	8	123	0	58	1	2	39
87	Portugal	314	7,361	42	6	8	5	39
88	Venezuela	24	461	2	24	2	4	67
89	Greece	63	3,312	67	3	3	1	27
90	Trinidad and Tobago	33	240	0	69	0	1	30
91	Libya	5	165	0	89	1	1	9
92	Oman	1	82	1	1	26	2	71
93	*Iran, Islamic Rep.*	95	619	86	0	1	0	13
94	*Iraq*	6	141	1	13	6	6	74
95	*Romania*	65	2,030	33	8	3	4	52
	Low- and middle-income	**3,984 t**	**180,158 t**	**28 w**	**5 w**	**14 w**	**6 w**	**46 w**
	Sub-Saharan Africa	**318 t**	**3,145 t**	**20 w**	**18 w**	**2 w**	**6 w**	**54 w**
	East Asia	**682 t**	**104,324 t**	**26 w**	**3 w**	**17 w**	**4 w**	**50 w**
	South Asia	**634 t**	**9,040 t**	**59 w**	**2 w**	**1 w**	**1 w**	**38 w**
	Europe, M.East, & N.Africa	**1,232 t**	**31,442 t**	**46 w**	**9 w**	**6 w**	**5 w**	**34 w**
	Latin America & Caribbean	**664 t**	**29,764 t**	**11 w**	**8 w**	**20 w**	**13 w**	**47 w**
	17 highly indebted	**890 t**	**37,392 t**	**16 w**	**7 w**	**20 w**	**12 w**	**45 w**
	High-income economies	**74,378 t**	**1,071,178 t**	**7 w**	**13 w**	**11 w**	**20 w**	**50 w**
	OECD members	**72,982 t**	**1,030,645 t**	**6 w**	**13 w**	**11 w**	**21 w**	**50 w**
	†Other	**1,396 t**	**40,533 t**	**26 w**	**7 w**	**18 w**	**1 w**	**48 w**
96	Spain	351	18,276	6	10	7	27	51
97	Ireland	310	9,662	8	22	12	1	57
98	†Saudi Arabia	3	1,263	0	61	6	1	32
99	†Israel	195	5,472	10	14	10	3	63
100	New Zealand	69	1,312	12	20	7	3	57
101	†Singapore	22	10,265	8	5	34	1	52
102	†Hong Kong	1,073	21,753	42	1	15	0	42
103	Italy	4,710	78,348	18	8	7	10	57
104	United Kingdom	7,470	70,427	6	18	10	12	55
105	Australia	308	4,265	2	33	5	10	49
106	Belgium[b]	4,496	56,557	9	20	6	20	45
107	Netherlands	3,385	47,039	8	31	9	7	45
108	Austria	925	19,002	11	9	12	6	63
109	France	5,526	85,237	7	18	9	21	45
110	Germany, Fed. Rep.	14,220	205,842	5	14	10	23	47
111	Finland	664	12,035	5	7	8	6	74
112	†Kuwait	5	141	0	25	8	14	52
113	Denmark	894	12,810	9	15	12	4	60
114	Canada	4,925	55,448	1	7	6	40	45
115	Sweden	2,705	31,648	2	8	9	21	60
116	Japan	4,568	148,150	2	3	17	33	45
117	†United Arab Emirates	0	355	9	19	7	6	60
118	Norway	747	6,026	3	22	9	8	58
119	United States	14,257	133,127	2	13	13	21	51
120	Switzerland	2,450	35,296	6	20	11	2	60
	Total reporting economies	**78,362 t**	**1,251,336 t**	**10 w**	**12 w**	**11 w**	**18 w**	**49 w**
	Oil exporters	**1,240 t**	**28,203 t**	**10 w**	**13 w**	**20 w**	**10 w**	**47 w**
	Nonreporting nonmembers	**955 t**	**7,866 t**	**10 w**	**23 w**	**6 w**	**9 w**	**53 w**

Note: Includes only high-income OECD economies.   a. Figures are for South Africa, Bostwana and Lesotho.   b. Includes Luxembourg.

Table 18. Balance of payments and reserves

		Current account balance (millions of dollars)				Net workers' remittances (millions of dollars)		Net direct private investment (millions of dollars)		Gross international reserves		In months of import coverage
		After official transfers		Before official transfers						Millions of dollars		
		1970	1987	1970	1987	1970	1987	1970	1987	1970	1987	1987
	Low-income economies									3,673 t	50,173 t	4.5 w
	China and India									1,023 t	33,965 t	6.4 w
	Other low-income									2,650 t	16,208 t	2.7 w
1	Ethiopia	−32	−264ª	−43	−475ª	..	..	4	..	72	245	2.3
2	Bhutan	..	−56	..	−56	..	..	..	..	..	..	..
3	Chad	2	−83	−33	−324	−6	−26	1	4	2	57	1.4
4	Zaire	−64	−705	−141	−851	−98	..	42	10	189	417	1.8
5	Bangladesh	−114ª	−309	−234	−966	0	617	..	2	..	876	3.5
6	Malawi	−35	−24	−46	−53	−4	..	9	..	29	58	1.8
7	Nepal	8ª	−133	−16ª	−194	..	..	..	..	94	251	4.9
8	Lao PDR	..	−114ª	..	−141ª	..	..	..	..	6	..	..
9	Mozambique	..	−372ª	..	−676ª	..	33ª	..	..	..	..	..
10	Tanzania	−36	−128ª	−37	−605ª	..	..	..	..	65	32	0.3
11	Burkina Faso	9	−124	−21	−124	16	110	0	..	36	328	4.4
12	Madagascar	10	−135ª	−42	−241ª	−26	..	10	..	37	185	3.1
13	Mali	−2	−111	−22	−313	−1	26	−1	4	1	25	0.5
14	Burundi	2ª	−132ª	−8ª	−185ª	−7ª	..	0ª	2ª	15	69	2.8
15	Zambia	108	21	107	−12	−48	1	−297	..	515	111	1.4
16	Niger	0	−67	−32	−201	−3	−43	0	..	19	254	6.4
17	Uganda	20	−107	19	−200	−5	..	4	1	57	55	1.0
18	China*	−81ª	300	−81ª	171	..	166	..	1,669	..	22,453	6.7
19	Somalia	−6	248ª	−18	−59ª	..	..	5	..	21	17	0.4
20	Togo	3	−73	−14	−147	−3	1	0	12	35	361	7.3
21	India	−386ª	−3,750ª	−592ª	−4,068ª	65ª	2,000ª	0ª	253ª	1,023	11,512	5.9
22	Rwanda	7	−131	−12	−250	−4	−15	0	23	8	164	4.6
23	Sierra Leone	−16	−5	−20	−9	0	0	8	−6	39	6	1.0
24	Benin	−3	−208ª	−23	−223ª	0	37ª	7	..	16	9	0.2
25	Central African Rep.	−12	−96ª	−24	−214ª	−4	−24ª	1	20ª	1	102	3.2
26	Kenya	−49	−497	−86	−639	..	..	14	..	220	294	1.4
27	Sudan	−42	−422ª	−43	−702ª	..	..	−1	..	22	12	0.1
28	Pakistan	−667	−336	−705	−719	86	2,172	23	62	195	1,441	2.2
29	Haiti	2	−31	−5	−158	13	58	3	5	4	26	0.6
30	Lesotho	18ª	−12	−1ª	−16	29ª	..	..	2	..	68	1.9
31	Nigeria	−368	−380	−412	−380	..	..	205	386	223	1,498	2.3
32	Ghana	−68	−275	−76	−275	−9	−2	68	5	43	332	3.0
33	Sri Lanka	−59	−378	−71	−572	3	348	0	29	43	310	1.4
34	Yemen, PDR	−4	−122	−4	−178	52	303	−1	..	59	117	2.1
35	Mauritania	−5	−73ª	−13	−164ª	−6	2ª	1	5ª	3	77	1.5
36	Indonesia	−310	−1,837	−376	−2,098	..	112	83	425	160	7,095	3.9
37	Liberia	−16ª	−118	−27ª	−163	−18ª	−51	28ª	39	..	1	0.0
38	Afghanistan	..	−556	..	−748	..	..	..	..	49	747	5.6
39	Burma	-63	−208ª	−81	−307ª	..	..	..	..	98	149	2.7
40	Guinea	..	−53ª	..	−114ª	..	..	..	5ª	..	..	..
41	Kampuchea, Dem.	..	..	..	..	..	..	..	..	..	..	..
42	Viet Nam	..	..	..	..	..	..	..	..	..	..	..
	Middle-income economies									16,606 t	133,497 t	3.5 w
	Lower-middle-income									7,024 t	64,672 t	3.4 w
43	Senegal	−16	−316ª	−66	−608ª	−16	10ª	5	−50ª	22	23	0.1
44	Bolivia	4	−485	2	−597	..	1	−76	22	46	530	5.2
45	Zimbabwe	−14ª	50	−13ª	−22	..	..	..	−24	59	370	2.7
46	Philippines	−48	−539	−138	−736	0	211	−29	186	255	2,312	2.7
47	Yemen Arab Rep.	−34ª	−607ª	−52ª	−607ª	45ª	428ª	..	−10ª	..	540	3.7
48	Morocco	−124	164	−161	164	27	1,587	20	57	142	752	1.5
49	Egypt, Arab Rep.	−148	−2,705ª	−452	−3,757ª	29	2,845ª	..	869ª	165	2,556	2.1
50	Papua New Guinea	−89ª	−326	−239ª	−530	..	..	..	71	..	467	3.2
51	Dominican Rep.	−102	−119	−103	−148	25	242	72	50	32	191	2.5
52	Côte d'Ivoire	−38	−624ª	−73	−641ª	−56	..	31	..	119	30	0.1
53	Honduras	−64	−183	−68	−330	..	..	8	36	20	114	1.0
54	Nicaragua	−40	−693	−43	−799	..	3	15	..	49	..	..
55	Thailand	−250	−586	−296	−723	..	..	43	270	911	5,206	4.1
56	El Salvador	9	127ª	7	−196ª	..	..	4	−41ª	64	413	3.7
57	Congo, People's Rep.	−45ª	−245	−53ª	−298	−3ª	−39	30ª	−40	9	9	0.1
58	Jamaica	−153	−96	−149	−160	29	44	161	−5	139	174	1.1
59	Guatemala	−8	−464	−8	−555	..	..	29	152	79	541	3.5
60	Cameroon	−30	−1,112ª	−47	−1,112ª	−11	3ª	16	31ª	81	78	0.3
61	Paraguay	−16	−411ª	−19	−422ª	..	..	4	9ª	18	514	4.2
62	Ecuador	−113	−1,176	−122	−1,251	..	..	89	75	76	692	2.4
63	Botswana	−30ª	597	−35ª	458	..	−29	6ª	125	..	2,057	17.6
64	Tunisia	−53	−62	−88	−99	20	486	16	92	60	616	1.9
65	Turkey	−44	−984	−57	−1,335	273	2,021	58	110	440	3,444	2.3
66	Colombia	−293	255	−333	255	6	616	39	349	207	3,416	5.2
67	Chile	−91	−811	−95	−871	..	..	−79	97	392	3,244	5.2
*	Data for Taiwan, China are:	1	17,925	2	17,917	..	..	61	14	627	80,460	22.5

Note: For data comparability and coverage, see the technical notes.   Figures in italics are for years other than those specified.

		Current account balance (millions of dollars)				Net workers' remittances (millions of dollars)		Net direct private investment (millions of dollars)		Gross international reserves		In months of import coverage
		After official transfers		Before official transfers						Millions of dollars		
		1970	1987	1970	1987	1970	1987	1970	1987	1970	1987	1987
68	Peru	202	−1,914	146	−1,419	..	..	−70	22	339	1,319	3.2
69	Mauritius	8	72	5	47	..	..	2	44	46	362	3.5
70	Jordan	−20	−350	−130	−350	..	844	..	33	258	910	2.6
71	Costa Rica	−74	−225	−77	−377	..	..	26	65	16	519	3.3
72	Syrian Arab Rep.	−69	−465	−72	−1,365	7	250	..	..	57	403	1.3
73	Malaysia	8	2,336	2	2,170	..	..	94	575	667	8,573	5.5
74	Mexico	−1,068	3,884	−1,098	3,509	..	..	323	3,248	756	13,692	6.2
75	South Africa	−1,215	3,027	−1,253	2,911	..	..	318	28	1,057	3,463	1.9
76	Poland	..	−578	..	−578	..	..	..	..	..	1,723	1.4
77	*Lebanon*	..	..	..	..	..	..	..	..	405	4,832	..
	Upper-middle-income									9,582 t	68,852 t	3.7 w
78	Brazil	−837	−1,275	−861	−1,275	..	..	407	582	1,190	7,477	3.0
79	Uruguay	−45	−124	−55	−132	..	..	..	−5	186	1,793	12.0
80	Hungary	−61	−676	−61	−676	..	..	..	..	697	3,067	2.9
81	Panama	−64	342	−79	229	..	..	33	−72	16	78	0.2
82	Argentina	−163	−4,285	−160	−4,285	..	..	11	−19	682	3,734	3.5
83	Yugoslavia	−372	819	−378	819	441	3,721	..	..	143	1,602	1.2
84	Algeria	−125	−406	−163	−406	178	434	45	−20	352	4,343	4.5
85	Korea, Rep.	−623	9,854	−706	9,835	..	−8	66	418	610	3,739	0.9
86	Gabon	−3	−210	−15	−231	−8	−143	−1	121	15	18	0.1
87	Portugal	−158a	641	−158a	309	523a	3,243	15a	306	1,565	13,039	9.9
88	Venezuela	−104	−1,125	−98	−1,103	−87	−34	−23	21	1,047	11,510	10.1
89	Greece	−422	−1,298	−424	−2,963	333	1,334	50	683	318	4,299	3.6
90	Trinidad and Tobago	−109	−184	−104	−184	3	..	83	−22	43	214	2.8
91	Libya	645	−54	758	−13	−134	−446	139	−80	1,596	7,581	15.4
92	Oman	..	−966	..	−966	..	−849	..	138	13	1,542	3.6
93	*Iran, Islamic Rep.*	−507	..	−511	..	..	..	25	..	217	..	..
94	*Iraq*	105	..	104	..	..	..	24	..	472	..	..
95	*Romania*	−23	1,489	−23	1,489	..	..	..	..	..	1,851	1.9
	Low- and middle-income									20,279 t	183,670 t	3.8 w
	Sub-Saharan Africa									2,028 t	8,030 t	2.1 w
	East Asia									2,885 t	50,401 t	3.9 w
	South Asia									1,453 t	14,547 t	4.6 w
	Europe, M.East, & N.Africa									7,375 t	56,700 t	3.4 w
	Latin America & Caribbean									5,481 t	50,529 t	4.7 w
	17 highly indebted									5,958 t	54,295 t	4.1 w
	High-income economies									75,457 t	892,235 t	4.2 w
	OECD members									72,938 t	832,318 t	4.1 w
	†Other									2,519 t	59,917 t	6.0 w
96	Spain	79	−51	79	−412	469	1,210	179	3,814	1,851	36,439	7.4
97	Ireland	−198	391	−228	−1,087	..	..	32	..	698	4,970	3.0
98	†Saudi Arabia	71	−9,571	152	−6,270	−183	−4,935	20	−1,175	670	24,909	7.9
99	†Israel	−562	−999	−766	−4,495	..	..	40	148	452	6,368	3.9
100	New Zealand	−232	−1,368	−222	−1,304	16	221	137	104	258	3,270	3.5
101	†Singapore	−572	539	−585	561	..	..	93	982	1,012	15,227	5.0
102	†Hong Kong	225	1,199	225	1,199	..	..	..	282	..	..	..
103	Italy	774	−1,059	1,096	1,213	446	1,214	498	1,742	5,547	62,489	4.8
104	United Kingdom	1,913	−2,621	2,316	2,738	..	..	−190	−16,345	2,918	50,918	2.4
105	Australia	−777	−8,688	−682	−8,611	..	..	778	57	1,709	12,584	3.5
106	Belgiumb	717	2,920	904	4,203	39	4	140	−411	2,947	25,899	2.6
107	Netherlands	−483	3,372	−511	4,427	−49	−236	−15	−5,505	3,362	37,225	3.8
108	Austria	−75	−226	−73	−155	−7	257	104	134	1,806	17,769	4.7
109	France	−204	−4,088	18	−1,030	−641	−2,055	248	−4,000	5,199	72,675	4.0
110	Germany, Fed. Rep.	852	44,956	1,899	55,599	−1,366	−3,673	−303	−7,064	13,879	124,834	5.0
111	Finland	−239	−1,938	−232	−1,633	..	..	−41	−809	455	7,364	3.5
112	†Kuwait	853a	4,414	853a	4,572	..	−1,102	−8a	−93	209	5,371	6.8
113	Denmark	−544	−2,951	−510	−2,798	..	..	75	..	488	10,854	3.3
114	Canada	1,056	−7,963	739	−7,498	..	..	566	−922	4,733	16,242	1.6
115	Sweden	−265	−853	−160	160	..	−16	−104	−2,844	775	11,112	2.4
116	Japan	1,980	87,660	2,160	90,410	..	..	−260	−18,330	4,876	92,702	5.2
117	†United Arab Emirates	75a	6,486	75a	6,486	..	..	4a	..	..	5,121	5.7
118	Norway	−242	−4,111	−200	−3,337	..	−55	32	−846	813	14,850	5.0
119	United States	2,330	−153,950	4,680	−141,760	−650	−890	−6,130	−2,470	15,237	161,738	3.4
120	Switzerland	72	5,879	114	5,834	−313	−1,413	..	26	5,317	67,791	10.2
	Total reporting economies									95,736 t	1,075,906 t	4.1 w
	Oil exporters									7,082 t	103,724 t	5.4 w
	Nonreporting nonmembers									..	..	..

a. World Bank estimates.　b. Includes Luxembourg.

Table 19. Official development assistance from OECD & OPEC members

		Amount									
		1965	1970	1975	1980	1983	1984	1985	1986	1987	1988[a]
OECD						**Millions of US dollars**					
97	Ireland	0	0	8	30	33	35	39	62	51	57
100	New Zealand	..	14	66	72	61	55	54	75	87	104
103	Italy	60	147	182	683	834	1,133	1,098	2,404	2,615	..
104	United Kingdom	472	500	904	1,854	1,610	1,429	1,530	1,737	1,865	2,615
105	Australia	119	212	552	667	753	777	749	752	627	1,091
106	Belgium	102	120	378	595	479	446	440	547	689	592
107	Netherlands	70	196	608	1,630	1,195	1,268	1,136	1,740	2,094	2,231
108	Austria	10	11	79	178	158	181	248	198	196	302
109	France	752	971	2,093	4,162	3,815	3,788	3,995	5,105	6,525	6,959
110	Germany, Fed. Rep.	456	599	1,689	3,567	3,176	2,782	2,942	3,832	4,391	4,700
111	Finland	2	7	48	110	153	178	211	313	433	610
113	Denmark	13	59	205	481	395	449	440	695	859	922
114	Canada	96	337	880	1,075	1,429	1,625	1,631	1,695	1,885	2,340
115	Sweden	38	117	566	962	754	741	840	1,090	1,337	1,534
116	Japan	244	458	1,148	3,353	3,761	4,319	3,797	5,634	7,454	..
118	Norway	11	37	184	486	584	540	574	798	890	988
119	United States	4,023	3,153	4,161	7,138	8,081	8,711	9,403	9,564	8,945	12,170
120	Switzerland	12	30	104	253	320	285	302	422	547	615
	Total	6,480	6,968	13,847	27,297	27,592	28,742	29,429	36,663	41,531	49,730
OECD						**As a percentage of donor GNP**					
97	Ireland	0.00	0.00	0.09	0.16	0.20	0.22	0.24	0.28	0.28	0.20
100	New Zealand	..	0.23	0.52	0.33	0.28	0.25	0.25	0.30	0.26	0.27
103	Italy	0.10	0.16	0.11	0.15	0.20	0.28	0.26	0.40	0.35	..
104	United Kingdom	0.47	0.41	0.39	0.35	0.35	0.33	0.33	0.31	0.28	0.32
105	Australia	0.53	0.59	0.65	0.48	0.49	0.45	0.48	0.47	0.33	0.46
106	Belgium	0.60	0.46	0.59	0.50	0.59	0.58	0.55	0.48	0.49	0.39
107	Netherlands	0.36	0.61	0.75	0.97	0.91	1.02	0.91	1.01	0.98	0.98
108	Austria	0.11	0.07	0.21	0.23	0.24	0.28	0.38	0.21	0.17	0.24
109	France	0.76	0.66	0.62	0.63	0.74	0.77	0.78	0.70	0.74	0.73
110	Germany, Fed. Rep.	0.40	0.32	0.40	0.44	0.48	0.45	0.47	0.43	0.39	0.39
111	Finland	0.02	0.06	0.18	0.22	0.32	0.35	0.40	0.45	0.50	0.59
113	Denmark	0.13	0.38	0.58	0.74	0.73	0.85	0.80	0.89	0.88	0.89
114	Canada	0.19	0.41	0.54	0.43	0.45	0.50	0.49	0.48	0.47	0.50
115	Sweden	0.19	0.38	0.82	0.78	0.84	0.80	0.86	0.85	0.88	0.87
116	Japan	0.27	0.23	0.23	0.32	0.32	0.34	0.29	0.29	0.31	..
118	Norway	0.16	0.32	0.66	0.87	1.10	1.03	1.01	1.17	1.09	1.12
119	United States	0.58	0.32	0.27	0.27	0.24	0.24	0.24	0.23	0.20	0.25
120	Switzerland	0.09	0.15	0.19	0.24	0.31	0.30	0.31	0.30	0.31	0.32
OECD						**National currencies**					
97	Ireland (millions of pounds)	0	0	4	15	26	32	37	46	34	..
100	New Zealand (millions of dollars)	..	13	55	74	91	95	109	143	146	..
103	Italy (billions of lire)	38	92	119	585	1,267	1,991	2,097	3,578	3,389	..
104	United Kingdom (millions of pounds)	169	208	409	798	1,062	1,070	1,180	1,194	1,151	..
105	Australia (millions of dollars)	106	189	402	591	802	873	966	1,121	895	..
106	Belgium (millions of francs)	5,100	6,000	13,902	17,399	24,390	25,527	26,145	24,525	25,835	..
107	Netherlands (millions of guilders)	253	710	1,538	3,241	3,411	4,069	3,773	4,263	4,242	..
108	Austria (millions of schillings)	260	286	1,376	2,303	2,838	3,622	5,132	3,023	2,478	..
109	France (millions of francs)	3,713	5,393	8,971	17,589	29,075	33,107	35,894	35,357	39,218	..
110	Germany, Fed. Rep. (millions of deutsche marks)	1,824	2,192	4,155	6,484	8,109	7,917	8,661	8,323	8,004	..
111	Finland (millions of markkaa)	6	29	177	414	852	1,070	1,308	1,587	1,902	..
113	Denmark (millions of kroner)	90	443	1,178	2,711	3,612	4,650	4,657	5,623	5,848	..
114	Canada (millions of dollars)	104	353	895	1,257	1,761	2,104	2,227	2,354	2,493	..
115	Sweden (millions of kronor)	197	605	2,350	4,069	5,781	6,129	7,226	7,765	8,477	..
116	Japan (billions of yen)	88	165	341	760	893	1,026	749	950	1,078	..
118	Norway (millions of kroner)	79	264	962	2,400	4,261	4,407	4,946	5,901	5,998	..
119	United States (millions of dollars)	4,023	3,153	4,161	7,138	8,081	8,711	9,403	9,564	8,945	..
120	Switzerland (millions of francs)	52	131	268	424	672	672	743	759	815	..
OECD						**Summary**					
	ODA (billions of US dollars, nominal prices)	6.48	6.97	13.86	27.30	27.59	28.74	29.43	36.66	41.53	49.73
	ODA as percentage of GNP	0.48	0.34	0.35	0.37	0.36	0.36	0.35	0.35	0.35	..
	ODA (billions of US dollars, constant 1980 prices)	20.90	18.34	22.00	27.30	27.87	29.03	29.14	30.55	30.76	..
	GNP (trillions of US dollars, nominal prices)	1.35	2.04	3.96	7.39	7.70	8.03	8.49	10.39	12.02	..
	GDP deflator[b]	0.31	0.38	0.63	0.99	0.99	0.99	1.01	1.35	..	..

		1976	1979	1980	1981	1982	1983	1984	1985	1986	1987
							Amount				
OPEC							Millions of US dollars				
31	Nigeria	80	29	35	143	58	35	51	45	52	30
84	Algeria	11	281	81	55	129	37	52	54	114	26
88	Venezuela	109	110	135	92	125	142	90	32	85	24
93	Iran, Islamic Rep.	751	−20	−72	−141	−193	10	52	−72	69	−10
94	Iraq	123	658	864	207	52	−10	−22	−32	−21	−35
98	Saudi Arabia	2,791	3,941	5,682	5,514	3,854	3,259	3,194	2,630	3,517	2,888
112	Kuwait	706	971	1,140	1,163	1,161	997	1,020	771	715	316
117	United Arab Emirates	1,028	968	1,118	805	406	351	88	122	91	19
91	Libya	98	145	376	257	44	144	24	57	68	76
	Qatar	180	282	277	246	139	20	10	8	19	4
	Total OAPEC	4,937	7,246	9,538	8,247	5,785	4,798	4,366	3,655	4,503	3,294
	Total OPEC	5,877	7,365	9,636	8,341	5,775	4,983	4,559	3,614	4,708	3,338
OPEC							As a percentage of donor GNP				
31	Nigeria	0.19	0.04	0.04	0.19	0.08	0.05	0.07	0.06	0.11	0.13
84	Algeria	0.07	0.90	0.20	0.13	0.31	0.08	0.10	0.10	0.18	0.04
88	Venezuela	0.35	0.23	0.23	0.14	0.19	0.22	0.19	0.07	0.17	0.06
93	Iran, Islamic Rep.	1.16	−0.02	−0.08	−0.13	−0.15	0.01	−0.01	−0.08	0.03	−0.01
94	Iraq	0.76	1.97	2.36	0.94	0.18	−0.09	−0.05	−0.08	0.04	0.06
98	Saudi Arabia	5.95	5.16	4.87	3.45	2.50	2.86	3.44	2.86	4.52	3.40
112	Kuwait	4.82	3.52	3.52	3.65	4.34	3.73	3.82	3.25	2.99	1.23
117	United Arab Emirates	8.95	5.08	4.06	2.57	1.39	1.30	0.32	0.29	0.34	0.08
91	Libya	0.66	0.60	1.16	0.81	0.15	0.51	0.08	0.58	0.13	0.30
	Qatar	7.35	6.07	4.16	3.50	2.13	0.39	0.17	0.18	0.08	0.08
	Total OAPEC	4.23	3.31	3.22	2.52	1.81	1.70	1.60	1.39	1.80	1.10
	Total OPEC	2.32	1.75	1.79	1.45	0.98	0.86	1.13	0.65	0.95	0.79

		1965	1970	1975	1980	1982	1983	1984	1985	1986	1987
						Net bilateral flows to low-income economies					
OECD							As a percentage of donor GNP				
97	Ireland	..	..	..	..	0.02	0.03	0.03	0.05	0.06	0.06
100	New Zealand	..	..	0.14	0.01	0.00	0.00	0.00	0.00	0.00	0.06
103	Italy	0.04	0.06	0.01	0.01	0.04	0.05	0.09	0.12	0.16	0.17
104	United Kingdom	0.23	0.15	0.11	0.11	0.07	0.10	0.09	0.09	0.09	0.09
105	Australia	0.08	0.09	0.10	0.04	0.07	0.05	0.06	0.05	0.04	0.08
106	Belgium	0.56	0.30	0.31	0.24	0.21	0.21	0.20	0.23	0.20	0.18
107	Netherlands	0.08	0.24	0.24	0.30	0.31	0.26	0.29	0.27	0.32	0.41
108	Austria	0.06	0.05	0.02	0.03	0.01	0.02	0.01	0.02	0.01	0.03
109	France	0.12	0.09	0.10	0.08	0.10	0.09	0.14	0.14	0.13	0.17
110	Germany, Fed. Rep.	0.14	0.10	0.12	0.08	0.12	0.13	0.11	0.14	0.12	0.13
111	Finland	..	..	0.06	0.08	0.09	0.12	0.13	0.17	0.18	0.20
113	Denmark	0.02	0.10	0.20	0.28	0.26	0.31	0.28	0.32	0.32	0.35
114	Canada	0.10	0.22	0.24	0.11	0.14	0.13	0.15	0.15	0.12	0.16
115	Sweden	0.07	0.12	0.41	0.36	0.38	0.33	0.30	0.31	0.38	0.29
116	Japan	0.13	0.11	0.08	0.08	0.11	0.09	0.07	0.09	0.10	0.13
118	Norway	0.04	0.12	0.25	0.31	0.37	0.39	0.34	0.40	0.47	0.42
119	United States	0.26	0.14	0.08	0.03	0.02	0.03	0.03	0.04	0.03	0.06
120	Switzerland	0.02	0.05	0.10	0.08	0.09	0.10	0.12	0.12	0.12	0.14
	Total	0.20	0.13	0.11	0.07	0.08	0.08	0.07	0.09	0.09	0.12

a. Preliminary estimates.   b. See the technical notes.

Table 20. Official development assistance: receipts

		Net disbursement of ODA from all sources							Per capita (dollars) 1987	As a percentage of GNP 1987
		Millions of dollars								
		1981	1982	1983	1984	1985	1986	1987		
Low-income economies		12,514 t	12,721 t	12,208 t	12,277 t	13,703 t	16,522 t	18,120 t	6.4 w	2.3 w
China and India		2,459 t	2,168 t	2,509 t	2,471 t	2,532 t	3,258 t	3,301 t	1.8 w	0.6 w
Other low-income		10,055 t	10,553 t	9,699 t	9,806 t	11,171 t	13,265 t	14,819 t	15.6 w	6.1 w
1	Ethiopia	245	200	339	364	715	636	635	14.3	11.8
2	Bhutan	10	11	13	18	24	40	42	31.3	16.7
3	Chad	60	65	95	115	182	165	198	37.6	20.3
4	Zaire	394	348	315	312	325	448	621	19.0	10.7
5	Bangladesh	1,104	1,341	1,049	1,200	1,152	1,455	1,637	15.4	9.3
6	Malawi	137	121	117	158	113	198	280	35.5	22.8
7	Nepal	181	200	201	198	236	301	345	19.6	12.7
8	Lao PDR	35	38	30	34	37	48	59	15.6	8.4
9	Mozambique	144	208	211	259	300	422	649	44.6	40.9
10	Tanzania	703	684	594	558	487	681	882	36.9	25.2
11	Burkina Faso	217	213	184	189	198	284	283	34.1	16.2
12	Madagascar	234	242	183	153	188	316	327	30.0	15.8
13	Mali	230	210	215	320	380	372	364	46.9	18.6
14	Burundi	121	127	140	141	142	187	192	38.5	15.3
15	Zambia	232	317	217	239	328	464	429	59.5	21.1
16	Niger	194	257	175	161	304	307	348	51.2	16.1
17	Uganda	136	133	137	163	182	198	276	17.6	7.2
18	China	477	524	669	798	940	1,134	1,449	1.4	0.5
19	Somalia	374	462	343	350	353	511	580	101.6	57.0
20	Togo	63	77	112	110	114	174	123	38.0	10.0
21	India	1,983	1,644	1,840	1,673	1,592	2,124	1,852	2.3	0.7
22	Rwanda	153	151	150	165	181	211	243	37.7	11.6
23	Sierra Leone	60	82	66	61	66	87	68	17.8	7.3
24	Benin	82	81	86	77	96	138	136	31.5	8.1
25	Central African Rep.	102	90	93	114	104	139	173	63.7	16.1
26	Kenya	449	485	400	411	438	455	565	25.6	7.0
27	Sudan	632	740	962	622	1,128	945	902	39.0	10.5
28	Pakistan	823	916	735	749	801	967	858	8.4	2.4
29	Haiti	107	128	134	135	153	175	218	35.4	9.7
30	Lesotho	104	93	108	101	94	88	108	66.5	29.4
31	Nigeria	41	37	48	33	32	59	69	0.6	0.3
32	Ghana	145	141	110	216	203	371	373	27.5	7.4
33	Sri Lanka	377	416	473	466	484	570	502	30.7	7.5
34	Yemen, PDR	87	143	106	103	113	71	80	35.2	8.1
35	Mauritania	214	187	176	175	207	221	178	95.6	19.0
36	Indonesia	975	906	744	673	603	711	1,245	7.3	1.8
37	Liberia	108	109	118	133	90	97	78	33.6	6.9
38	*Afghanistan*	23	9	14	7	17	2	45	2.4	..
39	*Burma*	283	319	302	275	356	416	364	9.3	..
40	*Guinea*	106	90	68	123	119	175	214	33.0	..
41	*Kampuchea, Dem.*	130	44	37	17	13	13	14	1.8	..
42	*Viet Nam*	242	136	106	110	114	147	116	1.8	..
Middle-income economies		11,895 t	10,092 t	9,502 t	9,839 t	10,032 t	11,121 t	12,219 t	13.4 w	0.8 w
Lower-middle-income		10,784 t	9,460 t	9,044 t	9,307 t	9,396 t	10,280 t	11,167 t	20.9 w	1.8 w
43	Senegal	398	285	323	368	295	567	642	92.4	13.6
44	Bolivia	169	148	174	172	202	322	318	47.3	7.1
45	Zimbabwe	212	216	208	298	237	225	295	32.6	5.0
46	Philippines	376	333	429	397	486	956	775	13.3	2.2
47	Yemen Arab Rep.	411	412	328	326	283	262	349	41.2	8.2
48	Morocco	1,037	774	398	352	785	419	401	17.2	2.4
49	Egypt, Arab Rep.	1,292	1,441	1,463	1,794	1,791	1,717	1,766	35.2	4.9
50	Papua New Guinea	336	311	333	322	259	263	322	87.0	10.6
51	Dominican Rep.	105	136	100	188	207	93	130	19.3	2.6
52	Côte d'Ivoire	124	137	156	128	125	186	254	22.8	2.5
53	Honduras	109	158	190	286	272	283	258	55.0	6.4
54	Nicaragua	145	121	120	114	102	150	141	40.2	4.4
55	Thailand	406	389	431	474	481	496	506	9.4	1.1
56	El Salvador	167	218	290	261	345	341	426	86.4	9.0
57	Congo, People's Rep.	81	93	108	98	71	110	152	75.2	7.0
58	Jamaica	155	180	181	170	169	178	169	70.4	5.9
59	Guatemala	75	64	76	65	83	135	241	28.5	3.4
60	Cameroon	199	212	129	186	159	224	213	19.6	1.7
61	Paraguay	54	85	51	50	50	66	82	20.9	1.8
62	Ecuador	59	53	64	136	136	147	203	20.5	1.9
63	Botswana	97	101	104	102	96	102	154	135.6	10.1
64	Tunisia	239	210	205	178	163	223	282	37.0	2.9
65	Turkey	728	647	356	242	179	339	417	7.9	0.6
66	Colombia	102	97	86	88	62	63	78	2.6	0.2
67	Chile	−7	−8	0	2	40	−5	21	1.7	0.1

Note: For data comparability and coverage, see the technical notes. Figures in italics are for years other than those specified.

									Per capita (dollars)	As a percentage of GNP
		Net disbursement of ODA from all sources								
		Millions of dollars							1987	1987
		1981	1982	1983	1984	1985	1986	1987		
68	Peru	233	188	297	310	316	272	292	14.4	0.6
69	Mauritius	58	48	41	36	28	56	65	62.5	3.7
70	Jordan	1,065	798	787	687	540	565	595	157.0	12.0
71	Costa Rica	55	80	252	218	280	196	228	87.5	5.3
72	Syrian Arab Rep.	1,500	962	813	641	610	728	697	61.9	2.9
73	Malaysia	143	135	177	327	229	192	363	22.0	1.2
74	Mexico	99	140	132	83	144	252	156	1.9	0.1
75	South Africa	..	..	..	..	..	..	..	..	..
76	Poland	..	..	..	..	..	..	..	..	..
77	*Lebanon*	455	187	127	77	83	62	100	37.5	..
	Upper-middle-income	**1,219 t**	**741 t**	**576 t**	**664 t**	**726 t**	**938 t**	**1,130 t**	**3.0 w**	**0.1 w**
78	Brazil	235	208	101	161	123	178	288	2.0	0.1
79	Uruguay	7	4	3	4	5	27	18	5.9	0.2
80	Hungary	..	..	..	..	..	..	..	..	..
81	Panama	39	41	47	72	69	52	40	17.7	0.7
82	Argentina	44	30	48	49	39	88	99	3.2	0.1
83	Yugoslavia	−15	−8	3	3	11	19	35	1.5	0.1
84	Algeria	167	136	95	122	173	165	222	9.6	0.3
85	Korea, Rep.	330	34	8	−37	−9	−18	11	0.3	0.0
86	Gabon	44	62	64	76	61	79	82	76.8	2.3
87	Portugal	82	49	43	97	101	139	65	6.4	0.2
88	Venezuela	14	13	10	14	11	16	19	1.0	0.0
89	Greece	13	12	13	13	11	19	34	3.4	0.1
90	Trinidad and Tobago	−2	6	5	5	7	19	34	28.0	0.8
91	Libya	11	12	6	5	5	11	6	1.6	0.0
92	Oman	231	133	71	67	78	84	16	11.7	0.2
93	*Iran, Islamic Rep.*	9	3	48	13	16	27	70	1.5	..
94	*Iraq*	9	6	13	4	26	33	91	5.3	..
95	*Romania*	..	..	..	..	..	..	..	..	..
	Low- and middle-income	**24,409 t**	**22,813 t**	**21,710 t**	**22,115 t**	**23,735 t**	**27,643 t**	**30,339 t**	**8.1 w**	**1.3 w**
	Sub-Saharan Africa	6,889 t	7,102 t	6,889 t	7,113 t	8,139 t	9,898 t	11,151 t	25.5 w	8.3 w
	East Asia	3,451 t	2,850 t	2,964 t	3,114 t	3,153 t	3,942 t	4,860 t	3.3 w	0.8 w
	South Asia	4,761 t	4,847 t	4,612 t	4,579 t	4,645 t	5,873 t	5,599 t	5.2 w	1.7 w
	Europe, M.East, & N.Africa	7,343 t	5,928 t	4,886 t	4,727 t	4,983 t	4,885 t	5,271 t	16.6 w	1.2 w
	Latin America & Caribbean	1,965 t	2,087 t	2,359 t	2,582 t	2,814 t	3,045 t	3,458 t	8.6 w	0.4 w
	17 highly indebted	**2,727 t**	**2,405 t**	**2,379 t**	**2,320 t**	**2,964 t**	**3,370 t**	**3,422 t**	**5.9 w**	**0.4 w**
	High-income economies	..	..	..	..	..	..	..	..	..
	OECD members	..	..	..	..	..	..	..	..	..
	†Other	843 t	954 t	1,421 t	1,353 t	2,060 t	2,055 t	1,434 t	50.3 w	0.7 w
96	Spain	2	22	0	0	0	0	0	0.0	0.0
97	Ireland									
98	†Saudi Arabia	30	57	44	36	29	31	22	1.8	0.0
99	†Israel	773	857	1,345	1,256	1,978	1,937	1,251	285.9	3.6
100	New Zealand									
101	†Singapore	22	20	15	41	24	29	23	8.9	0.1
102	†Hong Kong	9	8	9	14	20	18	19	3.5	0.0
103	Italy									
104	United Kingdom									
105	Australia									
106	Belgium									
107	Netherlands									
108	Austria									
109	France									
110	Germany, Fed. Rep.									
111	Finland									
112	†Kuwait	10	6	5	4	4	5	3	1.8	0.0
113	Denmark									
114	Canada									
115	Sweden									
116	Japan									
117	†United Arab Emirates	1	5	4	3	4	34	115	79.0	0.5
118	Norway									
119	United States									
120	Switzerland									
	Total reporting economies	**25,254 t**	**23,789 t**	**23,131 t**	**23,469 t**	**25,795 t**	**29,698 t**	**31,773 t**	**8.4 w**	**1.1 w**
	Oil exporters	4,768 t	4,282 t	3,864 t	3,991 t	3,960 t	4,452 t	5,181 t	9.0 w	0.8 w
	Nonreporting nonmembers	**75 t**	**77 t**	**88 t**	**107 t**	**110 t**	**149 t**	**165 t**	**4.0 w**	..

Table 21. Total external debt

		Long-term debt (millions of dollars)				Use of IMF credit (millions of dollars)		Short-term debt (millions of dollars)		Total external debt (millions of dollars)	
		Public and publicly guaranteed		Private nonguaranteed							
		1970	1987	1970	1987	1970	1987	1970	1987	1970	1987
Low-income economies											
China and India											
Other low-income											
1	Ethiopia	169	2,434	0	0	0	63	..	94	..	2,590
2	Bhutan	..	41	0	0	0	0	..	0	..	41
3	Chad	33	270	0	0	3	10	..	38	..	318
4	Zaire	311	7,334	0	0	0	833	..	462	..	8,630
5	Bangladesh	0	8,851	0	0	0	581	..	74	..	9,506
6	Malawi	122	1,155	0	0	0	110	..	98	..	1,363
7	Nepal	3	902	0	0	0	27	..	19	..	947
8	Lao PDR	8	736	0	0	0	0	..	0	..	736
9	Mozambique	..	..	..	..	..	..	..	..	..	..
10	Tanzania	250	4,068	15	11	0	65	..	192	..	4,335
11	Burkina Faso	21	794	0	0	0	0	..	67	..	861
12	Madagascar	89	3,114	0	0	0	144	..	119	..	3,377
13	Mali	238	1,847	0	0	9	75	..	94	..	2,016
14	Burundi	7	718	0	0	8	0	..	37	..	755
15	Zambia	623	4,354	30	0	0	957	..	1,089	..	6,400
16	Niger	32	1,259	..	254	0	91	..	75	..	1,679
17	Uganda	138	1,116	0	0	0	229	..	60	..	1,405
18	China	..	23,659	0	0	0	848	..	5,720	..	30,227
19	Somalia	77	2,288	0	0	0	154	..	92	..	2,534
20	Togo	40	1,042	0	0	0	78	..	103	..	1,223
21	India	7,838	37,325	100	3,442	0	3,653	..	1,950	..	46,370
22	Rwanda	2	544	0	0	3	0	..	39	..	583
23	Sierra Leone	59	513	0	0	0	83	..	63	..	659
24	Benin	41	929	0	0	0	0	..	204	..	1,133
25	Central African Rep.	24	520	0	0	0	37	..	28	..	585
26	Kenya	319	4,482	88	496	0	381	..	591	..	5,950
27	Sudan	307	7,876	..	372	31	859	..	2,019	..	11,126
28	Pakistan	3,064	13,150	5	56	45	804	..	2,280	..	16,289
29	Haiti	40	674	0	0	2	52	..	79	..	804
30	Lesotho	8	237	0	0	0	0	..	4	..	241
31	Nigeria	452	25,707	115	350	0	0	..	2,657	..	28,714
32	Ghana	488	2,207	10	30	46	779	..	108	..	3,124
33	Sri Lanka	317	4,109	..	117	79	234	..	273	..	4,733
34	Yemen, PDR	1	1,669	0	0	0	0	..	55	..	1,724
35	Mauritania	27	1,868	0	0	0	47	..	119	..	2,035
36	Indonesia	2,443	41,284	461	4,105	139	716	..	6,476	..	52,581
37	Liberia	158	1,152	0	0	4	291	..	175	..	1,618
38	*Afghanistan*	..	..	..	..	..	..	..	..	..	..
39	*Burma*	106	4,257	0	0	17	10	..	81	..	4,348
40	*Guinea*	312	1,617	0	0	3	30	..	138	..	1,784
41	*Kampuchea, Dem.*	..	..	..	..	..	..	..	..	..	..
42	*Viet Nam*	..	..	..	..	..	..	..	..	..	..
Middle-income economies											
Lower-middle-income											
43	Senegal	100	3,068	31	42	0	267	..	319	..	3,695
44	Bolivia	480	4,599	11	200	6	141	..	608	..	5,548
45	Zimbabwe	229	2,044	..	51	0	157	..	260	..	2,512
46	Philippines	625	22,321	919	1,516	69	1,194	..	4,931	..	29,962
47	Yemen Arab Rep.	..	2,155	0	0	0	2	..	232	..	2,389
48	Morocco	711	18,468	15	372	28	1,071	..	795	..	20,706
49	Egypt, Arab Rep.	1,713	34,515	..	1,098	49	182	..	4,469	..	40,264
50	Papua New Guinea	36	1,471	173	1,135	0	0	..	105	..	2,711
51	Dominican Rep.	212	2,938	141	133	7	284	..	341	..	3,695
52	Côte d'Ivoire	255	8,450	11	3,264	0	576	..	1,265	..	13,555
53	Honduras	90	2,681	19	115	0	68	..	439	..	3,303
54	Nicaragua	147	6,150	0	0	8	0	..	1,141	..	7,291
55	Thailand	324	14,023	402	3,108	0	916	..	2,664	..	20,710
56	El Salvador	88	1,597	88	70	7	6	..	89	..	1,762
57	Congo, People's Rep.	124	3,679	0	0	0	14	..	944	..	4,636
58	Jamaica	160	3,511	822	58	0	679	..	199	..	4,446
59	Guatemala	106	2,345	14	116	0	59	..	305	..	2,825
60	Cameroon	131	2,785	9	520	0	0	..	722	..	4,028
61	Paraguay	112	2,218	..	28	0	0	..	201	..	2,447
62	Ecuador	193	9,026	49	30	14	490	..	891	..	10,437
63	Botswana	17	514	0	0	0	0	..	3	..	518
64	Tunisia	541	6,189	..	226	13	271	..	224	..	6,909
65	Turkey	1,844	30,490	42	866	74	770	..	8,692	..	40,818
66	Colombia	1,297	13,828	283	1,524	55	0	..	1,654	..	17,006
67	Chile	2,067	15,536	501	2,466	2	1,465	..	1,772	..	21,239

Note: For data comparability and coverage, see the technical notes.   Figures in italics are for years other than those specified.

| | | Long-term debt (millions of dollars) | | | Use of IMF credit (millions of dollars) | | Short-term debt (millions of dollars) | | Total external debt (millions of dollars) | |
| | | Public and publicly guaranteed | | Private nonguaranteed | | | | | | | |
		1970	1987	1970	1987	1970	1987	1970	1987	1970	1987
68	Peru	856	12,485	1,799	1,433	10	845	..	3,295	..	18,058
69	Mauritius	32	545	0	46	0	150	..	34	..	775
70	Jordan	119	3,518	0	0	0	81	..	965	..	4,564
71	Costa Rica	134	3,629	112	290	0	132	..	676	..	4,727
72	Syrian Arab Rep.	233	3,648	0	0	10	0	..	1,030	..	4,678
73	Malaysia	390	19,065	50	2,610	0	0	..	..	..	..
74	Mexico	3,196	82,771	2,770	14,148	0	5,163	..	5,800	..	107,882
75	South Africa	..	..	..	..	..	..	..	..	..	..
76	Poland	..	35,569	..	0	..	0	..	6,565	..	42,135
77	*Lebanon*	64	236	0	0	0	0	..	260	..	496

Upper-middle-income

		1970	1987	1970	1987	1970	1987	1970	1987	1970	1987
78	Brazil	3,421	91,653	1,706	14,434	0	3,977	..	13,868	..	123,932
79	Uruguay	269	3,048	29	144	18	392	..	651	..	4,235
80	Hungary	..	15,931	0	0	0	809	..	2,217	..	18,957
81	Panama	194	3,722	0	0	0	346	..	1,256	..	5,324
82	Argentina	1,880	47,451	3,291	2,858	0	3,854	..	2,651	..	56,813
83	Yugoslavia	1,199	14,446	854	5,045	0	1,852	..	2,175	..	23,518
84	Algeria	937	19,240	0	0	0	0	..	3,641	..	22,881
85	Korea, Rep.	1,816	24,541	175	6,103	0	525	..	9,291	..	40,459
86	Gabon	91	1,605	0	0	0	60	..	406	..	2,071
87	Portugal	485	14,922	268	630	0	529	..	2,164	..	18,245
88	Venezuela	728	25,245	236	7,504	0	0	..	3,770	..	36,519
89	Greece	905	17,437	388	1,429	0	0	..	4,255	..	23,120
90	Trinidad and Tobago	101	1,635	0	0	0	0	..	166	..	1,801
91	Libya	..	..	..	..	..	..	..	..	..	..
92	Oman	..	2,474	0	0	0	0	..	405	..	2,879
93	*Iran, Islamic Rep.*	..	..	..	..	..	..	..	..	..	..
94	*Iraq*	..	..	..	..	..	..	..	..	..	..
95	*Romania*	..	5,425	0	0	0	507	..	730	..	6,662

Low- and middle-income
Sub-Saharan Africa
East Asia
South Asia
Europe, M.East, & N.Africa
Latin America & Caribbean

17 highly indebted

High-income economies
 OECD members
 †Other

		1970	1987	1970	1987	1970	1987	1970	1987	1970	1987
96	Spain										
97	Ireland										
98	†Saudi Arabia										
99	†Israel	2,274	16,767	361	5,729	13	0	..	3,837	..	26,332
100	New Zealand										
101	†Singapore	152	2,543	248	1,643	0	0	..	305	..	4,491
102	†Hong Kong										
103	Italy										
104	United Kingdom										
105	Australia										
106	Belgium										
107	Netherlands										
108	Austria										
109	France										
110	Germany, Fed. Rep.										
111	Finland										
112	†Kuwait										
113	Denmark										
114	Canada										
115	Sweden										
116	Japan										
117	†United Arab Emirates										
118	Norway										
119	United States										
120	Switzerland										

Total reporting economies
 Oil exporters

Nonreporting nonmembers

Table 22. Flow of public and private external capital

		Disbursements (millions of dollars)				Repayment of principal (millions of dollars)				Net flow[a] (millions of dollars)			
		Public and publicly guaranteed		Private nonguaranteed		Public and publicly guaranteed		Private nonguaranteed		Public and publicly guaranteed		Private nonguaranteed	
		1970	1987	1970	1987	1970	1987	1970	1987	1970	1987	1970	1987
Low-income economies													
China and India													
Other low-income													
1	Ethiopia	28	403	0	0	15	130	0	0	13	273	0	0
2	Bhutan	..	16	0	0	..	0	0	0	..	16	0	0
3	Chad	6	51	0	0	3	3	0	0	3	48	0	0
4	Zaire	32	493	0	0	28	127	0	0	3	365	0	0
5	Bangladesh	0	923	0	0	0	191	0	0	0	733	0	0
6	Malawi	40	132	0	0	3	45	0	0	37	87	0	0
7	Nepal	1	152	0	0	2	20	0	0	-2	133	0	0
8	Lao PDR	6	118	0	0	1	11	0	0	4	107	0	0
9	Mozambique	..	..	..	..	..	..	..	..	..	..	..	..
10	Tanzania	51	107	8	3	10	46	3	2	40	61	5	1
11	Burkina Faso	2	112	0	0	2	17	0	0	0	95	0	0
12	Madagascar	11	229	0	0	5	64	0	0	5	165	0	0
13	Mali	23	117	0	0	0	19	0	0	23	99	0	0
14	Burundi	1	140	0	0	0	27	0	0	1	113	0	0
15	Zambia	351	130	..	..	35	73	..	..	316	58	..	..
16	Niger	12	156	..	50	2	47	..	30	11	109	..	20
17	Uganda	27	187	0	0	4	46	0	0	23	141	0	0
18	China	..	5,704	0	0	..	1,774	0	0	..	3,930	0	0
19	Somalia	4	71	0	0	1	5	0	0	4	66	0	0
20	Togo	5	50	0	0	2	35	0	0	3	15	0	0
21	India	883	5,391	25	800	289	2,049	25	631	594	3,342	0	169
22	Rwanda	0	91	0	0	0	13	0	0	0	78	0	0
23	Sierra Leone	8	2	0	0	11	4	0	0	-3	-2	0	0
24	Benin	2	68	0	0	1	19	0	0	1	49	0	0
25	Central African Rep.	2	76	0	0	2	13	0	0	-1	63	0	0
26	Kenya	35	449	41	90	17	291	12	53	17	158	30	37
27	Sudan	53	169	..	..	22	30	..	..	30	139	..	..
28	Pakistan	489	941	3	41	112	792	1	15	378	148	2	26
29	Haiti	4	94	0	0	3	14	0	0	1	80	0	0
30	Lesotho	0	41	0	0	0	9	0	0	0	31	0	0
31	Nigeria	56	1,021	25	50	38	239	30	100	18	782	-5	-50
32	Ghana	42	365	..	0	14	117	0	8	28	248	..	-8
33	Sri Lanka	66	387	..	0	29	219	..	9	36	168	..	-9
34	Yemen, PDR	1	228	0	0	0	56	0	0	1	172	0	0
35	Mauritania	5	140	0	0	3	58	0	0	1	82	0	0
36	Indonesia	441	5,276	195	915	59	3,096	61	638	383	2,180	134	277
37	Liberia	7	32	0	0	11	5	0	0	-4	27	0	0
38	*Afghanistan*	..	..	..	..	..	..	..	..	..	..	..	..
39	*Burma*	22	336	0	0	13	114	0	0	9	222	0	0
40	*Guinea*	90	146	0	0	11	76	0	0	80	71	0	0
41	*Kampuchea, Dem.*	..	..	..	..	..	..	..	..	..	..	..	..
42	*Viet Nam*	..	..	..	..	..	..	..	..	..	..	..	..
Middle-income economies													
Lower-middle-income													
43	Senegal	19	360	1	6	5	161	3	8	14	199	-2	-2
44	Bolivia	55	209	3	0	17	74	2	0	38	134	1	0
45	Zimbabwe	..	278	..	..	5	274	..	..	..	3	..	..
46	Philippines	141	1,017	276	80	74	778	186	98	67	240	90	-18
47	Yemen Arab Rep.	..	115	0	0	..	100	0	0	..	15	0	0
48	Morocco	168	1,264	8	78	37	652	3	34	131	612	5	44
49	Egypt, Arab Rep.	397	1,291	..	245	309	778	..	150	88	513	..	95
50	Papua New Guinea	43	176	111	268	0	99	20	249	43	78	91	19
51	Dominican Rep.	38	144	22	0	7	68	20	14	31	76	2	-14
52	Côte d'Ivoire	78	602	4	900	29	289	2	591	49	314	2	309
53	Honduras	29	184	10	14	3	142	3	24	26	42	7	-10
54	Nicaragua	44	495	0	0	16	22	0	0	28	473	0	0
55	Thailand	51	1,311	169	577	23	1,102	107	789	28	209	62	-212
56	El Salvador	8	120	24	0	6	106	16	14	2	14	8	-14
57	Congo, People's Rep.	20	532	0	0	6	150	0	0	15	382	0	0
58	Jamaica	15	312	165	4	6	211	164	10	9	101	1	-6
59	Guatemala	37	125	6	0	20	147	2	3	17	-22	4	-3
60	Cameroon	29	302	11	217	5	203	2	210	24	99	9	7
61	Paraguay	15	214	..	0	7	128	..	3	8	86	..	-3
62	Ecuador	41	652	7	0	16	223	11	20	26	429	-4	-20
63	Botswana	6	102	0	0	0	38	0	0	6	64	0	0
64	Tunisia	89	806	..	43	47	591	..	68	42	215	..	-24
65	Turkey	329	4,182	1	435	128	2,741	3	279	201	1,441	-2	156
66	Colombia	253	1,217	0	79	75	1,264	59	140	177	-47	-59	-61
67	Chile	408	582	247	195	166	186	41	108	242	396	206	87

Note: For data comparability and coverage, see the technical notes. Figures in italics are for years other than those specified.

		Disbursements (millions of dollars)				Repayment of principal (millions of dollars)				Net flow[a] (millions of dollars)			
		Public and publicly guaranteed		Private nonguaranteed		Public and publicly guaranteed		Private nonguaranteed		Public and publicly guaranteed		Private nonguaranteed	
		1970	1987	1970	1987	1970	1987	1970	1987	1970	1987	1970	1987
68	Peru	148	491	240	106	100	251	233	10	48	241	7	96
69	Mauritius	2	70	0	22	1	45	0	3	1	25	0	19
70	Jordan	14	349	0	0	3	334	0	0	12	15	0	0
71	Costa Rica	30	86	30	0	21	61	20	16	9	25	10	−16
72	Syrian Arab Rep.	60	540	0	0	31	253	0	0	29	287	0	0
73	Malaysia	45	1,374	12	585	47	1,757	9	940	−2	−383	3	−355
74	Mexico	772	8,303	603	247	475	3,249	542	1,084	297	5,054	61	−837
75	South Africa	..	..	..	..	..	..	..	..	..	..	..	..
76	Poland	..	493	..	0	..	962	..	0	..	−469	..	0
77	*Lebanon*	12	13	0	0	2	17	0	0	10	−4	0	0

Upper-middle-income

		1970	1987	1970	1987	1970	1987	1970	1987	1970	1987	1970	1987
78	Brazil	892	1,555	900	0	256	2,942	200	740	637	−1,388	700	−740
79	Uruguay	37	237	13	125	47	134	4	19	−10	102	9	107
80	Hungary	..	3,168	0	0	..	2,097	0	0	..	1,070	0	0
81	Panama	67	139	0	0	24	158	0	0	44	−19	0	0
82	Argentina	482	2,916	424	200	344	507	428	188	139	2,409	−4	12
83	Yugoslavia	179	313	465	233	170	996	204	388	9	−683	261	−155
84	Algeria	308	4,196	0	0	34	3,543	0	0	274	653	0	0
85	Korea, Rep.	444	2,218	32	2,173	198	10,455	7	2,639	246	−8,237	25	−466
86	Gabon	26	265	0	0	9	13	0	0	17	252	0	0
87	Portugal	18	2,773	20	110	63	3,643	22	101	−45	−871	−1	9
88	Venezuela	226	315	67	0	42	1,209	25	380	184	−894	41	−380
89	Greece	163	2,676	144	100	62	2,294	37	285	101	383	107	−185
90	Trinidad and Tobago	8	129	0	0	10	263	0	0	−3	−134	0	0
91	Libya	..	..	..	..	..	..	..	..	..	..	..	..
92	Oman	..	342	0	0	..	436	0	0	..	−94	0	0
93	*Iran, Islamic Rep.*	..	..	..	..	..	..	..	..	..	..	..	..
94	*Iraq*	..	..	..	..	..	..	..	..	..	..	..	..
95	*Romania*	..	479	0	0	..	1,128	0	0	..	−649	0	0

Low- and middle-income
Sub-Saharan Africa
East Asia
South Asia
Europe, M.East, & N.Africa
Latin America & Caribbean

17 highly indebted

High-income economies
OECD members
†Other

		1970	1987	1970	1987	1970	1987	1970	1987	1970	1987	1970	1987
96	Spain												
97	Ireland												
98	†Saudi Arabia												
99	†Israel	410	1,052	123	794	26	1,080	36	548	385	−28	87	246
100	New Zealand												
101	†Singapore	61	443	53	320	6	307	49	265	55	136	5	55
102	†Hong Kong												
103	Italy												
104	United Kingdom												
105	Australia												
106	Belgium												
107	Netherlands												
108	Austria												
109	France												
110	Germany, Fed. Rep.												
111	Finland												
112	†Kuwait												
113	Denmark												
114	Canada												
115	Sweden												
116	Japan												
117	†United Arab Emirates												
118	Norway												
119	United States												
120	Switzerland												

Total reporting economies
Oil exporters

Nonreporting nonmembers

a. Disbursements less repayments of principal may not equal net flow because of rounding.

Table 23. Total external public and private debt and debt service ratios

		Total long-term debt disbursed and outstanding				Total interest payments on long-term debt (millions of dollars)		Total long-term debt service as a percentage of:			
		Millions of dollars		As a percentage of GNP				GNP		Exports of goods and services	
		1970	1987	1970	1987	1970	1987	1970	1987	1970	1987
Low-income economies											
China and India											
Other low-income											
1	Ethiopia	169	2,434	9.5	45.6	6	50	1.2	3.4	11.4	28.4
2	Bhutan	..	41	..	19.9	..	1	..	0.2	..	..
3	Chad	33	270	9.9	28.1	0	3	0.9	0.7	4.2	3.9
4	Zaire	311	7,334	9.1	139.5	9	119	1.1	4.7	4.4	12.8
5	Bangladesh	0	8,851	0.0	50.6	0	132	0.0	1.8	0.0	24.2
6	Malawi	122	1,155	43.2	98.3	4	26	2.3	6.0	7.8	23.3
7	Nepal	3	902	0.3	32.5	0	14	0.3	1.2	3.2	9.7
8	Lao PDR	8	736	..	105.1	0	2	..	1.9	..	..
9	Mozambique	..	..	..	..	..	..	..	..	..	..
10	Tanzania	265	4,079	20.7	144.1	8	38	1.6	3.0	6.3	19.2
11	Burkina Faso	21	794	6.6	44.0	0	14	0.7	1.7	6.8	..
12	Madagascar	89	3,114	10.4	163.2	2	83	0.8	7.7	3.7	35.3
13	Mali	238	1,847	71.4	95.7	0	13	0.2	1.7	1.4	9.9
14	Burundi	7	718	3.1	60.3	0	15	0.3	3.6	2.3	38.5
15	Zambia	653	4,354	37.5	227.5	..	..	..	..	..	..
16	Niger	..	1,513	..	72.6	..	73	..	7.2	..	46.9
17	Uganda	138	1,116	7.3	29.7	5	24	0.5	1.9	2.9	19.5
18	China	..	23,659	..	8.1	..	1,069	..	1.0	..	7.1
19	Somalia	77	2,288	24.4	236.9	0	4	0.3	0.9	2.1	8.3
20	Togo	40	1,042	16.0	90.6	1	29	1.0	5.5	3.1	14.2
21	India	7,938	40,767	14.9	16.5	193	1,517	0.9	1.7	23.6	24.0
22	Rwanda	2	544	0.9	26.1	0	7	0.1	1.0	1.2	11.3
23	Sierra Leone	59	513	14.3	54.6	3	1	3.1	0.5	10.8	..
24	Benin	41	929	15.1	56.5	0	15	0.6	2.0	2.4	15.9
25	Central African Rep.	24	520	13.5	49.2	1	9	1.7	2.1	5.1	12.1
26	Kenya	406	4,978	26.3	64.3	17	244	3.0	7.6	9.1	33.8
27	Sudan	..	8,248	..	101.9	..	..	..	..	..	..
28	Pakistan	3,069	13,205	30.6	38.2	77	386	1.9	3.5	23.6	26.3
29	Haiti	40	674	10.2	30.2	0	9	1.0	1.0	59.4	7.0
30	Lesotho	8	237	7.7	37.1	0	5	0.5	2.3	4.5	4.4
31	Nigeria	567	26,057	4.3	111.3	28	569	0.7	3.9	7.1	11.7
32	Ghana	498	2,237	22.9	45.3	12	58	1.2	3.7	5.5	20.3
33	Sri Lanka	..	4,226	..	64.7	..	126	..	5.4	..	20.2
34	Yemen, PDR	1	1,669	..	177.5	0	15	..	7.6	0.0	38.2
35	Mauritania	27	1,868	13.9	215.1	0	28	1.8	9.9	3.4	18.2
36	Indonesia	2,904	45,389	29.9	68.8	46	2,748	1.7	9.8	13.9	33.2
37	Liberia	158	1,152	39.2	108.4	6	6	4.3	1.0	8.1	2.5
38	*Afghanistan*	..	..	..	..	..	..	..	..	..	..
39	*Burma*	106	4,257	..	..	3	69	..	..	12.1	59.3
40	*Guinea*	312	1,617	..	..	4	35	..	..	..	..
41	*Kampuchea, Dem.*	..	..	..	..	..	..	..	..	..	..
42	*Viet Nam*	..	..	..	..	..	..	..	..	..	..
Middle-income economies											
Lower-middle-income											
43	Senegal	131	3,109	15.5	69.2	2	116	1.1	6.4	4.0	22.3
44	Bolivia	491	4,799	49.3	115.6	7	62	2.6	3.3	12.6	22.1
45	Zimbabwe	..	2,095	..	37.1	..	..	..	..	..	..
46	Philippines	1,544	23,837	21.8	69.4	44	1,497	4.3	6.9	23.0	25.7
47	Yemen Arab Rep.	..	2,155	..	46.6	..	45	..	3.1	..	24.8
48	Morocco	726	18,840	18.6	117.9	25	624	1.7	8.2	9.2	30.8
49	Egypt, Arab Rep.	..	35,613	..	108.7	..	806	..	5.3	..	21.5
50	Papua New Guinea	209	2,606	33.4	91.1	10	157	4.8	17.7	24.6	37.4
51	Dominican Rep.	353	3,071	26.1	66.3	13	106	2.9	4.1	15.2	..
52	Côte d'Ivoire	266	11,714	19.5	124.1	12	597	3.1	15.6	7.5	40.8
53	Honduras	109	2,796	15.6	73.6	4	92	1.4	6.8	5.0	26.1
54	Nicaragua	147	6,150	19.5	207.8	7	12	3.0	1.2	10.5	..
55	Thailand	726	17,131	10.2	36.2	33	1,057	2.3	6.2	14.0	20.6
56	El Salvador	176	1,667	17.3	36.0	9	76	3.1	4.2	12.0	21.0
57	Congo, People's Rep.	124	3,679	46.5	195.0	3	45	3.4	10.3	11.5	18.6
58	Jamaica	982	3,569	73.1	141.2	64	231	17.4	17.9	43.5	27.5
59	Guatemala	120	2,461	6.5	35.8	7	153	1.6	4.4	8.2	25.8
60	Cameroon	140	3,306	12.6	27.1	5	177	1.0	4.8	4.0	27.9
61	Paraguay	..	2,246	..	49.5	..	96	..	5.0	..	21.7
62	Ecuador	242	9,056	14.8	93.2	10	279	2.2	5.4	14.0	21.9
63	Botswana	17	514	21.2	38.2	0	32	0.7	5.2	1.0	3.7
64	Tunisia	..	6,415	..	69.7	..	340	..	10.8	..	29.4
65	Turkey	1,886	31,356	15.0	47.9	44	1,885	1.4	7.5	22.6	34.0
66	Colombia	1,580	15,352	22.5	45.3	59	1,177	2.8	7.6	19.0	36.3
67	Chile	2,568	18,002	32.1	103.6	104	1,420	3.9	9.9	24.5	26.4

Note: For data comparability and coverage, see the technical notes. Figures in italics are for years other than those specified.

	Total long-term debt disbursed and outstanding				Total interest payments on long-term debt (millions of dollars)		Total long-term debt service as a percentage of:			
	Millions of dollars		As a percentage of GNP				GNP		Exports of goods and services	
	1970	1987	1970	1987	1970	1987	1970	1987	1970	1987
68 Peru	2,655	13,918	37.3	31.2	162	203	7.0	1.0	40.0	12.9
69 Mauritius	32	591	14.3	34.1	2	31	1.4	4.6	3.2	6.5
70 Jordan	119	3,518	22.9	75.4	2	183	0.9	11.1	3.6	21.8
71 Costa Rica	246	3,919	25.3	95.9	14	139	5.7	5.3	19.9	14.3
72 Syrian Arab Rep.	233	3,648	10.8	15.3	6	112	1.7	1.5	11.3	16.5
73 Malaysia	440	21,675	10.8	74.3	25	1,461	2.0	14.3	4.5	20.0
74 Mexico	5,966	96,919	16.2	69.6	283	7,091	3.5	8.2	44.3	38.4
75 South Africa	. .	. .	. .	. .	. .	. .	. .	. .	. .	. .
76 Poland	. .	35,569	. .	55.7	. .	960	. .	3.0	. .	14.7
77 Lebanon	64	236	4.2	. .	1	13	0.2	. .	. .	. .

Upper-middle-income

78 Brazil	5,128	106,087	12.2	33.7	224	5,834	1.6	3.0	21.8	33.2
79 Uruguay	298	3,192	12.5	44.2	17	273	2.9	5.9	23.6	25.7
80 Hungary	. .	15,931	. .	63.5	. .	1,130	. .	12.9	. .	26.7
81 Panama	194	3,722	19.5	72.6	7	226	3.1	7.5	7.7	6.5
82 Argentina	5,171	50,309	23.8	65.5	338	3,775	5.1	5.8	51.7	52.0
83 Yugoslavia	2,053	19,491	15.0	32.2	104	1,717	3.5	5.1	19.7	19.4
84 Algeria	937	19,240	19.3	30.5	10	1,377	0.9	7.8	3.9	49.0
85 Korea, Rep.	1,991	30,644	22.3	25.8	76	2,375	3.1	13.0	20.4	27.5
86 Gabon	91	1,605	28.8	52.5	3	57	3.8	2.3	5.7	5.1
87 Portugal	753	15,552	12.1	44.6	34	1,232	1.9	14.3	8.7	38.9
88 Venezuela	964	32,749	7.6	67.8	53	2,518	0.9	8.5	4.3	32.4
89 Greece	1,293	18,866	12.7	40.4	63	1,260	1.6	8.2	14.7	37.8
90 Trinidad and Tobago	101	1,635	13.3	39.3	6	121	2.1	9.2	4.6	. .
91 Libya	. .	. .	. .	. .	. .	. .	. .	. .	. .	. .
92 Oman	. .	2,474	. .	33.9	. .	177	. .	8.4	. .	. .
93 Iran, Islamic Rep.	. .	. .	. .	. .	. .	. .	. .	. .	. .	. .
94 Iraq	. .	. .	. .	. .	. .	. .	. .	. .	. .	. .
95 Romania	. .	5,425	. .	. .	. .	503	. .	. .	. .	. .

Low- and middle-income
  Sub-Saharan Africa
  East Asia
  South Asia
  Europe, M.East, & N.Africa
  Latin America & Caribbean

17 highly indebted

High-income economies
  OECD members
  †Other

96 Spain										
97 Ireland										
98 †Saudi Arabia										
99 †Israel	2,635	22,495	47.9	67.2	34	1,864	1.7	10.4	6.8	25.3
100 New Zealand										
101 †Singapore	400	4,186	20.9	20.4	23	305	4.0	4.3	3.9	2.4
102 †Hong Kong										
103 Italy										
104 United Kingdom										
105 Australia										
106 Belgium										
107 Netherlands										
108 Austria										
109 France										
110 Germany, Fed. Rep.										
111 Finland										
112 †Kuwait										
113 Denmark										
114 Canada										
115 Sweden										
116 Japan										
117 †United Arab Emirates										
118 Norway										
119 United States										
120 Switzerland										

Total reporting economies
  Oil exporters

Nonreporting nonmembers

Note: Public and private debt includes public, publicly guaranteed, and private nonguaranteed debt; data are shown only when they are available for all categories.

Table 24. External public debt and debt service ratios

		External public debt outstanding and disbursed				Interest payments on external public debt (millions of dollars)		Debt service as a percentage of:			
		Millions of dollars		As a percentage of GNP				GNP		Exports of goods and services	
		1970	1987	1970	1987	1970	1987	1970	1987	1970	1987
	Low-income economies	..	218,245 t	..	28.4 w	..	16,834 t	..	2.2 w	..	15.7 w
	China and India	..	60,983 t	..	11.3 w	..	6,139 t	..	1.1 w	..	10.7 w
	Other low-income	10,422 t	157,261 t	15.5 w	68.8 w	720 t	10,696 t	1.1 w	4.7 w	7.1 w	21.9 w
1	Ethiopia	169	2,434	9.5	45.6	6	50	1.2	3.4	11.4	28.4
2	Bhutan	..	41	..	19.9	..	1	..	0.2	..	..
3	Chad	33	270	9.9	28.1	0	3	0.9	0.7	4.2	3.9
4	Zaire	311	7,334	9.1	139.5	9	119	1.1	4.7	4.4	12.8
5	Bangladesh	0	8,851	0.0	50.6	0	132	0.0	1.8	0.0	24.2
6	Malawi	122	1,155	43.2	98.3	4	26	2.3	6.0	7.8	23.3
7	Nepal	3	902	0.3	32.5	0	14	0.3	1.2	3.2	9.7
8	Lao PDR	8	736	..	105.1	0	2	..	1.9	..	..
9	Mozambique	..	..	..	..	..	..	..	..	..	..
10	Tanzania	250	4,068	19.5	143.7	7	37	1.3	2.9	5.3	18.5
11	Burkina Faso	21	794	6.6	44.0	0	14	0.7	1.7	6.8	..
12	Madagascar	89	3,114	10.4	163.2	2	83	0.8	7.7	3.7	35.3
13	Mali	238	1,847	71.4	95.7	0	13	0.2	1.7	1.4	9.9
14	Burundi	7	718	3.1	60.3	0	15	0.3	3.6	2.3	38.5
15	Zambia	623	4,354	35.7	227.5	29	56	3.7	6.7	6.4	13.5
16	Niger	32	1,259	5.0	60.4	1	60	0.4	5.1	4.0	33.5
17	Uganda	138	1,116	7.3	29.7	5	24	0.5	1.9	2.9	19.5
18	China	..	23,659	..	8.1	..	1,069	..	1.0	..	7.1
19	Somalia	77	2,288	24.4	236.9	0	4	0.3	0.9	2.1	8.3
20	Togo	40	1,042	16.0	90.6	1	29	1.0	5.5	3.1	14.2
21	India	7,838	37,325	14.7	15.1	187	1,247	0.9	1.3	22.2	18.9
22	Rwanda	2	544	0.9	26.1	0	7	0.1	1.0	1.2	11.3
23	Sierra Leone	59	513	14.3	54.6	3	1	3.1	0.5	10.8	..
24	Benin	41	929	15.1	56.5	0	15	0.6	2.0	2.4	15.9
25	Central African Rep.	24	520	13.5	49.2	1	9	1.7	2.1	5.1	12.1
26	Kenya	319	4,482	20.6	57.9	13	211	1.9	6.5	6.0	28.8
27	Sudan	307	7,876	15.2	97.3	13	18	1.7	0.6	10.7	6.8
28	Pakistan	3,064	13,150	30.6	38.0	77	381	1.9	3.4	23.5	25.9
29	Haiti	40	674	10.2	30.2	0	9	1.0	1.0	59.4	7.0
30	Lesotho	8	237	7.7	37.1	0	5	0.5	2.3	4.5	4.4
31	Nigeria	452	25,707	3.4	109.8	20	540	0.4	3.3	4.3	10.0
32	Ghana	488	2,207	22.5	44.7	12	56	1.2	3.5	5.5	19.2
33	Sri Lanka	317	4,109	16.1	62.9	12	120	2.1	5.2	10.9	19.2
34	Yemen, PDR	1	1,669	..	177.5	0	15	..	7.6	0.0	38.2
35	Mauritania	27	1,868	13.9	215.1	0	28	1.8	9.9	3.4	18.2
36	Indonesia	2,443	41,284	25.2	62.6	25	2,338	0.9	8.2	7.0	27.8
37	Liberia	158	1,152	39.2	108.4	6	6	4.3	1.0	8.1	2.5
38	*Afghanistan*	..	..	..	..	..	..	..	..	..	..
39	*Burma*	106	4,257	..	..	3	69	..	..	12.1	59.3
40	*Guinea*	312	1,617	..	..	4	35	..	..	..	..
41	*Kampuchea, Dem.*	..	..	..	..	..	..	..	..	..	..
42	*Viet Nam*	..	..	..	..	..	..	..	..	..	..
	Middle-income economies	28,807 t	668,122 t	11.5 w	44.8 w	4,193 t	85,269 t	1.7 w	5.7 w	11.7 w	23.9 w
	Lower-middle-income	16,847 t	378,385 t	13.5 w	57.5 w	2,392 t	36,189 t	1.9 w	5.5 w	12.6 w	21.7 w
43	Senegal	100	3,068	11.9	68.3	2	113	0.8	6.1	2.9	21.4
44	Bolivia	480	4,599	48.2	110.8	7	62	2.3	3.3	11.3	22.1
45	Zimbabwe	229	2,044	15.5	36.2	5	109	0.6	6.8	2.3	23.2
46	Philippines	625	22,321	8.8	65.0	26	1,365	1.4	6.2	7.5	23.2
47	Yemen Arab Rep.	..	2,155	..	46.6	..	45	..	3.1	..	24.8
48	Morocco	711	18,468	18.2	115.6	24	618	1.6	7.9	8.7	29.9
49	Egypt, Arab Rep.	1,713	34,515	22.5	105.4	56	716	4.8	4.6	38.0	18.5
50	Papua New Guinea	36	1,471	5.8	51.4	1	77	0.2	6.1	1.1	13.0
51	Dominican Rep.	212	2,938	15.7	63.4	4	94	0.8	3.5	4.4	..
52	Côte d'Ivoire	255	8,450	18.7	89.5	12	422	2.9	7.5	7.1	19.6
53	Honduras	90	2,681	12.9	70.6	3	86	0.8	6.0	2.9	23.0
54	Nicaragua	147	6,150	19.5	207.8	7	12	3.0	1.2	10.5	..
55	Thailand	324	14,023	4.6	29.6	16	845	0.6	4.1	3.3	13.6
56	El Salvador	88	1,597	8.6	34.5	4	74	0.9	3.9	3.6	19.4
57	Congo, People's Rep.	124	3,679	46.5	195.0	3	45	3.4	10.3	11.5	18.6
58	Jamaica	160	3,511	11.9	138.9	9	226	1.1	17.3	2.8	26.6
59	Guatemala	106	2,345	5.7	34.1	6	145	1.4	4.2	7.4	24.9
60	Cameroon	131	2,785	11.8	22.9	4	133	0.8	2.8	3.2	15.9
61	Paraguay	112	2,218	19.2	48.8	4	94	1.8	4.9	11.7	21.3
62	Ecuador	193	9,026	11.8	92.9	7	271	1.4	5.1	8.6	20.7
63	Botswana	17	514	21.2	38.2	0	32	0.7	5.2	1.0	3.7
64	Tunisia	541	6,189	38.6	67.2	18	322	4.7	9.9	19.7	26.9
65	Turkey	1,844	30,490	14.7	46.6	42	1,835	1.4	7.0	21.9	31.7
66	Colombia	1,297	13,828	18.5	40.8	44	1,108	1.7	7.0	11.7	33.4
67	Chile	2,067	15,536	25.8	89.4	78	1,181	3.1	7.9	19.2	21.1

Note: For data comparability and coverage, see the technical notes.   Figures in italics are for years other than those specified.

| | External public debt outstanding and disbursed | | | | Interest payments on external public debt (millions of dollars) | | Debt service as a percentage of: | | | |
| | Millions of dollars | | As a percentage of GNP | | | | GNP | | Exports of goods and services | |
	1970	1987	1970	1987	1970	1987	1970	1987	1970	1987
68 Peru	856	12,485	12.0	28.0	43	198	2.0	1.0	11.6	12.5
69 Mauritius	32	545	14.3	31.4	2	30	1.4	4.3	3.2	6.1
70 Jordan	119	3,518	22.9	75.4	2	183	0.9	11.1	3.6	21.8
71 Costa Rica	134	3,629	13.8	88.8	7	121	2.9	4.5	10.0	12.1
72 Syrian Arab Rep.	233	3,648	10.8	15.3	6	112	1.7	1.5	11.3	16.5
73 Malaysia	390	19,065	9.5	65.4	22	1,217	1.7	10.2	3.8	14.3
74 Mexico	3,196	82,771	8.7	59.5	216	5,722	1.9	6.4	23.6	30.1
75 South Africa	. .	. .	. .	. .	. .	. .	. .	. .	. .	. .
76 Poland	. .	35,569	. .	55.7	. .	960	. .	3.0	. .	14.7
77 *Lebanon*	64	236	4.2	. .	1	13	0.2	. .	. .	. .
Upper-middle-income	12,118 *t*	290,890 *t*	9.6 *w*	34.7 *w*	1,819 *t*	49,091 *t*	1.4 *w*	5.8 *w*	10.6 *w*	25.8 *w*
78 Brazil	3,421	91,653	8.2	29.1	135	4,714	0.9	2.4	12.5	26.7
79 Uruguay	269	3,048	11.3	42.2	16	270	2.7	5.6	21.7	24.4
80 Hungary	. .	15,931	. .	63.5	. .	1,130	. .	12.9	. .	26.7
81 Panama	194	3,722	19.5	72.6	7	226	3.1	7.5	7.7	6.5
82 Argentina	1,880	47,451	8.6	61.7	121	3,387	2.1	5.1	21.6	45.3
83 Yugoslavia	1,199	14,446	8.8	23.9	73	1,122	1.8	3.5	10.0	13.3
84 Algeria	937	19,240	19.3	30.5	10	1,377	0.9	7.8	3.9	49.0
85 Korea, Rep.	1,816	24,541	20.3	20.7	71	1,844	3.0	10.4	19.5	21.9
86 Gabon	91	1,605	28.8	52.5	3	57	3.8	2.3	5.7	5.1
87 Portugal	485	14,922	7.8	42.8	29	1,189	1.5	13.9	6.8	37.8
88 Venezuela	728	25,245	5.7	52.3	40	1,660	0.6	5.9	2.9	22.6
89 Greece	905	17,437	8.9	37.3	41	1,142	1.0	7.4	9.4	33.9
90 Trinidad and Tobago	101	1,635	13.3	39.3	6	121	2.1	9.2	4.6	. .
91 Libya	. .	. .	. .	. .	. .	. .	. .	. .	. .	. .
92 Oman	. .	2,474	. .	33.9	. .	177	. .	8.4	. .	. .
93 *Iran, Islamic Rep.*	. .	. .	. .	. .	. .	. .	. .	. .	. .	. .
94 *Iraq*	. .	. .	. .	. .	. .	. .	. .	. .	. .	. .
95 *Romania*	. .	5,425	. .	. .	. .	503	. .	. .	. .	. .
Low- and middle-income	47,066 *t*	886,367 *t*	12.7 *w*	39.2 *w*	5,389 *t*	102,104 *t*	1.5 *w*	4.5 *w*	11.2 *w*	22.0 *w*
Sub-Saharan Africa	5,374 *t*	103,874 *t*	13.1 *w*	80.8 *w*	472 *t*	5,235 *t*	1.2 *w*	4.1 *w*	5.3 *w*	14.7 *w*
East Asia	5,654 *t*	147,605 *t*	15.0 *w*	24.9 *w*	566 *t*	27,904 *t*	1.5 *w*	4.7 *w*	7.9 *w*	17.2 *w*
South Asia	11,327 *t*	68,696 *t*	15.1 *w*	21.6 *w*	724 *t*	5,355 *t*	1.0 *w*	1.7 *w*	17.9 *w*	20.8 *w*
Europe, M. East, & N. Africa	8,832 *t*	227,861 *t*	13.5 *w*	47.9 *w*	1,197 *t*	32,355 *t*	1.8 *w*	6.6 *w*	12.3 *w*	26.7 *w*
Latin America & Caribbean	15,878 *t*	338,331 *t*	10.5 *w*	45.5 *w*	2,430 *t*	31,256 *t*	1.6 *w*	4.2 *w*	13.1 *w*	26.5 *w*
17 highly indebted	17,923 *t*	402,171 *t*	9.8 *w*	47.5 *w*	2,789 *t*	36,251 *t*	1.5 *w*	4.3 *w*	12.4 *w*	24.9 *w*
High-income economies	. .	. .	. .	. .	. .	. .	. .	. .	. .	. .
OECD members	. .	. .	. .	. .	. .	. .	. .	. .	. .	. .
†Other	2,470 *t*	19,484 *t*	31.3 *w*	34.5 *w*	59 *t*	3,004 *t*	0.7 *w*	5.3 *w*	1.5 *w*	5.8 *w*
97 Spain										
98 Ireland										
99 †Saudi Arabia										
100 †Israel	2,274	16,767	41.3	50.1	13	1,372	0.7	7.3	2.8	17.8
101 New Zealand										
102 †Singapore	152	2,543	7.9	12.4	7	196	0.7	2.4	0.6	1.4
103 †Hong Kong										
104 Italy										
105 United Kingdom										
106 Australia										
107 Belgium										
108 Netherlands										
109 Austria										
110 France										
111 Germany, Fed. Rep.										
112 Finland										
113 †Kuwait										
114 Denmark										
115 Canada										
116 Sweden										
117 Japan										
118 †United Arab Emirates										
119 Norway										
120 United States										
121 Switzerland										
Total reporting economies	. .	. .	. .	. .	. .	. .	. .	. .	. .	. .
Oil exporters	. .	. .	. .	. .	. .	. .	. .	. .	. .	. .
Nonreporting nonmembers	. .	. .	. .	. .	. .	. .	. .	. .	. .	. .

Table 25. Terms of external public borrowing

		Commitments (millions of dollars)		Average interest rate (percent)		Average maturity (years)		Average grace period (years)		Public loans with variable interest rates, as a percentage of public debt	
		1970	1987	1970	1987	1970	1987	1970	1987	1970	1987
	Low-income economies	..	31,171 t	..	5.1 w	..	23 w	..	7 w	..	17.8 w
	China and India	..	17,141 t	..	6.2 w	..	19 w	..	5 w	..	19.0 w
	Other low-income	3,360 t	14,030 t	3.2 w	3.7 w	29 w	29 w	9 w	8 w	0.2 w	17.4 w
1	Ethiopia	21	561	4.4	4.4	32	24	7	6	0.0	5.8
2	Bhutan	..	13	..	1.0	..	40	..	10	..	0.0
3	Chad	10	116	5.7	1.3	8	34	1	8	0.0	0.1
4	Zaire	258	431	6.5	1.1	13	38	4	9	0.0	5.3
5	Bangladesh	0	1,009	0.0	1.1	0	42	0	10	0.0	0.0
6	Malawi	14	117	3.8	0.9	29	47	6	10	0.0	2.7
7	Nepal	17	163	2.8	0.9	27	45	6	10	0.0	0.8
8	Lao PDR	12	114	3.0	0.5	28	42	4	26	0.0	0.0
9	Mozambique	..	..	..	..	..	..	..	..	..	..
10	Tanzania	284	201	1.2	1.2	39	32	11	10	1.6	2.5
11	Burkina Faso	9	74	2.3	2.9	36	24	8	8	0.0	0.4
12	Madagascar	23	293	2.3	1.5	39	42	9	9	0.0	7.8
13	Mali	34	63	1.1	2.4	25	33	9	7	0.0	0.3
14	Burundi	1	30	2.9	2.2	5	35	2	9	0.0	0.0
15	Zambia	557	267	4.2	3.0	27	28	9	9	0.0	14.7
16	Niger	19	131	1.2	1.1	40	40	8	9	0.0	11.0
17	Uganda	12	248	3.8	2.5	28	29	7	7	0.0	0.0
18	China	..	9,210	..	6.6	..	15	..	4	..	28.2
19	Somalia	2	154	0.0	1.1	4	41	4	10	0.0	0.9
20	Togo	3	48	4.6	1.5	17	40	4	10	0.0	4.2
21	India	954	7,931	2.5	5.7	34	23	8	7	0.0	13.1
22	Rwanda	9	107	0.8	1.6	50	39	11	9	0.0	0.0
23	Sierra Leone	25	0	2.9	0.0	27	0	6	0	10.6	0.6
24	Benin	7	76	1.8	1.0	32	45	7	10	0.0	3.7
25	Central African Rep.	7	21	2.0	1.2	36	38	8	10	0.0	0.0
26	Kenya	50	286	2.6	1.4	37	37	8	10	0.1	4.0
27	Sudan	95	249	1.8	1.7	17	31	9	8	0.0	1.1
28	Pakistan	951	1,620	2.8	3.7	32	28	12	8	0.0	5.5
29	Haiti	5	182	4.8	1.4	10	37	1	9	0.0	1.3
30	Lesotho	0	42	5.0	3.1	25	29	2	7	0.0	1.2
31	Nigeria	65	78	6.0	7.2	14	18	4	5	2.7	49.5
32	Ghana	51	630	2.0	1.9	37	29	10	8	0.0	5.7
33	Sri Lanka	81	340	3.0	3.0	27	32	5	9	0.0	6.1
34	Yemen, PDR	63	209	0.0	2.7	21	25	11	8	0.0	0.0
35	Mauritania	7	124	6.0	1.0	11	45	3	10	0.0	6.7
36	Indonesia	520	5,262	2.6	6.1	35	20	9	7	0.0	26.2
37	Liberia	12	10	6.6	2.8	19	40	5	10	0.0	10.7
38	*Afghanistan*	..	..	..	..	..	..	..	..	..	..
39	*Burma*	48	383	4.1	1.8	16	36	5	10	0.0	0.8
40	*Guinea*	68	164	2.9	2.4	13	40	5	9	0.0	10.6
41	*Kampuchea, Dem.*	..	..	..	..	..	..	..	..	..	..
42	*Viet Nam*	..	..	..	..	..	..	..	..	..	..
	Middle-income economies	8,139 t	53,599 t	6.2 w	7.2 w	16 w	13 w	4 w	5 w	2.8 w	53.1 w
	Lower-middle-income	4,284 t	32,238 t	5.8 w	6.9 w	18 w	15 w	5 w	5 w	1.5 w	46.2 w
43	Senegal	7	443	3.8	3.3	23	32	7	8	0.0	4.1
44	Bolivia	24	301	1.9	6.7	48	26	4	6	0.0	29.1
45	Zimbabwe	..	410	..	7.6	..	12	..	4	0.0	26.6
46	Philippines	171	1,182	7.3	5.4	12	22	2	6	0.8	48.2
47	Yemen Arab Rep.	..	74	..	2.2	..	29	..	8	..	3.2
48	Morocco	187	1,425	4.6	7.8	20	19	3	5	0.0	31.1
49	Egypt, Arab Rep.	704	589	5.3	5.6	21	31	8	7	0.0	2.0
50	Papua New Guinea	91	258	6.4	4.0	22	21	8	6	0.0	31.9
51	Dominican Rep.	20	172	2.4	7.3	28	19	5	4	0.0	25.8
52	Côte d'Ivoire	71	490	5.8	6.6	19	18	5	6	9.1	51.4
53	Honduras	23	265	4.1	5.5	30	23	7	6	0.0	18.2
54	Nicaragua	23	350	7.1	4.1	18	17	4	4	0.0	22.1
55	Thailand	106	846	6.8	5.3	19	20	4	7	0.0	31.9
56	El Salvador	12	221	4.7	5.1	23	26	6	7	0.0	5.7
57	Congo, People's Rep.	31	258	2.8	7.8	17	15	6	4	0.0	40.4
58	Jamaica	24	369	6.0	6.8	16	15	3	3	0.0	25.3
59	Guatemala	50	189	3.7	4.7	26	27	6	7	10.3	30.9
60	Cameroon	42	412	4.7	6.5	29	18	8	5	0.0	5.9
61	Paraguay	14	150	5.7	5.9	25	21	6	5	0.0	13.7
62	Ecuador	78	1,045	6.2	7.3	20	17	4	4	0.0	68.9
63	Botswana	38	34	0.6	5.2	39	38	10	8	0.0	12.8
64	Tunisia	144	667	3.5	7.3	27	15	6	5	0.0	16.8
65	Turkey	484	6,287	3.6	6.7	19	11	5	4	0.9	31.8
66	Colombia	363	700	6.0	8.4	21	11	5	3	0.0	40.9
67	Chile	361	1,011	6.8	7.9	12	14	4	4	0.0	79.1

Note: For data comparability and coverage, see the technical notes. Figures in italics are for years other than those specified.

		Commitments (millions of dollars)		Average interest rate (percent)		Average maturity (years)		Average grace period (years)		Public loans with variable interest rates, as a percentage of public debt	
		1970	1987	1970	1987	1970	1987	1970	1987	1970	1987
68	Peru	125	317	7.4	6.6	14	16	4	4	0.0	33.3
69	Mauritius	14	97	0.0	8.2	24	18	2	3	6.0	14.1
70	Jordan	35	568	3.8	7.0	15	11	5	3	0.0	22.9
71	Costa Rica	58	102	5.6	6.7	28	20	6	5	7.5	53.8
72	Syrian Arab Rep.	14	257	4.4	6.9	9	20	2	3	0.0	0.8
73	Malaysia	84	957	6.1	6.0	19	13	5	4	0.0	49.7
74	Mexico	858	11,069	7.9	7.7	12	14	3	5	5.7	79.1
75	South Africa	..	..	..	..	..	..	..	..	..	..
76	Poland	..	558	..	6.5	..	6	..	3	..	64.5
77	*Lebanon*	7	37	2.9	7.6	21	26	1	3	0.0	11.9
	Upper-middle-income	3,867 *t*	21,371 *t*	6.7 *w*	7.6 *w*	14 *w*	10 *w*	4 *w*	4 *w*	4.5 *w*	61.8 *w*
78	Brazil	1,439	2,107	6.8	8.3	14	14	3	4	11.8	67.5
79	Uruguay	71	354	7.9	8.4	12	14	3	4	0.7	68.1
80	Hungary[a]	..	2,744	..	7.2	..	9	..	6	..	63.3
81	Panama	111	189	6.1	7.2	15	15	4	4	0.0	59.1
82	Argentina	494	3,322	7.3	8.2	12	12	3	5	0.0	84.1
83	Yugoslavia	199	214	7.1	8.4	17	14	6	3	3.3	52.9
84	Algeria	306	4,535	6.4	7.4	10	6	2	2	2.8	33.0
85	Korea, Rep.	691	1,295	5.8	7.0	19	17	6	4	1.2	30.5
86	Gabon	33	90	5.1	6.7	11	13	2	4	0.0	20.6
87	Portugal	59	2,188	4.3	7.3	17	10	4	5	0.0	42.8
88	Venezuela	198	260	7.8	8.3	8	17	2	3	2.6	89.1
89	Greece	246	2,881	7.2	7.1	9	8	4	5	3.5	56.1
90	Trinidad and Tobago	3	106	7.5	6.8	10	7	1	4	0.0	34.4
91	Libya	..	..	..	..	..	..	..	..	..	..
92	Oman	..	389	..	8.1	..	10	..	4	..	34.8
93	*Iran, Islamic Rep.*	..	..	..	..	..	..	..	..	..	..
94	*Iraq*	..	..	..	..	..	..	..	..	..	..
95	*Romania*	..	375	..	8.1	..	16	..	5	..	27.0
	Low- and middle-income	**12,453** *t*	**84,770** *t*	**5.1** *w*	**6.4** *w*	**21** *w*	**17** *w*	**6** *w*	**5** *w*	**1.7** *w*	**44.4** *w*
	Sub-Saharan Africa	**1,879** *t*	**7,006** *t*	**3.7** *w*	**3.4** *w*	**26** *w*	**29** *w*	**8** *w*	**7** *w*	**0.9** *w*	**21.7** *w*
	East Asia	**1,677** *t*	**19,155** *t*	**5.0** *w*	**6.3** *w*	**23** *w*	**17** *w*	**6** *w*	**5** *w*	**0.5** *w*	**34.0** *w*
	South Asia	**2,052** *t*	**11,467** *t*	**2.7** *w*	**4.7** *w*	**32** *w*	**27** *w*	**10** *w*	**7** *w*	**0.0** *w*	**8.6** *w*
	Europe, M.East, & N.Africa	**2,461** *t*	**24,232** *t*	**5.1** *w*	**7.1** *w*	**18** *w*	**11** *w*	**5** *w*	**4** *w*	**1.3** *w*	**36.8** *w*
	Latin America & Caribbean	**4,383** *t*	**22,910** *t*	**6.9** *w*	**7.6** *w*	**14** *w*	**15** *w*	**4** *w*	**5** *w*	**4.0** *w*	**68.3** *w*
	17 highly indebted	**4,784** *t*	**24,346** *t*	**6.9** *w*	**7.7** *w*	**14** *w*	**15** *w*	**4** *w*	**5** *w*	**3.9** *w*	**66.0** *w*
	High-income economies	..	..	..	..	..	..	..	..	..	..
	OECD members	..	..	..	..	..	..	..	..	..	..
	†Other	507 *t*	1,201 *t*	9.6 *w*	7.0 *w*	14 *w*	9 *w*	5 *w*	4 *w*	0.2 *w*	8.1 *w*
96	Spain										
97	Ireland										
98	†Saudi Arabia										
99	†Israel	438	853	10.0	7.7	13	10	5	3	0.0	6.1
100	New Zealand										
101	†Singapore	69	328	6.9	5.2	18	7	4	5	0.0	16.2
102	†Hong Kong										
103	Italy										
104	United Kingdom										
105	Australia										
106	Belgium										
107	Netherlands										
108	Austria										
109	France										
110	Germany, Fed. Rep.										
111	Finland										
112	†Kuwait										
113	Denmark										
114	Canada										
115	Sweden										
116	Japan										
117	†United Arab Emirates										
118	Norway										
119	United States										
120	Switzerland										
	Total reporting economies	..	..	..	..	..	..	..	..	..	..
	Oil exporters	..	..	..	..	..	..	..	..	..	..
	Nonreporting nonmembers	..	..	..	..	..	..	..	..	..	..

a. Includes debt in convertible currencies only.

Table 26. Population growth and projections

		Average annual growth of population (percent)			Population (millions)			Hypothetical size of stationary population (millions)	Assumed year of reaching net reproduction rate of 1	Population momentum 1990
		1965–80	1980–87	1987–2000	1987	2000[a]	2025[a]			
	Low-income economies	**2.3 w**	**2.0 w**	**1.9 w**	**2,824 t**	**3,625 t**	**5,161 t**			
	China and India	**2.2 w**	**1.6 w**	**1.5 w**	**1,866 t**	**2,279 t**	**2,893 t**			
	Other low-income	**2.6 w**	**2.8 w**	**2.6 w**	**958 t**	**1,346 t**	**2,268 t**			
1	Ethiopia	2.7	2.4	3.1	44	66	122	220	2040	1.9
2	Bhutan	1.6	2.0	2.4	1	2	3	5	2035	1.7
3	Chad	2.0	2.3	2.6	5	7	13	26	2045	1.8
4	Zaire	2.8	3.1	3.1	33	49	97	200	2045	1.9
5	Bangladesh	2.8	2.8	2.4	106	144	217	324	2025	1.9
6	Malawi	2.9	3.8	3.5	8	12	29	96	2060	1.9
7	Nepal	2.4	2.7	2.5	18	24	37	57	2030	1.8
8	Lao PDR	1.9	2.4	2.6	4	5	8	14	2030	1.8
9	Mozambique	2.5	2.7	3.2	15	22	42	87	2045	1.9
10	Tanzania	3.3	3.5	3.4	24	37	75	155	2045	2.0
11	Burkina Faso	2.1	2.6	2.9	8	12	23	48	2045	1.8
12	Madagascar	2.5	3.3	3.0	11	16	28	49	2035	1.9
13	Mali	2.1	2.4	3.0	8	11	24	59	2050	1.8
14	Burundi	1.9	2.8	3.2	5	7	14	29	2045	1.9
15	Zambia	3.0	3.6	3.5	7	11	23	50	2045	2.0
16	Niger	2.7	3.0	3.2	7	10	22	69	2060	1.9
17	Uganda	2.9	3.1	3.3	16	24	46	97	2045	2.0
18	China	2.2	1.2	1.3	1,069	1,269	1,528	1,681	2000	1.5
19	Somalia	2.7	2.9	3.0	6	8	16	37	2050	1.9
20	Togo	3.0	3.4	3.1	3	5	9	15	2035	2.0
21	India	2.3	2.1	1.8	798	1,010	1,365	1,766	2015	1.7
22	Rwanda	3.3	3.3	3.8	6	10	23	63	2055	1.9
23	Sierra Leone	2.0	2.4	2.6	4	5	10	24	2050	1.8
24	Benin	2.7	3.2	2.9	4	6	11	19	2035	2.0
25	Central African Rep.	1.8	2.5	2.6	3	4	6	11	2035	1.8
26	Kenya	3.6	4.1	3.9	22	37	83	196	2050	2.1
27	Sudan	2.8	3.1	2.7	23	33	56	98	2035	1.8
28	Pakistan	3.1	3.1	3.3	102	156	286	513	2040	1.9
29	Haiti	2.0	1.8	1.9	6	8	11	16	2025	1.7
30	Lesotho	2.3	2.7	2.6	2	2	4	6	2030	1.8
31	Nigeria	2.5	3.4	3.0	107	157	286	500	2035	1.9
32	Ghana	2.2	3.4	3.0	14	20	35	60	2035	1.9
33	Sri Lanka	1.8	1.5	1.1	16	19	23	26	1995	1.5
34	Yemen, PDR	2.1	2.9	3.0	2	3	6	11	2035	1.9
35	Mauritania	2.3	2.7	2.7	2	3	5	12	2050	1.8
36	Indonesia	2.4	2.1	1.7	171	214	279	345	2005	1.7
37	Liberia	3.0	3.3	3.0	2	3	6	11	2035	1.9
38	*Afghanistan*	2.4	..	..	..	..	..	..	..	..
39	*Burma*	2.3	2.2	2.2	39	52	72	97	2015	1.8
40	*Guinea*	1.9	2.4	2.4	6	9	16	34	2045	1.8
41	*Kampuchea, Dem.*	0.3	..	..	..	..	..	..	..	..
42	*Viet Nam*	..	2.6	2.4	65	88	127	168	2015	1.8
	Middle-income economies	**2.4 w**	**2.2 w**	**1.9 w**	**1,038 t**	**1,329 t**	**1,862 t**			
	Lower-middle-income	**2.5 w**	**2.3 w**	**2.1 w**	**610 t**	**795 t**	**1,145 t**			
43	Senegal	2.5	2.9	3.1	7	10	20	42	2045	1.9
44	Bolivia	2.5	2.7	2.7	7	10	16	25	2030	1.8
45	Zimbabwe	3.1	3.7	3.0	9	13	22	32	2025	2.0
46	Philippines	2.9	2.5	1.9	58	74	101	127	2010	1.8
47	Yemen Arab Rep.	2.8	2.6	3.1	8	13	23	44	2040	1.9
48	Morocco	2.5	2.7	2.4	23	32	47	64	2020	1.8
49	Egypt, Arab Rep.	2.2	2.7	2.3	50	67	99	137	2020	1.8
50	Papua New Guinea	2.3	2.7	2.5	4	5	8	12	2025	1.8
51	Dominican Rep.	2.7	2.4	1.8	7	9	11	14	2010	1.7
52	Côte d'Ivoire	4.2	4.2	3.6	11	18	36	83	2050	1.9
53	Honduras	3.2	3.6	2.9	5	7	11	17	2025	1.9
54	Nicaragua	3.1	3.4	3.0	4	5	9	13	2025	1.9
55	Thailand	2.9	2.0	1.5	54	65	82	98	2000	1.7
56	El Salvador	2.7	1.2	2.1	5	6	10	15	2025	1.7
57	Congo, People's Rep.	2.7	3.3	3.6	2	3	7	17	2050	1.9
58	Jamaica	1.5	1.4	0.8	2	3	3	4	2000	1.4
59	Guatemala	2.8	2.9	2.8	8	12	20	32	2030	1.8
60	Cameroon	2.7	3.2	3.2	11	16	33	67	2045	1.9
61	Paraguay	2.8	3.2	2.7	4	6	9	12	2025	1.8
62	Ecuador	3.1	2.9	2.2	10	13	19	24	2015	1.8
63	Botswana	3.5	3.4	2.3	1	2	2	3	2010	2.0
64	Tunisia	2.1	2.6	2.1	8	10	14	17	2010	1.8
65	Turkey	2.5	2.3	1.9	53	67	90	111	2010	1.7
66	Colombia	2.2	1.9	1.7	29	36	48	57	2005	1.7
67	Chile	1.7	1.7	1.4	13	15	19	21	2000	1.5

Note: For data comparability and coverage, see the technical notes.　Figures in italics are for years other than those specified.

		Average annual growth of population (percent)			Population (millions)			Hypothetical size of stationary population (millions)	Assumed year of reaching net reproduction rate of 1	Population momentum 1990
		1965-80	1980-87	1987-2000	1987	2000ᵃ	2025ᵃ			
68	Peru	2.8	2.3	2.1	20	26	36	46	2010	1.8
69	Mauritius	1.6	1.0	1.1	1	1	1	2	1985	1.6
70	Jordan	2.6	3.9	2.8	4	5	9	15	2035	1.9
71	Costa Rica	2.7	2.3	2.0	3	3	4	5	2005	1.7
72	Syrian Arab Rep.	3.4	3.6	3.7	11	18	37	69	2040	2.0
73	Malaysia	2.5	2.7	2.2	17	22	30	37	2010	1.7
74	Mexico	3.1	2.2	1.9	82	105	141	170	2005	1.8
75	South Africa	2.4	2.3	2.3	33	45	66	90	2020	1.8
76	Poland	0.8	0.8	0.5	38	40	44	47	1990	1.2
77	*Lebanon*	1.6	..	..	..	..	..	..	..	..
	Upper-middle-income	**2.1 w**	**1.9 w**	**1.7 w**	**432 t**	**539 t**	**726 t**			
78	Brazil	2.4	2.2	1.8	141	178	234	280	2005	1.7
79	Uruguay	0.4	0.5	0.7	3	3	4	4	2000	1.3
80	Hungary	0.4	−0.1	−0.2	11	10	10	10	2030	1.1
81	Panama	2.6	2.2	1.5	2	3	4	4	2000	1.6
82	Argentina	1.6	1.4	1.1	31	36	43	49	2005	1.4
83	Yugoslavia	0.9	0.7	0.6	23	25	27	28	2030	1.2
84	Algeria	3.1	3.1	3.1	23	34	56	84	2025	1.9
85	Korea, Rep.	2.0	1.4	1.0	42	48	56	57	2030	1.5
86	Gabon	3.6	4.3	2.6	1	1	3	6	2045	1.7
87	Portugal	0.6	0.4	0.1	10	10	10	9	2030	1.2
88	Venezuela	3.5	2.8	2.2	18	24	34	42	2010	1.8
89	Greece	0.7	0.5	0.2	10	10	10	9	2030	1.1
90	Trinidad and Tobago	1.3	1.6	1.2	1	1	2	2	2000	1.5
91	Libya	4.3	4.3	3.5	4	6	13	24	2040	1.9
92	Oman	3.6	4.6	3.6	1	2	4	8	2045	1.8
93	*Iran, Islamic Rep.*	3.2	3.0	3.0	47	69	113	171	2025	1.9
94	*Iraq*	3.4	3.6	3.4	17	26	49	83	2035	1.9
95	*Romania*	1.1	0.4	0.5	23	24	26	29	1985	1.2
	Low- and middle-income	**2.3 w**	**2.0 w**	**1.9 w**	**3,862 t**	**4,954 t**	**7,023 t**			
	Sub-Saharan Africa	**2.7 w**	**3.2 w**	**3.1 w**	**443 t**	**659 t**	**1,259 t**			
	East Asia	**2.3 w**	**1.5 w**	**1.5 w**	**1,513 t**	**1,825 t**	**2,261 t**			
	South Asia	**2.4 w**	**2.3 w**	**2.0 w**	**1,081 t**	**1,408 t**	**2,004 t**			
	Europe, M.East, & N.Africa	**2.0 w**	**2.1 w**	**2.0 w**	**390 t**	**505 t**	**743 t**			
	Latin America & Caribbean	**2.5 w**	**2.2 w**	**1.8 w**	**404 t**	**512 t**	**689 t**			
	17 highly indebted	**2.5 w**	**2.4 w**	**2.1 w**	**582 t**	**759 t**	**1,097 t**			
	High-income economies	**0.9 w**	**0.7 w**	**0.5 w**	**777 t**	**830 t**	**883 t**			
	OECD members	**0.8 w**	**0.6 w**	**0.4 w**	**747 t**	**787 t**	**814 t**			
	†Other	**3.6 w**	**3.0 w**	**2.5 w**	**31 t**	**42 t**	**69 t**			
96	Spain	1.0	0.5	0.3	39	40	41	37	2030	1.2
97	Ireland	1.2	0.6	0.5	4	4	4	5	1990	1.3
98	†Saudi Arabia	4.7	4.3	3.8	13	20	42	85	2045	1.8
99	†Israel	2.8	1.7	1.4	4	5	7	7	2005	1.5
100	New Zealand	1.3	1.0	0.6	3	4	4	4	2030	1.3
101	†Singapore	1.6	1.1	0.8	3	3	3	3	2030	1.3
102	†Hong Kong	2.0	1.6	1.0	6	6	7	7	2030	1.3
103	Italy	0.6	0.2	−0.1	57	57	53	42	2030	1.1
104	United Kingdom	0.2	0.1	0.1	57	57	57	54	2030	1.1
105	Australia	1.8	1.4	1.4	16	20	23	23	2030	1.4
106	Belgium	0.3	0.0	0.0	10	10	10	8	2030	1.1
107	Netherlands	0.9	0.5	0.3	15	15	15	13	2030	1.1
108	Austria	0.3	0.0	−0.1	8	7	7	6	2030	1.1
109	France	0.7	0.5	0.4	56	59	61	58	2030	1.1
110	Germany, Fed. Rep.	0.3	−0.1	−0.2	61	59	53	43	2030	1.0
111	Finland	0.3	0.5	0.2	5	5	5	4	2030	1.1
112	†Kuwait	7.1	4.5	3.1	2	3	4	6	2020	1.8
113	Denmark	0.5	0.0	−0.1	5	5	5	4	2030	1.0
114	Canada	1.3	1.0	0.8	26	29	31	29	2030	1.3
115	Sweden	0.5	0.1	0.0	8	8	8	8	2030	1.0
116	Japan	1.2	0.6	0.4	122	128	125	113	2030	1.1
117	†United Arab Emirates	15.3	5.2	2.4	1	2	3	3	2020	1.3
118	Norway	0.6	0.3	0.3	4	4	4	4	2030	1.1
119	United States	1.0	1.0	0.8	244	269	300	295	2030	1.3
120	Switzerland	0.5	0.3	−0.1	7	6	6	5	2030	1.0
	Total reporting economies	**2.1 w**	**1.8 w**	**1.7 w**	**4,640 t**	**5,783 t**	**7,906 t**			
	Oil exporters	**2.7 w**	**2.7 w**	**2.4 w**	**578 t**	**790 t**	**1,228 t**			
	Nonreporting nonmembers	**1.0 w**	**1.0 w**	**..**	**371 t**	**410 t**	**474 t**			

a. For the assumptions used in the projections, see the technical notes.

Table 27. Demography and fertility

		Crude birth rate per thousand population		Crude death rate per thousand population		Percentage of women of childbearing age		Total fertility rate			Percentage of married women of childbearing age using contraception[a]	
		1965	1987	1965	1987	1965	1987	1965	1987	2000	1970	1985
	Low-income economies	42 w	31 w	16 w	10 w	46 w	50 w	6.3 w	4.0 w	3.3 w		
	China and India	41 w	26 w	14 w	9 w	46 w	52 w	6.3 w	3.2 w	2.5 w		
	Other low-income	46 w	41 w	21 w	13 w	46 w	46 w	6.4 w	5.6 w	4.7 w		
1	Ethiopia	43	48	20	18	46	46	5.8	6.5	5.7	..	2
2	Bhutan	42	39	23	17	48	48	6.0	5.5	5.3	..	..
3	Chad	45	44	28	20	47	46	6.0	5.9	6.0	..	..
4	Zaire	47	45	21	14	46	45	6.0	6.1	5.8	..	1
5	Bangladesh	47	41	21	15	44	46	6.8	5.5	4.3	..	25
6	Malawi	56	53	26	20	46	44	7.8	7.6	7.6	..	..
7	Nepal	46	41	24	15	50	46	6.0	5.9	4.6	..	15
8	Lao PDR	45	42	23	16	47	47	6.2	5.7	5.0	..	..
9	Mozambique	49	45	27	17	47	46	6.8	6.3	6.1	..	..
10	Tanzania	49	50	22	14	45	43	6.6	7.0	6.0	..	..
11	Burkina Faso	48	47	26	18	47	46	6.4	6.5	6.2	..	..
12	Madagascar	47	46	22	14	47	44	6.6	6.4	5.1	..	..
13	Mali	50	51	27	20	46	45	6.5	7.0	6.9	..	6
14	Burundi	47	49	24	18	48	46	6.4	6.8	6.0	..	9
15	Zambia	49	50	20	13	45	44	6.6	6.8	6.0	..	..
16	Niger	48	51	29	20	43	44	6.8	7.0	7.2	..	..
17	Uganda	49	50	19	17	44	43	6.9	6.9	6.1	..	1
18	China	38	21	10	7	44	55	6.4	2.4	2.1	..	77
19	Somalia	50	49	26	19	45	44	6.7	6.8	6.5	..	2
20	Togo	50	49	23	14	46	44	6.5	6.5	5.2	..	..
21	India	45	32	21	11	47	48	6.2	4.3	3.1	12	35
22	Rwanda	52	52	17	18	45	43	7.5	8.0	7.2	..	1
23	Sierra Leone	48	48	32	23	47	46	6.4	6.5	6.5	..	4
24	Benin	49	48	25	16	44	44	6.8	6.5	5.2	..	6
25	Central African Rep.	34	43	24	16	47	46	4.5	5.8	5.2	..	..
26	Kenya	52	52	20	11	40	40	8.0	7.7	6.5	1	17
27	Sudan	47	44	24	16	46	45	6.7	6.4	5.4	..	..
28	Pakistan	48	47	21	12	43	46	7.0	6.7	5.4	..	11
29	Haiti	43	34	20	13	47	49	6.2	4.7	3.8	..	5
30	Lesotho	42	41	18	13	47	45	5.8	5.8	4.5	..	..
31	Nigeria	51	47	23	15	45	43	6.9	6.5	5.4	..	5
32	Ghana	47	46	17	13	45	44	6.9	6.4	5.1	..	..
33	Sri Lanka	33	23	8	6	47	53	4.9	2.7	2.1	..	62
34	Yemen, PDR	50	48	27	16	45	46	7.0	6.7	5.4	..	..
35	Mauritania	47	48	27	19	47	45	6.5	6.5	6.5	..	1
36	Indonesia	43	29	20	9	47	50	5.5	3.5	2.5	..	48
37	Liberia	46	45	21	13	46	44	6.3	6.5	5.2	..	7
38	*Afghanistan*	53	..	29	..	49	..	7.1	..	..	2	..
39	*Burma*	40	32	18	10	46	49	5.8	4.3	3.3	..	..
40	*Guinea*	46	47	30	23	47	46	5.9	6.2	6.2	..	..
41	*Kampuchea, Dem.*	44	..	20	..	47	..	6.3	..	..	..	..
42	*Viet Nam*	..	34	..	8	..	47	..	4.4	3.1	..	58
	Middle-income economies	38 w	30 w	13 w	8 w	45 w	49 w	5.5 w	3.9 w	3.1 w		
	Lower-middle-income	41 w	32 w	14 w	8 w	44 w	49 w	6.2 w	4.1 w	3.2 w		
43	Senegal	47	46	23	18	46	44	6.4	6.5	6.2	..	12
44	Bolivia	46	43	21	14	46	46	6.6	6.1	4.8	..	26
45	Zimbabwe	55	44	17	11	42	45	8.0	5.9	4.3	..	40
46	Philippines	42	30	12	8	44	49	6.8	3.9	2.7	2	44
47	Yemen Arab Rep.	49	48	27	16	46	44	7.0	7.0	5.7	..	..
48	Morocco	49	35	18	10	45	48	7.1	4.8	3.4	1	36
49	Egypt, Arab Rep.	44	36	19	10	43	47	6.8	4.8	3.6	..	32
50	Papua New Guinea	43	39	20	12	47	47	6.3	5.7	4.4	..	..
51	Dominican Rep.	47	31	14	7	43	50	7.0	3.8	2.7	..	50
52	Côte d'Ivoire	52	51	22	15	44	44	7.4	7.4	6.4	..	..
53	Honduras	51	40	17	8	44	45	7.4	5.6	4.2	..	35
54	Nicaragua	49	41	16	8	43	45	7.2	5.5	4.2	..	..
55	Thailand	41	25	10	7	44	53	6.3	2.8	2.2	15	65
56	El Salvador	47	36	14	8	44	45	6.7	4.9	3.8	..	48
57	Congo, People's Rep.	42	47	18	11	47	43	5.7	6.5	6.3	..	..
58	Jamaica	38	26	9	6	42	50	5.4	2.9	2.1	..	52
59	Guatemala	47	41	17	9	44	44	6.7	5.8	4.5	..	23
60	Cameroon	40	45	20	13	46	42	5.2	6.5	5.8	..	..
61	Paraguay	41	35	8	6	41	49	6.6	4.6	3.7	..	49
62	Ecuador	45	33	14	7	43	48	6.8	4.3	3.0	..	44
63	Botswana	53	35	19	10	45	45	6.9	5.0	3.1	..	29
64	Tunisia	44	30	17	7	43	49	7.0	4.1	2.8	10	41
65	Turkey	41	30	15	9	44	50	5.9	3.8	2.8	..	50
66	Colombia	45	26	14	7	43	52	6.3	3.2	2.4	..	63
67	Chile	34	24	11	6	45	53	4.9	2.7	2.1	..	..

Note: For data comparability and coverage, see the technical notes.   Figures in italics are for years other than those specified.

		Crude birth rate per thousand population		Crude death rate per thousand population		Percentage of women of childbearing age		Total fertility rate			Percentage of married women of childbearing age using contraception[a]	
		1965	1987	1965	1987	1965	1987	1965	1987	2000	1970	1985
68	Peru	45	31	17	9	44	49	6.7	4.1	2.9	..	46
69	Mauritius	36	20	8	7	45	54	5.0	2.1	2.1	..	78
70	Jordan	53	43	21	7	45	44	8.0	6.5	5.2	..	26
71	Costa Rica	45	28	8	4	42	52	6.4	3.3	2.4	..	66
72	Syrian Arab Rep.	48	45	16	7	41	43	7.6	6.8	5.5	..	..
73	Malaysia	41	31	12	6	43	51	6.3	3.8	2.8	7	51
74	Mexico	45	29	11	6	43	50	6.7	3.6	2.5	..	53
75	South Africa	40	35	16	10	46	47	6.1	4.5	3.5	..	..
76	Poland	17	16	7	10	47	48	2.5	2.2	2.1	..	..
77	*Lebanon*	41	..	13	..	42	..	6.2	..	..	55	..
	Upper-middle-income	33 w	27 w	11 w	8 w	46 w	50 w	4.7 w	3.5 w	2.8 w		
78	Brazil	39	28	11	8	45	51	5.7	3.5	2.5	..	65
79	Uruguay	21	19	10	11	49	46	2.9	2.6	2.1	..	..
80	Hungary	13	12	11	14	48	47	1.8	1.8	1.8	..	73
81	Panama	40	27	9	5	44	51	5.8	3.1	2.2	..	61
82	Argentina	23	21	9	9	50	47	3.1	3.0	2.3	..	..
83	Yugoslavia	21	15	9	9	50	50	2.7	2.0	2.0	59	..
84	Algeria	50	39	18	9	44	45	7.4	5.9	4.4	..	..
85	Korea, Rep.	36	20	11	6	46	55	4.9	2.1	1.9	32	70
86	Gabon	31	42	22	16	49	47	4.1	5.5	6.0	..	..
87	Portugal	23	12	10	10	48	48	3.1	1.5	1.6	..	..
88	Venezuela	42	31	8	5	44	50	6.2	3.8	2.7	..	..
89	Greece	18	12	8	10	51	47	2.3	1.7	1.7	..	..
90	Trinidad and Tobago	34	26	8	7	46	53	4.4	2.8	2.1	..	54
91	Libya	49	44	18	9	45	44	7.3	6.9	5.6	..	..
92	Oman	50	46	24	12	46	44	7.2	7.2	5.9	..	..
93	*Iran, Islamic Rep.*	46	41	18	9	42	47	7.1	5.6	4.4	..	..
94	*Iraq*	49	43	18	8	45	44	7.2	6.4	5.1	..	..
95	*Romania*	15	15	9	11	50	48	1.9	2.1	2.1	..	..
	Low- and middle-income	41 w	30 w	15 w	10 w	46 w	50 w	6.1 w	4.0 w	3.3 w		
	Sub-Saharan Africa	48 w	47 w	22 w	16 w	45 w	44 w	6.6 w	6.6 w	5.8 w		
	East Asia	39 w	23 w	11 w	7 w	45 w	54 w	6.2 w	2.7 w	2.3 w		
	South Asia	45 w	34 w	20 w	12 w	47 w	48 w	6.3 w	4.6 w	3.5 w		
	Europe, M.East, & N.Africa	35 w	31 w	15 w	10 w	46 w	47 w	5.1 w	4.3 w	3.7 w		
	Latin America & Caribbean	40 w	29 w	12 w	7 w	45 w	50 w	5.8 w	3.6 w	2.7 w		
	17 highly indebted	41 w	32 w	14 w	9 w	45 w	49 w	5.9 w	4.2 w	3.2 w		
	High-income economies	19 w	14 w	10 w	9 w	47 w	50 w	2.8 w	1.8 w	1.9 w		
	OECD members	19 w	13 w	10 w	9 w	47 w	50 w	2.7 w	1.7 w	1.7 w		
	†Other	36 w	30 w	11 w	7 w	45 w	48 w	5.5 w	4.6 w	4.1 w		
96	Spain	21	12	8	9	49	48	2.9	1.6	1.6	..	..
97	Ireland	22	17	12	9	42	48	4.0	2.3	2.1	..	..
98	†Saudi Arabia	48	42	20	8	44	42	7.3	7.2	5.9	..	..
99	†Israel	26	22	6	7	46	48	3.8	2.9	2.3	..	..
100	New Zealand	23	16	9	9	45	52	3.7	1.9	1.9	..	..
101	†Singapore	31	17	6	6	45	60	4.7	1.7	1.7	45	74
102	†Hong Kong	28	16	6	6	45	55	4.7	1.8	1.8	50	72
103	Italy	19	10	10	10	48	49	2.7	1.3	1.4	..	..
104	United Kingdom	18	13	12	12	45	48	2.9	1.8	1.8	..	..
105	Australia	20	15	9	8	47	52	3.0	1.9	1.9	67	..
106	Belgium	17	12	12	12	44	48	2.6	1.6	1.6	..	81
107	Netherlands	20	13	8	9	47	52	3.0	1.6	1.6	..	72
108	Austria	18	11	13	12	43	48	2.7	1.5	1.5	..	71
109	France	18	14	11	10	43	48	2.8	1.8	1.8	..	..
110	Germany, Fed. Rep.	18	10	12	12	45	49	2.5	1.4	1.4	..	78
111	Finland	17	12	10	10	48	50	2.4	1.6	1.6	..	77
112	†Kuwait	47	33	8	3	46	49	7.4	4.8	3.7	..	..
113	Denmark	18	11	10	12	47	50	2.6	1.5	1.6	67	..
114	Canada	21	15	8	8	47	53	3.1	1.7	1.7	..	73
115	Sweden	16	12	10	13	47	47	2.4	1.9	1.9	..	78
116	Japan	19	11	7	7	56	50	2.0	1.7	1.7	..	64
117	†United Arab Emirates	41	23	15	4	47	47	6.8	4.8	3.7	..	..
118	Norway	18	13	10	11	45	48	2.9	1.8	1.8	..	..
119	United States	19	16	9	9	45	51	2.9	1.9	1.9	65	68
120	Switzerland	19	12	10	10	48	50	2.6	1.6	1.6	..	70
	Total reporting economies	36 w	28 w	14 w	10 w	46 w	50 w	5.4 w	3.6 w	3.1 w		
	Oil exporters	45 w	36 w	18 w	10 w	45 w	47 w	6.4 w	4.8 w	3.8 w		
	Nonreporting nonmembers	20 w	20 w	8 w	10 w	47 w	47 w	2.7 w	2.5 w	2.3 w		

a. Figures include women whose husbands practice contraception; see the technical note.

Table 28. Health and nutrition

		Population per:				Daily calorie supply per capita		Babies with low birth weights (percent)
		Physician		Nursing person				
		1965	1984	1965	1984	1965	1986	1985
	Low-income economies	**9,790** w	**5,410** w	**6,010** w	**2,150** w	**1,993** w	**2,384** w	
	China and India	**2,930** w	**1,640** w	**4,420** w	**1,700** w	**2,001** w	**2,463** w	
	Other low-income	**28,190** w	**13,550** w	**10,170** w	**3,130** w	**1,976** w	**2,227** w	
1	Ethiopia	70,190	77,360	5,970	5,290	1,824	1,749	..
2	Bhutan	..	23,310	..	2,990	..	..	..
3	Chad	72,480	38,360	13,610	3,390	2,399	1,717	11
4	Zaire	35,130	..	..	..	2,187	2,163	..
5	Bangladesh	8,100	6,730	..	8,980	1,972	1,927	31
6	Malawi	47,320	11,560	..	3,130	2,244	2,310	10
7	Nepal	46,180	32,710	87,650	4,680	1,901	2,052	..
8	Lao PDR	24,320	1,360	4,880	530	1,956	2,391	39
9	Mozambique	18,000	37,950	5,370	5,760	1,979	1,595	15
10	Tanzania	21,700	..	2,100	..	1,832	2,192	14
11	Burkina Faso	73,960	57,180	4,150	1,680	2,009	2,139	18
12	Madagascar	10,620	10,000	3,650	..	2,462	2,440	10
13	Mali	51,510	25,390	3,360	1,350	1,859	2,074	17
14	Burundi	55,910	21,120	7,320	3,040	2,391	2,343	14
15	Zambia	11,380	7,100	5,820	740	..	..	14
16	Niger	65,540	38,770	6,210	450	1,994	2,432	20
17	Uganda	11,110	21,900	3,130	2,060	2,360	2,344	10
18	China	1,600	1,000	3,000	1,700	1,926	2,630	6
19	Somalia	36,840	16,090	3,950	1,530	2,167	2,138	..
20	Togo	23,240	8,720	4,990	1,240	2,378	2,207	20
21	India	4,880	2,520	6,500	1,700	2,111	2,238	30
22	Rwanda	72,480	34,680	7,450	3,650	1,665	1,830	17
23	Sierra Leone	16,840	13,630	4,470	1,090	1,837	1,855	14
24	Benin	32,390	15,940	2,540	1,750	2,009	2,184	10
25	Central African Rep.	34,020	23,070	3,000	2,170	2,135	1,949	15
26	Kenya	13,280	10,100	1,930	950	2,289	2,060	13
27	Sudan	23,500	10,110	3,360	1,250	1,938	2,208	15
28	Pakistan	..	2,900	9,910	4,900	1,761	2,315	25
29	Haiti	14,000	7,180	12,890	2,290	2,000	1,902	17
30	Lesotho	20,060	18,610	4,700	..	2,065	2,303	10
31	Nigeria	29,530	7,980	6,160	1,020	2,185	2,146	25
32	Ghana	13,740	14,890	3,730	640	1,950	1,759	17
33	Sri Lanka	5,820	5,520	3,220	1,290	2,153	2,401	28
34	Yemen, PDR	12,870	4,340	1,850	1,060	1,982	2,299	13
35	Mauritania	36,470	12,110	..	1,200	2,064	2,322	10
36	Indonesia	31,700	9,460	9,490	1,260	1,800	2,579	14
37	Liberia	12,360	9,240	2,290	1,360	2,154	2,381	..
38	*Afghanistan*	15,770	..	24,430	..	2,294	..	..
39	*Burma*	11,860	3,740	11,370	900	1,917	2,609	16
40	*Guinea*	54,430	57,390	4,750	6,380	1,923	1,777	18
41	*Kampuchea, Dem.*	22,410	..	3,670	..	2,276	..	..
42	*Viet Nam*	..	1,000	..	620	..	2,297	18
	Middle-income economies	**4,030** w	**2,390** w	**2,170** w	**980** w	**2,463** w	**2,855** w	
	Lower-middle-income	**5,370** w	**3,330** w	**1,810** w	**1,070** w	**2,394** w	**2,777** w	
43	Senegal	21,130	13,450	2,640	2,090	2,479	2,350	10
44	Bolivia	3,300	1,540	3,990	2,480	1,869	2,143	15
45	Zimbabwe	8,010	6,700	990	1,000	2,105	2,132	15
46	Philippines	..	6,700	1,130	2,740	1,924	2,372	18
47	Yemen Arab Rep.	58,240	6,270	..	2,680	2,008	2,318	9
48	Morocco	12,120	15,610	2,290	920	2,167	2,915	9
49	Egypt, Arab Rep.	2,300	790	2,030	800	2,400	3,342	7
50	Papua New Guinea	12,640	6,160	620	890	1,905	2,205	25
51	Dominican Rep.	1,700	1,760	1,640	1,210	1,872	2,477	16
52	Côte d'Ivoire	20,640	..	2,000	..	2,360	2,562	14
53	Honduras	5,370	1,510	1,530	670	1,963	2,068	20
54	Nicaragua	2,560	1,500	1,390	530	2,398	2,495	15
55	Thailand	7,160	6,290	4,970	710	2,101	2,331	12
56	El Salvador	..	2,830	1,300	930	1,859	2,160	15
57	Congo, People's Rep.	14,210	8,140	950	570	2,259	2,619	12
58	Jamaica	1,990	2,060	340	490	2,231	2,590	8
59	Guatemala	3,690	2,180	8,250	850	2,027	2,307	10
60	Cameroon	26,720	..	5,830	..	2,079	2,028	13
61	Paraguay	1,850	1,460	1,550	1,000	2,627	2,853	6
62	Ecuador	3,000	830	2,320	620	1,940	2,058	10
63	Botswana	27,460	6,910	17,720	700	2,019	2,201	8
64	Tunisia	8,000	2,150	..	370	2,202	2,994	7
65	Turkey	2,900	1,380	..	1,030	2,659	3,229	7
66	Colombia	2,500	1,190	890	630	2,174	2,543	15
67	Chile	2,120	1,230	600	370	2,592	2,579	7

Note: For data comparability and coverage, see the technical notes. Figures in italics are for years other than those specified.

		Population per:				Daily calorie supply per capita		Babies with low birth weights (percent)
		Physician		Nursing person				
		1965	1984	1965	1984	1965	1986	1985
68	Peru	1,650	1,040	900	. .	2,325	2,246	9
69	Mauritius	3,930	1,900	2,030	580	2,272	2,748	9
70	Jordan	4,710	1,140	1,810	1,300	2,314	2,991	7
71	Costa Rica	2,010	960	630	450	2,366	2,803	9
72	Syrian Arab Rep.	5,400	1,260	. .	1,440	2,195	3,260	9
73	Malaysia	6,200	1,930	1,320	1,010	2,247	2,730	9
74	Mexico	2,080	1,240	980	880	2,644	3,132	15
75	South Africa	2,050	. .	490	. .	2,623	2,924	12
76	Poland	800	490	410	190	3,229	3,336	8
77	Lebanon	1,010	. .	2,030	. .	2,489	. .	. .
	Upper-middle-income	2,430 w	1,170 w	2,590 w	870 w	2,556 w	2,970 w	
78	Brazil	2,500	1,080	3,100	1,210	2,402	2,656	8
79	Uruguay	880	510	590	. .	2,812	2,648	8
80	Hungary	630	310	240	170	3,171	3,569	10
81	Panama	2,130	980	1,600	390	2,255	2,446	8
82	Argentina	600	370	610	980	3,210	3,210	6
83	Yugoslavia	1,200	550	850	260	3,289	3,563	7
84	Algeria	8,590	2,330	11,770	330	1,681	2,715	9
85	Korea, Rep.	2,680	1,170	2,970	590	2,256	2,907	9
86	Gabon	. .	2,790	760	270	1,881	2,521	16
87	Portugal	1,240	410	1,160	. .	2,517	3,151	8
88	Venezuela	1,210	700	560	. .	2,321	2,494	9
89	Greece	710	350	600	450	3,049	3,688	6
90	Trinidad and Tobago	3,810	960	560	260	2,497	3,082	. .
91	Libya	3,860	690	850	350	1,925	3,601	5
92	Oman	23,790	1,700	6,420	770	. .	. .	14
93	Iran, Islamic Rep.	3,800	2,690	4,170	1,050	2,204	3,313	9
94	Iraq	5,000	1,740	2,910	1,660	2,150	2,932	9
95	Romania	760	570	400	280	2,978	3,373	6
	Low- and middle-income	8,300 w	4,630 w	5,030 w	1,860 w	2,116 w	2,509 w	
	Sub-Saharan Africa	33,840 w	23,760 w	5,460 w	2,130 w	2,096 w	2,101 w	
	East Asia	5,600 w	2,400 w	4,060 w	1,560 w	1,937 w	2,594 w	
	South Asia	6,220 w	3,570 w	8,380 w	2,710 w	2,060 w	2,228 w	
	Europe, M.East, & N.Africa	4,820 w	2,440 w	3,410 w	1,160 w	2,610 w	3,177 w	
	Latin America & Caribbean	2,370 w	1,230 w	2,090 w	1,010 w	2,457 w	2,701 w	
	17 highly indebted	7,930 w	3,440 w	2,460 w	1,160 w	2,422 w	2,635 w	
	High-income economies	940 w	470 w	470 w	130 w	3,083 w	3,375 w	
	OECD members	870 w	450 w	420 w	130 w	3,100 w	3,390 w	
	†Other	4,430 w	800 w	2,590 w	260 w	2,324 w	3,001 w	
96	Spain	800	320	1,220	260	2,822	3,359	. .
97	Ireland	950	680	170	140	3,546	3,632	4
98	†Saudi Arabia	9,400	690	6,060	320	1,853	3,004	6
99	†Israel	400	350	300	110	2,784	3,061	7
100	New Zealand	820	580	570	80	3,237	3,463	5
101	†Singapore	1,900	1,310	600	. .	2,297	2,840	7
102	†Hong Kong	2,520	1,070	1,250	240	2,504	2,859	4
103	Italy	1,850	230	790	. .	3,091	3,523	7
104	United Kingdom	870	. .	200	120	3,353	3,256	7
105	Australia	720	440	150	110	3,118	3,326	6
106	Belgium	700	330	590	110	. .	. .	5
107	Netherlands	860	450	270	170	3,108	3,326	4
108	Austria	720	390	350	180	3,231	3,428	6
109	France	830	320	380	110	3,217	3,336	5
110	Germany, Fed. Rep.	640	380	500	230	3,102	3,528	5
111	Finland	1,300	440	180	60	3,111	3,122	4
112	†Kuwait	790	640	270	200	2,945	3,021	7
113	Denmark	740	400	190	60	3,395	3,633	6
114	Canada	770	510	190	120	3,212	3,462	6
115	Sweden	910	390	310	100	2,888	3,064	4
116	Japan	970	660	410	180	2,687	2,864	5
117	†United Arab Emirates	. .	1,010	. .	390	2,705	3,733	. .
118	Norway	790	450	340	60	3,032	3,223	4
119	United States	670	470	310	70	3,224	3,645	7
120	Switzerland	710	700	270	130	3,412	3,437	5
	Total reporting economies	6,650 w	3,930 w	4,010 w	1,570 w	2,322 w	2,655 w	
	Oil exporters	17,940 w	5,120 w	5,740 w	1,010 w	2,128 w	2,738 w	
	Nonreporting nonmembers	770 w	2,210 w	370 w	290 w	3,130 w	3,358 w	

Table 29. Education

	Percentage of age group enrolled in education													
	Primary						Secondary						Tertiary	
	Total		Male		Female		Total		Male		Female		Total	
	1965	1986	1965	1986	1965	1986	1965	1986	1965	1986	1965	1986	1965	1986
Low-income economies	73 w	103 w	..	113 w	..	92 w	20 w	35 w	..	42 w	..	27 w	2 w	3 w
China and India	83 w	113 w	..	124 w	..	101 w	25 w	39 w	..	47 w	..	30 w	2 w	2 w
Other low-income	49 w	76 w	60 w	83 w	37 w	68 w	9 w	25 w	13 w	29 w	5 w	20 w	1 w	4 w
1 Ethiopia	11	36	16	44	6	28	2	12	3	14	1	9	0	1
2 Bhutan	7	23	13	29	1	17	0	4	0	7	..	1	..	0
3 Chad	34	43	56	61	13	24	1	6	3	10	0	2	..	0
4 Zaire	70	..	95	..	45	..	5	..	8	..	2	..	0	2
5 Bangladesh	49	60	67	69	31	50	13	18	23	24	3	11	1	5
6 Malawi	44	64	55	72	32	55	2	4	3	6	1	3	0	1
7 Nepal	20	79	36	104	4	47	5	25	9	35	2	11	1	5
8 Lao PDR	40	94	50	102	30	85	2	19	2	23	1	16	0	2
9 Mozambique	37	82	48	92	26	73	3	7	3	9	2	5	0	0
10 Tanzania	32	69	40	70	25	69	2	3	3	4	1	3	0	0
11 Burkina Faso	12	35	16	45	8	26	1	6	2	8	1	4	0	1
12 Madagascar	65	121	70	125	59	118	8	36	10	43	5	30	1	5
13 Mali	24	22	32	27	16	16	4	7	5	9	2	4	0	1
14 Burundi	26	59	36	68	15	50	1	4	2	6	1	3	0	1
15 Zambia	53	104	59	112	46	101	7	19	11	24	3	14	..	2
16 Niger	11	29	15	37	7	20	1	6	1	9	0	3	..	1
17 Uganda	67	..	83	..	50	..	4	..	6	..	2	..	0	1
18 China	89	129	..	137	..	120	24	42	..	48	..	35	0	2
19 Somalia	10	20	16	26	4	13	2	12	4	15	1	8	0	4
20 Togo	55	102	78	125	32	78	5	21	8	32	2	10	0	2
21 India	74	92	89	107	57	76	27	35	41	45	13	24	5	..
22 Rwanda	53	67	64	68	43	66	2	3	3	4	1	2	0	0
23 Sierra Leone	29	..	37	..	21	..	5	..	8	..	3	..	0	..
24 Benin	34	65	48	87	21	43	3	16	5	23	2	9	0	..
25 Central African Rep.	56	66	84	81	28	50	2	13	4	19	1	7	..	1
26 Kenya	54	94	69	97	40	91	4	20	6	25	2	15	0	1
27 Sudan	29	50	37	59	21	41	4	20	6	23	2	17	1	2
28 Pakistan	40	44	59	55	20	32	12	18	18	25	5	10	2	5
29 Haiti	50	78	56	83	44	72	5	18	6	19	3	17	0	1
30 Lesotho	94	115	74	102	114	127	4	22	4	18	4	26	0	2
31 Nigeria	32	..	39	..	24	..	5	..	7	..	3	..	0	3
32 Ghana	69	63	82	75	57	59	13	35	19	45	7	27	1	2
33 Sri Lanka	93	103	98	104	86	102	35	66	34	63	35	70	2	4
34 Yemen, PDR	23	..	35	..	10	..	11	..	17	..	5	..	..	..
35 Mauritania	13	46	19	57	6	35	1	15	2	21	0	8	..	0
36 Indonesia	72	118	79	121	65	116	12	41	18	45	7	34	1	7
37 Liberia	41	..	59	..	23	..	5	..	8	..	3	..	1	..
38 *Afghanistan*	16	..	26	..	5	..	2	..	4	..	1	..	0	..
39 *Burma*	71	..	76	..	65	..	15	..	20	..	11	..	1	..
40 *Guinea*	31	29	44	40	19	17	5	9	9	14	2	5	0	1
41 *Kampuchea, Dem.*	77	..	98	..	56	..	9	..	14	..	4	..	1	..
42 *Viet Nam*	..	100	..	107	..	94	..	43	..	44	..	41	..	..
Middle-income economies	93 w	104 w	99 w	108 w	86 w	100 w	26 w	54 w	30 w	62 w	22 w	56 w	6 w	18 w
Lower-middle-income	89 w	104 w	96 w	108 w	81 w	100 w	24 w	51 w	28 w	57 w	21 w	50 w	6 w	17 w
43 Senegal	40	55	52	66	29	45	7	13	10	18	3	9	1	2
44 Bolivia	73	87	86	93	60	82	18	37	21	40	15	34	5	19
45 Zimbabwe	110	129	128	132	92	126	6	46	8	55	5	37	0	4
46 Philippines	113	106	115	107	111	106	41	68	42	66	40	69	19	38
47 Yemen Arab Rep.	9	79	16	125	1	31	0	15	..	26	..	3	..	..
48 Morocco	57	79	78	96	35	62	11	34	16	39	5	27	1	9
49 Egypt, Arab Rep.	75	87	90	96	60	77	26	66	37	77	15	54	7	21
50 Papua New Guinea	44	..	53	..	35	..	4	..	6	..	2	..	..	2
51 Dominican Rep.	87	133	87	131	87	135	12	47	11	43	12	56	2	19
52 Côte d'Ivoire	60	78	80	92	41	65	6	20	10	27	2	12	0	3
53 Honduras	80	102	81	103	79	102	10	36	11	31	9	36	1	10
54 Nicaragua	69	98	68	93	69	103	14	42	15	27	13	57	2	9
55 Thailand	78	99	82	..	74	..	14	29	16	..	11	..	2	20
56 El Salvador	82	70	85	69	79	70	17	24	18	23	17	26	2	14
57 Congo, People's Rep.	114	..	134	..	94	..	10	..	15	..	5	..	1	..
58 Jamaica	109	..	112	..	106	..	51	..	53	..	50	..	3	4
59 Guatemala	50	76	55	82	45	70	8	20	10	..	7	..	2	9
60 Cameroon	94	107	114	116	75	97	5	23	8	29	2	18	0	2
61 Paraguay	102	99	109	102	96	97	13	30	13	30	13	29	4	10
62 Ecuador	91	114	94	..	88	..	17	55	19	..	16	..	3	33
63 Botswana	65	105	59	101	71	109	3	31	5	29	3	33	..	2
64 Tunisia	91	118	116	127	65	108	16	39	23	45	9	33	2	6
65 Turkey	101	117	118	121	83	113	16	44	22	56	9	33	4	10
66 Colombia	84	114	83	112	86	115	17	56	18	55	16	56	3	13
67 Chile	124	110	125	110	122	109	34	70	31	67	36	73	6	16

Note: For data comparability and coverage, see the technical notes.   Figures in italics are for years other than those specified.

		Percentage of age group enrolled in education												
		Primary						Secondary						Tertiary	
		Total		Male		Female		Total		Male		Female		Total	
		1965	1986	1965	1986	1965	1986	1965	1986	1965	1986	1965	1986	1965	1986
68	Peru	99	122	108	125	90	120	25	65	29	68	21	61	8	25
69	Mauritius	101	106	105	105	97	106	26	51	34	53	18	49	3	1
70	Jordan	95	..	105	..	83	..	38	..	52	..	23	..	2	..
71	Costa Rica	106	102	107	103	105	101	24	42	23	41	25	44	6	24
72	Syrian Arab Rep.	78	111	103	117	52	105	28	60	43	72	13	49	8	17
73	Malaysia	90	101	96	100	84	99	28	54	34	54	22	54	2	6
74	Mexico	92	114	94	115	90	113	17	55	21	56	13	54	4	16
75	South Africa	90	..	91	..	88	..	15	..	16	..	14	..	4	..
76	Poland	104	101	106	101	102	101	69	80	70	78	69	81	18	17
77	Lebanon	106	..	118	..	93	..	26	..	33	..	20	..	14	..
	Upper-middle-income	97 w	104 w	102 w	107 w	93 w	101 w	28 w	59 w	32 w	71 w	24 w	67 w	6 w	20 w
78	Brazil	108	105	109	..	108	..	16	36	16	..	16	..	2	..
79	Uruguay	106	110	106	111	106	109	44	71	42	..	46	..	8	42
80	Hungary	101	98	102	97	100	98	..	70	..	70	..	71	13	15
81	Panama	102	106	104	109	99	104	34	59	32	56	36	63	7	28
82	Argentina	101	109	101	109	102	109	28	74	26	68	31	79	14	39
83	Yugoslavia	106	95	108	95	103	94	65	82	70	84	59	80	13	19
84	Algeria	68	95	81	105	53	85	7	54	10	62	5	45	1	7
85	Korea, Rep.	101	94	103	94	99	94	35	95	44	98	25	93	6	33
86	Gabon	134	126	146	127	122	125	11	27	16	31	5	22	..	4
87	Portugal	84	117	84	131	83	123	42	52	49	47	34	56	5	13
88	Venezuela	94	110	93	110	94	110	27	46	27	41	28	50	7	26
89	Greece	110	106	111	106	109	106	49	88	57	89	41	87	10	24
90	Trinidad and Tobago	93	95	97	93	90	96	36	76	39	74	34	79	2	4
91	Libya	78	..	111	..	44	..	14	..	24	..	4	..	1	11
92	Oman	..	94	..	101	..	86	..	35	..	45	..	25	..	2
93	Iran, Islamic Rep.	63	117	85	127	40	107	18	47	24	56	11	38	2	5
94	Iraq	74	99	102	107	45	91	28	52	42	65	14	39	4	..
95	Romania	101	97	102	98	100	97	39	79	44	74	32	76	10	11
	Low- and middle-income	78 w	103 w	84 w	112 w	62 w	94 w	22 w	40 w	28 w	47 w	14 w	34 w	3 w	7 w
	Sub-Saharan Africa	41 w	66 w	52 w	73 w	31 w	58 w	4 w	16 w	6 w	20 w	2 w	12 w	0 w	2 w
	East Asia	88 w	123 w	..	131 w	..	117 w	23 w	45 w	..	50 w	..	39 w	1 w	5 w
	South Asia	68 w	84 w	83 w	98 w	52 w	69 w	24 w	32 w	36 w	41 w	12 w	22 w	4 w	5 w
	Europe, M.East, & N.Africa	83 w	97 w	94 w	104 w	71 w	91 w	32 w	56 w	38 w	62 w	26 w	49 w	7 w	13 w
	Latin America & Caribbean	98 w	108 w	99 w	110 w	96 w	108 w	19 w	48 w	20 w	54 w	19 w	56 w	4 w	20 w
	17 highly indebted	88 w	106 w	91 w	109 w	84 w	104 w	21 w	52 w	23 w	59 w	20 w	58 w	5 w	18 w
	High-income economies	105 w	102 w	106 w	103 w	105 w	102 w	62 w	92 w	63 w	91 w	60 w	93 w	21 w	39 w
	OECD members	107 w	102 w	107 w	103 w	106 w	102 w	63 w	93 w	64 w	92 w	61 w	94 w	21 w	39 w
	†Other	74 w	90 w	80 w	94 w	67 w	87 w	27 w	61 w	29 w	63 w	24 w	59 w	7 w	17 w
96	Spain	115	101	117	104	114	103	38	98	46	95	29	101	6	32
97	Ireland	108	100	107	100	108	100	51	96	53	91	50	101	12	22
98	†Saudi Arabia	24	71	36	78	11	65	4	44	7	52	1	35	1	13
99	†Israel	95	99	95	98	95	100	48	79	46	75	51	83	20	33
100	New Zealand	106	105	107	106	104	104	75	84	76	83	74	86	15	33
101	†Singapore	105	115	110	118	100	113	45	71	49	70	41	73	10	..
102	†Hong Kong	103	105	106	106	99	104	29	69	32	66	25	72	5	13
103	Italy	112	97	113	99	110	99	47	76	53	74	41	74	11	25
104	United Kingdom	92	106	92	105	92	106	66	85	67	83	66	87	12	22
105	Australia	99	106	99	106	99	105	62	96	63	95	61	98	16	29
106	Belgium	109	96	110	95	108	97	75	96	77	95	72	97	15	32
107	Netherlands	104	114	104	113	104	115	61	104	64	106	57	102	17	32
108	Austria	106	100	106	100	105	100	52	79	52	78	52	80	9	28
109	France	134	112	135	113	133	111	56	95	53	92	59	99	18	30
110	Germany, Fed. Rep.	..	97	..	97	..	97	..	72	..	71	..	74	9	30
111	Finland	92	104	95	104	89	104	76	102	72	95	80	110	11	35
112	†Kuwait	116	98	129	99	103	96	52	82	59	84	43	79	..	16
113	Denmark	98	98	97	98	99	98	83	105	98	105	67	105	14	29
114	Canada	105	105	106	106	104	104	56	103	57	103	55	103	26	55
115	Sweden	95	99	94	97	96	99	62	83	63	79	60	88	13	37
116	Japan	100	102	100	101	100	102	82	96	82	95	81	97	13	29
117	†United Arab Emirates	..	100	..	99	..	101	..	59	..	54	..	66	0	8
118	Norway	97	98	97	97	98	97	64	97	66	95	62	100	11	28
119	United States	..	102	..	103	..	101	..	100	..	100	..	100	40	59
120	Switzerland	87	..	87	..	87	..	37	..	38	..	35	..	8	23
	Total reporting economies	82 w	103 w	88 w	110 w	70 w	95 w	28 w	50 w	35 w	55 w	23 w	45 w	7 w	14 w
	Oil exporters	68 w	110 w	78 w	114 w	59 w	105 w	15 w	49 w	20 w	54 w	10 w	43 w	2 w	10 w
	Nonreporting nonmembers	102 w	105 w	103 w	..	102 w	..	66 w	92 w	60 w	..	72 w	..	27 w	21 w

Table 30. Income distribution and ICP estimates of GDP

		ICP estimates of GDP per capita, 1985 (US = 100)	Percentage share of household income, by percentile groups of households						
			Year	Lowest 20 percent	Second quintile	Third quintile	Fourth quintile	Highest 20 percent	Highest 10 percent
Low-income economies									
China and India									
Other low-income									
1	Ethiopia	1.6	..	..	..	..	..	..	..
2	Bhutan	..	..	..	..	..	..	..	..
3	Chad	..	..	..	..	..	..	..	..
4	Zaire	..	..	..	..	..	..	..	..
5	Bangladesh	..	1981-82	6.6	10.7	15.3	22.1	45.3	29.5
6	Malawi	3.6	..	..	..	..	..	..	..
7	Nepal	..	..	..	..	..	..	..	..
8	Lao PDR	..	..	..	..	..	..	..	..
9	Mozambique	..	..	..	..	..	..	..	..
10	Tanzania	2.6	..	..	..	..	..	..	..
11	Burkina Faso	..	..	..	..	..	..	..	..
12	Madagascar	3.9	..	..	..	..	..	..	..
13	Mali	2.4	..	..	..	..	..	..	..
14	Burundi	..	..	..	..	..	..	..	..
15	Zambia	4.7	1976	3.4	7.4	11.2	16.9	61.1	46.4
16	Niger	..	..	..	..	..	..	..	..
17	Uganda	..	..	..	..	..	..	..	..
18	China	..	..	..	..	..	..	..	..
19	Somalia	..	..	..	..	..	..	..	..
20	Togo	..	..	..	..	..	..	..	..
21	India	4.7	1975-76	7.0	9.2	13.9	20.5	49.4	33.6
22	Rwanda	3.8	..	..	..	..	..	..	..
23	Sierra Leone	3.0	..	..	..	..	..	..	..
24	Benin	6.5	..	..	..	..	..	..	..
25	Central African Rep.	..	..	..	..	..	..	..	..
26	Kenya	5.3	1976	2.6	6.3	11.5	19.2	60.4	45.8
27	Sudan	..	..	..	..	..	..	..	..
28	Pakistan	..	..	..	..	..	..	..	..
29	Haiti	..	..	..	..	..	..	..	..
30	Lesotho	..	..	..	..	..	..	..	..
31	Nigeria	7.2	..	..	..	..	..	..	..
32	Ghana	..	..	..	..	..	..	..	..
33	Sri Lanka	11.7	1980-81	5.8	10.1	14.1	20.3	49.8	34.7
34	Yemen, PDR	..	..	..	..	..	..	..	..
35	Mauritania	..	..	..	..	..	..	..	..
36	Indonesia	..	1976	6.6	7.8	12.6	23.6	49.4	34.0
37	Liberia	..	..	..	..	..	..	..	..
38	*Afghanistan*	..	..	..	..	..	..	..	..
39	*Burma*	..	..	..	..	..	..	..	..
40	*Guinea*	..	..	..	..	..	..	..	..
41	*Kampuchea, Dem.*	..	..	..	..	..	..	..	..
42	*Viet Nam*	..	..	..	..	..	..	..	..
Middle-income economies									
Lower-middle-income									
43	Senegal	7.0	..	..	..	..	..	..	..
44	Bolivia	..	..	..	..	..	..	..	..
45	Zimbabwe	9.9	..	..	..	..	..	..	..
46	Philippines	..	1985	5.2	8.9	13.2	20.2	52.5	37.0
47	Yemen Arab Rep.	..	..	..	..	..	..	..	..
48	Morocco	13.1	..	..	..	..	..	..	..
49	Egypt, Arab Rep.	15.8	1974	5.8	10.7	14.7	20.8	48.0	33.2
50	Papua New Guinea	..	..	..	..	..	..	..	..
51	Dominican Rep.	..	..	..	..	..	..	..	..
52	Côte d'Ivoire	10.2	1985-86	2.4	6.2	10.9	19.1	61.4	43.7
52	Honduras	..	..	..	..	..	..	..	..
54	Nicaragua	..	..	..	..	..	..	..	..
55	Thailand	17.0	1975-76	5.6	9.6	13.9	21.1	49.8	34.1
56	El Salvador	..	1976-77	5.5	10.0	14.8	22.4	47.3	29.5
57	Congo, People's Rep.	16.4	..	..	..	..	..	..	..
58	Jamaica	..	..	..	..	..	..	..	..
59	Guatemala	..	..	..	..	..	..	..	..
60	Cameroon	14.0	..	..	..	..	..	..	..
61	Paraguay	..	..	..	..	..	..	..	..
62	Ecuador	..	..	..	..	..	..	..	..
63	Botswana	16.1	..	..	..	..	..	..	..
64	Tunisia	19.8	..	..	..	..	..	..	..
65	Turkey	21.8	1973	3.5	8.0	12.5	19.5	56.5	40.7
66	Colombia	..	..	..	..	..	..	..	..
67	Chile	..	..	..	..	..	..	..	..

Note: For data comparability and coverage, see the technical notes. Figures in italics are for years other than those specified.

	ICP estimates of GDP per capita, 1985 (US = 100)	*Percentage share of household income, by percentile groups of households*						
		Year	Lowest 20 percent	Second quintile	Third quintile	Fourth quintile	Highest 20 percent	Highest 10 percent
68 Peru	..	1972	1.9	5.1	11.0	21.0	61.0	42.9
69 Mauritius	24.8	1980-81	4.0	7.5	11.0	17.0	60.5	46.7
70 Jordan	..	..	..	..	..	..	..	..
71 Costa Rica	..	1971	3.3	8.7	13.3	19.8	54.8	39.5
72 Syrian Arab Rep.	..	..	..	..	..	..	..	..
73 Malaysia	..	1973	3.5	7.7	12.4	20.3	56.1	39.8
74 Mexico	..	1977	2.9	7.0	12.0	20.4	57.7	40.6
75 South Africa	..	..	..	..	..	..	..	..
76 Poland	24.5	..	..	..	..	..	..	..
77 *Lebanon*	..	..	..	..	..	..	..	..

Upper-middle-income

	ICP estimates of GDP per capita, 1985 (US = 100)	Year	Lowest 20 percent	Second quintile	Third quintile	Fourth quintile	Highest 20 percent	Highest 10 percent
78 Brazil	..	1972	2.0	5.0	9.4	17.0	66.6	50.6
79 Uruguay	..	..	..	..	..	..	..	..
80 Hungary	31.2	1982	6.9	13.6	19.2	24.5	35.8	20.5
81 Panama	..	1973	2.0	5.2	11.0	20	61.8	44.2
82 Argentina	..	1970	4.4	9.7	14.1	21.5	50.3	35.2
83 Yugoslavia	29.2	1978	6.6	12.1	18.7	23.9	38.7	22.9
84 Algeria	..	..	..	..	..	..	..	..
85 Korea, Rep.	24.3	1976	5.7	11.2	15.4	22.4	45.3	27.5
86 Gabon	..	..	..	..	..	..	..	..
87 Portugal	33.8	1973-74	5.2	10.0	14.4	21.3	49.1	33.4
88 Venezuela	..	1970	3.0	7.3	12.9	22.8	54.0	35.7
89 Greece	35.5	..	..	..	..	..	..	..
90 Trinidad and Tobago	..	1975-76	4.2	9.1	13.9	22.8	50.0	31.8
91 Libya	..	..	..	..	..	..	..	..
92 Oman	..	..	..	..	..	..	..	..
93 *Iran, Islamic Rep.*	28.3	..	..	..	..	..	..	..
94 *Iraq*	..	..	..	..	..	..	..	..
95 *Romania*	..	..	..	..	..	..	..	..

Low- and middle-income
Sub-Saharan Africa
East Asia
South Asia
Europe, M.East, & N.Africa
Latin America & Caribbean

17 highly indebted

High-income economies
OECD members
†Other

	ICP estimates of GDP per capita, 1985 (US = 100)	Year	Lowest 20 percent	Second quintile	Third quintile	Fourth quintile	Highest 20 percent	Highest 10 percent
96 Spain	46.0	1980-81	6.9	12.5	17.3	23.2	40.0	24.5
97 Ireland	40.9	1973	7.2	13.1	16.6	23.7	39.4	25.1
98 †Saudi Arabia	..	..	..	..	..	..	..	..
99 †Israel	..	1979-80	6.0	12.0	17.7	24.4	39.9	22.6
100 New Zealand	60.9	1981-82	5.1	10.8	16.2	23.2	44.7	28.7
101 †Singapore	..	..	..	..	..	..	..	..
102 †Hong Kong	60.4	1980	5.4	10.8	15.2	21.6	47.0	31.3
103 Italy	65.6	1977	6.2	11.3	15.9	22.7	43.9	28.1
104 United Kingdom	66.1	1979	7.0	11.5	17.0	24.8	39.7	23.4
105 Australia	71.1	1975-76	5.4	10.0	15.0	22.5	47.1	30.5
106 Belgium	64.7	1978-79	7.9	13.7	18.6	23.8	36.0	21.5
107 Netherlands	68.2	1981	8.3	14.1	18.2	23.2	36.2	21.5
108 Austria	66.1	..	..	..	..	..	..	..
109 France	69.3	1975	5.5	11.5	17.1	23.7	42.2	26.4
110 Germany, Fed. Rep.	73.8	1978	7.9	12.5	17.0	23.1	39.5	24.0
111 Finland	69.5	1981	6.3	12.1	18.4	25.5	37.6	21.7
112 †Kuwait	..	..	..	..	..	..	..	..
113 Denmark	74.2	1981	5.4	12.0	18.4	25.6	38.6	22.3
114 Canada	92.5	1981	5.3	11.8	18.0	24.9	40	23.8
115 Sweden	76.9	1981	7.4	13.1	16.8	21.0	41.7	28.1
116 Japan	71.5	1979	8.7	13.2	17.5	23.1	37.5	22.4
117 †United Arab Emirates	..	..	..	..	..	..	..	..
118 Norway	84.4	1982	6.0	12.9	18.3	24.6	38.2	22.8
119 United States	100.0	1980	5.3	11.9	17.9	25.0	39.9	23.3
120 Switzerland	..	1978	6.6	13.5	18.5	23.4	38.0	23.7

Total reporting economies
Oil exporters

Nonreporting nonmembers

Note: ICP refers to the UN's International Comparison Program. Data are preliminary Phase V results; see the technical notes for details. All estimates in this table should be treated with caution.

Table 31. Urbanization

		Urban population			Percentage of urban population				Number of cities of over 500,000 persons	
		As percentage of total population		Average annual growth rate (percent)		In largest city		In cities of over 500,000 persons			
		1965	1987	1965-80	1980-87	1960	1980	1960	1980	1960	1980
	Low-income economies	**17** *w*	**30** *w*	**3.5** *w*	**8.8** *w*	**11** *w*	**13** *w*	**30** *w*	**43** *w*	**59** *t*	**165** *t*
	China and India	**18** *w*	**33** *w*	**3.0** *w*	**10.1** *w*	**6** *w*	**6** *w*	**36** *w*	**43** *w*	**49** *t*	**114** *t*
	Other low-income	**14** *w*	**24** *w*	**4.8** *w*	**5.6** *w*	**24** *w*	**29** *w*	**17** *w*	**43** *w*	**10** *t*	**51** *t*
1	Ethiopia	8	12	4.9	4.6	30	37	0	37	0	1
2	Bhutan	3	5	3.9	4.9	..	..	0	0	0	0
3	Chad	9	30	7.8	7.8	..	39	0	0	0	0
4	Zaire	26	38	4.5	4.6	14	28	14	38	1	2
5	Bangladesh	6	13	6.4	5.8	20	30	20	51	1	3
6	Malawi	5	13	7.5	8.6	..	19	0	0	0	0
7	Nepal	4	9	6.4	7.8	41	27	0	0	0	0
8	Lao PDR	8	17	5.2	6.1	69	48	0	0	0	0
9	Mozambique	5	23	9.4	10.7	75	83	0	83	0	1
10	Tanzania	5	29	10.8	11.3	34	50	0	50	0	1
11	Burkina Faso	5	8	4.1	5.3	..	41	0	0	0	0
12	Madagascar	12	23	5.4	6.4	44	36	0	36	0	1
13	Mali	13	19	4.3	3.4	32	24	0	0	0	0
14	Burundi	2	7	6.0	9.2	..	..	0	0	0	0
15	Zambia	23	53	7.2	6.6	..	35	0	35	0	1
16	Niger	7	18	7.0	7.5	..	31	0	0	0	0
17	Uganda	7	10	5.0	5.0	38	52	0	52	0	1
18	China	18	38	2.3	11.0	6	6	42	45	38	78
19	Somalia	20	36	5.5	5.5	..	34	0	0	0	0
20	Togo	11	24	6.6	6.9	..	60	0	0	0	0
21	India	19	27	3.9	4.1	7	6	26	39	11	36
22	Rwanda	3	7	7.5	8.1	..	..	0	0	0	0
23	Sierra Leone	15	26	4.3	5.0	37	47	0	0	0	0
24	Benin	11	39	9.0	7.9	..	63	0	63	0	1
25	Central African Rep.	27	45	4.3	4.7	40	36	0	0	0	0
26	Kenya	9	22	8.0	8.6	40	57	0	57	0	1
27	Sudan	13	21	5.7	4.2	30	31	0	31	0	1
28	Pakistan	24	31	4.3	4.5	20	21	33	51	2	7
29	Haiti	18	29	4.2	4.1	42	56	0	56	0	1
30	Lesotho	6	19	7.8	7.2	..	..	0	0	0	0
31	Nigeria	17	33	5.7	6.3	13	17	22	58	2	9
32	Ghana	26	32	3.2	4.1	25	35	0	48	0	2
33	Sri Lanka	20	21	2.3	1.2	28	16	0	16	0	1
34	Yemen, PDR	30	42	3.5	4.6	61	49	0	0	0	0
35	Mauritania	10	38	9.2	7.9	..	39	0	0	0	0
36	Indonesia	16	27	4.8	5.0	20	23	34	50	3	9
37	Liberia	22	42	6.2	5.9	..	..	0	0	0	0
38	*Afghanistan*	9	..	6.0	..	33	17	0	17	0	1
39	*Burma*	21	24	3.2	2.3	23	23	23	23	1	2
40	*Guinea*	12	24	5.3	5.7	37	80	0	80	0	1
41	*Kampuchea, Dem.*	11	..	−0.5	..	..	..	..	..	..	..
42	*Viet Nam*	..	21	..	3.9	..	21	..	50	..	4
	Middle-income economies	**42** *w*	**57** *w*	**3.9** *w*	**3.4** *w*	**29** *w*	**31** *w*	**34** *w*	**47** *w*	**51** *t*	**112** *t*
	Lower-middle-income	**39** *w*	**51** *w*	**3.8** *w*	**3.5** *w*	**31** *w*	**34** *w*	**32** *w*	**46** *w*	**29** *t*	**61** *t*
43	Senegal	33	37	2.9	3.8	53	65	0	65	0	1
44	Bolivia	40	50	3.1	4.4	47	44	0	44	0	1
45	Zimbabwe	14	26	6.0	6.3	40	50	0	50	0	1
46	Philippines	32	41	4.2	3.8	27	30	27	34	1	2
47	Yemen Arab Rep.	5	23	10.1	8.4	..	25	0	0	0	0
48	Morocco	32	47	4.3	4.5	16	26	16	50	1	4
49	Egypt, Arab Rep.	41	48	2.9	3.7	38	39	53	53	2	2
50	Papua New Guinea	5	15	8.1	4.8	..	25	0	0	0	0
51	Dominican Rep.	35	58	5.2	4.4	50	54	0	54	0	1
52	Côte d'Ivoire	23	44	7.5	6.9	27	34	0	34	0	1
53	Honduras	26	42	5.5	5.8	31	33	0	0	0	0
54	Nicaragua	43	58	4.7	4.7	41	47	0	47	0	1
55	Thailand	13	21	5.1	4.9	65	69	65	69	1	1
56	El Salvador	39	44	3.2	1.9	26	22	0	0	0	0
57	Congo, People's Rep.	34	41	3.4	4.6	77	56	0	0	0	0
58	Jamaica	38	51	2.9	2.6	77	66	0	66	0	1
59	Guatemala	34	33	2.7	2.9	41	36	41	36	1	1
60	Cameroon	16	46	8.1	7.4	26	21	0	21	0	1
61	Paraguay	36	46	3.8	4.6	44	44	0	44	0	1
62	Ecuador	37	55	4.7	5.0	31	29	0	51	0	2
63	Botswana	4	21	12.4	8.1	..	..	..	..	..	..
64	Tunisia	40	54	4.0	2.9	40	30	40	30	1	1
65	Turkey	34	47	4.2	3.4	18	24	32	42	3	4
66	Colombia	54	69	3.4	2.9	17	26	28	51	3	4
67	Chile	72	85	2.6	2.3	38	44	38	44	1	1

Note: For data comparability and coverage, see the technical notes. Figures in italics are for years other than those specified.

		Urban population				Percentage of urban population				Number of cities of over 500,000 persons	
		As percentage of total population		Average annual growth rate (percent)		In largest city		In cities of over 500,000 persons			
		1965	1987	1965–80	1980–87	1960	1980	1960	1980	1960	1980
68	Peru	52	69	4.3	3.2	38	39	38	44	1	2
69	Mauritius	37	42	2.5	0.8	..	..	..	..	..	..
70	Jordan	46	66	4.4	5.3	31	37	0	37	0	1
71	Costa Rica	38	45	4.0	1.8	67	64	0	64	0	1
72	Syrian Arab Rep.	40	51	4.6	4.5	35	33	35	55	1	2
73	Malaysia	26	40	4.5	5.0	19	27	0	27	0	1
74	Mexico	55	71	4.4	3.2	28	32	36	48	3	7
75	South Africa	47	57	3.3	3.3	16	13	44	53	4	7
76	Poland	50	61	1.9	1.5	17	15	41	47	5	8
77	*Lebanon*	50	..	4.5	..	64	79	64	79	1	1
	Upper-middle-income	**46** *w*	**66** *w*	**3.9** *w*	**3.2** *w*	**27** *w*	**27** *w*	**36** *w*	**49** *w*	**22** *t*	**51** *t*
78	Brazil	50	75	4.5	3.7	14	15	35	52	6	14
79	Uruguay	81	85	0.6	0.7	56	52	56	52	1	1
80	Hungary	43	59	2.0	1.4	45	37	45	37	1	1
81	Panama	44	54	3.5	3.0	61	66	0	66	0	1
82	Argentina	76	85	2.2	1.9	46	45	54	60	3	5
83	Yugoslavia	31	48	3.0	2.6	11	10	11	23	1	3
84	Algeria	38	44	3.7	3.9	27	12	27	12	1	1
85	Korea, Rep.	32	69	5.8	4.2	35	41	61	77	3	7
86	Gabon	21	43	6.7	6.7	..	..	..	..	..	..
87	Portugal	24	32	1.9	1.6	47	44	47	44	1	1
88	Venezuela	70	83	4.8	2.6	26	26	26	44	1	4
89	Greece	48	61	2.0	1.4	51	57	51	70	1	2
90	Trinidad and Tobago	30	67	5.7	3.9	..	..	0	0	0	0
91	Libya	26	67	9.8	7.0	57	64	0	64	0	1
92	Oman	4	10	7.4	8.8	..	..	..	..	..	..
93	*Iran, Islamic Rep.*	37	53	5.2	4.2	26	28	26	47	1	6
94	*Iraq*	51	72	5.3	4.9	35	55	35	70	1	3
95	*Romania*	38	49	3.0	0.3	22	17	22	17	1	1
	Low- and middle-income	**24** *w*	**37** *w*	**3.7** *w*	**6.3** *w*	**16** *w*	**18** *w*	**31** *w*	**44** *w*	**110** *t*	**277** *t*
	Sub-Saharan Africa	**14** *w*	**27** *w*	**5.5** *w*	**6.9** *w*	**28** *w*	**36** *w*	**7** *w*	**41** *w*	**3** *t*	**27** *t*
	East Asia	**19** *w*	**37** *w*	**3.1** *w*	**11.0** *w*	**11** *w*	**13** *w*	**41** *w*	**47** *w*	**46** *t*	**102** *t*
	South Asia	**18** *w*	**25** *w*	**4.0** *w*	**4.1** *w*	**11** *w*	**11** *w*	**25** *w*	**40** *w*	**15** *t*	**49** *t*
	Europe, M.East, & N.Africa	**37** *w*	**50** *w*	**3.5** *w*	**3.2** *w*	**28** *w*	**28** *w*	**31** *w*	**40** *w*	**22** *t*	**43** *t*
	Latin America & Caribbean	**53** *w*	**70** *w*	**3.9** *w*	**3.2** *w*	**27** *w*	**29** *w*	**32** *w*	**49** *w*	**20** *t*	**49** *t*
	17 highly indebted	**44** *w*	**60** *w*	**4.0** *w*	**3.8** *w*	**23** *w*	**25** *w*	**29** *w*	**49** *w*	**24** *t*	**62** *t*
	High-income economies	**71** *w*	**77** *w*	**1.4** *w*	**0.9** *w*	**19** *w*	**19** *w*	**47** *w*	**55** *w*	**107** *t*	**157** *t*
	OECD members	**72** *w*	**77** *w*	**1.3** *w*	**0.8** *w*	**18** *w*	**18** *w*	**47** *w*	**55** *w*	**104** *t*	**152** *t*
	†Other	**69** *w*	**83** *w*	**4.6** *w*	**3.6** *w*	**58** *w*	**49** *w*	**51** *w*	**54** *w*	**3** *t*	**5** *t*
96	Spain	61	77	2.2	1.4	13	17	37	44	5	6
97	Ireland	49	58	2.1	1.3	51	48	51	48	1	1
98	†Saudi Arabia	39	75	8.5	6.0	15	18	0	33	0	2
99	†Israel	81	91	3.5	2.1	46	35	46	35	1	1
100	New Zealand	79	84	1.6	1.1	25	30	0	30	0	1
101	†Singapore	100	100	1.6	1.1	100	100	100	100	1	1
102	†Hong Kong	89	93	2.1	1.7	100	100	100	100	1	1
103	Italy	62	68	1.1	0.6	13	17	46	52	7	9
104	United Kingdom	87	92	0.5	0.3	24	20	61	55	15	17
105	Australia	83	86	2.0	1.3	26	24	62	68	4	5
106	Belgium	93	97	0.4	0.2	17	14	28	24	2	2
107	Netherlands	86	88	1.2	0.5	9	9	27	24	3	3
108	Austria	51	57	0.8	0.6	51	39	51	39	1	1
109	France	67	74	1.2	0.6	25	23	34	34	4	6
110	Germany, Fed. Rep.	79	86	0.7	0.1	20	18	48	45	11	11
111	Finland	44	60	2.3	0.5	28	27	0	27	0	1
112	†Kuwait	78	95	8.3	5.2	75	30	0	0	0	0
113	Denmark	77	86	1.1	0.3	40	32	40	32	1	1
114	Canada	73	76	1.5	1.1	14	18	31	62	2	9
115	Sweden	77	84	0.9	0.2	15	15	15	35	1	3
116	Japan	67	77	2.1	0.8	18	22	35	42	5	9
117	†United Arab Emirates	41	78	17.5	4.5	..	..	..	..	..	..
118	Norway	48	74	3.0	1.0	50	32	50	32	1	1
119	United States	72	74	1.2	1.0	13	12	61	77	40	65
120	Switzerland	53	61	1.0	1.3	19	22	19	22	1	1
	Total reporting economies	**34** *w*	**44** *w*	**2.7** *w*	**4.5** *w*	**17** *w*	**18** *w*	**35** *w*	**46** *w*	**217** *t*	**434** *t*
	Oil exporters	**30** *w*	**46** *w*	**4.7** *w*	**4.7** *w*	**24** *w*	**26** *w*	**31** *w*	**49** *w*	**16** *t*	**50** *t*
	Nonreporting nonmembers	**52** *w*	**66** *w*	**2.2** *w*	**1.7** *w*	**9** *w*	**8** *w*	**20** *w*	**31** *w*	**31** *t*	**59** *t*

Table 32. Women in development

		Population: females per 100 males				Health and welfare								Education: females per 100 males			
		Total		Age 0–4		Life expectancy at birth (years)				Births attended by health staff (percent)	Maternal mortality (per 100,000 live births)	Infant mortality (per 1,000 live births)		Primary		Secondary[a]	
						Female		Male									
		1965	1985	1965	1985	1965	1987	1965	1987	1985	1980	1965	1987	1965	1986	1970	1986
	Low-income economies	**96** *w*	**96** *w*	**96** *w*	**94** *w*	**49** *w*	**62** *w*	**47** *w*	**60** *w*			**124** *w*	**76** *w*	..	**75** *w*	..	**60** *w*
	China and India	**94** *w*	**94** *w*	**94** *w*	**94** *w*	**51** *w*	**65** *w*	**48** *w*	**64** *w*			**114** *w*	**62** *w*	..	**74** *w*	..	**60** *w*
	Other low-income	**100** *w*	**100** *w*	**99** *w*	**97** *w*	**45** *w*	**55** *w*	**43** *w*	**53** *w*			**149** *w*	**103** *w*	**49** *w*	**75** *w*	**45** *w*	**59** *w*
1	Ethiopia	101	101	98	100	43	49	42	45	58	2,000[b]	166	154	38	63	32	64
2	Bhutan	98	94	95	94	40	47	41	49	3	..	173	128	..	54	..	31
3	Chad	104	103	100	100	38	47	35	44	..	700	184	132	..	39	9	*18*
4	Zaire	107	103	97	99	45	54	42	51	..	800[b]	142	98	48	75	26	*40*
5	Bangladesh	92	94	98	94	44	50	45	51	..	600	145	119	44	66	..	45
6	Malawi	108	104	105	98	40	48	38	44	59	250	201	150	..	78	39	51
7	Nepal	98	95	100	94	40	50	41	52	10	850	173	128	16	*41*	16	*30*
8	Lao PDR	98	99	98	98	..	50	..	47	..	..	..	110	59	*81*	34	*73*
9	Mozambique	104	103	100	100	39	50	36	47	28	479[b]	180	141	..	78	..	53
10	Tanzania	104	103	101	99	44	55	41	51	74	370[b]	139	106	60	100	38	62
11	Burkina Faso	103	102	100	100	40	49	37	46	..	600	195	138	48	59	33	*47*
12	Madagascar	103	102	102	99	44	55	41	52	62	300	203	120	83	..	70	*74*
13	Mali	108	107	108	100	39	49	37	46	27	..	207	169	49	59	29	43
14	Burundi	108	105	103	99	45	51	42	47	12	..	143	112	42	75	17	52
15	Zambia	102	103	98	98	46	55	42	51	..	110	123	80	78	90	49	58
16	Niger	103	102	98	100	38	46	35	43	47	420[b]	181	135	46	56	35	*39*
17	Uganda	102	102	100	99	47	50	43	47	..	300	122	103	..	82	31	54
18	China	94	94	95	93	59	71	55	68	..	44	90	32	..	82	..	69
19	Somalia	102	110	101	100	40	49	36	45	2	1,100	166	132	27	*52*	27	58
20	Togo	104	103	100	99	43	55	40	51	15	476[b]	156	94	42	62	26	31
21	India	94	93	94	94	44	58	46	58	33	500	151	99	57	*64*	*40*	48
22	Rwanda	103	102	101	100	51	50	47	47	..	210	141	122	69	97	44	29
23	Sierra Leone	104	104	101	100	34	42	31	40	25	450	210	151	55	..	40	..
24	Benin	104	104	104	100	43	52	41	49	34	1,680[b]	168	116	44	*50*	44	41
25	Central African Rep.	109	106	105	100	41	52	40	48	..	600	169	132	34	62	20	39
26	Kenya	100	100	99	98	49	60	45	56	.	510[b]	113	72	57	*93*	42	62
27	Sudan	100	99	98	97	41	51	39	49	20	607[b]	161	108	55	68	40	76
28	Pakistan	93	91	96	95	44	54	47	55	24	600	150	109	31	50	25	38
29	Haiti	105	104	98	98	46	56	44	53	20	340	180	117	..	87	..	88
30	Lesotho	111	108	102	102	50	57	47	54	28	..	143	100	157	*125*	111	*150*
31	Nigeria	103	102	100	99	43	53	40	49	..	1,500	179	105	63	79	51	..
32	Ghana	102	102	100	99	49	56	46	52	73	1,070[b]	121	90	71	77	36	*62*
33	Sri Lanka	93	98	97	96	64	73	63	68	87	90	63	33	86	93	101	109
34	Yemen, PDR	98	103	97	97	40	52	39	49	10	100	197	120	..	*36*	25	48
35	Mauritania	103	103	101	100	39	48	35	44	23	119	180	127	31	66	13	41
36	Indonesia	102	101	101	97	45	62	43	58	43	800	129	71	..	93	*64*	73
37	Liberia	99	97	100	99	45	56	42	53	..	173	139	87	..	..	30	..
38	*Afghanistan*	95	..	96	..	35	..	35	..	..	640	207	..	17	50	16	49
39	*Burma*	100	101	98	97	49	62	46	58	..	140	125	70	..	..	65	..
40	*Guinea*	101	102	101	100	36	44	34	41	..	..	197	147	..	44	*30*	33
41	*Kampuchea*	100	..	98	..	46	..	43	..	..	..	135	..	56	..	..	..
42	*Viet Nam*	..	105	..	97	..	68	..	64	100	110	..	46	..	*91*	..	90
	Middle-income economies	**100** *w*	**100** *w*	**97** *w*	**96** *w*	**59** *w*	**67** *w*	**55** *w*	**62** *w*			**99** *w*	**56** *w*	**78** *w*	**88** *w*	**88** *w*	**96** *w*
	Lower-middle-income	**100** *w*	**100** *w*	**97** *w*	**96** *w*	**57** *w*	**66** *w*	**53** *w*	**61** *w*			**108** *w*	**61** *w*	**76** *w*	**88** *w*	**83** *w*	**99** *w*
43	Senegal	102	102	101	100	42	49	40	46	..	530[c]	172	128	57	68	39	*50*
44	Bolivia	102	103	99	98	46	55	42	51	36	480	161	110	68	88	64	86
45	Zimbabwe	101	102	100	100	49	60	46	56	69	150[b]	104	72	..	95	63	68
46	Philippines	99	99	97	95	57	65	54	62	..	80	73	45	94	94	..	99
47	Yemen Arab Rep.	97	111	97	97	40	52	39	50	12	..	197	116	5	27	3	12
48	Morocco	100	100	98	96	51	63	48	59	..	327[b]	147	82	42	62	40	67
49	Egypt, Arab Rep.	98	97	95	95	50	62	47	59	24	500	173	85	64	77	45	..
50	Papua New Guinea	91	92	94	95	44	55	44	53	34	1,000	143	62	61	..	..	..
51	Dominican Rep.	97	97	97	97	57	68	54	64	57	56	111	65	..	96	..	*122*
52	Côte d'Ivoire	100	97	100	99	43	54	40	51	20	..	150	96	51	70	27	*41*
53	Honduras	99	98	97	96	51	66	48	62	50	82	130	69	..	100	..	..
54	Nicaragua	101	100	98	96	51	65	49	62	..	65	123	62	99	107	..	172
55	Thailand	100	99	96	96	58	66	53	63	33	270	90	39	89	..	69	..
56	El Salvador	99	103	97	96	56	67	52	58	35	74	122	59	91	99	77	94
57	Congo, Peoples Rep.	104	103	101	99	51	61	48	57	..	..	121	73	71	90	43	75
58	Jamaica	109	102	100	97	67	77	63	71	89	100	50	18	..	97	*111*	105
59	Guatemala	97	98	97	96	50	64	48	60	19	110	114	59	80	82	82	..
60	Cameroon	105	103	100	99	47	58	44	54	..	303	145	94	66	84	36	62
61	Paraguay	100	98	96	96	67	69	63	65	22	469	74	42	88	92	91	98
62	Ecuador	100	99	97	97	57	68	54	63	27	220	113	63	91	97	76	*100*
63	Botswana	122	110	103	100	49	62	46	56	52	300	113	67	129	108	..	111
64	Tunisia	96	98	96	95	51	66	50	65	60	1,000[c]	147	59	52	80	*44*	71
65	Turkey	96	94	97	97	55	66	52	63	78	207	165	76	66	89	37	59
66	Colombia	101	99	97	97	59	68	53	64	51	130	99	46	102	100	95	100
67	Chile	102	103	98	97	62	75	56	68	..	55	103	20	96	95	130	108

Note: For data comparability and coverage, see the technical notes. Figures in italics are for years other than those specified.

		Population: females per 100 males				Life expectancy at birth (years)				Births attended by health staff (percent)	Maternal mortality (per 100,000 live births)	Infant mortality (per 1,000 live births)		Education: females per 100 males			
		Total		Age 0–4		Female		Male						Primary		Secondary[a]	
		1965	1985	1965	1985	1965	1987	1965	1987	1985	1980	1965	1987	1965	1986	1970	1986
68	Peru	98	98	97	96	52	63	49	60	55	310	131	88	82	93	74	88
69	Mauritius	100	102	96	97	63	70	59	63	90	99	64	23	90	97	66	90
70	Jordan	94	94	96	96	51	68	49	64	75	..	114	44	72	91	53	96
71	Costa Rica	98	98	97	96	66	76	63	71	93	26	72	18	..	94	111	106
72	Syrian Arab Rep.	95	97	94	97	54	67	51	63	37	280	116	48	47	86	36	69
73	Malaysia	97	99	96	95	59	72	56	68	82	59	57	24	..	94	..	98
74	Mexico	100	100	96	96	61	72	58	65	..	92	82	47	..	95	..	88
75	South Africa	100	101	96	98	53	64	49	58	..	550[c]	125	72	..	..	..	..
76	Poland	106	105	95	95	72	76	66	68	..	12	42	18	..	94	251	265
77	Lebanon	99	..	96	..	64	..	60	..	..	..	57	..	..	..	77	..
	Upper-middle-income	101 w	100 w	96 w	96 w	61 w	69 w	58 w	64 w			88 w	50 w	82 w	..	92 w	..
78	Brazil	100	100	98	98	59	68	55	62	73	150	105	63	..	..	99	..
79	Uruguay	100	103	96	97	72	74	64	68	..	56	48	27	..	95	129	..
80	Hungary	107	107	94	96	72	74	67	67	99	28	39	17	94	95	202	187
81	Panama	96	96	96	96	64	74	62	70	83	90	58	23	93	92	102	109
82	Argentina	98	102	97	97	69	74	63	67	..	85	58	32	97	..	156	..
83	Yugoslavia	104	102	95	94	68	75	64	68	..	27	72	25	91	93	86	92
84	Algeria	99	101	97	95	51	64	49	61	..	129	155	74	62	79	40	72
85	Korea, Rep.	100	100	93	93	58	73	55	66	65	34	64	25	91	94	65	88
86	Gabon	104	104	100	100	44	54	41	51	..	124[b]	155	103	84	99	43	81
87	Portugal	110	107	95	94	69	77	63	70	..	15	65	16	95	91	98	116
88	Venezuela	97	98	96	96	64	73	60	67	82	65	67	36	98	96	102	119
89	Greece	106	103	94	93	72	79	69	74	..	12	34	13	92	94	91	102
90	Trinidad and Tobago	101	100	97	97	67	73	63	67	90	81	43	20	97	99	113	101
91	Libya	93	90	97	96	51	63	48	59	76	80	140	82	39	..	21	..
92	Oman	98	89	97	97	44	57	42	54	60	..	197	100	..	82	38	58
93	Iran, Islamic Rep.	99	97	99	94	52	64	52	62	..	..	154	65	46	87	49	67
94	Iraq	97	96	96	95	52	65	51	63	50	..	121	69	42	81	41	59
95	Romania	104	103	95	95	70	73	66	68	..	180	44	25	94	..	..	..
	Low- and middle-income	97 w	97 w	96 w	95 w	52 w	63 w	49 w	61 w			118 w	71 w	..	77 w	..	67 w
	Sub-Saharan Africa	103 w	102 w	100 w	99 w	44 w	52 w	41 w	49 w			160 w	115 w	56 w	76 w	40 w	56 w
	East Asia	96 w	96 w	95 w	94 w	54 w	69 w	50 w	66 w			93 w	40 w	..	85 w	..	72 w
	South Asia	94 w	94 w	95 w	94 w	45 w	57 w	46 w	57 w			147 w	102 w	54 w	63 w	40 w	47 w
	Europe, M.East, & N.Africa	101 w	99 w	96 w	95 w	59 w	66 w	56 w	62 w			115 w	65 w	65 w	80 w	81 w	97 w
	Latin America & Caribbean	100 w	100 w	97 w	97 w	60 w	69 w	56 w	63 w			95 w	56 w	..	..	103 w	..
	17 highly indebted	100 w	100 w	98 w	97 w	57 w	65 w	53 w	60 w			107 w	64 w	80 w	88 w	87 w	92 w
	High-income economies	104 w	104 w	96 w	95 w	74 w	79 w	67 w	73 w			25 w	10 w	..	94 w	..	99 w
	OECD members	104 w	105 w	96 w	95 w	74 w	79 w	68 w	73 w			24 w	9 w	..	95 w	..	99 w
	†Other	95 w	87 w	96 w	95 w	63 w	72 w	59 w	65 w			72 w	38 w	..	88 w	68 w	92 w
96	Spain	106	104	96	94	74	80	68	74	96	10	38	10	93	94	..	102
97	Ireland	99	99	96	94	73	76	69	71	..	7	25	7	..	95	..	101
98	†Saudi Arabia	96	84	97	97	49	65	47	62	78	52	150	71	29	80	16	70
99	†Israel	98	100	95	94	73	77	70	74	99	5	27	12	..	97	133	122
100	New Zealand	99	102	95	95	74	78	68	72	99	14	20	11	94	95	..	98
101	†Singapore	94	96	95	93	68	76	63	70	100	11	26	9	85	89	103	102
102	†Hong Kong	97	95	95	92	71	79	64	73	..	4	28	8	..	91	74	105
103	Italy	104	106	95	95	73	80	68	74	..	13	36	10	93	95	86	95
104	United Kingdom	106	105	95	95	74	78	68	72	98	7	20	9	..	..	..	..
105	Australia	98	100	95	95	74	80	68	73	99	11	19	10	95	94	..	98
106	Belgium	104	105	95	95	74	78	68	72	100	10	24	10	94	96	..	96
107	Netherlands	100	102	95	96	76	80	71	74	..	5	14	8	95	98	91	112
108	Austria	114	110	96	94	73	78	66	71	..	11	28	10	95	94	95	93
109	France	105	105	96	95	75	80	68	74	..	13	22	8	95	94	..	110
110	Germany, Fed. Rep.	111	109	95	95	73	78	67	72	..	11	24	8	94	96	92	98
111	Finland	107	107	96	96	73	79	66	72	..	5	17	7	..	95	..	113
112	†Kuwait	64	76	97	98	64	75	61	71	99	18	66	19	76	95	73	89
113	Denmark	102	103	95	96	75	78	71	73	..	4	19	8	96	96	102	105
114	Canada	99	102	95	94	75	80	69	73	99	2	24	8	94	93	95	95
115	Sweden	100	102	95	95	76	80	72	73	100	4	13	6	96	95	..	107
116	Japan	104	103	96	95	73	81	68	75	100	15	18	6	96	95	101	99
117	†United Arab Emirates	72	46	96	96	59	73	55	69	96	..	108	26	..	94	52	97
118	Norway	101	102	95	95	76	80	71	74	100	4	17	8	..	96	97	103
119	United States	103	105	96	95	74	79	67	72	100	9	25	10	..	94	..	97
120	Switzerland	105	105	96	95	75	80	69	74	..	5	18	7	..	97	..	99
	Total reporting economies	99 w	98 w	96 w	95 w	56 w	66 w	53 w	63 w			98 w	60 w	..	80 w	..	73 w
	Oil exporters	101 w	99 w	98 w	97 w	50 w	62 w	48 w	58 w			134 w	75 w	..	87 w	56 w	77 w
	Nonreporting nonmembers	116 w	111 w	96 w	96 w	72 w	73 w	64 w	65 w			33 w	27 w	..	..	..	..

a. See the technical notes.   b. Data refer to maternal mortality in hospitals and other medical institutions only.   c. Community data from rural areas only.

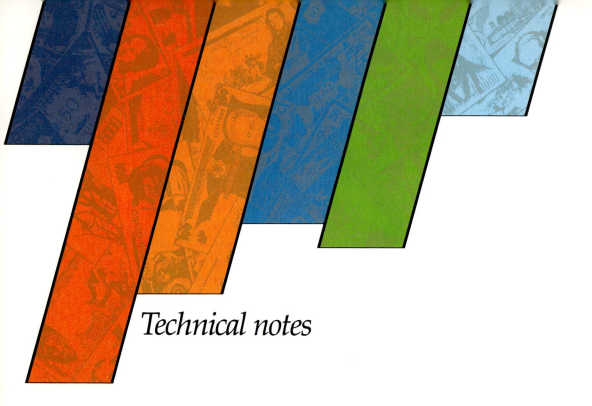

Technical notes

This twelfth edition of the World Development Indicators provides economic and social indicators for selected periods or years in a form suitable for comparing economies and groups of economies.

The main criterion of country classification is GNP per capita, and this edition introduces new country groupings. The main tables now include country data on 120 economies rather than the 129 presented in the previous edition. Since only sparse data are available for nonreporting non-member economies, these countries are not included in the main tables. Summary measures for them are shown in the main tables where available, and selected country data are presented in Box A.2 in the technical notes. Box A.1, Basic indicators for economies with populations of less than 1 million, has been expanded to cover 55 economies. See the definitions and data notes at the beginning of the main report for details of country composition of the new groups and other related information.

The tables have been rearranged thematically, so the table order has changed since the last edition. Note also that two tables have been modified: Table 17, OECD imports of manufactured goods: origin and composition, and Table 30, Income distribution and ICP estimates of GDP. Table 17 provides data on South-North and North-North manufactured trade, and Table 30 now includes International Comparison Program (ICP) estimates

of GDP as a percentage of the United States' GDP. The table on labor force has been dropped in this year's edition because of the lack of new data. This table will be reinserted when the 1990 round of census results has been tabulated and collected by the International Labour Office (ILO).

This makes a total of 32 main tables in which the statistics and measures have been chosen to give a broad perspective on development.

Considerable effort has been made to standardize the data; nevertheless, statistical methods, coverage, practices, and definitions differ widely. In addition, the statistical systems in many developing economies are still weak, and this affects the availability and reliability of the data. Moreover, intercountry and intertemporal comparisons always involve complex technical problems, which cannot be fully and unequivocally resolved. The data are drawn from sources thought to be most authoritative, but many of them are subject to considerable margins of error. Readers are urged to take these limitations into account in interpreting the indicators, particularly when making comparisons across economies.

To facilitate international comparisons, national accounts constant price data series based on years other than 1980 have been partially rebased to the 1980 base. This is accomplished by *rescaling*, which moves the year in which current and constant price versions of the same time series have the same value, without altering the trend of either. Components of GDP are individually rescaled and are summed up to provide GDP and its subaggregates. In this process, a rescaling deviation may occur between constant price gross domestic product by industrial origin and GDP by expenditure. Such rescaling deviations are absorbed under the heading *private consumption, etc.,* on the assumption that GDP by industrial origin is a more reliable estimate than GDP by expenditure.

This approach takes into account the effects of changes in intersectoral relative prices between the original and the new base period. Because private consumption is calculated as a residual, the national accounting identities are maintained. It does, however, involve incorporating in private consumption whatever statistical discrepancies arise for *expenditure* in the rebasing process. The value added in the services sector also includes a statistical discrepancy as reported by the original source.

The summary measures are calculated by simple addition when a variable is expressed in reasonably comparable units of account. Indicators that do not seem naturally additive are usually combined by a price weighting scheme. It should be emphasized, however, that use of a single base year raises problems over a period encompassing profound structural changes and significant changes in relative prices, such as have occurred from 1965 to 1987.

The World Development Indicators, unlike the *World Tables,* does not present time series. For summary measures that cover many years, it is important that the calculation is based on the same country composition over time and across topics. The World Development Indicators does so by permitting group measures to be compiled only if the country data available for a given year account for at least two-thirds of the full group, as defined by the 1980 benchmarks. So long as that criterion is met, uncurrent reporters (and those not providing ample history) are, for years with missing data, assumed to behave like the sample of the group that does provide estimates. Readers should keep in mind that the purpose is to maintain an appropriate relationship across topics, despite myriad problems with country data, and that nothing meaningful can be deduced about behavior at the country level by working back from group indicators. In addition, the weighting process may result in discrepancies between summed subgroup figures and overall totals. See the introduction to the *World Tables* for further details.

All growth rates shown are calculated from constant price series and, unless otherwise noted, have been computed using the least-squares method. The least-squares growth rate, r, is estimated by fitting a least-squares linear regression trend line to the logarithmic annual values of the variable in the relevant period. More specifically, the regression equation takes the form: $\log X_t = a + bt + e_t$, where this is equivalent to the logarithmic transformation of the compound growth rate equation, $X_t = X_o (1 + r)^t$. In these equations, X is the variable, t is time, and $a = \log X_o$ and $b = \log (1 + r)$ are the parameters to be estimated; e is the error term. If b^* is the least-squares estimate of b, then the annual average growth rate, r, is obtained as $[\text{antilog} (b^*)] - 1$, and multiplied by 100 to express it in percentage terms.

Table 1. Basic indicators

Population estimates for mid-1987 are based on data from the Population Division of the United Nations (U.N.) or from World Bank sources. These are normally projections, usually based on data from the most recent population censuses or surveys, which, in some cases, are neither recent nor very accurate. *Note* that refugees not permanently settled in the country of asylum are generally considered to be part of the population of their country of origin.

The data on *area* are from the Food and Agriculture Organization (FAO). For basic indicators on economies with populations of less than 1 million, see the table in Box A.1. For selected indicators on nonreporting nonmember economies, see the table in Box A.2.

Gross national product (GNP) measures the total domestic and foreign value added claimed by residents and is calculated without making deductions for depreciation. It comprises GDP (defined in the note for Table 2) plus net factor income from abroad, which is the income residents receive from abroad for factor services (labor and capital) less similar payments made to nonresidents who contributed to the domestic economy.

GNP per capita figures in U.S. dollars are calculated according to the *World Bank Atlas* method. The Bank recognizes that perfect cross-country comparability of GNP per capita estimates cannot be achieved. Beyond the classic, strictly intractable, index number problem, two obstacles stand in the way of adequate comparability. One concerns the GNP and population estimates themselves. There are differences in national accounting and

Box A.1. Basic indicators for countries with populations of less than 1 million

		Population (thousands) mid-1987	Area (thousands of square kilometers)	GNP per capita[a] Dollars 1987	Average annual growth rate (percent) 1965-87	Average annual rate of inflation[a] (percent) 1965-80	Average annual rate of inflation[a] (percent) 1980-87	Life expectancy at birth (years) 1987
1	Guinea-Bissau	922	36	160	−1.9	. .	39.2	39
2	Gambia, The	797	11	220	1.2	8.3	13.8	43
3	São Tomé and Principe	115	1	280	−0.1	. .	4.9	65
4	Maldives	196	b	300	1.9	. .	4.7	59
5	Comoros	426	2	370	0.6	. .	6.6	56
6	Guyana	797	215	390	−4.4	8.1	13.6	66
7	Solomon Islands	293	28	420	. .	. .	6.8	66
8	Kiribati	66	1	480	. .	5.7	5.7	53
9	Cape Verde	344	4	500	. .	. .	13.9	65
10	Western Samoa	166	3	550	. .	. .	11.2	65
11	Swaziland	712	17	700	2.4	9.1	10.2	55
12	Tongo	100	1	720	. .	. .	8.1	66
13	St. Vincent and the Grenadines	120	b	1,000	1.2	11.1	4.6	69
14	Belize	176	23	1,240	1.9	7.4	1.1	67
15	Grenada	100	b	1,340	. .	11.2	4.9	69
16	St. Lucia	142	1	1,400	2.3	9.4	3.9	70
17	Dominica	80	1	1,440	0.1	12.9	5.7	74
18	Fiji	722	18	1,570	2.2	10.4	5.8	70
19	St. Kitts and Nevis	44	b	1,700	3.3	9.3	5.2	68
20	Suriname	420	163	2,270	1.8	. .	4.1	67
21	Antigua and Barbuda	83	b	2,540	0.6	9.1	6.1	73
22	Seychelles	67	b	3,120	3.1	12.9	3.7	70
23	Malta	345	b	4,190	7.6	3.5	1.8	73
24	Cyprus	680	9	5,200	. .	. .	6.8	76
25	Barbados	254	b	5,350	2.4	11.2	6.1	75
26	Puerto Rico[c]	3,343	9	5,530	. .	. .	4.5	75
27	Bahamas	240	14	10,280	0.9	6.4	6.3	70
28	Qatar	332	11	12,430	. .	. .	. .	69
29	Brunei	235	6	15,390	. .	. .	−4.4	74
30	Iceland	246	103	16,600	3.4	26.9	41.3	77
31	Luxembourg	371	3	18,550	4.2	6.7	5.5	74
32	*American Samoa*	36	b	d	. .	. .	. .	. .
33	*Aruba*	60	b	e	. .	. .	. .	. .
34	*Bahrain*	445	1	e	. .	.	−2.8	71
35	*Bermuda*	56	b	e	. .	8.1	10.7	. .
36	*Channel Islands*	136	. .	e	. .	. .	. .	76
37	*Djibouti*	370	22	f	. .	. .	. .	47
38	*Equatorial Guinea*	389	28	g	. .	. .	. .	46
39	*Faeroe Islands*	47	1	e	. .	. .	. .	. .
40	*Fed. States of Micronesia*	90	. .	f	. .	. .	. .	. .
41	*French Guiana*	. .	90	d	. .	7.4	. .	. .
42	*French Polynesia*	179	4	e	. .	. .	. .	72
43	*Gibraltar*	30	b	d	. .	. .	. .	. .
44	*Greenland*	54	342	e	. .	. .	. .	. .
45	*Guadeloupe*	337	2	d	. .	8.7	. .	73
46	*Guam*	128	1	d	. .	. .	. .	72
47	*Isle of Man*	63	. .	e	. .	. .	. .	. .
48	*Marshall Islands*	. .	. .	f	. .	. .	. .	. .
49	*Macao*	429	b	d	. .	. .	. .	71
50	*Martinique*	329	1	d	. .	9.2	. .	74
51	*Netherlands Antilles*	190	1	e	. .	. .	. .	66
52	*New Caledonia*	158	19	e	. .	. .	. .	68
53	*Reunion*	566	3	d	. .	. .	. .	71
54	*Vanuatu*	150	15	g	. .	. .	4.6	63
55	*Virgin Islands (U.S.)*	110	b	e	1.9	6.0	4.5	73

Note: Countries in italics are those for which 1987 GNP per capita cannot be calculated; figures in italics are for years other than those specified.
a. See the technical note to Table 1.   b. Less than 500 square kilometers.   c. Population is more than 1 million.   d. GNP per capita estimated to be in the upper-middle-income range.   e. GNP per capita estimated to be in the high-income range.   f. GNP per capita estimated to be in the lower-middle-income range.   g. GNP per capita estimated to be in the low-income range.

demographic reporting systems, and in the coverage and reliability of underlying statistical information between various countries. The other relates to the conversion of GNP data, expressed in different national currencies, to a common denomination—conventionally the U.S. dollar—to compare them across countries.

Recognizing that these shortcomings affect the comparability of the GNP per capita estimates, the World Bank has introduced several improvements in the estimation procedures. Through its regular review of member countries' national accounts, the Bank systematically evaluates the GNP estimates, focusing on the coverage and concepts employed and, where appropriate, making adjustments to improve comparability. As part of the review, Bank staff estimates of GNP (and sometimes of population) may be developed for the most recent period. The Bank also systematically assesses the appropriateness of official exchange rates as conversion factors. An alternative conversion factor is used (and reported in the *World Tables*) when the official exchange rate is judged to diverge by an exceptionally large margin from the rate effectively applied to foreign transactions. This applies to only a small number of countries.

The *Atlas* conversion factor for any year is the average of the exchange rate for that year and the exchange rates for the two preceding years, after adjusting them for differences in relative inflation between the country and the United States. This three-year average smooths fluctuations in prices and exchange rates for each country. The resulting GNP in U.S. dollars is divided by the midyear population for the latest year to derive GNP per capita.

Some sixty low- and middle-income economies have suffered declining real GNP per capita in constant prices. In addition, terms of trade changes affect relative income levels as do currency fluctuations, which have been sharp during the decade. Hence the levels and ranking of GNP per capita estimates have sometimes changed in ways not necessarily related to the relative domestic growth performance of the economies considered.

The following formulas describe the procedures for computing the conversion factor for year t:

$$(e^*_{t-2,t}) = \frac{1}{3} \left[e_{t-2} \left(\frac{P_t}{P_{t-2}} \middle/ \frac{P^\$_t}{P^\$_{t-2}} \right) + e_{t-1} \left(\frac{P_t}{P_{t-1}} \middle/ \frac{P^\$_t}{P^\$_{t-1}} \right) + e_t \right]$$

and for calculating GNP per capita in U.S. dollars for year t:

$$(Y^\$_t) = (Y_t / N_t \div e^*_{t-2,t})$$

where

Y_t = current GNP (local currency) for year t
P_t = GNP deflator for year t
e_t = annual average exchange rate (local currency/U.S. dollar) for year t
N_t = midyear population for year t
$P^\$_t$ = U.S. GNP deflator for year t.

Because of problems associated with the availability of comparable data and the determination of conversion factors, information on GNP per capita is not shown for nonreporting nonmarket economies.

The use of official exchange rates to convert national currency figures to the U.S. dollar does not attempt to measure the relative domestic purchasing powers of currencies. The United Nations International Comparison Program (ICP) has developed measures of real GDP on an internationally comparable scale using purchasing power parities (PPPs) instead of exchange rates as conversion factors; see Table 30 for the most recent ICP estimates. Information on the ICP has been published in four studies and in a number of other reports. The most recent study is Phase V, parts of which have already been published by the European Communities and the OECD.

The ICP has now covered more than 70 countries in five phases, at five-year intervals. The Bank is currently reviewing the data and methodology underlying the latest estimates and will include an updated comparison of ICP and *Atlas* numbers in a future edition of the *Atlas* or another statistical publication.

The ICP figures reported in Table 30 are preliminary and may be revised. The United Nations and its regional economic commissions, as well as other international agencies, such as the European Communities, the Organisation for Economic Co-operation and Development, and the World Bank, are working to improve the methodology and to extend annual purchasing power comparisons to all countries. However, exchange rates remain the only generally available means of converting GNP from national currencies to U.S. dollars.

The *average annual rate of inflation* is measured by the growth rate of the GDP implicit deflator for each of the periods shown. The GDP deflator is first calculated by dividing, for each year of the period, the value of GDP at current values by the value of GDP at constant values, both in national currency. The least-squares method is then used to calculate the growth rate of the GDP deflator for the period. This measure of inflation, like any other, has limitations. For some purposes, how-

Box A.2. Selected indicators for nonreporting nonmember economies

	USSR		Democratic People's Republic of Korea		German Democratic Republic		Czechoslovakia		Cuba	
	1965	1987	1965	1987	1965	1987	1965	1987	1965	1987
Population (millions)	232	283	12	21	17	17	14	16	8	10
Urban population (percentage of total)	52	67	45	66	73	77	51	67	58	73
Life expectancy at birth (years)	69	69	57	69	70	73	69	71	67	75
Crude birth rate (per thousand)	18	19	39	29	17	14	16	14	34	17
Crude death rate (per thousand)	7	10	12	5	14	13	10	12	8	6
Population per physician	480	..	..	420	870	440	540	280	1,150	530
Total fertility rate	2.5	2.4	5.6	3.6	2.5	1.8	2.4	2	4.4	1.9
Infant mortality per 1,000 live births	28	25	64	33	25	9	26	13	38	13
Low birth weight (percent)	..	6	..	..	..	6	..	6	..	8
Daily calorie supply, per capita	3,205	3,399	2,329	3,232	3,204	3,814	3,383	3,448	2,374	3,124
Food production index (1979–81 = 100)	85	112	72	110	73	114	73	119	82	108
Education, primary (female)	103	..	..	..	111	103	97	98	119	101
Education, primary (total)	103	106	..	..	109	103	99	97	121	105
Area (thousands of square kilometers)	..	22,402	..	121	..	108	..	128	..	111
Population projected to year 2000 (millions)	..	307	..	28	..	17	..	16	..	12

Note: For data comparability and coverage, see the technical notes. Figures in italics are for years other than those specified.

ever, it is used as an indicator of inflation because it is the most broadly based deflator, showing annual price movements for all goods and services produced in an economy.

Life expectancy at birth indicates the number of years a newborn infant would live if patterns of mortality prevailing for all people at the time of its birth were to stay the same throughout its life. Data are from the U.N. Population Division, supplemented by World Bank estimates.

The *summary measures* for GNP per capita and life expectancy in this table are weighted by population. Those for average annual rates of inflation are weighted by the 1980 share of country GDP valued in current U.S. dollars.

Tables 2 and 3. Growth and structure of production

Most of the definitions used are those of the U.N. *System of National Accounts* (SNA), series F, no. 2, revision 3. Estimates are obtained from national sources, sometimes reaching the World Bank through other international agencies but more often collected by World Bank staff during missions.

World Bank staff review the quality of national accounts data and in some instances, through mission work or technical assistance, help adjust na-

tional series. Because of the sometimes limited capabilities of statistical offices, strict international comparability cannot be achieved, especially in economic activities that are difficult to measure, such as the informal sector or subsistence agriculture.

GDP measures the total for final use of output of goods and services produced by an economy, by residents and nonresidents, regardless of the allocation to domestic and foreign claims. It is calculated without making deductions for depreciation. While SNA envisages estimates of GDP by industrial origin to be at producer prices, many countries still report such details at factor cost, which differs from producer prices because of the treatment of certain commodity taxes at the sector level. Overall, GDP at producer prices is equal to GDP at purchaser values, less import duties. For individual sectors, say agriculture, values at producer prices differ from purchaser values because of indirect taxes minus subsidies and, at least in theory, because purchaser prices include retail and wholesale service and transport costs. International comparability of the estimates is affected by the use of differing country practices in valuation systems for reporting value added by production sectors. As a partial solution, GDP estimates are shown at purchaser values if the components are

	Angola		Bulgaria		Albania		Mongolia		Namibia		
	1965	1987	1965	1987	1965	1987	1965	1987	1965	1987	
	5	9	8	9	2	3	1	2	1	1	Population (millions)
	13	26	46	68	32	35	42	51	28	54	Urban population (percentage of total)
	35	45	69	72	66	72	57	64	45	56	Life expectancy at birth (years)
	49	47	15	13	35	27	42	39	46	45	Crude birth rate (per thousand)
	29	20	8	12	9	6	12	8	22	13	Crude death rate (per thousand)
	13,150	17,780	600	280	2,100	..	710	100	..	..	Population per physician
	6.4	6.4	2.1	1.9	5.3	3.3	5.8	5.4	6.1	6.1	Total fertility rate
	193	137	31	15	87	39	90	45	146	106	Infant mortality per 1,000 live births
	..	17	..	..	..	7	..	10	..	..	Low birth weight (percent)
	1,897	2,716	3,452	3,642	2,389	2,713	2,597	2,847	1,904	1,824	Daily calorie supply, per capita
	126	87	78	104	85	95	138	101	114	88	Food production index (1979–81 = 100)
	26	..	102	102	87	93	97	103	..	..	Education, primary (female)
	39	93	103	103	92	96	98	102	..	..	Education, primary (total)
	..	1,247	..	111	..	29	..	1,565	..	1,824	Area (thousands of square kilometers)
											Population projected to year 2000
	..	13	..	9	..	4	..	3	..	2	(millions)

on this basis, and such instances are footnoted. However, for a few countries in Tables 2 and 3, GDP at purchaser values has been replaced by GDP at factor cost. *Note* that in editions before 1986, *GDP at producer prices* and *GDP at purchaser values* were referred to as *GDP at factor cost* and *GDP at market prices*, respectively.

The figures for GDP are dollar values converted from domestic currencies using single-year official exchange rates. For a few countries where the official exchange rate does not reflect the rate effectively applied to actual foreign exchange transactions, an alternative conversion factor is used (and reported in the *World Tables*). *Note* that this table does not use the three-year averaging technique applied for GNP per capita in Table 1.

Agriculture covers forestry, hunting, and fishing, as well as agriculture. In developing countries with high levels of subsistence farming, much of agricultural production is either not exchanged or not exchanged for money. This increases the difficulty of measuring the contribution of agriculture to GDP and reduces the reliability and comparability of such numbers. *Industry* comprises value added in mining; *manufacturing* (also reported as a subgroup); construction; and electricity, water, and gas. Value added in all other branches of economic activity, including imputed bank service charges,

import duties, and any statistical discrepancies noted by national compilers, are categorized as *services, etc.*

Partially rebased 1980 series in domestic currencies, as explained above, are used to compute the growth rates in Table 2. The sectoral shares of GDP in Table 3 are based on current price series.

In calculating the *summary measures* for each indicator in Table 2, partially rebased constant 1980 U.S. dollar values for each economy are calculated for each of the years of the periods covered; the values are often aggregated across countries for each year; and the least-squares procedure is used to compute the growth rates. The average sectoral percentage shares in Table 3 are computed from group aggregates of sectoral GDP in current U.S. dollars.

Table 4. Agriculture and food

The basic data for *value added in agriculture* are from the World Bank's national accounts series at current prices in national currencies. The value added in current prices in national currencies is converted to U.S. dollars by applying the single-year conversion procedure, as described in the technical note for Tables 2 and 3.

The figures for the remainder of this table are

from the Food and Agriculture Organization (FAO).

Cereal imports are measured in grain equivalents and defined as comprising all cereals in the *Standard International Trade Classification* (SITC), revision 2, groups 041–046. *Food aid in cereals* covers wheat and flour, bulgur, rice, coarse grains, and the cereal component of blended foods. The figures are not directly comparable since cereal imports are based on calendar-year data, whereas food aid in cereals is based on data for crop years reported by donor countries and international organizations, including the International Wheat Council and the World Food Programme. Furthermore, food aid information by donors may not correspond to actual receipts by beneficiaries during a given period because of delays in transportation and recording, or because it is sometimes not reported to the FAO or other relevant international organizations. The earliest available food aid data are for 1974. The time reference for food aid is the crop year, July–June.

Fertilizer consumption measures the plant nutrients used in relation to arable land. Fertilizer products cover nitrogenous phosphate, which includes ground rock phosphate and potash fertilizers. Arable land is defined as land under temporary crops (double-cropped areas are counted once), temporary meadows for mowing or pastures, land under market or kitchen gardens, land temporarily fallow or lying idle, as well as land under permanent crops. The time reference for fertilizer consumption is the crop year, July–June.

The *index of food production per capita* shows the average annual quantity of food produced per capita in 1985–87 in relation to that produced in 1979–81. The estimates are derived by dividing the quantity of food production by the total population. For this index *food* is defined as comprising nuts, pulses, fruits, cereals, vegetables, sugar cane, sugar beet, starchy roots, edible oils, livestock, and livestock products. Quantities of food production are measured net of animal feed, seeds for use in agriculture, and food lost in processing and distribution.

The *summary measures* for fertilizer consumption are weighted by total arable land area; the *summary measures* for food production per capita are weighted by population.

Table 5. Commercial energy

The data on energy are primarily from U.N. sources. They refer to commercial forms of pri-

mary energy—petroleum and natural gas liquids, natural gas, solid fuels (coal, lignite, and so on), and primary electricity (nuclear, geothermal, and hydroelectric power)—all converted into oil equivalents. Figures on liquid fuel consumption include petroleum derivatives that have been consumed in nonenergy uses. For converting primary electricity into oil equivalents, a notional thermal efficiency of 34 percent has been assumed. The use of firewood, dried animal excrement, and other traditional fuels, although substantial in some developing countries, is not taken into account because reliable and comprehensive data are not available.

Energy imports refer to the dollar value of energy imports—section 3 in the SITC, revision 1—and are expressed as a percentage of earnings from merchandise exports.

Because data on energy imports do not permit a distinction between petroleum imports for fuel and for use in the petrochemicals industry, these percentages may overestimate the dependence on imported energy.

The *summary measures* of *energy production* and *consumption* are computed by aggregating the respective volumes for each of the years covered by the periods and then applying the least-squares growth rate procedure. For *energy consumption per capita*, population weights are used to compute *summary measures* for the specified years.

The *summary measures* of *energy imports as a percentage of merchandise exports* are computed from group aggregates for energy imports and merchandise exports in current dollars.

Table 6. Structure of manufacturing

The basic data for *value added in manufacturing* are from the World Bank's national accounts series at *current* prices in national currencies. The figures shown are dollar values converted from national currencies by using single-year official exchange rates. For a few countries where the official exchange rate does not reflect the rate effectively applied to actual foreign exchange transactions, an alternative conversion factor is used.

The data for *distribution of value added* among manufacturing industries are provided by the United Nations Industrial Development Organization (UNIDO), and distribution calculations are from national currencies in current prices.

The classification of manufacturing industries is in accord with the U.N. *International Standard Industrial Classification of All Economic Activities* (ISIC). *Food and agriculture* comprise *ISIC division 31; tex-*

tiles and clothing, division 32; *machinery and transport equipment,* major groups 382–84; and *chemicals,* major groups 351 and 352. *Other* comprises wood and related products (division 33), paper and related products (division 34), petroleum and related products (major groups 353–56), basic metals and mineral products (divisions 36 and 37), fabricated metal products and professional goods (major groups 381 and 385), and other industries (major group 390). When data for textiles, machinery, or chemicals are shown as not available, they are also included in *other.*

Summary measures given for value added in manufacturing are totals calculated by the aggregation method noted in the front of the technical notes.

Table 7. Manufacturing earnings and output

Four indicators are shown—two relate to real earnings per employee, one to labor's share in total value added generated, and one to labor productivity in the manufacturing sector. The indicators are based on data from UNIDO, although the deflators are from other sources, as explained below.

Earnings per employee are in constant prices and are derived by deflating nominal earnings per employee, by the country's consumer price index (CPI). The CPI is from the IMF's *International Financial Statistics* (IFS). *Total earnings as percentage of value added* are derived by dividing total earnings of employees by value added in current prices, to show labor's share in income generated in the manufacturing sector. *Gross output per employee* is in constant prices and is presented as an index of overall labor productivity in manufacturing with 1980 as the base year. To derive this indicator, UNIDO data on *gross output per employee* in current prices are adjusted using the implicit deflators for value added in manufacturing or in industry taken from the World Bank's national accounts data files.

To improve cross-country comparability, UNIDO has, where possible, standardized the coverage of establishments to those with 5 or more employees.

The concepts and definitions are in accordance with the *International Recommendations for Industrial Statistics* published by the United Nations. *Earnings* (wages and salaries) cover all remuneration to employees paid by the employer during the year. The payments include (a) all regular and overtime cash payments and bonuses and cost of living allowances; (b) wages and salaries paid during vacation and sick leave; (c) taxes and social insurance contributions and the like, payable by the employ-

ees and deducted by the employer; and (d) payments in kind.

The value of *gross output* is estimated on the basis of either production or shipments. On the production basis it consists of (a) the value of all products of the establishment, (b) the value of industrial services rendered to others, (c) the value of goods shipped in the same condition as received, (d) the value of electricity sold, and (e) the net change in the value of work-in-progress between the beginning and the end of the reference period. In the case of estimates compiled on a shipment basis, the net change between the beginning and the end of the reference period in the value of stocks of finished goods is also included. *Value added* is defined as the current value of gross output less the current cost of (a) materials, fuels, and other supplies consumed, (b) contract and commission work done by others, (c) repair and maintenance work done by others, and (d) goods shipped in the same condition as received.

The term *employees* in this table combines two categories defined by the U.N., *regular employees* and *persons engaged.* Together these groups comprise regular employees, working proprietors, active business partners, and unpaid family workers; they exclude homeworkers. The data refer to the average number of employees working during the year.

Tables 8 and 9. Growth of consumption and investment; structure of demand

GDP is defined in the note for Table 2, but for these two tables it is in purchaser values.

General government consumption includes all current expenditure for purchases of goods and services by all levels of government. Capital expenditure on national defense and security is regarded as consumption expenditure.

Private consumption, etc., is the market value of all goods and services purchased or received as income in kind by households and nonprofit institutions. It excludes purchases of dwellings, but includes imputed rent for owner-occupied dwellings (see Table 10 for details). In practice, it includes any statistical discrepancy in the use of resources. At constant prices, this means it also includes the rescaling deviation from partial rebasing.

Gross domestic investment consists of outlays on additions to the fixed assets of the economy, plus net changes in the level of inventories.

Gross domestic savings are calculated by deducting total consumption from gross domestic product.

Exports of goods and nonfactor services represent the value of all goods and nonfactor services provided to the rest of the world; they include merchandise, freight, insurance, travel, and other nonfactor services. The value of factor services, such as investment income, interest, and labor income, is excluded.

The *resource balance* is the difference between exports of goods and nonfactor services and imports of goods and nonfactor services.

Partially rebased 1980 series in constant domestic currency units (see above) are used to compute the indicators in Table 8. Table 9 uses national accounts series in current domestic currency units. The growth rates in Table 8 are calculated from the constant 1980 price series; the shares of GDP in Table 9, from current price series.

The *summary measures* are calculated by the method explained in the note for Tables 2 and 3.

Table 10. Structure of consumption

Percentage shares of selected items in total household consumption expenditure are computed from SNA-defined details of GDP (expenditure at national market prices), often as collected for International Comparison Program (ICP) Phases IV (1980) and V (1985). For countries not covered by the ICP, less detailed national accounts estimates are included, where available. The intention is to present a general idea of the broad structure of consumption. The data cover 83 countries (five more than last year's edition, including Bank staff estimates for China) and refer to the most recent estimates, generally for a year between 1980 and 1985, inclusive. Where they refer to earlier years, the figures are shown in italics. *Consumption* here refers to private (nongovernment) consumption as defined in the SNA and in the notes to Tables 2, 4, and 9, except that education and medical care comprise government as well as private outlays. This ICP concept of "enhanced consumption" reflects who uses rather than who pays for consumption goods, and improves international comparability because it is less sensitive to differing national practices regarding the financing of health and education services.

A major subitem of *food* is presented: *cereals and tubers.* The subitem comprises the main staple products: rice, flour, bread, all other cereals and cereal preparations, potatoes, yams, and other tubers. For high-income OECD economies, however, this subitem does not include tubers. *Gross rents, fuel and power* consist of actual and imputed rents, and repair and maintenance charges, as well as the

subitem *fuel and power* (for heating, lighting, cooking, air conditioning, and so forth). *Note* that this item excludes energy used for transport (rarely reported to be more than 1 percent of total consumption in low- and middle-income economies). As mentioned above, *medical care* and *education* include government as well as private consumption expenditure. *Transport and communication* also includes the purchase of *motor cars*, which are reported as a subitem. *Other consumption*, the residual group, includes beverages and tobacco, nondurable household goods and household services, recreational services, and services supplied by hotels and restaurants. It also includes the separately reported subitem, *other consumer durables*, comprising household appliances, furniture, floor coverings, recreational equipment, and watches and jewelry.

Estimating the structure of consumption is one of the weakest aspects of national accounting in low- and middle-income economies. The structure is estimated through household expenditure surveys and similar survey techniques. It therefore shares any bias inherent in the sample frame or population. For example, some countries limit surveys to urban areas or, even more narrowly, to capital cities. This tends to produce exceptionally low shares for *food* and high shares for *transport and communication, gross rents, fuel and power,* and *other consumption*, which includes meals purchased outside the home. Controlled food prices and incomplete national accounting for subsistence activities also contribute to low food shares.

Table 11. Central government expenditure

The data on central government finance in Tables 11 and 12 are from the IMF *Government Finance Statistics Yearbook, 1988* and IMF data files. The accounts of each country are reported using the system of common definitions and classifications found in the IMF *Manual on Government Finance Statistics* (1986).

For complete and authoritative explanations of concepts, definitions, and data sources, see these IMF sources. The commentary that follows is intended mainly to place these data in the context of the broad range of indicators reported in this edition.

The shares of total expenditure and revenue by category are calculated from series in national currencies. Because of differences in coverage of available data, the individual components of central government expenditure and current revenue shown in these tables may not be strictly comparable across all economies.

Moreover, inadequate statistical coverage of state, provincial, and local governments dictates the use of central government data; this may seriously understate or distort the statistical portrayal of the allocation of resources for various purposes, especially in countries where lower levels of government have considerable autonomy and are responsible for many economic and social services. In addition, *central government* can mean either of two accounting concepts: *consolidated* or *budgetary*. For most countries, central government finance data have been consolidated into one overall account, but for others only the budgetary central government accounts are available. Since all central government units are not included in the budgetary accounts, the overall picture of central government activities is incomplete. Countries reporting budgetary data are footnoted.

It must be emphasized that for these and other reasons the data presented, especially those for education and health, are not comparable across countries. In many economies private health and education services are substantial; in others public services represent the major component of total expenditure but may be financed by lower levels of government. Caution should therefore be exercised in using the data for cross-country comparisons.

Central government expenditure comprises the expenditure by all government offices, departments, establishments, and other bodies that are agencies or instruments of the central authority of a country. It includes both current and capital (development) expenditure.

Defense comprises all expenditure, whether by defense or other departments, on the maintenance of military forces, including the purchase of military supplies and equipment, construction, recruiting, and training. Also in this category are closely related items such as military aid programs.

Education comprises expenditure on the provision, management, inspection, and support of pre-primary, primary, and secondary schools; of universities and colleges; and of vocational, technical, and other training institutions. Also included is expenditure on the general administration and regulation of the education system; on research into its objectives, organization, administration, and methods; and on such subsidiary services as transport, school meals, and school medical and dental services. *Note* that Table 10 provides an alternative measure of expenditure on education, private as well as public, relative to household consumption.

Health covers public expenditure on hospitals, maternity and dental centers, and clinics with a major medical component; on national health and medical insurance schemes; and on family planning and preventive care. *Note* that Table 10 provides a more comprehensive measure of expenditure on medical care, private as well as public, relative to household consumption.

Housing and community amenities and social security and welfare cover expenditure on housing, such as income-related schemes; on provision and support of housing and slum clearance activities; on community development; and on sanitary services. They also cover compensation for loss of income to the sick and temporarily disabled; payments to the elderly, the permanently disabled, and the unemployed; family, maternity, and child allowances; and the cost of welfare services, such as care of the aged, the disabled, and children. Many expenditures relevant to environmental defense, such as pollution abatement, water supply, sanitary affairs and refuse collection, are included indistinguishably in this category.

Economic services comprise expenditure associated with the regulation, support, and more efficient operation of business; economic development; redress of regional imbalances; and creation of employment opportunities. Research, trade promotion, geological surveys, and inspection and regulation of particular industry groups are among the activities included.

Other covers items not included elsewhere; for a few economies it also includes amounts that could not be allocated to other components (or adjustments from accrual to cash accounts).

Total expenditure (as a percentage of GNP) is more narrowly defined than the measure of general government consumption (percentage of GDP) given in Table 9, because it excludes consumption expenditure by state and local governments. At the same time, central government expenditure is more broadly defined because it includes government's gross domestic investment and transfer payments.

Overall surplus/deficit is defined as current and capital revenue and grants received, less total expenditure and lending minus repayments.

Summary measures for the components of central government expenditure are computed from group totals for expenditure components and central government expenditure in current dollars. Those for total expenditure as a percentage of GNP and for overall surpus/deficit as a percentage of GNP are computed from group totals for the above total expenditures and overall surplus/deficit in current dollars, and GNP in current dollars, respectively. Since 1987 data are not available for more than half the countries, by weighting, 1986 data are used for the summary measures in Tables 11 and 12.

Table 12. Central government current revenue

Information on data sources and comparability is given in the note to Table 11. Current revenue by source is expressed as a percentage of total current revenue, which is the sum of tax revenue and nontax revenue and is calculated from national currencies.

Tax revenue comprises compulsory, unrequited, nonrepayable receipts for public purposes. It includes interest collected on tax arrears and penalties collected on nonpayment or late payment of taxes and is shown net of refunds and other corrective transactions. *Taxes on income, profit, and capital gain* are taxes levied on the actual or presumptive net income of individuals, on the profits of enterprises, and on capital gains, whether realized on land sales, securities, or other assets. *Social security contributions* include employers' and employees' social security contributions, as well as those of self-employed and unemployed persons. *Domestic taxes on goods and services* include general sales, turnover or value added taxes, selective excises on goods, selective taxes on services, taxes on the use of goods or property, and profits of fiscal monopolies. *Taxes on international trade and transactions* include import duties, export duties, profits of export or import monopolies, exchange profits, and exchange taxes. *Other taxes* include employers' payroll or labor taxes, taxes on property, and taxes not allocable to other categories. They may include negative values that are adjustments, for instance, for taxes collected on behalf of state and local governments and not allocable to individual tax categories.

Nontax revenue comprises receipts that are not a compulsory nonrepayable payment for public purposes, such as administrative fees or entrepreneurial income from government ownership of property. Proceeds of grants and borrowing, funds arising from the repayment of previous lending by governments, incurrence of liabilities, and proceeds from the sale of capital assets are not included.

Summary measures for the components of current revenue are computed from group totals for revenue components and total current revenue in current dollars; those for current revenue as a percentage of GNP are computed from group totals

for total current revenue and GNP in current dollars. Since 1987 data are not available for more than half the countries, by weighting, 1986 data are used for the summary measures for Tables 11 and 12.

Table 13. Money and interest rates

The data on monetary holdings are based on the IMF's *International Financial Statistics* (*IFS*). *Monetary holdings, broadly defined*, comprise the monetary and quasi-monetary liabilities of a country's financial institutions to residents other than the central government. For most countries, monetary holdings are the sum of *money* (*IFS* line 34) and *quasi-money* (*IFS* line 35). *Money* comprises the economy's means of payment: currency outside banks and demand deposits. *Quasi-money* comprises time and savings deposits and similar bank accounts that the issuer will readily exchange for money. Where nonmonetary financial institutions are important issuers of quasi-monetary liabilities, these are also included in the measure of monetary holdings.

The growth rates for monetary holdings are calculated from year-end figures, while the average of the year-end figures for the specified year and the previous year is used for the ratio of monetary holdings to GDP.

The *nominal interest rates of banks*, also from *IFS*, represent the rates paid by commercial or similar banks to holders of their quasi-monetary liabilities (deposit rates) and charged by the banks on loans to prime customers (lending rate). They are, however, of limited international comparability partly because coverage and definitions vary, and partly because countries differ in the scope available to banks for adjusting interest rates to reflect market conditions.

Since interest rates (and growth rates for monetary holdings) are expressed in nominal terms, much of the variation between countries stems from differences in inflation. For easy reference, the Table 1 indicator of recent inflation is repeated in this table.

Table 14. Growth of merchandise trade

The statistics on merchandise trade, Tables 14 through 17, are primarily from the U.N. trade data system, which accords with the U.N. *Yearbook of International Trade Statistics*—that is, the data are based on countries' customs returns. However, more recent statistics are often from secondary sources, notably the IMF, as indicated in footnoted cases. World Bank estimates are also reported. Secondary sources and World Bank estimates are based on aggregated reports available before the detailed reports submitted to the U.N. appear. In some cases, these permit coverage adjustments for significant components of a country's foreign trade not subject to regular customs reports. Such cases are identified in the country notes to the *World Tables*. Values in these tables are in current U.S. dollars.

Merchandise exports and imports, with some exceptions, cover international movements of goods across customs borders. Exports are valued f.o.b. (free on board) and imports, c.i.f. (cost, insurance, and freight), unless otherwise specified in the foregoing sources. These values are in current dollars; *note* that they do not include trade in services.

The *growth rates of merchandise exports and imports* are in constant terms and are calculated from quantum indexes of exports and imports. Quantum indexes are obtained from the export or import value index as deflated by the corresponding price index. To calculate these quantum indexes, the World Bank uses its own price indexes, which are based on international prices for primary commodities and unit value indexes for manufactures. These price indexes are country-specific and disaggregated by broad commodity groups. This ensures consistency between data for a group of countries and those for individual countries. Such data consistency will increase as the World Bank continues to improve its trade price indexes for an increasing number of countries. These growth rates can differ from those derived from national practices because national price indexes may use different base years and weighting procedures from those used by the World Bank.

The *terms of trade*, or the net barter terms of trade, measure the relative movement of export prices against that of import prices. Calculated as the ratio of a country's index of average export prices to its average import price index, this indicator shows changes over a base year in the level of export prices as a percentage of import prices. The terms of trade index numbers are shown for 1985 and 1987, where 1980 = 100. The price indexes are from the source cited above for the growth rates of exports and imports.

The *summary measures* for the growth rates are calculated by aggregating the 1980 constant U.S. dollar price series for each year and then applying the least-squares growth rate procedure for the periods shown. *Note* again that these values do not include trade in services.

Tables 15 and 16. Structure of merchandise trade

The shares in these tables are derived from trade values in current dollars reported in the U.N. trade data system and the U.N. *Yearbook of International Trade Statistics*, supplemented by other secondary sources and World Bank estimates as explained in the note to Table 14.

Merchandise exports and imports are defined in the note to Table 14.

The categorization of exports and imports follows the *SITC*, series M, no. 34, revision 1. Estimates from secondary sources also usually follow this definition.

In Table 16, *fuels, minerals, and metals* are the commodities in *SITC* section 3 (mineral fuels and lubricants and related materials) divisions 27 and 28 (minerals and crude fertilizers, and metalliferous ores) and division 68 (nonferrous metals). *Other primary commodities* comprise *SITC* sections 0, 1, 2, and 4 (food and live animals, beverages and tobacco, inedible crude materials, oils, fats, and waxes) less divisions 27 and 28. *Machinery and transport equipment* are the commodities in *SITC* section 7. *Other manufactures* represent *SITC* sections 5 through 9 less section 7 and division 68. *Textiles and clothing*, representing *SITC* divisions 65 and 84 (textiles, yarns, fabrics, and clothing), are shown as a subgroup of *other manufactures*.

In Table 15, *food* commodities are those in *SITC* sections 0, 1, and 4 and division 22 (food and live animals, beverages, oils and fats, and oilseeds and nuts), less division 12 (tobacco). *Fuels* are the commodities in *SITC* section 3 (mineral fuels, lubricants and related materials). *Other primary commodities* comprise *SITC* section 2 (crude materials, excluding fuels), less division 22 (oilseeds and nuts) plus divisions 12 (tobacco) and 68 (nonferrous metals). *Machinery and transport equipment* are the commodities in *SITC* section 7. *Other manufactures*, calculated residually from the total value of manufactured imports, represent *SITC* sections 5 through 9, less section 7 and division 68.

The *summary measures* in Table 15 are weighted by total merchandise imports of individual countries in current dollars; those in Table 16, by total merchandise exports of individual countries in current dollars. (See the note to Table 14.)

Table 17. OECD imports of manufactured goods: origin and composition

The data is from the U.N., reported by high-income OECD countries, which are the OECD members excluding Greece, Portugal, and Turkey.

The table reports the value of *manufactured imports* of high-income OECD countries by the economy of origin, and the composition of such imports by major manufactured product groups.

It replaces an earlier one on the origin and destination of manufactured exports, which was based on exports reported by individual economies. As there was a lag of several years in reporting by many developing economies, estimates based on various sources were used to fill the gaps. Until these estimates can be improved, this present table, based on up-to-date and consistent but less comprehensive data, is included instead. Manufactured imports of the predominant markets from individual economies are the best available proxy of the magnitude and composition of the manufactured exports of these economies to all destinations taken together.

Manufactured goods are the commodities in *SITC*, revision 1, sections 5 through 9 (chemical and related products, basic manufactures, manufactured articles, machinery and transport equipment, and other manufactured articles and goods not elsewhere classified) excluding division 68 (nonferrous metals). This definition is somewhat broader than the one used to define *exporters of manufactures.*

The major manufactured product groups reported are defined as the following: textiles and clothing (*SITC* 65 and 84), chemicals (*SITC* 5), electrical machinery and electronics (*SITC* 72), transport equipment (*SITC* 73), and others, defined as the residual.

Table 18. Balance of payments and reserves

The statistics for this table are mostly as reported by the IMF but do include recent estimates by World Bank staff and, in rare instances, the Bank's own coverage or classification adjustments to enhance international comparability. Values in this table are in current U.S. dollars.

The *current account balance after official transfers* is the difference between exports of goods and services (factor and nonfactor) as well as inflows of unrequited transfers (private and official), and imports of goods and services as well as unrequited transfers to the rest of the world.

The *current account balance before official transfers* is the current account balance that treats net official unrequited transfers as akin to official capital movements. The difference between the two balance of payment measures is essentially foreign aid in the form of grants, technical assistance, and food aid, which, for most developing countries, tends to make current account deficits smaller than the financing requirement.

Net workers' remittances cover payments and receipts of income by migrants who are employed or expect to be employed for more than a year in their new economy, where they are considered residents. These remittances are classified as private unrequited transfers, and are included in the balance of payments current account balance, while those derived from shorter-term stays are included in services, as labor income. The distinction accords with internationally agreed guidelines, but many developing countries classify workers' remittances as a factor income receipt (and hence a component of GNP). The World Bank adheres to international guidelines in defining GNP and, therefore, may differ from national practices.

Net direct private investment is the net amount invested or reinvested by nonresidents in enterprises in which they or other nonresidents exercise significant managerial control, including equity capital, reinvested earnings, and other capital. The net figures are obtained by subtracting the value of direct investment abroad by residents of the reporting country.

Gross international reserves comprise holdings of monetary gold, special drawing rights (SDRs), the reserve position of members in the IMF, and holdings of foreign exchange under the control of monetary authorities. The data on holdings of international reserves are from IMF data files. The gold component of these reserves is valued throughout at year-end (December 31) London prices: that is, $37.37 an ounce in 1970 and $484.10 an ounce in 1987. The reserve levels for 1970 and 1987 refer to the end of the year indicated and are in current dollars at prevailing exchange rates. Because of differences in the definition of international reserves, in the valuation of gold, and in reserve management practices, the levels of reserve holdings published in national sources do not have strictly comparable significance. Reserve holdings at the end of 1987 are also expressed in terms of the number of months of imports of goods and services they could pay for, with total imports level for 1987.

The *summary measures* are computed from group aggregates for gross international reserves and total imports of goods and services, in current dollars.

Table 19. Official development assistance from OECD and OPEC members

Official development assistance (ODA) consists of net disbursements of loans and grants made on concessional financial terms by official agencies of the members of the Development Assistance Committee (DAC) of the Organisation for Economic Co-operation and Development (OECD) and members of the Organization of Petroleum Exporting Countries (OPEC), to promote economic development and welfare. While this definition aims at excluding purely military assistance, the borderline is sometimes blurred; the definition used by the country of origin usually prevails. ODA also includes the value of technical cooperation and assistance. All data shown are supplied by the OECD, and all U.S. dollar values are converted at official exchange rates.

Amounts shown are net disbursements to developing countries and multilateral institutions. The disbursements to multilateral institutions are now reported for all DAC members on the basis of the date of issue of notes; some DAC members previously reported on the basis of the date of encashment. *Net bilateral flows to low-income economies* exclude unallocated bilateral flows and all disbursements to multilateral institutions.

The nominal values shown in the summary for ODA from high-income OECD countries were converted at 1980 prices using the dollar GDP deflator. This deflator is based on price increases in OECD countries (excluding Greece, Portugal, and Turkey) measured in dollars. It takes into account the parity changes between the dollar and national currencies. For example, when the dollar depreciates, price changes measured in national currencies have to be adjusted upward by the amount of the depreciation to obtain price changes in dollars.

The table, in addition to showing totals for OPEC, shows totals for the Organization of Arab Petroleum Exporting Countries (OAPEC). The donor members of OAPEC are Algeria, Iraq, Kuwait, Libya, Qatar, Saudi Arabia, and United Arab Emirates. ODA data for OPEC and OAPEC are also obtained from the OECD.

Table 20. Official development assistance: receipts

Net disbursements of ODA from all sources consist of loans and grants made on concessional financial terms by all bilateral official agencies and multilateral sources to promote economic development and welfare. They include the value of technical cooperation and assistance. The disbursements shown in this table are not strictly comparable with those shown in Table 19 since the receipts are from all sources; disbursements in Table 19 refer only to those made by high-income members of the OECD and members of OPEC. Net disbursements equal gross disbursements less payments to the originators of aid for amortization of past aid receipts. Net

disbursements of ODA are shown per capita and as a percentage of GNP.

The *summary measures* of per capita ODA are computed from group aggregates for population and for ODA. *Summary measures* for ODA as a percentage of GNP are computed from group totals for ODA and for GNP in current U.S. dollars.

Table 21. Total external debt

The data on debt in this and successive tables are from the World Bank Debtor Reporting System, supplemented by World Bank estimates. That system is concerned solely with developing economies and does not collect data on external debt for other groups of borrowers, nor from economies that are not members of the World Bank. The dollar figures on debt shown in Tables 21 through 25 are in U.S. dollars converted at official exchange rates.

The data on debt include private nonguaranteed debt reported by twenty-four developing countries and complete or partial estimates for an additional twenty-five countries.

Public loans are external obligations of public debtors, including the national government, its agencies, and autonomous public bodies. *Publicly guaranteed loans* are external obligations of private debtors that are guaranteed for repayment by a public entity. These two categories are aggregated in the tables. *Private nonguaranteed loans* are external obligations of private debtors that are not guaranteed for repayment by a public entity.

Use of IMF credit denotes repurchase obligations to the IMF for all uses of IMF resources, excluding those resulting from drawings in the reserve tranche and on the IMF Trust Fund and the Structural Adjustment Facility. It is shown for the end of the year specified. It comprises purchases outstanding under the credit tranches, including enlarged access resources, and all of the special facilities (the buffer stock, compensatory financing, and Extended Fund Facility). Trust Fund and Structural Adjustment Facility loans are included individually in the Debtor Reporting System and are thus shown within the total of public long-term debt. Use of IMF credit outstanding at year-end (a stock) is converted to U.S. dollars at the dollar-SDR exchange rate in effect at year-end.

Short-term external debt is debt with an original maturity of one year or less. Available data permit no distinctions between public and private nonguaranteed short-term debt.

Total external debt is defined for the purpose of this report as the sum of public, publicly guaranteed, and private nonguaranteed long-term debt, use of IMF credit, and short-term debt.

Table 22. Flow of public and private external capital

Data on *disbursements* and *repayment of principal* (amortization) are for public, publicly guaranteed, and private nonguaranteed long-term loans. The *net flow* estimates are disbursements less the repayment of principal.

Table 23. Total external public and private debt and debt service ratios

Total long-term debt data in this table cover public and publicly guaranteed debt and private nonguaranteed debt. The ratio of debt service to exports of goods and services is one of several conventional measures used to assess the ability to service debt. The average ratios of debt service to GNP for the economy groups are weighted by GNP in current dollars. The average ratios of debt service to exports of goods and services are weighted by exports of goods and services in current dollars.

Table 24. External public debt and debt service ratios

External public debt outstanding and disbursed represents public and publicly guaranteed loans drawn at year-end, net of repayments of principal and write-offs. For estimating external public debt as a percentage of GNP, the debt figures are converted into U.S. dollars from currencies of repayment at end-of-year official exchange rates. GNP is converted from national currencies to U.S. dollars by applying the conversion procedure described in the technical note to Tables 2 and 3.

Interest payments are actual payments made on the outstanding and disbursed public and publicly guaranteed debt in foreign currencies, goods, or services; they include commitment charges on undisbursed debt if information on those charges is available.

Debt service is the sum of actual repayments of principal (amortization) and actual payments of interest made in foreign currencies, goods, or services on external public and publicly guaranteed debt. Procedures for estimating total long-term debt as a percentage of GNP, average ratios of debt service to GNP, and average ratios of debt service to exports of goods and services are the same as those described in the note to Table 23.

The *summary measures* are computed from group aggregates of debt service and GNP in current dollars.

Table 25. Terms of external public borrowing

Commitments refer to the public and publicly guaranteed loans for which contracts were signed in the year specified. They are reported in currencies of repayment and converted into U.S. dollars at average annual official exchange rates.

Figures for *interest rates, maturities,* and *grace periods* are averages weighted by the amounts of the loans. Interest is the major charge levied on a loan and is usually computed on the amount of principal drawn and outstanding. The maturity of a loan is the interval between the agreement date, when a loan agreement is signed or bonds are issued, and the date of final repayment of principal. The grace period is the interval between the agreement date and the date of the first repayment of principal.

Public loans with variable interest rates, as a percentage of public debt, refer to interest rates that float with movements in a key market rate; for example, the London interbank offered rate (LIBOR) or the U.S. prime rate. This column shows the borrower's exposure to changes in international interest rates.

The *summary measures* in this table are weighted by the amounts of the loans.

Table 26. Population growth and projections

Population growth rates are period averages calculated from midyear populations.

Population estimates for mid-1987 are based on official estimates made by country statistical offices, the U.N. Population Division, and the World Bank. They take into account the results of recent population censuses, which, in some cases, are neither recent nor accurate. *Note* that refugees not permanently settled in the country of asylum are generally considered to be part of the population of their country of origin.

The *projections of population* for 2000, 2025, and the year in which the population will eventually become stationary (see definition below) are made for each economy separately. Information on total population by age and sex, fertility, mortality, and international migration is projected on the basis of generalized assumptions until the population becomes stationary. The base-year estimates are from updated printouts of the U.N. *World Population Prospects: 1988,* recent issues of the U.N. *Population* and *Vital Statistics Report*, World Bank country data, and national censuses and surveys.

The *net reproduction rate* (NRR), which measures the number of daughters a newborn girl will bear during her lifetime, assuming fixed age-specific fertility and mortality rates, reflects the extent to which a cohort of newborn girls will reproduce themselves. An NRR of 1 indicates that fertility is at replacement level: at this rate women will bear, on average, only enough daughters to replace themselves in the population.

A *stationary population* is one in which age- and sex-specific mortality rates have not changed over a long period, while age-specific fertility rates have simultaneously remained at replacement level (NRR=1). In such a population, the birth rate is constant and equal to the death rate, the age structure is constant, and the growth rate is zero.

Population momentum is the tendency for population growth to continue beyond the time that replacement-level fertility has been achieved; that is, even after the NRR has reached 1. The momentum of a population in any given year is measured as a ratio of the ultimate stationary population to the population of that year, given the assumption that fertility drops to replacement level by that year and remains there. For example, the 1990 population of India is projected to be 848 million. If the NRR were to drop to 1 by 1990, the projected stationary population would be 1,448 million— reached in the middle of the twenty-second century—and the population momentum would be 1.7.

A population tends to grow even after fertility has declined to replacement level because past high growth rates will have produced an age distribution with a relatively high proportion of women in, or still to enter, the reproductive ages. Consequently, the birth rate will remain higher than the death rate, and the growth rate will remain positive for several decades.

Population projections are made component by component. Mortality, fertility, and migration are projected separately and the results are applied iteratively to the 1985 base year age structure. For the projection period 1985 to 2005, the changes in mortality are country specific: increments in life expectancy and decrements in infant mortality are based on previous trends for each country. When female secondary school enrollment is high, mortality is assumed to decline more quickly. Infant mortality is projected separately from adult mortality.

Projected fertility rates are also based on previous trends. For countries in which fertility has started to decline (fertility transition), this trend is assumed to continue. It has been observed that no country with a life expectancy of less than 50 years experienced a fertility decline; for these countries the average decline of the group of countries in fertility transition is applied. Countries with below-replacement fertility are assumed to have constant total fertility rates until 1995–2000 and then to regain replacement level by 2030.

International migration rates are based on past and present trends in migration flows and migration policy. Among the sources consulted are estimates and projections made by national statistical offices, international agencies, and research institutions. Because of the uncertainty of future migration trends, it is assumed in the projections that net migration rates will reach zero by 2025.

The estimates of the size of the stationary population and the assumed year of reaching replacement-level fertility are speculative. *They should not be regarded as predictions*. They are included to show the implications of recent fertility and mortality trends on the basis of generalized assumptions. A fuller description of the methods and assumptions used to calculate the estimates will be available from the World Bank's forthcoming *World Population Projections*, 1989–90 edition.

Table 27. Demography and fertility

The *crude birth and death rates* indicate respectively the number of live births and deaths occurring per thousand population in a year. They come from the sources mentioned in the note to Table 26.

The *percentage of women of childbearing age* provides a more complete picture of fertility patterns. Comparison of 1965 and 1987 data adds an interesting aspect to the pattern of reproduction during the past two decades. *Childbearing age* is generally defined as 15 to 49.

The *total fertility rate* represents the number of children that would be born to a woman if she were to live to the end of her childbearing years and bear children at each age in accordance with prevailing age-specific fertility rates. The rates given are from the sources mentioned in Table 26.

The *percentage of married women of childbearing age using contraception* refers to women who are practicing, or whose husbands are practicing, any form of contraception. Contraceptive usage is generally measured for women age 15–49. A few countries use measures relating to other age groups such as 15 to 44, 18 to 44, and 19 to 49.

Data are mainly derived from the World Fertility Surveys, the Contraceptive Prevalence Surveys, the Demographic and Health Surveys, World Bank country data, and the U.N. publication *Recent Levels and Trends of Contraceptive Use as Assessed in 1983*. For a few countries for which no survey data are available, program statistics are used; these include Bangladesh, India, and several African countries. Program statistics may understate contraceptive prevalence because they do not measure use of methods such as rhythm, withdrawal, or abstinence, or contraceptives not obtained through the official family planning program. The data refer to rates prevailing in a variety of years, generally not more than three years prior to the year specified in the tables.

All *summary measures* are country data weighted by each country's share in the aggregate population.

Table 28. Health and nutrition

The estimates of *population per physician and nursing person* are derived from World Health Organization (WHO) data. The data refer to a variety of years, generally no more than two years prior to the year specified. The figure for *physicians*, in addition to the total number of registered practitioners in the country, includes medical assistants whose medical training is less than that of qualified physicians, but who nevertheless dispense similar medical services, including simple operations. The numbers include "barefoot doctors." *Nursing persons* include graduate, practical, assistant, and auxiliary nurses, as well as paraprofessional personnel such as health workers, first aid workers, traditional birth attendants, etc. The inclusion of auxiliary and paraprofessional personnel provides more realistic estimates of available nursing care. Because definitions of doctors and nursing personnel vary—and because the data shown are for a variety of years—the data for these two indicators are not strictly comparable across countries.

The *daily calorie supply per capita* is calculated by dividing the calorie equivalent of the food supplies in an economy by the population. Food supplies comprise domestic production, imports less exports, and changes in stocks; they exclude animal feed, seeds for use in agriculture, and food lost in processing and distribution. These estimates are from the FAO.

The percentage of *babies with low birth weights* relates to children born weighing less than 2,500 grams. Low birth weight is frequently associated with maternal malnutrition, and tends to raise the risk of infant mortality and to lead to poor growth in infancy and childhood, thus increasing the inci-

dence of other forms of retarded development. The figures are derived from WHO and UNICEF sources and are based on national data. The data are not strictly comparable across countries, as they are compiled from a combination of surveys and administrative records and other such sources.

The *summary measures* in this table are country figures weighted by each country's share in the aggregate population.

Table 29. Education

The data in this table refer to a variety of years, generally not more than two years distant from those specified, and are mostly from Unesco. However, disaggregated figures for males and females sometimes refer to a year earlier than that for overall totals.

The data on *primary school enrollments* are estimates of children of all ages enrolled in primary school. Figures are expressed as the ratio of pupils to the population of school-age children. While many countries consider primary school age to be 6 to 11 years, others do not. The differences in country practices in the ages and duration of schooling are reflected in the ratios given. For some countries with universal primary education, the gross enrollment ratios may exceed 100 percent because some pupils are younger or older than the country's standard primary school age. The data on *secondary school enrollments* are calculated in the same manner, but again the definition of secondary school age differs among countries. It is most commonly considered 12 to 17 years. Late entry of more mature students, as well as repetition and the phenomenon of *bunching* in final grades, can influence these ratios.

The *tertiary enrollment* ratio is calculated by dividing the number of pupils enrolled in all postsecondary schools and universities by the population in the 20–24 age group. Pupils attending vocational schools, adult education programs, two-year community colleges, and distance education centers (primarily correspondence courses) are included. The distribution of pupils across these different types of institutions varies among countries. The *youth* population, that is 20 to 24 years, is used as the denominator since it represents an average tertiary level cohort. Although in higher-income countries, youths age 18 to 19 may be enrolled in a tertiary institution (and are included in the numerator), in both low- and middle-income and high-income economies, many people older than 25 years are also enrolled in such institutions.

The *summary measures* in this table are country enrollment rates weighted by each country's share in the aggregate population.

Table 30. Income distribution and ICP estimates of GDP

The data in this table refer to the distribution of total disposable household income accruing to percentile groups of households ranked by total household income, and ICP estimates for GDP.

The first column presents preliminary results of the U.N. International Comparison Program (ICP), Phase V, for 1985. ICP recasts traditional national accounts through special price collections and disaggregation of GDP by expenditure components. Reviewed ICP results are expected to be available by the end of 1989. The figures given here are subject to change and should be regarded as indicative only. ICP Phase V details are prepared by national statistical offices and coordinated by the U.N. Statistical Office (UNSO) with support from other international agencies, particularly the Statistical Office of the European Communities (EUROSTAT) and the Organisation for Economic Co-operation and Development (OECD). The World Bank, the Economic Commission for Europe (ECE), and the Economic and Social Commission for Asia and the Pacific (ESCAP) also contribute to this exercise.

A total of 64 countries participated in the ICP Phase V exercise but preliminary results are available for only 57. For four of these countries (Bangladesh, Nepal, Pakistan, and the Philippines), total GDP data were not available, and comparisons were made for consumption only; two countries with populations of less than 1 million—Luxembourg, with 81.3 as its estimated index of GDP per capita; and Swaziland, with 13.6—have been omitted from this table. Data for the remaining seven countries, all Caribbean, are expected later in the year.

Although the GDP per capita figures are presented as indexes to the U.S. value, the underlying data are expressed in U.S. dollars. However, these dollar values, which are different from those shown in Tables 1 and 3 (see the technical notes for these tables), are obtained by special conversion factors designed to equalize purchasing powers of currencies in the respective countries. This conversion factor, commonly known as the purchasing power parity (PPP), is defined as the number of units of a country's currency required to buy the same amounts of goods and services in the domestic market as one dollar would buy in the United States. The computation of PPP involves obtaining implicit quantities from national accounts expenditure data and specially collected price data, and revaluing the implicit quantities in each country at a single set of average prices. The PPP rate thus equalizes dollar prices in every country, and intercountry comparisons of GDP based on them reflect differences in quantities of goods and services free of any price level differentials. This procedure is designed to bring intercountry comparisons in line with intertemporal real value comparisons that are based on constant price series.

The figures presented here are the results of a two-step exercise. Countries within a region or group such as the OECD are first compared using their own group average prices. Next, since group average prices may differ from each other, making the countries belonging to different groups not comparable, the group prices are adjusted to make them comparable at the world level. The adjustments, done by UNSO, are based on price differentials observed in a network of "link" countries representing each group. However, the linking is done in a manner that retains in the world comparison the relative levels of GDP observed in the group comparisons.

The two-step process was adopted because the relative GDP levels and ranking of two countries may change when more countries are brought into the comparison. It was felt that this should not be allowed to happen *within* geographic regions; that is, that the relationship of, say, Ghana and Senegal should not be affected by the prices prevailing in the United States. Thus overall GDP per capita levels are calculated at *regional* prices and then linked together. The linking is done by revaluing GDPs of all the countries at average "world" prices and allocating the new regional totals on the basis of each country's share in the original regional total that was based on regional prices.

Such a method does not permit the comparison of more detailed quantities (for example, food consumption). Thus these subaggregates and more detailed categories are calculated by the *world* prices. Therefore these quantities are indeed comparable internationally, but they do not add up to the indicated GDPs, because they are calculated at a different set of prices.

Some countries belong to several regional groups. Some groups have priority; others are equal. Thus fixity is always maintained between members of the European Communities, even within the OECD and world comparison. For Finland and Austria, however, the bilateral relationship that prevails within the OECD comparison is also the one used within the global comparison. However, a significantly different relationship (based on Central European prices) prevails in the comparison within that group, and this is the relationship presented in the separate publication of the European comparison.

For further details on the ICP procedures, readers may consult the ICP Phase IV report: *World Comparisons of Purchasing Power and Real Product for 1980* (New York: United Nations, 1986).

The *income distribution* data cover rural and urban areas and refer to different years between 1970 and 1986. The data are drawn from a variety of sources, including the Economic Commission for Latin America and the Caribbean (ECLAC), Economic and Social Commission for Asia and the Pacific (ESCAP), International Labour Office (ILO), the Organisation for Economic Co-operation and Development (OECD), the U.N. *National Account Statistics: Compendium of Income Distribution Statistics*, 1985, the World Bank, and national sources.

In many countries the collection of income distribution data is not systematically organized or integrated with the official statistical system. The data are derived from surveys designed for other purposes, most often consumer expenditure surveys, that also collect some information on income. These surveys use a variety of income concepts and sample designs, and in many cases their geographic coverage is too limited to provide reliable nationwide estimates of income distribution. Therefore, while the estimates shown are considered the best available, they do not avoid all these problems and should be interpreted with extreme caution.

The scope of the indicator is similarly limited. Because households vary in size, a distribution in which households are ranked according to per capita household income, rather than according to total household income, is superior for many purposes. The distinction is important because households with low per capita incomes frequently are large households, whose total income may be high, while conversely many households with low household incomes may be small households with high per capita incomes. Information on the distribution of per capita household income exists for only a few countries and is infrequently updated; for this reason this table is unchanged from last year's version. The World Bank's Living Standards Measurement Study and the Social Dimensions of Adjustment project, covering Sub-Saharan African countries, are assisting a few selected countries to improve their collection and analysis of data on income distribution.

Table 31. Urbanization

The data on *urban population as a percentage of total population* are from the forthcoming U.N. publication, *The Prospects of World Urbanization*, supplemented by data from the World Bank.

The growth rates of urban population are calculated from the World Bank's population estimates; the estimates of urban population shares are calculated from the sources cited above. Data on urban agglomeration in large cities are from the U.N. *Patterns of Urban and Rural Population Growth, 1980*.

Because the estimates in this table are based on different national definitions of what is *urban*, cross-country comparisons should be interpreted with caution. Data on urban agglomeration in large cities are from population censuses, which are conducted at five- or even ten-year intervals.

The *summary measures* for urban population as a percentage of total population are calculated from country percentages weighted by each country's share in the aggregate population; the other *summary measures* in this table are weighted in the same fashion, using urban population.

Table 32. Women in development

This table provides some basic indicators disaggregated to show differences between the sexes to illustrate the condition of women in society. It reflects their demographic status and their access to some health and education services. Statistical anomalies become even more apparent when social indicators are analyzed by gender, because reporting systems are often weak in areas related specifically to women. Indicators drawn from censuses and surveys, such as those on population, tend to be about as reliable for women as for men; but indicators based largely on administrative records, such as maternal and infant mortality, are less reliable. Currently more resources are being devoted to developing better statistics on this topic, but the reliability of data, even in the series shown, still varies significantly.

The first four columns show the ratios of females to males for the total population and for the under-five age group. In general, throughout the world, more males are born than females. Under good nutritional and health conditions and in times of peace, male children have a higher death rate than females, and females tend to live longer. In the industrial market economies, these factors have resulted in ratios of about 103 to 105 females per 100 males in the general population. The figures in these columns reveal that there are cases where the number of females is much smaller than what would be a normal demographic pattern. In some countries, the apparent imbalance may be the result of migration (for example, Kuwait and United Arab Emirates), where males enter the country to work on contracts. In others, male out-migration or the disproportionate effect of war creates a reverse imbalance of fewer than expected males and may partly hide, or compensate for, the excessive female mortality.

Typically, however, in the absence of such factors, a female-to-male ratio significantly below 100 in the general population of a country reflects the effects of discrimination against women. Such discrimination affects mostly three age groups: very young girls, who may get a smaller share of scarce food or receive less prompt costly medical attention; childbearing women; and to a lesser extent the resourceless elderly. This pattern of discrimination is not uniformly associated with development. There are low- and middle-income countries (and within countries, regions) where the composition of the population is quite "normal." In many others, however, the numbers starkly demonstrate the need to associate women more closely with development.

The health and welfare indicators in the next five columns draw attention, in particular, to the conditions associated with childbearing. This activity still carries the highest risk of death for women of reproductive age in developing countries. The indicators reflect, but do not measure, both the availability of health services for women and the general welfare and nutritional status of mothers.

Life expectancy at birth is defined in the note to Table 1.

Births attended by health staff show the percentage of births recorded where a recognized health service worker was in attendance. The data are from the World Health Organization (WHO) and supplemented by UNICEF data. *Maternal mortality* usually refers to the number of female deaths that occur during childbirth, per 100,000 live births. Because "childbirth" is defined more widely in some countries, to include complications of pregnancy or of abortion, and since many pregnant women die because of lack of suitable health care, maternal mortality is difficult to measure consistently and reliably across countries. The data in these two series are drawn from diverse national sources and collected by WHO, although many national administrative systems are weak and do not record vital events in a systematic way. The data are de-

rived mostly from official community reports and hospital records, and some reflect only deaths in hospitals and other medical institutions. Sometimes smaller private and rural hospitals are excluded, and sometimes even relatively primitive local facilities are included. The coverage is therefore not always comprehensive, and the figures should be treated with extreme caution.

Clearly, many maternal deaths go unrecorded, particularly in countries with remote rural populations; this accounts for some of the very low numbers shown in the table, especially for several African countries. Moreover, it is not clear whether an increase in the number of mothers in hospitals reflects more extensive medical care for women or more complications in pregnancy and childbirth because of poor nutrition, for instance. (See Table 28 for low birth weight data.)

These time series attempt to bring together readily available information not always presented in international publications. WHO warns that there are "inevitably gaps" in the series, and it has invited countries to provide more comprehensive figures. They are reproduced here, from the 1986 WHO publication *Maternal Mortality Rates*, supplemented by the UNICEF publication *The State of the World's Children 1989*, as part of the international effort to highlight data in this field. The data refer to any year from 1977 to 1984.

The *infant mortality* rate is the number of infants who die before reaching one year of age, per thousand live births in a given year. The data are from the U.N. publication *Mortality of Children under Age 5: Projections, 1950–2025* as well as from the World Bank.

The *education* indicators, based on Unesco sources, show the extent to which females are enrolled at school at both primary and secondary levels, compared with males. All things being equal, and opportunities being the same, the ratios for females should be close to 100. However, inequalities may cause the ratios to move in different directions. For example, the number of females per 100 males will rise at secondary school level if male attendance declines more rapidly in the final grades because of males' greater job opportunities, conscription into the army, or migration in search of work. In addition, since the numbers in these columns refer mainly to general secondary education, they do not capture those (mostly males) enrolled in technical and vocational schools or in full-time apprenticeships, as in Eastern Europe.

Bibliography

Production and domestic absorption	U.N. Department of International Economic and Social Affairs. Various years. *Statistical Yearbook.* New York. U.N. Department of International Economic and Social Affairs. Various years. *World Energy Supplies.* Statistical Papers, series J. New York. FAO, IMF, UNIDO, and World Bank data; and national sources.
Fiscal and monetary accounts	International Monetary Fund. 1988. *Government Finance Statistics Yearbook.* Vol. XII. ———. Various years. *International Finance Statistics.* Washington, D.C. U.N. Department of International Economic and Social Affairs. Various Years. *World Energy Supplies.* Statistical Papers, series J. New York. IMF data.
Trade and balance of payments	International Monetary Fund. Various years. *International Financial Statistics.* Washington, D.C. U.N. Conference on Trade and Development. Various years. *Handbook of International Trade and Development Statistics.* Geneva. U.N. Department of International Economic and Social Affairs. Various years. *Monthly Bulletin of Statistics.* New York. ———. Various years. *Yearbook of International Trade Statistics.* New York. FAO, IMF, U.N., and World Bank data.
External finance	Organisation for Economic Co-operation and Development. Various years. *Development Co-operation.* Paris. ———. 1987. *Geographical Distribution of Financial Flows to Developing Countries.* Paris. IMF, OECD, and World Bank data; and the World Bank Debtor Reporting System.

Human resources

U.N. Department of International Economic and Social Affairs. Various years. *Population and Vital Statistics Report*. New York.

———. 1980. *Patterns of Urban and Rural Population Growth*. New York.

———. 1984. *Recent Levels and Trends of Contraceptive Use as Assessed in 1983*. New York.

———. 1988. *Mortality of Children under Age 5: Projections 1950–2025*. New York.

———. Forthcoming. *The Prospects of World Urbanization*. New York.

———. Updated printouts. *World Population Prospects: 1988*. New York.

Food and Agriculture Organization. 1981. *Fertilizer Yearbook 1982*. Rome.

———. 1983. *Food Aid in Figures* (December). Rome.

Institute for Resource Development/Westinghouse. 1987. *Child Survival: Risks and the Road to Health*. Columbia, Md.

Sivard, Ruth. 1985. *Women—A World Survey*. Washington, D.C.: World Priorities.

U.N. Department of International Economic and Social Affairs. Various years. *Demographic Yearbook*. New York.

———. Various years. *Statistical Yearbook*. New York.

U.N. Educational, Scientific, and Cultural Organization. Various years. *Statistical Yearbook*. Paris.

UNICEF. 1989. *The State of the World's Children 1989*. Oxford: Oxford University Press.

World Health Organization. Various years. *World Health Statistics Annual*. Geneva.

———. 1986. *Maternal Mortality Rates: A Tabulation of Available Information*, 2d edition. Geneva.

———. Various years. *World Health Statistics Report*. Geneva.

FAO and World Bank data.

Country classifications: *World Development Report 1988* and selected international organizations

World Development Report 1988[a]	**International Monetary Fund**	**United Nations**[b]	**United Nations Conference on Trade and Development**	**General Agreement on Tariffs and Trade**
Industrial market economies	*Industrial countries*	*Developed market economies*	*Developed market economies*	*Developed countries*
OECD (excluding Greece, Portugal, and Turkey)	North America Canada USA	Northern America Canada USA	North America Canada USA	North America Canada USA
	Europe EC (excluding Greece and Portugal) EFTA	Europe EC EFTA	Europe EC EFTA	Western Europe EC EFTA
		Other Europe Faeroe Islands Gibraltar Malta	Other Europe Faeroe Islands Gibraltar	Other Western Europe
		Africa South Africa	Africa South Africa	Africa South Africa
	Asia Japan	Asia Israel Japan	Asia Israel Japan	Asia Australia Japan New Zealand
	Oceania Australia New Zealand	Oceania Australia New Zealand	Oceania Australia New Zealand	
Developing economies	*Developing countries*	*Developing market economies*	*Developing market economies*	*Developing economies*
Latin America and the Caribbean	Western Hemisphere	Americas (excluding Northern America)	America CACM CARICOM LAIA Other	Latin America
Europe (including Cyprus, Greece, Hungary, Malta, Poland, Portugal, Romania, Turkey, and Yugoslavia)	Europe	Europe Yugoslavia	Europe Malta Yugoslavia	
Middle East and North Africa	Middle East (including Egypt)			Middle East
Sub-Saharan Africa	Africa (including South Africa)	Africa Northern Other CEUCA ECOWAS Rest of Africa (excluding South Africa)	Africa North Other CEPGL CEUCA ECOWAS Other (excluding South Africa)	Africa (excluding South Africa)
South Asia East Asia	Asia (excluding Middle East but including Oceania)	Asia Western Asia Other Asia Oceania	Asia West South and South-East Oceania	Asia (excluding Australia, Japan, New Zealand, and China and other Asian centrally planned economies)
High-income oil exporters	*Twelve major oil exporters*[c]	*OPEC*	*Major petroleum exporters*[d]	
Nonreporting nonmembers	*USSR and other nonmembers not included elsewhere*	*Centrally planned economies* Asia (including China) Europe and USSR (including Hungary, Poland, and Romania)	*Socialist countries* Asia Eastern Europe (including Hungary, Poland, and Romania)	*Eastern trading area* China and other Asian centrally planned economies Eastern Europe and USSR (including Hungary, Poland, and Romania)

Country classifications *(continued)*

World Development Report 1988[a]	**International Monetary Fund**	**United Nations**[b]	**United Nations Conference on Trade and Development**	**General Agreement on Tariffs and Trade**
Other analytical groups				
Developing economies	*Developing countries*	*Developing countries*	*Developing countries*	*Developing economies*

Low-income
    China and India
    Other low-income
Middle-income
    Lower middle-income
    Upper middle-income
	Low-income countries, excluding China and India[e]	Least developed countries[f]	Least developed countries[f]
			
			Income groups based on 1980 GDP per capita:
			    less than $500
			    $500 to $1,500
			    more than $1,500
				Least developed countries[f]

Oil exporters[a] Exporters of manufactures[a] Highly indebted countries[a] Sub-Saharan Africa[a]	Oil exporters[g] Exporters of manufactures[h] Fifteen heavily indebted countries[j] Sub-Saharan Africa[k]		Major exporters of manufactures[i]	Fifteen highly indebted countries[j]

Notes: CACM, Central American Common Market; CARICOM, Caribbean Community; CEPGL, Communauté économique des pays des Grands Lacs (Economic Community of the Great Lakes Countries); CEUCA, Customs and Economic Union of Central Africa; EC, European Communities; ECOWAS, Economic Community of West African States; EFTA, European Free Trade Association; LAIA, Latin American Integration Association; OECD, Organisation for Economic Co-operation and Development; OPEC, Organization of Petroleum Exporting Countries. For details, see the IMF's *Directory of Regional Economic Organizations and Intergovernmental Commodity and Development Organizations.*

a. See *World Development Report 1988,* page xi, for details. For this year's groupings, see the "Definitions and data notes" at the front of this volume.

b. The United Nations uses the detailed groupings shown for presenting many types of economic statistics. It uses more general geographical groupings for other types of statistics—for details, see the U.N. publication *Standard Country or Area Codes for Statistical Use* (series M, no. 49, rev. 2).

c. Includes Algeria, Indonesia, Islamic Republic of Iran, Iraq, Kuwait, Libya, Nigeria, Oman, Qatar, Saudi Arabia, United Arab Emirates, and Venezuela.

d. High-income and developing oil exporters (excluding Cameroon), Angola, and Egypt.

e. IMF member countries whose per capita GDP, as estimated by the World Bank, did not exceed the equivalent of $425 in 1986.

f. Includes Afghanistan, Bangladesh, Benin, Bhutan, Botswana, Burkina Faso, Burma, Burundi, Cape Verde, Central African Republic, Chad, Comoros, Democratic Yemen, Djibouti, Equatorial Guinea, Ethiopia, Gambia, Guinea, Guinea-Bissau, Haiti, Kiribati, Lao People's Democratic Republic, Lesotho, Malawi, Maldives, Mali, Mauritania, Mozambique, Nepal, Niger, Rwanda, Samoa, São Tomé and Principe, Sierra Leone, Somalia, Sudan, Togo, Tuvalu, Uganda, United Republic of Tanzania, Vanuatu, and Yemen.

g. Twelve major oil exporters plus Cameroon, Congo, Ecuador, Gabon, Mexico, and Trinidad and Tobago.

h. Exporters of manufactures and Turkey.

i. Includes Argentina, Brazil, Hong Kong, Korea, Singapore, Taiwan Province of China, Turkey, and Yugoslavia.

j. Highly indebted countries, excluding Costa Rica and Jamaica.

k. Sub-Saharan Africa excluding Nigeria.